THEONOMY IN CHRISTIAN ETHICS

THIRD EDITION

GREG L. BAHNSEN

CMP

Covenant Media Press, Nacogdoches, TX

2002

TO JONATHAN

our beloved "gift from God" while
this volume was in preparation,
praying that the inscription
"Non Sub Homine Sed Sub Deo Et Lege"
may be realized during his lifetime
in home, church, and state.

First edition, 1977
Second edition, 1984
Third edition, 2002

759651—www.cmfnow.com.

ISBN: 0-9678317-3-3

"A new and more powerful proclamation of that law is perhaps the most pressing need of the hour; men would have little difficulty with the gospel if they had only learned the lesson of the law. . . . So it always is: a low view of law always brings legalism in religion; a high view of law makes a man a seeker after grace. Pray God that the high view may again prevail."

J. Gresham Machen, *What is Faith?*, pp. 141-142

"Do we then nullify the Law through faith? May it never be! On the contrary, we establish the Law."

Romans 3:31 (NASV)

"For the love of God is this, that we keep His commandments; and His commandments are not burdensome."

1 John 5:3

"Where there is no vision, the people perish: but he that keepeth the law, happy is he."

Proverbs 29:18 (AV)

"There is no alternative but that of theonomy and autonomy."

Cornelius Van Til, *Christian Theistic Ethics*, p. 134

Table of Contents

VI. ANTITHESIS

VII. APPLICATION OF THE THESIS TO THE STATE

VIII. INDIFFERENCE TO THE THESIS DISPELLED

IX. APPENDICES

X. INDICES

Publisher's Preface

Dr. Greg Bahnsen left this world for His eternal reward in Christ on December 11, 1995. We that remain are grateful to him for his labor, scholarship, love, and most of all, for his faithfulness to Christ. *Theonomy in Christian Ethics* started as aquiet masters thesis in fulfillment of a Master of Theology degree from Westminster Theological Seminary in 1973. First published in 1977, this volume unexpectedly shook the theological establishment in its call for a return to God's law as the only perfect standard of righteousness for civil ethics. Twenty-five years later it continues to challenge the church to unashamedly embrace the "Word of God, contained in the Scriptures of the Old and New Testaments as the only rule of faith and life."

This 25th anniversary edition of *Theonomy in Christian Ethics* offers a third preface by Dr. Kenneth L. Gentry, Jr., a larger, reformatted page over previous editions, and a few minor changes and added.notes.

Randy Booth

Director—Covenant Media Foundation

Acknowledgements

This 25th anniversary, third edition of *Theonomy in Christian Ethics* would not have been possible without the generous support of Ken Hall and several other friends of Covenant Media Foundation. Thanks to Ed Walsh for scanning the original text. We are especially grateful for those who volunteered their labors to proofread and index: David Alders, Virginia Bahnsen, Marinell Booth, Christin Booth, James Bramer, Paul Heidmann, Kevin Johnson, Richard and Camala Klaus, Megan Lindsay, Jeff Niell, and Gary St. John.

FOREWORD

IN 1872, Robert L. Dabney, writing on the "Theology of the Plymouth Brethren" commented with dismay on the strange interpretation given to the Christian hope by "the Pre-Advent theory" of that body.[1] The glorious, full-bodied hope of Scripture had been reduced to an expectation concerning the millennium, and an erroneous one at that. We feel something of the same dismay when we see how so many Christians who profess to believe the whole counsel of God, and profess their faith in the Bible "from cover to cover," casually dismiss a major and most vital aspect thereof, the law of God.

If law be separated from grace, then grace also disappears, for the Bible knows no antinomian grace. The redeeming work of Jesus Christ, and the necessity of His atoning death on the cross, attest to the absoluteness of God's law: it could not be set aside. The redemptive work of Christ did not end the function of the law but rather re-established man in obedience to the law. We are redeemed, St. Paul made clear, "That the righteousness of the law might be fulfilled in us" (Rom. 8:4).

Adam was created in the image of God to exercise dominion over the earth and to subdue it to God's purposes through man as God's priest, prophet, and king. As priest, man was ordained to dedicate himself and his activities to the triune God. As king, man was to rule the earth as God's vicegerent, and, as prophet, to interpret all things in terms of God's sovereign word. By his fall, man's calling was deflected and perverted, and, instead of the Kingdom of God, the Kingdom of Man became his goal, and towers of Babel have, in one form or another, consistently occupied his energies.

By redeeming and restoring man in God's image, Jesus Christ restored man to his creation mandate, to subdue the earth by means

---

[1] See Robert L. Dabney, *Discussions: Evangelical and Theological,* reprint, 2 vols. (London: Banner of Truth Trust, [1890] 1967), 1:168-213.

of science, agriculture, the arts, commerce and industry, education, and every other legitimate human pursuit, and to exercise dominion over all things under God. The purpose of the law has from the beginning been this task. Salvation is by the grace of God through faith, and sanctification is by law. Because God's law has been abandoned by the modern church, both evangelical and reformed, it has, *first,* restricted holiness to things personal. Clearly, sanctification inescapably begins in the heart of man, but it cannot rest there. The man who is being progressively sanctified will inescapably sanctify his home, school, politics, economics, science, and all things else by understanding and interpreting all things in terms of the word of God and by bringing all things under the dominion of Christ the King. Holiness is not restricted to man alone in Scripture, and the prophetic vision of Christ's Kingdom is emphatic on this point:

> In that day shall there be upon the bells of the horses, HOLINESS UNTO THE LORD; and the pots in the LORD'S house shall be like the bowls before the altar.
>
> Yea, every pot in Jerusalem and in Judah shall be holiness unto the LORD of hosts: and all they that sacrifice shall come and take of them, and seethe therein: and in that day there shall be no more the Canaanite in the house of the LORD of hosts (Zech. 14:20-21).

As T. V. Moore noted, "The idea is, absolute and universal consecration to the Lord."[2]

Where God's law is honored, no man can regard himself as meeting God's requirements of holiness who gives his children to a godless school system to educate, or who feels that a secular state is acceptable to a Christian. God's law requires obedience by all men and institutions at all times.

---

[2] Thomas V. Moore, *The Book of Zechariah* (London: The Banner of Truth Trust, 1958), p. 236.

Second, since God's law is God's program for conquest in His name, where antinomianism in any degree prevails a pessimistic eschatology will likewise prevail, because the heart of biblical eschatology has been denied. The second coming and the last judgment give us the triumph of God's law and Kingdom, and who can dare to face that day who despises that law beforehand?

The history of Puritanism in America is very telling at this point. Law, an optimistic, biblical eschatology, and social power went hand in hand. The decline of one was the decline of all. The word of God is a seamless garment, and men who deny its law deny its eschatology also, and are deprived of God's power. It is not surprising, therefore, that this is an era of impotence in the church. That impotence will no more be cured by frantic and earnest prayer meetings than was the problem of Baal's prophets by their shouts, "O Baal, hear us" (1 Kings 18:26). True faith means law-obedience, and obedience spells power and blessing. Deuteronomy 28 tells us precisely, and for all time, how prayers are answered and a people blessed. There was a time when civil magistrates in the United States, from the president down, took their oath of office with the Bible opened to this chapter, because they knew what the law of God meant. Holiness and blessing are tied to the law, not to religious exercises (Deut. 28:8, 9) which substitute religiosity for faith in the Lord and obedience to His sovereign word.

The purpose of Chalcedon is, among other things, to restore knowledge of God's law-word to every area of life and to develop its implications for every discipline of study. Towards this end, Greg L. Bahnsen's study of *Theonomy in Christian Ethics* has been written. The issue, as Bahnsen so tellingly states it, is between theonomy (God's law) and autonomy (self-law). Modern autonomous man is aided and abetted in his apostasy from God by the antinomianism of the church, which, by denying God's law, has, in theology, politics, education, industry, and all things else, surrendered the field to the law of the fallen and godless self, to autonomy. Answers to the crisis of the modern age are futile if they refer Scripture only to matters of faith and then look to the constructs of autonomous man for answers. Too many church-men have been less honest than modern unbelievers, because they have restricted Scripture to matters of "faith" and created a mythical world of common grace where autonomous man and his anti-theistic law principles prevail. Against such unbelief and heresy, this study is an important and major defense of the faith and an extension to its full force of the crown rights of King Jesus.

Rousas John Rushdoony
October 26, 1971

PREFACE TO THE THIRD EDITION

SINCE 1977 *Theonomy in Christian Ethics* has served as the defining intellectual cornerstone for establishing *the* key distinctive of Christian Reconstructionism. Christian Reconstructionism as a distinctive school of thought within the Reformed tradition is founded upon five basic theological premises: (1) Calvinistic soteriology; (2) covenantal theology; (3) postmillennial eschatology; (4) presuppositional apologetics; and (5) theonomic ethics: the cornerstone of Reconstruction thought.[1] Undoubtedly the most distinctive aspect of the movement is the topic of this book: theonomic ethics, which establishes the whole revelation of God in Scripture (including the Mosaic law) as the source of a truly Christian ethic in all of life—private and public, cultural and political, social and judicial.[2]

I first became aware of the theonomic approach to ethics in 1975 when I transferred to Reformed Theological Seminary (Jackson, Mississippi) after my middler year at Grace Theological Seminary (Winona

---

[1] Some theologians recognize all five of these points, e.g., J. G. Child, "Christian Reconstruction Movement," in David J. Atkinson, David F. Field, et al. *New Dictionary of Christian Ethics & Pastoral Theology* (Downers Grove, IL.: InterVarsity, 1995), 227. Other writers not within the movement lay out only a few of these points, but interestingly, they do recognize these issues. For instance, "these foundational ideas underlie the Reconstructionist agenda: (1) a presuppositional apologetic; (2) a belief that Old Testament law applies today, in 'exhaustive' and 'minutial' detail; and (3) postmillennialism." Daniel G. Reid, Robert D. Linder, et. al, eds., *Concise Dictionary of Christianity in America* (Downers Grove, IL.: InterVarsity, 1995), 285.

[2] A common error of some theonomy opponents is to assume that theonomy entails postmillennialism. The two theological constructs, however, are distinct; in no way do they stand or fall together. Postmillennialism is concerned with "what *will* be"; theonomy focuses on "what *should* be." Many theonomists are amillennialists; few postmillennialists are theonomists.

Lake, Indiana). Through my personal, extracurricular study at Grace I became frustrated with dispensationalism and intrigued by covenant theology. At my new seminary I encountered their new professor, Greg L. Bahnsen, Associate Professor of Apologetics. I had him for several classes—most significantly his courses on "History and Eschatology" and "Christian Theistic Ethics." My first introduction to his book *Theonomy in Christian Ethics* was quite unusual: the ethics class was assigned readings in it *before* it was published. We had to read trimmed, loose page proofs stored in small boxes in the reference room of the seminary library (my wife, Melissa, was a reference librarian there and well remembers shuffling those little boxes in and out to students). We were reading the book even *before* it was "hot off the press."

Thus, upon transferring from the fundamentalist, dispensational seminary to the reformed, covenantal one, I encountered quite unexpected and rather startling implications of a rigorously covenantal Calvinism: its application to the field of ethics, i.e., theonomy. To put it mildly, I not only resisted Bahnsen's theonomic perspective at first, but was quite alarmed by it. Nevertheless, sitting under Bahnsen's careful, deliberate, coherent, rigorous, and compelling instruction, many of my classmates and I were eventually "converted" to theonomic ethics before the course was completed. Some of the students back then later became well-known exponents of theonomy, including Gary DeMar, David Chilton, and Richard Flinn. During my student days at RTS (1975–77) I grew to greatly admire Bahnsen's theological prowess, philosophical precision, and instructional clarity. After those days and up until his untimely death on December 11, 1995, I treasured my relationship with him, not only holding him as my mentor and rejoicing to work with him as a co-laborer in theology, but delighting in a close friendship: Bahnsen and I co-authored *House Divided: The Break-up of Dispensational Theology*, served on the adjunct faculty of Christ College, and jointly spoke at several conferences. I invited him to speak at my church on several occasions and he invited me to join him as an instructor on the staff of his Southern California Center for Christian Studies. Working with him in these various ministerial endeavors was a great privilege and high honor. He had a greater impact on my theological commitments than any other scholar I could name. And I know many Christians who would gladly affirm the same.

Unfortunately though, theonomic ethics does not sit well with the modern values of personal peace and affluence. Its absolutistic character stands like the Rock of Gibralter against the relentless, ever changing waves of the do-your-own-thing approach to life. Sadly, even within conservative and evangelical, as well as reformed Christian circles, theonomy has generated an enormous backlash and vigorous opposition. Even worse, the great majority of Bahnsen's opponents have never taken the time to read through his extensive and detailed argument presented in *Theonomy in Christian Ethics*, the Bible of theonomic ethics.

I even remember being astounded during a theological examination in my first presbytery in the Presbyterian Church in America. The examiner, an ordained minister, was challenging a ministerial candidate regarding the matter of theonomy. In his inquiry the minister could not even pronounce "theonomy" so he spelled it out! I arose to ask the examiner if he had read *Theonomy in Christian Ethics* which explains the position; he confessed that he had not but that he knew it was wrong. And this type of uninformed and highly emotional response is not unique in the ongoing debate over theonomic ethics.

Perhaps the most bizarre review of the book was by (maverick) reformed Old Testament scholar, Meredith G. Kline. His review opened with scathing emotion-laden denunciations of Greg Bahnsen and theonomy—intermixed with admissions that the repugnant outlook of theonomy was inherent in the Westminster Confession of Faith itself. Kline's first sentence complains about "the over-heated typewriter of Greg Bahnsen." His second sentence laments "the tragedy of Chalcedon" (i.e., his name for the theonomic movement) which promotes "a delusive and grotesque perversion" of Scripture. Kline even notes of this "grotesque perversion": "Ecclesiastical courts operating under the Westminster Confession of Faith are going to have their problems, therefore, if they should be of a mind to bring the

Chalcedon aberration under their judicial scrutiny."[3] Why? As he well notes: "Chalcedon is not without roots in respectable ecclesiastical tradition. It is in fact a revival of certain teachings contained in the Westminster Confession of Faith."[4]

Despite the wide-spread emotionally-charged and ecclesiastically-encouraged response to theonomy, various well-respected evangelical scholars recognize the theonomic approach as a viable option in the debate, even though they themselves do not adopt it. For instance, note the following comments:

- Ronald Nash, a reformed theologian at Reformed Theological Seminary, Orlando, writes that: "For one thing, the people called theonomists don't appear to be dangerous. Efforts to show that they are dangerous do more, I suspect, to dishonor the people raising the charges."[5]

- Mark Noll, McManis professor of Christian Thought, Wheaton College, observes that theonomy insists "on carefully formulated theological foundations for political action" by which it "pushes toward a more self-conscious political reflection than is customary in the evangelical tradition."[6]

- Carl F. H. Henry, in his landmark *God, Revelation, and Authority* series, expresses appreciation for *Theonomy in Christian Ethics*: "By a wealth of biblical data Greg L. Bahnsen establishes that God's commands impose universal moral obligation; that God's ethical standards ought universally to inform

---

[3] Meredith G. Kline, "Comments on an Old-New Error: A Review Article," in *Westminster Theological Journal* 41:1 (Fall, 1978), 173.

[4] Kline, "Old-New Error," 173.

[5] Ronald H. Nash, *Great Divides: Understanding the Controversies That Come Between Christians* (Colorado Springs, CO.: NavPress, 1993), 176.

[6] Mark A. Noll, *The Scandal of the Evangelical Mind* (Grand Rapids: Eerdmans, 1994), 225.

civil legislation; that civil magistrates are ideally to enforce God's social commands and that Christians are involved in covenantal use of divine law (*Theonomy in Christian Ethics*)."[7]

• J. G. Child commends theonomy, for "forcing Christians to grapple with the OT's contribution to Christian ethics and a just society, and by offering insightful biblical solutions to the problems of the modern world, the Reconstrucionists have enriched the church."[8]

• D. Claire Davis, Professor of Church History at Westminster Seminary, notes: "Theonomy can be of great service precisely within the context of the constitution of the American republic." Later he continues: "It is easy to argue that the Westminster Confession's commitment to the general equity of Old Testament law provides ample justification for theonomic clarification of that equity."[9]

• Even in the introductory note to *Theonomy: A Reformed Critique,* a full-scale reformed critique of theonomy, the editors can conclude: "Although this volume is a critique of theonomy, several of the chapters have concluded on a positive note of appreciation for what the theonomists have contributed to our understanding of God's law."[10]

Consequently, I am delighted that Covenant Media Press has undertaken the task of republishing this irreplaceable classic on biblical

---

[7] Carl F. H. Henry, *God Who Stands and Stays* (Part Two), vol. 6 of *God, Revelation and Authority* (Waco, Tex.: Word, 1983), 447.

[8] J. G. Child, "Christian Reconstruction Movement," 227.

[9] Will S. Barker and W. Robert Godfrey, *Theonomy: An Informed Critique* (Grand Rapids: Zondervan, 1990), 392, 394.

[10] Will S. Barker and W. Robert Godfrey, eds., *Theonomy: An Informed Critique* (Grand Rapids: Zondervan, 1990), 385.

ethics, which has become a widely-cited reference work.[11] In this new edition the text remains largely unchanged, except for the correction of several typos, the provision of a cleaner type-font and more white space (for reader comfort)—and in adding a few updated reference works. Once again the opponents of theonomy have at their disposal the whole system clearly presented. I hope this time around they read it.

KENNETH L. GENTRY, JR., TH.D.
June 7, 2001
Bahnsen Theological Seminary
Placentia, California

---

[11] D. J. Moo, "Law," in Michael B. Green, Scot McKnight, I. Howard Marshall, eds., *Dictionary of Jesus and the Gospels: A Compendium of Contemporary Biblical Scholarship* (Downers Grove, IL.: InterVarsity, 1992), 461. J. G. Child, "Christian Reconstruction Movement," in *New Dictionary of Christian Ethics & Pastoral Theology*, 227. P. A. Marshall, "Theonomy," in *New Dictionary of Christian Ethics & Pastoral Theology*, 845. Joe M. Sprinkle, "Law," in Walter A. Elwell, ed., *Evangelical Dictionary of Biblical Theology* (Grand Rapids: Baker, 1996), 470. J. H. Gerstner, "Law in the NT," in Geoffrey W. Bromiley, ed., *The International Standard Bible Encyclopedia,* 2d ed. (Grand Rapids: Eerdmans, 1982), 3:91. Thomas D. Ice, "Reconstructionism, Christian," in Mal Couch, *Dictionary of Premillennial Theology* (Grand Rapids: Kregel, 1996), 362. J. R. McQuilkin, "Reformed Ethics," Roland Kenneth Harrison, ed., *Encyclopedia of Biblical and Christian Ethics*, (2d. ed.: Nashville: Nelson, 1992), 348. David Clyde Jones, *Biblical Christian Ethics* (Grand Rapids: Baker, 1994), 113–15.

PREFACE TO THE SECOND EDITION

SINCE the publication of this book six years ago, a multitude of related and unrelated books, along with studies and actions within churches and schools, have revived serious interest in the current normativity of God's law. *Theonomy in Christian Ethics,* in tandem with other "Reconstructionist" publications,[1] has proved to be one more stimulus to reflection and discussion. It has generated further articles and books in which its conclusions are incorporated, taken note of, or positively applied to concrete moral issues of our day.[2] It has also been angrily opposed.[3] The "theonomic perspective" has been studied by two presbyteries, made the crux of an ordination battle, examined by the 1979 General Assembly of the Presbyterian Church in America,[4]

---

[1] For many "reconstructionists" the works of R. J. Rushdoony (even when they disagreed with details) have had a formative influence, for instance his popular essays, *Law and Liberty* (Fairfax, VA: Thoburn Press, 1971), and his massive study, *Institutes of Biblical Law* (Nutley, NJ: Craig Press, 1973). In 1974 Dr. Gary North began to publish and edit for the Chalcedon Foundation *The Journal of Christian Reconstruction* (Box 158, Vallecito, CA 95251).

[2] E.g., Gary North, *Unconditional Surrender: God's Program for Victory* (Tyler, TX: Geneva Press, 1981); Gary DeMar, *God and Government: A Biblical and Historical Study,* Biblical Worldview Library (Atlanta: American Vision Press, 1982); Carl F. H. Henry, *God, Revelation and Authority,* vol. 6 (Waco, TX: Word Inc., 1983), pp. 447-49; my subsequent book, *Homosexuality: A Biblical View* (Grand Rapids: Baker Book House, 1978); David Chilton, *Productive Christians in an Age of Guilt Manipulators,* 2nd ed. (Tyler, TX: Institute of Christian Economics, 1982).

[3] E.g., Walter J. Chantry, *God's Righteous Kingdom* (Edinburgh: Banner of Truth Trust, 1980).

[4] "No particular view of the application of the judicial law for today should be made a basis for orthodoxy or excluded as heresy" *(Minutes,* pp. 41, 115, 194-95: Resolution 6-45). A Study Committee in Evangel Presbytery (P.C.A.) took essentially the same stand (reversing a previously negative action) in June, 1979, and acknowledged the "Clear Benefits" which had come from theonomy: namely, that it drives us "to *all* the Scripture, to deal with ethics, to sound exegesis, to a Biblical

and publicly debated at the 1981 Evangelical Theological Society Meeting in Toronto.[5] In each case the strength or acceptability of the viewpoint, reflecting a modern defense of traditional Reformed and Puritan sympathies,[6] has been evident.

Enthusiastic conviction and emotional criticism have both accompanied this book, making it a center of informed (and sometimes uninformed)[7] ethical discussion in Reformed circles. Popular interest appears to have demanded a third printing of it—despite its academic cast (exegetical and logical reasoning), its length and detail (amounting to overkill at points), and its ponderous and polemical prose.

---

emphasis on the law of God, to study earnestly the ways and means of *applying* scriptural data and principles once they are understood" ("Report of the Committee to Study 'Theonomy,' " June 5, 1979, pp. 6-8). Both reports balanced popular reservations about the theonomic position with supportive considerations. The attempt to block the ordination of a theonomic candidate in Gulf Coast Presbytery (P.C.A.) was overturned by the 1982 General Assembly.

[5] Tape: "The Bahnsen-Feinberg Debate," available from Covenant Media Foundation (800/553-3938), catalog #GB340. The catalog also lists many summaries and explanations of the theonomic position, along with seminary courses and individual topics in Christian ethics.

[6] See the "Symposium on Puritanism and Law," *The Journal of Christian Reconstruction* 5, no. 2 (Winter, 1978-79), *passim,* but especially James B. Jordan's "Calvinism and 'The Judicial Law of Moses,' " pp. 17-48. Even a vehement critic like Meredith G. Kline is compelled to admit that the theonomic position was that of the Westminster Standards: "Comments on an Old-New Error," *Westminster Theological Journal* 41, no. 1 (Fall, 1978): 173, 174.

[7] The P.C.A. pastor who campaigned to disinvite a theonomic speaker from the Pensacola Theological Institute (by distributing a critique written by Robert Strong) and to block ordination of a theonomic candidate (rendered ineffective by the General Assembly) responded to Dr. Joseph Kickasola's inquiry about the basis of his criticisms that he had *not* read the book and did not *need* to in order to see that it was wrong! Chantry tells his readers that they need not check out or study the works of his opponents *(op. cit.,* pp. 11, 12). And Evangel Presbytery's study committee acknowledged that a previous, prejudicial action "was taken without proper study and deliberation"; the committee said, "We admit that many of our minds were made up before we began this study. . . .The vast majority of us voting with the majority had never seen, much less read, a copy of the book" (Report, pp. 4, 14, 15).

The continuing call for this volume has been a surprise to the author, but a gratifying one. This reprinting provides opportunity for a variety of observations about the theonomic viewpoint and opposition to it.

Analysis of the Position

Since "theonomy" simple means "God's law" and has been used in connection with diverse ethical writers (e.g., Geesink, Van Til, Barth, Tillich), the title *Theonomy in Christian Ethics* does not tell us what specific view is taken of the place of God's law in Christian living. Nevertheless, common parlance (if not partisan antipathy) has come to conventionally label the distinctive theses of this book (the ethical perspective of "Reconstructionism") as the "theonomic position." It would be beneficial if its teaching could be summarized.

Before offering an outline, we must be warned that some people have been kept from an accurate analysis of theonomic ethics—sometimes by the author's manner of expression, sometimes because the order of discussion (especially qualifications) is not that expected by some readers, and sometimes because the book has simply not been read, or read completely, or read at a safe distance from distorting preconceptions and prejudices. For instance, a combination of such factors has misled some to maintain that *Theonomy,* because it often speaks of our obligation to the exhaustive details of God's law ("every jot and tittle"), cannot allow any change or advance over the Old Testament at any point, even by God Himself, and must follow without exception every single Old Testament precept strictly, literally (even the cultural trappings necessitate *verbatim* application), and without qualification or modification.[8]

---

[8] For the elements of this composite and grotesque misrepresentation: Robert Strong, "*Theonomy:* Expanded Observations" (privately distributed, 1978), pp. 3-4; Aiken Taylor, "Theonomy Revisited," *The Presbyterian Journal* 37, no. 32 (Dec. 6, 1978): 12, 13; Paul Fowler, "God's Law Free From Legalism" (privately distributed, 1980), pp. 16-27, 84; Report of the Committee to Study 'Theonomy' (Evangel Presbytery, P.C.A., 1979), p. 4; Kline, *op. cit.,* pp. 188, 189; John Zens, "The Believer's Rule of Life" *Baptist Reformation Review* 8, no. 4 (1979): 15, 17, and "This is My

These false depictions cannot be justified from a careful reading of the book. There are no fewer than seventy pages that refer to the progress of revelation and redemptive history, God's right to change the law, exceptions to general continuity, laws which are laid aside, or advances over the Old Covenant. I mentioned "radical differences," "legitimate and noteworthy discontinuities," and laws which have "become obsolete." What *is* championed is "the presumption" of moral continuity between the Testaments. It was clearly spelled out that "if we are to submit to God's law, then we must submit to every bit of it *(as well* as its *own* qualifications)." Because "*only God* has the authority and prerogative to discontinue the binding force of anything He has revealed," we should live by the Old Testament law "except where expressly indicated otherwise."[9]

Furthermore, it should be perfectly plain to any student of Scripture, theonomic or not, that God requires obedience to the underlying principles illustrated by Scripture's cultural expressions. *Theonomy* plainly observed: "the case law illustrates the application or qualification of the principle laid down in the general commandment," and it is "the underlying principle (of which the case law was a particular illustration)" which "has abiding ethical validity."[10] We are not bound to the cultural details of flying axheads and rooftop railings, but to the principles about unpremeditated homicide and safety precautions, etc. Those who have ridiculed the theonomic position for requiring observance of ancient cultural details[11] should give responsible reflection to

---

Beloved Son . . .Hear Him," 7, no. 4 (1978): 24; Gary Long, "Biblical Law and Ethics: Absolute and Covenantal" (paper presented to a Council on Baptist Theology, Dallas, 1980; details of subsequent publication unavailable), pp. 15, 21, 23, 31; Lewis Neilson, *God's Law in Christian Ethics* (Cherry Hill, NJ: Mack Publishing Co., 1979), pp. 37, 54; Leonard Coppes, "Review of *Theonomy,*" *Blue Banner of Faith and Life* 33, no. 1 (Jan., 1978): 30-31; Chantry, *op. cit.,* pp. 43, 47.

[9] See for quotations: pages 92, 211, 304, 306, 307, 356, 417.

[10] See pages 306-08, 516-17.

[11] E.g., Aiken Taylor, "Theonomy and Christian Behavior," *The Presbyterian Journal* 37 (Sept. 13, 1978): pp. 18, 19. At the 1983 General Assembly of the Orthodox Presbyterian Church one delegate, without benefit of adequate research and reason-

their ill-conceived criticism. Such disdain would *equally* ridicule New Testament ethical directives with their cultural trappings as though "Go and do likewise" at the end of the story of the good Samaritan (Luke 10:37) literally obligates us to pour oil and wine on the wounds of half-dead victims of robbery on the Jericho road today, setting them on donkeys (not in cars) and paying for their stay at roadside inns with (literal) denarii. Critical ridicule which is blind to this feature of Biblical interpretation in general is too superficial and inconsistent to warrant serious attention.

A Reformed Seminary professor once told me that what bothered him about *Theonomy* was its repeated stress on obeying "every jot and tittle" of the Old Testament. His complaint was ultimately, then, with the language *Jesus chose to use* in teaching His attitude toward the law (Matt. 5:18). Even though He would qualify it elsewhere, Christ used a *categorical* declaration, expecting it to be our *operating assumption.* Christians can legitimately echo His teaching, likewise acknowledging the qualifications given elsewhere in Scripture. Others have not been kept from discerning my intention (and, I believe, that of Jesus):

> He seems to be arguing that every OT rule is a phrasing for Jewish culture of some principle of mercy, justice and/or truth. And what we need to do is to go to every one of those rules, find that specific or general principle and apply it to our own societies.[12]

The following analysis draws together, clarifies, and states in distilled form the vital teachings elaborated in the full text of *Theonomy in*

---

ing, attempted to discredit an endorsement of the Old Testament prohibition on usury (within the kingdom) by facetiously moving that a loan be secured by pledge of the clerk's left shoe, to be returned prior to sunset—amusing, but with dense understanding of the issues.

[12] William F. Luck, "Book Review: *Theonomy in Christian Ethics*," *Journal of the Evangelical Theological Society* 23, no. 1 (March 1980): 76.

Christian Ethics:

1. Since the Fall it has always been unlawful to use the law of God in hopes of establishing one's own personal merit and justification, in contrast or complement to salvation by way of promise and faith; commitment to obedience is but the lifestyle of faith, a token of gratitude for God's redeeming grace.

2. The word of the Lord is the sole, supreme, and unchallengeable standard for the actions and attitudes of all men in all areas of life; this word naturally includes God's moral directives (law).

3. Our obligation to keep the law of God cannot be judged by any extrascriptural standard, such as whether its specific requirements (when properly interpreted) are congenial to past traditions or modern feelings and practices.

4. We should presume that Old Testament standing laws[13] continue to be morally binding in the New Testament, unless they are rescinded or modified by further revelation.

5. In regard to the Old Testament law, the New Covenant surpasses the Old Covenant in glory, power, and finality (thus reinforcing former duties). The New Covenant also supercedes the Old Covenant shadows, thereby changing the application of sacrificial, purity, and "separation" principles, redefining the people of God, and altering the significance of the promised land.

6. God's revealed standing laws are a reflection of His immutable moral character and, as such, are absolute in the sense of being non-arbitrary, objective, universal, and established in advance of particular circumstances (thus applicable to general types of moral situations).

7. Christian involvement in politics calls for recognition of God's transcendent, absolute, revealed law as a standard by which to judge all social codes.

---

[13] "Standing law" is used here for *policy* directives applicable over time to classes of individuals (e.g., do not kill; children, obey your parents; merchants, have equal measures; magistrates, execute rapists), in contrast to particular directions for an individual (e.g., the order for Samuel to anoint David at a particular time and place) or positive commands for distinct incidents (e.g., God's order for Israel to exterminate certain Canaanite tribes at a certain point in history).

8. Civil magistrates in all ages and places are obligated to conduct their offices as ministers of God, avenging divine wrath against criminals and giving an account on the Final Day of their service before the King of kings, their Creator and Judge.

9. The general continuity which we presume with respect to the moral standards of the Old Testament applies just as legitimately to matters of socio-political ethics as it does to personal, family, or ecclesiastical ethics.

10. The civil precepts of the Old Testament (standing "judicial" laws) are a model of perfect social justice for all cultures, even in the punishment of criminals.

This summary highlights the fact that theonomic ethics, proceeding in terms of salvation by grace alone, (1) is committed to developing an overall Christian world-and-life view (2) according to the regulating principle of *sola Scriptura* (3) and to the hermeneutic of covenant theology (4) instead of dispensationalism (where Old Covenant commandments are deemed abrogated unless repeated in the New Testament).[14] Changes in covenantal administration that are warranted by Scripture (cf. 4) are recognized with the coming of the new and better covenant in Christ (5). Relativism (situationism) is repudiated, and the divinely revealed ethic is not reduced to a parochial or tribal perspective in the evolutionary history of ethics; (6) God's word advances universal justice, not a double-standard of morality.

Rejecting legal positivism, theonomic ethics favors the idea of a "law above the (civil) law" as a protection against the tyranny of rulers and anarchy of reformers (7). Because Christ is Lord over all (cf. 2), it follows that even civil magistrates are His servants and owe obedience to His revealed standards for them (8). There is no justification (cf. 4) for exempting civil authorities from responsibility to the universal standards of justice (cf. 6) found in God's Old Testament revelation (9). Therefore, in the absence of biblically grounded argumentation that

---

[14] E.g., Charles Ryrie, "The End of the Law," *Bibliotheca Sacra* 124 (1967): 239-42.

releases the civil magistrate from Old Testament social norms (cf. 4, 5), it follows from our previous premises that in the exercise of their offices rulers are morally responsible to obey the revealed standards of social justice in the Old Testament law (10). The New Testament explicitly confirms this inference by making magistrates avengers of wrath on evil-doers (Rom. 13:4), making it a lawful use of God's law to restrain the publicly unruly (1 Tim. 1:8-10), and saying that in this law, "every transgression and disobedience received its just recompense of reward" (Heb. 2:2). The law was never viewed as defining justice *exclusively* within the narrow confines of Israel. "All of the statutes" revealed by Moses for the covenant nation were a *model* to be emulated by the *non-covenantal* nations as well—were "your wisdom and understanding in the sight of the peoples, who shall say . . . what great nation is there that has statutes and ordinances so righteous as all this law" (Deut. 4:6-8). Accordingly, the Mosaic law was a standard by which *unredeemed* Canaanite tribes were punished (Lev. 18:24-27) and which "non-theocratic" *rulers* were called to obey (Ps. 119:46; Prov. 16:12) or prophetically denounced for violating (Isa. 14:4-11; Jer. 25:12; Ezek. 28:1-10; Amos 2:1-3; etc.).

My book *The Authority of God's Law Today* (Texas: Geneva Press [708 Hamvassy Road, Tyler, TX 75701], 1983) explains the position outlined above, providing a popular presentation of theonomic ethics that is much shorter and less technical than *Theonomy*. It also summarizes replies to critics of the position.[15]

Differences in Exegesis, Application

Our outline of the theonomic perspective indicates that it pertains to fundamental, underlying ethical principles and is not, as such, committed to distinctive interpretations and applications of the Old

[15] Theonomic ethics is also condensed in my lengthy essay, "God's Law and Gospel Prosperity," which is available from Covenant Media Foundation. This essay was abbreviated for publication as "The Authority of God's Law" in *The Presbyterian Journal* 37, no. 32 (Dec. 6, 1978): 9-12, 21-22. (See also footnote no. 5 above.)

Testament moral directives. In the nature of the case, these principles leave plenty of room for disagreements in biblical exegesis (for prescriptive premises), observation of the world (for factual premises), and reasoning (for logically drawing an application). Thus theonomists will not necessarily agree with each other's every interpretation and ethical conclusion. For instance, many (like myself) do not affirm R. J. Rushdoony's view of the dietary laws, Gary North's view of home mortgages, James Jordan's stance on automatic infant communion (without sessional examination), or David Chilton's attitudes toward bribery and "ripping off" the unbeliever.[16] Nevertheless, all share the basic perspective reflected in the above ten propositions. *Theonomy* does not make the determination of our moral obligations or the elucidation of God's commands a cut-and-dried, easy, obvious, or simplistic task. It rather advocates a basic *approach* to ethical questions which still requires (even if it does not always get) skilled exegesis and sensitive application. It does not automatically remove all difficulties in ethical reasoning, and theonomists certainly do not "have all the answers"! I have made such observations before.[17]

Misrepresentations by Critics

Often enough critics of the theonomic position have unfairly attributed to it claims which are *quite contrary* to what it teaches or which do *not logically follow* from the ten propositions outlined above. Such inaccurate representations may make criticism easier, but simultaneously make it irrelevant since it misses the intended target.

A case in point are theonomic beliefs about the nature, coming, and effects of God's kingdom—something touched upon in over ninety

---

[16] Rushdoony, *Institutes,* pp. 297-302; North, "Response to John Mitchell on Usury" (essay distributed by Chalcedon [Box 158, Vallecito, CA 95251] 1977), p. 4; Jordan, "Theses on Paedocommunion," *The Geneva Papers,* special edition (from Geneva Divinity School, Tyler, TX, 1982); Chilton, *op. cit.,* pp. 74, 138.

[17] See pages xxxv, xxxvi, 454, 532.

references in *Theonomy*.[18] These pages indicate that theonomists reject any combination of grace and self-effort (works) in salvation, finding even the dynamic for sanctification in the Holy Spirit's internal work. The kingdom of God, an international community of faith, comes by the Spirit's gracious power working through evangelistic preaching and Christian nurture. As converts strive to grow in holiness, they desire to keep God's commandments—recognizing the literary, logical, and hermeneutical differences between laws of a summary nature ("moral") and those of an explanatory and illustrative nature ("judicial"). Because they want to obey God in all areas of life (home, church, and even state), Christians will seek to persuade their civil leaders to honor the principles of those laws from God (and only those) which are relevant to the power of the sword in Scripture. They realize this is what *ought* to take place, whether or not they have the millennial confidence that such reform efforts *will* see success in the long run.

Therefore, it is mean, illogical, and inexcusable propaganda for some theonomic critics to dismiss it as allegedly: (1) Judaizing the New Testament, (2) making the law our dynamic of sanctification, (3) denying any distinction between moral and judicial laws, (4) taking the civil use of God's law as the way of bringing in His kingdom, (5) wishing to impose the kingdom by the sword, (6) asking the state to enforce all the Mosaic laws and curb all outward evil, (7) shifting emphasis from personal piety, evangelism, and the church so as to stress instead the cultural mandate, politics, and capital punishment, (8) demanding postmillennial eschatology, or (9) viewing America as God's chosen nation.[19]

---

[18] Especially in the Preface and chapters 1, 4, 7, 8, 9, 19, 20, 23, 25, and Appendix 2.

[19] Such false portrayals are set forth, for instance, by: Aiken Taylor, "Theonomy and Christian Behavior," p. 9; Gary Long, *op. cit.*, p. 23; Paul Fowler, *op. cit.*, pp. 3, 29, 30, 39ff., 46, 59; Walter Chantry, *op. cit.*, pp. 17, 21, 23, 25, 26, 29, 37, 43, 54, 61, 99, 100, 111; Meredith G. Kline, *op. cit.*, pp. 172, 174, 186-87, 178-86; Robert Strong, *op. cit.*, pp. 1-2; Lewis Neilson, *op. cit.*, pp. 15, 20, 21, 23, 28, 49 and chap. 3; Donald Dunkerley, "What is Theonomy?" (privately distributed from McIlwain Memorial

Three more major misrepresentations, dealing with the status of Old Covenant Israel, deserve special mention. Some claim (10) that theonomists seek to establish a church-state today. Others allege the opposite: (11) that *Theonomy* says the Old Covenant form of the kingdom has not changed, wherein separation of the religious cult (strictly equated with the New Covenant church) from the state (which was no different from civil rule in any other nation) was total and rigid—making Israel's church-state relationship identical with the relationship called for today. Finally, it has been pretended (12) that *Theonomy* overlooks or logically denies the typological character of the Old Covenant economy as a special redemptive-historical prototype of Christ's coming kingdom.[20] Once again, however, a *multitude* of references from *Theonomy* disprove such false reports; for example, in a response to Kline I could allude to over fifty places in the book which countered his characterization.[21] That is hardly acceptable performance for scholarly circles. Let it suffice to observe here that chapter 20 argues from Old and New Testaments in favor of an institutional separation of church and state; acknowledging "legitimate and noteworthy differences" between the Old Covenant order and the situation today, I maintained that "a parallel" exists with the church-state relation, but *not* an equation. Finally, "with respect to typology, it might be suggested that Israel as a nation is a type of the church of Christ. There

---

Presbyterian Church, Pensacola, FL, in 1978), p. 3; R. Laird Harris, "*Theonomy in Christian Ethics:* A Review," *Presbyterian* 5, no. 1 (Spring, 1979): 1, 9, 14, 15; Jerram Barrs, Tape: "The Law of Moses Today" (Hampshire, GB: L'Abri Cassettes [no. 98.4], 1978); John Van Til, "Books: *God's Righteous Kingdom*, by Walter Chantry," *Christianity Today*, 25, no. 18 (Oct. 23, 1981): 72.

[20] Counterfeit claims of this nature are pushed, for instance, by Chantry, *op. cit.*, p. 52; Long, *op. cit.*, p. 23; Kline, *op. cit.*, pp. 173, 175-78, 181-82; Fowler, *op. cit.*, pp. 3, 29-31, 33, 37, 56-58; Harris, *op. cit.*, p. 11; O. Palmer Robertson, Tapes: "Analysis of Theonomy" (Mt. Olive Tape Library tapes no. OR1O7Al, A2, A3 [Mt. Olive, MS 39119], 1979); H. Hanko, "An Exegetical Refutation of Postmillennialism," *Protestant Reformed Theological Journal* 11, no. 2 (April, 1978), p. 40.

[21] Greg L. Bahnsen, "M. G. Kline on Theonomic Politics: An Evaluation of His Reply," *Journal of Christian Reconstruction* 6, no. 2 (Winter, 1979-80), pp. 195-221.

is certainly scriptural warrant for that comparison."[22] Such were the book's own words. And these views falsely attributed to theonomic ethics are *not logically essential* to it (as analyzed above) to begin with, anyway.

Critical discussions of *Theonomy* which relied at heart entirely upon these last two kinds of misrepresentation must be judged failures through inaccuracy: for instance Robertson's (where the identity of cultic-civic relations between Old and New Covenants was called *Theonomy's* distinctive thesis and foundational problem)[23] and Fowler's (where a "sharp" church-state separation was exaggerated so much that *Theonomy* allegedly allowed *nothing unique* about Israel's civil order).[24] A similar attack on a straw man is found in Kline's surprisingly vehement and vitriolic review article, where readers were misled about *Theonomy's* view of Israel's typological significance.[25] Kline barely touched the actual theonomic position anywhere—and not at all when speaking of its "radical fault." He seemed to reason fallaciously that *some* discontinuity between Old Covenant Israel and modern nations proves *complete* discontinuity and that any typological value in Israel's

---

[22] See for these quotations: pages 401-02, 417, 440.

[23] O. Palmer Robertson, Tapes: "Analysis of Theonomy." Crucial conceptual ambiguities further hamper this treatment (e.g., the Israelite *state* was a "redemptive community" with a "cultic dimension" in all its laws, which can be applied only with "flexibility" today). Since Robertson questions the continuing validity of laws which are "civil" in nature, how can he rescue the sixth and eighth commandments of the Decalogue? His attempts to make the penal sanctions ceremonial in nature or applicable today to excommunication or the last judgment are already refuted in *Theonomy,* pp. 434-35.

[24] Paul Fowler, "God's Law Free From Legalism," pp. 29, 31, 37, 56. Fowler arrogantly declared that his characterization *could not* be *unjust* since he constructed it from quotations (p. 58). It may be replied that he should have attended to *further* quotations from the same source.

[25] Meredith G. Kline, "Comments on an Old-New Error." Forecasting the perceived weakness of his effort, Kline would not publish his article in the *Westminster Theological Journal* without assurances from its editor (his former student) that no replies to it would be allowed. Readers were left with maximal rhetoric and minimal proof as a result.

civil policy meant it was *merely* typological (and not also definitive of justice). Kline's major conceptual error is to speak as though civil "justice" in the same kind of case can be completely different in two cultures ("cultural relativism"). The critical arguments he advanced against theonomic ethics had already been answered in the book, and he attempted *no biblical demonstration* of anything contradictory to the book's conclusions anyway.

Efforts at Refutation

Critics who aim to disprove the validity of some *portion* of the law by *appealing to some special feature* (F) about Old Testament Israel must (1) define clearly what is meant by F, (2) delineate on principle the intended segment of the law, (3) show that F was actually and uniquely the case, and especially (4) demonstrate that the validity of this portion of the law rested solely on F. Popular discussions which appeal to a word like 'theocracy' often fail at step *1,* unwittingly begging the question. By nowhere indicating why laws were included or excluded from his categorization of "religious crimes," Neilson stumbled at step *2.*[26] The downfall of many discussions has been step *3.* Neilson and Fowler were mistaken to think everything in Israel was fused into a "church-state" (Uzziah the king would then hardly have been culpable for doing priestly work), and Robertson and Harris incorrectly claimed that all citizens had to be members of the sacred community by circumcision (thereby disenfranchising women and sojourners, who had the same civic protections and duties as circumcised native men).[27] Finally, the arguments of men like Fowler (even *if* Israel were a church-state) and like Kline (rightly taking Israel as a redemptive type and holy nation) are without cogency because the unique features to which they appeal were *not necessary* to the Mosaic law's validity—given the fact (observed

---

[26] Neilson, *op. cit.,* pp. 5-10, 23.

[27] Fowler, *op. cit.,* pp. 89-93; Neilson, *op. cit.,* pp. 25, 34, 35; Harris, *op. cit.,* p.13; Robertson, tapes referred to earlier. See chapter 20 in *Theonomy.*

above) that all of its statutes were a moral standard published for "non-theocratic" nations *as well as* for Israel.[28]

Critics like Jon Zens thus aim to lay aside the *whole* Mosaic law by *appealing to* the establishment of *the New Covenant,* arguing that a new covenant brings a new law-code and saying we must now heed Christ rather than Moses.[29] This approach carries little plausibility, though, when we recall that Christ and His apostles endorsed the validity of every Old Covenant Scripture, command, word, letter, and stroke (1 Tim. 3:16-17; James 2:10; Matt. 4:4; 5:18-19)! The *New* Covenant itself writes *the law* known in the *Old* Covenant (in Jeremiah's day) on our hearts today (Jer. 31:33; Heb. 8:10). Christ, you see, directs us to obey Moses as well!

Exegetical attempts to thwart theonomic conclusions have been linguistically, logically, and hermeneutically flawed. Fowler's (revised) treatment of Matthew 5:17-20 made it refer to Christ's foreshadowed redemptive work, but only by suppressing the immediate context (which obviously deals with the ethic of His followers). By making "one jot or one tittle" the antecedent of "all things" in verse 18, his interpretation violated Greek grammar, and the verse was made self-contradictory by Fowler assigning contrary referents to the temporal clauses and over-looking the absence of any subordinating conjunction between them.[30]

---

[28] This thesis is demonstrated in chapter 18 of *Theonomy;* it undermines Carl Henry's reasoning, *op. cit.,* p. 448. Henry also overlooks the book's argument against the claim that the Mosaic penal sanctions represented "heightened retribution" (pp. 456-58).

[29] See many of the articles Zens has written or published as editor of *Baptist Reformation Review,* especially: "Is There a 'Covenant of Grace'?" (vol. 6, no. 3), "Crucial Thoughts Concerning 'Law' in the New Covenant" (vol. 7, no. 3), "This is My Beloved Son. . . . Hear Him" (vol. 7, no. 4), "The Believer's Rule of Life" (vol. 8, no. 4), and " 'As I Have Loved You': The Starting Point of Christian Obedience" (vol. 9, no. 2). See also Gary Long, "Biblical Law and Ethics: Absolute and Cov-enantal."

[30] Fowler, *op. cit.,* pp. 71-75, 80. (His *original* paper denied that v. 19 spoke of the law's minutiae!) Cf. Blass and DeBrunner's *A Greek Grammar* (University of Chicago Press, 1961), section 135.

Contrary to linguistic usage and local context, Long's study pressed "Law or Prophets" (v. 17) to denote literary *types* (commands, prophecies) and not merely canonical divisions (e.g., the Pentateuch). He also mistakenly attributed *relative negation* to verse 17 ("not to abrogate, but to fulfill"), for it lacks the paradoxical introductory formula found with its use elsewhere (e.g., Mark 9:37; John 12:44).[31] Fowler and Long both find themselves unable to weaken the law's endorsement in this passage by *exegetical* considerations and are forced in the end to import theological considerations (drawn from *other* passages) to argue for their qualifications on it.

Chantry aimed to dismiss the judicial law (but *not* the *whole* Mosaic code) by reasoning (illogically) from Galatians 3:15-4:11 that the dismissed "schoolmaster" was harsh, the Mosaic judicial law was harsh, and so Paul's dismissed "schoolmaster" must have been the judicial law.[32] One could analogously argue: red is a color, blue is a color, and so red is blue. The Mosaic code was *not* harsh (cf. Ps. 19). Paul spoke of "rudiments" (4:3, 9; cf. Col. 2:16-20), including feasts and circumcision (2:14; 4:10), which were a "tutor to Christ" by teaching we are "justified by faith" (3:24). Only the *ceremonial* law fits this description. Poythress suggested that new (civil?) sanctions of providing for one's enemies (Matt. 5:21-22, 38-43 with Rom. 12:17-21) have now, with Christ's intensified presence, replaced the Mosaic penal code.[33] This is hardly credible (is the *state* to feed and pray for the rapist as "punishment"?), and it misses the very reason (given in the verses *immediately following* those cited by Poythress) why we do not avenge ourselves: because God has appointed a *sword-bearing* magistrate to "avenge wrath against evil-doers" (Rom. 13:4). Nor is Poythress correct to make the Mosaic law depend on the Levitical priesthood. Deuteronomy 17:8-13 simply required appellate experts in the law (here Levites, but every

---

[31] Long, *op. cit.,* pp.14-20, 30-34. In Matthew 5:17 Christ *twice denies* what Long claims He was (relatively) doing: abrogating the Old Covenant laws.

[32] Chantry, *op. cit.,* pp. 111-12, 117 (cf. pp. 108-10, 121, 123).

[33] Vern Poythress, Tape: "A Critique of Theonomy" (Philadelphia: Westminster Media, 1979); cf. Harris, *op. cit.,* pp. 11, 13.

system of law has the same), and the "change of law" in Hebrews 7:12 *just is* the *individual* change of tribal prerequisite for priests (as the context shows: vv. 11-16), *not* an *entire* revolution of moral regime *accompanying* it.

Attempts have been made to counter theonomic ethics by various fallacious moves. Appeals to New Testament silence[34] are refuted by the established *presumption* of moral continuity (Deut. 4:2) and by the fact that the New Testament is *not* silent (Matt. 15:3-4; Heb. 2:2; Rom. 13:4; 1 Tim. 1:8-10). Neilson has vainly argued that when supposed evidence *for* theonomic ethics in the New Testament is laid aside, one (surprisingly?) does not get the (subjective) *impression* from the rest of the New Testament that the Mosaic civil code is endorsed for today.[35] Aiken Taylor, though, has used perhaps the least acceptable method of all, pointing to what he feels are *horrid examples* of what the law required, then holding up the use of these commands today to virtual ridicule.[36] Even if he could demonstrate that such laws are invalidated today (and he has failed to do so), he still owes them respect as the holy word of God (at least intended for Israel to keep). We dare not become those who "speak against and judge the law" (James 4:11).

Finally, Harris fears that terrible consequences (e.g., an inquisition) might result from unbelievers' striving to submit to the Mosaic judicial laws; instead he would have them rule nations by the compass of common grace and general revelation, which is to say by the voice of conscience.[37] This suggestion not only wrongly assumes that natural revelation communicates a different moral standard than special revelation (contrary to Rom. 1-3), it actually turns us over to the *worst kind of tyranny*—political might which is *unrestrained* by an *objective*, publicly

---

[34] E.g., Neilson, *op. cit.*, pp. 11, 14, 19, 23, 27, 29, 30, 38, 39, 45, 47, 51; Fowler, *op. cit.*, pp. 52-56; Dunkerley, *op. cit.*, p. 2; Strong, *op. cit.*, pp. 2-4; Henry, *op. cit.*, p. 448.

[35] Neilson, *op. cit.*, pp. 11-12, 24-31, 39-41, 48, 50-53.

[36] Taylor, "Theonomy and Christian Behavior," pp. 18, 19; "Theonomy Revisited," p. 13.

[37] Harris, *op. cit.*, pp. 10, 12, 13, 14; cf. Henry, *op. cit.*, p. 449.

accessible, written standard by which even the state's actions can be judged. If we will not have *inscripturated* morality *from God* as our socio-political standard, we have *no principle* to protect us from those who wish to *play god.*

A detailed answer to all of the critics of theonomic ethics can be found in my book, *The Debate Over God's Law.*[38] After six years of listening to them closely, I am more than ever convinced that whatever mistakes have been made are not big and obvious, but extremely subtle. Our national experience increasingly confirms my belief that we need something very much like what I try to say herein.

Greg L. Bahnsen
Orange, California
July 4, 1983

---

[38] This book was never published. However, much of the material responding to critics of *Theonomy* was later published in the book: *No Other Standard: Theonomy and Its Critics*, (Institute for Christian Economics, Tyler, TX: 1991).

PREFACE TO THE FIRST EDITION

CENTRAL to the theory and practice of Christian ethics, whether personal or social, is every jot and tittle of God's law as laid down in the revelation of the Older and New Testaments. The Christian is obligated to keep the whole law of God as a pattern of sanctification, and in the realm of human society the civil magistrate is responsible to enforce God's law against public crime. These themes, as elementary as they may seem, have been my concern in the present study.

I have not attempted to offer a commentary on the particulars of God's law as found in the Bible. While such a discussion of the specific commandments of God would follow naturally upon the conclusion of this study, it is not the primary purpose of the study itself. Instead I aim to demonstrate from Scripture that we have an ethical obligation to keep all of God's law. It is this formal requirement, rather than the details of the law or even the procedure for activating society and its rulers to observe that law, that I have taken as the subject matter for analysis. If Christians do not first realize their obligation and privilege to keep the law of God in its entirety they will not proceed to implement such obedience (by the enabling power of the Holy Spirit) in their own lives as well as the lives of their neighbors. Moreover, the failure to recognize that the Lord requires us to obey His word in exhaustive detail is itself a failure in Christian morality—not simply an insignificant slip in abstract, mental theologizing. Thus I have seen fit to concentrate in this book on the issue of formal obligation in ethics: the normative perspective, the authoritative guide, in godly morality.

Two comments follow from the foregoing observations. First, the reader is cautioned not to mistake what is taught herein with whatever distortions or abuses of the theonomic principle that might be unearthed in the history of the church. I am defending what I take to be the biblical position respecting ethics, not any particular past theological school or social group. Abuses and misuses of the thesis propounded in this study must be recognized as just that: abuses and misuses. Second, the present study leaves a great deal to be explored and discussed in Christian ethics as well as extensive room for disagreement in the area of exegeting, understanding, and applying God's law in specific situations. Two people can submit to the exhaustive theonomic principle in Christian ethics while disagreeing on a particular moral question (e.g., whether a certain biblical command is ceremonial or moral, whether lying is ever condoned by God, etc.). Thus agreement with the thesis of this book is not contingent upon agreement in every particular moral issue or specific interpretation of a scriptural text.

Although there may be some differences among those adhering to a theonomic ethic, they who wish to follow the whole of God's law as their moral principle are definitely set apart in theological-ethical alignment from those pseudo-teachers who impugn the integrity of God's word and the validity of His law, and the unorthodox churchmen who replace God's direction with that of man or who presume to amend the stipulations of the Lord, and those who force Scripture onto a dispensational Procrustean bed, and finally the proponents of redirecting the focus of Christian life and behavior into a narrow ecclesiasticism. The advocates of a theonomic ethic, contrary to many popular theological fads, hold that God's commandments (inclusive of the Older Testament) are neither mere artifacts in a religious museum nor suspended ideals (over an age of parenthesis) appropriate only for the coming day of consummation.

The biblical backing for theonomic ethics is rehearsed in the following pages. And because it has not been possible within the limits of space to transcribe fully every scriptural citation to which reference is made, the reader is encouraged to examine the following treatise with the Bible in hand. The full force of any argument is naturally dulled if the reader is unfamiliar with the text cited, and the author's thought is better understood (as well as evaluated) if all the biblical references are looked up as the reader progresses through the present study. It is my prayer that, in so doing, readers will be led to respond to God's word (rather than the author's opinions) and return Christian ethics to its proper position of strength and direction in the home, church, and state through submission as redeemed men, in the power of the Holy Spirit, to every stipulation of God's revealed law. This is the best way to manage our lives because it is God's way to manage our lives. Because God does not merely love us in some vague and general way, He has delivered to us more than simply a few general and vague moral principles; instead He has set down specific and extensive commands since He cares for *every specific* of our lives as His people. Because He has first loved us we must love Him—by keeping His commandments. Hence the examination which follows, although being apologetical in mood, is nonetheless a rehearsal of God's love for us; should it be treated only as an academic argument, the following study would, to the extent it faithfully teaches the word of Christ, be deprived of both spiritual power and the ability to generate wonder and gratitude in response to the thoroughgoing love of God for us.

According to God's word our love for the Lord (expressed in obedience to His law) should eventuate in love for our neighbors. Consequently, the Christian has a duty, not only personally and privately to do that which is pleasing in the sight of God, but to exercise *public* and *social* responsibility as well. We must endeavor to do that which is best for the welfare of our neighbor, and theonomic ethics maintains that this welfare is produced and guarded by the stipulations of God's law. Hence my present thesis is not restricted to the individual's personal obligation to keep God's law, but I have gone on to discuss the public obligation to promote and enforce obedience to God's law in society as well. It is perhaps here that many will be challenged to re-think their initial ideas. Since the common practice is to ignore God's law in social and political matters, we are often lulled into thinking that there is no other way of doing things than according to the basic (antinomian) *status quo.* It is a difficult thing to re-orient your thinking so as to make every thought subject to the word of Christ, and the author certainly felt that difficulty when the time came to recognize inconsistency and unfaithfulness to Scripture in his own social ethic. However, difficult though it be, the Christian (especially in this day) must come to grips with the full obligations of the Christian ethic. God's law requires some very stern, although blessed, things to be done in society; His commandments require us to change many things that are now commonplace in social behavior and political policy. Yet, once you stand back and think about it, it is not really so startling that God's standards should entail radical readjustment of fallen ideas, new patterns of social behavior, a turning of the world upside-down. The reader should be willing to investigate the idea that God's law as revealed in Scripture ought to direct society and the civil magistrate today. A society which is to reflect *Christian* morality is a society which has the full, distinctive *law of God* for its direction. Should the reader disagree, I would have to ask, why should it be important for Christians to exercise social responsibility (loving their neighbors)—even within the power structure—if what they do in society and the state is to be guided by the same standards which non-Christians apply?

Enough has now been said about the purposes and themes of the present publication to indicate to the reader what this book is about and basically where the author stands. With respect to the production of this volume I have many thanks to extend. The patience and encouragement of my wife, Cathie, were invaluable over the months during which I labored on the manuscript (as well as on my master's thesis in theology which has been worked into portions of the book). I am very thankful for the writings of R. J. Rushdoony as well as for his personal discussions with me on the subject of God's law. Past authors such as Calvin and Fairbairn, as well as current writers like Kevan, H. Ridderbos, Cornelius Van Til, and especially John Murray, have been of great instructional value to me along the way to authoring this study. My personal thanks is also extended to instructor John Frame of Westminster Theological Seminary for the education of my thinking which he effected; his courses and personal conversations have been, not only an aid in grounding and clarifying my thesis, but even more "theology" (or "doctrine") in that best sense in which he defines it. Standing on the shoulders of these, my mentors, if I disagree with any element of their thinking, it is hopefully only in terms of principles which they have taught me that I have differed in that slight degree. The many fruitful discussions and technical aid of my very good friends,

Dennis Johnson and Roger Wagner, will always be remembered with appreciation; specifically I thank Dennis Johnson for proofreading the manuscript, and Roger Wagner for his extensive and inestimable help in compiling the Scripture Index. I am also grateful to Jim Jordan for his unselfish assistance in compiling one of the indices, and to Mrs. Paul Picard for valuable secretarial help in preparing the indices for printing.

GREG L. BAHNSEN
November 7, 1972 (Election Day)
North Wales, Pennsylvania

During the past four years while this manuscript was in the printer's hands, our nation has seen how important it is to have a "law above the law."

Jackson, Mississippi
July 4, 1976

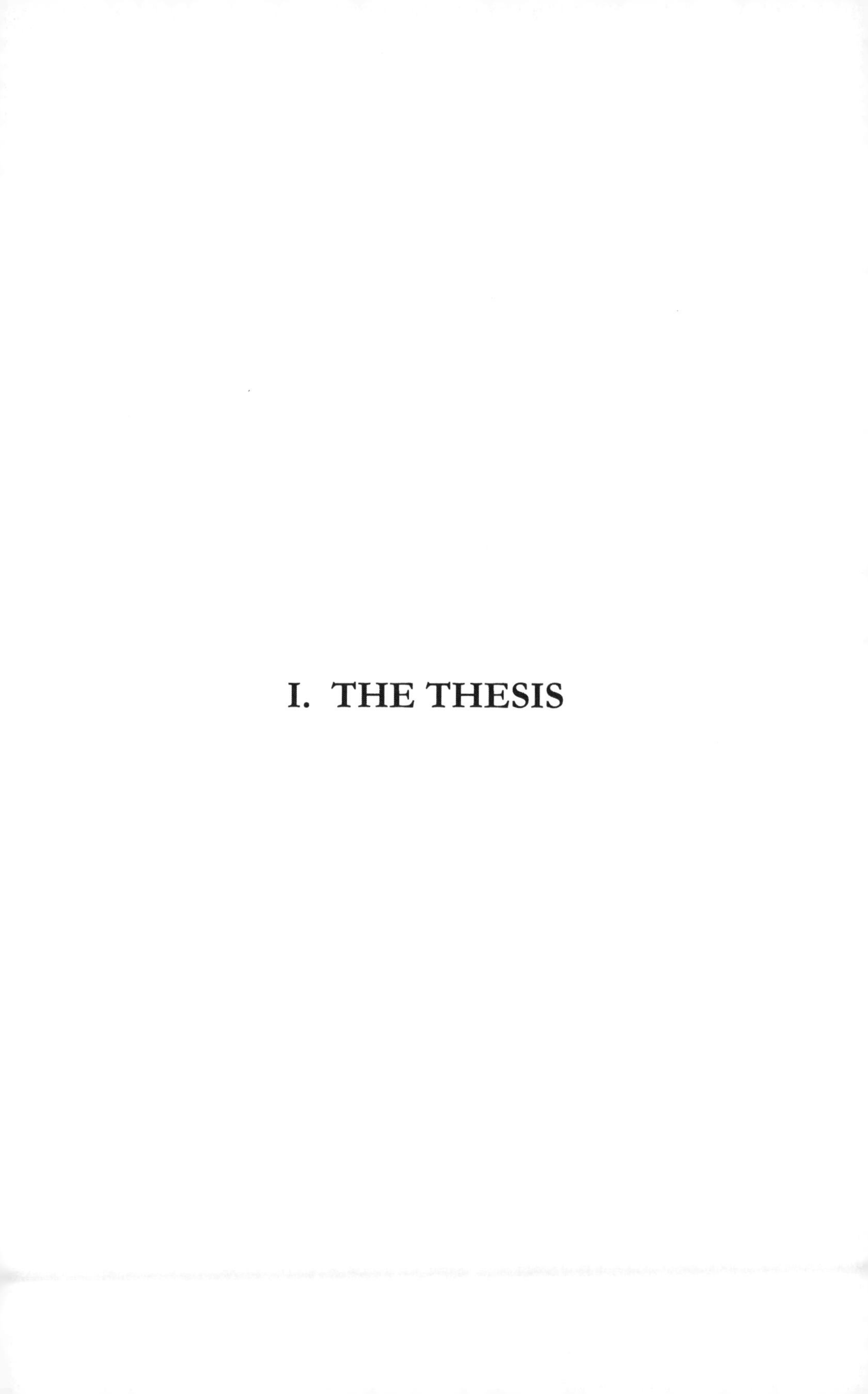

I. THE THESIS

Chapter 1
INTRODUCTION:

THE PROBLEM

AS the early church formulated its creeds it simultaneously reformulated civil law. Such a correlation was inevitable since, against the ancient pagan tradition that located the source of authority and morality in the *polis,* orthodox Christian creedalism asserted the sovereignty of the Creator over history and the incursion of the Messianic God-man into history. Thus the early creeds were a declaration concerning, not only theology proper, but eschatology and ethics; the course of history and the source of ethical authority were both found in the transcendent and immanent, self-contained ontological Trinity. The word of this God was clearly pertinent to every aspect of man's historical existence since Christ, the Word of God, was seen as prophet, priest, and king over man and history. The sovereignty of the state was challenged by the sovereign rule of Christ, and canon law endeavored to bring all of life under the norms of God's law. Western liberty, constitutionalism, and morality stem from the early creeds of Christendom as the alternative to the messianic claims of the secular state. Whereas the Roman senate had to approve the gods (thus bringing Tertullian's ridicule), the Christian creeds affirmed God's authority over all creation, attributing all authority in heaven and earth to Christ. Therefore, the state had only a *derivative* authority as a minister of justice under Christ and His word. The political source of law, then, traced back, not to Caesar, but ultimately to Christ and God's law.[1]

During a time of increasing nominalism the medieval church of Rome steadily divorced canon law from the revealed law of Scripture.

[1] Rousas John Rushdoony, *The Foundations of Social Order: Studies in the Creeds* and *Councils of the Early Church* (Presbyterian and Reformed Publishing Co., 1968), passim.

This procedure facilitated the growing absolutism of the state, as did also the dichotomy between the realms of nature and grace posited by Aquinas. Nominalism and dualism contributed to the separation of natural reason and scriptural revelation, which in turn assigned matters of politics to a realm independent of God's word and its norms. The Reformation took a decided stand against this trend, challenging both antinomianism and totalitarianism in the name of God's law. John Calvin broke with the view that the state was autonomous, arguing for the sole rule of Christ over both church and state (as well as the non-interference between the official bodies). He reopened the way to a Christian view of the state, taking it to be subject, not to the church, but only to the laws of God. Since all authority in human society derived from God, held Calvin, religious influence should be brought to bear on the magistrates, and God should be held the "president and judge" of all elections. The Kingly rule of Christ over even the state, taken to be a minister of justice, was reaffirmed.[2] Calvin maintained that "a perfect pattern of righteousness stands forth in the law . . . one everlasting and unchangeable rule to live by"; this holy standard "is just as applicable to every age, even to the end of the world."[3] His conviction is reflected in the Geneva Confession of Faith of 1536, a confession intended for the entire community:

> Because there is one only Lord and Master who has dominion over our consciences, and because his will is the only principle of all justice, we confess all our life ought to be ruled in

---

[2] Herman Dooyeweerd, *The Christian Idea of the State*, trans. John Kraay, University Series: Historical Studies, ed. Rousas J. Rushdoony (Nutley, New Jersey: The Craig Press, 1968), pp.18-20; J. Marcllus Kik, *Church and State: The Story of Two Kingdoms* (New York: Thomas Nelson and Sons, 1963), pp. 83-85; John T. McNeill, *The History and Character of Calvinism* 2nd ed. (New York: Oxford University Press, 1967 [reprinted 1970]), pp. 184-190.

[3] John Calvin, *Institutes of the Christian Religion*, trans. Ford Lewis Battles, ed. John T. McNeill, The Library of Christian Classics, Vols. 20, 21, eds. John Baillie, John T. McNeill, and Henry P. Van Dusen (Philadelphia: The Westminster Press, 1967), (Book II, Chapter VII, section 13)20:362.

> accordance with the commandments of his holy law in which is contained all perfection of justice, and that we ought to have no other rule of good and just living, nor invent other good works to supplement it than those which are there contained, as follows: Exodus 20: "I am the Lord thy God, who brought thee," and so on.[4]

In article 21 of the same confession Calvin wrote that magistrates, in performing their office, serve God and follow a Christian vocation: Christians were bound to obey the ruler's statutes unless they contravened the commandments of God. Hence Calvin saw the law of God as directing life into the paths of righteousness; it was taken to be as applicable to the individual believer as to the society in which he lived, in which society it served to restrain the public evil of men. Consequently, in his commentary on Psalm 72 Calvin wrote:

> By the terms *righteousness* and *judgment,* the Psalmist means a due and well-regulated administration of government, which he opposes to the tyrannical and unbridled license of heathen kings, who, despising God, rule according to the dictates of their own will. . . . From the words we learn by the way, that no government in the world can be rightly managed but under the conduct of God, and by the guidance of the Holy Spirit. . . . But in requesting that the righteousness and judgment of God may be given to kings, he reminds them that none are fit for occupying that exalted station, except in so far as they are formed for it by the hand of God. . . . David teaches us that the people would enjoy prosperity and happiness, when the affairs of the nation were administered according to the principles of righteousness. . . . But it is a truth

---

[4] J. K. S. Reid, trans., "The Geneva Confession of 1536," *Reformed Confessions of the 16th Century: Edited, with Historical Introductions*, ed. Arthur C. Cochrane (Philadelphia: The Westminster Press, 1966), Article 3, pp. 120-121.

> which ought to be borne in mind, that kings can keep themselves within the bounds of justice and equity only by the grace of God; for when they are not governed by the Spirit of righteousness proceeding from heaven, their government is converted into a system of tyranny and robbery.[5]

The words of David to which Calvin refers are a prayer that God would give His law judgments unto the king; quite properly Calvin took this both typically (referring to the Messiah) and ethically (referring to those who rule in the temporal realm). The use of God's law by the civil magistrate is graphically portrayed in a painting by Paul Robert which is in the old Supreme Court Building, Lausanne, Switzerland; it is titled *Justice Instructing the Judges* and portrays Justice as pointing her sword to a book upon which are the words "The Law of God."[6] Such was the legacy of the Reformation. In agreement with the orthodox creeds of the early church, the Reformers maintained that state government was a vicegerent of God and His absolute law—rather than God and morality being the arbitrary tools of an absolute state (as in Machiavelli's *The Prince*,[7] first written in 1513).

In antipathy to the idea that the state is obligated to be subservient to God's authority and direction, the Enlightenment reasserted the autonomy of the modern state.

> In the seventeenth century, for the first time in a thousand years in Western history, a deliberate attempt was made on a grand scale to organize a religiously neutral civilization—a

---

[5] John Calvin, *Commentary on the Book of Psalms*, trans. James Anderson, Calvin's Commentaries, vol. 3 (Grand Rapids: Wm. B. Eerdmans Publishing Co., 1845 [reprinted 1948, 1963]), pp. 102, 103, 104-5.

[6] Francis A. Schaeffer, *Escape From Reason* (Chicago: InterVarsity Press, 1968), pp. 80-81.

[7] Niccolo Machiavelli, *The Prince and the Discourses*, trans. Luigi Ricci (rev. E. R. P. Vincent), The Modern Library of the World's Best Books (New York: The Modern Library, Random House, Inc., 1940).

political, economic, ethical and intellectual structure independent of Christianity. This great transformation was effected in the seventeenth and eighteenth centuries by the movement sometimes described as the *Enlightenment*. . . . Modern Western culture, whatever its positive meaning, may be distinguished from that of earlier phases by its emancipation from explicit Christian direction. . . . The basis for political decisions in this modern system was to be dynastic or national power and glory. . . . But the point that concerns us here is that the international law has been conceived as independent of Christianity, and that with certain exceptions, the states inhabited by Christians have thus made their decisions on avowedly a-Christian grounds in this modern period.

In their domestic policies also, these modern Western states have no longer recognized Christian criteria for policy. . . . But the emergence and prevalence of the theory of "sovereignty" show that in fact the modern state has insisted on its independence of and superiority to Christian direction. The actual criterion has been the military, commercial, and general economic welfare of the state. The modern state has generally declined to serve as the "secular arm" of a Christian society, and the political influence of the Christian churches has been confined to secondary and indirect manifestations. Modern political thought has found the governing sanctions for political association in the nature of man in general, without benefit of biblical revelation or ecclesiastical authorities. . . . Modern Christians have generally thought and acted in politics independently of their faith. . . . Whichever way they turned, however, these states have generally conceived their decisions as having been formed by natural reason apart from any specifically Christian direction. . . . And the nineteenth century continued the trend toward the religious neutrality of the state.[8]

---

[8] James Hastings Nichols, *History of Christianity 1650-1950: Secularization of the West* (New York: The Ronald Press Co., 1956), pp. 6, 7, 8.

The modern period, marked by increasing criticism of biblical Christianity[9] and a philosophically imposed cleavage between facts and values,[10] witnessed the merging of the notions of power and authority in politics.[11] No longer was government seen as resting upon the shoulder of the God-man, the Messianic Prince of Peace, but civil authority was taken to be the result of an ancestral or limiting-concept "social

---

[9] For instance, cf. Colin Brown, *Philosophy and the Christian Faith: A Historical Sketch from the Middle Ages to the Present Day* (London: Tyndale Press, 1969); Oswald T. Allis, *The Old Testament: Its Claims and Its Critics* (Presbyterian and Reformed Publishing Co., 1972), chap. 4; Werner Georg Kümmel, *The New Testament: The History of the Investigation of its Problems*, trans. S. MacLean Gilmour and Howard C. Kee (New York: Abington Press, 1972).

[10] Cf. W. T. Jones, *A History of Western Philosophy,* (New York: Harcourt, Brace and World, Inc., 1952), 2:847-870; James H. Olthuis, *Facts, Values and Ethics* (Assen: Van Gorcum and Co., 1968); Remkes Kooistra, *Facts and Values,* Christian Perspective Series (Hamilton, Ontario: Guardian Publishing Co., 1963); Frank H. Knight, *Freedom and Reform: Essays in Economics and Social Philosophy* (New York: Harper and Brothers, 1947), chap. 9 ("Fact and Value in Social Science"); C. E. M. Joad, *Guide to the Philosophy of Morals and Politics* (London: Victor Gollancz, 1947).

[11] E.g., "The fundamental character of the State is not right but might. . . . Through law the coercive power of the state becomes a moral entity." Emil Brunner, *The Divine Imperative* trans. Olive Wyon (Philadelphia: The Westminster Press, 1947), pp. 446, 452; or (for a different approach to power) ". . . the Soveraigne power of all Civil Authority is founded in the consent of the people. . . . Magistrates have received their power from the people. . . ." Roger Williams, *The Bloudy Tenet of Persecution,* ed. Samuel L. Caldwell, The Complete Writings of Roger Williams (New York: Russell and Russell, Inc., 1963), 3:214, 355; cf. George Bernard Shaw, *Major Barbara,* ed. Elizabeth T. Porter, Crofts Classics (New York: Appleton-Century-Crofts, 1971); Friedrich Nietzsche, *The Will to Power: An Attempted Transvaluation of All Values*, trans. Anthony M. Ludovici, ed. Oscar Levy, 2 vols., The Complete Works of Friedrich Nietzsche, vols. 14, 15 (London: George Allen and Unwin Ltd., 1909 [1924]); J. L. Talmon, *The Origins of Totalitarian Democracy* (London: Secker and Warburg, 1952); Carlton Kemp Allen, *Law in the Making,* 6th ed. (Oxford: Clarendon Press, 1958), pp. 2 ff.; Nathaniel Micklem, *Law and the Laws: Being the Marginal Comments of a Theologian* (Edinburgh: W. Green, 1952), pp. 51 ff.; Gordon H. Clark, *Dewey,* ed. David H, Freeman, International Library of Philosophy and Theology: Modern Thinkers Series (Philadelphia: Presbyterian and Reformed Publishing Co., 1960), p. 33.

contract," thus centering in the sovereign consent of the governed.[12]

> In the view of historians, the general pattern of the Age of Reason can now be identified. . . . The special effort of the Enlightenment was to find a foundation in every field, from the profane sciences to revelation, from music to morals, and theology to commerce, such that thinking and action could be made independent of speculative metaphysics and supernatural revelation. . . . In politics the conception of divine right and supernatural providence were replaced by the "social contract," so that governments could be evaluated as instruments of human desire. In moral philosophy the effort was made to base moral codes on Natural Law or the well established facts of human psychology.[13]

Emancipated from its ministry of justice under God's rule, the modern state has turned away from Scripture's moral law as the standard of political and legal obligation within society. Instead, direction is thought to be provided by the sovereign will of whoever can seize and hold onto power—illustrated by the French (1789) and Russian (1917) Revolutions, both of which were followed by deliberate attempts on the part of the state to dissolve the influence of God's word, now completely, in public affairs as a matter of policy.[14] The history and

---

[12] Cf. Thomas Hobbes, *Leviathan or the Matter, Form and Power of a Commonwealth, Ecclesiastical and Civil,* ed. Henry Morley, 2nd ed. (London: George Routledge and Sons, 1886); John Locke, *The Second Treatise of Civil Government, and a Letter Concerning Toleration,* ed. John W. Gough (Oxford: Basil Blackwell, 1947); Jean-Jacques Rousseau, *The Social Contract, trans.* G. D. H. Cole, ed. Ernest Rhys, Everyman's Library (New York: E. P. Dutton and Co. Inc., 1913 [reprinted 1935]); John Wiedhofft Gough, *The Social Contract: A Critical Study of Its Development,* 2nd ed. (Oxford: Clarendon Press, 1957); Peter Laslett, ed., *Philosophy, Politics and Society: A Collection* (New York: The Macmillan Co., 1956).

[13] Charles Frankel, cited by Evan Runner in "Scriptural Religion and Political Task," *Christian Perspectives 1962*, ed. Paul G. Schrotenboer (Hamilton, Ontario: Guardian Publishing Co., Ltd., 1962), p. 199.

[14] E. L. Hebben Taylor, *The Christian Philosophy of Law, Politics and the State: A*

political development of the modern "neutral" states has only confirmed the dictum of William Penn: "Men must choose to be governed by God or they condemn themselves to be ruled by tyrants." However, even in those countries where overt revolution has not broken out and in those lands where a hostile dictatorship has not been established, there has been a steady movement toward social pragmatism and messianic ideals[15] —so that the state is viewed as the sole originator of law, and its legislation aims to create a perfect social order by rehabilitation of criminals, pervasive welfare and revenue sharing, guardianship of the world and foreign aid, all of which are done irrespective of justice and questions of moral obligation in order to realize the "higher" principle of love. Thus the idea is reintroduced that law is grounded, not in the word of Christ, but in the arbitrary saving deeds of Caesar.

Concomitant with the progressive growth of large government and neutral statism has been the development of emphasis on personal freedom in Western culture. Since the rule of Christ and God's law has been restricted to *individual* commitment and (if anywhere) *private* conscience, man has seen himself as free to generate or reject, as his own ethical authority, moral ideals and obligation. Individualism and liberty become the only absolutes which govern interpersonal relations.[16] To "be yourself" and do what is dictated by desire is the

Study of the Political and Legal Thought of Herman Dooyeweerd of the Free University of Amsterdam, Holland as the Basis for Christian Action in the English-Speaking World (Nutley, New Jersey: The Craig Press, 1969), p. 6 (cf. pp. 238-243).

[15] Cf. J. L. Talmon, *Political Messianism: The Romantic Phase* (New York: Frederick A Praeger Inc., Publishers, 1961); Rousas John Rushdoony, *Politics of Guilt and Pity* (Nutley, New Jersey: The Craig Press, 1970); M. Stanton Evans, *The Liberal Establishment* (New York: Devin-Adair, 1965).

[16] For varying emphases within this motif consult: Marshall Cohen (ed.), *The Philosophy of John Stuart Mill: Ethical, Political and Religious,* The Modern Library of the World's Best Books (New York: Modern Library, Random House Inc., 1961); John Dewey, "Individualism Old and New," *John Dewey's Philosophy*, ed. Joseph Ratner (New York: Random House Inc., 1939); Jean-Paul Sartre, *Being and Nothingness*, trans. Hazel Barnes (New York: Philosophical Library, 1956); "Existentialism is a Humanism," *Existentialism from Dostoevsky to Sartre*, ed. Walter Kaufmann (London: Meridan Books, 1957); see also Sartre's trilogy of novels: *Age of Reason, The Reprieve, Troubled Sleep* as

goal of life; thus responsibilities and standards of justice come to be seen as shackles. Such thinking has gained widespread endorsement, being promoted in secular schools and represented in popular culture. When this is placed in the context of a socio-political order which affirms moral neutrality and is governed by arbitrary standards of crime and penology, the resultant increase in reprobate behavior, defiance of law, and indifference or disrespect for God are to be expected.[17] Thus there is a crescendo in the crime rates of all major cities of the world (which cannot be documented in a way which shall not be virtually outdated by the time records are tallied and reported) and a continuing expression of group anarchy or terrorism (which, due to the overwhelming number of such incidents, tragically dulls the consciences of the world population and loses its shock value). In the face of these situations (crime and lawless behavior) neither the government of the United States nor the Christian church of said nation have done what is requisite in the way of supplying an antidote.

The Age of Enlightened Reason has played itself out into a degenerated ethical state; alleged moral neutrality and lawless assumptions have engendered a clash between statism and anarchy. The Supreme Court of the United States has meanwhile abolished capital punishment (1972) and legitimized abortion (1973), thus adding to the moral decay of this nation. The Church of Christ, then, lives in a time which is in many respects parallel to the moral environment of the Roman world to which the apostle Paul addressed himself and the Romanist empire against which the Reformers worked. The follower of Christ today confronts a political tradition which has divorced itself from God's sovereign authority over it, a long developing attitude of

---

well as his play *The Flies* (many publications); J. Malina and J. Beck (eds.), *Paradise Now* (New York: Vintage Press, 1971). For a popular exposition, well illustrated, of the contemporary expression of counter-culture individualism, dissent, and resultant violence: Os Guinness, *The Dust of Death: A Critique of the Establishment and the Counter Culture – and a Proposal for a Third Way* (Downers Grove: InterVarsity Press, 1973), pp. 76-191.

[17] Romans 1:18-32.

autonomy in social affairs, and now specific acts by his government that violate the revealed law of God. Here, we might be inclined to think, is the precise "problem" which the present study introduces and seeks to resolve.

But attenuation is required. It would not be sufficient simply to observe the influence of the early church and the Reformation in the civil realm and then to summarize (in broad strokes) three centuries of socio-political thought which has eroded respect and submission to God's law on the part of present-day rulers and citizens alike. To discern adequately the present state of affairs one must also take note of attitudes and thinking on the part of the current church.

The Failure of the Theologians

The church is called to function as a preservative in society ("the salt of the earth"),[18] and thus the early church and Reformers maintained, among other things, that the civil "magistrate" is also a "minister" of God[19] and as such responsible to His authority and law. Previously the autonomous *polis* and natural reason, taken to be the source and authority for political law, were challenged by the church, but today the church has largely succumbed to the idea that God's law is extraneous, not only to personal morality, but to matters of statesmanship and civil government. The theologians of this century have offered no serious alternative to the world, giving the impression that "the salt has lost its saltiness." For instance, in a book on the very topic of *The Christian in Politics* we read these words by Walter James:

> The Christian is called upon to act beside other men and no assurance is given him that he will sense God's purpose better than they. He can no more aim to be a Christian statesman than a Christian engineer. . . . He stands on a par with the

[18] Matthew 5:13.

[19] Romans 13:4, 6.

> non-Christian. . . . His religion will give him no special guidance in his public task. . . . [20]

In addition to not having anything to speak before kings[21] because of its endorsement of neutralism in civil affairs, the modern church has shown itself to be as antinomian in its theory of ethics as the autonomous secular man. As a result the church fails to challenge "the powers that be" with the "power (authority)" of Christ[22] or to offer restorative guidance to its society.[23] Therefore, to understand more clearly the precise problem with which this study deals we need to survey (by representative examples) the present theological situation as it bears upon ethics. In the subsequent sketch those authors and works mentioned have been selected, not (necessarily) as exemplifying the most rigorous thinking within their respective schools, but on the basis of their popular influence within corresponding circles (i.e., because they are central advocates of different movements, from academicians to laymen, which are endorsed somewhere in Christendom).

The business of "Christian ethics" has justly fallen into disrepute in the course of the past hundred years or so. The absence of a theologically viable, philosophically vigorous, and socially adequate ethic in the Christian church today is the embarrassing result of a disengagement from scriptural theology and assimilation with humanism that

---

[20] Walter James, *The Christian in Politics* (London: Oxford University Press, 1962), p. 191.

[21] Cf. Psalm 119:46.

[22] Romans 13:1 (ἐξούσια) with Matthew 28:18 (ἐξούσια).

[23] Matthew 28:20 with Acts 3:21. Until the "consummation of the age" the church is to work toward the "restoration (restitution, re-establishment) of all things" which the prophets foretold (speaking of these days, Acts 3:24) by teaching the nations to observe all the commandments of Him who has been given dominion and a kingdom that all nations should serve Him (Matt. 28:18-19 with Dan. 7:14). For a few relevant passages where the prophets foretold this worldwide, blessed rule of the Messiah (in fulfillment of the Abrahamic covenant; cf. Gen. 12:3; Acts 3:25), see Psalm 47, 67, 72; Isaiah 2:2-5; 11:6-10; 65:17-25; Jeremiah 31:33-34; Daniel 2:44-45; Habakkuk 2:12-14; in these passages the social, cultural, and political effects are noteworthy.

took root in the last century. Even early twentieth century liberalism, with its singular interest in Christian morality, ran its status-quo ethic headlong into the brink of arbitrariness by rejecting the authority of Scripture. On the other hand, fundamentalism's dispensational approach to Scripture and its parenthesis view of the church was tied to a withdrawal into individualistic, reactionary moral rules which produced, in overall cash value, socio-political impotence; such salt which had lost its saltiness was appropriately thrown away and trodden upon by men. Yet neo-orthodoxy, with its reduction of "thus saith the Lord" to "it seems to me," completely failed to produce a theological position with informative and normative significance. Recent theologies which have cropped up in the wake of neo-orthodoxy have been recognized as a mere echo of the present decadent society.

With painful irony we note the words of Dietrich Bonhoeffer: "Man has learned to cope with all questions of importance without recourse to God. . . . [God] is teaching us that we must live as men who can get along very well without him." The pathos of these words is that they were penned in Bonhoeffer's *Letters and Papers from Prison*[24]—penned after Hitler's Gestapo, learning to get along very well without God, had imprisoned Bonhoeffer, thereby preventing the completion of his book on *Ethics*[25] and resulting in his hanging in 1945. When the questions of ethics are answered without recourse to God, the following views of the state become inevitable:

> The State incarnates the Divine Idea upon earth (Hegel).
>
> The State is the supreme power, ultimate and beyond repeal, absolutely independent (Fichte).
>
> Everything for the State; nothing outside the State; nothing against the State (Mussolini).

---

[24] Dietrich Bonhoeffer, *Letters and Papers from Prison*, trans. Reginald H. Fuller, ed. Eberhard Bethge (London: SCM Press, 1953), pp. 145, 164.

[25] Dietrich Bonhoeffer, *Ethics*, 6th ed., ed. Eberhard Bethge, trans. Neville Horton Smith (New York: The Macmillan Co., 1965), p. 11.

> The State dominates the nation because it alone represents it (Hitler).
>
> The State embraces everything, and nothing has value outside the State. The State creates right (Franklin Delano Roosevelt).[26]

Thus Bonhoeffer's assertion represented the very outlook which condoned his immoral execution. The source of moral authority and law within a society will either be theistic or political; when the former is repudiated, the latter allows of no logical barrier from tyranny.

However, the Christian today is told by the professional theologians that, for various reasons, he cannot turn to the words of Christ for direction in public matters. Reinhold Niebuhr discredits the full relevance of Jesus' teaching and ethic since they were predicated upon the expectation of history's soon termination.[27] Paul Ramsey says that Jesus dealt only with the simplest moral situations in person-to-person contexts.[28] Roger Mehl sees Jesus' message as a-historical, spiritual, and existential—certainly not social or concrete.[29] Rudolf Bultmann gives his popular support to all three of these ideas,[30] and the cumulative result is that the believer cannot expect to be any better off than the modern secularist when it comes to the complex and concrete moral questions of history and politics.

Our hope for a theological ethic which is socially adequate is not greatly kindled even when we look to those who (formally) promote a culture transformed by Christ. For H. Richard Niebuhr the relativity

---

[26] For the above quotes see Albert Jay Nock, *Our Enemy the State* (Idaho: Caxton Printers, 1959).

[27] Reinhold Niebuhr, *An Interpretation of Christian Ethics* (New York: Harper and Brothers, 1935), pp. 67-71.

[28] Paul Ramsey, *Basic Christian Ethics* (New York: Charles Scribner's Sons, 1950), p. 167.

[29] Roger Mehl, "The Basis of Christian Social Ethics," *Christian Social Ethics in a Changing World,* ed. John C. Bennett (New York: Association Press, 1966), pp. 44 ff.

[30] Rudolf Bultmann, *Theology of the New Testament*, trans. Kendrick Grobel (New York: Charles Scribner's Sons, 1951), p. 25.

of all our actions and decisions is evident, and thus the will of God cannot be identified with any one ethical answer or else the Creator/creature distinction (e.g., God-autonomous value/human-finite value) has been violated. Consequently "when we think of our duties in the historical process or in the social structure" we must take account of the relativity of our reasoning, historico-cultural relativity, and finally the "relativity of values." Niebuhr promotes a communal faith of intense loyalty which is mated to objective uncertainty and divorced from belief in the trustworthiness of any writings; such faith cannot be made explicit in creeds he says. And it is *this* faith which "forms the basis for our reasoning in culture; for our efforts to define a rational justice; for our endeavors after a rational political order. . . ."[31] Of course it is not at all clear why this should be considered *Christ* transforming culture since His words have been made as irrelevant to present circumstances as they are in the previously cited theologians.

Absolute value and justice cannot be founded upon Niebuhr's incorrigible relativism, and normative ethics is pushed out of the picture altogether in Joseph Fletcher's situationism.[32] Fletcher promotes an antimoralistic ethic for Christians where decisions ought never be made prescriptively; in Fletcher's own words, "Law ethics is still the enemy." Fletcher collapses the standard of ethics into moral motive and eliminates a goal for ethics completely; consequently he facilitates anarchism as much as Bonhoeffer played into the hands of statism.

The worst of both these worlds is expressed in D. L. Munby's *The Idea of a Secular Society*.[33] Upon the premise of God's omni-hiddenness, Munby maintains that Christians should not only accept a religiously neutral society which is free from political enforcement of any moral bias and pragmatic in its approach to ethics, but they should actively

---

[31] H. Richard Niebuhr, *Christ and Culture*, Harper Torchbooks: The Cloister Library (New York: Harper and Row Publishers, 1956), pp. 234-237, 246, 255.

[32] Joseph Fletcher, *Situation Ethics: The New Morality* (Philadelphia: The Westminster Press, 1966) and *Moral Responsibility* (Philadelphia: The Westminster Press, 1967).

[33] Denys Lawerance Munby, *The Idea of a Secular Society and Its Significance for Christians* (New York: Oxford University Press, 1963).

seek to secularize (and not Christianize) their culture. Hence we can move from H. Richard Niebuhr's brand of Christ transforming culture to transfigured secularism without difficulty. And the church has joined hands with the Enlightenment in emancipating society and politics from explicit biblical direction; the voices from both church and state have merged in repudiating God's law as a criterion for personal and civic morality.

In this way society loses moral corrective and endorses secular *anomia* as the theologians of our time fail to offer God's authoritative guidance, social norms for justice and love, or ethical motive and goal. The Christian ethicist is bound to be discouraged whether he looks to modern Protestantism, Roman Catholicism, or Fundamentalism, not to mention the Lutheran and Reformed schools of thought. An antidote for the declining strength of biblical ethics in its personal relevance and in its social applicability (i.e., the "political function" of the law in "its constraining influence in the unregenerate world")[34] is not to be readily found in modern theology.

The United Presbyterian Church in the U.S.A. has given an expression of the church's mission of reconciliation and a declaration against threatening evil as our times require in its *Confession of 1967* (cf. 9.06; 9.02). As a document which alleges to ground the church's duty exclusively in obedience to Jesus Christ (9.03) we would expect it to promote a relevant Christian ethic. However, it docs not discuss the law of God infallibly revealed in the pages of Scripture (indeed, God's "law" is not even mentioned), define sin thereby, or relate the Christian life and mission to inspired ethical norms laid out in God's word. While this confession speaks of such things as rebellion, guilt, wrong, evil, judgment, legal penalty, integrity, goodness, justice, direction, duties, and will of God, it completely neglects that substantial portion of Scripture which makes these concepts meaningful—God's law. The idea of obedience to Christ thereby analyzes into a mist (and mysticism) wherein every man finally does what is right in his own eyes.

---

[34] Carl F. H. Henry, *Christian Personal Ethics* (Grand Rapids: William B. Eerdmans Publishing Co., 1957), p. 355.

Looking for an improved point of view we turn to Jürgen Moltmann and find him saying that:

> Promise and command, the pointing of the goal and the pointing of the way, therefore belong immediately together. . . .The covenant must be understood as . . . a "contract requiring adherence." . . . To this extent the promise of the covenant and the injunctions of the covenant have an abiding and guiding significance. . . .[35]

But far from laying a foundation for a normative ethic centering in the covenantly revealed law of God, Moltmann dissolves God's law into a category of Christian eschatology and leaves the kingdom of God to human building.

> In this conjunction with the promises of the covenant, the commandments . . . are not legal conditions or what theologians commonly call "law." If the commandments are the ethical side of the promise and obedience is the fruit of hope, then the commandments are just as little rigid norms as the promises are. . . . They are not abstract norms of ideal orders that always exist and reflect their images in time, but they are a real foreshadowing of the historic prospects. . . . The commandments have accordingly just as much a future tenor as the promises. . . . Then "the redemption of the world is left to the power of our conversion. God has no wish for any other means of perfecting his creation than by our help. He will not reveal his kingdom until we have laid its foundations."[36]

---

[35] Jürgen Moltmann, *Theology of Hope: On the Ground and the Implications of a Christian Eschatology*, trans. James W. Leitch (New York: Harper and Row Publishers, 1967), pp. 120, 121.

[36] Ibid., pp. 122, 124.

Thus obscuring the logic of ethical discourse and forcing God's word into the mold of his own theology, Moltmann translates the law of God out of its proper normative context into a category of the future so that the relevance of rigid commands from God is suspended and law collapses into promise (being only illustrative and anticipatory). By giving the law of God a "future tenor," man is set free to establish autonomously the kingdom of God upon the law of the vassal rather than the law of the King. Regrettably, Moltmann's reference to Scripture comes after certain extra-scriptural premises have been determined. The result of such a methodology (whether one is dealing with a soteric antagonism of law to grace, near Eastern treaty forms, or the Marxism of Ernst Bloch) is a depreciation of the current validity or relevance of God's law for ethics and a baptism of those determinations with biblical language. By providing a goal for ethics without a corresponding and proper standard for ethics (just as Fletcher provides a motive without a standard), Moltmann's outlook manifests a frightening parallel to the end-justifies-means morality of Marxism.

Turning from modern Protestantism and *The Secular City* wherein "speaking about God in a secular fashion is thus a political issue [which] entails our discerning where God is working and then joining His work" and thereby altering the word "God" as the times require,[37] we come to modern Romanism only to find the same outlook. Current Roman Catholic thinking is permeated with an ethical orientation. Gregory Baum explains that:

> . . . the new theologians think of theology as establishing some kind of correlation . . . between the normative revelation of the past and the ongoing revelation present in human experience, personal and social. . . . But the Church's awareness, created by Christ, appoints her to enter into dialogue and cooperation with other people, to serve the mystery of

---

[37] Harvey Cox, *The Secular City: Secularization and Urbanization in Theological Perspective* (New York: The Macmillan Co., 1965), pp. 256-257.

> redemption present among them, to effect the formation of a new consciousness in humanity and thus to create a more truly human future for mankind.[38]

In the new theism of Roman Catholic thinking there is recognition that "many Christians can no longer accept the radical division of life into the sacred and the profane. . . ."[39] Does this signalize an exodus from the secular city then? Not at all.

> What is wrong, for today, in the traditional manner is the objectification of God. . . . God is not objective: God cannot become an object of man's mind, of which he can acquire some knowledge, however analogous, and about which he is able to make true statements. . . . God does not exist: he is not an object of which existence may be predicated. . . . The doctrine of God is the Good news that humanity is possible . . . a commitment to the critical and constructive process, by which man assumes responsibility for his future, personal and social. . . . By believing in God's transcendence man affirms his hope in the future, in his own human future.[40]

In *The Future of Belief* Leslie Dewart proposes that Christian faith compels disbelief in God in any absolute sense.[41] In Dewart's "relative theism" there is a redefinition (transmogrification) of God's attributes, leaving an echo of Hegel's view of the state.

> . . . the Christian conception of God might stress a point the moral and practical implications of which have been somewhat

---

[38] Gregory Baum, "Toward a New Catholic Theism," *The Ecumenist, A Journal for Promoting Christian Unity*, 8 (4, 1970), 54.

[39] Ibid., p. 56.

[40] Ibid., p. 55.

[41] Leslie Dewart, *The Future of Belief* (New York: Herder and Herder), pp. 204-205.

> neglected: that the reality of God, implying the real possibility of a world totally open to God, implies therefore a world totally open to *future creation by man.*[42]

The true character of this new Roman Catholic outlook and its implications for social ethics is clearly set forth in the position of Johannes B. Metz:

> All this demands the development of theology as eschatology. . . .For it is only in the eschatological horizon that the world appears as a becoming reality whose development is entrusted to the freedom of men. . . .The universal transformation of the world through an offensive of human freedom upon it characterizes that process which we call secularization. . . . THIS IMPLIES INTRINSICALLY A KIND OF "POLITICAL THEOLOGY." . . . The theology of the world is neither a purely objective theology of the cosmos nor a purely transcendental theology of personal existence, but rather and above all *political theology.*[43]

By rejecting the objective, absolute, living God, modern Romanism has found the source of direction and morality in the *polis* just as did the ancient world. A humanistic eschatology has replaced the normative law revealed by God so that we are ushered into the threat of secularized statism again. The law of man has replaced the law of God.

The repudiation of divinely established ethical norms is not amended even in the more conservative, transcendental Thomism of Bernard J. F. Lonergan. While he holds out for "a true value,"[44] he still

---

[42] Ibid., p. 193.

[43] Johannes B. Metz, "Creative Hope," *New Theology No. 5,* eds. Martin E. Marty and Dean G. Peerman (New York: The Macmillan Co., 1968), pp. 135, 136, 138.

[44] Bernard J. F. Lonergan, *Insight: A Study of Human Understanding*, 3rd ed. (New York: Philosophical Library, 1970), p. 605.

does not present objective standards for ethics. Instead of having a "code of laws" define virtue, it is found in the changing circumstances of human experience and development.

> It is to be insisted that the good of order is not some design for utopia, some theoretic ideal, some set of ethical precepts, some code of laws, or some super-institution. It is quite concrete. . . . One works out an ideal of human reality and achievement, and to that ideal one dedicates oneself. As one's knowledge increases, as one's experience is enriched, as one's reach is strengthened or weakened, one's ideal may be revised and the revision may recur many times.
>
> In such vertical liberty, whether implicit or explicit, are to be found the foundations of the judgments of value that occur . . . they attain their proper context, their clarity and refinement, only through man's historical development and the individual's personal appropriation of his social, cultural, and religious heritage . . . a rounded moral judgment is ever the work . . . as Aristotle would put it, of a virtuous man. . . . "Virtue, then, is a state of character concerned with choice, lying in a mean, i.e., the mean relative to us. . . ."[45]

So in the viewpoint of modern Protestants and Roman Catholics we oscillate between personal relativism and secular statism. What is common to the assortment of viewpoints is the negative attitude (indifference or hostility) toward the revealed law of God found in Scripture. Christian ethics, left to these thinkers, would fail to reach a suitable concurrence of moral standard, motive, and goal; and social relevance could be found only by standing on the same ground with the secular humanist and pursuing political tasks in oblivion of God's word. In the law of God, however, the modern Christian could find

---

[45] Bernard J. F. Lonergan, *Method in Theology* (New York: Herder and Herder, 1972), pp. 49, 40, 41n.

authoritative norms and guidance, a motive for obedience in loving God and neighbor, and the goal of God's glory and Christ's kingdom; further, in God's law there is found the proper separation of *polis* and *ecclesia* without sacrificing socio-political relevance. We turn our attention, then, to Fundamentalistic, Lutheran, and Reformed thinking to see how each responds to the law of God and its bearing on ethics and to see if these schools are restoring health to theological ethics in this day.

In the course of the last fifty years Fundamentalism has come to be characterized by the dispensationalism of Dr. C. I. Scofield, editor of the *Scofield Reference Bible.* In the notes for this Bible Scofield quite plainly assigns the law of God to the temporally-limited fifth dispensation which extends from Sinai to Calvary, concluding "The Christian is not under the conditional Mosaic Covenant of works, the law, but under the unconditional New Covenant of grace."[46] In this scheme of thought the law of God *ex hypothesi* could not be the foundation of Christian ethics, for:

> The Scriptures divide time . . . into seven unequal periods, usually called "Dispensations." . . . These periods are marked off in Scripture by some change in God's method of dealing with mankind, in respect of the two questions: of sin, and of man's rcsponsibility.[47]

Obviously then, godly ethics today would not be guided by the way in which God dealt with the Old Testament Israelites. Scofield's negative attitude toward the law goes beyond this historical division; even at Mount Sinai Israel should have had nothing to do with God's proposal of law—instead of humbly pleading for a continued relation of grace,

---

[46] C. I. Scofield et. al. (eds.), *Scofield Reference Bible* (New York: Oxford University Press, 1909), pp. 94, 95.

[47] C. I. Scofield, *Rightly Dividing the Word of Truth* (New Jersey: Loizeaux Brothers, 1896), p. 12.

they presumptuously answered: "All that the Lord hath spoken we will do."[48] Obedience to God's law is to be scorned today and should have been then as well. Nothing could be more significant for Christian ethics than the contrast Scofield drew between man under law and man under grace: "The sacrificial death of the Lord Jesus Christ introduced the dispensation of pure grace . . . instead of God REQUIRING righteousness, as under Law."[49] Thus in the booklet, *Rightly Dividing the Word of Truth*, Scofield declared:

> The most obvious and striking division of the Word of Truth is that between Law and Grace. Indeed, these contrasting principles *characterize* the two most important dispensations—the Jewish and the Christian. . . . Scripture never, in *any* dispensation *mingles* these two principles. Law always has a place and work distinct and wholly diverse from that of grace. . . . Everywhere the Scriptures present law and grace in sharply contrasted spheres. *The mingling of them in much current teaching of the day spoils both*. . . .Three errors have troubled the Church touching the right relations of law and grace: . . .The third is Galatianism, or the *mingling* of law and grace—the teaching . . . that grace is given to enable an otherwise helpless sinner to keep the law. . . . Law has but one language. . . . It speaks only to condemn. . . . It is purely and only a ministration of condemnation and death. . . . It is reserved to modern nomolators to wrench these holy and just but deathful tables from underneath the mercy-seat and the atoning blood, and erect them in Christian churches as the rule of Christian life. . . . It is not, then, a question of dividing what God spoke from Sinai into "Moral Law" and "Ceremonial Law"—the believer does not come to that mount at all.[50]

---

[48] Ibid., p. 14.

[49] Ibid.

[50] Ibid., pp. 34, 35, 36, 38, 42, 44.

Clearly then, dispensationalism is as antagonistic as modern Protestantism and Romanism, though for different reasons, to the law of God. Ironically, for all its endeavor to distance itself from legalism, Fundamentalism introduced a form of legalism all its own: the pious "do not's" of man—a moral code as arbitrary as it was anachronistic. As always, when God's law is rejected, the law of man (embodied in the state, or the church, or the individual himself) is substituted; will worship preempts God's standards for behavior.

The more recent expressions of Fundamentalism found in such places as the *New Scofield Reference Bible*[51] and Charles Ryrie's *Dispensationalism Today*[52] have not corrected Scofield's negative attitude toward the Mosaic Law. The *New Scofield* still asserts that the Christian is not under the provisional Mosaic Law, and Ryrie even disqualifies the Sermon on the Mount as having any primary application to current Christian ethics. Ryrie temporally restricts the law of God to a dispensation extending from Sinai to Calvary and contrasts it to the dispensation of grace wherein faith is the new test laid upon God's people. The distinctive characteristic of the covenant of law according to the *New Scofield* is that requirement precedes promise. In *The Basis of Premillennial Faith* Ryrie listed as one of the contrasts between the Mosaic covenant and the New covenant the latter's advantage of not being under the law.[53] John F. Walvoord incriminates covenant theologians for the alleged error of disregarding the legal and nongracious character of the Mosaic covenant, thereby failing to contrast its ministry of death to the New Testament.[54] Therefore, with its continued dismissal of the law of God in ethics, Fundamentalism expressed both a "spiritualized" form of *situation* ethics and "Christianly submissive" *statism*. The

---

[51] E. Schuyler English et. al. (eds.), *The New Scofield Reference Bible* (New York: Oxford University Press, 1967).

[52] Charles Ryrie, *Dispensationalism Today* (Chicago: Moody Press, 1965).

[53] Charles Ryrie, *The Basis of Premillennial Faith* (New York: Loizeaux Brothers, 1953), cf. pp. 108-125.

[54] John F. Walvoord, *The Millennial Kingdom* (Grand Rapids: Zondervan Publishing House, 1959), p. 91.

Christian individual receives no concrete direction, and the social problems and political difficulties of the day fail to be biblically challenged.

Modern day Lutheranism propounds a view of God's law which is as unsatisfactory as that of dispensationalism. The late Werner Elert (formerly professor of systematic theology at the University of Erlangan), writing on *Law and Gospel*, declares that they are in dialectical opposition to one another; indeed, "they are as opposed to one another as death and life."[55] While long ago the Lutherans officially recognized the law of God as providing a functional theological ethic which was authoritative, corrective, and relevant to personal and social morality,[56] Elert dashes any hope for such a project in the current day:

> And here once more it becomes irrefutably clear that law and promise . . . are irreconcilably opposed to one another. . . . In this new order, however, the law no longer has any voice whatsoever. . . . The disciple of Jesus . . . no longer has any need whatsoever for the law's threats or its promises of reward. . . . The Holy Spirit's entry into the world marks the beginning of the Christian church. Since that time the church lives no longer under law. . . . That means it lives in freedom. . . . When we look to Christ, the law has absolutely no validity. . . . The irreconcilable opposition of law and gospel remains also for the Christian.[57]

The law serves only in the destruction of the old man, says Elert, but cannot serve in the construction of the new man (i.e., traditionally termed "the third use of the law").[58] Another Lutheran theologian,

---

[55] Werner Elert, *Law and Gospel*, trans. Edward H. Schroeder, ed. Franklin Sherman, Facet Books: Social Ethics Series, No. 16 (Philadelphia: Fortress Press 1967), p. 48.

[56] Cf. "The Formula of Concord (The Epitome)," in Philip Schaff, *The Creeds of Christendom with a History and Critical Notes*, 4th ed., Vol. III (Grand Rapids: Baker Book House, 1877 [reprinted 1966]), Article VI, pp. 130-135.

[57] Elert, *op. cit.,* pp. 28, 30, 33, 34, 42.

[58] Ibid., pp. 33, 36, 43.

Martin Scharlemann (professor of exegetical theology at Concordia Seminary), tells us that "there are two elements in Scripture: Law and Gospel. Each has its own kind of authority, which must be carefully distinguished from the other."[59] The Christian is to live under one, and not the other. Yet another Lutheran theologian, John Warwick Montgomery (professor of church history at Trinity Evangelical Divinity School), claims that the law primarily drives us to Christ so that we can (as contrite) be picked up by grace; certainly law and grace should not be merged or confused (e.g., seeing Christ as a new Moses or preaching law to those already convicted of sin). It is most important that the gospel predominate over the law.[60] However, neither systematics, exegesis, nor the history of Christian thought point to the appropriateness of this restriction of the law's function and disparagement of its positive application today.

Paul Althaus, recognizing that the Bible clearly purports to direct Christian living, attempts to remain true to the Lutheran dichotomy of law and gospel by distinguishing "command" (God's will for us) from "law" (a special form of that will).[61] The "commands" of God are actually the summons to life and love, God's offer to be man's God, a challenge to accept freedom and permission to live in God's love.[62] Law, by contrast, is what became of God's command through the fall; it distorts the command, always accuses man, demands greater purity than the command (indeed, an impossible purity), and applies always and only to the sinner before acceptance of the gospel.[63] The gospel puts an end to the law, and through the gospel the law again becomes

---

[59] Martin Schlarlemann, "Biblical Authoroity," *Christianity Today*, XVII (3, 1972), 134.

[60] John Warwick Montgomery, "An Exhortation to Exhorters," *Christianity Today*, XVII (12, 1973), 607.

[61] Paul Althaus, *The Divine Command: A New Perspective on Law and Gospel*, trans. Franlkin Sherman, ed. Franklin Sherman. Facet Books: Social Ethics Series, No. 9, (Philadelphia: Fortress Press, 1966), p. 2.

[62] Ibid., pp. 9-10, 28-29.

[63] Ibid., pp. 12, 22-23, 31, 27.

command; this command has a place in the Christian life, not as making works follow causally upon faith, but as showing the works in which faith finds living expression.[64] The arbitrariness and tendentious character of this scheme should be obvious; indeed, it should be obvious to Althaus himself, for he admits that: the distinction between law and command cannot be derived from the terms themselves as used in Scripture (or the Lutheran confessions!), the law is interchangeable with command and applied to the Christian life at points in Scripture, the actual contents of law and command are identical, the law cannot be distinguished from command by the law's negative form since gospel commands take negative form also, and the command (with its life and love) is still heard in the law.[65] Althaus' distinction, then, has been qualified so extensively that it virtually vanishes. However, the problem with the ethical scheme suggested by Althaus is not simply that he refuses to apply the term "law" to the Christian life, but that *in fact* there is no absolutely authoritative law (or call it "command") for the Christian life. While the believer is "well advised" to consider the biblical illustrations of God's will, just as he might also consider the lives of the saints, these ethical admonitions (e.g., the Decalogue) are "aids and correctives" or teaching examples, but *never* "legal prescriptions."[66] The threat of relativism or autonomy is clear when Althaus declares:

> The Christian ethic is an ethic of the Spirit . . . This guidance by the Holy Spirit implies that God's concrete commanding cannot be read off from a written document, an inherited scheme of law. I must learn afresh every day what God wants of me. For God's commanding has a special character for each individual: it is always contemporary, always new. God commands me (and each person) in a particular way, in a different way than he commands others. And his command is spoken afresh in each situation. . . . The living and spiritual

[64] Ibid., pp. 22-23, 26, 28-29, 41.

[65] Ibid., pp. 3, 13, 26, 20-21.

[66] Ibid., pp. 44-47.

> character of the knowledge of what God requires of me in the present moment must not be destroyed by rules and regulations.[67]

While in actual practice the modern day Lutheran may wish to avoid concrete sins (e.g., murder, stealing, adultery) as much as in classic Reformed theology, nevertheless an ethical system such as that propounded by Althaus shows that *in principle* there is nothing to which appeal can be made in order to prevent these concrete sins in any unqualified and pre-established fashion. The general Lutheran disclaimer of any "third use" of the law of God has regrettable implications for their "first use" of the law (i.e., the political use). A contemporary proponent of Luther's doctrine of two kingdoms, the "kingdom of the right hand" (redemption) and the "kingdom of the left hand" (creation), is Helmut Thielicke. He seems ready to admit that those dangers which men like Troeltsch, Wunsch, Barth, and Deutelmoser have seen in Luther's doctrine (e.g., a double morality—one for each kingdom—as well as the secularization of the state so that it is ethically autonomous) are "theological possibilities"; however, Thielicke thinks that, outside of Luther's unguarded expressions, Luther has two safeguards against abuse: the office holders of the state should remember that their *purpose* is to preserve peace (so that men can have the opportunity to accept the gospel) and that they should be *motivated* by love.[68] Yet Thielicke suspects that this is not quite enough, for the commandments are not used to *call into question* the *activities* of the kingdom of the left (only their motivation); "there is still the possibility that in Luther the temporal kingdom is understood to be too isolated, too insulated, vis-a-vis the Law of God."[69] Thielicke then offers his own *social* proposal, and it is a proposal that parallels Althaus' suggestion for the use of God's commandments in the Christian's *personal* life (viz., that they are not

[67] Ibid., pp. 43, 45.

[68] Helmut Thielicke, *Theological Ethics*, Vol. I, ed. William H. Lazareth (Philadelphia: Fortress Press, 1966), pp. 359-378.

[69] Ibid., p. 379.

positive legal prescriptions but only corrective illustrations that advise us). Thielicke holds that, just as God's commandments necessarily suffer refraction when entering the order of this age, so the laws of jurisprudence and politics are alien so far as the kingdom of God is concerned. Relying heavily upon the negative form of the Decalogue, Thielicke says that the Law does not show us what is right but only what is naturally wrong. Thus the Decalogue can point out political wrong for a Christian (it illustrates the natural decadence and dehumanization to which the state is prone) but gives no specific program; Christianity cannot solve our political problems. While there are non-Christian forms of politics, there can be no such thing as "Christian politics"; the Christian can only commend such concrete structures or orders as may befit the time and occasion. "The commandment of God has no abiding affinity either to a specific economic order or to a specific political order."[70] Therefore, we are left with the same rejection of the *positive* and *guiding* function of God's law as we were in the life of the individual believer. There are no unqualified and preestablished rules for the kingdom of the left, and the authority of God's revealed law is reduced to that of a corrective illustration—resulting in the odd asymmetry that politics is subject to one value predicate ("non-Christian") but not its opposite. One wonders if there is any sense in which a biblical and concrete guideline can be suggested by the Christian to modern society under the terms specified by modern Lutherans; private and public morality are not, but vaguely, called back from the dangers of autonomy.

Recalling what was said above about the stand that the Reformation took (e.g., John Calvin) with respect to the law of God and public life, we turn to current Reformed writers hoping to find the theologically viable, philosophically vigorous and socially adequate ethical system needed by the church at the present time. Yet with disappointment we must acknowledge the failure of much contemporary Reformed thinking to maintain a proper view of the law of God, its authority, present

---

[70] Ibid., p. 449; cf. pp. 379-382, 439-451.

validity, relevance, and salutary effects. E. J. Carnell wrote that concern for law was inherently low in moral worth.[71] Forgetting that even unfallen Adam needed special revelation pertaining to ethics, Carnell thought that "if we were moral by nature, we would do the right out of a necessity that is unconscious of law."[72] With his tendency to subordinate the standard of ethics to the motive for ethical behavior Carnell was implicitly led into subjectivism with respect to the knowledge of God's will: "Degrees of moral peace measure the degree to which our affections conform to the will of God."[73] Consequently Carnell answered the question of moral standard by turning the authority structure of Christianity upside-down. He claimed that it was erroneous to view the law of love as a religious summary of the Ten Commandments, that the Old Testament ethic was in itself no better than that of Plato and Aristotle, that the New Testament stands in judgment over the Old Testament ethic, that Israel shared in the standards of cruelty which then prevailed, and thus that certain Mosaic laws had to pass away with the old economy.[74] Carnell's concern for "Christian social action" was of limited value, for he erected *abstract and indeterminate* principles of "human equality" and "love" as limiting concepts for morality, asserting that "sanctification does not mean that a believer keeps the law or performs good works. . . .The emphasis is on the creative work of the Spirit."[75] The inevitable outcome in Carnell's system was that man became the ultimate moral judge: "Jesus is a good man because he verified everything that a decent society means by goodness."[76] When the seed of excluding God's law once gets into a system of thought, it is finally harvested in unethical self-sufficiency.

---

[71] Edward John Carnell, *Christian Commitment: An Apologetic* (New York: The Macmillan Co., 1957), pp. 161, 289.

[72] Ibid., p. 196.

[73] Ibid., p. 221.

[74] Edward John Carnell, *The Case for Orthodox Theology* (Philadelphia: The Westminster Press, 1959), pp. 55-56.

[75] Ibid., p. 73.

[76] Ibid., p. 82.

Another method for spurning God's law is to relativize it into a time-bound illustration of how a broad ethical principle was applied in ancient times. Some segments of the Reformed church today use such a method to affirm a commitment to God's law while simultaneously rendering it anything but germane to current life. In the 1971 report of the Christian Reformed Church on "The Nature and Extent of Biblical Authority" there is an expressed desire to honor the comprehensive character of biblical authority and thus to have a mature witness to secular society; however, the very foundation of that witness and authority is undermined when the report says:

> . . . the Bible was originally addressed to definite situations and to people living under particular circumstances. These situations and circumstances affect what is said and how it is said. For example, commandments and exhortations given at a certain time and place are not necessarily universally applicable. The entire legal structure of the Old Testament applied then and there but after the fulfillment in Christ no longer now and here. Not that we no longer learn from that legal structure, but even where it still instructs us the manner in which it applies has drastically changed. This is so because of the fulfillment of the law in Christ, but also because the circumstances under which the Old Testament people lived are no longer those under which we live . . . All of these observations which stem from the character of the Bible as an historical book are important for our understanding of the nature and extent of biblical authority. Because the Bible is an historical record it is important to take into account the distinction between what it meant originally and what it continues to mean.[77]

[77] "The Nature and Extent of Biblical Authority" (Grand Rapids: Board of Publications of the Christian Reformed Church, 1971), pp. 469, 470; cf. p. 489.

So also the "reformational" movement centering in the "Philosophy of the Cosmonomic Idea" would desire to make Christianity pertinent to every area of current life. But for all of its interest in the "law" of God, this movement is opposed to going to the inscripturated laws of God's word to find direct ethical guidance. Again the reason offered is that God's commandments are time-bound and culturally relativized:

> . . . because my twentieth century situation and the ancient parallel made abstractly ideal jibe of sorts only after a dozen qualifications, the binding force is lost. . . . It is not: Thus says the Lord to Seerveld—. . . . The great commandment relativizes every other commandment the Scriptures contain. . . . These dynamic directives of Scripture . . . are religious *principles, beginnings* that want to take on concrete form in our lives. . . . All the other ordinances are nothing more than concrete outworkings, positivizations of this Directive within a particular period of history. None of them can be literally followed or applied today, for we live in a different period of history in a different culture.[78]

The echo of situationism is not stifled when De Graff says "it is our religious calling to give concrete form to these directives for our times in our situations."[79] There are no concrete, pre-established ethical norms—just religious motives, the broad commandment, and new situations in which we must find the particular application. Scripture shows us how the broad commandment was applied in one culture and thus can be used for illustrative purposes, but "for the rest . . . we are referred to and are dependent upon God's revelation that comes to us in

---

[78] A. H. De Graff and C. G. Seerveld, *Understanding the Scriptures: How to Read and Not to Read the Bible,* Christian Perspective Series 1969 (Hamilton, Ontario: The Association for the Advancement of Christian Scholarship, 1968), pp. 68, 35.

[79] Ibid., p. 37.

creation."[80] Hence the significance of the "*cosmo*-nomic" designation of this philosophy. The ironic thing is that this "reformational" movement appears to be paralleling the emphasis on *natural* law of the medieval scholastics—an emphasis repudiated and countered by the Reformation in its stress upon God's revealed law in *Scripture*. According to De Graff, however, the Bible does not contain any moral lessons; indeed, to keep the law is not a matter of rules or obeying the letter of the law at all. The Bible is not even a book from which we can deduce some moral applications.[81] Therefore, the Bible is assigned to a position of concrete, ethical irrelevance for the current day, and the expressions of personal and socio-political antinomianism are not biblically challenged.

When we come to the writings of Meredith G. Kline we find superb ammunition for dealing with the documentary hypothesis and the late canon views of the Old Testament; however, what Kline has written in the area of ethics cannot be so enthusiastically endorsed. By means of his discussion of covenant-canons and of "intrusion ethics" Kline would dismiss the Older Testamental life norms, in particular the community life norms, from present day application.[82] The church would then have little, if anything, to urge upon the civil magistrates of our time since the social aspects of God's law are not valid today—another illustration of the depreciation of God's law in Reformed circles. In addition to the indirect rebuttal provided by the present treatise, a short critique of Kline's viewpoint on ethics will be found in an appendix at the end of the book.

Finally, even in the writings of those Reformed theologians who maintain the validity of God's law for contemporary ethics there is a general tendency to draw back from following out the full implications of that position for socio-political affairs in the present age. The law's validity is commonly reduced to its personal and individualistic use,

---

[80] Ibid.

[81] Ibid., pp. 2, 18, 21, 29, 31.

[82] Meredith G. Kline, *The Structure of Biblical Authority* (Grand Rapids: William B. Eerdmans Publishing Co., 1972), pp. 94-110, 154-171.

while the magistrate is released from his own obligation to enforce the penal sanctions of the law against its social violators. While it is good that these writers urge the individual Christian to acknowledge his responsibility to the law of God (a matter into which the present study will also delve), it is inconsistent to stop from applying that law to society. And to apply God's law to society involves enforcing penal sanctions—either God's own directives or the arbitrary punishments of statesmen. Not to apply God's law to society and not to enforce penal sanctions renders the state as a judicial body useless. So once again the threat of statism or anarchy rears its ugly head. Furthermore, the social necessity, relevance, and adequacy of Christian ethics again becomes doubtful. Therefore, even in the writings of Reformed theologians today we fail to find the ethical health and biblical challenge to society which typified the Reformers.

And so, having surveyed the attitudes toward God's law which are expressed by the theologians of this century (whether modernistic Protestant, Roman Catholic, Fundamentalistic, Lutheran, or Reformed), we can see why the current moral problems in the United States (and reflected throughout the world) go beyond the general lawlessness of society and the autonomous attitudes of politicians. Whereas the Reformers sought to sanctify their culture by bringing the inscripturated law of God to bear upon both the individual and the civil magistrate, the church today has either joined hands with the Enlightenment in insisting that the individual and state be free from scriptural direction or has declared that the law of God is no longer valid at least in its socio-political details (e.g., its penal sanctions). Either way there is little, if any, concrete biblical challenge addressed to the citizens and rulers of this country. Attenuation has revealed that the worst part of this silence is the current conviction among theologians that God's law no longer binds the individual or the civil magistrate. Secularization and autonomous politics have become the order of the day. Christendom seems to have taken a negative (or truncated) view of the commandments of God's written word. Thus the dilemma facing it is expressed in these words by Michael Novak: "The choice seems to be between an irrelevant religion and an effective secular morality."[83] It is precisely this dilemma which the present study intends to counter, hoping that the personal and political relevance of Reformed Christianity can once again (through biblical direction) effectively challenge secular morality as it finds in the state, private conscience, or natural law the source of ethical normativeness. Speaking of the urgent necessity for a biblical social ethic, Dr. Visser't Hooft has well said:

> It is strange that after these many centuries of church history we have to admit that in this respect the Bible is still very largely a closed book. We have only the vaguest ideas about its message concerning the abiding realities of social and political life. We operate with a few obvious texts or a few general principles, but we know next to nothing about the biblical witness with regard to such basic elements of our common life as property, justice, work, soil, money.[84]

Theoretical Framework

The central concern of this treatise can be expressed in the term "theonomy," a compound of the Greek words for "God" and "law." However, in using this term it is necessary that the position taken herein be sharply contrasted to that of Paul Tillich, a writer who also expressed his concern for ethics in terms of the word "theonomy."[85] For Tillich "theonomy" represents a law which is not imposed from outside the human person (i.e., "heteronomy") and is not simply the rule of oneself by oneself (i.e., "autonomy"). When man locates the moral law within his own heart under the impact of the "Spiritual Presence," then we are dealing with "theonomy" according to Tillich. I would

---

[83] Michael Novak, *Belief and Unbelief, a Philosophy of Self-Knowledge* (New York: The New American Library, 1965), p. 139.

[84] W. A. Visser 't Hooft, *The Kingship of Christ: An Interpretation of Recent European Theology* (New York: Harper and Brothers, 1948), p. 144.

[85] Paul Tillich, *Systematic Theology*, Vol. III (Chicago: The University of Chicago Press, 1963), part IV, sect. III, B.2-C.3, pp. 249-275.

question why Tillich, in rejecting any authoritatively revealed law from outside of man, should want to speak of "God's law" ("theonomy") at all; he could just as well speak of a qualified, indeed a vaguely religious, autonomy. Tillich fully admits that "actual theonomy is autonomous ethics under the Spiritual Presence."[86] Moreover, he approves of any propounding of autonomy over against heteronomy, thus showing the ultimate character of his "transmoral morality."[87] In terms of the theoretical framework of this treatise, Tillich's scheme would still be considered *self-law.* By "theonomy" I will mean that verbalized law of God which is imposed from outside man and revealed authoritatively in the words of Scripture. While the Holy Spirit inspired the Scriptures and must enable our obedience to them, He is not the law itself. Men who were carried along by the Spirit of God spoke the law from God. This law cannot be identified with self-law but is genuine "theonomy."

Consequently, this study presupposes the full inspiration of the Bible as defined in the Westminster Confession of Faith and Catechisms. The Bible is taken to be self-attestingly true, uniquely authoritative, necessary and sufficient for all matters of faith and godliness, and perspicuous in its saving message. The unity of all the scriptures found in the canon and their inerrancy (in opposition to higher or negative criticism) is also assumed. Moreover, the views on Trinitarian Theology, creation, anthropology, and sovereign, gracious soteriology as taught in the Westminster Standards are taken for granted in this study. Hence, while I will be dealing with the moral and political aspects or implications of scriptural passages, I forthrightly reject any reduction of the sacred message to moralism or politics. Although the moral and political effects and teachings of the Scripture cannot be excised or ignored, the central thrust of the Bible is recognized to be the accomplishment and application of salvation to God's people. Furthermore, this study shall operate outside of any radical dichotomy between *Historie* and *Geschichte,* nature and freedom, the spiritual and the historical-social, or the realm of I-Thou and the realm of I-it.

---

[86] Ibid., p. 268.

[87] Ibid., pp. 266-268.

Preliminary Survey of the Solution

In the pages that follow, my concern will be to show from God's word that the Christian is obligated to keep the whole law of God as a pattern of sanctification and that this law is to be enforced by the civil magistrate where and how the stipulations of God so designate. That is to say, "theonomy" has a central and irradicable place in any genuinely Christian ethic—any moral system claiming the support of Scripture. The Older Testament commandments are not mere artifacts in a religious museum, nor are they ideals suspended over an age of parenthesis and appropriate only for the coming day of consummation. They are the living and powerful word of God, directing our lives here and now. The moral behavior and ethical relations within society desired by God are discernable in the full law of God as revealed in the scriptures of the Older and New Testaments; in these pages we see the pattern of personal and social action that desperately calls for adherence in our day. When that pattern is followed, when we learn to think God's thoughts after Him (loving His law, obeying His voice), then our lives and our nation will be well pleasing in the Lord's sight and benefited with His blessing. This calls for following the biblical pattern of ethics in its far-reaching details, not arbitrarily cutting our obedience short at some point dictated by personal desire or preconceived political outlook. Because God loves us in a very extensive and specific fashion (caring for every detail of our lives) and because He expects all-encompassing devotion from us (loving Him with all our heart, soul, mind and strength; glorifying Him by our eating or drinking or whatever we do), He did not deliver to us merely some broad and general moral principles, but He revealed very extensive, specific, and all-encompassing commands. Theonomy is crucial to Christian ethics, and all the details of God's law are intrinsic to theonomy. Here is the heart of the present thesis.

While facile armchair analyses of the moral anarchy of our day are easily spawned, it is not so much the diagnosis as it is the prescribed antidote that modern man needs. He is ever so aware that things are not right; he knows that the legislative schemes of the politicians and the moral rearmament plans of the humanists alike do not work. The moral degeneracy of personal lives as well as the public depravity of our society keep accelerating. The lawless assumptions of man without God have resulted in a dreadful stalemate between the anarchy of the radicals and the latent totalitarianism of the statists. Man is aware that absolute morality is becoming a matter for ridicule as anachronistic, and he sees the effects of the new immorality in himself, his friends, and his society. Very few people genuinely appreciate the outcome.

The Christian surely must diagnose the problem biblically; he must give God's analysis of the source and character of man's disease. But that analysis would be cruel, if not useless, without the accompanying antidote. Man must be given God's answer—not emotive slogans, but the realistic and thorough "recovery plan" of Scripture. A summary of that plan is found in Ephesians 2:8-10, "you are saved by grace through faith; and this is not from yourself, it is God's gift, not of works lest any man should boast." Theonomy is not a scheme for personal self-justification. God's grace, expressed in the accomplished and applied redemption of Jesus Christ, alone can save us. The Savior is not embraced but by faith; one's works cannot earn his salvation. However, all too often Christians leave matters at that point, failing to see that God not only forgives the sinner, but also develops his "new life" according to the (previously spurned) pattern of holiness. God remedies not only our legal guilt (justification) but also our moral pollution (sanctification). Ephesians 2 goes on to say: "For we are His workmanship, created in Christ Jesus *unto good works,* that God ordained beforehand that we should walk in them." Theonomy is the Christian's pattern of sanctification. The believer's life is comprised not only of repentance and faith, but also of continual growth into conformity with the stature of Christ.

Moreover, Christians are not withdrawn individualists who, being smug with their own private morality, let their society continue its moral decline and its suffering in the darkness of sin. The law of God has social, interpersonal, and political directions as well as dictates for the individual heart. The Christian is remiss if he, retreating into a quietistic, pietistic ecclesiology which will not give God's directives to the world, refuses to heed the whole law of God with its extra-personal, extra-ecclesiastical content. The believer is not true to the Great Commission if he plans to disciple the nations without teaching the nations to obey the law of God as well as to observe the ecclesiastical sacraments (read Matt. 28:18-20). If the believer is going to be a trustworthy physician, then, he will give the unbelieving world not only a diagnosis of its moral dilemma, but especially the gracious antidote from God—*all* of that antidote (not just believism without subsequent obedience, and not just obedience to God's law in personal, private matters), which means the gospel with the entirety of God's law. The physician who gives only a portion of the remedy is untrue to *his patient;* but when the physician is the Christian taking God's remedy to sinners, and when he holds back from giving the full remedy, he is also tragically untrue to *his Lord.*

It is the place of God's law, all of God's law, then, that is the subject matter of this study. I will first lay out fundamental scriptural support for the thesis to be discussed. The ensuing discussion will clarify the thesis against misconceptions, show why God's law is integral to biblical Christianity, reply to alleged conflicts, and then briefly confirm the thesis from further passages and summarize.

The next section of the book has an apologetical cast. I shall attempt to show that there is really no other ethical answer but that which is authoritatively revealed in God's word. One must choose theonomy *or* autonomy, but autonomy is morally crippled. So also are half-way measures between theonomy and autonomy; the blending of the two yields subtle antinomianism. The next major section of the treatise goes on to discuss the applicability of God's law to social concerns; in particular I will aim to demonstrate that the civil magistrate is obligated to enforce God's law in public matters. Then finally, from the double perspective of command and blessing, I will explain why the reader cannot be indifferent to what has been written. My conclusion: "The wise in heart will receive commandments" (Prov. 10:8, AV).

Now, as preparation for the upcoming and foundational chapter of the book, let us reflect upon the Christian's previously mentioned obligation to influence his society, to keep it from moral decay, to work toward the eradication of public unrighteousness. As the believer grows in sanctification he reflects more clearly the glory which belongs to Christ, the Light of the World; by following Him we have the light of life (John 8:12 and 1:4). Hereby *we* are the light of the world, reproving its darkness (Eph. 5:11), and instructing it in the paths of righteousness (Ps. 51:13). If we reflect the glory of Christ's light, if we are truly His disciples and friends, if He is really the author of our eternal salvation, then we will obey the Lord's commandments (John 14:15; 15:9-10, 13-14; 1 John 2:3-4; Matt. 7:21 ff.; Luke 8:21; Heb. 5:9). Those who have been redeemed by Christ desire to obey their King as grateful subjects. In the Sermon on the Mount Christ our Lord commands us to be the light of the world and salt of the earth (Matt. 5:13-16). But *how* do we let our light shine before men? What are we to do in order that we be preservatives in the immoral world? Our good motives would be powerless without a correct blueprint, a guide to Christ-honoring behavior. So what pattern should we follow in order to be the light of the world?

One way to answer this question would be to look to the way that Jesus, the Light of the world, lived. He was concerned to obey every detail of God's law. A *second way* to answer our question would be to consider the Older Testamental background to Christ's statement that we are the ligh of the world. This can be found in Isaiah 51:4-8; especially note these words hich parallel verses 14, 17, and 18 of Matthew 5:

> Attend unto me, O my people . . . a law shall go forth from me, and I will establish my justice for a light of the peoples . . . the heavens shall vanish away like smoke, and the earth shall wax old like a garment . . . but my righteousness shall not be abolished. Hearken unto me, ye that know righteousness, the people in whose heart is my law . . . my righteousness shall be forever. . . .

In this passage the justice of God's law is the light of the world, and to know righteousness is to have God's law. This righteous law will *not be abrogated* because it *stands forever*. Therefore, if we are to be the light of the world we should contemplate and obey the law of God, for that law shows His righteousness and justice; and it shall not be abolished. A *third way* in which we can find the answer to the question posed above (how are we to be the light of the world?) is simply to read on in the Sermon on the Mount, for Christ goes on from verses 13-16 to answer our question in verses 17-20. Here He sets before us the way of personal holiness and social sanctification, and here He indicates what our Christian attitude should be toward the Older Testament law of God. The life of Christ's disciple is not governed by the commandments of men (e.g., Matt. 15:9; Titus 1:14) but by the law of God. Autonomy (self-law) is out of place in Christian ethics. Therefore, we turn to "Theonomy" as it is taught in Matthew 5:17-19

Chapter 2

THE ABIDING VALIDITY OF THE LAW IN EXHAUSTIVE DETAIL (Matthew 5:17-19)

THE *locus classicus* pertaining to Jesus and the law is Matthew 5:17-20; in this familiar section Jesus speaks openly of His relation to the law of the Older Testament, the status of that law, and what the response of His disciples should be to that law. The theonomy of true kingdom righteousness is the heart of His teaching here.

Joachim Jeremias outlines the three basic interpretive approaches to the Sermon on the Mount,[1] labeling them "the perfectionist conception," "the theory of the impossible ideal," and "the interim-ethic." In the first case Jesus is seen as laying down an obedience ethic as rigid as that of the Older Testament. The second view holds that Jesus knows that we cannot keep His intensified demands and so intends to move us to despair in order that we would appreciate God's mercy. In the third case the Sermon represents a kind of martial law, a set of exception laws valid only in a time of crisis, imposed by Jesus because he expected the end of the world in the near future. Carl F. H. Henry goes into a thorough discussion and refutation of the various theological approaches to the Sermon on the Mount.[2] To Jeremias' outline he would add the humanist repudiation of the Sermon, the liberal approach which says that Jesus is presenting the "brave news" of salvation

---

[1] Joachim Jeremias, *The Sermon on the Mount,* trans. Norman Perrin, ed., John Reumann, Facet Books: Biblical Series, No. 2 (Philadelphia: Fortress Press, 1963), pp. 1-12.

[2] Carl F. H. Henry, *Christian Personal Ethics* (Grand Rapids: William B. Eerdmans Publishing Co., 1957), pp. 278-308.

by good works, the dispensational interpretation which sees a code of ethics valid only for a future millennial kingdom in the Sermon on the Mount, and the existential interpretation which holds that Jesus is offering a disposition of mind and not concrete normative laws. Henry comes to the conclusion that the historic Reformed approach to the Sermon on the Mount is the only one which does full justice to all the data.[3] According to this view the unity of the Divine covenant with man is presupposed; thus the Sermon expresses the only righteousness acceptable to God in this or in any age. Jesus offers a closer definition of the constant Divine moral requirement and does not depart from either the creation ethic or that of the Old Testament; consequently, the Sermon is relevant as the standard of conduct, convicting men of sin, restraining public wickedness, and ruling the life of the believer. "The Sermon brings into clear relief the eternal oneness of the law."[4] Henry offers a summary of the defects in the other approaches to Matthew 5-7 by saying:

> The existential view errs in holding that the Sermon is not intended as practical legislation clearly defined in propositional form. The dispensational view errs in holding that the Sermon was given as practical legislation to be fulfilled primarily in the future millennial age. The humanist is wrong in holding that it has been outmoded by evolutionary progress; and the interim-ethic school is wrong in its position that the Sermon is discredited by its eschatological factor; the liberal is wrong when he treats the Sermon as an ethic independent of supernatural redemption; the dispensationalist is wrong when he assigns it only a secondary relevance for this age; and the existentialist is wrong when he finds its relevance only in the sphere of attitude and not at all as practical legislation. The humanist, liberal, and interim ethic views are wrong in

---

[3] Ibid., pp. 308-326.

[4] Ibid., p. 310.

> supposing that man in his present state can fulfill the requirements of the Sermon. . . . Some dispensational writers imply that during the millennial age. . . . some will attain salvation on the basis of fulfillment. This is despite the emphasis of the Gospel that the salvation of sinners is solely on the ground of grace. The existential view proclaims, and rightly so, the impossibility of the man in sin himself fulfilling the Sermon's requirements. . . .[5]

Even Jeremias, who maintains that the Sermon is *not* law *but* gospel (a choice the necessity of which is repudiated on the Reformed view), admits that "a real element of validity" must be found in Jesus' endorsement of the central theme of Judaism, viz., "the inexorable nature of the law of God." "It is also quite valid to say . . . that both Jesus and late Judaism are firmly rooted in the Old Testament."[6] Moreover, against any view which would assign the Sermon to a *personalistic* ethic which operates without law demands,[7] Herman Ridderbos rightly insists that one cannot eliminate *any* section of life as not belonging to the scope of the Sermon; it cannot be solely referred to future salvation, present asceticism, social revolution, distinct persons, or distinct phases of life:[8] indeed, one must not think that it is valid only for the church or for personal relations.[9] Therefore, against those who say we must emphasize Jesus Himself and *not* the practicality of the law when we come to the Sermon,[10] against those who say that the law has

[5] Ibid., pp. 308-309.

[6] Jeremias, *op. cit.,* pp. 4, 2.

[7] E.g., R. F. Collins, "Christian Personalism and the Sermon on the Mount," *Andover Newton Quarterly,* 10 (1, 1969), pp. 19-30.

[8] Herman N. Ridderbos, *When the Time Had Fully Come: Studies in New Testament Theology* (Grand Rapids: William B. Eerdmans Publishing Co., 1957), pp. 31-37.

[9] Herman Ridderbos, *Matthew's Witness to Jesus Christ: The King and the Kingdom,* World Christian Books (New York: Association Press, 1958), p. 33.

[10] E.g., M. Corbin, "Nature et signification de la Loi evangelque," *Recherches de Science Religieuse,* 57 (1, 1969), pp. 5-48.

absolutely no validity when we look at Jesus,[11] and against those who maintain that the gospel remits the severity of the moral law,[12] it should be emphasized that law and gospel are not irreconcilably opposed to each other in the New Covenant since Jesus is both the law's "fulfillment" and the heart of the gospel.[13] Therefore, we must not hesitate to see in the Sermon on the Mount a proclamation of the absolute moral will of God.[14]

The central demand of Jesus' commandments, especially in the Sermon on the Mount, is that of righteousness: Matthew 5 deals with the righteousness that Christ's disciples must have in order to enter the kingdom of heaven (Matt. 5:20), Matthew 6 continues the theme of righteousness and ends with the summary: "seek first the kingdom of God and His righteousness" (Matt. 6:33), and persecution for the sake of righteousness is interchangeable with persecution for the sake of the kingdom (cf. Matt. 5:10 and Luke 18:29).

> It may rightly be said, therefore, that kingdom and righteousness are synonymous concepts in Jesus' preaching. The one is unthinkable without the other. . . . In all these places, righteousness means the sum total of God's demand imposed upon all who would enter the kingdom.[15]

---

[11] E.g., Werner Elert, *Law and Gospel* trans. Edward H. Schroeder, ed. Franklin Sherman, Facet Books: Social Ethics Series, No. 16 (Philadelphia: Fortress Press, 1967), p. 42.

[12] E.g., Thomas Watson, *The Ten Commandments,* rev. ed. (London: The Banner of Truth Trust, 1965 [original edition 1692]), p. 47.

[13] Cf. J. G. Kooren, "Wet en Evangelie," *Homiletica en Biblica,* 22 (9, 1963), pp. 200-205.

[14] Cf. J. Schmid, "Ich aber sage euch. Der Anruf der Bergpredigt," *Bibel und Kirche*, 19 (3, 1964), pp. 75-79.

[15] Herman Ridderbos, *The Coming of the Kingdom,* trans. H. de Jongste, ed. Raymond O. Zorn (Philadelphia: The Presbyterian and Reformed Publishing Co., 1962 reprinted 1969), p. 286.

The righteousness which reflects God's nature, the righteousness which is demanded by our love and discipleship to Christ, the righteousness which characterizes the kingdom of God, the righteousness which makes us the light of the world and salt of the earth is described in the Sermon on the Mount; it is capsulated in Matthew 5:17-20. In light of the fact that Jesus intends to relate His conception of righteousness to the law of the Older Covenant in Matthew 5:17-20, it is not without significance that the literary framework of the Sermon seems to imitate or be patterned after the first giving of the law at Sinai (Ex. 20-23). Both are divine pronouncements from a mountain having similar form and intent;[16] the giving of a general principle and following of it with case law particularizations is present in both Exodus 20 ff. and Matthew 5:17 ff. [17]

Since no important textual-critical qualifications need to be made in our common manuscript rendition of the passage under

---

[16] Austin Farrer, *St. Matthew and St. Mark*, 2nd ed., (London: Dacre Press, 1954 [reprinted 1966]), pp. 160 ff.

[17] Some have viewed the whole gospel of Matthew as structured after a Pentateuchal motif, e.g., Benjamin W. Bacon, *Studies in Matthew* (New York: Henry Holt and Co., Inc., 1930) even though a man like W. D. Davies is not entirely convinced of it, cf. *The Setting of the Sermon on the Mount* (Cambridge: The University Press, 1964), pp. 14-93. Others have found the Sermon on the Mount itself to be structured according to a Pentateuch ordering, e.g., Jeremias, *op. cit.,* pp. 13-14; and some have even seen the five discourse themes paralleling the five themes of the Pentateuchal books, e.g., E. M. Skibbe, "Pentateuchal Themes in the Sermon on the Mount," *Lutheran Quarterly,* 20 (1, 1968) 44-51. C. H. Dodd finds in the very event of delivering a message from a mount a correspondence to Moses bringing the law from a mount (in Dodd's case, Jesus is seen as bringing a new law) cf. *Gospel and Law: The Relation of Faith and Ethics in Early Christianity* (New York: Columbia University Press, 1951 [reprinted 1968]), pp. 62-63. In all of this the point to be recognized is that the whole sermon is subsumed under the category of law and demand, cf. Hans Windisch, *The Meaning of the Sermon on the Mount,* 2nd ed., trans. S. MacLean Gilmour (Philadelphia: The Westminster Press, 1951), p. 66. Moreover, Matthew 5:17-20 is the key to the Sermon as a whole, cf. Eduard Thurneysen, *The Sermon on the Mount* 5th ed., trans. William Childs Robinson and James M. Robinson (Richmond: John Knox Press, 1964), p. 48. Therefore, in approaching this passage one should expect a significant legal pronouncement.

consideration we can move immediately into an exegetico-theological examination of it.[18] A general survey of the basic interpretations that have been assigned to Matthew 5:17-20 could appropriately precede a more technical consideration. Not all commentators have been willing to see these words of Jesus as straightforward and fully meant. They have suggested that this passage is simply an emphatic expression of Jesus' deep loyalty to His Jewish heritage in general,[19] or that this is sheer hyperbole indicating what is preferable to the unrestraint present in certain iconoclastic elements in the crowd,[20] or that Jesus was merely attempting to enlist the support of the Jewish leaders early in His ministry, or that Jesus was following His typical didactic method of making far-reaching statements and then leaving it up to His hearers to discover the limitations and qualifications in their own thought and experience.[21] Beyond the doubtful factuality of these observations (e.g., was Jesus seeking the support of the Pharisees in verse 20? Did Jesus

---

[18] It has been suggested that Matthew's account of the Sermon on the Mount is actually a compilation of individual sayings of Christ since the parallels found in Luke's gospel appear scattered throughout the ministry of Christ; cf. Jeremias, *op. cit.*, pp. 14-19. However, it is not at all clear why Jesus could not have repeated points at different times in His ministry (indeed, it would seem highly likely, given changing audiences and localities) or why, if there is a divergence between Matthew and Luke, Luke is not the one who altered the chronological order (after all, Luke had to piece the history of Christ together from many sources, but Matthew was an eyewitness). Moreover, even granting the *possibility* that Matthew has artificially devised a sermon from separate sayings it still has to be *demonstrated* that this possibility was an actual occurrence, and noting how smoothly the Sermon reads it is not likely that anyone is going to show it to be reflecting such a genetic history. Thus it is only appropriate that we read and interpret the Sermon as a consistent and continual message from Christ.

[19] Floyd V. Filson, *A Commentary on the Gospel According to St. Matthew,* ed. Henry Chadwick, Harper's New Testament Commentaries (New York: Harper and Brothers Publishers, 1960) and *Jesus Christ the Risen Lord* (New York: Abingdon Press, 1956), p. 100.

[20] W. D. Davies, *Christian Origins and Judaism* (Philadelphia: The Westminster Press, 1962), p. 52.

[21] Alfred Plummer, *An Exegetical Commentary on the Gospel According to S. Matthew* (New York: Charles Scribner's Sons, 1909), pp. 74-75.

really esteem sinners capable of qualifying God's pronouncements? etc.), none of these considerations sufficiently explain the explicitness of Jesus' assertions about the law's validity—that it extends to the minutest part and will hold until the universe passes away.

It has been suggested that in Matthew 5:17-48 Jesus brings the Old Testament concepts of righteousness and justice to full maturity by stressing their "interiority"; He thereby implies that the Christian ethical ideal is immeasurably higher than that of the scribes and Pharisees.[22] However, while Jesus stressed inward heart attitude in contrast to the Pharisees, so did the Older Testament! God had already revealed His abhorrence of any merely outward performance of religious duties and His desire for the heartfelt response of inward sanctification from His people (cf. Isa. 1:10-20; Ps. 51:16, 17). In the Book of the Law God says, "And these words which I am commanding you today shall be on your heart. . . . You shall therefore impress these words of mine on your heart and on your soul. . . . the word is very near you, in your mouth and in your heart, that you may observe it" (Deut. 6:6; 11:18; 30:14, NASV). The applications of the law's interiority mentioned by Jesus in the antitheses of Matthew 5 have parallels in the Older Testament. Although Jesus rebukes the Pharisees for failing to see this, the interpretation before us of Matthew 5:17-20 still fails to go far enough. The main element of Jesus' teaching in Matthew 5:17-20, its boldest feature, has been overlooked. This feature (viz., the abiding validity of the law in exhaustive detail) is actually an integral and necessary part of the observation that Jesus corrects the Pharisaic externalism.

Others have said that Jesus came to deliver a New Torah which would replace the Old, but Jesus realized that He could make no public annulment of the law (even though the sheer pressure of human need led Him to break it openly!) until His blood had been shed and the New Covenant ratified. He could not assume the authority to explicitly

[22] A. George, "Soyez parfaits comme votre Pere celeste (Matth. 5.17-48)," *Bible et Vie Chretienne,* 19 (1957), 85-90.

utter the law's abrogation; only His death could do that. The life and words of Jesus replace the Old Law with the principle of freedom, a new order infused with the Spirit and perfected inwardly.[23] Even if it could be demonstrated that this explanation does not flatly contradict the actual assertions of Matthew 5:17-20, it would nevertheless fail to see the emphatic authority (presently in hand)[24] to which Jesus draws attention in our passage: the pattern of "you heard that it was said . . . *but I say*" is utilized extensively. Jesus had assumed the very most authoritative teaching stance (e.g., "*truly* I say to you") and could have abrogated the law if that had been His divine desire. The explicit and emphatic affirmation of the law's authority does not allow one to take "fulfillment" in verse 17 as any sort of euphemism for "relaxation" or "invalidation."[25] At the same time in which God promised *a new* covenant He indicated that, far from being different from the first covenant, the ethical stipulations of that new covenant would be the same as the original law; God says He will write the law on His people's hearts, not change the law. The "newness" of the new covenant is not constituted by a new law; the old law has perpetual sanction (cf. Jer. 31:33-34). Although this "New Torah" interpretation of Matthew 5:17-20 fails to see that Jesus' death was in conformity to the law (Gal. 3:10, 13; Heb. 9:22) and not the abrogation of it, and that the Spirit which grants us freedom fulfills the law through us because the law is the pattern of true freedom (Rom. 8:4; Ps. 119:45; James 1:25), its most

---

[23] Davies, *Christian Origins, op. cit.*, p. 56; cf. Alexander Jones, *Gospel According to St. Matthew: A Text and Commentary for Students* (New York: Sheed and Ward Inc., Publishers, 1965), p. 79.

[24] Note Matthew 7:28; cf. Ned Bernard Stonehouse, *The Witness of Matthew and Mark to Christ,* 2nd ed. (Grand Rapids: William B. Eerdmans Publishing Co., 1958), pp. 198-199; Schmid, *loc. cit.*; David Brown sees Christ wielding "supreme legislative authority" here, *The Four Gospels: A Commentary, Critical, Experimental, and Practical* (London: The Banner of Truth Trust, 1864 [reprinted 1969]), p. 30; J. A. Alexander takes Christ's words in the Sermon to be solemnly propounded with divine authority, *The Gospel According to Matthew* (New York: Scribner, Armstrong, and Co., 1873), p. 127.

[25] Stonehouse, *op. cit.*, p. 202.

obvious fault is that it misses the forthright emphasis Jesus places on the element of continuity. Far from criticizing the Older Testament, Jesus asserts its eternal validity. Verses 17-18 teach that everything Christ is going to teach is in absolute harmony with the entire Older Testamental law (while being in antipathy to the Pharisees: verses 19-20).

A technical analysis of Matthew 5:17-19 can secure a proper understanding of its teaching. Μὴ νομίσητε is a prohibition (expressed by means of an aorist subjunctive and the negative); it means "do not think." If Christ's enemies had basely slandered Him by stating that His teachings were at variance with the law[26] this is not indicated in the text, for the aorist tense gives the verb an ingressive force: "do not (begin to) think," as opposed to "stop thinking" (which would require prohibition expressed in the present tense). The implication is that Christ knew the danger that His hearers or scribal opponents might misunderstand or willfully distort His doctrine of the law, so He commands them not even to start thinking that the Messiah abrogates the law.

Καταλῦσαι is a telic infinitive indicating that Christ did not come "*in order to* annul," "make invalid," or "repeal" the law. The sense of καταλύω is that of dissolving, or dismantling (the destruction of something by separating its pieces)[27] —the word is particularly used of the destruction, pulling down, of an established building (cf. Matt. 24:2; 26:61; 27:40; Mark 13:2; Luke 21:6; Acts 6:14; 2 Cor. 5:1; Gal. 2:18).

---

[26] As suggested and implied by the following: John Calvin, *Commentary on a Harmony of the Evangelists, Matthew, Mark, and Luke,* Vol. I, trans. William Pringle, Calvin's Commentaries (Grand Rapids: William B. Eerdmans Publishing Co., 1845 [reprinted 1948, 1963]), pp. 275-276; Plummer, *op. cit.,* p. 75; John Brown, *Discourses and Sayings of Our Lord Jesus Christ,* Vol. I, 2nd ed. (London: The Banner of Truth Trust, 1852 [reprinted 1967]), pp. 168-169; Thomas Walker, *The Teaching of Jesus and the Jewish Teaching of His Age* (London: George Allen and Unwin Ltd., 1923), p. 262; Charles Augustus Briggs, *The Ethical Teaching of Jesus* (New York: Charles Scribner's Sons, 1904), p. 143.

[27] Cf. Alexander, *op. cit.,* p. 126; cf. William F. Arndt and F. Wilbur Gingrich, *A Greek-English Lexicon of the New Testament and Other Early Christian Literature* (Chicago: The University of Chicago Press, 1957), p. 415.

This is the meaning of the word as it is used in language pertaining to physical objects. It is evident that καταλύω must also carry a figurative usage, for the literal ("empiricalistic") sense will not fit numerous contexts in which "to dismantle" appears.[28] In the *Gospel According to the Ebionites*,[29] for example, καταλύω is used in reference to τὰς θυσίας ("the sacrifices"); here we are not to understand the dismembering or dissecting of sacrificial animals, but rather the *abolishing* of the sacrificial system. This same figurative sense appears in a legal context (parallel to that of Matt. 5:17 ff.) in 2 Maccabees 2:22; here καταλύω, being placed in contrast to "restore," means essentially the same thing as it does in Matthew 5:17. The phrase from 2 Maccabees reads ". . . and restored the laws that were about to be *abolished*." Καταλύω is used in 2 Maccabees 4:11 to speak of abolishing or overthrowing the lawful institutions, and the Didache utilizes the same word in speaking of those who undermine apostolic teaching (11: 2). Καταλύω never takes the meaning of "disobey, or violate"; "to dismantle (καταλύω) the law" is not an idiomatic expression for transgressing the commandments.[30] In Matthew 5:17 Jesus uses a vivid metaphor (drawn from the language sphere of physical objects) to teach that His relationship to the law is *not* one of invalidation or abrogation.[31] Here καταλῦσαι means "to abrogate, to set aside in the exercise of legislative authority."[32] The Messiah has no intention of undoing the will of His Father as it is found in the law and prophets.

---

[28] That is, "to dissolve the law" is not akin to the burning of books (cf. Acts 19:19) in some literalistic sense; cf. John Brown, *op. cit.*, p. 167.

[29] Cited in Arndt and Gingrich, *loc. cit.*

[30] John Murray, *Principles of Conduct: Aspects of Biblical Ethics* (Grand Rapids: William B. Eerdmans Publishing Co., 1957), p. 149; 4 Maccabees 5:33 may be a rare exception.

[31] J. A. Alexander correctly observes that the legal context requires such a translation, *loc. cit.*

[32] Alexander Balmain Bruce, "The Synoptic Gospels," ed. W. Robertson Nicoll, *The Expositor's Greek Testament* Vol. I (New York: George H. Doran Co., [n.d.]), p. 104.

Τὸν νόμον comprises more than simply those aspects of the Mosaic legislation (i.e., "the Law") which have permanent moral application and sanction; the class of commandments traditionally termed "ceremonial" or "ritual" is also within the scope of the term.[33] Nothing in the text supports a restriction of this term's referent to the moral law. Jesus is saying that He did not come to abrogate *any* part of the law. Christ stands in a positive relation to God's law, "not the smallest ceremonial or national ordinance being destroyed in its ultimate idea."[34] Calvin points out that the meaning of the ceremonies is eternal, while their outward form and use are temporal; consequently Christ confirms even the ceremonial law. "That man does not break ceremonies, who omits what is shadowy, but retains their effect."[35] The Levitical ordinances were patterned after a heavenly model (Heb. 8:4-5; 9:23) and thereby typologically foreshadowed the Messiah and His atoning work (Heb. 10:1). These ceremonial laws are organically connected with Christ and His work in salvation history. The truth depicted in these ritual commands is embodied in Christ and is valid yet today. Only the pre-incarnation *use* of these ceremonial procedures is removed for the Christian in the New Covenant—because they were observed once for all by and in the person and work of Christ. The principle involved in these particular ordinances is confirmed, not repealed, in Christ's coming. Hence τὸν νόμον in Matthew 5:17 includes *all* of God's stipulations as revealed in "the Law" of the Older Testament.[36]

---

[33] Cf. Henrich August Wilhelm Meyer, *Critical and Exegetical Hand-book to the Gospel of Matthew*, ed. George R. Crooks, Meyer's Commentary on the New Testament, 6th ed., trans. Peter Christie rev. Frederick Crombie and William Stewart (New York: Funk and Wagnalls Publishers, 1890), p. 120.

[34] John Peter Lange, *The Gospel According to Matthew: Together with a General Theological, and Homiletical Introduction to the New Testament*, 3rd ed., trans. and ed. Philip Schaff (12th ed.), A Commentary on the Holy Scriptures: Critical, Doctrinal and Homiletical, Vol. I of the New Testament (New York: Charles Scribner's Sons, 1899), p. 109.

[35] Calvin, *op. cit.,* p. 280.

[36] Murray, *op. cit.,* pp. 149-151; Arthur W. Pink, *Exposition of the Sermon on the Mount* (Philadelphia: Bible Truth Depot, 1950), p. 50; D. Martin Lloyd-Jones, *Studies*

Προφῆται can refer to a division of the Older Testamental Scriptures (e.g., Matt. 11:13; Luke 16:16; Acts 13:15; 24:14; Rom. 3:21) or can even denote the whole Scripture (e.g., Luke 24:25; John 6:45; Heb. 1:1). Being placed next to τὸν νόμον in Matthew 5:17, προφήτας most likely indicates the contents of those books other than the Pentateuch (cf. Matt. 7:12; 22:40). Jesus phrases His teaching in such a way as to embrace the entire canon of the Older Testament; none of the existing Scriptures are abrogated by His advent or redemptive work. Although Matthew 5:17 is the only place in the New Testament where the disjunction ἤ is used between "law" and "prophets," Matthew is merely putting variety into his expression (not indicating distinctive emphasis),[37] for ἤ can be used where one related or similar term can take the place of or support the other. Matthew uses it in this way in Matthew 10:11, 14, 37; 17:25, and when he intends the distinctive sense of "either . . . or . . ." he always uses ἤ twice in the phrase (Matt. 6:24 and 12:33). Moreover, it has been observed that ἤ is used in Matthew 5:17 simply as better suiting the negative form of expression used by Jesus (". . . not . . . law or prophets" better expresses the negative correlative than ". . . not . . . law and prophets").[38] So "law or prophets" in Matthew 5:17 functions just as "law and prophets" elsewhere in Scripture.

There is no reason to see any *distinctive* mention of the predictive prophecies of the Older Testament in Matthew 5:17 or its context. Besides, since nobody would have expected the self-proclaimed Messiah to turn back the prophecies referring to Himself, it would hardly call for a specific and emphatic pronouncement to correct an unheld opinion. Meyer concurs in this judgment:

---

in the Sermon on the Mount, Vol. I (Grand Rapids: William B. Eerdmans Publishing Co., 1959), pp. 184 ff.

[37] As suggested by some commentators, e.g., Meyer, *loc. cit.*

[38] Henry Alford, *The Greek Testament: With a Critically Revised Text a Digest of Various Readings, Marginal References to Verbal and Idiomatic Usage, Prolegomena, and a Critical and Exegetical Commentary*, Vol. I, ed. and rev. Everett F. Harrison (Chicago: Moody Press, 1958), p. 42.

> We are not to think of their [the O.T.] *predictions as such* (the Greek Fathers, Augustine, Beza, Calovius, and others; also Tholuck, Neander, Harnack, Bleek, Lechler, Schegg, and others), as nobody could imagine that *their* abrogation was to be expected from the Messiah, but, as the connection with νόμος shows . . . their contents as *commands*. . . . [39]

There *is* reason to hold that the phrase "law or prophets" is best taken as focusing on the *ethical stipulations* contained in the canon of the entire Older Testament.[40] The context of Matthew 5:17 clearly demonstrates that both "the law" and "the prophets" refer to divine demand and not prophecy or promise. Verse 16 preceding deals with "good works"; indeed, throughout the entire sermon Jesus speaks as the Messiah who promulgates God's will (cf. Matt. 7:28 f.). Verses 21-48 correct misinterpretations of the divine demands. Matthew 7:12 (cf. Matt. 22:40) uses "the law and prophets" exclusively of moral demands. And most telling is the fact that verses 18 and 19 following, which explain and apply verse 17 of Matthew 5, mention only the *law*. The entire passage is concerned primarily with Christ's *doctrine, not* His *life*.[41] Of course His doctrine and manner of life are a unity, and His life exemplifies His teaching; however, not every verse of Scripture teaches every element of Christian truth. The concern of Matthew 5:17 is Christ's *doctrine* as it bears upon theonomy (God's law). While "law or prophets" broadly denotes the Older Testament Scriptures, Jesus' stress is upon the ethical content, the commandments, of the Older Testament.

---

[39] Meyer, *loc. cit.*

[40] It is so obvious that the context is dealing with moral imperatives and not predictions that some have (wrongly) used this fact to excise the word "prophets" as out of place, e.g., Willoughby C. Allen, *A Critical and Exegetical Commentary on the Gospel According to S. Matthew*, eds. Charles Augustus Briggs, Samuel Rolles Driver, and Alfred Plummer, The International Critical Commentary (New York: Charles Scribner's Sons, 1925), p. 46.

[41] "Here he treats of doctrine, not of life," Calvin, *op. cit.*, p. 275.

The concern of Jesus in Matthew 5:17-19 is to make clear that His purpose is *not* to abrogate the Older Testamental law.[42] The clause following the one under investigation repeats this thought again, thus giving it emphasis: "Do not begin to think that I came in order to abrogate the law or the prophets: *I did not come to abrogate. . . .*" According to J. A. Alexander, in saying this Christ's purpose was to do away with the delusion that the Messianic age meant "a change of moral principles, a relaxation of the claims of justice, and a greater license of indulgence in things hitherto forbidden."[43] So also Calvin:

> With respect to doctrine, we must not imagine that the coming of Christ has freed us from the authority of the law: for it is the eternal rule of a devout and holy life, and must, therefore, be as unchangeable, as the justice of God, which it embraced, is constant and uniform.[44]

If the Messiah did not come to dissolve or abrogate the standing law of the Older Testament, then what relation does He sustain to that law? While Jesus stresses that He did not come with the end in mind of invalidating the law, He states that, conversely, He came πληρῶσαι ("to fulfill"). Undoubtedly, πληρῶσαι is the most crucial word for our understanding of this passage. It is a telic infinitive (aorist) expressing the purpose of Christ's coming with respect to God's law. There have been a variety of suggested senses for "fulfill" in this passage. Does it

---

[42] Thus one cannot agree with Dodd that the Church is to bear witness to the aboriginal law of man's creation in his heart (cf. Romans 2), *op. cit.*, p. 82; nor is John Trapp right in saying that we are now bound only by the law of nature common to Jew and Gentile and not the Mosaic legislation, cf. *Commentary on the New Testament* (Evansville, Indiana: The Sovereign Grace Book Club, 1647 [reprinted 1865, 1958]), pp. 59-60.

[43] Alexander, *op. cit.*, p. 125.

[44] Calvin, *op. cit.*, p. 277.

indicate that Jesus puts an end to,[45] replaces,[46] supplements (adds to),[47] intends to actively obey,[48] enforce[49] or confirms and restores the law?

---

[45] E.g., R. A. Hawkins, "Covenant Relations of the Sermon on the Mount," *Restoration Quarterly,* 12 (1, 1969), 1-9.

[46] E.g., A. B. Bruce, *loc. cit.*; cf. W. D. Davies, *Christian Origins, loc. cit.* Windisch sees Christ as presenting "anti-Jewish, anti-Mosaic Christian legalism," *op. cit.*, p. 131; B. Haring says a New Law founded on the beatitudes is set against the Old Testament covenant law, "The Normative Value of the Sermon on the Mount," *Catholic Biblical Quarterly*, 29 (3, 1967), 375-385.

[47] E.g., Plummer, *op. cit.,* p. 76; W. D. Davies, *Setting of the Sermon, op. cit.*, pp. 100-102; R. V. G. Tasker, *The Gospel According to St. Matthew: An Introduction and Commentary*, ed. R. V. G. Tasker, The Tyndale New Testament Commentaries, Vol. I (Grand Rapids: William B. Eerdmans Publishing Co., 1961), p. 67; E. H. Plumptre, *The Gospel According to St. Matthew, St. Mark, and St. Luke*, ed. Charles John Ellicott, A Bible Commentary for Bible Students, Vol. VI (London: Marshall Brothers, Ltd., [n.d.]), p. 54; John Brown, *op. cit.,* p. 170; David Thomas, *The Genius of the Gospel: A Homiletical Commentary on the Gospel of St. Matthew*, ed. William Webster (London: Dickinson and Higham, 1873), pp. 41-44; J. Oswald Dykes, *The Manifesto of the King: An Exposition of the Sermon on the Mount* (London: James Nisbet and Co., 1881), p. 206; Martin Dibelius, *The Sermon on the Mount* (New York: Charles Scribner's Sons, 1940), pp. 22-23, 71; Windisch, *op. cit.,* pp. 126, 131; Alan Hugh M'Neile, *The Gospel According to St. Matthew: The Greek Text with Introduction, Notes, and Indices* (London: Macmillan and Co., Ltd., 1915), pp. 57-58; Theodore H. Robinson, *The Gospel of Matthew*, ed. James Moffat, The Moffatt New Testament Commentary (London: Hodder and Stoughton, 1928 [reprinted 1936]), p. 35; J. Y. Campbell, "Fulfill," *A Theological Word Book of the Bible*, ed. Alan Richardson (London: SCM Press Ltd., 1950 [reprinted 1956]), p. 88; Jones, *op. cit.*, pp. 22-23; Meyer, *op. cit.*, p. 121; see also the New English Bible, and the translations of Weymouth, Phillips, and Ronald Knox. Many of these authors go beyond the idea of a (bare) increment of commands to the idea of transcending by internalization, deepening the principles, developing the ideal reality, raising to a higher plane by the spirit, probing to the comprehensive character by working out the spirit, etc.

[48] E.g., Lloyd-Jones, *loc. cit.;* Pink, *op. cit.*, p. 52; R. Mackintosh, "Fulfillment," *A Dictionary of Christ and the Gospels.* Vol. I, ed. James Hastings (New York: Charles Scribner's Sons, 1906), p. 627; C. A. Briggs, *op. cit.*, p. 144; Thurneysen, *op. cit.,* p. 48; Patrick Fairbairn, *The Revelation of Law in Scripture: Considered with Respect Both to its own Nature and to its Relative Place in Successive Dispensations* (Grand Rapids: Zondervan Publishing House, 1869 [reprinted 1957]), p. 233; Geerhardus Vos, *Biblical Theology: Old and New Testaments* (Grand Rapids: William B. Eerdmans Publishing Co., 1948 [reprinted 1966]), p. 388.

[49] E.g., J. A. Alexander, *op. cit.*, p. 127; B. B. Warfield, "Jesus' Mission According

The attempt to answer this question by discovering the underlying Aramaic from which Matthew translated his gospel[50] is ill founded. The extant text of Matthew bears the marks of an original Greek composition and shows no evidence of translation Greek. Moreover, there is no agreement as to what the Aramaic original would have been, some holding that Matthew mistook the original form, others that he mistranslated it, and there is even a major textual variant (which inserts the negative, "not") in the supposedly Talmudic rendition of Matthew 5:17! With there being no concrete evidence for an Aramaic original it is not surprising that the attempt to render it is wholly conjectural. All the arguments for an Aramaic prototype of the Greek gospel according to Matthew have been adequately answered elsewhere.[51] The Greek gospel by Matthew is canonical for the Christian people of God in this age, and it must be from this source that we derive our doctrine and direction.[52] Accordingly, is πληρόω in Matthew 5:17 to be taken in the

---

to His Own Testimony," *The Princeton Theological Review*, XIII (4, 1915), 557-559; cf. Windisch, *op. cit.*, pp. 66-67; see also the translation by Goodspeed.

[50] As in W. D. Davies, *Christian Origins, op. cit.*, pp. 32-33; Günther Bornkamm, Gerhard Barth and Heinz Joachim Held, *Tradition and Interpretation in Matthew*, trans. Percy Scott (London: SCM Press Ltd., 1963), p. 67; Joseph K. Klausner, *Jesus of Nazareth: His Life, Times and Teaching*, trans. Herbert Danby (Boston: Beacon Press, 1925), p. 45; and especially Joachim Jeremias. *Unknown Sayings of Jesus,* 2nd ed., trans. Reginald H. Fuller (London: SPCK, [1957] 1964), pp. 24-25 and cf. *The Sermon on the Mount, op. cit.*, pp. 15-16.

[51] See Donald Guthrie, *New Testament Introduction*, Vol. I (Chicago: Inter-Varsity Press, 1965), pp. 44-45; Everett F. Harrison, *Introduction to the New Testament* (Grand Rapids: William B. Eerdmans Publishing Co., 1964), pp. 153-159; cf. R. V. G. Tasker, *op. cit.*, p. 13.

[52] Passing note might be made of the fact that when one searches for the Aramaic background he comes, or can come, to the conclusion that Christ's original words meant "confirm, validate"; cf. Gustaf Dalman, *Jesus-Jeshua: Studies in the Gospels*, trans. Paul P. Levertoff (New York: The Macmillan Co., 1929), p. 61. This is the conclusion which one should reach, I shall subsequently argue, when he studies the Greek text itself (our only legitimate and concrete data). With respect to the possible Aramaic allusion to Matthew 5:17 in Shabbath 116b, "I came not to destroy the Law of Moses nor [a variant reading says 'but'; however, 'nor' is the correct reading, cf. Dalman, *op. cit.*, p. 57] to add to the law of Moses," the one thing that is quite clear

sense of ending, replacing, supplementing, obeying, enforcing or confirming the ethical stipulations of the Older Testament?

The first suggestion (i.e., "put an end to"), although not uncommonly held, would attempt to force a distinction between the conceptions of "dismantling" (καταλύω) and "abrogating" (πληρόω) the law (e.g., to abrogate the law in effect while repudiating the spirit of a destroyer,[53] or loosening the law without violence or selfish intent).[54] It has already been shown, however, that καταλύω means "abrogate, invalidate" in reference to the law. Hence the proponents of this interpretation (i.e., that "fulfill" connotes a particular *mode* of "abrogating") would have Jesus saying, "I came not to abrogate the law, *but* to put it to an end"—a not so subtle contradiction![55] Furthermore, when πληρόω is used in the New Testament in the sense of "finish, or end" it always appears in a context where the thought of advancement, or moving on, as well as a temporal element, are explicit (cf. Luke 7:1; Acts 12:25; 13:25; 14:26; Rev. 6:11); both these elements are absent in the present passage with reference to the fulfilling done by Jesus. Some

---

from the context is that Gamaliel is citing this saying in order to prevent the sly judge from doing away with any Old Testament prescription, and so confirmation of the Law must be at least implicit in the saying; cf. *Shabbath*, Vol. II, trans. H. Freedman, The Babylonian Talmud: Seder Mo'ed, ed. I. Epstein (London: The Soncino Press, 1938).

[53] A. B. Bruce, *op. cit.*, p. 104.

[54] E. Lyttelton *Studies in the Sermon on the Mount* (London: Longmans, Green, and Co., 1905), pp. 130-131.

[55] It is of interest that when the liberalizing interpretation of this passage is set forth it leads to the conclusion that the passage lacks unity and actually reflects three schools of thought: rabbinic orthodoxy (vv. 18-19), Marcionism (vv. 21-48), along with liberal Judaism (v. 17); cf. Bennet Harvie Branscomb, *Jesus and the Law of Moses* (New York: Harper and Brothers, 1930), pp. 213 ff. Of course this fragmenting line of thought does not give the passage the benefit of the doubt by adequately checking other senses of "fulfill" to see if they keep unity in the pericope; moreover, the fragmented character of the passage has a *prima facie* case against it in the conjunctions used between verse 17 and verse 18, and between verse 18 and verse 19—either the speaker, the recorder, or the editor thought the three assertions to be coherent with each other!

have maintained that the fulfillment mentioned in Matthew 5:17 points to Christ abolishing the ceremonial laws and returning to the purity of the Torah alone,[56] that there can be no doubt but that He came to abrogate the law of Moses as part of a temporary and typical economy,[57] or that the outer shell of the Old Testament law had to be destroyed in the fulfillment of that law.[58] The problem with these views is that they overlook the scope of the "law" dealt with by Christ in this passage. Above we noted that "law or prophets" applies to the *whole* law of God found throughout the Older Testament (therefore, *more* than simply the ritual ordinances). That this is the referrent is corroborated in verse 18 following. The set of antitheses given by Christ in verses 21-48 also demonstrate to us that He is thinking of the moral law as much as anything else in verse 17. (And even *if* Christ were referring only to the ceremonial law in Matthew 5:17, these views would have Jesus contradicting Himself again: "I did not come to abrogate the ceremonies, but to abolish them"!) But perhaps the view could be rehabilitated by holding that Jesus came not to abrogate or attack the validity or "lawfulness" of the law in the *past* period of redemptive history (for which it was intended) but now puts an end to that *era* governed by the law. Besides suffering from the defect of imposing theological prejudice upon πληρῶσαι and infusing it with content that it cannot sustain, this view simply fails to take cognizance of verse 18 immediately following where Jesus clearly states that the law He is discussing remains valid "until heaven and earth pass away." Furthermore, one must take account of the strong adversative ἀλλὰ standing between καταλῦσαι and πληρῶσαι, as well as Jesus' double assertion that He came not to abrogate the law—both appearing in the very verse under discussion.

The second interpretation suggested (i.e., "replace") holds basically that Jesus brings in the law of the Spirit which cancels the law of

---

[56] E.g., G. H. Tavard, "Christianity and Israel: How did Christ Fulfill the Law?" *Downside Review* 75 (1957), 55-68.

[57] John Brown, *op. cit.*, p. 168.

[58] Dykes, *op. cit.*, p. 211.

the letter; as mentioned above, the "New Torah" replaces the old. Millar Burrows says that Jesus, like the Old Testament prophets, is teaching an attitude rather than a moral code.[59] However, this overlooks the fact that the law of God was the basis for the prophetic announcements against the people, rulers, or nations (hence the covenantal "lawsuit" of the prophets) in the Old Testament. Ethical imperatives and references to the law of God are not lacking in the prophets, and thus we cannot dismiss the idea of a moral *code*. Hence Burrows would want to maintain that Jesus, like the Old Testament prophets, urged the law of the Spirit and not that of the letter; Christ brought a "Spiritualized" Torah in place of the Mosaic Law. This view shares the same crucial defects as the "New Torah" view discussed previously; thus, it also must be rejected. Matthew 5:17 must be interpreted on the principle of *continuity* with the Older Testament, for Jesus authoritatively affirms the eternal validity of the law in verse 18. The comments of Calvin and Geerhardus Vos are appropriate here:

> By these words [Matthew 5:17] he [Christ] is so far from departing from the former covenant, that on the contrary, he declares that it will be confirmed, and ratified, when it shall be succeeded by the new.[60]

> Jesus never loses sight of the continuity that ought to exist in revelation. The old is not ruthlessly sacrificed to the new, purely on account of the latter's newness. The idea is always that the old had the seeds of the new in itself. For this reason also a revolutionary discarding of the Old Testament is out of the question.[61]

---

[59] Millar Burrows, *An Outline of Biblical Theology* (Philadelphia: The Westminster Press, 1946), pp. 160-161.

[60] Calvin, *op. cit.*, p. 277.

[61] Vos, *op. cit.*, p. 387.

To *replace* the Mosaic law Jesus would perforce *abrogate* that law; yet the suggestion that "fulfill" connotes "putting an end to" has been dismissed already. The final problem with the interpretation of πληρόω as "replace" is that πληρόω never assumes that meaning in the New Testament or early Christian literature.

According to the third suggestion (i.e., that "fulfill" takes the sense of "supplement" or "add to") Jesus begins where the law of the Older Testament leaves off and completes it; He delivers the more perfect will of God. Supposedly Jesus brings the written law to completion by drawing out its latent principles and "filling it out." The central thought is that of perfecting the law of the Older Testament. Jesus consummates the law, going beyond the narrowness of the letter and bringing it to its destined goal. As Greenwood put it, Jesus considered the Mosaic Law inadequate and desired to perfect it.[62] However, the Holy Spirit inspired the Psalmist to write that the law (in his own day) was "perfect, complete" (Ps. 19:7 f; 119:128). Out of the ranks of those who take πληρῶσαι to mean "supplement and perfect" the Older Testamental law, John Broadus appears to be the only commentator who realized the defect in his view, that it contravened the Older Testament's own testimony to its perfection; Broadus had to admit the truth of the Older Testament's self-evaluation as perfect, "yet for a higher and more spiritual dispensation its principles might be developed into greater completeness."[63] However, this was simply an admission on Broadus' part that his position is inherently self-contradictory; in order to avoid the *material* inconsistency of saying the Older Testament is, and is not, complete or perfect, Broadus had to appeal to a contradiction in *terms*

---

[62] D. Greenwood, "Moral Obligation in the Sermon on the Mount," *Theological Studies*, 31 (2, 1970), 301-309.

[63] John A. Broadus, *Commentary on the Gospel of Matthew*, ed. Alvah Hovey, An American Commentary on the New Testament (Philadelphia: American Baptist Publication Society, 1886), p. 99. N.B.: "different" or "excellent" (cf. Heb. 1:4; 8:6) are comparative adjectives while "complete" or "perfect" are not; there may be degrees of difference and excellence, but not of completeness and perfection (only of the *course toward* completeness, e.g., "more complete" in the sense of "closer to being complete").

(viz., "greater completeness"). Moreover, his answer erroneously assumes that, in contrast to the New Testament perfection, the Older Testament was a dispensation deficient in inward spirituality as to its legislation. The Older Testamental law did *not* fall short of informing God's people of the need for inward heart righteousness in contrast to mere external legalism: for example, "Behold, thou desirest truth in the inward parts, and in the hidden part thou shalt make me know wisdom. . . . Create in me a clean heart, O God, and renew a right spirit within me. . . . The sacrifices of God are a broken spirit, a broken and contrite heart" (Ps. 51:6, 10, 17); "I delight to do thy will, O my God; yea thy law is within my heart" (Ps. 40:8); compare 1 Samuel 15:22; Psalm 37:31; Isaiah 1:10-20. Therefore, Jesus can rebuke the Pharisees and hold them guilty for their hypocritical legalism. If the Older Testamental law is viewed (wrongly) as lacking the inward spirituality provided by the "higher righteousness" of the New Testament, then, as the Jewish writer, Friedlander, will be quick to point out, Jesus is being terribly unfair in condemning the righteousness of the scribes and Pharisees (cf. Matt. 5:20) as merely external.[64] After all, they were living up to the righteousness of God *as far as it had been revealed* to them. However, the Pharisees were not being judged *ex post facto* by the (allegedly higher) standard of righteousness to apply in the New Testament. Had they truly known God's *Older* Testamental law their behavior would have been completely different—not a matter of mere externals, for the demand of inward righteousness was already present in the Older Testament's legislation. Ernest Kevan expresses the proper view of what Jesus was doing in the Sermon on the Mount by saying that Jesus was not adding new laws but simply expounding a proper understanding of the old laws.[65] Jesus did not need to perfect the law, although He did have to remind His hearers and restore (or reassert) the demand for inward purity from the Older Testament. Moreover, it would not

---

[64] Gerald Friedlander, *The Jewish Sources of the Sermon on the Mount* (New York: KTAV Publishing House, Inc., 1969), pp. 35-36.

[65] Ernest F. Kevan, *The Moral Law (God's Law)* (Jenkintown, Pennsylvania: Sovereign Grace Publishers, 1963), p. 70.

be feasible to maintain that Christ came to *expand* the law, for in what way does He expand the *ceremonial* law?[66] It is special pleading to ask that the restorative rituals (i.e., ceremonial law) not be considered part of "the law or prophets" Christ came to fulfill according to Matthew 5:17; yet it is difficult to see that Christ was supplementing them with new laws in any way (note that the substitution of one outward *form* of the ritual for another, e.g., the Lord's Supper for Passover, is substitution and not material supplementation; the principle or meaning of the Passover meal is confirmed and unchanged, for only the historical perspective—looking ahead to the accomplishment of redemption, or looking back to it—has been altered). Furthermore, πληρόω, used to mean "bring to completion, finish something already begun," does not appear in the synoptic gospels at all (and its only use in John is with reference to the emotion of joy in an idiomatic sense—"my joy is fulfilled"). Jesus does not add to the law, nor does He delete from the law; rather, He gives that law the rightful measure, use, and understanding which it had demanded all along.[67]

> Moreover, any exegesis which explains the text as if it meant a quantitative supplement of the law does not do justice to the meaning of the words . . . "fulfillment" does not mean "completion of the law as the source of our knowledge of the divine will," but the effectual assertion of the demands of the law. The word suggests a vessel that is being filled. The "vessel" of the law is given its rightful measure. For this purpose Jesus has come.[68]

---

[66] C. G. Montefiore, *The Synoptic Gospels: Edited with an Introduction and a Commentary*, Vol. II, 2nd ed. (London: Macmillan and Co.. Ltd., 1927), p. 48.

[67] Although the word does not mean "complete or perfect" here, we could still note that even if it did, "fulfill" would be something much different from setting the law aside (i.e., it assumes the *validity* of the foundation); cf. Broadus, *loc. cit.*

[68] Ridderbos, *The Coming of the Kingdom, op. cit.,* p. 294.

The next proposed interpretation of πληρῶσαι in Matthew 5:17 is that Jesus here states His intention to carry out or obey the law in His own life; thus, "I came not to abrogate the law, but personally to obey it." Although πληρόω can refer to the keeping or doing of a commandment (e.g., 1 Macc. 2:55; Rom. 13:8; 8:4; Matt. 3:15), the fact that three commonly circulated words more directly and explicitly expressed that thought and were at hand for Matthew or Christ to use makes this interpretation seem unlikely at the outset. Πράσσω was often used in moral contexts (e.g., Acts 26:20; Rom. 9:11; 2 Cor. 5:10); in Romans 2:25 it clearly means "to practice the law." Φυλάσσω is used often in the sense of "to keep a law (from being broken), to observe or follow a commandment" (e.g., 1 Tim. 5:21; Luke 18:21; Acts 7:53; 21:24; Gal. 6:13; Rom. 2:26); special note should be made of Matthew's use of this word for "keeping" of the commandments in the story of the rich young ruler (19:20). Ποιέω is also frequently used to indicate obedience to commandments or the law (e.g., Matt. 7:12; 12:50; John 4:34; 6:38; 7:17, 19; 9:31; Rom. 2:14; Gal. 3:12; 5:3; Eph. 6:6; Heb. 10:7; 9:36; 13:21; 1 John 2:17). It is used *in the immediate context* of Matthew 5:17 in this way (Matt. 5:19). The availability and clarity of these other words should at least make us ask why πληρόω would be selected and put to such service. More importantly, however, is the fact that the *context* of Matthew 5:17 indicates that πληρόω refers to Jesus' work as a *teacher*. There are no allusions to predictions of the Older Testament and the question of Jesus' good works or of His own ethical holiness in behavior is not really at stake in this passage. But the issues of moral *authority*, pronouncement, and direction *are* prominent. The teaching of Jesus, not His doing of the law, is decisive here; the context speaks of Jesus' doctrine, not His life. The main problem with John Trapp's idea that in Matthew 5:17 Christ is saying that He came to accomplish the mission given to Him by the Father[69] is that it imposes John 17:4 onto the verse without warrant; Jesus' saying has its own context and integrity in Matthew 5:17, and that context deals not with inter-Trinitarian counsel, but with the Older Testamental law. The *object* of πληρωῶσαι (note:

[69] Trapp, *op. cit.*, p. 59.

not τελείωσες*)* in Matthew 5:17 is not τὸ ἔργον ὃ δέδωκας ("the work which you gave") but τὸν νόμον ἤ τούς προφήτας ("the law and the prophets"). And, as we were saying, the passage is not dealing with Jesus' own obedience to the law but with His doctrine or legislation with respect to the law. Furthermore, not only must we recall that Jesus is speaking to the *legislative* issue of the possible abrogation of the law (i.e., whether it is rescinded or not after the Messiah's advent), but also that the idea of fulfillment by *doing* is usually expressed in the passive voice, whereas in Matthew 5:17 πληρόω appears in the active voice. Therefore, in Matthew 5:17 we are concerned with the Messianic attitude toward, and interpretation of, the law—not Jesus' own personal obedience to the commandments.[70]

J. A. Alexander's interesting suggestion that πληρῶσαι in Matthew 5:17 means "to cause it [the law] to be better kept and carried out"[71] is picked up by the later Princeton theologian B. B. Warfield, who says that to fulfill the law is to make it perfectly obeyed, "to get the law kept."[72] That is, Christ came to enforce the law, to work it into the actual living of His disciples, to give the power of New Covenant obedience. These things are most certainly true about the work of Christ, and they correspond nicely to the promise of Jeremiah 31:33 and the words of Romans 8:4 (where the Spirit "fulfills" the righteousness of the law within us); this idea would also have some partial support from the context of Matthew 5:17, for Jesus does want men to see the "good works" of His disciples (v. 16) and does want people to do and teach the least of the commandments (v. 19). However, this is not the exact teaching of the specific Scripture found at Matthew 5:17 (although it can easily be found elsewhere in Scripture and harmoniously

---

[70] Ironically, Fairbairn rightly insists on the distinction between καταλύω in verse 17 and λύω in verse 19; however, he has their meanings exactly and erroneously reversed (taking the former to be "violate" and the latter to be "annul"). Consequently he is unnecessarily forced to hold that "fulfill" denotes "obedience," the idea of substantiating the law by doing it; cf. *op. cit.*, p. 224.

[71] J. A. Alexander, *loc. cit.*

[72] Warfield, *op. cit.*, pp. 558, 559.

related to Matthew 5:17 to be sure). Where verse 19 deals with the doing and teaching of the commandments it also begins with the conjunction "therefore"; the point of obedience, then, is an *extension* from the preceding teaching about "fulfillment" of the law in verse 17 (and the explanation for that fulfillment in verse 18). We must then find out more exactly what the "fulfillment" itself is. Note should also be made of the fact that the doing and teaching of the law in verse 19 is *not* a matter of doing and teaching *in general,* but rather the emphasis lies upon doing and teaching *the least* commandments—implying that, while Christ certainly deals with obedience to the law, it is still something about the *law itself* (e.g., its proper extent, its improper distortion by tendentious excising) that is at the front of His consideration. Further, attention should be given the fact that, while πληρόω can be used for one's *own* obedience to a command, it is never used elsewhere for someone inducing *another* person to obey a command (Rom. 8:4 carries the idea of enforcement of righteousness, but it gets that *nuance* not so much from πληρώθη itself but from the conjoining prepositional phrase ἐν ἡμῖν, "in us"). And yet another reason why we should see Matthew 5:17 as saying something a bit different than what Warfield suggests can be found in contrast to Warfield's assertion that "what Jesus is primarily concerned for here, is not the completer formulation of the law but its better keeping."[73] This is not precisely the case. Christ's *primary* concern at this point was the validity and meaning of the Older Testament law. From the antitheses listed in verses 21-48 we see that Christ was concerned to show how the meaning of the law was being distorted (and thus its finer points overlooked). In verse 17 itself the issue is not one of obedience or transgression; rather it is directly a *legislative* matter (note the meaning of καταλύω as "abrogate"). Quite clearly the focus of Jesus' teaching is upon the law and *its own* attributes (abiding validity, precise extent, genuine meaning, etc.) and not so much the obedience as such (or disobedience) of His disciples. Furthermore, not only is the stress upon the law (not the disciples), but the emphasis in verse 17 is upon the *relation* which *Christ Himself* has to that law (not

---

[73] Ibid., p. 557.

the relation which the disciples have to the law, or even the relation that the disciples have to Christ). Consequently, for these contextual and lexical reasons we cannot agree with Warfield's interesting exposition of Matthew 5:17 at the point where he deals with πληρῶσαι.[74] (It is noteworthy that this preceding interpretation, as also the suggestion that Jesus is asserting His intention to obey the law, would both presuppose the *abiding validity* of the Older Testament law—which, in the long run, is the point that is crucial to the development of the present thesis.)

The establishment of God's will as *the* work of Christ plays an important part in Matthew's Christology;[75] accordingly, Matthew Henry

---

[74] It hardly needs mention that if the preceding series of suggestions as to the meaning of πληρῶσαι in Matthew 5:17 cannot be accepted, then any combination of those suggestions will *a priori* be unacceptable as well; a leaky bucket will not hold water any better if you simply contribute more faults or leaks to it. It has not been uncommon for writers (and preachers!) to assign a multiplicity of meanings to "fulfill" in this one verse and then support the variety of resultant doctrinal observations by appeal to Scripture *elsewhere* (e.g., Christ is the substance of the typology of the O.T. ceremonial law; Christ kept the whole law, both actively and passively; Christ enforces the obedience of the law in His people; etc.). However, this is still eisegesis, even though what you are pouring into the verse comes from other well-founded scriptural teachings. A few writers who expand the meaning of "fulfill" in order to accomodate a number of well-intended, but conflicting, interpretations are: Adam Clarke, *The New Testament of our Lord and Saviour Jesus Christ: The Text . . . With a Commentary and Critical Notes; Designed as a Help to a Better Understanding of the Sacred Writings*, Vol. I, rev. ed. (New York: Abingdon Press, c. 1830 [n.d. for reprint]), p. 69; J. N. D. Anderson, *Morality, Law and Grace* (Downers Grove, IL: InterVarsity Press, 1972), pp. 118-119; Basil F. C. Atkinson, "The Gospel According to Matthew," *The New Bible Commentary*, 2nd ed., eds. F. Davidson, A. M. Stibbs, and E. F. Kevan (Grand Rapids: William B. Eerdmans Publishing Co., 1954 [reprinted 1965]), p. 779—with whom Carl Henry concurs, *op. cit.*, p. 319; Lloyd-Jones, *op. cit.*, pp. 189-195. Of course the problem is only compounded when, in giving a multiple-meaning interpretation of "fulfill" in Matthew 5:17, the proper meaning is left out of the list altogether—which is what we find in C. I. Scofield et. al. (eds.), *The Scofield Reference Bible* (New York: Oxford University Press, 1909), p. 1000.

[75] Matthew 5:21-48; cf. Bornkamm, Barth and Held, *op. cit.,* p. 68.

writes that the gospel is not the repeal of the law, but *its re-establishment.*[76] Jesus says in Matthew 5:17 that He came to confirm and restore the full measure, intent, and purpose of the Older Testamental law. He sees the whole process of revelation deposited in the Older Testament as finding its validation in Him—its actual embodiment (cf. John 1:17).[77] Jesus' own teaching represents a proclamation of the full implications of the commandments God delivered in the Older Testament in opposition to the legalistic scribal interpretations; His teaching demonstrates that God's law is more exacting and comprehensive than the current shallow and externalistic interpretations would lead people to think. Πληρόω is subject to the norm both of literal Older Testamental wording and the meaning of salvation manifested in Jesus Christ. Therefore, πληρόω should be taken to mean "confirm and restore in full measure." We must not think that the coming of Christ has invalidated the previous law of God, for "the word of the Lord *abides* forever" (1 Peter 1:24-25).

Perhaps the best indicator of the meaning that should be extracted from πληρόω in Matthew 5:17 is its antithesis to καταλύω.[78] The verse clearly states that the purpose of Jesus' coming was *not to abrogate* the law, and it is certain that the meaning of πληρῶσαι is in

---

[76] Cited in Pink, *op. cit.*, p. 57.

[77] Murray, *op. cit.*, pp. 149-150.

[78] Gerhard Delling wants to maintain that the meaning cannot be determined by contrast with καταλύω because in verse 19 λύω is set in contrast to both "teaching" and "doing"; cf. "πληρόω," *Theological Dictionary of the New Testament*, 1968, VI, ed. Gerhard Friedrich, trans., and ed. Geoffrey W. Bromiley (Grand Rapids: William B. Eerdmans Publishing Co.), p. 293. However, Delling has committed the error of assuming that the complex word will be identical in meaning with one of its simple elements; he has, aside from that, assumed that word meaning is to be found in word disection rather than the use (function) of the word in the contexts where it appears. Consequently, it is not surprising (to get to the most crucial problem in Dellings' pronouncement) that he has overlooked the "patent distinction" between λύω and καταλύω, as John Murray calls it; cf. *op. cit.*, p. 153. One does not look to the contrasts in verse 19 to determine the contrast in verse 17 for the simple reason that there is no contrasting word common to both verses (καταλύω with πληρόω in v. 17; ποιέω and διδάσκω with λύω in v. 19).

strict contrast to καταλῦσαι, as the strong adversative ἀλλά testifies. In Blass and Debrunner's *A Greek Grammar of the New Testament and Other Early Christian Literature* we read:

> 'Αλλὰ usually refers to a preceding negative ("but"). This relationship can also be expressed, though more weakly, by dev. A distinction is to be observed between general contrast (δέ) and that which is directly contrary (ἀλλά).[79]

Consequently, the meaning of πληπῶσαι will be *directly contrary* to that of καταλῦσι (cf. the directly adversative sense of ἀλλά in the identical syntactical structure of Matt. 10:34).

We should recall that Jesus is *not* talking about *transgressing* the law; καταλύω is taken to mean "invalidate, annul, abrogate" in this verse, and the context is one of doctrinal teaching, not behavior. The issue before us is the validity of the law and what Jesus should pronounce about it; legislative exposition, not activity, is the subject of Matthew 5:17. Our task, then, is to find out what will constitute a *suitable* contrast to καταλύω. From the outset it is clear that the thought of "performing or obeying" the law is a mismatched contrast to "not abrogating" the law.[80] These are different spheres of reference. The two phrases are distinguishable (i.e., "obeying" is *other* than "abrogating") but not strictly *contrary* since they fail to represent different positions under the same determinable issue or topic; they do not speak to the same exact question. This is similar to the following muddled shifting of categories: "he is not Russian, *but* third to bat"; "she is not left handed, *but* very sad"; "he did not come to repudiate the Koran, *but* to play the piano." *Obeying* a law is contradictory to *repealing* a law only in the shallow

---

[79] F. Blass and A. Debrunner, *A Greek Grammar of the New Testament and Other Early Christian Literature*, trans., and rev. Robert W. Funk (Chicago: The University of Chicago Press, 1961), p. 231.

[80] As observed by J. A. Alexander, *op. cit.*, p. 126, as well as M. Dibelius, *op. cit.*, p. 71.

sense of otherness; in this sense "drinking milk" is just as much a contradiction to "repealing a law" as "obeying a law." To assign the sense of "obedient behavior" to "fulfill" in Matthew 5:17, then, would muddle the contradiction intended within the legislative category of καταλῦσαι τὸν νόμον. Any semantic term proposed as an elucidation of "fulfill" in Matthew 5:17 must be, not merely *different* from "abrogate" in some possible sense, but interchangeable in all contexts *salva veritatae* with precisely "*not* abrogate."

Since the appropriate sphere of reference for καταλῦσαι is that of legal pronouncement (and not personal activity) the hypothetical question to which Matthew 5:17 addresses itself (and which we can use in order to clarify the intended contrast) is not "how will you *behave* with respect to the law?" but rather "what is your *attitude* toward the law?" This question, due to the contrast required for καταλῦσαι, deals with the law's validity and not so much with Jesus' personal liking or disliking of the law. Hence Matthew 5:17 is hypothetically answering the question, "Is the law still *binding* after your messianic advent?"[81] The effort of specifying this question is expended only in order to *clarify* the category of discourse involved in Matthew 5:17 and to help us ascertain the sense of "fulfill" which will appropriately contrast "abrogate."

In order to translate the Greek word πληρόω into its proper English equivalent it is just as necessary to understand linguistic usage of the English language as it is to have a lexigraphical understanding of the Greek word in mind. A survey of authorities in English word usage[82] will demonstrate that the general idea of keeping a law is not set

---

[81] Dykes poses this as the unexpressed question that Jesus intended to answer: "what must we understand you to make of all this former revelation and these existing laws?" *op. cit.*, p. 204.

[82] E.g., S. I. Hayakawa, *Use the Right Word: Modern Guide to Synonyms and Related Words* (United States: Funk and Wagnalls, 1968); Rose F. Egan, (ed.), *Webster's Dictionary of Synonyms* (Springfield, Mass, G. and C. Merriam C. Publishers, 1951); Albert H. Morehead (ed.), *The New American Roger's College Thesaurus* (New York: The New American Library of World Literature, 1958).

out as a contrast (properly speaking) to the idea of not repealing a law. The words generally equivalent to "obey" have as their contrasting antonyms "violating, falling short of," etc. If a direct contrast to καταλῦσαι is to be retained, then the general sense of fulfillment by performance of the law cannot be assigned to πληρῶσαι. None of the words denoting "abrogation" in English are listed with antonyms expressing "obedience" or its synonyms. Webster records the contrasts to "invalidate" as "enforce, implement"; over against "abrogate" stand "ratify, confirm, establish, fix, set"; and "abolish" is contrary to "establish." Hayakawa isolates the antonym of "destroy" as "establish"; he lists the contrasts of "void, abolish, abrogate, annul, cancel, invalidate, negate, nullify, repeal, rescind, revoke" as "endorse, establish, uphold, validate, recover, renew, reinstate." Note should be made of the fact that the thought of *confirming* (or establishing) constantly recurs in this catalogue of antonyms for "abrogate," etc. The conclusion of our line of thought to this point, then, is that although the general notion of obedience does not suitably contrast what καταλύω must mean in Matthew 5:17, the meaning of "confirm" very adequately accommodates the requisite antithesis. "The exact opposite to καταλῦσαι is to 'establish,' to 'ratify.' "[83]

Examination of the use of πληρόω in Greek will demonstrate that this word took the meaning of "confirm" or "establish" in certain instances. At least twice the Septuagintal Old Testament explicitly uses πληρόω in the definite sense of confirming-establishing. The Greek rendering of 3 Kings 1:14 in the LXX (1 Kings in AV) is: καὶ ἰδοὺ ἔτι λαλούσης σου ἐκεῖ μετὰ τοῦ βασιλέως καὶ ἐγὼ εἰσελεύσομαι ὀπίσω σου καὶ πληρώσω τοῦς λόγους σοῦ. The translation is clearly "And behold while you are speaking with the king I will come in after you and *confirm* your words." The translation of 1 Maccabees 2:55 (LXX) is "Joshua, while he *confirmed* the word, was made ruler in Israel"; here πληρόω is used. Taken in historical perspective this activity of Joshua's obviously refers to his taking a stand for God's ability to grant Israel their promised land (cf. Gen. 12:7; 13:15; 15:7, 18; 17:8) while the other

[83] Cited by Warfield, *loc. cit.*

spies cowered before the size and might of the Canaanites (see Num. 14:8 f.). It is not that Joshua obeyed the word (for the word was one of promise, not a demand), but that he confirmed it by his testimony. In 4 Maccabees 12:14 we read that in martyrdom men "fulfill" righteousness before God; yet martyrs are not actively involved in performing a deed, accomplishing a task or doing the law; rather they have something *done to* them. The fact that these individuals are selected for execution, and the fact that they endure it without apostasy, *confirms* that they are righteous. The point is not that they needed to be martyred to complete certain holiness-requirements before God, but that in God's sight their holy character is fully established by enduring martyrdom. Thus 4 Maccabees 12:14 should be seen as saying that certain people "confirmed their righteousness before God" by their martyrdom, *not* that they "obeyed their righteousness before God." (The LXX also exhibits πληρόω as meaning "establish, set" e.g., in 1 Kings 20:3 and Song of Solomon 5:14; the word takes the sense of "ordain" in Num. 7:88; Judges 17:5, 12; 3 Kings 13:33; 2 Chron. 13:9 and Sirach 45:15.) Viewed theologically, even when πληρόω is used of the actualization of a prophecy (as it often is) the word has the unmistakable connotation of "confirmation." A primary purpose of prophecy was the accreditation of a messenger from God or of his (His) message; prophecy was meant to inspire faith in those who witnessed its fulfillment. Jesus indicates this in John 14:29, "And now I have told you before it comes to pass, that when it comes to pass, you may believe" (cf. John 13:19). This double sense for πληρόω (i.e., actualization and confirmation) is witnessed in the LXX and extensively in the New Testament.[84] Since the Septuagint was translated *circa* 250 B.C., from at least that time on the use of πληρόω to mean "confirm" was in circulation. The Septuagint was well known to Palestinian Jews; hence the use of πληρόω for "confirm" was available to Jesus and Matthew.

A few New Testament passages can also be adduced to demonstrate that πληρόω can take the sense of "confirm, establish." James

---

[84] Cf. 1 Kings 2:27; 8:15, 24; 2 Chronicles 6:4, 15; 36:21-22; Matthew 1:22; 2:15, 17, 23; 8:17; 12:17; 13:35; 21:4; 26:54, 56; 27:9; Mark 14:49; 15:28; Luke 1:20; 4:21; 24:44; John 12:38; 13:18; 15:25; 17:12; 18:9, 32; 19:24, 36; Acts 1:16; 3:18; 13:27.

2:23 says, "The scripture was fulfilled saying, Abraham believed God, and it was imputed to him for righteousness." The quotation from the Older Testament to which James alludes is Genesis 15:6; yet the activity of Abraham which James has in mind is Abraham's willingness to offer up Isaac (James 2:21), and this does not occur in Genesis until chapter 22. Abraham's activity does not fulfill a prophecy, for the statement in Genesis 15:6 is an assertion, not a prediction. What James tells us, therefore, is that Abraham *confirmed* his imputed righteousness by obedience to God; this is the theme of James 2:14-26. In 2 Corinthians 10:6 Paul states that he will take action against all disobedience, but (because of his gentleness toward the Corinthians) only "when your obedience is fulfilled." Punishment will be restrained until it is not needed, that is, when the obedience of his readers is a standing fact. Obedience is not established as such until it is completed; to "fill up" obedience is equivalent to confirming or establishing obedience. The same idea is expressed in Revelation 3:2 where Christ says that He has not found the Sardisians' "works having been fulfilled before God." Their efforts to date had not confirmed a status of obedient servants in God's sight and judgment. Hence they must endeavor to "establish" their works (plural; not "work" in the sense of "mission") before God. In Romans 15 Paul says that, lest he *build* upon another man's *foundation* (v. 20), he has *established* the gospel message from Jerusalem to around Illyricum (v. 19). In saying that he has "fulfilled the gospel" Paul is not reflecting upon the fulness with which he preached nor upon preaching to every single person in every locality.[85] Without going into another man's territory Paul had *established* the message of Christ's gospel throughout the area between Jerusalem and Illyricum by making it known to people through his preaching and ministry (cf. Col. 1:25). Therefore, the New Testament, in agreement with the Septuagint, is found to use πληρόω with a variety of meanings, and one of those is that of "establish" or "confirm."

---

[85] John Murray, *Epistle to the Romans,* Vol. II (Grand Rapids: William B. Eerdmans Publishing Co., 1965), pp. 214-215.

Given the preceding contextual and lexigraphical considerations πληρῶσαι in Matthew 5:17 must be taken to mean "to confirm." The translation of the verse thus reads: "Do not (begin to) think that I came in order to abrogate the law or the prophets; I did not come to abrogate *but* to confirm." Such a translation should not be regarded as novel in any way; it has well-established roots in the history of translation and commentary. We noted above that Calvin said "By these words [Matthew 5:17] . . . he declares, that it [the former covenant] will be *confirmed and ratified,* when it shall be succeeded by the new."[86] Windisch parallels this comment: "The Messiah declares that the law in all its parts is to retain its validity. . . . Quite in accordance with Jewish expectations, he *confirms* the authority of the Torah."[87] In 1837 George Campbell rendered the verse in this way in his translation of the Gospels from Greek: "I am come not to subvert, but to *ratify.*"[88] In 1864 David Brown translated ἀλλὰ πληρῶσαι "but to *establish* them."[89] Charles Spurgeon commented upon this verse: "The law of God he *established* and *confirmed.* . . . Our king has not come to abrogate the law, but to *confirm* and *reassert* it."[90] In the present day Herman Ridderbos, in writing on the "Significance of the Sermon on the Mount" said that "there is no antithesis, either, between the principles of the Law of Moses and the Sermon on the Mount. The latter does not abolish the former, but *confirms* it."[91] In the International Critical Commentary on Matthew, W. C. Allen said that the editor of this gospel took πληρόω in 5:17 to have the sense of "reaffirming" the Law of Moses.[92] And John Murray says in his discussion of Matthew 5:17 and the analysis of

---

[86] Calvin, *op. cit.*, p. 277.

[87] Windisch, *op. cit.*, p. 125.

[88] George Campbell, *op. cit.*, p. 541.

[89] David Brown, *op. cit.*, p. 30.

[90] C. H. Spurgeon, *The Gospel of the Kingdom: A Popular Exposition of the Gospel According to Matthew*, (London: Passmore and Alabaster, 1893), p. 25.

[91] Ridderbos, *When the Time Had Fully Come*, *op. cit.*, p. 42.

[92] Allen, *op. cit.*, p. 46; however, I do not agree with Allen's critical view of the integrity, authenticity, and genetic history of Matthew's gospel.

the word πληρόω there: "Jesus refers to the function of *validating* and *confirming* the law and the prophets. . . ."[93] Therefore, the sense of "confirming, validating, ratifying, establishing" has been recognized as applying to "fulfill" in Matthew 5:17 by past and present biblical scholars, and this thesis is not setting forth a brand new suggestion for handling that verse. What has been attempted is the demonstration of sufficient and necessary grounds for translating πληρῶσαι in the sense of "confirm" over against the other alternatives. Given the corruption that the ethical stipulations of the Older Testament had suffered at the hands of the scribes and Pharisees[94] (which Jesus will go on to comment upon), it can be seen why the word πληρόω was used instead of the simpler and less expressive (or pithy) word ἵστημι. The Pharisees had reduced and cheapened the law to mere externalism; however, Jesus gave it back its proper measure. Hence He did not merely "establish" the law (in a pioneering sense) but confirmed and restored it to full measure. As Ridderbos has observed, "fulfill" in Matthew 5:17 does not mean to abolish or replace the Mosaic law, but to make plain its full demand, true content, and purpose in contrast to the Jewish interpreters;[95] such was the effect of Christ's confirmation of the Older Testament law. Πληρόω has a wealth of connotations (not associated with ἵστημι) which make it the most appropriate word for the context of Matthew 5.

Verse 18 of Matthew 5 goes on to *strengthen* the teaching of verse 17. Only obstinacy or theological bias prevents some commentators

---

[93] Murray, *Principles of Conduct, op. cit.*, p. 150 (here, as in the preceding seven citations, emphasis has been supplied).

[94] When Fairbairn says that πληρόω is not to be taken as "confirm, ratify" because God's word *needs no* ratification, it is just this fact of persistent distortion and false expectation that he does not take into account. Christ continued the authority of the Older Testament, not because *it* needed to be bolstered (far from it: v. 18), but because *men* were (and are) so proned to cease accounting the law as binding upon them.

[95] Ridderbos, *When the Time Had Fully Come, op. cit.*, p. 37; *Matthew's Witness to Christ, op. cit.*, p. 32.

from seeing the complete harmony between Matthew 5:17 and 18. Verse 18 gives the reason for the teaching in verse 17; the two verses are connected with the conjunction "for" (γάρ). This conjunction draws attention to what follows and signifies a matter of serious importance in the subject matter at hand. "Truly" (ἀμήν) adds emphasis to that importance. Jesus is impressing the following assertions upon us with supreme authority. The reason why Jesus could not presume to invalidate the law is that the law remains binding until the end of the world. And far from undervaluing the precise details of the Older Testamental law, Christ heightens their importance by affirming that they are as crucial to the law and as abiding as are the general standards. Even the minutiae of the law have significance according to our Lord. Verse 18 has led some commentators to see here the most extreme acceptance of rabbinic Judaism enunciated in the New Testament, the work of an overly active Judaistic evangelist, or an alteration of the original text by the Judaizers (e.g., the antinomian heretic Marcion, who rejected the Older Testament altogether, maintained that this passage, before corruption, read: "Do you think that I came to fulfill the law or prophets? I came not to fulfill but to destroy them").[96] Although they give it the wrong interpretation, the fact that Jesus (or some editor) was concerned with the very *details* of the law is clearly acknowledged by these commentators!

Ἰῶτα ἓν ἤ μία κεραία emphasizes minute detail. Due to its repetition, the word "one" receives stress. The Greek ἰῶτα represents yod, the smallest letter in the Hebrew alphabet. About this letter Rabbi Alexander (in the Canticles Rabba 5:11) said, "If all men in the world were gathered together to destroy yod which is the smallest letter in the law, they would not succeed."[97] It is this same inviolable nature of

---

[96] Cf. C. F. D. Moule, *The Birth of the New Testament* (New York: Harper and Row Publishers, Inc., 1962), p. 73; Karl Reinhold Kostlin, *Der Ursprung und die Komposition der synoptischen Evangelien* (Stuttgart, 1853), pp. 55-56; also passim A. B. Bruce, *op. cit.*, and R. V. G. Tasker, *op. cit.*

[97] Cited by Friedlander, *op. cit.*, p. 33.

the details of the law which Jesus teaches; however, He does not append the illustration of a human attempt to cancel the law because His statement is broader and more absolute—there is absolutely *nothing* which could be supposed to invalidate the law (not even the Messianic advent!) until the very end of the world and final consummation. There is dispute over the actual denotation of κεραία (literally "horn"). Some take it to be the small projection which distinguishes certain Hebrew letters,[98] but since this mark can greatly alter the meaning of a sentence and verse 18 envisages only minor detail, others have taken it to be a stroke placed over certain words in the Hebrew Old Testament. It is the point of *slightness* that Jesus brings forcefully before us.[99] Not even the very least extensive number of the very least significant aspect of the Older Testamental law will become invalid until heaven and earth pass away! This statement is underscored in its importance by the double negative (οὐ μὴ) and use of ἀμήν at the head of the sentence. It is hard to imagine how Jesus could have more intensely affirmed that *every bit* of the law remains binding in the gospel age.

It is not surprising that the Messiah should have such a regard for the law, for Deuteronomy 8:3, 6 states clearly that man is to live by *everything* that proceeds out of the mouth of the Lord, and 2 Timothy 3:16 says that *every scripture* is God breathed. It is inconceivable that He who is the Word and Truth of God should turn aside from God's truthful word. While Jesus definitely warns against any hypocritical appeal to the Older Testamental law, He never warns against the complexity and complicated content of the revealed divine will. He appeals to the (apparently) most minor items of God's revealed will throughout His ministry, both in defense of Himself and in teaching others. "Jot and tittle" then, not broad vague principles,[100] are the characteristic of a Christ-like ethic.

---

[98] E.g., Adam Clarke, *op. cit.*, pp. 69-70.

[99] Thus it has even been argued, not convincingly, that ἰῶτα and κεραία are a repetition of the same denotation; cf. W. Auer, "Iota unum aut unus apex non praeteribit a lege. . . (Mt. 5,18)," *Bibel und Kirche*, 14 (4, 1959), 97-103.

[100] As suggested by Allen, *op. cit.*, p. 46, saying that only "general scope and purport" is permanent.

> Too often the person imbued with meticulous concern for the ordinances of God and conscientious regard for the minutiae of God's commandments is judged as a legalist, while the person who is not bothered by details is judged to be the practical person who exemplifies the liberty of the gospel. Here Jesus is reminding us of the same great truth which he declares elsewhere: "He that is faithful in that which is least is faithful also in much, and he that is unjust in the least is unjust also in much" (Luke 16:10). The criterion of our standing in the kingdom of God and of reward in the age to come is nothing else than meticulous observance of the commandments of God in the minutial details of their prescription and the earnest inculcation of such observance on the part of others.[101]

He who believes the word of God must affirm its precise contents, and he who follows the Christian ethic must seek to observe the full and exact details of God's law.

In order to properly understand Christ's declaration about the temporal length of the law's validity in exhaustive detail it is helpful to look at the common Jewish teaching on that same point. Wisdom 18:4 speaks of "the incorruptible light of the law" given to the world through Israel, and Tobit 1:6 talks of "fulfilling the law that binds all Israel perpetually." Of this incorruptible, perpetual law 2 Esdra 9:37 says, "The Law perishes not, but remaineth in its honor," and Baruch 4:1 parallels this in declaring "This is the book of the commandments of God, the Law that stands forever." In the Midrash Coheleth 71:4 we read, "The law shall remain in perpetuity forever," and Josephus calls the Mosaic law "immortal" (*Against Apion* II. 277). Rabbi Shemoth got even more specific: "Not a letter shall be abolished from the law forever" (VI), and Va'era of the Exodus Midrash harmonized by maintaining that "The smallest tittle will not be erased from thee." These

[101] Murray, *Principles of Conduct, op. cit.*, p. 154.

last statements sound much like what Christ Himself declared on the Mount. So also does the statement from Rabbi Bereshith in the Midrash for Genesis sound similar to Christ's teaching, especially in that there is a common standard of comparison: "To everything is its own end, the heaven and the earth have their own end; only one thing is excepted which has no end, and that is the law." In the *Biblical Antiquities* of Philo it is said that "It is an everlasting Law by which God will judge the world. Men will not be able to say 'We have not heard!'"(XI:2) and "It is an eternal commandment which shall not pass away" (XI:15). Christ also speaks of the commandments not "passing away." However, there is an even more impressive parallel between Matthew 5:18 and Philo's *On the Life of Moses*; there Philo says that the Mosaic laws are "firm, unshakable, immovable . . . remain secure from the day when they were first enacted to now, and we may hope that they will remain for all future ages as though immortal, so long as the sun and moon and the whole heaven and universe exist . . . not even the smallest parts of the ordinances has been disturbed" (II. 14-15).[102] From the fact that Christ's words so closely resemble what must have been the pervasive Jewish teaching on the length of the law's validity, and from the fact that He did not go on to qualify or redefine His terms (or explain that there was a broader model that His hearers had to keep in mind as modifying His apparent agreement with the common teaching) we can expect that the above quotations help us to understand (in the historical and literary-pedagogical context of the saying) what Christ was actually telling His audience in Matthew 5:18.

---

[102] For the above quotes see: *Genesis*, Vol. I, trans. H. Freedman; *Exodus*, trans. S. M. Lehrman, found in Midrash Rabbah, Vols. I, III, eds. H. Freedman and Maurice Simon (London: Soncino Press, 1939); *Josephus*, Vol. I, trans. J. Thackeray and Vol. VI, trans. Ralph Marcus, both in The Loeb's Classical Library, eds. T. E. Page, E. Capps, and W. H. D. Rouse (Cambridge: Harvard University Press, 1926 and 1937 respectively); *Philo*, Vol. VI, trans. F. H. Colson, The Loeb Classical Library (ibid.), 1935; *The Biblical Antiquities of Philo*, trans. M. R. James, The Library of Biblical Studies, ed. Marry M. Orlinsky (New York: KTAV Publishing House, Inc., 1917 [reprinted 1971]); Alexander Jones (ed.), *The Jerusalem Bible* (Garden City: Doubleday and Co., Inc., 1966); Alien, *op. cit.*, p. 45; Meyer, *op. cit.*, p. 122.

"Until heaven and earth pass away" was probably a formula commonly used by Jesus to express the unchangeableness of the divine word. The "heaven and earth" was a regular allusion for stability (e.g., Eccl. 1:4; cf. Baruch 3:32) and thus the cosmic order stood as a standard for comparison—especially of the durability of God's word and covenant love (e.g., Ps. 119:89-92; Isa. 40:8; 51:6; 54:9-10; Jer. 31:35-36; 33:20-21, 25-26). Jesus contrasts the passing away of the heaven and earth to the immutability of His word (e.g., Matt. 24:35), and Luke 16:17 actually expresses the thought of Matthew 5:18 in terms of such comparison ("It is *easier* for heaven and earth to pass away than for one tittle of the law to fall"). Thus we can see what Christ is stating. He states that the law will remain valid *at least* as long as the physical universe lasts, that is, until the end of the age or world. Given the cultural-literary milieu it is quite likely that this phrase was a graphic and strong way of saying "never."[103] Christ certainly taught that heaven and earth would pass away (e.g., Matt. 24:35); yet the idiomatic use of the phrase for strong comparison should not be overlooked in understanding His words. Christ was not likely discoursing on the exact status of the law in the consummation age here[104] but simply emphasizing its continual validity during *this* age by means of a strong literary device. Even when we do take into account the actual ending of heaven and earth we see that Scripture teaches it to be at the return of Christ: there will be a great conflagration and noise (2 Peter 3:10) and separation of mankind into those who no longer experience death and those who experience the second death eternally (Rev. 21:1-8; cf. Isa. 66:22-24). At least until that point the details of the law will remain. Thus Carl Henry correctly comments that Jesus teaches us that the Torah has "a basis firmer than the stability of the space-time universe."[105] "The word of our God shall stand forever" (Isa. 40:8). Παρέλθῃ is used twice in this verse: first of the physical universe, and second of the smallest details of

---

[103] Broadus, *op. cit.*, p. 100; A. B. Bruce, *op. cit.*, p. 104.

[104] As Calvin properly observed in disdaining the "ingenious refinements" of the scholastics, *op. cit.*, p. 278.

[105] Carl F. H. Henry, *op. cit.*, p. 329.

God's law. Both times it means "pass away," the first in the sense of "come to an end" or "disappear," the second in the sense of "lose force, become invalid." The parallel found in Luke 16:17 draws out this distinction well; there the κεραία is said not to "*fall*" (from πίπτω, "become invalid, come to an end").[106] Jesus is saying that the exhaustive particulars of God's law have "imperishable validity for all time."[107] The double negative associated with the minutiae of the law in regard to their invalidation is (with the aorist subjunctive) the most definite form of negation concerning the future; it is also the classical way of strengthening the negative. The details of the law will *by no means* become invalid until heaven and earth pass away. The same thought is implied in Deuteronomy 11:20 f.: "And you shall write them on the doorposts of your house and on your gates, so that your days and the days of your sons may be multiplied on the land which the Lord swore to your fathers to give them, as *long as the heavens remain above the earth*" (NASV). Jesus and the law harmonize as to the length of the law's validity.

Particular note should be made of the misleading rendering given to ἕως ἄν πάντα γένηται in many translations of the New Testament (e.g., AV, RSV, NEB, NASV); it is often taken to mean "until all is fulfilled or accomplished." This makes it appear that "all" refers to the commandments of the law; however, it cannot do so since νόμος is masculine gender while πάντα is neuter gender. The translation of "fulfilled" or "accomplished" is simply spurious; furthermore, such a translation is deceptive since a completely different word (πληρόω) receives the translation of "fulfill." As George Campbell observed, "till all be fulfilled" is a mistranslation for "till everything comes to pass."[108] Some interpreters have wrung out this small phrase, attempting to exact from it more content than it was meant to communicate.

---

[106] Cf. Arndt and Gingrich, *op. cit.*, p. 665.

[107] John Smith, *The Integrity of Scripture* (London: Hodder and Stoughton, 1902), p. 104.

[108] George Campbell, *op. cit.*, p. 88.

Davies says that it refers to Jesus' death upon the cross,[109] and this parallels the New English Bible's translation "until all that must happen has happened," as well as Plumptre's application of this phrase to "the great facts of his messianic work."[110] Lytellton says this applies to all the events which bring out the meaning of the old dispensation Scriptures and illumine them; [111] Jones makes the phrase refer to the law and translates "until its purpose is achieved,"[112] and John Brown refers the phrase to the passing away of the Mosaic economy.[113] (All these variations only demonstrate the inevitable results of eisegesis—or the exegesis of one's *theological scheme* in the name of exegeting a Bible *text;* a verse like Matt. 5:18, with its unparticularized πάντα, is prey for such treatment.) Now such views might be appropriate pertaining to a verse like Matthew 24:34 from the Olivet Discourse (which reads πάντα ταῦτα), but they are unjustified in Matthew 5:18; the former has a definite referent and antecedent, while the latter does not (it does not even qualify a noun adjacent to it as does Matt. 24:34).[114] Nothing in the context or vocabulary of Matthew 5:18 warrants the induction of speculative meaning; a phrase as colorless and abstract as πάντα should not be particularized, personalized, and steered into this theological preconception. Furthermore, if this formula is taken to refer to an event in the present order, then the entire verse would be made self-contradictory; we know from the previous ἕως clause that the details of the law remain in force as long as the world lasts. Davies' only defense is to retreat to the claim that "heaven and earth" figuratively refer to the period before Christ's death. Besides arguing from one unclear point to another, this move by Davies and others (e.g.,

---

[109] W. D. Davies, *Christian Origins, op. cit.*, pp. 60, 65; *Setting of the Sermon, op. cit.*, p. 334.

[110] Plumptre, *op. cit.*, pp. 14-16.

[111] Lyttelton, *op. cit.*, pp. 129-130.

[112] Alexander Jones, *The Jerusalem Bible,* New Testament, *op. cit.*, p. 22.

[113] John Brown, *op. cit.*, pp. 171-173.

[114] Note also in the case of Luke 21:32 that, while it reads ἕως ἄν πάντα γένηται, nevertheless verse 31 preceding specifies "these" things.

John Brown) suffers from the fact that parallels for such usage of ὁ οὐρανὸς καὶ ἡ γῆ are not available. Indeed, it is impossible to take the phrase "the heaven and the earth" as designating the previous dispensation or age (the Old Testament economy, alternately). That phrase is *not* a translation of κόσμος which *could* (but does not necessarily) become interchangeable with αἰών. And in biblical usage the phrase *could not* be a technical designation for the time period prior to Christ's advent. For instance, God is said to have created heaven and earth (Ex. 20:11; 31:17; 2 Kings 19:15; 2 Chron. 2:12; Ps. 115:15; 121:2; 124:8; 134:3; 146:6; Isa. 37:16; Jer. 32:17; Acts 4: 24); this is obviously an allusion to the origin of the spatial and material universe (especially since He is said to have done it in six days—which is hardly equivalent to a few thousand years of history before Christ!). Heaven and earth are also called as witnesses (Deut. 4:26; 31:28), said to sing (Jer. 51:48), and be regulated by ordinances (Jer. 33:25); reading these statements in context makes it impossible to see them as referring to a period of history which witnesses, sings, and obeys. When Paul refers to God as "Lord of heaven and earth" (Acts 17:24), or when Jesus prays "O Father, Lord of heaven and earth" (Matt. 11:25), are they referring to a bygone God? The most dramatic refutation of Davies' suggested interpretation of "heaven and earth" comes in Matthew 28:18. The decisive event of redemptive history with which Davies is concerned has taken place; Christ is risen from the dead as all-glorious Messiah and Lord. But then note what Christ declares: "All power has been given to me in heaven and on earth." Can even Davies think that here Christ has gained authority in the dispensation prior to His incarnation? By infusing the phrase "heaven and earth" in Matthew 5:18 with an unparalleled and unwarranted meaning Davies has strained his outlook to the breaking point. Moreover, the words seem to dictate a more concrete sense, and there is nothing in the words of the phrase (*even* taken figuratively) which suggest any element of *specific* temporality or, much more, *personal* identity and activity (e.g., that of specific ending at the time when the Christ lays down His life at the cross).

Ἕως is used with the aorist subjunctive and ἄν to indicate that the commencement of an event is dependent upon certain circumstances (cf. Matt. 2:13; 5:26; 22:4; Mark 6:10; 9:1; Luke 21:32; Acts 2:35; 1 Cor. 4:5; Heb. 1:13). In Matthew 5:18 the commencement of the law's passing away is made dependent upon πάντα γένηται. Πάντα, when used without an article or preposition indicates "all things, everything" (as in Matt. 11:27; John 1:3; 3:35; 21:17; 1 Cor. 2:10; 15:27, 28; Eph. 1:22a; Rev. 21:5); it is to be taken in this absolutely general sense unless the context dictates some antecedent *whole* of which πάντα constitutes the complete parts (e.g., Matt. 18:26; 22:4; Mark 4:34; Luke 1:3; Rom. 8:28; 2 Cor. 6:10; Gal. 4:1; Phil. 2:14; 1 Thess. 5:21; 2 Tim. 2:10; 1 John 2:27). It has already been observed that πάντα does not agree in gender with "law," nor does it with "prophets," "heaven," "earth," "jot or tittle." Consequently, the views of Meyer and Broadus, viz. that πάντα γένηται refers to all the prescriptions of the law being realized and nothing being left unobserved[115] (Broadus says the ceremonial shadows must become substance, the civil regulations ground Christian legislation, and the moral precepts be kept by every new generation)[116] cannot be sustained as they wrongly make "law" an antecedent to "all things." To hold that "all" refers to law and prophets would, moreover, create a trivial tautology (i.e., "the law and prophets will not become invalid until all the law and prophets becomes invalid"); the same holds true for "jot and tittle." And even if this consideration be overlooked, making "*all*" refer to the law would place an unwarranted strain upon γένηται and reforge it to mean πληρόω.[117] There are no grounds, moreover, for taking "all" to refer to the *whole* of Christ's redemptive work or sacrifice. Ἕως ἄν πάντα γένηται states unconditionally "until all things have taken place (are past)." Thus this phrase is functionally equivalent to "until heaven and earth pass away." These two ἕως clauses parallel (a common literary device) and explain each other. The teaching of this verse, therefore, receives *another* note of

---

[115] Meyer, *op. cit.*, pp. 122-123.

[116] Broadus, *op. cit.*, p. 100.

[117] E.g., as done by Hermann Olshausen, *Biblical Commentary on the New Testament*, Vol. I, 4th ed., trans., and ed. A. C. Kendrick (New York: Sheldon and Co., 1872), p. 303.

emphasis: by this parallel restatement, as well as by ἀμήν, by repetition of the word "one," by reference to the smallest parts of the alphabet, and by the double negative. With divine authority Christ says, "for truly I say to you, until heaven and earth pass away, (i.e.) until everything has taken place, not one iota or one horn will by any means become invalid (pass away from the law)." J. A. Alexander correctly views Christ as stating the "immutability of God's law," even as applying to the ceremonial law, from which there is no deviation since its purpose is answered in Christ; the meaning of this verse, he said, was that "the law shall abide in its integrity without the least deduction from its actual contents and substance as a well-known systematic whole."[118] Allen's summary of Christ's teaching on the law is to the point: "So long as the world lasted its [the law's] authority was to be permanent."[119] *Every* single stroke of the law must be seen by the Christian as applicable to *this* very age between the advents of Christ.[120]

Verse 18 expresses what was anticipated in the Older Testament. Deuteronomy 18:18 foretold that Christ should have God's words in His mouth: "I will raise up a prophet from among their countrymen like you, and I will put My words in his mouth, and he shall speak to them all that I command him" (NASV). As Moses is revealing to the people the Book of the Law, God's Word, he relates God's promise to send a Prophet who shall *wholly* speak God's Word. The Book of the Law specified that "You shall not add to the word which I am commanding you, nor take away from it, that you may keep the commandments of the Lord your God" (Deut. 4:2, NASV). Consequently, the

---

[118] J. S. Alexander, *op. cit.*, pp. 128-129.

[119] Allen, *op. cit.*, p. 45.

[120] Henry Alford's comment should be noted well: ". . . it is always in *contempt and setting aside of the Old Testament* that rationalism has begun. First, its *historical truth*—then its *theocratic dispensation* and the *types* and *prophecies* connected with it are swept away; so that Christ came to fulfil nothing, and becomes only a teacher or a martyr: and thus the way is paved for a similar rejection of the New Testament. . . . It should be a maxim for every expositor and every student that Scripture is a *whole*, and stands or falls together" *op. cit.,* p. 43.

Messiah-Prophet declares that every written stroke of God's law continues in force until the consummation of all things. He makes no deletion. Deuteronomy 12:28 says "Be careful to listen to *all* these words which I command you, in order that it may be well with you and your sons after you *forever,* for you will be doing what is good and right in the sight of the Lord your God" (NASV). In speaking to all those who are sons of Abraham by faith in the Messiah (cf. Gal. 3:7) Jesus binds us to *all* the commandments of God *forever.* The *poetry* of the Older Testament also extols the eternality of the Lord's commandments. "All His precepts are trustworthy. They are established forever and ever, to be performed with faithfulness and uprightness" (Ps. 111:7 f., RSV). "Thy testimonies are fully confirmed; Holiness befits Thy house, O Lord, for evermore" (Ps. 93:5, NASV). "All Thy commandments are truth. Of old I have known from thy testimonies, that Thou has founded them forever" (Ps. 119:152, NASV). Indeed, every jot and tittle holds forever: "The sum of Thy word is truth, and *every one* of Thy righteous ordinances is *everlasting*" (Ps. 119:160, NASV). The Older Testamental *prophets* confirm this truth. Although human life may be short and fragile, "the word of our God stands forever" (Isa. 40:8); Isaiah does not disqualify the prescriptions of Yahweh (e.g., 1:10). The ethical stipulations of the covenant are part of that word of Yahweh which endures forever. Thus the righteous law of God shall not be abolished (51:6). In the last prophet of the Older Testament, continuing responsibility to the law is left ringing in our ears. Against the background of God's immutability (Mal. 3:6) and in the context of Messianic prophecy and promise (Mal. 3:1 ff.; 4:5 f.) the prophet speaks from God: "Remember the law of Moses My servant, even the statutes and ordinances which I commanded him in Horeb" (Mal. 4:4). The Son of God does not break with the word of His Father; what Jesus teaches in Matthew 5:18 is in full accord with the prescription, praise, and prophets of the Older Testament. Until the world draws to an end not one slightest stroke of the law shall be invalidated.

Calvin has accurately analyzed the point which Christ makes:

> When the Lord testifies that he "came not to abolish the law but to fulfill it" and that "until heaven and earth pass away. . . not a jot will pass away from the law . . ." (Matt. 5:17-18), he sufficiently confirms that by his coming nothing is going to be taken away from the observance of the law. And justly—inasmuch as he came rather to remedy transgressions of it. Therefore through Christ the teaching of the law remains inviolable; by teaching, admonishing, reproving, and correcting, it forms us and prepares us for every good work (cf. 2 Tim. 3:16-17).[121]

B. B. Warfield's summary was also right on the mark: "it is asserted with an emphasis which could not be made stronger, that the law in its smallest details remains in undiminished authority so long as the world lasts."[122] Honeyman comes right to the heart of Christ's teaching in Matthew 5:17-18:

> The attitude towards the Law expressed by Jesus in Matt. v. 15-20 is one of unqualified acceptance and approval. The Law is to he observed in every detail and there is no suggestion that there is any limit in time to its observance. The Law is eternal, and its most minute prescription retains its validity . . . so long as the created world endures, to the end of time.[123]

The foregoing interpretation of Matthew 5:17, 18 is verified by the passage immediately following it. The word "therefore" at the

---

[121] Ford Lewis Battles (trans.), *Calvin: The Institutes of the Christian Religion,* ed. John T. McNeill. The Library of Christian Classics, Vol. XX, eds. John Baillie, JohnT. McNeill, and Henry P. Van Dusen (Philadelphia: The Westminster Press, 1967), Book II, chap. VII, section 14, p. 363.

[122] Warfield, *op. cit.*, p. 558.

[123] A. M. Honeyman, "Matthew v. 18 and the Validity of the Law," *New Testament Studies: An International Journal*, I (1954-1955), 141.

beginning of verse 19 indicates that what follows can assist us in determining the meaning of what has just been said by demonstrating the practical consequences of that teaching. "Therefore, whoever shall loosen one of these least commandments and shall teach men so shall be called least in the kingdom of heaven, but whoever shall do and teach them shall be called great in the kingdom of heaven." Christ is reflecting upon the criterion of personal standing *within* the kingdom (not the way of entrance *into* the kingdom) and says that a person's relation to the kingdom of God is determined by meticulous observance of the least details of the law.[124] God's law is weighty with relevance for sanctification. The breaking of the very least stipulation of the law generates God's displeasure; taking an erroneous teaching position with respect to the details of the law (e.g., that the exhaustive details of God's law no longer bind Christians or this period of history) does the same. While the smallest items of the law are significant for the kingdom of God and its righteousness, the righteousness of the scribes is said to have absolutely *no* affinity whatsoever with the kingdom (v. 20). This is an important distinction to make. The mistake of the Pharisees was *not* concern for detail; it was externalism, humanistic traditionalism, and hypocrisy. *Their* kind of concern for detail led them to miss the whole genius of kingdom righteousness; hence they made God's law void by their own traditions.[125]

Now *if* the Messianic advent of Jesus had the effect of ending the binding force of the Older Testamental law, how could He go on to teach that acknowledgment of, and obedience to, the very minutiae of that law led to personal exaltation from God and that the opposite attitude led to debasement? Any orthodox view of Scripture and consistent hermeneutic forces one to see that Matthew 5:17-18, in light of 5:19, represents Christ as confirming the entire Older Testamental law.

The antecedent referent of "these" in verse 19 is clearly the jot and tittle of the law mentioned in verse 18. Τούτων stands with τῶν ἐλαχίστων: "these least." Thus it is readily associated with the

---

[124] Murray, *Principles of Conduct, op. cit.*, pp. 152-153.

[125] Ibid., pp. 155-157.

emphasis on minuteness in the former phrase. Verse 19 teaches, then, that the smallest part of the law of God is a canon for determining personal standing in the kingdom of heaven. In the subsequent verses of Matthew 5 Christ goes on to attack the Pharisees for their "unlawful" legalism; as R. V. G. Tasker puts it: "Jesus insists that in His teaching He is in no way contradicting the Mosaic law, though He is opposed to the legalistic type of religion that the scribes had built upon it."[126] Jesus showed them the radicalism of the law but by no means superceded it; the law was far more comprehensive than the Pharisees had supposed. Jesus contradicts the scribal interpretations (and distortions) of the law which had been heard by the people and handed down upon the authority of what the elders had said.[127] Jesus shows in case(-law) after case(-law) how the scribes had overlooked so many jots and tittles of God's holy law that they abused it to their own selfish ends.

Jesus, the awaited Messiah, rectifies the fallen standard of the law; He confirms its exhaustive details and restores a proper conception of kingdom righteousness. Vos puts it well in saying:

> He once more made the voice of the Law the voice of the living God, who is present in every commandment, so absolute in his demands, so personally interested in man's conduct, so all-observant that the thought of yielding to him less than the whole inner life, the heart, the soul, the mind, the strength, can no longer be tolerated. Thus quickened by the spirit of God's personality, the law becomes in our Lord's hands a living organism. . . .[128]

---

[126] R. V. G. Tasker, *op. cit.*, p. 64.

[127] Cf. Stonehouse. *op. cit.*, pp. 199-209; Murray, *Principles of Conduct, op. cit.*, pp. 157-180; Ridderbos, *Matthew's Witness to Christ op. cit.*, pp. 31-32; Carl F. H. Henry, *op. cit.*, pp. 306-307; Fairbairn, *op. cit.*, pp. 229-230; cf. J. Hering, "Le Sermon sur la Montagne dans la nouvelle traduction anglaise de la Bible," *Revue d' Histoire et de Philosophie Religieuses* 42 (2-3, 1962), 122-132.

[128] Geerhardus Vos, *The Teaching of Jesus Concerning the Kingdom of God and the Church* (Grand Rapids: William B. Eerdmans Publishing Co., 1951), p. 109.

II. MISCONCEPTIONS OF THE THESIS ERADICATED

Chapter 3

PHARISAISM REPROVED

JESUS' attitude toward the law of the Older Testament is one of confirmation, and He expects His followers to have an earnest and scrupulous concern for that law. However, it would be all too easy for people to associate such concern for the law with those who, while making a *boast* of their *lawfulness,* were actually ungodly and *lawless.*

Antithesis Between Christ and the Pharisees

Christ goes on, therefore, in Matthew 5 to make it clear that the model for Christian obedience to God's law is *not* Pharisaical legalism; their type of interest in the law *excludes* one from the kingdom of heaven. Matthew 5:20 is offered as the explanation for verse 19 preceding. Why must one practice and teach the details of God's law? Because *then* your righteousness will exceed that of the scribes and Pharisees who have no part in the kingdom. Strange as it may seem, the problem with the Pharisees is that they did *not* observe the Older Testamental law! Their legalism was illegal. While relaxing the hold of even a minor stipulation of God's law leads to a low position in the kingdom of heaven, misconceiving the nature of obedience prevents entrance into the kingdom altogether. A righteous observance of God's holy standards for human behavior would far surpass the righteousness and "legality" of the scribes. Jesus repudiates the perverse externalistic interpretations of the Pharisees, their exegetical distortions of the law, and their works-righteousness scheme of justification.

If a man is to be truly law-abiding, he must keep the law *as delivered* by God and *in the way specified* by God. A smorgasbord approach to the law is abusive; it leads to externalism, self-righteousness, and *autonomy*. Twisting what the law says is a satanic pretension and slanderous to God's revelation. Using the law as a means of salvation is high-handed flattery and disdain for God's grace. On the other hand, willing submission to every ordinance of God as actually revealed, and obedience in gratitude for God's gracious salvation, are recognition of a creaturely position before God and honoring to *His* name. The Pharisees appealed to the law in a way calculated to help them escape the real and original demand of God, and they did it under the hypocritical veneer of "righteousness" and "piety." This precludes kingdom enrollment. Hence Jesus continues the Sermon on the Mount with a warning against the lawless self-righteousness of the Pharisees.

First He states the general principle that Pharisaism has no affiliation with the righteousness of God's kingdom (v. 20). He follows the declaration with a number of concrete examples of this fact. These radical commands (vv. 21-48) do not supercede the Older Testamental law; they illustrate and explain it. The scribes had neglected the radicalism of the law, and Jesus discloses this to the people. Jesus does not criticize the *law* at all; rather, He severely reproves *Pharisaical* applications of the law. He makes it clear that the Pharisees overlook the weightier matters of the law altogether (cf. Matt. 23:23). The law demanded inner sanctification and its outward expression; the scribes and Pharisees disregarded the former and perverted the latter. In six antitheses between His teaching and the scribal interpretations Christ demonstrates His confirmation of the Older Testamental law and simultaneously substantiates His allegation against the Pharisees. Verses 21-48 of Matthew 5 are thus similar to case-law applications of the general principle announced in verses 17-20; in this they parallel the Older Testamental structure of Ten Words (general commandments) followed by particular explanatory cases (cf. Exodus 20-23). Ridderbos observes,

> Sometimes the fulfillment of the law formulated by Jesus in his commandments consists in a deepening, a refinement, a qualitative reduction of a particular sin to its root and origin; at others it contains the rejection of the atomistic conception

> of sin and righteousness, and sets God's demand in the light of the *original* meaning of *the whole* of all the divine commandments.[1]

The importance of a contextual exegesis of the antitheses of Matthew 5 can be made immediately apparent. Due to their nature as *particular* applications of God's demand for *specific* situations (and not unqualified general principles) they have a certain one-sidedness; possible exceptions are not detailed in this sermon format. Note, for instance, that while Matthew 5:16 exhorts us to let our good works be seen before men, Matthew 6:1 warns us against letting our goodness be done before men. Matthew 7:1 warns against a judgmental attitude, but Matthew 7:6 demands that we regard certain people as dogs and swine. Is Jesus contradicting Himself? Hardly. There is a certain motive for doing good deeds in public which is condemned, another which is commended: we must seek God's glory and not self-acclaim. Judgment must begin with oneself, and then it can (indeed, must) be exercised toward others. Now if no regard for context and the whole of Christ's teaching were exercised, *we* would fall under the *same* indictment brought against the Pharisees! We would suit our own bias by picking and choosing certain case law particulars to escalate into unqualified principles. Instead, the part must be viewed in light of the whole demand of God; each passage must be read seeking the intention of the author. Not every antithesis of Matthew 5 addresses the whole of life or the complexity of God's law. The commandments of Matthew 5 are absolute in their *intended* application, but not *all* possible applications are dealt with at once. (Contextual interpretation, not ethical relativity, is being argued for here; given its intended meaning and application the demand of God's commandment is unswerving.) And so we should be ready to recognize in the sermon recorded at Matthew 5 the use of understandable homiletical techniques (e.g., hyperbole) and

---

[1] Herman Ridderbos, *The Coming of the Kingdom*, trans. H. de Jongste, ed. Raymond O. Zorn (Philadelphia: The Presbyterian and Reformed Publishing Co., 1962 reprinted 1969), p. 312.

not merely expect unqualified and universal dictates. Jesus forbids taking an oath, and He says this with emphasis ("make no oath at all" NASV); however, He Himself takes an oath (Matt. 26:64). Now a Pharisee would seize upon the formal statement of Christ and apply it without regard for what *kind* of oath-making, or what *motive* for oath-making, Jesus originally had in mind. By contrast he who wants to be obedient to the law would seek to find out what the divine demand specifically means and thus actually requires. Another example of the need for contextual exegesis is Jesus' exhortation to turn the other cheek (Matt. 5:39); yet He protests when someone slaps His face at His trial before the High Priest (cf. John 18:23) rather than turning the other cheek. We are bound to misinterpret the antitheses of Matthew 5 if we do not take account of their life setting and textual context.

In light of the previous remarks it would be ill-advised to see Matthew 5:21-48 (as many are prone to do today) as a series of dissents from the law. We have seen in Matthew 5:17-19 that Jesus confirms the law in exhaustive detail; if He then goes on to contravene the Older Testamental law, He would steer Himself into diametrical opposition with His emphatic assertions in the previous verses. So, in these antitheses Jesus restores the original demand of the law and, thereby, reproves the Pharisees.

Furthermore, if these antitheses do not represent restorations of the law but annulments of the law (as antinomians suggest), then is not Christ's rebuke and condemnation of the Pharisees terribly unfair? *If* the Pharisees were indeed *keeping* the law of God and the problem with their lives was the *law's* defectiveness (not their own personal depravity), then why does Christ denounce *them* in verse 20 rather than the imperfect law? The Pharisees, according to the antinomian interpretation of the antitheses, would have been doing everything they could according to the light given them; what fault could God find with this? How were the Pharisees to guess that God's word was imperfect and would mislead them? No, everything about this interpretation is muddled. God's law is *not* imperfect, and the Pharisees would not have been reproved for full *obedience* to God's revealed will! Christ upbraided the *scribes* because *they* were at fault, were *not* obedient to God's will, and actually *distorted* the true law of God. The condemnation of the Pharisees is just, for they had defected from God's law. Christ proves this point by confirming the law in a number of examples.

Another general indication that Christ is *not* diverging from the law in the antitheses of Matthew 5 is the fact that three of these antitheses *plainly presuppose* the authority of the Older Testamental law; in fact all of the antitheses assume the validity of the law, but even the antinomians cannot miss the *explicit* endorsement and full implications of the law being propagated in half of the antitheses. It is not the holy law of God with which Jesus takes difference, but the oral traditions, the unwritten law based on man's word, the Pharisees had made void the word of God, His law.

However, the very passage itself requires the same view to be taken. In these antitheses Christ is contrasting what has been *said* and *heard* by someone to His own teaching. Note the emphatic, "But *I* say to you" which points toward a contrast of *persons*. In verses 17-18 Christ is definitely referring to the *written* law ("jot and tittle"), but in verses 21-48 He refers to what has been *said;* what is written and what is orally spoken have different referents. Christ does not set Himself against the word of God written, but to the word of man spoken. The person of Christ and that of the Pharisees clash in these antitheses (at the end of the discourse the people are astonished because Christ taught as one having authority and *not as the scribes,* Matt. 7:28 f.). What Christ says is opposed to what the *Pharisees* say, but it confirms what is *written* in the jot and tittle of the law. Jesus is contrasting the law of God to the tradition of the elders (as in Matt. 15:2 f.).

That Jesus is opposing the scribal interpretations of the law (the halacha) and not the law itself is sufficiently proven by the ἐρρέθη and the ἀρχαίοις in the phrase "it was said by them of old." It is not the contents of what was written of old but those *persons of old* that Jesus opposes. It was the rabbinic practice to appeal for authority to what was said of old (e.g., "Rabbi Eleazar said this, Rabbi Judah also said that; all our rabbis agree that . . ."). The scribes commonly cited what the old rabbis said, but Jesus repudiated it with his own personal authority. Τοὶς ἀρχαίοις is used in Scripture as a *substantive* adjective having reference to men only in Matthew 5 (although it can be used *adjectivally,* when there is no connection with the law, to qualify a reference to the prophets, cf. Luke 9:8, 19, the two uses are clearly unparallel). In Jewish writings the phrase "those of old" refers to the *rabbis* in connection with the law, and their own comments are even distinguished *from* the law (e.g., Tanchuma 202a: "A man should not say, I shall not keep the commandments of those of old because they do not belong to the Tora").[2] The Talmud and Midrashim repeatedly appeal to the "words of them of old." Consequently, it seems best to see Jesus referring to those scribes who propagated the oral traditions and interpretations of the law rather than those ancestral Jews who received the law from God.

᾽Ερρέθη is never used elsewhere by Jesus as a discrete formula for introducing quotations from the Older Testament; He commonly uses formulas like "it stands written" instead. The lone instance of a form similar to ἐρρέθη being used by Jesus in this capacity (Luke 4:12) is, in context, conspicuously parallel to "it stands written" (cf. vv. 4, 8; Matt. 4:7). Indeed the New Testament never uses εἶπον or its derivatives to preface a citation of the Older Testament without explicitly specifying that the source of the quotation is God, Scripture, or an inspired writer (e.g., Matt. 1:22; 4:14; 22:31; Luke 2:24) or at least clearly indicating the same in immediate context (Rom. 4:18; 9:12; Heb. 4:3). However, in Matthew 5 there is a noticeable absence of any evident attribution of the sayings to a divine origin. By itself, the indefinite "it was said" is too general a phrase to signify a citation of God's word; if used in Matthew 5 to adduce Scripture texts, then it patently fails to fit the pattern discerned elsewhere when derivatives of ἐρρέθη are put to such service.

The suggestion that "you heard that it was said" is a phrase pointing to the common custom of reading the Scriptures aloud in the synagogue still fails to account for the non-specified speaker or source of reading; *Scripture* is never treated in this fashion elsewhere, but the halacha

---

[2] Quoted ibid., p. 298.

is. Furthermore, the word that is used in the New Testament for the public reading of God's word is never ἐρρέυη, but ἀναγινώσκω (see Luke 4:16; Acts 15:21; 13:27; 2 Cor. 3:15; Col. 4:16; 1 Thess. 5:27; also refer to Arndt and Gingrich). Another point to remember is that what Jesus quotes as having been said does *not* correspond precisely to the Older Testamental law which has affinities to it; in fact, at one point not only does what is quoted have additions to the Older Testamental law, it blatantly contradicts the law of God (cf. Matt. 5:43). All of the foregoing factors, taken in connection with Jesus' polemic against the Pharisaical teaching and practice of "righteousness" in Matthew 5:19-20, definitely point to representations of scribal interpretations to the law. Hence we should not see these antitheses as Jesus' own evaluation of the law itself.

The way in which the antitheses are introduced as well as their context prevent us from seeing Jesus as annulling the Older Testamental law; it is the misrepresentation of the law on the part of the scribes and Pharisees which is set right. An examination of these antitheses, albeit short, will bear this out.[3]

Hatred and Lust

The first antithesis (Matt. 5:21-26) draws out the full implications of the sixth commandment against the stunted interpretation given by the scribes. Rabbinical tradition had restricted guilt and punishment simply to the *overt* act of killing. It would even *lighten* the sentence of death for the overt act many times![4] Jesus says, "you are familiar with what the scribes have said about the commandment 'thou shalt not kill' and how murder brings you into God's dreadful judgment, *but I* tell you that murder is a disposition of the heart as well." The scribes had

---

[3] See also John Murray, *Principles of Conduct: Aspects of Biblical Ethics* (Grand Rapids: William B. Eerdmans Publishing Co., 1957), pp. 160-178, and Ned Bernard Stonehouse, *The Witness of Matthew and Mark to Christ*, 2nd ed. (Grand Rapids: William B. Eerdmans Publishing Co., 1958), pp. 196-209.

[4] A. Edersheim, *History of the Jewish Nation* (Grand Rapids, 1954), pp. 373 ff.

not even touched upon the sin of unholy anger; yet this is the root of murder and warrants everlasting punishment. Neither had the rabbis condemned abusive language; Christ does. The full wealth of the sixth commandment had been overlooked; in fact, direct portions of the law had been selectively ignored by the rabbis in their sly interpretations of the prohibition against killing. Jesus restores the law; He confirms what the Older Testament had stated so well: "do not devise evil in your hearts against one another" (Zech. 7:10 and 8:17, NASV); "There are six things which the Lord hates, yes, seven which are an abomination to Him: haughty eyes, a lying tongue, and *hands that shed innocent blood, a heart that devises wicked plans . . .*" (Prov. 6:16-18, NASV). The inner heart attitude is definitely affected by the sixth commandment, but the scribes dealt only with the overt act of murder. Jesus reminds them of the further implications of the sixth commandment; not only does it prohibit certain things, it also commands a positive attitude toward your brother (Matt. 5:23-26). The Pharisees had certainly not taught or exemplified this, but Christ unpacks the commandment for His audience: pursue peace with all men, let no one be defiled by any root of bitterness growing up and causing trouble (cf. Heb. 12:12 f.), for ethical integrity and acceptable worship are inseparable. You cannot have a right attitude toward God when your heart is evil against your brother; hence the sixth commandment should have been explained as demanding love toward our neighbors, and not simply as prohibiting physical killing.

Without detailing all the implications as He just has, Christ makes the same point with respect to the seventh commandment (Matt. 5:27-30). The people had heard what the scribes said about adultery (i.e., how it had been condemned only in its overt manifestation), but Christ again demands that the heart be pure as well. Adultery can occur as the heart's desire; this is just as detestable as the external act. In fact, lewdness is the heart-source of the final act. So with forceful hyperbole Jesus says that nothing is too precious to keep if it causes one to sin; better to pluck out the eye than to lust after a woman. The scribes had not been as true to the intent of the seventh commandment as this. They had no excuse for overlooking the sin of lust, for it was plainly prohibited in the Older Testament (e.g., Prov. 6:25, "Lust not after her beauty in thy heart" ASV; cf. Job 31:1) and specifically in the Decalogue ("thou shalt not covet thy neighbor's wife," Ex. 20:17). Thus Christ introduced here no new standard of morality; He simply reinforced the norms of the Older Testamental law. In *both* of the first two antitheses Christ affirms what the Older Testament had taught: evil comes from the thoughts of man's heart (Gen. 6:5), and thus the law of God touches upon the inner disposition as well as outward behavior (cf. Ex. 20:3, 17 which show God's concern for *inner* purity). Christ brings no radically new teaching; He forcefully confirms the old.

Divorce and Fornication

When we turn to the antithesis on divorce we again find no grounds for asserting that Christ breaks with the outlook of God's inspired word. While some have alleged to find a repudiation of Older Testament morality here, in actuality it was the hard-hearted and distorted interpretation put forward by the Pharisees that Christ reproved, not the law itself. Christ clearly maintains the Older Testament's disapprobation for *adultery* in this antithesis since He argues *against* divorce by saying that adultery is its (morally intolerable) outcome (Matt. 5:32; cf. 19:9). His declaration not only presupposes the gravity of the offense of adultery, but simultaneously presents the utter sanctity of the marriage bond. The marriage union is so inviolable that only fornication can qualify as grounds for breaking it. Rather than loosening God's law, Christ confirms its indignation toward both divorce and (its ensuing evil) adultery.

However, it might be suggested that, while Christ did not in any way relax the law,[5] nevertheless He altered it by abrogating the alleged

[5] This is an important concession. One must admit that, if anything, the Older Testament law has been intensified rather than slackened. Thus no ground is afforded here for arguing that God's law has been abrogated elsewhere. The principle of *relaxing* the stipulations of God's law cannot be *generalized* from an instance of *strengthening* those stipulations! To grant that Christ did not relax the law is to concede that one's moral obligation extends *at least* as far as the demands made by the Older Testament.

permissiveness of the Older Testament with respect to *divorce.* The supposition is that by strengthening the law He contradicted the attitude of Moses. Of course it is immediately doubtful whether the assumption of the Older Testament's permissive stance on divorce is accurate. Marriage is therein presented as a creation ordinance whereby a husband and wife cleave together as one inseparable flesh (Gen. 2:24); one finds extensive legislation which bears on chastity and marriage (e.g., Lev. 20; Num. 5; Deut. 22), including the possible deprivation of one's right to divorce (Deut. 22:19, 29). Moreover, Malachi 2:16 declares "For the Lord God of Israel says that He *hates* divorce." This hardly represents a lax attitude! One *does* discover a liberal view of divorce, though, if he looks to the Hillel school of *rabbinic* interpretation. Its teaching seemed to prevail in Christ's day,[6] permitting a man to divorce his wife for talking too loud,[7] for poor preparation of his meal, or even for not being as beautiful as another woman.[8] From Matthew 5:31-32 and 19:3-9[9] we can see that the Pharisees would misinterpret Deuteronomy 24:1-4 (not unlike many today) and improperly appeal to it in order to support their loose policy on divorce: maintaining that it merely taught the necessity of a divorce certificate and that a man, then, could divorce his wife for any cause. It is helpful to study the passages from Matthew 5 and 19 in connection with each other. Christ there redressed this scribal abuse of Deuteronomy 24 and confirms the original teaching of God's holy law.

The Pharisees had severely *distorted* the law's teaching on divorce. *First,* the emphasis in their exposition and the concern of their debates were misplaced. While Jesus stressed the hallowed nature of the marriage

---

[6] William Hendriksen, *New Testament Commentary: Exposition of the Gospel According to Matthew* (Grand Rapids: Baker Book House, 1973), p. 714.

[7] Ibid.

[8] J. R. Willis, "Adultery," A *Dictionary of Christ and the Gospels*, ed. James Hastings (New York: Charles Scribner's Sons, 1921), Vol. I, p. 30.

[9] For a harmonization of Mark 10:2-12 and Luke 16:18 with the account given in Matthew 19, see John Murray's *Divorce* (Philadelphia: Presbyterian and Reformed Publishing Co., 1961), pp. 43-54.

covenant, the scribes were more interested in the "bill of divorcement" (which the Mosaic law mentioned only *in passing*)[10] and the *exception* to God's basic creation ordinance[11] (which was given as a last moral resort and rectifying procedure in the post-fall world). So Jesus drove them back to study *every* jot and tittle of God's law. *Secondly,* the text of Matthew 5:31 shows that the Pharisees were prone to misquote Scripture, for it represents neither the Hebrew nor the Septuagintal rendering of Deuteronomy 24. "The saying of the scribes, which has been quoted, is a *mutilation* of the legal precept, which had become traditional in the service of their lax principles."[12] So Jesus drove them back to a *correct* reading of every jot and tittle of God's law. *Thirdly,* the Pharisees misinterpreted the teaching of Deuteronomy 24:1-4 in favor of their loose view of divorce. They presented it as saying that *if* a man takes any disliking toward his wife, *then* he has the right to put her away with a certificate of divorce. However, this is *not* what the law stated. Instead it was given to *prohibit remarriage* between the divorced parties. "In these verses . . . all that is done is, that in case of a divorce a reunion with the divorced wife is forbidden."[13]

> Verses 1-3 are protasis and verse 4 is the apodosis. The effect of this construction is that *if* a man puts away his wife and she remarries another, the former may not under any conditions take her again to be his wife. This is the *law* which the passage establishes.[14]

---

[10] Hendriksen, *op. cit.*, p. 305.

[11] "The only source of dispute among them was as to what constituted a valid reason or just cause [for divorce]." W. W. Davies, "Divorce in OT," *The International Standard Bible Encyclopaedia*, ed. James Orr, (Grand Rapids: Wm. B. Eerdmans Publishing Co., 1939), Vol. II, p. 864.

[12] Henrich August Willhelm Meyer, *Critical and Exegetical Hand-Book to the Gospel of Matthew*, ed. George R. Crooks, Meyer's Commentary on the New Testament, 6th ed., tran. Peter Christie (New York: Funk and Wagnalls, 1890), p. 132.

[13] C. F. Keil and F. Delitzsch, *Biblical Commentary on the Old Testament,* Vol. III, tran. J. Martin (Grand Rapids: Wm. B. Eerdmans Publishing Co., 1971 reprint), p. 417.

[14] John Murray, "Divorce," *The Encyclopedia of Christianity*, Vol. III, ed. Philip E. Hughes (Delaware: The National Foundation for Christian Education, 1972), p. 420; cf. *Divorce, op. cit.*, pp. 3-7.

This understanding of the legal precept is substantiated by Jeremiah 3:1, "If a man put away his wife, and she go from him, and become another man's, will he return unto her again?" Therefore, one can see that the Pharisees had corrupted the law with respect to divorce (by misplaced emphasis, inaccurate quotation, and tendentious interpretation) just as they had distorted it on the other points which Jesus took up in the antitheses of Matthew 5. Hence Jesus, having told His audience what had been said by them of old, went back to every jot and tittle of God's law on the subject of divorce. "It is clear that here again, as previously, Jesus goes back, beyond rabbinical opinions, to the original intention of the law."[15]

Jesus' teaching about divorce, in contrast to that of the scribes, is consonant with the attitude of the Older Testament, and He intended for His hearers to understand that fact. When the Pharisees tried to trap Him with a question about the proper grounds for divorce (Matt. 19:3), He inferred that they should *already* know the answer to their question. Jesus indicates that He is not a moral innovator; He simply confirms what God's law had already taught, answering the question of the Pharisees with "Have you not read?" (Matt. 19:4). The earliest stage in the progressive unfolding of God's revelation provided an answer for the Pharisees. *From the very beginning* God's law had taken a strict view of marriage. Christ indicates that divorce would be a violation of this creation ordinance (cf. Gen. 2:24) and therefore inconsistent with the standard of holy living, God's revealed will (Matt. 19:4-6). From the most rudimentary stage of revelation the scribes should have understood that God would take displeasure with divorce, and thus a man cannot presume to divorce his wife for just *any* cause.

> Manifestly Christ does not concede that they interpreted Moses rightly. . . . He refers to that constitution of the marriage tie which was original, which preceded Moses, and was

---

[15] Hendriksen. *op. cit.*, p. 304.

> therefore binding when Moses wrote, to show that it was impossible he could have enacted what they claimed.[16]

But the Pharisees still missed the point, as we can see from their response in Matthew 19:7. "So accustomed to talking about divorce and neglecting the divine marriage ordinance have the Pharisees become, that even now they refuse to take to heart Christ's exposition."[17] From the fact that the Mosaic stipulations give instructions about divorce the Pharisees insinuate that Jesus is contradicting the law. Instead of dealing with their muddled thinking and re-emphasizing that, in light of the creation ordinance at Genesis 2:24, their interpretation of the law at Deuteronomy 24:1-4 could not be correct (after all, how could they pit Moses against Moses?), Jesus answers their question directly (in Matt. 19:8) and then proceeds to confirm the *full* teaching of Deuteronomy 24:1 (in 19:9; cf. 5:32).

Jesus first explains why the Mosaic law gives instructions on divorce even though "from the beginning it has not been so." Moses "allowed" (or gave the right for)[18] divorce in view of their

---

[16] Robert L. Dabney, *Lectures in Systematic Theology* (Grand Rapids: Zondervan Publishing House, 1878, reprinted 1972), pp. 408, 409.

[17] Hendriksen, *op. cit.*, p. 716.

[18] Some commentators have mistakenly viewed this word as indicating deprecated toleration of a positive evil (i.e., reluctantly forbearing something against which you have strong scruples or detest). Such a connotation must be read *into* the word. It is used quite simply for the giving of candid permission (without overtones of disapprobation). When ἐπιτρέπω is used elsewhere in the NT there is no reason to think that the person using it intends to communicate the notion of tolerating something he is severely disinclined to approve of or something that he considers definitely improper. It is primarily used for the gaining of *authorization from a superior*. Thus Pilate "allowed" Joseph to bury Jesus (John 19:38), the chief captain "permitted" Paul to address the people (Acts 21:39-40), Agrippa granted Paul the legal prerogative of speaking for himself (Acts 26:1), Julius very considerately "allowed" Paul to go to his friends for care (Acts 27:3), the officer "permitted" Paul to dwell by himself (Acts 28:16), and a disciple requested that Jesus give him leave to perform (from the disciple's perspective) the morally proper duty of burying his father (Matt. 8:21). In the sense of the expression, "God willing," the word is used of God in

"hard-heartedness." Although in the unfallen world of Genesis 2 divorce was not envisaged, after man's fall into sinful depravity divorce was then introduced as a moral redress (Deut. 24:1-4). The Mosaic law went beyond the original command and provided direction for just requital when God's commandments were violated. The "hardheartedness" of the people which required such legislation refers to being in an unregenerate state (Deut. 10:16), unwilling to hear God's word (Ezek. 3:7), wholly disinclined to good (Prov. 17:20), and deserving the burning wrath of God for evil devices (Jer. 4:4). That is, hardheartedness was not the condition of man from the beginning but became his status in the state of sin. Hence Jesus answers the Pharisees by pointing to the people's depraved nature, and His point was that man's fallen condition occasioned divorce legislation which would have been irrelevant at the beginning (i.e., prior to the fall). Further illustrations of such a point can be found in the law's directions pertaining to capital punishment and burial (e.g., Gen. 9:6; Deut. 21:23; cf. Gen. 3:19), oppressive labor, war, and crop protection (e.g., Deut. 20:19-20; 24:15; cf. Gen. 3:17-19), dress requirements (e.g., Deut. 22:5; cf. Gen. 3:21), and the husband's rule over the wife (e.g., Num. 30:6-16; Prov. 19:13-14; cf. Gen. 3:16). There is nothing unethical about capital punishment, burial, unoppressive labor, war, ecology, clothing, or a husband's authority when any of them are used properly; however, from the

---

1 Cor. 16:7 and Heb. 6:3. In the LXX it is used for the giving of authority over one's possessions (Gen. 39:6), granting a queen's request (Est. 9:14), and commissioning a man to speak (Job 32:14). And outside of biblical literature the word can even mean "to order, instruct." Therefore, it is unwarranted to maintain that, in Matt. 19:8, Jesus represents the Mosaic law as "tolerating with disapproval" an immoral activity, viz. divorce. The verse simply reports that Moses *authorized* the use of divorce. One should note, in passing, that the commentators who read the connotation of disapproval-of-an-immoral-activity into the word, ἐπιτρέπω, fail to justify their view that an all holy God could enact an immoral law. *How*, one must ask in astonishment, could the God who is "of purer eyes than to behold evil and cannot look on iniquity" (Hab. 1:13), the just Lord who "will do no iniquity" (Zeph. 3:5), tolerate the legalization of immorality in His law, which is itself perfect, right, pure, and righteous altogether (Ps. 19:7-9)? Even leaving *linguistic* considerations aside, this *theological* difficulty with the view is insurmountable.

beginning there would have been no need for legislation touching on these points. So it is with divorce. When resorted to under appropriate circumstances it is no more an inherent evil than these other things, for notice that the Lord God can apply the divorce legislation even to Himself (Jer. 3:8; Isa. 50:1)! Divorce, as Jesus teaches them, came in because of the hardheartedness of the people; it would not be needed in an unfallen world, and thus was not countenanced from the beginning (Matt. 19:8). Deuteronomy 24:1-4 is not a contradiction of the creation ordinance in Genesis 2:24, but rather an extension of it to cover further circumstances. Therefore, the Pharisees were mistaken in their insinuation that Jesus repudiated the law at Deuteronomy 24:14 by appealing to Genesis 2:24 in answering their question as to whether a man had the right to put his wife away for just any cause.

Thus far we have noted that a *lax* attitude toward divorce is not found in Jesus or the Older Testament but in the doctrine of the Pharisees, that the Pharisees *distorted* the law (through inaccurate emphasis, quotation, and interpretation), that Jesus appealed to the Older Testament to *substantiate* His moral evaluation of divorce, and that He *refuted* any insinuation to the effect that He contravened one portion of the Older Testament by appealing to another portion. From this we should go on to observe that, while the Pharisees challenged Christ with their mistaken view of Deuteronomy 24:1-4, Christ *confirmed* the *full* details of that very passage from the law and thus disproved the position that a man can divorce his wife for any cause (Matt. 5:32 and 19:9). The scribes had, *in general,* perverted Deuteronomy 24:1-4, using it to encourage a liberal view of divorce, whereas a fair reading makes clear that the passage itself *discourages* divorce[19] by encumbering technicalities[20] and its prohibition of remarriage (thereby warning against hasty divorce).[21] Then even further and more *specifically,* the Pharisees had

---

[19] Murray, *Divorce, op. cit.*, p. 14.

[20] Meredith G. Kline, *Treaty of the Great King: The Covenant Structure of Deuteronomy: Studies and Commentary* (Grand Rapids: Wm. B. Eerdmans Publishing Co., 1963), pp. 114-115.

[21] Hendriksen, *op. cit.*, p. 305.

misused Deuteronomy 24:1-4 by *ignoring* the sole, proper ground which it set forth as justifying the husband's disfavor and subsequent divorcing of his wife. The cause of his disfavor could *not* legitimately be just *any*thing, but according to Deuteronomy 24:1 it had to be some "indecent (unclean, shameful, abhorrent) thing." It has been correctly observed that Christ uses the word "fornication" in Matthew 5:32 and 19:9 to explain or interpret "unclean thing" in Deuteronomy 24:1 and thereby "acknowledges the permanent validity of that Law thus interpreted in a strict sense."[22] By making fornication the only exception to the general disapprobation of divorce, Christ was harmonizing with the Mosaic law which made indecent or unclean behavior the only legal cause for divorce.

The word "fornication" in Matthew 5:32 and 19:9 is not synonymous with "adultery";[23] while it is inclusive of adultery,[24] it is not restricted to adultery.[25] The same is true of "indecent (unclean) thing" in

---

[22] W. C. Allen, *A Critical and Exegetical Commentary on the Gospel According to S. Matthew*, eds. Charles Augustus Briggs, Samuel Rolles Driver, and Alfred Plummer, The International Critical Commentary (New York: Charles Scribner's Sons, 1925), p. 484. Although I would make it clear that I disagree sharply with Allen's view of the authenticity and integrity of Matthew's gospel, at this point the issue is the *meaning* of the term as used in the gospel account (no matter to whom we attribute it).

[23] Meyer, *op. cit.*, p. 132. "Fornication" is clearly differentiated from "adultery" in Matt. 15:19; 1 Cor. 6:9; Gal. 5:19; Heb. 13:4. A specific and different word for adultery was available and even used by Christ *in the very passages* in question. Jesus would *not*, if He intended to denote adultery alone, have to leave that fact to questionable inference. He could simply have used the exact word.

[24] "Every form of unchastity is included in the term 'fornication.'" F. E. Hirsch, "Crimes," *International Standard Bible Encyclopaedia, op. cit.*; see also W. F. Arndt and F. W. Gingrich, *A Greek-English Lexicon of the New Testament and Other Early Christian Literature* (Chicago: University of Chicago Press, 1957) at πορνεία: "every kind of unlawful sexual intercourse." Cf. ". . . fornication, including what is now technically called adultery" John D. Davis, *A Dictionary of the Bible*, 4th ed. (Philadelphia: The Westminster Press, 1929), "Divorce," p. 180.

[25] Cf. Hauck/Schulz, πορνεία, *Theological Dictionary of the New Testament*, Vol. VI, ed. Gerhard Friedrick, tran. G. W. Bromiley (Grand Rapids: Eerdmans, 1968).

Deuteronomy 24:1; while it is inclusive of adultery,[26] it is not restricted to adultery.[27] A study of the original word for "indecent thing" (along with its Greek equivalent) and "fornication" is very helpful at this point, for it discloses that in the biblical literature (viz., Hebrew OT, Greek LXX and NT) the two terms and their cognates are virtually *coextensive*

---

[26] It is a strange logic indeed which some commentators have used in maintaining, because adultery under certain specified conditions receives the death penalty (Deut. 22:22; Lev. 20:10), that the "indecent thing" of Deut. 24:1 cannot include adultery (seeing that the indecent thing is not punished by death). But there is *no* reason to think that "Under all circumstances adultery requires execution" follows from "Under some circumstances adultery requires execution"; no standard logic warrants such a deduction. However, without that deduction (based on the Scriptures adduced above) the view that Deut. 24:1 cannot be inclusive of adultery is simply a *non-sequiter*. Why should we think that a law which deals with a crime under particular conditions automatically rules out any other mention of a response to the same crime under other conditions? Indeed, we know that the Older Testament does *not* follow any such principle. Deut. 22:20-21 specifies that a harlot is to be executed; however, Lev. 21:7 tells us that a priest is prohibited from marrying a harlot. Now why (*if* the foregoing principle were valid) would Lev. 21:7 bother to say this? If the woman was known to be a harlot, then she would be executed and removed, leaving *no reason* to tell the priest to avoid marrying her. Thus the principle under question must be faulty. The fact is that adultery was not always punishable by death in the Older Testament. For instance, the case where an adulteress is not taken in the act but found out by a voluntary ordeal before the priest (that is, a case without legal evidence that can be adjudicated by the civil authorities) is not treated by the infliction of capital punishment (Num. 5:11-31). Thus Deut. 24:1-4 could very well include cases of adultery which are not covered by other laws. The fact that such cases may be few in number would be no reason to say that "indecent thing" *cannot* refer to adultery. Authorities in these areas have maintained that the reference of Deut. 24:1 to adultery is not inconsistent with the specification of capital punishment for adultery elsewhere: e.g., John Lightfoot, *Horae Hebraicae et Talmudicae, Works*, ed. Pitman (London, 1823), Vol. XI. pp. 116-117. And in fact legal divorce for adultery was practiced by the Jews before Christ's day: *The Cyclopaedia of Biblical Literature,* ed. John Kitto (New York: American Book Exchange, 1880), Vol. I, p. 78. All the rabbins would admit that adultery could be redressed by divorce: Willis, *loc. cit.* And some rabbins would even *restrict* the word, "indecent thing," to *adultery*: Keil and Delitsch, *loc. cit.* Obviously then, the word *can* apply to adultery and was used to do so.

[27] It refers more generally to "some gross indecency, some singular impropriety" according to E. Neufeld, *Ancient Hebrew Marriage Laws* (London, 1944), p. 179.

in their applications. They both denote generic, ethically abhorrent misbehavior with a focus on sexual immorality. The word for "indecent (shameful) thing" is used in referring to human nakedness (e.g., Ex. 22:27; Isa. 20:2) and the genital organs (e.g., Ex. 20:26; 1 Cor. 12:23; Rev. 16:15), and thus the focus of its use on sexual immorality (e.g., "to make naked," Lev. 20:18-19) is understandable. It should be observed that the focus on sexual immorality pertains to a broad understanding of sexual sins; that is, beyond adultery it could include rape (e.g., Gen. 34:7) as well as illicit sexual relations with one's own wife (e.g., Lev. 18:19). *Both* "fornication" and "indecent thing" have such a focus on sexual licentiousness of various sorts. They are both used to denote incest (e.g., Lev. 18:6; Acts 15:29; 1 Cor. 5:1), whoredom (e.g., Ezek. 23:18; Gen. 38:24; 1 Cor. 6:15-16; 7:2) and homosexuality (e.g., Gen. 9:22; Ezek. 22:10; Rom. 1:27; Jude 7). Beyond this sexual focus, however, both terms are used for more general abhorrence or generic misbehavior of a serious kind. "Indecent thing" is the term used of excrement in Deuteronomy 23:14. It is applied to shameful, public disgrace (e.g., Deut. 25:3; Isa. 20:4), perversity (e.g., 1 Sam. 20:30), and rebellious dishonor for authority (e.g., Ezra 4:14). The LXX root for "indecent thing" is used in the New Testament and early Christian literature for behavior which is somehow shameful, unpresentable, disgraceful, indecent, dishonorable, without proper deportment, propriety, decorum, good order or repute.[28] In 1 Corinthians 13:5 it means "*To behave unseemly* (cf. 7:36), to treat somebody in a wrong way. Perhaps the reference is to the many irregularities at Corinth."[29] The word is placed in contrast to "that which is decent, becoming, of good repute" in 1 Corinthians 7:35-36; thus indecent behavior is the *antithesis* of walking *becomingly*—which, following a discussion of keeping God's

---

[28] See Arndt and Gingrich, *op. cit.*, at ἀσχημονέω etc. and contrast εὐσχημονέω, etc.; cf. οχῆμα.

[29] F. W. Grosheide, *Commentary on the First Epistle to the Corinthians: The English Text with Introduction, Exposition, and Notes*, ed. F. F. Bruce, The New International Commentary on the New Testament (Grand Rapids: Wm. B. Eerdmans Publishing Co., 1953), p. 307.

law, is explained in Romans 13:13 as *not* walking in carousing, drunkedness, illicit sexuality, licentiousness, contentiousness or jealousy (which sins, through double-negation, would characterize "unseemly" behavior). Analogously, the Greek word for "fornication" is also used in *general* reference to shameful behavior. In the LXX it is applied to the provoking of the Lord with distrust and murmering (e.g., Num. 14:33), and to an arrogant way of life (such as Babylon's) which knows no fear of God (e.g., Isa. 47:10); metaphorically it refers to apostasy (e.g., Jer. 2:20), idolatry (e.g., Jer. 3:9; Hos. 5:4; 9:1), and idolatrous witchcraft (e.g., 2 Kings 9:22). Likewise, in the New Testament it serves to mention heretical or apostate teaching and its accompanying deeds (e.g., idolatrous associations) (Rev. 2:21). It includes the unclean things, defilements, and abominations of secular, ungodly Rome (Rev. 17:4; 19:2). It also refers to profane apostasy (Heb. 12:16) and idolatrous fornication (1 Cor. 10:8). Thus "fornication" can function as a generic term for immoral behavior (and is translated as "immorality" or "debauchery," "impurity" in many versions).[30] In Romans 1:29 the term[31] is grouped with other *general* terms for wickedness (e.g., "unrighteousness," "covetousness," "evil") as distinguished from, and introductory of, a list of *specific* sins. Again, in 2 Corinthians 12:21, "fornication" is placed in conjunction with the general designations, "uncleanness" and "debauchery" and separated from a preceding list of specific misdeeds. The same kind of arrangement (viz., placing "fornication" with the less concrete expressions instead of with particular, distinct transgressions) is found in Ephesians 5:3. In the above three cases there is no need to see a specific sexual reference at all. First Thessalonians 4:3 identifies abstaining from fornication with sanctification as a whole, thereby pointing to the general nature of the former; the sense of "fornication" is further clarified by the parallel contrast

---

[30] E.g., at 2 Cor. 12:21 cf. RSV, Twentieth Century NT, and Phillips; at Eph. 5:3 cf. RSV, NASV, Today's English Version, and NT Translation by Ronald Knox; at 1 Thess. 4:3 cf. RSV, Twentieth Century NT, and Today's English Version; and at Heb. 12:16 cf. RSV, NASV, New English Bible, Today's English Version, Phillips, and New Translation by O. M. Norlie.

[31] According to some, but not all, early manuscripts.

between *uncleanness* and sanctification in verse 7. The fornication mentioned in this passage can be made manifest not only in sexual immorality (cf. v. 5) but also in defrauding your brother (cf. v. 6). Therefore, from a linguistic perspective "fornication," just like "unclean thing," can be a generic indication for misbehavior of a shameful or abhorrent nature. While including (and even focusing on) sexual immorality, these two terms are not restricted to that denotation. This is evident from a theological viewpoint as well. Fornication, which Jesus taught to be the *sole* ground for divorce, must be inclusive of desertion unless you (wrongly) assume that Jesus and Paul can contradict each other, for in 1 Corinthians 7:15 Paul establishes desertion[32] as a legitimate cause for divorce.[33] We must conclude, then, that "fornication" and "indecent thing" are similar expressions, being coextensive in application, and denoting unclean behavior of an inordinately immoral nature.

Therefore, in Matthew 5:32 and 19:9, Christ confirms every jot and tittle of the law's teaching by, in harmony with Deuteronomy 24:1, restricting the ground for divorce to fornication. The lax view of the Pharisees which was based on extensive distortion of the law was confuted by the teaching of the Messiah, who not only substantiated His position from the Older Testament and controverted the insinuation that He repudiated the Mosaic law, but also disproved the Pharisaical viewpoint by specifically confirming and insisting upon the full details of Deuteronomy 24:1.

---

[32] To belabor the obvious, we would observe that desertion (even if in fact, it implies adultery) is a *different* act from adultery and is *itself* a grave moral offense (viz., insubordination) which need not derive its shamefulness from any implied sequel. Legally-established-adultery is dealt with as a separate kind of case from implied-adultery in God's law (cf. Deut. 22:13-22 with Num. 5:11-31). Thus desertion, in order to he redressed, need not and should not automatically be treated *as* implied adultery; desertion can be redressed simply as *desertion*. It is a crime in its own right.

[33] It is noteworthy here that 'played the harlot' is used in some Greek versions of the Older Testament to denote the insubordinate desertion of the Levite's concubine in Judges 19:2 (as indicated in the Berkeley Version as well as the Harper Study Bible).

> Thus Jesus, by making the inclusive term *fornication* the ground for divorce, reaffirmed the Mosaic law of Deuteronomy 24:1, in opposition to the interpretations of the day, which stressed the fact that the wife "find no favor in his eyes," without emphasizing that this had to rest on the fact of "uncleanness" or "fornication" as the reason for the disfavor.[34]

As with the other antitheses, so with the subject of divorce, Jesus would say "Do not begin to think that I have come to abrogate the law or the prophets, for not one jot or tittle shall be invalidated until heaven and earth pass away" (cf. Matt. 5:17-18).

The person who may be avid to solicit from Matthew 5:32 a divulgence of Messianic impugning of God's law might say at this point that, even though Christ does not break with the law's view of fornication and divorce, He still renounced the punishment for adultery prescribed in the Older Testament. Of course such a claim would be patently false. In fact Jesus did *not* broach the subject of the Older Testament's punishment for adultery and then express personal disapproval. The subject matter of the declaration in Matthew 5:32 (cf. 19:9) is *divorce* and its proper *ground, not* adultery and its proper punishment. Jesus expounded upon the evil of fornication, not the punitive aspect of adultery. He repudiated the Pharisees, not the law. Hence it is totally unwarranted to maintain that Christ expressly abrogated the law's penal sanction against adultery. However, our hypothetical opponent might (shifting ground) then say that Christ *implicitly* invalidated the punishment of God's law for adultery; supposedly, by making divorce the recourse for fornication Jesus *implied* that capital punishment is not the recourse for adultery. This allegation would be equally erroneous. One certainly cannot *deduce by good and necessary consequence* (cf. Westminster Confession of Faith, I.6) from Matthew 5:32 that the law's requital for

---

[34] Rousas John Rushdoony, "Fornication," *The Encyclopedia of Christianity*, Vol. IV, ed. Philip E. Hughes (Delaware: The National Foundation for Christian Education, 1972), p. 232.

adultery has been nullified. To attempt such a deduction would automatically be a commission of the formal fallacy of *quaternio terminorum;* that is, the key terms of the conclusion ("adultery," "death penalty") would be different from the key terms of the premises ("fornication," "divorce"). This is just to say, then, that the conclusion would *not* be founded upon the premises. Thus Matthew 5:32 does not *imply* the abrogation of the law's penal sanction against adultery. What is specifically mentioned and denied is what has been *said* by the men of old about *divorce,* not what stands *written* in God's law about *adultery.* Christ does not speak to the issue of the penal sanction for adultery at all (i.e., He does not aim to answer the question, "what is your attitude toward the execution of adulterers?"); He speaks to the issue of the grounds for divorce (i.e., gives His attitude toward the distorted view of the Pharisees). Consequently, He *neither expressly nor implicitly* abrogates the law of God with respect to the former issue. A nullification of the penal sanction against adultery might be founded on another text, but it could only be *read into* Matthew 5:32 and 19:9.

The main point here is to enjoin our recognition of the clear *aim* of Matthew 5:32, rather than concentrating to the point of distortion on the *way* in which it leads to its aim. The teaching here on fornication is itself without a doubt important; however, it should be recognized that the subject of fornication is brought in to serve the end of stressing the utter sanctity of the marriage bond. *How* binding is marriage? Jesus answers that only the *most severe* sort of situation, viz. fornication, is sufficient to dissolve the marriage contract. Recognizing this central thrust of Matthew 5:32 will deter us from trying to find there a relaxation of divine disfavor toward such behavior as directly assaults the holiness of the marriage covenant (e.g., adultery). One could hardly expect Jesus, at one and the same time, to set forth both the strengthening and slackening of disapprobation for violations of marital sanctity (i.e., detesting fornication as the destruction of the marriage bond, but removing penal sanction against that violation of marriage found in fornication in the form of adultery). Recognizing the main thrust of Matthew 5:32 will also deter us from constraining it to answer questions (e.g., how should the civil magistrate treat adultery?) other than those to which it addresses itself (e.g., what cause could be grave enough to warrant a rupture of the marriage tie?).

However, couldn't the opponent argue that, since fornication is inclusive of adultery, Jesus would not have even mentioned divorce as a redress to fornication unless He meant to contravene the punishment for adultery provided by God's law? In answer, no, this would *not* be evident at all. To say that *fornication* is the *exclusive ground* for divorce is *not* the same as saying that *divorce* is the *exclusive requital* for fornication. The latter does not follow properly from the former, as the following examples demonstrate. From the fact that being elected president is the exclusive warrant for governing the use of the presidential seal, it does not follow that governing the use of the presidential seal is the exclusive privilege gained by being elected president. Or again: if hitting five hundred homeruns were the only qualification for selection to some baseball Hall of Fame, it would not follow that selection to that Hall of Fame is necessarily the only reward reaped for hitting those homeruns. An example, from the perspective of demerit now, might be: the fact that violating a traffic law is the only reason for making you stand trial in traffic court is surely no guarantee to you that such a trial will be the only detriment you would suffer (e.g., your car might also get demolished). So we see that fornication's being the exclusive ground for divorce does not imply that divorce is the sole requital for fornication. For instance, the fact that a wife has grounds for divorce in her husband's adulterous relations does not mean that the state cannot *also* have grounds for retaliating against the adulterous offender. The fact that adultery is contained in the larger class of crimes, fornication, does not imply even remotely that Christ abrogated the penal sanction against adultery (by confirming the Older Testament's teaching that fornication is the only basis for divorce). Since the *Older* Testament allows *both* divorce for fornication and execution for adultery, the two norms cannot be viewed as contradictory in the *New* Testament either.

For an abrogation of the penal sanction against adultery the hypothetical opponent would have to show that Jesus introduced divorce as the only redress for adultery in direct contrast to the law of God. However, Jesus did *not introduce* divorce for adultery; this was both *recognized* by the rabbins and practiced before Christ's day.[35] Jesus did *not* introduce divorce as the *only* redress for adultery, as we have just seen; there is no textual or logical reason to hold that Matthew 5:32 teaches an *exclusive* requital for any crime. Jesus did *not* introduce divorce as the only redress to *adultery*. His subject matter was the pertinence of *fornication* with respect to divorce, and when He did go on to identify the sin of adultery as following upon illegal divorce, He made no mention whatsoever of the method of redressing this adultery (since that was not the topic for discussion, as it was in the *pericope adulterae* of John 8:3-11).[36] Finally, Jesus did *not* introduce divorce as the only redress to adultery *in contrast to the law of God*. In the first place, Jesus was evaluating not the Older Testamental law but the *Pharisaical* interpretations of it; and secondly, different circumstances involved in the adultery, its discovery, and its recompense were countenanced by the Older Testament (e.g., Num. 5:11-31).[37] The law did not have one exclusive pattern

---

[35] Lightfoot, *loc. cit.;* Willis, *loc. cit.;* Keil and Delitzsch, *loc. cit.; Cyclopaedia of Biblical Literature, loc. cit.*

[36] It will be shown subsequently that this passage *also* bears up every jot and tittle of the law rather than nullifying the holy provisions of the Older Testament.

[37] It might even be the case that the law expressly provides divorce as the requital for some forms of adultery. For instance, Leviticus 18:18 prohibits taking one woman (as a rival) in addition to another woman (cf. John Murray, *Principles of Conduct: Aspects of Biblical Ethics.* Grand Rapids: Wm. B. Eerdmans Publishing Co., 1957, pp. 251-254; Murray suggests that the verse speaks, not of a man marrying two *sisters,* but of a man taking *any two women* to wife). From a monogamous perspective this might be viewed as a form of adultery with respect to the first wife. Leviticus 18:18 speaks of this situation as uncovering her "shame," the Hebrew root being the same as that for "shameful thing" in Deuteronomy 24:1. This suggests that the behavior described would qualify as a matter of shame (indecency) and thereby grounds for divorce. Interestingly, if this supposition is not true, then the crime prohibited in Leviticus 18:18 is given no penal redress at all in the law (which, in comparing Lev. 18:6-20 with 20:10-21, seems highly unlikely). Another case might be found in the

for handling instances of adultery; thus *neither* testament need be read as giving one exclusive, uniform treatment for adultery in general. Therefore, Jesus did not at all do what our hypothetical opponent must *demonstrate* that He did if the opponent is to substantiate his repudiation of the penal sanction against adultery.[38] Just as the death penalty for

---

situation where an adulteress has no witness against her and is not taken in the act (Num. 5:13), but is found out by means of ordeal before the priest (Num. 5:27). While she is afflicted with bodily ailment and social adjuration, the law does not authorize executing her (probably in light of the lack of legal evidence, e.g., eyewitnesses or absence of tokens of virginity: cf. Deut. 22:17-22). In this case the woman, having been involved in a matter of abhorrence, could possibly be divorced by her (innocent) husband even though not executed. A further case might be found in Leviticus 20:21, where the "shameful" act of taking your brother's wife is punished not with execution but divine intervention to produce childlessness; it seems the brother who had been wronged here would have grounds for divorce according to Deuteronomy 24:1. This example could possibly be expanded to cover verses 19-20 of Leviticus 20 as well. Keil and Delitzsch say about vv. 19-21: "No civil punishment, on the other hand, to be inflicted by the magistrate or by the community generally, was ordered to follow marriage with an aunt, the sister of father or mother (ver. 19, cf. chap. xviii. 12, 13), with an uncle's wife (ver. 20, cf. chap. xviii. 4), or with a sister-in-law, a brother's wife (ver. 21, cf. chap. xviii. 16). In all these cases the threat is simply held out, 'they shall bear their iniquity,' and (according to vers. 20, 21) 'die childless'; that is to say, God would reserve the punishment to Himself" (*Biblical Commentary on the Old Testament,* Vol. II, tran. James Martin. Grand Rapids: Wm. B. Eerdmans Publishing Co., 1971 reprint, pp. 427-428). In these cases, while there might be no magisterial punishment, it does not seem unreasonable to think that the offended parties (uncle and brother) could have recourse to *divorce* against their adulterous spouses.

[38] It is worth noting that, even if (contrary to what has been established above) Christ gave divorce instead of execution as the only recompense for adultery, a commentator or ethicist would not have done all his work if he did not take into consideration the *historical* as well as grammatical context of Jesus' words (i.e., did not follow the grammatical-historical method of biblical interpretation). At the time in which Christ spoke, the Jews were under Roman subjugation. Thus they were tied to Roman legal practice when it came to capital punishment; John 18:31 makes it clear that they could not carry out the stipulations respecting capital crimes while Rome occupied Palestine. In a society where the sword-bearer (cf. Rom. 13:1-4) does not execute adulterers as required by God's moral law, then what can the disciple of Christ do? Jesus would supply an answer: follow out the principle of the

adultery appears to have been a *pre*-Mosaic requirement (cf. Gen. 38:24), so there is no reason to suppose that it has lost its sanction *after* the passing of the Mosaic economy. It reflects the unchanging justice of God.

Since no word of God can be turned back except by divine authority,[39] and since Jesus did *not* introduce divorce in Matthew 5:32 as the exclusive requital for adultery in contrast to the Older Testament (as just seen), Christians who allow their doctrinal affirmations to be determined and circumscribed by the principle of *sola scriptura*[40] have no moral warrant or authority to maintain that the penal sanction of God's inspired law against adultery has been nullified. "Whosoever therefore shall loosen one of these least commandments, and shall teach

---

Older Testament sanction against adultery to the *degree* that you legitimately can. The Older Testament explained the purpose of execution as purging evil from God's kingdom; we note this rationale with regard to adulterers in particular (Deut. 22:24). In the Christian's *home* there must be a purging, a sending-away of the evil-doer, just as Paul exhorts the *church* (who cannot rightly do what pagan Roman officials of the state failed to do) to purge or send-away the adulterer from its midst (cf. 1 Cor. 5:1, 4-5, 13). By means of divorce and excommunication the believer and the church keep God's law to the extent that they can with respect to the adulterer. As the kingdom of God is manifest in the home and church adulterers therein must be purged away. So also in the state (over which Christ also rules as absolute King) the offender should be purged away; the magistrate bears not the sword in vain as he avenges God's wrath against adulterers (cf. Rom. 13:4). Therefore, in Matthew 5:32 and 19:9, Christ need not be seen as denying the moral appropriateness and magisterial obligation of executing adulterers, but as merely explaining how to handle adulterous situations in a pagan society or under ungodly rulers. Of course, while this historical note is significant in placing Jesus' words in proper *perspective* and harmonizing them with God's law, the most vital point to remember is that His *words* do *not assert* what is often claimed for them (viz., that they abrogate the penal sanction of the Older Testament and replace it with divorce as the proper and exclusive requital for adultery).

[39] Cf. Deut. 4:2; Ps. 119:160; Isa. 51:6; Matt. 4:4: John 10:35; 2 Tim. 3:16-17; etc.

[40] "The *whole* counsel of God concerning *all* things necessary for His own glory, man's salvation, faith and *life,* is either *expressly* set down in Scripture, or by good and *necessary consequence* may be deduced from Scripture: unto which *nothing* is to be added ..." (Westminster Confession of Faith, I. 6).

men so, shall be called least in the kingdom of heaven" (Matt. 5:19, ASV). Surely, after such a strong declaration, Jesus would not immediately go on to loosen a commandment of God's law (viz., Deut. 22:22; Lev. 20:10). Nor should we go on to do so. Matthew 5:32 and 19:9 are silent on the question of penal sanction for adultery, and one cannot rightly *infer* an abrogation of God's eternal, holy law *from silence;* to allow otherwise would be to allow *man's* say so to become the voice of authority, as well as to tolerate informal fallacies in one's reasoning (e.g., *argumentum ad ignorantiam,* if not also *converse accident*). Thus we should concur with Meyer in his comment upon Christ's specification of fornication as the sole ground for divorce: "The exception which Jesus here makes cannot become devoid of meaning by means of Lev. xx.10."[41] The renowned presbyterian theologian, Robert L. Dabney, correctly concluded, "The laws of Moses, therefore, very properly made adultery a capital crime; nor does our Savior . . . repeal that statute, or disallow its justice"; modern legislation which ignores the Mosaic stipulation is "drawn rather from the grossness of Pagan sources."[42]

With respect, then, to the antithesis on divorce in Matthew 5:31-32, we find every reason to believe that Jesus is contradicting the teaching of the scribes and Pharisees (what "has been said") and not the holy law of God (what "stands written"). We find no adequate reason or justification for the allegation that He breaks here with the outlook of God's inspired law in any way. Jesus required His audience to take account of every jot and tittle of God's law, to see the utter sanctity of marriage, to recognize (in harmony with Deut. 24:1-4) only fornication as a ground for divorce, and to uphold the full and accurate understanding of the Older Testament morality. Let us be sure that we are part of His audience by hearing and heeding His word (cf. Matt. 7:24; John 10:27). Christ in no way (expressly or implicitly) regards the Mosaic law as inferior to New Testament standards. "To say . . . that Jesus *breaks* with Moses is unwarranted."[43] Instead we must concur that:

---

[41] Meyer, *op. cit.*, p. 133.

[42] Dabney, *op. cit.*, p. 407. Dabney's reference is to the even stronger passage about the woman taken in adultery.

[43] Meyer, *op. cit.*, p. 339.

> Here, by means of a few simple words, Jesus discourages divorce, refutes the rabbinical misinterpretation of the law, reaffirms the law's true meaning (cf. Matt. 5:17, 18), censures the guilty party, defends the innocent, and through it all upholds the sacredness and inviolability of the marriage bond as ordained by God.[44]

Oaths, Retaliation, and Enemies

The next antithesis in Matthew 5 deals with taking oaths (vv. 33-37). The quotation to which Christ alludes and which the people had heard from the old scribes is not a precise rendition of the Older Testament. There is abundant evidence in the Babylonian Talmud, tractate Shebu'oth, that the scribes had held that a substitution for God's name in adjuration exempted one from the penalty attaching to perjury when God's name had been used in the oath.[45] This was a vain scribal effort to avoid reckoning with God in one's assertions. The substitutes for God's name would secure emphasis for the person's statement without obligating him to the truth, or so the Pharisees thought. Christ makes it clear that all these substitutes have an unavoidable God-ward reference anyway. Furthermore, resort to this kind of subterfuge implies that your simple word is not sufficiently credible, but rather suspect. With rhetorical hyperbole our Lord prohibits all such oath-taking; there is to be absolutely no disguised, needless, irreverent and surreptitious swearing. Note that it is Pharisaical oath-making that Jesus prohibits, not lawful oath-making. A *civil* context is different from the interpersonal one to which Christ here addresses Himself. Christ consented to the oath form of asseveration in Matthew 26:63, 64. That Christ does *not* mean to condemn all oaths without qualification should be clear to us from *God's* example of taking an oath (Gen. 22:16; Ps. 110:4; Heb. 6:17 f.) as well as the apostle Paul's frequent and appropriate taking of an oath (Rom. 1:9; 2 Cor. 1:23; Phil. 1:8; 1 Thess. 2:5, 10). Jesus exposed

---

[44] Hendriksen, *op. cit.*, p. 306.

[45] See Murray, *Principles of Conduct*, *op. cit.*, p. 169.

scribal oath-making as unlawful and thereby restored the law's intent. Although lawful oaths may be taken in court, in normal circumstances our simple word should be trustworthy and sufficient.

It would be wrong to see Jesus annulling the Older Testamental law with respect to the *ius talionis* in Matthew 5:38-42, but it is correct to see Him correcting the Pharisaical abuse of that law. The Pharisees were wont to appeal to the Older Testamental principle of *equitable* punishment in civil court in order to justify *personal* revenge and vindictiveness. Christ is speaking to the situation of interpersonal relations and prohibits the exacting of due punishment for wrongs suffered. In civil jurisprudence there is still to be an "eye for an eye, etc." but between individuals there is to be forbearance. Jesus attacks the use of the *ius talionis* for revenge instead of for retribution; in private life the methods of civil jurisprudence do not apply. The Older Testament applies the principle of an "eye for an eye" to court-room contexts, that is, when public justice was being exacted; Jesus did not repudiate this use of the *ius talionis.* Again using hyperbole, Jesus stresses willingness to suffer personal loss as a characteristic Christian virtue; such a disposition did not describe the Pharisees. Paul's word in Romans 12:18 f. is parallel to what Jesus teaches: "beloved, never take your own revenge." To see Jesus annulling the Older Testamental law here would imply that Jesus is saying that there is no longer any need for public justice—a totally unacceptable implication. Moreover, could Jesus be against the *ius talionis* and still need to go to the cross for our sins? If God does not evaluate "an eye for an eye" as a righteous standard of judgment and penalty, then Jesus would not have to die as a *substitute* taking the punishment due for our sins. So any antinomian interpretation of Matthew 5:38-42 cannot do justice to Christian social morality or soteriology.

The final antithesis of Matthew 5 probably best shows the nature of Pharisaical interpretation and distortion of God's law; it also strongly confirms our thesis that Jesus is reproving the scribal view of the law and not abrogating the law itself in the antithesis of Matthew 5. Whereas the law specified that God's people were to love each other, it did not command them to hate their enemies. The scribes had affixed this man-made commandment to hate your enemies to God's law of loving neighbor. Not only was this an improper inference and gross failure to understand the nature of God on the part of the scribes, it was in blatant contradiction to the word of the Older Testament! Proverbs 25:21 says, "If your enemy is hungry, give him food to eat; and if he is thirsty give him water to drink." The Pharisees were not even close to approximating this loving attitude; rabbinic teaching even *commanded* hate in certain instances,[46] as well as demonstrating an unloving disposition in attitude and practice. Jesus confirms the true intent of the Older Testamental law and restores its proper interpretation. Christians are to be as loving and fair as is their Heavenly Father; this is what the law requires. Hence this is what Christ requires.

So we see in Matthew 5:21-48 examples of how Christ confirms the Older Testamental law and reproves the Pharisaical use of it; the antitheses are case law applications of the principle enunciated in Matthew 5:17-20. Christ did not come to abrogate the law; far from it! He confirmed it in full measure, thereby condemning scribal legalism and showing us the pattern of our Christian sanctification.

Matthew 5 is not the only passage in which Christ condemns the externalism and anthropo-centrism of the Pharisees; He also does so in Matthew 23. It might appear initially that Jesus contradicts His attitude toward the Pharisees when in verse 3 He commands His hearers to observe what the scribes bid them. The context makes it clear, however, that Jesus is telling the crowd to observe the teaching of the scribes *to the extent* that they *legitimately* sit in Moses' seat. His hearers are to obey all the *lawful* things that the Pharisees require. The Mosaic law is to be obeyed, but note this qualification: the scribes do not always represent the truth or a proper interpretation of the law. They follow the traditions of the elders instead (Matthew 15:1-20). They appeal to the older rabbinic precepts (Matthew 5:21 ff.). Furthermore, they do not practice what they preach and are vain and self-exalting (rather

---

[46] Cf. Stonehouse, *op. cit.*, p. 200n.

than God-revering and righteous). Because of their authority, when they are a stumbling block to conversion and salvation (v. 13) theirs is the greater condemnation (if verse 14 is original) and their converts are the two-fold children of hell; scribal legalism spells spiritual death. These Pharisees are blind guides, hypocrites who leave behind the more important, intrinsic, and weightier matters of the law while straining legalistically at embellished tradition. The scribes and Pharisees are white-washed graves, unclean and dead within (v. 27) and *lawless* to the core (v. 28). Given this warning qualification, Jesus says to follow and heed the lawful and proper teaching of those who presume to sit legitimately in Moses' seat. Jesus does not give unqualified endorsement to the Pharisees, and He does not oppose the law. In Matthew 23:4, 23 we get a capsulated evaluation of the scribal treatment of the law of God. The Pharisees lay grievously heavy burdens on the people; these are comprised of the rabbinic additions to the law, the man-made commandments which were intended to be a hedge around the law; the scribal precepts are burdensome, but God's law is not (1 John 5:3). Secondly, in their casuistry the scribes totally missed the law's call for judgment, mercy, and faith; the Pharisees were ungracious and self-righteous. In this they missed the heart of the law. If a person truly follows God's law he will look to Christ in faith for his salvation, be truly discerning and merciful toward others; far from being antagonistic to love, the law of God is the concrete expression of love, and love is the summary of the law.

In Matthew 15:2, 6 and Mark 7:5 ff. Jesus strongly opposes the traditions of "them of old" to the law of God; in these passages the hypocrisy of the Pharisees is clearly revealed. Christ does not commend the scribes for their type of concern with the law because, by contrast, only those who hear God's word and keep it are blessed (Luke 11:28, cf. James 1:22-24). By the tradition of the elders (self-law) the Pharisees both invalidate and transgress the true law of God (Matthew 15:3, 6). So although they think that they merit God's blessing, the Pharisees really exclude themselves from God's favor by their unlawful legalism which will not hear what *God* has to say nor obey it in love. Autonomy and self-righteousness makes theonomy void.

Paul also opposed Judaistic legalism; many of the disparaging comments he makes about law-keeping are directed against the Judaizers who abused God's law by making it a way of justification. Paul, in agreement with Jesus, takes a stand against the Judaistic interpretation of the law as a means of salvation. The law itself is not a hostile force to man, but whoever expects his salvation by way of the law will be deceived and lost. Legalistic justification, such as that attempted by the Pharisees, will damn a man; hence Paul constantly warns against trusting in the law. This explains his negative comments about the law.[47] The view of the law entertained both by the Pharisees and Judaizers was hopeless and antagonistic to God's grace; they were setting out to establish their own righteousness, but there was no hope that they could. The law was always an instrument of condemnation to such legalists. Vos states this point accurately:

> The apostle's polemic against the Jewish legalism proceeds along two distinct lines of attack. In the first place, it is rejected because utterly impractical and futile, because it has never led and can never lead to the end for which the Jewish mind pursues it. In the second place, not satisfied with this practical dismissal of it, Paul condemns it on the fundamental ground of its irreligious character and tendency.[48]

We conclude then that the New Testament theonomy is not to be identified with that of the Pharisees and Judaizers. Christ binds us His people to the law of God as revealed in the Older Testament, but we must steer clear of the type of legalism which does not receive God's law the way it was intended or follow it in the manner it prescribes. Externalism, legalism, and autonomy are all contrary to God's law.

---

[47] See H. Ridderbos' excellent article, "The Law of God in Paul's Doctrine of Salvation," in *When the Time Had Fully Come* (Grand Rapids: Eerdmans, 1957), pp. 61-77.

[48] Geerhardus Vos, "The Alleged Legalism in Paul's Doctrine of Justification," *Princeton Theological Review*, I (April, 1903), p. 167.

When, in opposition to the Pharisees, Christ reproves a legalistic concern with outward behavior alone and emphasizes the need for heartfelt obedience and inner purity, He is *not* going *beyond* the law and its Older Testamental demands (as many are inclined to think today). The stress on inner heart attitude in Jesus' commandments is no more than the confirmation of the letter of the law. Professing themselves to be experts in the law, the scribes and Pharisees showed themselves to be ignorant of the law's demands. The Older Testament, which the scribes had at their disposal, is replete with indications that the man who is truly righteous has *his heart* affected by the law. The Pharisees should have read in 1 Chronicles 28:9 that the Lord searches the heart and knows its every intent; therefore, to please God they must serve Him with a *willing* mind and with the *whole* heart, just as David instructs Solomon. In the Book of the Law the scribes could have read of God's longing for His people to have revering and obedient hearts: "Oh that they had such a heart in them that they would fear Me and keep all My commandments always" (Deut. 5:29, NASV). The main theme of Deuteronomy had been missed by the Pharisees: "And you shall love the Lord your God with all your heart and with all your soul and with all your might. And these words which I am commanding you today shall be on your heart" (Deut. 6:5 f. NASV). God commanded His people to impress His law on their hearts and souls (Deut. 11:18); He both *demanded* that the people circumcise their hearts and *promised* that *He* would circumcise their hearts (Deut. 10:16 and 30:6-10). Yet the Pharisees could worry about nothing more than circumcision in the flesh. The Psalms teach that God's law is *in the heart* of the righteous, who delights to do God's will (Ps. 37:31; 40:8); the Psalmist's prayer is that God would incline his heart to the law, and his resolve is to keep the law with his whole heart (Ps. 119:34, 36, 69, 80). And this concern for the law which is advocated in the Older Testament is not one of begrudging and burdensome slavery; the obedience which God blesses must be a *willing* obedience (cf. Isa. 1:19). If our religious duties are not done in gratefulness, faith, and love, then they might just as well not be done at all, for God abhors a mere outward and hypocritical performance (e.g., Isa. 1:10-20), while desiring inner sanctification (e.g.,

Ps. 51: 16 f.). God's law was to be written on the heart and treasured as the apple of one's eye (Prov. 7:1-3); such an interest in the law was *not* deadening: "keep my commandments and *live.*" The commandment and law of the father and mother was to be God's law (see Deut. 6:7), and this was to be bound upon the heart for guidance, protection, and discipline in the way of life (Prov. 6:20-23). The Lord's commandments were to be kept, then, with the heart, for they were kindness, truth, and peace (Prov. 3:1-3); and obedience to the law was not advocated as a means of self-trust or works-salvation, for in the same place where heartfelt obedience is commanded it is said, "*Trust in the Lord with all your heart,* and do not lean on your own understanding. In all your ways *acknowledge Him,* and *He* will make your paths straight" (Prov. 3:6 f.).

The Older Testament itself condemns the anthropo-centrism and externalism of the scribes and Pharisees; Christ restores the theonomy of the Older Testament and thereby confirms its disapprobation of Pharisaism. Christ did not bring in a change from law to spirit; He effectually pressed home the spiritual demand of the law. He did not transcend a legalistic testament but substantiated that the Older Testament was not legalistic.

> We must reject any antithesis between "the ethics of law and the ethics of disposition" as the basic scheme of Jesus' moral teaching. It is true that Jesus again and again has strongly emphasized the necessity of a heart disposition to please God in contrast to an external view of the law. He makes the possibility of a good deed dependent upon a good disposition of the heart, found especially in the sayings about the tree and its fruit (Matt. 7:17 ff.; 12:33 ff.). But all this does not in the least cancel God's law as an external authority and source of knowledge, nor does it replace this law by man's good disposition. When Jesus puts the Pharisees to blame because they only teach the people the letter of the law relating to the exterior action (of manslaughter, adultery, etc.), and do not

indicate the disposition of the heart as the real origin of wickedness; he does not go back to what lies behind the law, but maintains the latter in its deepest meaning and purport. The disposition of the heart (indicated in whatever way it may be) is not some attribute transcending the law, but is subjected to the law and demanded by the law.[49]

[49] Ridderbos, *op, cit.*, pp, 306 f.

Chapter 4

THE LAW'S INABILITY TO JUSTIFY AND EMPOWER

NOT only did the Pharisees demonstrate their unlawful legalism by concern merely for external behavior, they also abused the law by not using it in the manner God intended. The Pharisees had set out to establish their own righteousness by means of the law; they expected that God would justify them on the basis of the moral merit they had earned. The Pharisees attempted to justify *themselves* by means of the law; theirs was a works-salvation scheme to the core.

The prologue to the Ten Commandments should have sufficiently shown the Pharisees that salvation was an act of God's grace. Indeed, the *entire* Older Testament, as it takes the form of a covenant document,[1] was a testimony to God's *gracious* dealings with His people. Justification was not by the law in the Older Testament, and the scribes of the law should have known this fact well. The violation of the law by our first parents, Adam and Eve, rendered it impossible that either they or their descendants should ever be justified on the ground of their own personal righteousness.[2] If there was to be salvation at all, it would necessarily be according to God's mercy and based on *His* righteousness. In telling about the Messiah who shall bring salvation for God's people, Jeremiah calls Him "The Lord our righteousness" (Jer. 23:6). Justification is grounded in the righteousness of the Lord, accounted as our own. Thus the theology of the Older Testament testified

---

[1] Cf. Meredith G. Kline, *The Structure of Biblical Authority* (Grand Rapids: Wm. B. Eerdmans, 1972), pp. 35-38, 45-68.

[2] Cf. John Murray, *The Imputation of Adam's Sin* (Grand Rapids: Wm. B. Eerdmans, 1959), pp. 19-21, 71-95.

that salvation is by grace through faith.[3] It could not be otherwise, as is explained by the Psalmist's plea: "Enter not into judgment with Thy servant, for in Thy sight shall no man living be justified" (Ps. 143:2). The Pharisees were deluded to think that they could establish their own righteousness by the law; the Scriptures taught them otherwise.

Abel, Enoch, and Noah were all clear illustrations that man gains favor with God, not by works, but by faith (Gen. 4:4; 5:24; 6:8-9 with Heb. 11:4-7). But if the scribes overlooked these examples how could they miss the example of Abraham, in whom they boasted as their father? Genesis 15:6 clearly teaches that righteousness was *imputed by faith:* "then he believed in God, and it was imputed to him for righteousness."[4] Forgiveness and redemption are with *the Lord* (Ps. 130:4, 7), and those who take refuge in the Son are blessed (Ps. 2:12). Note David's eloquent expressions of Older Testamental soteriology: "For *Thy name's sake,* O Lord, Pardon my iniquity, for it is great" (Ps. 25:11). "Be *gracious* to me, O God, according to Thy lovingkindness; According to the greatness of Thy compassion blot out my transgressions" (Ps. 51:1, NASV). "How blessed is the man to whom the Lord does not impute iniquity" and "he who *trusts in the Lord* lovingkindness shall surround him" (Ps. 32:2, 10, NASV). Both the nature and necessity of substitutionary atonement were plainly taught in Isaiah 53:5 f.: "He was wounded for our transgressions, He was crushed for our iniquities; the chastening for our peace fell upon Him, and by His scourging we are healed. All we like sheep have gone astray, each of us has turned to his own way, but the Lord has caused all our iniquity to fall on Him." Only grace could secure justification for the sinner in the Older Testament; the law here could personally avail nothing. The experts in the law should have so taught. The law convicts of sin and leads the redeemed in the paths of righteousness. However, in reference to personal

---

[3] Cf. J. Barton Payne, *The Theology of the Older Testament* (Grand Rapids: Zondervan, 1962), pp. 232 ff., 304 ff.

[4] Cf. John Murray, *The Epistle to the Romans* (Grand Rapids: Wm. B. Eerdmans, 1959), pp. 130-132, 343-344, 353-355, 358-359; also M. G. Kline, "Abram's Amen," *Westminster Theological Journal,* XXXI, No. 1 (Nov., 1968), pp. 1-11.

justification the Pharisees should have testified "my hope is from Him. He *only* is my rock and my salvation. . . . On God my salvation and glory rest; the rock of my strength, my refuge is in God" (Ps. 62:5-8, NASV). They should have driven home the words of the prophet: "In the Lord have I righteousness and strength. . . . In the Lord shall all the seed of Israel be justified. . . . This is the heritage of the servants of the Lord, and their righteousness is of me, saith the Lord. . . . I will greatly rejoice in the Lord, my soul shall be joyful in my God; for he hath clothed me with the garments of salvation, he hath covered me with the robe of righteousness" (Isa. 45:24 f.; 54:17; 61:10, AV). Accordingly, the people under the Older Testament were justified by imputed righteousness from the Lord. "The salvation of the righteous is from the Lord" (Ps. 37:39). The ancient Pharisees, as well as modern dispensationalists,[5] failed to see this. Therefore, their view of the law was *unlawful.*

The law does *not* save a man, but it *does* show him *why* he needs to be saved and *how* he is to walk after he is saved.

Because God's moral nature, His holiness, is revealed in the law, the law accuses and convicts its reader of sin. "By the law is the knowledge of sin. . . . I had not known sin but by the law" (Rom. 3:20; 7:7, AV). And this is so because "sin is the transgression of the law" (1 John 3:4). Where there is no law there can be no transgression (Rom. 4:15). As the sinner compares his life to the demands of the law he finds himself sold under sin and lost. The magnitude of his sinfulness is glaring because "it stands written that accursed is everyone who continues not in *all* the things having been written in the book of the law to do them" (Gal. 3:10) and "whoever keeps all the law, but stumbles in *one point* has become guilty of all" (James 2:10). The law, then, works wrath against the sinner (Rom. 4:15). Hence it should be plain that "no man is justified by the law in the sight of God" (Gal. 3:11; cf. 2:16). To use the law as a means of justification is an unlawful use of the law (cf. 1 Tim. 1:8). Moralism is not the biblical way of salvation. Instead, "a

---

[5] E.g., C. I. Scofield, *Rightly Dividing the Word of Truth* (New Jersey: Loizeaux Brothers, 1896), pp. 14 f., 34 f.

man is justified by faith without the deeds of the law" (Rom. 3:28, AV). The law cannot give life to man, or else righteousness would have been by the law (Gal. 3:21). Although the law itself is a way of life, it cannot restore life lost because of sin; hence, for the *transgressor* of the law, the law is a way of condemnation and death. So conspicuous is the law's function of indicting men of sin that Paul can often use "sin" and "law" as synonyms; for example, "sin shall not have dominion over you, for you are not under law but under grace" (Rom. 6:14). To be *under* the law is to be dominated by sin; not being able to live by the law, the man who is under it as a way of salvation dies, and sin is then victorious. To be saved by grace includes dying to sin as well as to the law (Rom. 7:4; Gal. 2:19). The law represents a curse and indicting conviction of sin to all men. Thereby the law is a schoolmaster which leads sinful man to Christ, the sinless One (see Gal. 3:24); by its oppressive and condemning yoke the law drives us to our emancipation in Christ.[6] Consequently the Scriptures uniformly represent justification by the works of the law as a way of *death* which is contrary to justification by Christ (who perfectly kept the law), the way of *life.*

Christ's perfect obedience to the law of God secures our release from the necessity of personally keeping the law as a condition of justification. "And may be found in Him, not having a righteousness of my own derived from the law, but that which is through faith in Christ, the righteousness which comes from God on the basis of faith" (Phil. 3:9, NASV). Our righteousness before God must be that which is *imputed* to us, the righteousness of Christ who was sinless before the law.[7] We who were once disobedient cannot be saved on the basis of deeds which we have done; rather, we are justified by God's grace (Titus 3:3-7). Christ justifies us from all the things which the *Mosaic law was not able* to justify us (Acts 13:38 f.; cf. Rom. 3:28; 10:4; Acts 2:38; 10:43). Being

---

[6] Cf. J. Gresham Machen, *What Is Faith?* (Grand Rapids: Wm. B. Eerdmans, 1925), ch. IV, "Faith Born of Need."

[7] Cf. James Buchanan, *The Doctrine of Justification* (Banner of Truth Trust, [1867] 1961), ch. XII, "Justification: Its Immediate and only Ground, the Imputed Righteousness of Christ."

released from the law as a way of justification also means being released from the penalty which attaches to failure to keep the law. Although faith does not nullify the law (see Rom. 3:31), it does release us from the law's condemnation. Instead of appearing before God in our own unrighteousness earned under the law, we are presented to God in the righteousness of Jesus Christ which is received as a free gift of God's grace. Second Chronicles 26:20 should be a lesson to us; God struck Uzziah with leprosy for offering incense without a priest, and so much worse it shall be for us if we attempt to "obediently" come to God without the intercession of the spotless One, Jesus Christ. Horatius Bonar expressed this truth beautifully:

> Not what my hands have done can save my guilty soul;
> Not what my toiling flesh has borne can make my spirit whole.
> Not what I feel or do can give me peace with God;
> Not all my prayers and sighs and tears can bear my awful load.
>
> Thy grace alone O God to me can pardon speak;
> Thy pow'r alone O Son of God can this sore bondage break.
> No other work, save thine, no other blood will do;
> No strength, save that which is divine, can bear me safely through.

Due to the lingering influence of the Pharisees among Christians, especially as manifest in the teaching of the Judaizers, the New Testament Scriptures gave a great deal of space to refuting the view that the law is a way of *justification*,[8] especially in Acts 15, Galatians, Hebrews,

[8] In fact, so emphatic is this note in the New Testament that many have erroneously inferred that the Christian should have absolutely *nothing* to do with the Older Testamental law of God. Although such people fail to note the positive teaching on the law in the New Testament (witness Matt. 5:17-19), they do prove that one can hardly use the New Testament to ground any hope of earning his salvation through self-righteous obedience to the law.

and Romans 8. The first general assembly of the Christian Church was occasioned by the heresy of the Judaizers (follow Acts 15). These false teachers were requiring observance of the ceremonial law for salvation; in particular, they taught that the Gentiles had to be circumcised (v. 1). Justification must be *by the law* according to the *Pharisaical* converts (v. 5); this squares with what we know about the doctrine of the Pharisees elsewhere. Reminiscent of our Lord's words in Matthew 23:4, Peter says that the Pharisees are known to lay heavy and grievous burdens on the people; but neither the believers under the Older Testament nor the New Testament Christians were able to bear this load. So since these believers had not been able to justify themselves by the law, why should this yoke be laid upon the Gentiles (vv. 10-11)? James sums up the issue by saying that they must refuse to require legalistic justification from the Gentiles. *All* men who are saved must be saved by God's free grace; the only yoke they must accept is that easy one given by Christ (cf. Matt. 11:29 f.).

But there was still a practical problem to be dealt with: how can the Jewish Christians who were brought up to detest certain things cope with Gentile believers who do not share this disapprobation? In order to facilitate harmony among believers, therefore, James recommends that the Gentile converts respect their Jewish brethren's scruples. The things which James says should be avoided, then, are not to be viewed as the only portions of the law which are still binding on New Testament Christians. These things would not be morally binding at all due to their ceremonial nature. Yet expediency called for the Jerusalem Council to request the Gentiles to avoid meat which had idolatrous associations or which was not drained of its blood as well as to conform to the Jewish social code respecting the relation between the sexes.[9] That is, while neither Jew nor Gentile are required to keep the

---

[9] "Fornication" here denotes a violation of the degrees of consanguinity prohibited in Leviticus 18, as F. F. Bruce points out: *Commentary on the Book of Acts* (Grand Rapids: Wm. B. Eerdmans, 1954), p. 315, and *New Testament History* (New York: Doubleday & Co., 1971), p. 287. Such a use of the word is reflected in the Zadokite *Covenant of Damascus*, iv. 17 ff.; cf. 1 Cor. 5:1.

ceremonial law as a way of justification, in Acts 15:20 three stipulations are set forth in order to improve social relations between believers of widely divergent cultural backgrounds. Therefore, the Judaizers who had taught that the Gentiles must keep the ceremonial law in order to be saved were unorthodox; they subverted and unsettled these Christians (v. 24). On the other hand, at the Holy Spirit's guidance, and in order to smooth the path of fellowship between Jewish and Gentile Christians, the Gentiles were requested by the Jerusalem Council to abstain from certain things (vv. 28-29). This is wise and expedient advice, but it does not imply that believers are obligated to keep the ceremonial provisions of the Mosaic law as such, much less that justification requires it. With respect to justification, the Jerusalem Council ruled out the works of the law as its proper ground.

Paul expresses the same doctrinal point of view in the letter to the Galatian churches, which we can here survey. Paul's theme throughout Galatians is the inadequacy of the law for salvation. In opposition to the heretical teachers who were demanding observation of the Mosaic ceremonial law, Paul teaches that the law is neither able to justify a man nor able to give men requisite spiritual power. The Judaizers who were troubling the Galatian Christians were particularly concerned with circumcision and the observation of special days and seasons (Gal. 4:10, 21; 5:2; 6:12 ff.). The Galatians were turning aside to a way of salvation dependent on these. But Paul would not stand for any combining of the Christian gospel with the Jewish ceremonies; faith alone could save a sinner and not obedience to outdated rituals. Paul himself could readily understand the heresy of the Judaizers, for he had once been a fanatic for the Jewish halacha (1:14); but now he has been called by God's *grace* (1:15). Paul knew all too well the impotence of the law; it could not give him the power to truly serve God. He had to *die* to the law in order to *live* unto God; and this death was brought about *through* the law. The law had executed Paul because he was unable to keep it; the letter killed him (cf. 2 Cor. 3:6). Now the law can no longer manipulate him, for he is a dead servant; nothing more can be exacted of him. The law was in no position to grant man what it demanded of him. It did not supply the power to obey. The fault, of course, is wholly that of the sinner; the law simply guides or condemns—dependent on the spiritual condition of the person in question. Paul, being a sinner, suffered under the law, but having died to it as a way of salvation he could live unto God. Hence Paul would not rely upon the works of the law for justification any longer; to do so would make grace void. If a sinner could attain righteousness through the law, then Christ died needlessly (2:21). Only the Holy Spirit of God can bring power to obey to the sinner, and that Holy Spirit was received not by law-works but by faith (3:2). The law is simply not a quickening power; it is without power because of sin (Rom. 8:3), and therefore unable to impart life and righteousness (Gal. 3:21).

Thus anyone who seeks justification before God out of obedience to the law lies under the law's curse. Paul directs this comment against the self-righteous legalism of the Judaizers and Jewish rabbis. They should have known that nobody shall be justified by the law, for the Older Testament clearly said that the righteous shall live by *faith* (Gal. 3:10-12). Although the law is not against the promises of God (3:21)—since they both aim at the same thing—the fulfillment of the promise cannot be made dependent upon obedience to the law, for in redemptive history the law came after the promise (3:15-22). Grace (the promise) and law (the demand) cannot be mixed together as ways of salvation; the man who is saved by grace cannot have anything added to his salvation by law. The promise *grants* what the law could only aim at: righteousness and salvation. The law served to make transgression and sin obvious; the law brought out sin more and more. It manifests man's inability to attain salvation by shutting up all men under sin, in order that the necessity of Christ's coming might be understood (3:19, 22). Before the coming of Christ, sin and the law held man in bondage; it prepared him, or oriented him, for salvation in Christ. Now that we have been saved by grace through faith, the law has served out its *tutorial* function (although we must remember that the law has *more* functions to serve, e.g. 1 Tim. 1:9 f., etc.). The law brought bondage, but Christ brings redemptive freedom from sin and death (3:23-29). Christ did this by subjecting Himself *to the law*; He then redeems those who are enslaved to the law and under its curse (4:4-6; cf. 3:13), making them ethically able to respond to God's will. How could anyone then wish to return to *bondage* under the ceremonial law (4:9 f.)! If those individuals who want to be under the law as a way of salvation would truly *listen to the law*, then they would *not* submit to the Judaizers and their slave principle (4:21-31); by so doing they stand to lose their inheritance. Christ set us free from the guilt-establishing and deadening power of the law; but if we submit to a legalistic soteriology then we must take the whole law for our reckoning (and with it, its curse) because salvation by grace is an *exclusive* principle (5:1-3). Galatians 5:4 makes it unmistakably clear that Paul has been dealing in this epistle with the way of *justification*; if one takes the law as his salvation, then he has precluded grace.

The book of Hebrews is also very much concerned with the law, especially in its ceremonial aspects. The epistle intends to demonstrate that Christ is superior to the angels, to the priesthood, to the older covenant, etc. In the course of its argument the book explains that the law had no power to make anything perfect (Heb. 7:19; cf. 10:1). By contrast, the gospel is able to accomplish what the law could not; it offers power, profit, perfection and direct access to God. Thus the good news of God's grace offers a better hope, for by it Christians are *enabled* to draw near unto God through their mediator-priest, Jesus Christ. It would be definite spiritual regression to return to the older and impotent covenant; therefore, the readers of Hebrews must press on in the faith dependent upon Jesus Christ for salvation. All other alternatives, even that of obedience to the law, would fail to make them perfect.

Paul's main theme in Galatians had been the inability of the law to justify and empower; in Romans he particularly stresses that there can be salvation *despite* transgression of God's perfect law. In order to establish this, however, Paul needs to show that no one can rely upon the law for his personal salvation; consequently Paul stresses the negative element of the law: its condemning role. "By the works of the law no flesh will be justified in His sight, for through the law comes the knowledge of sin" (Rom. 3:20, NASV). Since all are unrighteous (3:23) the law will justify none. And because justification is a *gift* of God's grace, obedience to the law can contribute absolutely nothing (3:21-24). "We maintain that a man is justified by faith *apart from* the works of the law" (3:28). Paul laments over Israel's total misapprehension of the way of justification in chapter 9, verses 31 and following; they should have seen that it is by faith and not the law (cf. 3:27-4:25). Israel had missed God's provision of grace and so failed to submit genuinely to God's righteous law. Because they sought to establish their own righteousness in opposition to God's, Israel's zeal for God was totally ignorant (10:2-3). Paul expresses himself succinctly in Romans 10:4. Christ is, *for believers,* the end of using the law as a way of attaining righteousness. This parallels the message of Galatians (see especially 2:21 and 5:4): righteousness by law conflicts with righteousness by faith. For a person to choose the former he would have to be ignorant of the law's impotence due to his sin. The Christian believer is not the servant of sin, in other words, "under the law," but he is redeemed and renewed by God's grace; this is the guarantee that sin will not have dominion over him (Rom. 6:14). Grace grants the power which the law fails to provide. "But now we have been released from the law, having died to that by which we were bound, so that we serve in newness of the Spirit and not in oldness of the letter" (7:6). Because of the weakness of sinful human nature the law could not overcome sin's power, but in the believer the power of the Holy Spirit frees him from the power of sin unto death, thereby enabling him to accomplish what the law demands (8:1-4). The conclusion of the matter, then, is that a man must trust in God's grace and Christ's righteousness rather than in his own works, which only condemn him under the law's curse; the letter is unto death, but the Spirit gives new life and spiritual power.

Therefore when this treatise affirms the continuing validity of every stroke of God's law based on scriptural authority (e.g., Matt. 5:17 ff.), this teaching must be kept in proper perspective. Scripture uniformly views the law as a standard of righteousness after which we should pattern our sanctification and Christian life, but *justification* is *never* by our obedience to the law (after the fall of Adam and Eve). The Pharisees and Judaizers both missed this important truth and thereby unlawfully abused the law of God.

It is necessary for us to *distinguish* between *two types* of forensic religion: that of Judaistic legalism and that of the Scriptures. In the former *self-* righteousness is generated. In the latter Christ perfectly obeys the law's demands and qualifies as an atoning substitute for those who have violated the law, and then in gratitude to God for His grace Christians pattern their lives after the law as the expression of God's holy will. Before the law the sinner is guilty and powerless to obey its demands, but in the gospel he is forgiven and empowered (cf. Rom. 3:19-26; 8:1 ff.). When Paul says that we are not under the law but under the Spirit, he has in mind that we are no longer obligated to the law in regard to the accomplishment of righteousness or doing of God's commandments; instead, we are dependent upon the Spirit who renders us capable of doing what God demands (cf. Gal. 5:18 with Rom. 8:4). A proper understanding of the law's abiding *validity* must be accompanied with a recognition of the law's *inabilities.*

The modern view, however, which says that the letter of the law inadequately expresses the contents of righteousness would be completely alien to Paul. He declares that the law is *holy* (Rom. 7:12) but that we who are sinners by nature fall under the law's curse. Christ took that curse upon Himself, and thc Spirit works through us *to obey* that holy law. This is the forensic religion of divine revelation. Paul is careful not to give the impression that the law itself is evil or inglorious (see 2 Cor. 3:7 f.). He refutes his antinomian opponents who would make him as a minister of the new covenant a despiser of grace. But since the law came from God, Paul appropriately states that it came in glory. Nevertheless, the law is not to he exalted at the expense of the gospel. The gospel far *excels* in glory because it has renewing *power.* Although Moses' glory faded, the glory of the good news in the face of Jesus Christ does not (2 Cor. 4:6).

Therefore, whether we turn to Acts 15, Galatians, Hebrews, or Romans, those who have been saved by God's grace should see the grave impropriety of stressing legal obligation in such a way that the good news of God's merciful forgiveness and monergistic regeneration is assigned to the periphery of their attention. A proper reading of *the law itself* would prevent any such imbalance. As did Paul, so must we recognize that *the law's abiding validity does not obviate its crucial inadequacies:* as a mere ethical stipulation it cannot empower us to obey it, and thus it cannot serve to justify us before God. Consequently we *glory in the gospel* of Christ and His Spirit as accomplishing what the law could not; that is, we magnify the gospel as the *power of God unto salvation* unto all who believe, for therein is revealed the *righteousness of God unto our justification* (Rom. 1:16 f.).

III. THE THESIS AS INTEGRAL TO CHRISTIANITY

Chapter 5

THE INTEGRITY OF THE LAW

HAVING stated that the law is impotent to deliver a man from the bondage of sin, Paul asks in Romans 7:7, "What shall we say then? Is the law sin?" His answer is an emphatic, "May it never be!" Our reasoning fails to be scriptural if we see the inability of the law to justify the sinner as carrying with it the inference that the law is thereby discarded or abrogated (see Rom. 3:31; 7:12, 14, 16, 19, 21). We must ask ourselves, how could it be that the standard of *God's unchanging holiness* should ever be deprived of its sanctity and validity? Christ our Lord and Saviour has clearly taught us that this law shall never fail to be binding upon us (Matt. 5:17-18). This divine pronouncement should be sufficient to deter us from that erroneous dispensational conclusion that the Christian has no obligation to the law of God after the advent of the Messiah. It was the Messiah who confirmed the law and renounced any view which holds that His coming had the effect of abrogating it.

The law of God expresses God's holy nature to man. It does so due to its intimate relation to the person of God. The Decalogue, which summarily comprehends the whole law of God, was appropriately written by the very finger of God (Ex. 31:18; 32:16; Deut. 4:13; 9:10; 10:4). It thereby shares its Author's perfection. The ark of the covenant represented God's presence and typified God's throne in the Holy of Holies; it was alternately called "the ark *of God*" (1 Sam. 3:3). Deuteronomy 10:5 (cf. 31:25 f.) tells us that the law was placed in this ark of the covenant; hence God's law was identified with His presence. In Exodus 24:3-8 Moses sprinkled sacrificial blood on *the altar,* which represented God the sovereign author of the covenant, and upon the people, thus bringing them into covenant relation with God. In relating this event Hebrews 9:19 reads "For when every commandment had been spoken by Moses to all the people according to the law, he took the blood of the calves and goats . . . and sprinkled both *the book* itself and all the people, saying, 'This is the blood of the covenant. . . .' " Here the Book of the Law is taken to fittingly represent God in the covenantal transaction.

The law reflects not only the *presence* but the *moral character* of God. "We know that the law is good," says Paul (1 Tim. 1:8; cf. Rom. 7:12, 16); a good thing can be produced only by that which in itself is good (Matt. 7:16-18; 12:33), and God alone is good (Mark 10:18). In detailing what He requires of man the Lord has revealed what is good (Mic. 6:8), and the Psalmist declared, "Thou art good and doest good; teach me thy statutes" (Ps. 119:68, AV). Deuteronomy expressed the same: "Be careful to listen to all these words which I command you, in order that it may be well with you and your sons after you forever, for you will be doing what is good and right in the sight of the Lord your God" (12:28, NASV). God alone *is good;* yet because the law reflects His moral goodness, it too is designated "good." Consequently, we are exhorted to imitate what is good, for he that does good is of God (3 John 11; cf. Heb. 13:21). Because the law is the law *of God* it is good as God is good; therefore, to impugn the goodness of the law is to impugn the goodness of God Himself.

The same comments can be made with respect to the *perfection* of God and His law. Our heavenly Father is perfect (Matt. 5:48); God and His ways are perfect, righteous, and just (Deut. 32:4). So then, the way of the Lord is perfect (Ps. 18:30), and the will of God is the good, the acceptable, and the perfect (Rom. 12:2). To be perfect is to walk before God (Gen. 17:1). In the midst of the law we are commanded to be perfect before the Lord our God (Deut. 18:13), and the New Testament exhorts us to stand perfect in all the will of God (Col. 4:12). The Psalmist declares that "the law of the Lord is perfect" (Ps. 19:7), which is echoed in James 1:25. Hence Jesus, at the end of a long passage expounding upon the *law*, commanded us to "be perfect as your heavenly Father is perfect" (Matt. 5:48). The law shares God's goodness and perfection.

The divine origin and character of the law is indicated in the fact that the attributes of God are applied to the law. "The law is *Spiritual*" (Rom. 7:14) and as such is from the Spirit of God (John 4:24), and bears the imprints of His character. We read in Revelation 15:4 that God alone is holy; yet Paul can say that the *law* of the Lord is *holy* (Rom. 7:12) because it transcribes the moral perfection of God. Having concluded that the law is holy, Paul affirms that sin, not the law, is to blame for spiritual death (Rom. 7:13). As holy, just, and good, the law exhibits the moral excellence of God (cf. Rom. 7:7). The doing of all God's commandments would make one holy before Him (Num. 15:40), and according to Leviticus 11:44 we are commanded to be holy since God is holy. Leviticus 20:7-8 reads: "Sanctify yourselves, therefore, and be ye holy, for I am the Lord your God. And ye shall keep my statutes and do them" (AV). The holiness of God is manifest in the holiness of His law. God's name is holy and inspires *reverence* (Ps. 111:9); His law inspires the same (Ps. 119:38, 63, 79). "And now, Israel, what does the Lord your God require from you, but to reverence (fear) the Lord your God, to walk in all His ways and love Him . . . to keep the Lord's commandments and His statutes" (Deut. 10:12 f.). The Older Testamental Wisdom tells us that "the fear of the Lord is to hate evil" (Prov. 8:13), and evil consists in forsaking God's law (Ps. 119:53). So then, the one who genuinely fears the Lord delights in His commandments (Ps. 112: 1) and keeps His precepts (Ps. 119:63).

> It is the apprehension of God's glory that commands our totality commitment to him, totality trust and obedience. The fear of God is but the reflex in our consciousness of the transcendent perfection which alone could warrant and demand the totality of our commitment in love and devotion . . . (Mark 12:30). It is the transcendent perfection of God . . . that validates this totality demand. The fear of God in us is that frame of heart and mind which reflects our apprehension of who and what God is. . . . The commandments of God are the concrete expressions to us of God's glory and

> will. If we are committed to him in devotion and love, we shall love his commandments, too. The fear of God and the love of God are but different aspects of our response to him in the glory of his majesty and holiness (cf. Deut. 6:2, 4, 14). "The fear of the Lord is clean, enduring for ever: the judgments of the Lord are true and righteous altogether. More to be desired are they than gold, yea, than much fine gold: sweeter also than honey and the honeycomb. Moreover by them is thy servant warned: and in keeping of them there is great reward."[1]

To treat or consider the law as less than holy is to have a blasphemous attitude toward God Himself and to fail to properly reverence Him.

The will of God is the perfect reflection of His holiness, justice, and goodness; it is "the good, the acceptable, and the perfect," says Romans 12:2. Hence God's will can be identified with God's law (cf. Rom. 7:12). The law or commandments often stand as the manifestation of God's prescriptive will in the New Testament (Matt. 7:21; 12:50; 21:31; Luke 12:47; John 4:34; 7:17; 9:31; Acts 13:22; Rom. 2:18; Eph. 5:17; 6:6; Col. 4:12; 1 Thess. 4:3; 5:18; Heb. 10:10; 13:21; 1 Peter 4:2; 1 John 2:17; 5:14). Because the Lord is *righteous* (Ps. 116:5; 129:5; 145:17; Ezra 9:15; Jer. 12:1; Lam. 1:18; Dan. 9:7, 14), He instructs sinners in the way and loves righteous deeds (Ps. 11:7; 25:8). The will of God is generally summarized in Psalm 45:6 f., "Thy throne, O God, is forever and ever; a scepter of uprightness is the scepter of Thy kingdom. *Thou hast loved righteousness, and hated wickedness*" (NASV). The way of the Lord, then, is to do righteousness and justice (Gen. 18:19). If a man walks in the Lord's statutes and ordinances, he, too, is righteous (Ezek. 18:9), for righteous and true are the Lord's ways (Rev. 15:2). The 119th Psalm particularly stresses the righteousness of God's law (vv. 3, 137 f., 144): "I esteem all thy precepts concerning all things to be right" (v. 128,

---

[1] John Murray, *Principles of Conduct: Aspects of Biblical Ethics* (Grand Rapids: William B. Eerdmans Publishing Co., 1957), p. 242.

AV); "All Thy commandments are righteousness" (v. 172, NASV). God's will for us, therefore, is to emulate His righteousness by living according to the pattern of His righteous law. The New Testament reflects the same viewpoint. Because God is seen as righteous (cf. John 17:25; Rom. 1:17; 3:25 f.; Eph. 4:24; 1 John 2:29), righteousness is viewed as the opposite of lawlessness (2 Cor. 6:14; Heb. 1:9). The fruit of the Holy Spirit is righteousness, for the Spirit fulfills the law in us (Eph. 5:9; Rom. 8:4). Thus the doers of the law are righteous (Rom. 2:13). Anyone who does not practice righteousness is not of God (1 John 3:10) because the commandments of His law are righteous (Rom. 7:12).[2] Therefore, the people who know righteousness are those in whose heart is God's law (Isa. 51:7); this is true in all generations, under both covenants, and for all men. Therefore, the man who is *of God* pursues *righteousness* and *godliness* (1 Tim. 6:11 f.), as they are expressed in God's law.

Further attributes of God which are applied to the law are *justice* (Ps. 25:8-10; Prov. 28:4-5; Zech. 7:9-12), *truth* (Ps. 25:10; 119:142, 151; Rev. 15:3), *faithfulness* (Ps. 93:5; 111:7; 119:86), and *purity* (Ps. 119:140). This law which is viewed as having divine integrity is not some allegedly New Testament law of the inner disposition or spirit; it is identical with the Mosaic commandments: "Thou didst come down on Mount Sinai, and didst speak with them from heaven; Thou didst give to them just ordinances and true laws, good statutes and commandments" (Neh. 9:13). The Older Testamental law which Christ confirmed from the Mount in Matthew 5:17 ff. is thus the transcript of God's holiness and the standard for human righteousness.

Consequently, a man's attitude toward the law is an index of his relation to God. While the godly and righteous people of God *delight* in the law, the man who has a mind set on sinful human nature does not subject himself to the law (Rom. 8:7). To distinguish between the righteous and the wicked is to distinguish between those who serve God and those who do not serve Him (Mal. 3:18), and *serving* God

[2] The Greek word for "righteous" (δίκαιος) is even *defined* by Arndt and Gingrich as "conforming to the laws of God and living in accordance with them."

means obeying His commandments (Josh. 22:5). The first Psalm clearly defines the difference between the godly and the wicked; the righteous delight in the law of the Lord and keep it, but the ungodly are not so. The book of Proverbs abounds in contrasts between the wicked and the righteous (e.g., 10:6, 9, 21-32; 11:21, 23; 15:9, etc.); the godly man has gladness, hope, prosperity, and God's favor, but the paths of the unrighteous man are all destruction and misery. The law is the criterion which defines who is *wicked.* The wicked man does not seek God (Ps. 10:4) and transgresses the law (Ps. 37:38). The one who does not reverence God, who ceases to do good, and who is flattered with lawlessness is wicked (Ps. 36:1-4). To forsake the law, therefore, is to praise the wicked (Prov. 28:4). Psalm 119 informs us that the wicked forsake God's law (v. 53), are not in accord with the law (v. 85), and are far from the law (v. 150). The implication is the same in verses 101, 104, 115, 121, 163; verse 155 leaves nothing to implication: "Salvation is far from the wicked, for they do not seek Thy statutes" (NASV). Paul is in harmony with the Psalmist and says that to break the law is to dishonor God (Rom. 2:23), that not being subject to the law is open hostility to God (Rom. 8:7). Obedience to the law was intended to result in life (Rom. 7:10; cf. Lev. 18:5), but the wages of transgression against that law is death (Rom. 6:23).

We see, then, that the continuous witness of God's inscripturated revelation is to the divine integrity of God's law. The law came from God. It suitably represented His covenantal presence. It shares His goodness, perfection, holiness, righteousness, justice, truth, faithfulness, and purity. It defines what it is to fear and serve the Lord. It communicates God's prescriptive will for His people and delineates between the godly and the wicked. It is not surprising, then, that David said he would *worship* the commandments; such are their divine character ("I shall lift up my hands to Thy commandments, which I love; and I will meditate on Thy statutes," Ps. 119:48, NASV). On the other hand, turning one's heart away from obedience to God's law is epitomized by the worship of other gods (Deut. 30:17). Accordingly, to *follow* God or have Him as one's *Lord* entails obedience to His law. "With all my heart I have *sought Thee;* do not let me wander from *Thy commandments"* (Ps. 119:10). "You have today declared the Lord to *be your God,* and that you would *walk in His ways* and keep His statutes, His commandments and His ordinances, and listen to His voice" (Deut. 26:17, NASV). "Only be very *careful to observe the commandment* and the law which Moses the servant of the Lord commanded you, to love the Lord your God and walk in all His ways and keep His commandments and *hold fast to Him and serve Him* with all your heart and all your soul" (Josh. 22:5, NASV; cf. Ps. 119:10, 21, 125; Deut. 11:28).

The point is made well by the fact that to remember the *Lord's name* prompts the keeping of His law (cf. Ps. 119:55). Indeed, the test for whether someone genuinely *knows* the Lord or not is obedience to the law of God: "By this we know that we have known Him, if we keep His commandments. The one saying 'I have known Him' and not keeping His commandments is a liar" (1 John 2:3 f.). Observation of the law is indispensable to knowing God; a person cannot be devoted to God without being willing to emulate God's moral perfection as expressed in the law. One does not know *about* God if he is unfamiliar with the law which *characterizes* His moral nature, but even more one does not have the intimate, *loving,* covenant relation to God of "Knowing the Lord" unless he is compliant with God's *desires* as revealed in His law. In order to be perfect as our heavenly Father is perfect we must have a guide to the standard of moral perfection. To set down the pattern of sanctification (that is, to disclose God's nature) is the unique prerogative of God; only He can tell us what He is like and what He expects. That information is imparted through God's holy and inspired law. Thus to depreciate this law would be to impinge upon God's unique prerogatives, submitting to the satanic temptation to "be like God determining good and evil" (Gen. 3:5) for oneself. Such is the epitome of rebellion against God's very person. Obviously, then, to set aside, repudiate, or alter the law is blasphemy, an attitude that ought never to be found in God's people.

Although the law can be abused and unlawfully used as a way of justification, let us remember that *sin,* not the perfect law of God, works spiritual death and bondage. The law retains its divine integrity.

Being God-breathed, the law has the authority of God standing behind it. It can often be substituted for God Himself in Scripture. The law has divine attributes predicated of it, and it demarcates between reverence for and rebellion against God. Finally, as the self-revelation of God, the law has eternal validity. All biblical Christians should see in the law not a passing stage of morality, but the transcript of God's eternal holiness and the permanent standard for human righteousness.

Chapter 6

MESSIANIC OBEDIENCE AND THE ATONEMENT

IN reflecting the moral perfection of God the law exposes our sinfulness by sharp contrast. We have no reason to hope that God, who is immutably righteous, will lower His ethical norms in order to accommodate our unrighteousness. However, God does credit the perfect obedience of Christ to our account, thereby being just and the justifier of His people (cf. Rom. 3:26). Herein the law takes on a two-fold significance for Christians; *first,* obedience to the law by the Messiah plays an integral part in the accomplishment of salvation, and *second,* followers of Christ thus have set before them the example and goal of lawful living by their Lord.

As the law speaks God's holy nature, it is only to be expected that the Son of God, who is the exact representation of God's nature (Heb. 1:3), should embody the law in His own person. He is called "the Lord our righteousness" (Jer. 33:16), and as such He is the model of the law. Accordingly, Christ qualifies as a substitute for sinners by perfectly obeying each and every commandment of God; He can challenge His enemies, saying, "Which one of you convicts Me of sin?" (John 8:46). Only our blessed Lord can truly say, "I have kept My Father's commandments and abide in His love" (John 15:10); He was tempted in all points and is yet without sin (Heb. 4:15). Because He is holy, innocent, undefiled and separate from sinners, He has no need to offer up sacrifices for His own sins; having kept the law without any miscarriage He is made perfect forever (Heb. 7:26-28). Therefore, Christ could offer Himself without spot to God in order to cleanse us of our sins (Heb. 9:14).

The Older Testament had promised such a Deliverer. Isaiah wrote that "He will delight in the fear of the Lord. . . . And righteousness will be the belt about His loins" (Isa. 11:3, 5). It was foretold that He who would faithfully sit upon the Davidic throne would be prompt in righteousness (Isa. 16:5); this was fulfilled in the Messiah-King, Jesus Christ (Isa. 9:6-7; Luke 2:11). The Older Testament established that the Messiah's life would be the active counterpart of the written law, the will of God which is set down in the scroll of the book. Certainly the Incarnate Word would embody the written word: "Behold, I come; in the scroll of the book it is written of me; I delight to do Thy will, O my God; Thy law is within my heart" (Ps. 40:7 f.); Hebrews 10:4-10 unquestionably applies this to Jesus Christ, our sacrifice for sins. Thereby we learn that only the *Obedient One* could atone for disobedience.

Though the law was weak through the flesh, Christ condemned sin in the flesh (Rom. 8:3) by His perfect compliance with the law of God. Christ was *made* under the law (Gal. 4:4) and carefully *observed* it to the minutest detail (cf. Matt. 8:4; 9:20; 14:36; 17:24 ff.; 21:12 ff.; Mark 11:16; Luke 2:22 ff.; etc.). Since many could be justified before God only by the lawful obedience of One, our Saviour said that it was fitting for Him to fulfill all righteousness—in other words, to perform all the law's demands (Matt. 3:15). Christ received *authority* from the Father because of His righteous deeds (cf. Rev. 2:26 f.). Even the *words* which Christ spoke were in obedience to His Father: "The Father Himself who sent Me has given Me commandment, what to say, and what to speak. And I know that His commandment is eternal life; therefore the things I speak, I speak just as the Father has told Me" (John 12:49 f.).

It is thus in the fullest accord with the Older Testamental promise, the righteous character, the works and the words of Christ that by His teaching He bound others also to the law of God (Matt. 5:17 ff.; 7:12; 19:17; 22:40; 24:12). God's law was the sole, presupposed *foundation* for Christ's ethical exhortation and instruction:

> The norms of the righteousness demanded by Jesus are not founded in an earthly ideal of God's kingdom, nor in the

> future and transcendent character of the kingdom. God's will expressed in Jesus' commandments is not subordinated to certain creaturely values, nor is it to be derived from the latter, nor does it consist in their negation. It rests solely in God's own communication. Jesus' "ethics" does not consist in some doctrine concerning "goods," nor in asceticism. It is the "ethics" of *obedience* in the full sense of the word. That which is "righteousness," and may be taught as such, is always to be traced back to God's own words. This fundamental notion is the great presupposition of the remarkable fact that again and again Jesus speaks of "God's will" without any further explanation (Matt. 7:21; 12:50; 18:14; 21:31; Luke 12:47, 48), the "commandment" or "God's commandments" (Matt. 15:3; Mark 7:8, 9; Matt. 19:17; Mark 10:19; Luke 18:20), "God's word" (Matt. 15:6; Luke 11:28), as that which man has to "fulfill," to "do," to "keep," and which as such is known, or at least can be known. If, therefore, the question is asked by what Jesus' commandments are regulated, the ultimate answer is only this: *by God's will as it is revealed in his law*. . . . Jesus' ethical preaching does not have a deeper ground than the law as the revelation of God's will to Israel, the people of the covenant. Again and again it is the law, and only the law, the meaning and purpose of which is also the meaning and purpose of Jesus' commandments.[1]

The *whole* of Christ's life—His behavior, teaching, and saving work—was patterned after God's holy commandments. He willingly humbled Himself by becoming obedient even to the very point of suffering the *penalty* prescribed by the law for sin, indeed death as a criminal (Phil. 2:8). Christ obeyed the fullest *intention* of the law in the fullest *extension* of His life. "There was no other good enough to pay the price of sin."

---

[1] Herman Ridderbos, *The Coming of the Kingdom*, trans. H. de Jongste, ed. Raymond O. Zorn (Philadelphia: The Presbyterian and Reformed Publishing Co., 1962 reprinted 1969), p. 290 f.

Christ is our great High *Priest* who sacrifices Himself to discharge the curse of law (Gal. 3:13; Heb. 2:17-3:1; 4:14-5:10). He functions as a *prophet* of the law, properly interpreting it and freeing it from the overlaid traditions of men (e.g., Matt. 15:1-20). And because the Son of God has heeded the law and hated all *lawlessness*, God has exalted Him as the Anointed *King* (Heb. 1:8 f.). The three-fold office of Christ is unified around the permanent expression of God's will, His holy law.

The Scriptures regard *the work* of Christ as that of obedience. Christ defined the purpose of His coming in this way: "I have come down from heaven to do the will of Him who sent Me" (John 6:38). In the capacity of a suffering *servant* Christ accomplished the work of our atonement (Isa. 52:13-53:12). With reference to the pivotal event in the accomplishment of redemption, Christ spoke of obedience to His Father's *commandment* (John 10:17 f.). Christ was subjected to the law in order to redeem us who are under its curse (Gal. 4:5); learning obedience in the things which He suffered (Heb. 5:8 f.), Christ could justify us by His obedience (Rom. 5:19). God could only forgive sins in a manner which is consistent with His holiness; in salvation righteousness and peace must kiss each other (Ps. 85:9 f.). Consequently, salvation without justification is impossible, and justification without righteousness is inconceivable. There must be perfect righteousness in the reign of God's grace for our salvation. Therefore, Scripture centers on the *obedience* of Christ—both active and passive—because it is the necessary requirement for the full justification of sinners.

The extent of Christ's righteous obedience is seen in the fact that He both actively obeyed the prescriptive as well as passively obeying the penal requirements of the law, the former in order to qualify as a substitute, the latter in order to atone for sin. Having obeyed the law in its moral requirements in order that His perfect righteousness might be imputed to us, He came under the law's curse and condemnation so that our transgressions could be forgiven. Sin must, of necessity, meet divine judgment (cf. Nah. 1:2-3; Hab. 1:13); however, long ago God instituted a system of sacrifice whereby the sin and liability of the one offering the sacrifice was imputed to the animal victim, who then endured the penalty of sin in substitution for the actual offender. Christ was this substitutionary sacrifice in the accomplishment of our redemption (Isa. 53:6; John 1:29; Heb. 9:6-15; 10:3-18; 13:10-13; 1 Cor. 5:7; 2 Cor. 5:21; 1 Peter 1:18 f.). The new covenant, instituted by Christ's death and resurrection, is in accord with the law's stipulation that without shedding of blood there is no forgiveness for sin (Heb. 9:22). Hence the New Testament declares that it is Christ's shed blood which cleanses us from sin (Matt. 26:28; 1 John 1:7), thereby demonstrating the crucial *continuity* between Older and New Testaments. According to Colossians 2:14, Christ cancelled the handwriting against us (our certificate of indebtedness) which is a result of the commandments (that is, the law especially in its legal requirement of death for the sinner), which were opposed to us (because of our failure to comply with the law and its stipulated punishment); He has removed it by nailing it to the cross. Christ, by His perfect life, was the only One who did not deserve to die; by being our substitutionary sacrifice, Christ nailed our death certificate to His cross (see also 1 Peter 2:24, plus Rom. 6:23 with 1 John 3:4 for the same thought).

Therefore, although *our own* obedience to the law cannot be used as a way of justification, we are saved by the *imputed* obedience of the Messiah (1 Cor. 1:30; Phil. 3:9), an obedience to *both* the prescriptive and penal requirements of God's law. With its customary accuracy the Westminster Confession states: "The Lord Jesus, by His perfect obedience, and sacrifice of Himself, which He through the eternal Spirit, once offered up unto God, hath fully satisfied the justice of His Father; and purchased, not only reconciliation, but an everlasting inheritance in the kingdom of heaven, for all those whom the Father hath given unto Him" (chapter VIII, section V). Hence the nature of the atonement (with respect to sacrifice, propitiation, reconciliation and redemption) is integrated under the rubric of *obedience* [2] So important is the law in our salvation that our justification is grounded in Christ's obedience to it (Rom. 5:17-19); we are saved by grace no doubt, but by

[2] John Murray, *Redemption Accomplished and Applied* (Grand Rapids: Eerdmans Publishing Co., 1955), pp. 19-24.

a grace made possible through the lawful obedience of God's Son. Our *faith in Christ* is counted for righteousness, thereby justifying us freely by God's grace *through Christ's righteousness,* which is declared for the remission of our sins (Rom. 4:5-8; 3:22-25; 5:17-19). "He made the one who did not know sin to be sin on our behalf in order that we might become the righteousness of God in Him" (2 Cor. 5:21). Christ's atoning work, then, does not entail the relaxation of the law's demand for righteousness, but rather accentuates it. Christ, who suffered as the righteous for the unrighteous (1 Peter 3:18), *is* the believer's righteousness (1 Cor. 1:30).

Consequently, *far from revoking* the law, grace *confirms* the law and points one to the law: saving faith in Christ establishes the law (Rom. 3:31), and the gracious *promises* of God were realized and confirmed by Christ becoming the minister of the circumcision-covenant (Rom. 15:7-9). There is no antagonism between law and grace fostered by either our Lord or the atonement. By His substitutionary atonement Christ did *not* cancel the holy law of God; instead, He cancelled only the curse which the law attaches to us because of our disobedience: "Christ redeemed us from the *curse of the law*" (Gal. 3:13). By nailing our indictment to His cross He blotted out our trespasses (Col. 2:14). Therefore, "there is now no condemnation to those who are in Christ Jesus" (Rom. 8:1). It is the *condemning* aspect of the law which is nullified by Christ's perfect obedience to that law; the law itself with all its integrity, remains in force while our *guilt* is removed. Our atonement by means of the Messiah's obedience *presupposes* the law's permanent validity; the law could not be put aside, and hence it was *necessary* for atonement to be accomplished in accord with the law's demands (Heb. 9:22-26).

Furthermore, the Holy Spirit causes the believer in his sanctification to grow in *likeness* and obedience to Christ, "to the measure of the stature which belongs to the fullness of Christ" (Eph. 4:13; cf. v. 15; Gal. 4:19). Consequently, the life of a Christian is not characterized by flight from the law of God or renunciation of its obligation, but rather by progressive conformity to the character of his Savior, who necessarily complied with the law's every demand. *Union* with Christ, which underlies our salvation, entails the requirement of sharing His righteous character—of *identifying* with His lawful obedience. "Have this attitude in yourselves which was also in Christ Jesus, who . . . humbled Himself by becoming *obedient* . . ." (Phil. 2:5, 8, NASV). Christ, who did no sin, has left us an *example* that we should *follow His steps* (1 Peter 2:21). *Those who have been saved by Christ's obedience must strive to imitate the same obedient spirit.* "Hereby we know that we are in him: he that saith he abideth in him ought himself also to walk even as he walked" (1 Jn. 2:5 f., ASV). Therefore, not only does gracious atonement presuppose the law's permanent validity (seeing that it behooved Christ to obey its every demand), but because the salvation procured by Christ assumes our union with Him in order for its effective application, the atonement must of necessity be followed by our adherence to God's law (1 Cor. 6:15-20). Our character must come to be like His in moral uprightness.

In the last chapter we observed that the law is the transcript of God's holiness. In this chapter we have seen how God's law is crucial to Christ's atoning work. In the next chapter we shall note the centrality of the law in the sanctifying ministry of the Holy Spirit. In this way whether one considers the character of the Father, the ministry of the Son, or the work of the Spirit, he will be confronted with the abiding validity of God's law as integral to Trinitarian Christianity.

Chapter 7

SANCTIFICATION BY THE HOLY SPIRIT

JUST as the Son delights in the holy law of His Father, even so the Spirit of God promotes the law as the pattern of our sanctification. Neither the Son nor the Spirit can be placed in opposition to the Father's law; if this were not so the unity of the Trinity would be dissolved.

Salvation Necessitates Sanctification

In two previous chapters the gracious nature of justification has been emphasized. The removal of man's guilt and his securing of a right standing in the sight of God comes, not by his own personal works of the law, but only through the imputation of Christ's righteousness (His perfect obedience, both active and passive, to every demand of God's law). The sinner's legal condition is changed by God's judicial act, grounded in the "alien" righteousness of Christ, so that God's people are entitled to the eternal enjoyment of God's presence. Man does not *earn* his new standing in God's eyes; it is established solely by God's own gracious work. Thus *faith* is justification's proper instrument.

Not infrequently this cardinal doctrine of the Protestant Reformation has been accused of thwarting the exercise of holy living and impeding good works. However, such allegations are groundless. Man's need for salvation arises not simply from his *guilt*, but also from his *moral pollution*. B. B. Warfield observed,

> It is uniformly taught in Scripture that by his sin man has not merely incurred the divine condemnation but also corrupted

> his own heart; that sin, in other words, is not merely guilt but depravity: and that there is needed for man's recovery from sin, therefore, not merely atonement but renewal; that salvation, that is to say, consists not merely in pardon but in purification. Great as is the stress laid in the Scriptures on the forgiveness of sins as the root of salvation, no less stress is laid throughout the Scriptures on the cleansing of the heart as the fruit of salvation. Nowhere is the sinner permitted to rest satisfied with pardon as the end of salvation; everywhere he is made poignantly to feel that salvation is realized only in a clean heart and a right spirit.[1]

Recognizing this fact, the Protestant Reformers did not, by their preaching of the doctrines of grace, promote loose living. Salvation required for them the deliverance from sin's bondage as well as sin's curse. Hence justification, though distinct from sanctification, could not be separated from sanctification.

> In clear accord with the teaching of Scripture, Protestant theology insists that justification underlies sanctification, and not *vice versa.* But it has never imagined that the sinner could get along with justification alone. It has rather ever insisted that sanctification is so involved in justification that the justification cannot be real unless it be followed by sanctification.[2]

A definite understanding of the coordination (and in *some* respects, identification—1 Cor. 15:45; 2 Cor. 3:17) of the saving activities of the Son and the Spirit prevents Reformed theology from compromising either the foundational requirement that guilty man become just be-

---

[1] "On the Biblical Notion of 'Renewal,' " reprinted in *Biblical and Theological Studies,* ed. S. G. Craig (Philadelphia: The Presbyterian and Reformed Publishing Co., 1952), p. 352.

[2] Ibid., p. 374.

fore God or the subsequent demand that man's indwelling sin be eliminated as he lives unto righteousness. Berkhof correctly notes,

> The Reformers in speaking of sanctification emphasized the antithesis of sin and redemption. . . . They made a clear distinction between justification and sanctification, regarding the former as a legal act of divine grace, affecting the judicial status of man, and the latter, as a moral or re-creative work, changing the inner nature of man. But while they made a careful distinction between the two, they also stressed their inseparable connection. . . . Justification is at once followed by sanctification, since God sends out the Spirit of His Son into the hearts of His own as soon as they are justified, and that Spirit is the Spirit of sanctification.[3]

In a fine article, "The Moral Effects of a Free Justification," Robert Dabney maintained that the Reformed doctrine of justification brought with it the greatest *guarantee* of holiness in the lives of those who are justified:

> United to Christ by faith, believers share his spiritual life as surely as they share the merit of his justifying righteousness. Just as surely as the body of the Redeemer was emancipated from the grave, so surely are their souls, by that death of the Lord, emancipated from the corruption and bondage of sin, if they cleave to him by faith. It is as impossible that the glorified Saviour can suffer and die again, after he proclaimed "It is finished," as that the believer, who is in Christ by faith, can still live in Satan's bondage. . . . This plan of gratuitous justification is the most efficient ministry of holiness, because it sets in the strongest possible light the demands of the di-

[3] L. Berkhof, *Systematic Theology,* 4th ed., (Grand Rapids: Wm. B. Eerdmans Publishing Co., 1939), p. 530.

> vine holiness, the inflexibility of the law, the absolute necessity of conformity thereto, and the evil of sin; and because it supplies the generous incentive of devotion as our motive to duty.[4]

Central to the Reformed doctrines of atonement and justification is an insistence on the abiding validity of God's holy law. Therefore, it would be highly incongruous that the demands of the law should be relaxed upon the occasion of either the atonement or personal justification; it is rather the case that atonement and justification must issue in a sanctified life according to God's law. Sanctification follows *from the very nature* of the atonement and justification as law-oriented. Charles Hodge had a clear insight into this fact:

> It is not the system which regards sin as so great an evil that it requires the blood of the Son of God for its expiation, and the law as so immutable that it requires the perfect righteousness of Christ for the sinner's justification, which leads to loose views of moral obligation; these are reached by the system which teaches that the demands of the law have been lowered, that they can be more than met by the imperfect obedience of fallen men, and that sin can be pardoned by priestly intervention. This is what logic and history alike teach.[5]

The continuing *demand* of the law, which is attested by the doctrines of atonement and justification, entails the believer's obligation to be *sanctified.* Conversely, the believer's obligation to be sanctified entails the continuing demand of God's law, as Dabney correctly commented:

---

[4] Reprinted in *Discussions: Evangelical and Theological* (London: The Banner of Truth Trust, 1967), Vol. I, pp. 95, 99.

[5] Charles Hodge, *Systematic Theology* (Grand Rapids: Wm. B. Eerdmans Publishing Co., 1871-73), Vol. III, p. 241.

> Redemption would be a mockery without sanctification; for sin itself, and not the external wrath of God, is the cause of misery here, and eternal death hereafter. Hence, to deliver the fallen son of Adam from his guilt, and leave him under the power of corruption, would be no salvation. . . . The chief ultimate end of redemption, which is God's glory (Rom. xi:36; Is. lxi:3; Eph. i:6), would be utterly disappointed, were believers not required to depart from all sin. For God's holiness, His consummate attribute, would be tarnished by taking to His favour polluted creatures. This point suggests, also, the second, where God points to His own perfect holiness as the reason for the purification of His people. No argument could be plainer. An unholy creature has no place in the favour and bosom of a holy God. . . . God's law is as immutable as His nature; and no change of relation whatever, can abrogate it as a rule of right action.[6]

To be sanctified is to be "set apart" *by* and *unto* God, so that the Christian is recreated after the image of God in righteousness and true holiness and empowered by the Holy Spirit to die progressively unto sin and live more and more in conformity with God's will. It is easy to see that sanctification, then, requires the law of God as the *standard* for God's holiness and will; it *defines* that sinfulness unto which we are to die. Therefore, the necessity of sanctification and the validity of the law mutually imply each other.

To summarize what has been said to this point, we can say that salvation is not exhaustively circumscribed by God's pardon of, and the imputation of Christ's righteousness to, the sinner; salvation continues beyond the *point* of justification into the *process* of sanctification, a process which begins with a *definitive break* with the bondage of sinful depravity and matures by *progressively preparing* the Christian to enjoy

---

[6] Robert L. Dabney, *Lectures in Systematic Theology* (Grand Rapids: Zondervan Publishing House, [1878] reprinted 1972), p. 664.

eternal life with God by the internal purifying of his moral condition.[7] Because salvation involves accepting Christ as *both* one's Savior and Lord (Acts 16:31), and because the reception of God's Son entails the reception of the Spirit of His Son as well (Rom. 8:9-10), justification cannot be divorced from sanctification. It is precisely the scriptural teaching with respect to the atonement and justification that both *require* and *guarantee* sanctification, which in turn implies (just as it is implied by) the abiding validity of God's law.

Before going on to the next point in our discussion we should pause to rehearse the scriptural backing for the necessity of sanctification. It is the perfect obedience of God's Son that is imputed to the Christian in justification, and sanctification can be understood as a progressive growth toward the *personal realization* of that level of righteousness which has been imputed to the believer. As Scripture puts it, God has predestined His people to be conformed to the image of His Son (Rom. 8:29), to be built up into the stature of Christ (Eph. 4:13). Christians are called into *union* with Christ (1 Cor. 1:9); however, evil cannot dwell with God (Ps. 5:4). Therefore, union with Christ requires that the believer be dead to sin, that his old man be crucified, and that sin no longer have dominion over him (Rom. 6:2-6, 14).

Those who love the Lord must hate evil (Ps. 97:10) and separate themselves from ungodliness (Deut. 7:2-4; 2 Cor. 6:17; Eph. 5:11). Only then can they be set apart unto God or "sanctified." "Pursue after sanctification *without which no one will see God*" (Heb. 12:14). One of the clearest explanations and exhortations to sanctification is found in 2 Corinthians 7:1, "Therefore, having these promises, beloved, let us cleanse ourselves from all defilement of flesh and spirit, perfecting holiness in the fear of God" (NASV). Elsewhere we are commanded to evidence public righteousness (Eph. 6:14), to be without offense and filled with the fruit of righteousness (Phil. 1:9-11), to supply to

---

[7] A clear, brief explanation of the distinction between definitive and progressive sanctification can be found in John Murray's article, "Sanctification," in *Basic Christian Doctrines,* ed. Carl F. H. Henry (Grand Rapids: Baker Book House, 1962), pp. 227-233.

ourselves virtue and godliness (2 Peter 1:5-8), to present our bodies as holy sacrifices, to abhor evil and cling to good (Rom. 12:1-3, 9-21), to think on the pure, right, honorable and true (Phil. 4:4-9), and to be diligent to be found spotless and blameless (2 Peter 3:14). That is, those who have been saved by the work of Christ are called to put on a new self created after the *image* of their Creator (Col. 3:1-10) in righteousness and holiness (Eph. 4:17-32). In short, the Christian is to be an *imitator* of God (Eph. 5:1), *to be holy* in all manner of living *even as He is holy* (1 Peter 1:14-15).

This inescapable requirement of holiness or sanctification is *not* contradictory to salvation by grace through faith (Eph. 2:8-9); we are not saved *by* obedience, but *unto* obedience. "We are His workmanship created in Christ Jesus unto good works" (v. 10). God's gracious salvation delivers one from the bondage of sin and enables him to walk in the liberty of God's holy law (Gal. 5:13-14). Immediately after his strong affirmation to Titus that we are saved by God's mercy, not by works done in righteousness which we did ourselves, Paul went on to assert with confidence and emphasis that those who trust God must be careful to maintain good works (Titus 3:5-8). Quite clearly we are justified by faith—that is, by *living* faith, and "faith without works is dead" (James 2:26). Living, saving faith is working faith (cf. Gal. 5:6). Such faith is a gracious gift from God, who also *works in* His people to make them perfect in every good work to do His will (Heb. 13:20 f.). These passages plainly testify that salvation is invariably accompanied by good works, deeds performed in obedience to God's law. Just as the eternal salvation which was promised under the Older Testament (Isa. 45:17) carried with it an obligation to obey God's commandments (Isa. 48:18; cf. Deut. 5:29), so also under the New Covenant Christ "became the author of eternal salvation unto *all those who obey Him*" (Heb. 5:9). Christ cannot be Savior if He is not also Lord, and thus obedience is characteristic of those who benefit from the Lord's salvation. Justification must be followed by sanctified growth in holiness (conformity to God's image), and sanctification is *manifest* in obedience to God's word: "Therefore, putting aside all filthiness and all that remains of wickedness, humbly receive the implanted word which is able to save your souls. And prove yourselves *doers of the word*" (James 1:21 f.).

So then, there are many angles from which the Christian can approach the subject. Whether he considers his union with Christ, his recreation according to the image of his holy Creator, the goal of God's merciful salvation, the nature of justifying faith, or the obligation of those who are saved to obey God's word, the Christian cannot overlook the clear teaching of Scripture that salvation necessitates sanctification. One has to be *deceived* to think that the unrighteous could possibly inherit the kingdom of God (1 Cor. 6:9 f.). The sad fact is that, along with the toning down or virtual elimination of the need for repentance in the proclamation of the gospel which characterizes so much of modern day evangelism, a neglect of the Christian's duty to pursue sanctification and a failure to discern the Lordship of the Savior is symptomatic of the theological deception currently at large in Christendom. Here we have the heresy of "easy believism," with its corollary motto "we are under grace, not law." The erroneous presupposition of this outlook and message is that grace and law, promise and demand, trust and obedience are mutually exclusive categories. The review of biblical teaching provided above demonstrates the contrary: namely, that these categories are *mutually inclusive* of each other. There is an inseparable connection between justification and sanctification, such that our salvation secures release not only from the guilt of sin, but also from its power and effects. Therefore, as Dabney put it, redemption would be a mockery without sanctification. *Without it no man can see the Lord* (Heb. 12:14)—not even those who (merely) *profess* to have saving faith. There can be no substitute for diligent striving after growth in holiness as the work of God's Spirit in the believer (rather than the spurious notion of the experience of a "second blessing" which is charismatic in nature). The Savior's word stands written, "Blessed are the *pure in heart:* for *they shall see God*" (Matt. 5:8; cf. Ps. 24:3 f; 51:10 f.).

God's Spirit as the Dynamic of Sanctification

A discerning reader will realize that a grave problem arises from the absolute demand for sanctification in those who are to be saved. We have observed in a previous chapter that the law of God expresses His unchanging holiness and thus stands as a permanent obligation upon His people, who are called to be like Him. Notice has also been taken of the fact that the nature of Christ's atonement presupposes the abiding validity of the law's demand, just as the biblical doctrine of justification also reveals the law's immutability. Finally, in the section above, it was demonstrated that man's moral pollution must be transformed into personal holiness if he is to see God; justification and sanctification require each other. These considerations place the inflexible obligation of moral uprightness in the strongest possible light; there is no way around the exacting requirement of lawful obedience and the unmitigated demand for righteousness of character. However, given certain anthropological facts revealed in Scripture, God's absolute demand for holiness can be for man nothing but a Sisyphian task. The reflective person will admit in all honesty that, for him moral perfection is impossible to achieve; the frustrating fact is that we cannot even begin to approach that high level or morality dictated in God's law. None of us are sufficient to the task of imitating the obedience of Christ. Our grandest efforts are still woefully inadequate, and the more determined we are to meet God's demand in ourselves the greater the inner tension and despair becomes. God has required sanctification, but we are unable to comply. With man the stipulation is an impossible one.

The level of perfection required by God is that of His own holiness (Lev. 19:2; Matt. 5:48; 1 Peter 1:15-16); that holiness is revealed in His law, and thus we are obligated to observe every stipulation of the law. However, we all have a different law (principle) in ourselves, one which wars against holiness and brings us captive under the law of sin (Rom. 7:23). We have been *slaves* of sin (Rom. 6:16-20), the fruit of which is death. As Paul puts it in Ephesians 2:1, we are "dead in trespasses and sin." How then can we find a resolution to the tension?

How can those who are utterly unable to correct their depraved and disobedient hearts meet God's unmitigated demand for complete holiness like unto His own? How can those who are dead *in* sin come to be dead *to* sin?

When one dies to sin he no longer lives in it (Rom. 6:2). The only way that this can be accomplished, this task which is impossible for man, is by the God through whom all things are possible—even giving life to the dead (Rom. 4:17). Paul explains that those who have died to sin are those who are in union with Jesus Christ in virtue of His death and resurrection (Rom. 6:3-4); just as Christ was raised from the dead, so also believers in Him can walk in *newness of life*. Christians have been made *dead to the law's curse* in that they have been united to Christ, who was raised from the dead; no longer do they bring forth the deadly fruit of sin, then, but instead they bring forth fruit unto God (Rom. 7:4). Because of Christ's powerful resurrection, those in union with Him have passed from death unto life, from bondage unto freedom, from depravity to renewal. Christ's resurrection guarantees that death and sin shall no more have dominion over us (Rom. 6:8-9, 13-14). We have been created *in* Christ Jesus *unto* good works (Eph. 2:10); the end achieved by union with the Savior is an obedient life of righteous deeds which are now pleasing to God. Our new lives are made possible by the *resurrection power* of Jesus Christ, a mighty strength which works in those united to Him (Eph. 1:19-20; Phil. 3:10). Christ indwells the believer through faith (Gal. 2:20; Eph. 3:17; Col. 1:27), and thereby the Christian dies to the law in order that the Holy Spirit might live within him effecting righteous living unto God (Rom. 8:10; Gal. 2:19). Christ's victory over sin and death means the victory of the believer over the same, for when the resurrected Lord dwells in His people, He does so with mighty *power* (Eph. 3:20; cf. 2 Cor. 13:3-4), a power which frees them from sin, makes them servants of God, and brings forth the fruit of *sanctification* and eternal life (Rom. 6:22).

The way in which this union with the resurrected Lord is effected, and the bond of that union, is found in the Holy Spirit. Those who are no longer in the deathly bondage of an unrighteous nature have the

Spirit of Christ dwelling in them (Rom. 8:9). Indeed, so intimate is the cooperation between the Son and the Spirit in our regeneration and sanctification that Paul can actually say that Christ is "life-giving Spirit" (1 Cor. 15:45). The Holy Spirit who raised Jesus from the dead (Rom. 1:4; 1 Tim. 3:16; 1 Peter 3:18) dwells in us with that same resurrection power (Rom. 8:11). Therefore, the law of the Spirit of life in Christ Jesus has made us free from the law of sin and death (Rom. 8:2). And thus the Holy Spirit who brings us into union with Christ, the resurrected Savior, is then mighty power at work in our sanctification—our death to sin and our life of righteousness. How well the Westminster Confession of Faith puts it, saying:

> They, who are once effectually called, and regenerated, having a new heart, and a new spirit created in them, are further sanctified, really and personally, through the virtue of Christ's death and resurrection, by His Word and Spirit dwelling in them: the dominion of the whole body of sin is destroyed, and the several lusts thereof are more and more weakened and mortified; and they more and more quickened and strengthened in all saving graces, to the practice of true holiness, without which no man shall see the Lord (13.1).

Christ sends the Spirit into our hearts working resurrection power in us, uniting us to Himself, and raising us to a new life of holiness. That is why the primal emphasis in sanctification belongs to the saving work of the Savior; sanctification is the extension of His gracious economy so that, not only are we released from the guilt of sin but also its power.

> This is why the resurrection of Christ is the dynamic of the biblical ethic; the resurrected Lord is *life-giving* Spirit and therefore communicates life to those who are in him. . . . This is but another way of saying that the dynamic of the biblical

> ethic is the Holy Spirit as the Spirit of Christ, sent forth in accordance with the promise of the Father. . . . It is scarcely necessary to draw attention to the relation which the Holy Spirit sustains to ethical life—it is only they who are after the Spirit, who have the mind of the Spirit, who are in the Spirit, who are indwelt by the Spirit of God and have the Spirit of Christ, who are able to do that which is well-pleasing to God.[8]

The uniform scriptural perspective is that God's Spirit is necessary for the process of sanctification (1 Peter 1:2) and bringing about the conditions of holiness (cf. Rom. 15:16). It must be the *Lord* who sanctifies, both in the Older Testament (Ex. 31:13) and in the New (1 Thess. 5:23).

Having exhorted us to apply our energies to sanctification, the Scripture still makes it clear that we cannot accomplish this task on our own. Self-sanctification in an unqualified sense is ruled out. "Are you so foolish? Having begun by the Spirit, are you now being perfected by the flesh?" (Gal. 3:3). Of course we are not. The Spirit of the Lord is the source of believing obedience to God's law: "But we all, with unveiled face beholding as in a mirror the glory of the Lord are being transformed into the same image from glory to glory, just as from the Lord the Spirit" (2 Cor. 3:18, NASV). God had promised His Spirit for this very purpose (Ezek. 36:27). Christians who are saved by God's sovereign grace will recognize that "it is God who is at work within you, both to will and to work His good pleasure" (Phil. 2:13). We cannot possibly obey God's law unless we abide in our Saviour and Lord, Jesus Christ: "Abide in Me, and I in you. As the branch cannot bear fruit of itself, unless it abides in the vine, so neither can you unless you abide in Me. I am the vine, you are the branches; he who abides in Me and I in him bears much fruit; for apart from Me you can do nothing" (John 15:4 f., NASV). Consequently we recognize that our adequacy is

---

[8] John Murray, *Principles of Conduct* (Grand Rapids: Wm. B. Eerdmans, 1957), pp. 223-224.

from God (2 Cor. 3:5), that it is the Lord who strengthens us (Phil. 4:13). God is the One who equips us in every good thing to do His will and works in us that which is pleasing in His sight through Jesus Christ; hence, to *Him* belongs all glory forever and ever (Heb. 13:21). *Both* our justification by Christ and our sanctification through the Spirit are *by grace and in conformity to the law.* Since it is the God of peace who sanctifies us entirely (1 Thess. 5:23), self-confident moralism which leads to spiritual pride is ruled out; the law can never be abused to that end, either in justification or sanctification. Our sanctification in obedience to the law which is produced by God's grace must have the same effect as does our justification by that grace: both prompt humility, gratefulness, and love. Just as the righteousness which justifies us comes from God, so does the strength to keep the law which sanctifies us.

The Spirit Does Not Replace the Law

In living the Christian life before God, then, it is essential that we be people of the Word of God written. We cannot take it into our own hands to draw the blueprints for Christian ethics; instead of seeking to establish our own righteous pattern of life we must submit to God's (cf. Rom. 10:3). In this present day there is a grave heresy which has permeated large areas of the Christian Church; it claims that the Christian life of victory is produced solely by an inward guidance of the Holy Spirit. In matters of Christian ethics, whether it be in reference to how to love one's neighbor or to deciding if any particular activity is wrong, many Christians claim that for moral authority they depend only upon the guidance of the Spirit. Whichever way the Spirit "moves" them is the way which they trust to be right. Now even the most elementary biblical doctrine should dissuade these subjective moralists, for who among sinfully depraved men can trust his inner inclinations? On such a basis as has been described how could one possibly test the spirits to see if they be from God or Beelzebub? Does such a way of life affirm the sufficiency of God's *canonical* word? Does Scripture describe the work of the Spirit as that of mystical guidance? All these questions are fundamental and to be answered negatively. An amazing irony is to be found in the fact that many such "Spiritualistic" groups boast in being preachers of God's Word and adamant opposers of modernism while, in point of fact, they have a *great deal* in common with liberal theology as regards ethics; the post-Kantian theologian is ear-marked by his making *religious experience,* not the revealed word, his authority (this is variously labeled as insight, piety, intuition, practical reason, mystical rapport, valuation, spiritual vitality, guiding light, etc.).

The same general defects afflict both "Spiritualistic Fundamentalism" and all varieties of modern unorthodoxy in theology. For claiming to receive guidance from an inner revelation of God's Spirit, all these people are amazingly reluctant to specify what God said. One must wonder, when a person cannot clearly relate what the content of God's message was, whether the inner revelation was clear even to the person who supposedly received it. Besides, what shall we do when two different people falteringly express what the Spirit's direction was and their accounts radically differ? Does God contradict Himself, or is Christianity the original source of situational ethics? Furthermore, the test for whether the Spirit had genuinely given the direction followed by a person would have to be another subjective evaluation; such an inner regress easily facilitates self-justification or rationalization. Also, if the direction needed in making ethical decisions is found in a mere "feeling," what assurance has the person that this "feeling" is due to God's influence and not *simply* to his disagreeable breakfast? It is further disquieting when one finds a person led by the "Spirit" to do what the written word of God, inspired by the Holy Spirit, prohibits—which is too often the case. One would think that, since Christ, the Spirit, and the Scriptures form an inseparable unity (as Calvin ably defended), it would be impossible to isolate one from the others and make it disagree with them. But if these immense practical problems are not enough to stop one from "lording the Spirit over the Word," the biblical problems are overwhelmingly stronger. According to Scripture *the written word* contains the message from God; the function of the Spirit is to illumine the mind of the reader. The Scripture does not regenerate and enlighten the blinded eyes, nor does the Spirit do the work of the written word. *The Spirit always witnesses to the word.* The Spirit does not speak from Himself, but speaks what He hears (John 16:13); the Spirit of truth will glorify and disclose the Son and the Son's words (John 16:14). "When the Helper comes, whom I will send to you from the Father, that is the Spirit of truth, who proceeds from the Father, *He will bear witness of Me*" (John 15:26, NASV). Having stated that if anyone loves Him he will keep His word (which is really the Father's word), Christ tells His disciples that the Holy Spirit will teach them all things and bring to their remembrance all that Christ said (John 14:23-26). The Spirit of truth bears witness concerning the Son; it is the written word that supplies the content of what Christians know (1 John 5:7-13). The Westminster Confession and its scriptural support should be heeded when it says, "The whole counsel of God concerning *all things necessary* for His own glory, man's salvation, faith and life is either expressly set down in *Scripture,* or by good and necessary consequence may be deduced from *Scripture* . . . . The supreme Judge by which all controversies of religion are to be determined . . . doctrines of men and private spirits are to be examined, and in whose sentence we are to rest, can be no other but *the Holy Spirit speaking in the Scripture*" (Chapter I, sections VI and X). The Spirit cannot be divorced from the word.

The Spirit Not Opposed to thc Law

In Ezekiel 36:27 the Holy Spirit is promised in order that we might obey the law: "And I will put My Spirit within you and cause you to walk in My statutes, and you will be careful to observe My ordinances" (NASV). Galatians 5:18-23 explains that to be *led by the Spirit* is not to be under the curse, bondage, impotence, and death of the law (which had been described in the preceding sections of Galatians); the demand of the law remains, but now the *power* needed to obey is provided by the Spirit of God. The law could not be against those who walk by the Spirit, for they are fulfilling the law (see vv. 14, 23). Far from *distracting* from the law, then the Spirit enables us to *observe* the law as we should. Instead of being condemned and held in bondage by the old *letter* of the law, we now serve in the newness of the Holy *Spirit* (Rom. 7:6); we are released from guilt and set free to obedience. The letter of the law without the power of God's Holy Spirit is a word of condemnation and death to us, but the Spirit gives life and ethical ability. Here we find the proper contrast between the law and the Spirit: namely, the law is not a *quickening* Spirit.

However, the fact that the letter *kills* but the Spirit *enlivens* (2 Cor. 3:6) in no way discredits or stigmatizes the law. Philip E. Hughes rightly observes:

> The Apostle does not mean that the law is in and of itself something evil and death-dealing. On the contrary, he taught that it was holy and good, and indeed "unto life" (Rom. 7:10 ff.), and he approved the doctrine of the Old Testament Scriptures that "the man that doeth the righteousness which is of the law shall live thereby" (Romans 10:5; Galatians 3:12; cf. Leviticus 18:5; Nehemiah 9:29; Ezekiel 20:11, 13, 21; Proverbs 4:4; 7:2; also Romans 2:13). It is, moreover, the plain teaching of our Lord (cf. Matthew 19:17; Luke 10:28). Paul is a faithful follower of his Master in that he nowhere speaks of the law in a derogatory manner. Christ, in fact, proclaimed that He had come to fulfil the law, not to destroy it (Matthew 5:17). So also the effect of Paul's doctrine was to establish the law (Romans 3:31). There is no question of an attack by him on the law here [i.e., 2 Corinthians 3:6], since, as we have previously seen, the law is an integral component of the new no less than it is of the old covenant.[9]

The law exposes sin and demands death, but it was not *designed* to kill. The law came in glory (2 Cor. 3:7); not it, but our *sin* falls short of God's glory (Rom. 3:23). The surpassing glory of the new covenant is that it brings with it the spiritual power to comply with the glorious law of God.

---

[9] P. E. Hughes, *Paul's Second Epistle to the Corinthians* (Grand Rapids: Eerdmans Publishing Co., 1962), pp. 96 f.

Therefore, we conclude that the Holy Spirit is *not* against the holy law of God—contrary to what so many are wont to suggest in this day. What the Father spoke and the Son lived is not downgraded by the Spirit who proceeds from both the Father and Son. Herman Ridderbos says:

> What is true of Paul's Christological utterances about the law is also true of his pneumatological utterances. Quite definitely the possibility of *doing* what the law requires lies in this that true believers are in the Spirit and live through the Spirit (Galatians 5:25). The fact remains, however, that the work of the Spirit consists in working out the law of God in the life of the believers (Romans 8:4). Therefore we do not find in Paul's epistles a spiritualistic way of thinking, which, in regard to the *contents* of the will of God, makes a contrast between "law" and "Spirit," "external ordinance" and "internal disposition." To Paul it is quite evident that the norm of the Christian life is in the law as an expression of the will of God. Only in this way is it possible to explain why Paul in his Epistle to the Galatians, for instance, in which he makes the sharpest pronouncements about the negative significance of the law, nevertheless, without further explanation declares that love is indispensable because it is the fulfillment of the law. Only the Spirit can arouse the love, and without the Spirit the law is powerless as a result of the flesh (Romans 7:13-25; 8:4). However, the law as good and holy commandment is not suspended by the Spirit. It is the Spirit who writes the law in the hearts (2 Corinthians 3), and the fruits of the Spirit are the good works which the law prescribes.[10]

The truly biblical Christian should not promote any Spirit/law dichotomy in his personal ethics; the Spirit, whose nature is holy,

[10] Herman Ridderbos, *When the Time Had Fully Come: Studies in New Testament Theology*, (Grand Rapids, Wm. B. Eerdmans, 1957), pp. 75-76.

sanctifies us according to the pattern of holiness to which the law of God gives expression.

Sanctification Necessitates the Law

God *exhorts* us to renewal (Rom. 12:2), as well as making provision that we *be renewed* (Eph. 4:24; Col. 3:10). We are exhorted not to let sin reign over us (Rom. 6:12), but then God goes on to assure us that according to His sovereign will it *shall not* have dominion over us (v. 14). Genuine ethical freedom can be attained in no other way but in allowing God to control you such that He Himself supplies what He demands. Sanctification requires exertion (e.g., 2 Peter 1:5-7), but it must be exertion *enabled* by the Holy Spirit. The Spirit must regenerate and renew us (Titus 3:5), overcome our sinful natures (Rom. 8:5-13), free us from the works of the flesh (Gal. 5:17), lead us and produce His fruits in us (Rom. 8:14; Gal. 5:16, 25).

The freedom which the Spirit brings us can never be operative, however, apart from the Word of God which reveals the law of righteousness to us. Genuine freedom is enslavement to God, being free to follow His direction and obey His will. The Holy Spirit brings liberty (2 Cor. 3:17) in order that we might keep the *law* of liberty (James 1:25; 2:8, 11-12). Ethical power and freedom are not an occasion for sin but rather for law-keeping (Gal. 5:13-14). Becoming free from sin is coincident with becoming the servant of God who serves His law (Rom. 6:22; 7:25). Hence Scripture teaches that the indwelling of the Holy Spirit has the effect of preventing us from sinning—which is to say, from violating God's law (1 John 3:4, 9; 5:18). Any view of sanctification, therefore, which aims to replace the law with the Spirit is at odds with God's clear word. God's Spirit who brings us liberty does so by transforming us into the image of Christ (2 Cor. 3:17-18). The freedom of the Christian man is bounded by the limits of Christ's stature and image; hence freedom does not burst the controls of God's holy law. Salvation is thus not for freedom from the law, but only from its curse. Christ came and condemned sin in the flesh precisely "*in order that the requirement of the law might be fulfilled in us who walk after the Spirit*"

(Rom. 8:4). The Law-word of God and the Spirit of God are mutually necessary for, and support each other in, the process of sanctification.

Therefore, recognizing that the Spirit bears witness to the word, we should not trust ourselves (or our "feelings" of spiritual guidance) to draw up the blueprint of Christian ethics. The pattern of our sanctification must be learned from the word of God written. Christian morality has an objective standard of righteousness on which it depends for guidance in ethical decisions. Early in the Bible it is revealed to us that sanctification must be *according to the law of God*: "And you shall keep My statutes and practice them; I am the Lord who sanctifies you" (Lev. 20:8, NASV). The law is the transcript of God's holiness and the pattern for human righteousness. Our example in sanctification is the obedient Son; we are to be conformed to His image, and thereby we shall be holy as our heavenly Father is holy. The Older Testament agrees perfectly with the New Testament that the Father is the pattern of our sanctification: "You shall be holy, for I the Lord your God am holy" (Lev. 19:2; 11:44, 45; Matt. 5:48; 1 Peter 1:15 f.). Christ, the highest revelation of what God is (Heb. 1:3), is an example to us of complete obedience to God's law. Consequently, the law as the self-revelation of God's holiness (see discussion of the law's integrity above) must be taken as the ethical roadmap of the Christian walk. If we are to be *like God* (in the way He requires), then our lives must conform to God's law. Theonomy is the manual of Christian living; autonomy is the way of spiritual death.

Scripture says that the Holy Spirit *regenerates* us in order that we who were once disobedient and spiritually dead might live in accord with God's law. "And I shall give them one heart, and shall put a new spirit within them. And I shall take the heart of stone out of their flesh and give them a heart of flesh, that they may walk in My statutes and keep My ordinances and do them. Then they will be My people and I shall be their God" (Ezek. 11:19 f., NASV). Romans 8:13 says that we shall *live* if we put to death those practices which are characteristic of the body of sin by means of the Holy Spirit (cf. Rom. 6:6; Col. 3:5). The whole process of our salvation from beginning to end, and the core of our spiritual life are *positively* related to the law. Grace and law are not enemies, but pursued in their respectively proper places are both vital elements in the Christian life and God's plan.

The Test of the Spirit's Work

Having made obedience to the law a test of Christian discipleship, John writes in 1 John 2:5 f., "Whoever keeps His word, in him the love of God has truly been perfected. By this we know that we are in Him: the one who says he abides in Him ought himself to walk in the same manner as He walked" (NASV). The fruit of the Spirit is love (Gal. 5:22), and John says that God's love is perfected in those who obey the word (i.e., commandments; see context). To love Christ is to emulate His life, and He says that those who love Him should keep His commandments (John 14:15), which are the jot and tittle of the Older Testamental law (Matt. 5:17 f.).

The mind that is set on the Spirit is life and peace (Rom. 8:6). Having set forth the law of God to the people, Moses says that he has set before them life and blessing (Deut. 30:15 f.). It comes as no surprise, therefore, that the law has the fullest normative relevance for those who are led by the Spirit; by the strength which God's Spirit brings we keep the law (Rom. 8:4). Just as the test of love and discipleship to the Son, the test of knowing God and revering Him, is obedience to the law, so also the *mark of the Spirit's indwelling* is observance of God's commandments. "And the one who keeps His commandments abides in Him, and He in him. And we know by this that He abides in us, by the Spirit which He has given us" (1 John 3:24, NASV). The Spirit, Christ, and the word cannot be separated in our Christian experience.

The fruit of the Holy Spirit's indwelling and power is love according to Galatians 5:22, and the love of God has been poured out within our hearts through the Holy Spirit given us, says Romans 5:5. Because God first loved us, we ought also to love (1 John 4:10 f.); Christ's redeeming love should constrain our obedience (2 Cor. 5:14 f.). Hence the *criterion of love,* both to God and to brother, just as the test of the Spirit's indwelling is obedience to the law (1 John 5:3; 2 John 5 f.). The law shows what love is, and the Spirit gives us the ability to love and obey.

The sanctification which is wrought by Christ and the Spirit of the Lord (cf. 2 Cor. 3:18) makes us the brethren of Christ in the household of God: "For both He who sanctifies and those who are sanctified are all from one Father, for which reason He is not ashamed to call them brethren" (Heb. 2:11, NASV). We are of the Father, just as Christ is of the Father, if we keep His commandments. Christ says we are His brethren if we do His Father's will (Matt. 12:50) as expressed in the written word (Luke 8:21). Sanctification in God's law makes us children of God and brethren of Christ, just as obedience to the law demonstrates that we love our other Christian brethren (1 John 5:2). Being led by the Spirit of God and being indwelt with His power makes the Christian a follower of God's holy law, thereby granting life, peace, and love to this brother of Christ in the household of God the Father.

The progressive sanctification of the Christian life then, is inseparably tied to the law of God, and has as its outcome righteousness characteristic of God and the joy of eternal salvation. John Calvin aptly summarizes:

> The whole life of Christians ought to be a sort of practice of godliness, for we have been called to sanctification (I Thess. 4:7; cf. Eph. 1:4; I Thess. 4:3). Here it is the function of the law, by warning men of their duty, to arouse them to a zeal for holiness and innocence.[11]

---

[11] Ford Lewis Battles (trans.), *Calvin: The Institutes of the Christian Religion,* ed. John T. McNeill, The Library of Christian Classics, Vol. XX, eds. John Baillie, John T. McNeill, and Henry P. Van Dusen (Philadelphia: The Westminster Press, 1967), Book III, chap. XIX, section 2, p. 835.

The Spirit, Law, and Means of Grace

Corroboration of the vital importance the law of God has for the Christian's sanctification is found in its significance for the means of grace. Growth in the Christian life is occasioned by prayer, the word, and the sacraments; however, these means of grace are effective only when there is obedience to the law of God. It is the prayer of a *righteous* man that can accomplish much according to James 5:16, and, since we have seen that the pattern of righteousness is the law, we would expect that effective prayer must be related to obedience. This is what John explicitly states: "And whatever we ask we receive from Him because we keep His commandments and do the things that are pleasing in His sight" (1 John 3:22). When Peter says that the Lord attends to the prayer of the righteous but His face is against evil-doers (1 Peter 3:12), or when John says that God does not hear sinners, but only those who are God-fearing and do His will (John 9:31), they are only applying the trenchant teaching of Proverbs 28:9 from the Older Testament: "He who turns away his ear from listening to the law, even his prayer is an abomination" (NASV). God's Wisdom says that God answers the prayer of the righteous while He is far from the wicked who spurn His law and direction; so the Lord laughs at their calamity (Prov. 15:29; 1:24 ff.). The testimony of God's Praisebook is that "if I regard wickedness in my heart, the Lord will not hear" (Ps. 66:18, NASV). The prophets concur that the Lord hides His face when those who practice evil deeds pray to God (Mic. 3:4; Isa. 59:2); "They made their hearts like flint so that they could not hear the law and the words which the Lord of hosts had sent by His Spirit through the former prophets . . . and it came to pass that just as He called and they would not listen, even so they called and I would not listen, says the Lord of hosts" (Zech. 7:12 f.). When God's people turn from their wicked ways and have God's word abiding in them, then God hears their prayers and grants their petitions (2 Chron. 7:14; John 15:7).

Obedience is also an indispensable ingredient in the acquiring of knowledge from reading God's word. A short survey of the Scriptures will show this to be the consistent teaching of God, in Older as well as

New Testaments. The *wisdom* literature of the Old Testament particularly stresses *practical morality*, in other words, the conduct which God desires. The wise man is righteous (Prov. 9:9; 10:31), for wisdom is the opposite of wickedness (Prov. 10:23)—in the logic of Scripture this does not constitute a confusion of the ethical with the epistemological, for they are inter-related. Discernment and understanding come from keeping the law (Prov. 28:5-7); obedience leads to good understanding and wisdom (Ps. 111:10). Understanding, insight and wisdom come from observing God's precepts (Ps. 119:98-100), hence observing the commandments can be placed in parallel to knowing God (cf. 1 Chron. 28:8 f.). A lack of knowledge comes from forgetting God's law and not keeping it (Hos. 4:1-2, 6; 6:6). Jeremiah emphasizes this theme: one cannot be wise and not be following God's ordinances (8:7-8), the wise man will boast in understanding the Lord who delights in righteousness (9:23 f.), to know the Lord is to live a godly life (22:16). Taking Christ's yoke upon oneself (i.e., being obedient to His will) makes it possible to learn from Him who alone knows and reveals the Father (Matt. 11:27-29). John goes to lengths to bring out the vital connection between obedience and understanding. Any man who is willing to do God's will shall know and understand Christ's teaching (John 7:17). *Abiding* in the word (not simply hearing it) leads to a knowledge of the truth (John 8:31 f.); doing evil deeds precludes knowledge of the Father, but keeping God's word produces knowledge (John 8:41, 55). Truth is inseparable from living in the way (John 14:6). Because the Spirit of truth *abides* in us we can receive His instruction (John 14:17), and having a disclosure of Jesus depends on keeping His commandments (John 14:21). One must be *ethically regenerate* if he is to have the Spirit of truth disclose knowledge or witness to him (John 15:26 with 16:8, 13). The indispensable requirement for knowing and understanding the word, then, is *keeping* the word (John 17:6-8); hence the *process* of *sanctification* is in the *word* which is truth (John 17:17; cf. Ps. 119:142, 160). The knowledge of God and salvation depend on keeping His commandments; hereby we do not need a teacher (1 John 2:3-5, 27-29). Paul's point would be the same; for him, the "truth" is to be "obeyed" (Rom. 2:8). Spiritual maturity, love to God, and an obedient attitude (cf. Phil. 2:5, 8) are requisite for a spiritual knowledge of God's revelation (1 Cor. 2:6-16). *Having righteousness* produces a knowledge of Jesus Christ (Phil. 3:8 f.), and increasing in knowledge and understanding of God is based on walking worthy and bearing fruit in good works (Col. 1:9-11). The word of Christ dwells richly with all wisdom in those who show good behavior (Col. 3:16 with James 3:13). Repentance and turning away from an evil will (i.e., satanically controlled) leads to a genuine knowledge of the truth (2 Tim. 2:25 f.). Peter underscores what these other authors have written; genuine knowledge is to be added to the foundation of moral excellence (2 Peter 1:3, 5, 8), but the sensuality, greed, corrupt desires and self-will of the unrighteous leads to a maligning of the truth, a speaking of vain and false words, an unreasonableness of thought, and an absence of knowledge (read 2 Peter 2).

A man cannot expect to have effective prayer or proper understanding of God's word if he departs from the law of God. The same is true of the sacraments; they are ineffective if used in disobedience. To partake of the Lord's Supper one must examine himself to make sure that he does not partake in an unworthy manner (1 Cor. 11:27-32); testing oneself to see if he be in the faith means seeing to it that one does no wrong but rather does what is right (2 Cor. 13:5-7). We cannot celebrate the Passover of the Son if we go on willfully sinning; we must be disciplined of the Lord out of His law in order that we can share His holiness (Heb. 10:26, 29; 12:10 with Ps. 94:12). Consequently the Lord's table is to be guarded by the minister of the supper with words such as:

> It is my solemn duty to warn the uninstructed, the profane, the scandalous, and those who secretly and impenitently live in any sin, not to approach the holy table lest they partake unworthily, not discerning the Lord's body, and so eat and drink condemnation to themselves. Nevertheless, this warning is not designed to keep the humble and contrite from the table of the Lord . . . we who are invited to the supper . . .

> humbly resolve to deny ourselves, crucify our sinful natures and follow Christ as becomes those who bear His name. . . .[12]

We come to the sacrament of the Lord's Supper as those who are justified freely by God's grace, but as those who strive to be holy before God in gratitude for our salvation. Similar words must be spoken with reference to Christian baptism. We who are buried with Christ in baptism are spiritually circumcised, signifying the cutting off of the sinful human nature (Col. 2:11-13); being raised with Christ we must seek those things which are above, in accord with godly holiness (Col. 3:1-17). The washing of baptism should have the effect of cleansing and sanctifying us (Eph. 5:25 f.) or else the baptism is meaningless for us. Our baptism must have the effect of causing us to walk in newness of life (Rom. 6:3 f.), which means that sin (the transgression of the law) should no longer reign in our lives (Rom. 6:5-13). Words which appropriately accompany the sacrament of baptism, then, would be:

> And since baptized persons are called upon to assume the obligations of the covenant, baptism summons us to renounce the devil, the world and the flesh and to walk humbly with our God in devotion to His commandments.[13]

None of the means of God's grace can have the result of building us up in the faith if we do not strive to be obedient to the commandments of God. Disobedience to the law makes our prayer abominable, prevents us from understanding the word, makes us unworthy partakers of the Lord's Supper, and is a forsaking of our covenant obligation in baptism. We who are saved by God's grace must be careful to live by that grace in conformity with God's holy standard of morality, the law.

---

[12] From the "Forms of Public Profession of Faith, Baptism, the Lord's Supper, and Services of Ordination and Installation of Church Officers" of the Orthodox Presbyterian Church.

[13] Ibid.

We have seen, then, that the Spirit is not antagonistic to the law of God, that we are to work toward realizing the level of righteousness imputed to us in our practical living by the Spirit's power, that we are to imitate Christ's obedience, that the indwelling of the Spirit is attested by obedience to God's law, that the pattern of our sanctification is the law of God (reflecting God's holiness), that sanctification by the Spirit produces life, peace, love, and a family relationship to Christ, and that the means of grace which are calculated to build us up in the faith are ineffective without obedience to the law. In short, the law is indispensable in sanctification.

Chapter 8

COVENANTAL UNITY

Proper Expectations

IN what has preceded, the law of God has been variously demonstrated as binding today. Since the law was introduced in Scripture as the stipulation of a gracious covenant, it should never have been expected that the inauguration of the New Covenant would abrogate the Older Testamental law. Those ethical stipulations which came with the Older Testament are the same moral standards which guide us under the New Covenant. As Christ said in Matthew 5:17 f., the epochal advent of the awaited Messiah did not have the effect of abrogating the law; rather the Mediator of the better covenant *confirmed* the Older Testamental *law*. Romans 15:8 tells us that Christ became the minister of the circumcision-covenant in order to *confirm* the *promises* given to the fathers. In biblical perspective, grace and promise are not antithetical to law and demand. The law and the gospel both aim at the same thing; what the law was unable to bestow upon us, the gospel has the power to grant. Hence Paul can say, "Is the law contrary to the promises of God? May it never be!" (Gal. 3:21).

In line with this fact we must be careful not to use the "newness" of the New Covenant to dismiss or repress the law's demands on our lives. It is imperative to see the novelty of the New Covenant as what the Scriptures express it to be, and not what our own imagination can excogitate according to some ungrounded "hermeneutical assumption." Orthodox theology, with its dogma of the immutability of God, should recognize as an interpretative principle the unity and continuity of all God's inscripturated revelation; only the Author of Scripture can discontinue what He has said previously. We must presuppose unity in the word of God, which stands to all generations, and not discontinuity, for who among men can presume to alter the word of the living God? Thus God alone can pronounce what is new about the New Covenant, and He has not revealed (in the pages of Scripture at any rate) that after Christ's advent there is a *new law.* To approach the New Testament with the premise that only that which is *repeated* from the Old Testament is still binding is faulty procedure; everything God has said should be that by which man lives (Matt. 4:4), not simply those things which God has spoken *twice* (and at the right places). We must live by *every* Scripture unless God explains otherwise, and with respect to the law of the Older Covenant Scriptures we have no annulment, but rather an emphatic confirmation.

One could anticipate that the law of the Mosaic covenant would have permanent validity from the fact (1) that the *other* Older Testamental covenants have continuing significance in the New Covenant (e.g., Adamic covenant—Rom. 16:20; Noahic covenant—2 Peter 3:5-9; Abrahamic covenant—Rom. 4:16 f.; Davidic covenant—Rom. 15:12) and (2) that God has such a character that He does not alter the covenant words which have gone forth from His lips (e.g., Ps. 89:34). The covenants preceding the Mosaic covenant all contained the element of law (Adam—Gen. 3:19; Noah—Gen. 9:6; Abraham—Gen. 17:14), and the succeeding Davidic covenant as well as the history, poetry, and prophets of the later Old Testament continue emphasis upon the law (e.g., 2 Sam. 7:14; Ps. 119:97; Hos. 8:12). Accordingly New Testament morality also stresses the law (e.g., Rom. 3:31; James 2:8-11; 2 Peter 2:21; 1 John 5:3) in a way which covenant consciousness would lead us to presume. The New Covenant presents no new covenental law or moral order, just as the Older Testament predisposes one to expect: "He is the Lord our God; His judgments are in all the earth. Remember *His covenant forever,* the word which He commanded to a thousand generations, the covenant which . . . He confirmed to Israel as an everlasting covenant" (1 Chron. 16:14-17, NASV). The perpetuity of God's commandments follows from the eternality of His covenant of which they comprise an inalienable part.

> Now we can clearly see from what has already been said that all men adopted by God into the company of his people since the beginning of the world were *covenanted to him by the same law* and by the bond of the same doctrine as obtains among us. [1]

Key Continuities

Both the Older and New Covenants have the *aim* of constituting a kingdom of priests and a holy nation (Ex. 19:5 f.; 1 Peter 2:9). Sin is defined in both covenants as a transgression of the *commandments* implicit in the covenant (Josh. 7:11; Isa. 24:5; Hos. 6:7; 1 John 3:4); to violate God's law is to break the covenant.

Both covenants were *monergistic* covenants of *grace*. This fact is openly admitted with respect to the New Testament, but many close their eyes to it in the Older Testament. God's dealings at Sinai were preceded by His grace at the Red Sea (Ex. 14:13; 15:2; cf. 19:4; 20:2), and the revelation from Sinai was by grace (Ex. 19:4; cf. Lev. 11:45). The testament was devised, declared, and commanded by *God* (Ex. 19:5-8; 20:1; 24:3-7; Deut. 4:13 f.). It was subsequently preserved by God's grace as often as Israel failed (Ex. 32:11 f.; 33:13 f.). When Israel would have perished in the wilderness they were graciously saved by looking in faith upon the brazen serpent (Num. 21:9; cf. John 3:14). Mercy was seen to be the unique prerogative of God (Ex. 33:19; cf. Joel 2:14; Jonah 3:9), and the fundamental recourse of men under the law was to God's undeserved mercy, especially as it was shown to the patriarchs (Ex. 32:13; 33:13 f.). Read the accounts of Joseph's brothers, of Simeon and Levi, of Reuben or Judah (Gen. 37, 34, 35, 38) and recall that God nevertheless raised these men up as the heads of Israel. What about David? He received pardon even for shedding innocent

---

[1] Ford Lewis Battles (trans.), *Calvin: The Institutes of the Christian Religion,* ed. John T. McNeill, The Library of Christian Classics, Vol. XX, eds. John Baillie, John T. McNeill, and Henry P. Van Dusen (Philadelphia: The Westminster Press, 1967), Book II, chap. 10, section 1, p. 428.

blood and adultery (2 Sam. 11-12). Moses even promises that God will graciously deliver an entire nation of apostates (Ex. 30). The promises of gracious forgiveness were numerous in the Older Testament (e.g., Jer. 3:1, 12; Ezek. 18:23, 32; 33:11; 1 Kings 8:46 ff.; even Num. 28:3 ff.). God's restoration of the patriarchs and of Israel was thus by His grace, and *not* according to merit. Although grace is more fully realized in the New Testament, it was certainly known in the Older Testamental period—just as was God's *truth* known in the Older Testament but more fully realized in the New (John 1:17). All success was seen by the Israelites as a direct work of the Lord (Deut. 20:3 f.). It was never the righteousness or greatness of Israel that made the Lord grant them blessing and favor (see Deut. 7:7; 8:17; 9:4).

The ministry of Moses was exercised by faith (Heb. 11:24-29), and Joshua and Caleb were heroes for their faith in God (Num. 32:12). In the Older Covenant, as in the New, faith and salvation (Ex. 19) precede moral works (Ex. 20). Consequently the gracious promise of God was never voided by the law of God (Gal. 3:17).[2] The primary requirement of the law was circumcision of the heart (Deut. 10:16) and seeking God with one's whole person (Deut. 4:29); fundamental to the keeping of the law was faith (Deut. 1:32; 9:23; 10:12; especially 6:2). Even the ceremonies of the Older Testament were effective only when they were a manifestation of faith. Confession of sin had to precede them (Lev. 5:5 f.), and when performed by the wicked they were viewed as an abomination (Prov. 15:8; 21:27).

Hence the Older Covenant had the same *goal, definitions, principles, operating power*, and *foundation* as the New Covenant. Consequently, even though the Jews were disobedient and unfaithful, in the Older Covenant and revelations *they had the gospel preached to them* (Heb. 4:2, 6), and some of them could be selected as prime examples of faith—for instance Abraham who is the *father* of the faithful (Heb. 11:8-19; Rom. 4:11; Gal. 3:6-9). Jesus Himself states that the *law* had as its *weightier* matters mercy and faith (Matt. 23:23)! Because dispensationalism fails

---

[2] See appendix 1 for a discussion of Galatians 3:17 in its scriptural context.

to see this it characterizes the Mosaic period as law in contrast to grace, and the gospel period as grace in contrast to law; the inevitable result of such a false antithesis is that dispensationalism is led into a false view of the law's place in the sphere of grace.

Although it is undeniable that God's deliverance of Israel was *gracious* and that the Sinaitic covenant was one characterized by *grace,* nevertheless *obedience* to God's *law* was appropriately demanded: "Cursed is the man who does not heed the words of this covenant which I commanded your forefathers in the day I brought them out of the land of Egypt, from the iron furnace, saying Listen to My voice, and do according to all which I command you; so you shall be My people and I will be your God" (Jer. 11:3 f., NASV). Yet because the Sinaitic covenant presupposed redemption, we conclude that law observance does *not* imply a covenant of works. Grace is the foundation, and holiness the character, of all covenant relationships with God. Abraham was to "keep the covenant" by obeying God's voice (Gen. 17:9; 18:19), and the Mosaic covenant in which God's holiness is the governing principle and demand (cf. Lev. 19:2; etc.) promises the same intimate fellowship which was offered to Abraham: "I will be your God and you will be My people" (Gen. 17:7; Ex. 6:7; Deut. 29:13). Without holiness no man can see God (cf. Heb. 12:14). Hence any *covenant* relationship demands *obedience* to God's statutes. No man can disobey God and expect to commune with Him. Our first father Adam experientially learned this truth; to our benefit, our second federal head, Christ, understood the conditions of covenant fellowship well. The fellowship of God's covenant is consummated in holy obedience to His laws (Lev. 26:3, 11 f.); He tabernacles among an obedient and blessed people. The New Covenant also centers on the promise that God's tabernacle is with men, that He will be their God (Rev. 21:3). Under the New Covenant, no less than the Older, continued blessing rests upon perseverance of the saints (Col. 1:22 f.; Heb. 3:14; 6:11 f.; Phil. 3:13 f.; etc.). Obedience is the necessary and proper expression of gratitude and love to God in a covenant which was conceived in pure grace. The New Testament saint, no less than the Older Testamental saints or Adam in paradise, is committed to obey the law of His gracious God.

If a man disobeys God's law, he has *broken* covenant with God, and his covenant sign loses its value; this is just as true under the New Covenant as under the Older. If the Gentile now gratefully keeps the law he is regarded as a part of God's one covenant people (e.g., Gal. 6:16). Obedience demarcates between those who do and do not partake of God's covenant privileges (Rom. 2:25-29). So with respect to the law, when we exalt Christ as the mediator of the New Covenant, it is not necessary to defame Moses; in the New Covenant the law is not dismissed, but substantiated (Heb. 10:1). The old foreshadowed the new (cf. Heb. 8:5; Col. 2:17). Just as the reality is more permanent than the shadow, the New Covenant presses home the demands of the law more severely than does the Older. The economy which Jesus inaugurated cannot then be characterized by ethical or penal laxity!

Covenant Renewals

Matthew 5:17 f. fits readily into the pattern of *covenant renewals* throughout the Scriptures. In the covenant form of Deuteronomy (or Exodus 20 ff.), after the self-identification of the Lord of the covenant and a review of His gracious dealing with His vassal people, stipulations are laid down for the people to observe. These laws fundamentally demanded loyalty and love and then went on to detail specific commands which showed to the vassal people the pattern of grateful response for the Lord's grace. Throughout the later history of the covenant people this covenant was repeatedly held forward as binding on the Lord's vassals, the primary mark of the covenant being its laws. At the time of entering the promised land it was said, "Only be thou strong and very courageous, that thou mayest observe to do according to all the law which Moses My servant commanded thee; turn not from it to the right hand or to the left . . . for then thou shalt make thy way prosperous, and then thou shalt have good success" (Josh. 1:7 f., AV). See also Joshua 8:30-35. At the dedication of the temple the covenant received much attention (1 Kings 8:21; 2 Chron. 5:10; 6:11). The covenant was renewed in 2 Kings 17, and it brought revival in later years (2 Kings 14:6; 18:6; 22-23). It is the covenant and its law which again receive attention and renewal at the rededication of the temple (Neh. 8). Throughout the entire Older Testament the covenant and its lawful precepts was continually held to have abiding validity for God's people (see Isa. 8:16-20; Dan. 9:3 f.); in fact, the law was to be confirmed by public reading every seven years (Deut. 31:10-13). And prophetic promise was given of covenant renewal (Isa. 55:3; Jer. 31-33). It is into this pattern of covenant renewal that Matthew 5:17 f. is organically integrated. The Older Testamental law was declared to have exhaustive validity under the New Covenant by the covenant mediator, our Lord.

The Newness of the New

The same law which was written at Sinai is internally written by the finger of God on the fleshly tables of the human heart in the New Covenant. The gospel makes the law neither evil nor obsolete; on the contrary, to disregard the law would be to undermine the whole structure of Christian redemption. Hence Paul can contrast Sinai with the New Covenant in 2 Corinthians 3 *without* doing despite to the law. Certainly the New Covenant is *better* than the older one, but its improvement does *not* consist in prompting unrighteousness and injustice by abrogating God's holy law. The New Covenant is better *because it brings the power of obedience* with it by the agency of the Holy Spirit.

> The establishment of the new covenant, however, implies neither the abrogation nor the depreciation of the Mosaic law. This is plainly shown by the terms in which God announces His new covenant: "I will put *my law* in their inward parts" (Jeremiah 31:33), and by the object it is intended to achieve: "that they may walk in *my statutes,* and keep *my ordinances,* and do them" (Ezekiel 11:20). There is no question of a new law or of no law. Neither God changes nor His law. The difference between the old and new covenants is that under the former that law is written on tablets of stone, confronting man as an external ordinance and condemning him

> because of his failure through sin to obey its commandments, whereas under the latter the law is written internally within the redeemed heart by the dynamic regenerating work of the Holy Spirit, so that through faith in Christ, the only law-keeper, and inward experience of His power man no longer hates but loves God's law and is enabled to fulfill its precepts.[3]

There was no power or perfection with the former covenant, but now we have a better hope which *enables* us to draw near to God (Heb. 7:19). Hebrews 8:6-8 explains that the New Covenant has *better promises* than the Older Covenant which was not faultless. However, we must be careful to see that the fault rested upon the sinful covenant *people;* God found fault "*with them*" (v. 8). The Older Covenant was not sufficient to make provision against the faultiness of the people. Both the newness and superiority of the New Covenant reside in its *success,* its accomplishment of the covenant promise of fellowship with Yahweh, our Lord.

Consultation with Jeremiah 31:33 ff. or its quotation in Hebrews 8:8 ff. will establish that the New Covenant does not bring a new law which replaces and abrogates the old. Instead new depth and wealth is given to the covenant promise, "I will be to them a God, and they shall be to me a people." This is seen in *three main provisions:* internalization and ability to keep the law of God, the overwhelming prosperity of gospel preaching, and the actual accomplishment of redemption for God's elect.

This is the covenant which God has made with Israel in these days. First the law of God (i.e., the well known and commonly identified law of the Older Testament) is written upon the heart and placed in the mind of God's elect people (Heb. 8:10; Jer. 31:33). Under the Older Covenant the law had been weak through sinful human nature (cf. Rom. 8:3), but now there is to be no condemnation of the believer

[3] P. E. Hughes, *Paul's Second Epistle to the Corinthians* (Grand Rapids: Eerdmans Publishing Co., 1962), pp. 94.

because the Holy Spirit indwells him and enables him to obey God's statutes (Ezek. 11:19 f.; 36:26 f.; Rom. 8:1). What was once merely on stone tablets is now written on the heart, indicating that the power to comply is being given, for "out of the heart are the issues of life" and "as a man thinketh in his heart so is he" (Prov. 4:23; 23:7). The proper spiritual response to God's law is now insured by internal renovation of the believer's heart and mind. Note that there is absolutely no indication of, or justification for seeing here, a new set of commandments; the Older Testamental law was perfect and holy, and as such needed no change. It is the human heart that needs regeneration and change.

Second, whereas the law did not convert and justify *even one* sinner, the power of the new covenant is manifest in the fact that *everyone* will know the Lord (Heb. 8:11; Jer. 31:34). This does not refer to the previous failings of *priestly* education, for the provision has reference to *each man's* teaching of his neighbor. What the New Covenant promises is that teaching will now be so *prosperous* that in some future day everyone will be converted by it. The day is coming when, in the power of the Holy Spirit, *all* citizens and relatives, from the small to the great, will know the Lord (i.e., love, serve, and understand Him). Nor can this second provision of the New Covenant be understood as referring to a *more intimate* "knowledge" of God (as many have suggested), for it is the *quantitative* element that is brought to the foreground in the biblical passages. Also it will be quite clear to anybody who consults a concordance that people in the Older Testament were said to *know* the Lord already (e.g., 1 Chron. 28:8 f.; Jer. 9:24; 22:16; etc.). Granted that our knowledge about God is qualitatively better after the revelation of the Son, we must still see that it is not this fact which is stressed in Jeremiah 31 or Hebrews 8. To know the Lord in the sense being spoken of in the second provision of the New Covenant is synonymous with being saved (cf. John 17:3). The power and prosperity of the New Covenant is dramatically evidenced in the hyperbole that there will someday be no need to evangelize any longer; no man will need to exhort his neighbors or relatives to know Yahweh, *for they all shall know Him*. This accords well with the testimony of Scripture elsewhere. Revelation 19 metaphorically describes the stupendous victory of gospel preaching done by the church led by their Captain, Jesus Christ; the sword with which they conquer the nations proceeds out of the mouth, i.e., is the powerful word of God's gospel being heralded to the world (cf. Eph. 6:17; Heb. 4:12). Isaiah prophesied that "the earth will be full of the knowledge of the Lord as the waters cover the sea" (Isa. 11:9). The Great Commission will one day be fulfilled, a day in which *all nations* (not just representative individuals in them) shall have been discipled. Scripture often brings together the first and second provisions of the New Covenant. For instance, the Great Commission includes the first provision of the New Covenant as well: all nations are to be taught to observe Christ's commandments, in other words, all the law of God (Matt. 28:19 f.; cf. Matt. 5:17 f.). The power and presence of Christ is the seal and guarantee of the Great Commission's success (Matt. 28:18, 20); Christ shall be exalted as Lord, and in love to Him all nations shall observe His law. Isaiah 2:2 f. relates the same two promises: "In the last days the mountain of the *house of the Lord* (i.e., the church) will be established as the chief of the mountains . . . and *all nations* will stream to it, and many peoples will say 'Come let us go up to the mountain of the Lord . . . that He may teach us concerning His ways, and that we may walk in His paths, for *the law* will go forth from Zion' " (NASV). The kingdom of Christ the Savior will be a stone not cut with human hands (i.e., worked by the power of God's Spirit, not human might) that crushes the world empires and grows to be a mountain which *fills the whole earth* (Dan. 2:31-45).[4] The New Covenant will bring with it the power to convert sinners to God; its prosperity will be overwhelming—such is God's promise, and if the Spirit can convert one individual sinner, why should we hesitate to see Him having the power to effect a worldwide revival? This could not be expected under the Older Covenant, but it is guaranteed under the New.

The foundation for the first two provisions of the New Covenant is given in the third provision (which is introduced with the explanatory "for"): God will make a full satisfaction for sin (Heb. 8:12;

---

[4] See also Psalm 86:9; 22:27; 2:8; 47; 72; Isaiah 54:13; Numbers 14:21; Joel 2:28; John 6:45; 1 Corinthians 15:25 f.

Jer. 31:34). Sins will be blotted out and remembered no more; God will be merciful and forgiving toward those who had been lawless (cf. Heb. 10:15-17). Forgiveness from God, of course, was not a new thing (e.g., Ex. 34:6 f.; Isa. 44:22; Mic. 7:18 f.), and the extent of His forgiveness, which the New Covenant mentions, had already been stated in the Older Testament (Isa. 43:25). What the New Covenant brings is the *assurance* of redemption's *accomplishment* and the *power* to justify. In an unqualified fashion God writes the promise of forgiveness right into the very terms of the covenant; He declares the sovereignty of His grace. We get a sense of the "newness" of this provision if we contrast Hebrews 10:3 with 7:27; under the old order there was continual reminder of sins and the necessity of sacrificing over and over again, *but Christ accomplishes* salvation once for all. Hence God can give the assured word of pardon to His people. The Older Covenant did not have promises like these three!

We see that although the New Covenant in no way changes the Older Testamental law of God, it does have wonderful new promises of power and prosperity. The novelty of the New Covenant, according to God's word, is found in the granting of power to obey God's law, in the overwhelming victory of gospel preaching, and in the full and actual accomplishment of redemption. Christ shall present full atonement for our sins, the gospel shall be believed in all the world, and believers will be enabled by the Holy Spirit to live according to God's holy statutes. Hebrews 8:13 says that the old age is past, but the age of the Son is here to stay; the kingdom of God has superseded the time of expectation (Luke 16:16), for grace and truth have been realized by Jesus Christ (John 1:17). We live under the wonderful and powerful New Covenant, not under the weak covenant of external law and unfulfilled promise. This in no way dismisses the *validity* of God's holy law, however; rather, just because the law is *necessarily* valid, it is placed *within* our hearts. The promises of the New Covenant are not against the law of the Older Covenant (in its entirety).[5]

---

[5] It is not the case that the New Testament believer is solely under obligation to the Ten Commandments; no support for such a restriction can be properly found here. The reason why only the Decalogue is alluded to in Jeremiah 31 and Hebrews

Harmony of Gospel and Law

There are many indications in Scripture that the New Covenant does not depreciate the Mosaic law. The law's demands are intimately associated with the covenant established by Christ. First, the "law of God" is identical with the "law of Christ" (1 Cor. 9:21; cf. Gal. 5:23; 6:2). Second, Christ is the paradigm of obedience to the law; yet His life is *our* example of holiness. Third, the law has always had validity only as it related to Christ. Without Christ the Older Testamental law is empty; the Jews failed to see that it referred to Christ (John 5:45 f.). The law is not to be used in neglect of Christ's proper place (e.g., Gal. 2:21; 5:4). Fourth, Christ's death, which ratifies the New Covenant, was in accord with the demands of the Older Testamental law (Heb. 9:22; Matt. 26:28; 1 John 1:7). Fifth, the coming of the Gentiles into covenant relationship with God under the new order (Eph. 2:11-18) does not infer that the moral law given to the Jews was extraneous to the heart of God's relationship to men (Rom. 2:26 f.). Paul makes it clear throughout his writings that the *gracious, universal* salvation which is assured in the New Covenant does *not* imply antinomianism (Rom. 3:31; 6:15 ff.; 7:4 ff.; 8:4; Gal. 5:13 ff.).

So the advent and work of Christ in effecting a new testament of life should not set up a moral system in opposition to the law of God found in the Older Testament. The letter of the law in the Older Covenant killed, but this is no reason to suppose that the New Covenant of life has nothing to do with the letter of the law; after all, the *gospel* is a *two*-edged sword which *also* deals a death blow to those which refuse to believe it (cf. Rom. 1:16 f. and 2 Thess. 1:7-8, plus the numerous *commands* to believe the gospel, with 2 Cor. 2:15 f.; 1 John 3:23; John 3:36; 8:24; Heb. 11:6). Although the letter of the law *always* kills sinners

---

8 is in order to facilitate the intended contrast of *stone* to *heart*. Furthermore, the Decalogue has a *summary* nature: it briefly comprehends the whole law of God without going into detail. So the New Covenant does *not* carry with it an obligation *merely* to the Ten Commandments; it is not only the Decalogue which the covenant mediator ratifies, but *every jot and tittle* of the law, whether written on stone (like the summary words) or not (like the case law applications and elaborations).

and under it there is no hope of cure (cf. Gal. 3:10), the gospel only sometimes kills sinners; whereas under the law man was always guilty, now under the gospel he can be forgiven and empowered. The consequences of despising the gospel, however, are even *more dreadful* than those of despising the law, for the privileges associated with the gospel are more awesome (Heb. 12:18 ff.; cf. 2:2-4). The punishment of the apostate under the new order is much sorer than under the old, and the equity of this terrifying judgment under the New Covenant is established by *appeal to the Older Covenantal law* (read Heb. 10:26-29)—thereby assuming its foundational validity. Since the New Covenant brings with it further and worse punishment, we certainly should not see a turning back from the judicial tone, the law and penal sanction, of the Older Covenant. To the contrary, there is an intensification of it!

In 1 Timothy 1:5-10 Paul stresses that the law and the gospel have full agreement. He says there that the aim of the command to conform with orthodox doctrine is identical with the aim of the law. The "command" might refer to a synecdoche for the law,[6] or the practical instruction of the gospel,[7] or the apostolic orders as in 1 Timothy 1:18 and 1 Thessalonians 4:2, but most likely it refers to the substance of the charge mentioned in verse 3 preceding (cf. παραγγείλης and παραγγελίας).[8] Gospel doctrine brings about the goal of the law, for right doctrine necessitates right living (cf. Acts 15:9; 24:14-16; Rom. 13:10; Gal. 5:6; 2 Tim. 1:13; 2:19-22; Ps. 19:8; 119:66, 80, 121-128). Faithful teaching aims at love, a pure heart, and a good conscience, as does the law of God. Anticipating the rebuttal of his opponents that *they* have the support of the law, Paul urges Timothy to demonstrate

---

[6] John Calvin, *Second Epistle of Paul the Apostle to the Corinthians and the Epistles to Timothy, Titus and Philemon* (Grand Rapids: Eerdmans, printed 1964), p. 191.

[7] A. Plummer, "Pastoral Epistles," *The Expositor's Bible*, volume VI, ed. W. R. Nicoll (Hartford: S. S. Scranton, n.d.), p. 396 f.; and A. M. Stibbs, *New Bible Commentary* 2nd ed. F. Davidson (Grand Rapids: Eerdmans, 1954), p. 1065.

[8] This is also the view taken by John Trapp, *Commentary on the New Testament* (Evansville: Sovereign Grace, printed 1958), p. 637.

that there is a complete agreement between the law and the gospel which he has taught. By contrast, the opponents do *not* understand the law and so abuse it. Ironically these unorthodox teachers have a desire to be *authorities* (rabbis) of the law! While pretending to teach the law, they who understand neither faith nor doctrine are at odds with the law; their commentary on the law is ignorant, worthless, vain chatter. But,

> Lest his derogatory reference to would-be law-teachers should be misunderstood, Paul declares that the law is good and that it supports and complements the gospel by forbidding everything that is opposed to its wholesome teaching.[9]

The law is only good, says Paul, when used "lawfully" (the use of the cognate adverb here implies using the law in *its* intended way or purpose). The law has many functions, but Paul mentions simply its restraining role in 1 Timothy 1:5-10. Interestingly, the list in verses 9-10 follows the order of the Decalogue (citing the worst examples of violation for emphasis). The *lawful* use of *the law,* then, is *harmonious* with the *gospel* of the *New Covenant.* Calvin has accurately commented:

> Here he (i.e., Paul in 1 Timothy) declares that his Gospel, far from contradicting the law, is its best confirmation. He says that in his preaching he supports the sentence which the Lord has pronounced in His law against all those things that are contrary to sound doctrine. From this it follows that those who draw back from the Gospel do not hold to the heart of the law but merely pursue its shadow.[10]

From the above comments we must conclude that the New Covenant and the law of the Older Covenant have many elements in com-

[9] Stibbs, *op. cit.*, p. 1066.

[10] Calvin, *op. cit.*, p. 194.

mon and are perfectly consistent with each other. The New Covenant cannot be used to beat down the demands of God's law as it is found throughout the Older Testament. As Dr. Machen has written, "The gospel does not abrogate God's law, but it makes men love it with all their hearts."[11] And in his *Institutes of the Christian Religion* (II. IX.4) John Calvin declared, "we infer that, where the whole law is concerned, the gospel differs from it only in clarity of manifestation."[12] A scriptural consideration of the doctrine of the covenant, then, should lead one to agree with our Lord's words in Matthew 5:17 f.

Unfortunately this fact must be explicitly stated in this day because there are some who would "argue" that a consideration of the development of covenantal teaching in the Bible vitiates the obligation to keep the details of the Older Testamental law except for its general, core precepts.[13] Some would argue that the details of Old Testament law have expired under the New Covenant, appealing to the "sense" of the covenant, the "feeling" for its newness in Christ, the alleged "tenor" of the New Testament, and supposed hermeneutical assumptions that must be *inferred* to be the beliefs, yet unrecorded, of the scriptural writers. Now, without minimizing the solid contribution and value of the historico-theological method and Biblical Theology, we must squarely face the fact that the sort of argument suggested here is biblical interpretation at its worst. The "unwritten Torah" of the ancient Jews, and the church *tradition* of the Roman Catholics are devices similar to these modern, generalized feelings which have been used to distort, alter, and nullify the Word of God. Jesus condemned the Pharisees for such a method: letting man's autonomous thinking dismiss the truth and obligation of God's clearly spoken word. The intended

---

[11] J. G. Machen, *What Is Faith?* (Grand Rapids: Eerdmans Publishing Co., 1925), p. 192.

[12] Calvin, *Institutes, op. cit.*, p. 427.

[13] Of course, without a definite criterion of continuity and discontinuity, such a position is quite *ambiguous.* And it is hard to imagine how an independent, *non-question-begging* criteria might be established which will avoid dispensationalism. What would the mark of requisite *generality* be in order to preserve an Older Testament command's obligatoriness into the new age?

outcome of any argument like that posed above would be the contravention of Jesus' direct statements in Matthew 5:17 f. to the effect that every bit of God's law is binding today. Not many will want to grant that a consideration of the New Testament "tenor" or a "feeling" for covenantal development could carry *this much weight*—enough to reverse the straight-forward assertions of God's word. Historical considerations and covenant analogies do not have any significant qualification or alteration to make of the explicit and categorical assertions of Christ speaking in Scripture. A "Biblical Theology" which contravenes the clear pronouncements of Scripture is not worthy of its name.

The Kingdom: Its Fellowship, Literature, and Life

Obedience to the law of God is so integral and significant to the development of the *kingdom of God* that to expect its renunciation in the epoch of the New Covenant, where the Messianic Kingdom is established with power, is scurrilous and incongruous. God's "kingdom" means nothing if it does not mean that He exercises *dominion* in every aspect of the lives of His subjects. Even Adam, who was created perfect, needed moral guidance by special revelation from God; to this law he was bound as a condition of fellowship and continued blessing. Each man has the law of God implanted in his nature, as the Gentiles demonstrate (Rom. 2:14 f.); this is so because we are all created as God's image. In his original state man had an unmediated knowledge of God's moral nature because he was created as the image of God (Gen. 1:27), but since that time this "innate" knowledge has been distorted and suppressed (Rom. 1:18 ff.).

Even before the law was delivered at Sinai, the law was in the world (Rom. 5:13 f.; Gal. 3:19); that is, between Adam and Moses God's law was binding. Abraham was chosen by God in order that he might keep God's way and righteousness, and Abraham, who is the father of the faithful (Gal. 3:6-9), kept God's commandments, statutes and laws (Gen. 18:19; 26:5). Later when the people of God were wandering in the wilderness the Bible says that God was testing their heartfelt obedience (Deut. 8:2). The Lord's expectation of His people is *summarized* in the demand of obedience to Him (Deut. 10:12 f.). The Psalmist recognized that simply because the Lord was his God he should be taught to do the Lord's will; this is what the creature's attitude should always be toward his Creator (Ps. 143:10). Moral purity has been required of God's people in every age, generation, and historical period.[14] Moral obligation has formed an inevitable concomitant of faith throughout the entire Older Testament and its theological-covenantal development. In other words, *holiness* (which is defined by God's law) has always been necessary for covenant fellowship.[15] It is not at all surprising then that lawlessness and disobedience lead to captivity for the Jews and removal from the promised land.[16] Only when the people of God had learned the lesson of obedience to God's law could they be delivered according to the promise (Deut. 30:1-3). It was prophesied that there would be a righteous remnant who should preserve God's law in the midst of the apostasy; *they* would be waited upon by the Lord (Isa. 8:16). Finally, in the ultimately restored kingdom, obedience to the law would continue to be characteristically required by God (Zech. 8:14-17). The ethical requirements of the Older Covenant are thus carried into the New by virtue of the very nature of covenantal fellowship with the Creator, our King.

Even the main divisions of Older Testamental *literature* were vitally connected to the law of God. The first division of Scripture is denominated "*the Law.*" The Psalms of praise and Proverbs of wisdom in the "*Writings*" have great concern for the law; in the Psalter the behavior and destiny of the good and evil man is a main theme, while

---

[14] Read Gen. 2:15-17; 6:8 f., 22; 7:1; 17:1; 18:19; 39:9; Deut. 6:4-15; Lev. 11:44; 18:5; 19:2; 1 Sam. 15:22; Ezra 7:23-26; Neh. 8-10; Job 1:1; Ps. 5:4-7; 25:10, 14; 34:14-16; 103:18; Prov. [cf. the decalogue], especially 1:1-3; 22:19; Eccles. 12:13; Isa. 11:3-5; Jer. 7:5; Ezek. 17:22; Hos. 6:6; Amos 5:24; Mic. 6:8; Zeph. 3:13; Zech. 7:9, 16 f.

[15] Read J. B. Payne's excellent survey and discussion of this point in "Morals," *The Theology of the Older Testament* (Grand Rapids: Zondervan Publishing Co., 1962), pp. 315-350.

[16] See Isa. 1:23; 3:12-15; 10:1-3; 28:14-15; 29:20 f.; 52:5; 59:14 f.; Jer. 5:28; Hos. 5:1, 10; 7:3; Amos 3:10 f.; 4:1 f.; 5:11 f.; 6:12 f.; Mic. 3:1-3, 9-11; 7:3 f.; cf. Neh. 9:34-37.

the wisdom literature is strongly ethical in character and emphasizes the righteous conduct which God desires. Biblical "*Prophecy*" is based on and developed out of the law (e.g., Isa. 8:20; Dan. 9:4 ff.). Moses, who delivered the law, was a qualitatively esteemed prophet in his own right (Num. 12: 7; Deut. 34:10). Prophetic indictments against the people of God were based on the law of God; these prophets acted as God's "prosecuting attorneys" who appropriately indict and condemn lawlessness. The prophesied rule of the coming Messiah was primarily characterized as one of lawfulness (Isa. 9:6 f.; 42:1; 60:17).

Hence in the entire Older Testament *life* was to be centered around God's commandments (Deut. 8:3, 6). The law was to govern in the home, in education, in behavior and thought (Deut. 6:4-9; 11:18-21; Ex. 13:9, 16). Not obeying God was identical with forgetting one's redemption (Deut. 8:11-17). Obedience was more highly esteemed and desired than sacrifice (1 Sam. 15:22; Jer. 7:22); thus God's people were called upon to offer up the sacrifice of righteousness (Ps. 4:5). The law taught one to put his confidence in God (Ps. 78:1-7), with lawful obedience being the subsequent response to God's grace (read Ps. 103). Revering and loving God were associated with obedience to God's law (Deut. 10:12 f.), and by obeying Him God's people became a peculiar treasure (Ex. 19:5).

We see, then, that the law was neither the meritorious *ground* of blessing in the Older Testament, nor was it anything like a *burden* to God's people. It is not surprising that we should read of the desire to be taught God's statutes under these circumstances (e.g., Ps. 119:12, etc.). The book of Deuteronomy and the 119th and 19th chapters of Psalms give us a clear insight into the Older Testamental evaluation of the law. The law is perfect (Ps. 19:7), faithful (Ps. 119: 86), righteous, pure, and true (Ps. 19:8 f.; 119:9, 128, 137, 138, 140, 142, 144, 151, 172). It is enlightening and makes one wise (Ps. 19:7 f.; 119:66, 98 f.; 119:66, 98-100, 104). The law inspires reverence for God (Ps. 119:38, 63, 79); it leads to repentance, revival, and restoration (Ps. 19:7, 12; 119:25, 37, 40, 93, 107, 149). The law restrains sin (Ps. 119:11), is wondrous (Ps. 119:18, 27), and is the source of blessedness (Ps. 19:11; 119:1 f.). The law brings strength (Ps. 119:28), peace (Ps. 119:165), liberty (Ps. 119:45), comfort (Ps. 119:50, 52), and hope (Ps. 119:43, 114). One's response to the law, then, should be grateful praise (Ps. 19:62; 119:164, 171), delight, joy, and love (Ps. 119:14, 16, 19 f., 24, 35, 40, 47, 70, 77, 92, 97, 111, 127, 131, 143, 159, 174).

The New Testament and Covenant continue the same demand for obedience. Entrance to the kingdom is dependent upon attesting obedience (Matt. 7:21), and the kingdom itself is *synonymous* with *righteousness;* the kingdom (and its commandments) is not solely future, but absolutely demands that everything be subjected to it in this *current* age.[17]

> The will of God finds expression in the revelation of the law. This is why *the preaching of the kingdom is also that of the law.* So we should not be surprised that Jesus as the Christ not only proclaims the coming of the kingdom as the fulfillment of the great time of salvation and as the fulfillment of Scripture (Mark 1:15; Luke 4:21), but that he also gives supreme emphasis to the *fulfillment of the law* as the purpose of his messianic coming and as the content of the gospel of the kingdom.[18]

The early preachers of the gospel of the kingdom declare that man's duty is to obey God (cf. Acts 5:29). Without the obedience of kingdom righteousness Christ cannot be one's Savior (Heb. 5:9). Grateful obedience leads to wisdom (Matt. 7:24), a family relationship with Christ (Matt. 12:50), and divine fellowship (John 14:23). The Spirit which indwells God's people prompts this obedience (Rom. 8:2, 4). And such obedience is the key to spiritual knowledge (John 7:17). All men are exhorted to seek first the kingdom of God and *its righteousness* (Matt.

---

[17] Read Herman Ridderbos, *The Coming of the Kingdom*, trans. H. de Jongste, ed. Raymond O. Zorn (Philadelphia: The Presbyterian and Reformed Publishing Co., 1962 reprinted 1969), p. 312.

[18] Ibid., pp. 291 f. (emphasis mine).

6:33). The chastening of God which comes in the form of affliction or persecution makes one righteous, obedient to the law, and worthy of the kingdom (Heb. 12:11; Ps. 119:67, 71; Matt. 5:10-12; 2 Thess. 1:4 f.). The kingdom, righteousness, and law-keeping are inseparable and mutually inclusive. The Messianic kingdom is to be advanced in the earth *along with* the teaching of obedience to the *law* of God (Matt. 28:19 f.). When Christ returns in judgment He will take vengeance upon all those who do not *obey* the gospel (2 Thess. 1:7 f.).

Even this very rough sketch of the place obedience has in the kingdom of God and its prominence throughout the Scriptures is enough to dissuade us from any "hermeneutical feeling" or evaluation of the New Testament's "tenor" that would infer the abrogation of any of the slightest commands of God's law under the New Covenant.[19] Continued blessing for Adam in paradise, Israel in the promised land, and the Christian in the kingdom has been seen to be dependent upon persevering obedience to God's will as expressed in His law. There is complete covenantal *unity* with reference to the law of God as the standard of moral obligation throughout the *diverse* ages of human history.

---

[19] As the history of theology evidences, it is just when men are willing to depart from Scripture's *explicit* statements in favor of their generalized, undeniably subjective, assessments of the *implicit* message or meaning of the Bible that doctrinal deviation begins to cut its wide swath. Of course, it is amazing how the imagined, transtextual "tenor" of the Bible (or N.T.) always seems to correlate so exactly with the theological milieu, ecclesiastical background, and personal opinions of the one who assesses this "tenor"; one's own predispositions and the ideological status quo are easily read into this not so clearly defined and defended "*tenor.*" There is a sober lesson here for contemporary evangelical and Reformed teachers; that which we disapprobate in unorthodox theologians is all too easily and unwittingly pressed into service against teaching that is uncongenial to our preconceived opinions. Resort is then made to "tenor" over against *text.*

IV. SUPPOSED CONFLICTS WITH THE THESIS RESOLVED

Chapter 9

THE CEREMONIAL (RESTORATIVE) LAW

ABOUT this point the question may have arisen, what about the laws in the Older Testament dealing with sacrifices, the temple, etc.? According to the foregoing thesis, *every* jot and tittle of the Lord's law is binding upon God's people in all ages. Does this mean that New Testament Christians are required to observe the Older Testamental *ritual?* The answer to this question is yes and no. Yes, Christians under the New Covenant are still responsible to offer blood atonement for their sins and tend to the obligations of the temple, etc.; however, we must be mindful of the fact that the *way* or *manner* in which Christians do these things under the New Covenant is *not* identical with the Older Testamental observation of the ritual and ceremony.

Christ is the once-for-all sacrifice for Christians. He is also the presence of God among His people (i.e., the temple; "Immanuel"), and the Holy Spirit's indwelling makes each Christian the temple of God. Thus the Older Testamental ceremonies were *foreshadows* of the person and work of Christ. The ceremonial law was nothing less than "the gospel in figures." With Christ's obedient life, sacrificial death, and the accomplishment of salvation under the New Covenant, the ceremonies have been finally observed for all God's people. *The meaning of the ceremonial laws received permanent validity and embodiment in Christ, His work, and His saving economy.* The purpose of the ceremonies, then, was realized in the New Testament. Christ released us from the relative and provisional bondage of which the Mosaic ritual was the instrument. The ceremonial observations were stop-gap and anticipatory; Christ and the New Covenant are the *fulfilled reality.* Therefore, all Christians have had the ceremonial laws observed for them finally and completely *in Christ.*

The book of Hebrews especially emphasizes the completion of the ceremonies in Christ. F. F. Bruce has commented:

> In this epistle, moreover, the law is not a principle set in opposition to the grace manifested in Christ's saving work, but rather an anticipatory sketch of that saving work. Here we find a concern with the sacrificial cultus rather than with the "tradition of the elder," with the ritual law as a means of access to God rather than with the moral law as a way of life. . . . In Hebrews the law is a pattern or preliminary blueprint of the redemptive order introduced by Christ.[1]

The Levitical priesthood, representing the Mosaic system of ceremonial redemption, could not bring perfection and so was *intended* to be superseded (Heb. 7:11 f., 28). The people of God were subjected to a law or principle of ceremonial redemption with reference to the priesthood, says the author of Hebrews, but when Jesus instituted a change in the priesthood (for He was of the tribe of Judah, not Levi) the ceremonial principle was altered as well. This was inevitable because the ceremonial priests remained powerless to effect the perfect inward cleansing required. The former commandment with reference to ceremonial matters was set aside, then, in order that God's people might have a better hope, for the ceremony was imperfect and kept men at a distance from God (Heb. 7:18 f.). The commandment which was annulled was "a commandment with respect to flesh" (i.e., concerning external qualification of physical descent of the priests in the tribe of Levi; cf. vv. 11-13 earlier in chapter 7, plus the NASV and RSV rendition of v. 16). This law made nothing perfect; but Christ, who is a priest after the order of Melchizedek, does. Lest a contradiction with Matthew 5:17 f. be generated at this point, let us note that such a change in stipulation is *also* a confirmation of the Older Testamental law as

---

[1] F. F. Bruce, *The Epistle to the Hebrews* (Grand Rapids: Eerdmans Publishing Co., 1964), pp. 28 f., 198 n.

implied in Psalm 110:1, 4. The *ineffective* priesthood has been superseded by the *better hope*; hence the ceremonial system is now antiquated. The perfect has come, thus making the sacrificial, priestly, temple system irrelevant (Heb. 8:13). The ceremonial system of the Older Covenant has become obsolete and grown old; it is ἀφανισμός, which (in its verbal form) is used of legislation which becomes inoperative because it is no longer relevant to changed circumstances.[2] After Christ and the inauguration of the New Covenant the Older Testamental way of observing the ceremonial laws is irrelevant. What need has a Christian for a Levitical priest, physical temple, and bleating lamb when Christ, his great high priest, perfect sacrifice and spiritual temple, has performed all things necessary for his salvation?

The ceremonial observations no longer apply, but their meaning and intention have been eternally validated. The earlier sacrificial ritual was a foreshadow pointing to Christ (Heb. 10:1), and no repetition of a mere shadow can amount to the substantial reality! That which is the foundation of the *new economy,* in which the outward performance of the ceremonial ritual is not observed, is the *obedience of Christ* (cf. Heb. 10:8 f.). His obedience makes it no longer necessary for us to obey the ceremonial law in the way which the saints living in the period of *expectation* did. Ephesians 2:14-16 says that Christ has put the principle of commandments contained in ordinances "out of gear."[3] Christ has

---

[2] Ibid., p. 177 n.

[3] In this context the ceremonial law is dealt with as it applies to the separation of Jews and Gentiles. The Jews were culturally taught God's requirement of separation by means of certain prohibitions against (a) unclean animals (Lev. 11:1-47, esp. vv. 44-45; Deut. 14:1-21, esp. vv. 2, 21; carefully note Lev. 20:22-26 and Acts 10:9-43), and (b) certain kinds of mixing (Lev. 19:1-2, 19; Deut. 22:9-11; note 2 Cor. 6:14-17). Paul's point in Ephesians 2 is that with the coming of Christ this legal system of *national* separation has been disengaged; the Jews and Gentiles are *now* brought together in Christ (2:11-13) and made fellow-heirs of salvation (3:1-7). God's requirement of separation is no longer national (the shadow) but spiritual (the reality). The *physical* separation of Israel, Yahweh's bride, typified the *spiritual* separation of the church, Christ's bride, from the unbelieving world. The ceremonial (typological) system of ordinances retains its meaning, but is altered in its manner of observation.

broken down the barrier between Jews and Gentiles of which the dividing wall in the temple was the symbol. It should be quite clear that the law which represents enmity and separation between Jews and Gentiles is the *ceremonial* law, for the moral law does not distinguish between these groups (all men are responsible to the moral law and are condemned under it: Rom. 1-3). It is *this ceremonial system*[4] which Christ has made ineffective. The ritual ordinances of the Older Testament typified Christ and His saving economy; they were foreshadows based on a heavenly exemplar. Christ does not abrogate their *meaning* and intention; rather, He makes their old manner of *observation* irrelevant, for circumstances have radically changed. The perfect has come, salvation has been actually accomplished, the substance of the shadows has appeared. The obedience of Christ and His saving work has satisfied the obligation of observing the ceremonies for me; if I were to continue the ritual observances under the New Covenant, I would be despising the final accomplishment of salvation in Christ. I would be substituting the symbol for the Saviour.

Basically, the Older Testamental ceremonial law dealt with the priesthood, ceremonial atonements, sacrifice, circumcision, ritual feasts,

---

[4] It is not only the *content* of the stipulations envisioned by Paul, but also the *phraseology* pertaining to them, which indicates that Paul's referent is the ceremonial system. "The law of commandments in ordinances" does *not* refer to each and every command revealed in the Older Testament; rather, Paul speaks of "*the law* of commandments"—i.e., the *principle*, order, policy, or system of commandments. Further, the stipulations he has in mind are the "commandments contained *in ordinances*"—that is, in "decrees" (laws imposed by authority, but *not* in virtue of *intrinsic* rightness; e.g., Luke 2:1; Acts 17:7; Acts 16:4; and LXX), thus referring to the ceremonial law. Colossians 2:14 speaks of these "ordinances" as the "shadow of things to come" (v. 17), and specific ceremonial illustrations are given (vv. 11, 16). Paul's wording indicates that he is thinking foremost of the ceremonial law: cf. F. W. Grosheide, *De Brief Van Paulus Han De Efeziers* (Van Kampen, 1960), p. 45. "In fact the law with its detailed ordinances of ceremonies and regulations about the clean and the unclean had the effect of imposing a barrier and of causing enmity between Jews and Gentiles" (F. Foulkes, *The Epistle of Paul to the Ephesians*, Grand Rapids: Wm. B. Eerdmans, n.d., p. 82).

and ritual places. To observe these ceremonies demonstrated *faith* in the *coming* Messiah, for they typified Christ.

> [The ceremonial system] contained also an elaborate system of symbols, wherein spiritual truths were significantly set forth by outward visible signs, the vast majority of which were types, or prophetic symbols, setting forth the person and work of Christ and the benefits of his redemption.[5]
>
> This revealed law is called moral, because it concerns character, questions of right and wrong, holiness and sin. It is distinguished from the ceremonial law, foretelling and prefiguring the redemption of Christ, [showing] the preparatory form of the mystery of salvation.[6]

False reliance upon the performance of these rituals for their own sake was excluded (e.g., Amos 5:21; Isa. 1:11-15; 1 Sam. 15:22; Ps. 15:2; Hos. 6:6; etc.). As indicated earlier, the ceremonies had to be preceded by a confession of sin and were effective only when they manifested faith. Therefore, the heavenly blueprint of redemption was manifested in the ceremonial ordinances. Just as Christ ministers in the heavenly reality of which the tabernacle was a shadow copy (Heb. 8:5), so the force and effect of *all* the ceremonies depends on *Him*. In and of themselves the ceremonies accomplished nothing (cf. Heb. 10:4), but by Christ believers are justified from all things which the Mosaic law was without ability to justify (Acts 13:38 f.).

Realizing this truth, Paul can ask with rhetorical abhorrence: "How can you desire to be enslaved again to the weak and worthless rudiments

---

[5] A. A. Hodge, *The Confession of Faith: A Handbook of Christian Doctrine Expounding the Westminster Confession* (London: Banner of Truth Trust, reprinted 1958), p. 255; cf. Westminster Confession at chap. 19, sec. 3.

[6] A. A. Hodge and J. A. Hodge, *The System of Theology Contained in The Westminster Shorter Catechism Opened and Explained* (New York: A. C. Armstrong and Son, 1888), p. 83.

of the (ceremonial) law?" (cf. Gal. 4:9 f.). Paul declares in Galatians 5:2-4 that to observe the ceremonial law after the inauguration of full salvation by Christ is to exhibit a legalistic soteriological motive; to continue the ceremonies under the New Covenant is to evidence misunderstanding of what these ritual ordinances actually meant. Christ condemned the Pharisees for distortion and misunderstanding of the moral law (Matt. 5:17 ff.), and Paul condemned the Judaizers for distortion and misunderstanding of the ceremonial law (Gal. 5:1 ff.). In both cases self-righteousness and willful misunderstanding of God's revelation led to antinomianism (even though a boast was made of legalism)! The ancient observation of the ceremonial law is simply irrelevant after Christ.

However, the *meaning* and intention of these laws is equally valid under the Older and New Covenants, even though the former manner of observation is now "out of gear." The restorative law of the Older Testament declared that there is no remission of sin apart from the shedding of blood (Lev. 17:11; Heb. 9:22). The truth of this law, its axiomatic content, could not be set aside, even though the way in which it is observed could. The meaning was secure. "Therefore, it was *necessary*" that the Older Testament copies be cleansed with blood *because* they anticipated the cleansing of the heavenly things by Christ's sacrifice (Heb. 9:23-24). Christ did *not cancel* the requirement of the restorative ceremonies; He once and for all kept them so that we might observe them *in Him*. He is our sacrificed passover (1 Cor. 5:7), our redemptive lamb (1 Pet. 1:19), etc. It is "impossible" to be saved now by any other sacrifice (Heb. 10:4).

A final observation must be made about the ceremonial (or restorative, typological) law in Scripture in light of certain modern claims to the effect that the ceremonial/moral law distinction is an arbitrary distinction invented by the theologians. This attitude is seriously mistaken. The distinction *must* be drawn between *ceremonial* and *moral* laws, and one must recognize that the former's manner of *observation* is today altered. Recall that:

1. The Christian is morally obligated to observe every jot and tittle of the Older Testament law (Matt. 5:17-19); to disobey any point is to violate the whole law (James 2:10).

2. There is a *system* (or interrelated set) of ceremonial laws (cf. Eph. 2:15).

3. The observation of this system of ordinances (redemptive ceremonies) was intended to be superseded (Heb. 7:11-12, 18-19); it was a foreshadow of Christ's saving economy and has become obsolete with His historical work (Heb. 10:1; 8:13).

4. Thus the continued observation of this system of shadows is to miss their true import, is diametrically opposed to Christian faith, and evidences condemning bondage (Gal. 4: 9-10; 5:2-4).

5. Therefore, in order to walk righteously before our God and not violate His requirements at any point, we *must* identify and distinguish ceremonial observance *from* moral requirement.

In view of these things we conclude that the distinction between moral and ceremonial laws is not one which the New Testament theologian today arbitrarily foists upon the Older Testament. Recognition of such a distinction (between morality *per se* and cult) can be illustrated in the Older Testament itself (e.g., unique capital crimes— Lev. 10:8-11; Num. 4:15; typological requirements—Ex. 25:40; special food restrictions to teach separation from pagans—[in context] Lev. 20:25-26; Deut. 14:21,[7] godly living distinguished from cultic performance—1 Sam. 15:22; Isa. 1:11-17; Hos. 6:6; Amos 5:21-24; Mic. 6:6-8; sacrificial laws given, not to define sin as the other laws do, but to atone for existing sin—Lev. 4:35; etc.). Moreover, modifications in the immutable Torah were expected by the rabbis with respect to the Older Testament festivals, cleanness and purity rules, and sacrifices.[8] Furthermore, the early church

[7] Ibid., pp. 226-227; cf. Hengstenberg, *op. cit.*, p. 330.

[8] W. D. Davies, *The Sermon on the Mount* (Cambridge: The University Press, 1966), pp. 51-55.

shows evidence of having accepted the ceremonial/moral law distinction very early in the extant noncanonical writings (e.g., the *Didascalia Apostolorum,* early in the third century A.D., distinguished between the perennial Decalogue and the temporary ceremonies). Secondly, then, it should be noted that this distinction has a rationale behind it (i.e., follows a consistent rule) and is thus not arbitrary. The following outline can briefly summarize that rationale, namely, a distinction between laws reflecting God's *justice* and those based upon His *redemptive* purposes—i.e., moral law and restorative law, the former *defining* sin while the latter aims at salvation from sin. This shows the *basic* purposes of each:

I. Moral Law (reflecting God's absolute righteousness and judgment, but not showing the means of salvation *per se* for sinners)
    A. It guides life into the paths of righteousness
        1. by defining holiness and sin
        2. by restraining evil (through penal sanctions, etc.)
    B. It *drives* us to Christ and gracious restoration (since we are condemned as sinners therein)
II. Restorative Law (reflecting the mercy of God and His electing love; it reflects the Messiah's saving person, work, and redemptive economy, but not God's absolute justice *per se)*
    A. It directs the visible, redeemed community (either Israel or the church; e.g., passover, the Lord's Supper)
        1. by defining the redemptive process of historical restoration (e.g., necessity of sacrifice for atonement, etc.)
        2. by defining *further* sins *for the community* (e.g., the sin of refusing the Lord's Supper) and restrains impurity by ecclesiastical discipline (e.g., "cutting off" a person according to the Levitical code,[9] or barring one from Lord's Supper in the Christian church)

---

[9] Cf. Shearer, *op. cit.*, p. 146; H. B. Clark, *Biblical Law*, 2nd ed. (Portland: Binsfords & Mort, 1944), p. 52.

B. It (typologically) *points* us to Christ and His redemption

The preceding outline is not intended to be watertight in separating the moral from restorative law (e.g., moral law has typological elements, like marriage reflecting the relation between God and Israel, Christ and the church; restorative law has morally obligatory elements), but it does indicate the *first order* functions of the two classes of commands in the Bible. Due to the historical base which the restorative law has (dealing with the history of redemption as it does) it can take *various forms* in different eras; primarily these changes in outward observance are due to the two different historical perspectives on the work of Christ (looking ahead to the accomplishment of redemption or looking back to it; e.g., the Older Testament sacrifices were anticipatory, while the Lord's Supper is, among other things, a memorial). The New Testament shows the Christian how to "see" the ceremonial laws fulfilled in Christ and His redemptive economy (e.g., passover is seen in the Lord's supper). Thus the change in outward form of observance is grounded finally in the teaching of God's word and is not arbitrarily brought to the data of the Bible as an extraneous model. Hence also the New Testament is showing the believer how it is that the ceremonial law is *not abrogated* but fulfilled in Christ for us; as Hengstenberg says, the ceremonial law was not abrogated, for it embodies a moral law with divestable outward form (the duration of the whole law being founded upon Matt. 5:17-19).[10]

It is not within the purview of this work to distinguish all the typological laws from all the precepts having abiding moral force. But as we said above, particular Older Testamental laws are not concluded to be ceremonial on the basis of any imaginative construction of typological meaning. Only scriptural authority is sufficient to alter the observance of any law from God, and only Scripture can be taken as the basis for characterizing any law as typological or ceremonial (passages such as Acts 10:9-15; Col. 2:16 f.; and the book of Hebrews are paradigm

---

[10] E. W. Hengstenberg, *History of the Kingdom of God Under the Old Testament*, Vol. I (Cherry Hill, N.J.: Mack Publishing Co., 1871 [reprinted 1972]), pp. 325-326.

examples). Biblical Christians must not only face up to their obligation to keep the entire law of God, they must also take responsibility to do their exegetical homework so as to determine *which* laws are to be continually observed as abidingly moral.

Chapter 10

ALLEGED NEGATIVE PASSAGES

OUR thesis has been that the New Testament Christian is obligated to every jot and tittle of the Older Testamental law; our Lord's teaching, the unity of the covenant, the nature of sanctification, our Lord's example, plus numerous texts pointing to the integrity of the law confirm this thesis. The preceding portions of this treatise have demonstrated the *validity* of the law as well as its proper *place* and *function*. The Christian who is concerned for biblical orthodoxy has been given good reason to consider himself responsible for the exhaustive details of God's law. However, the reader who has come to this treatise with something of an antinomian inclination will more than likely be troubled with the passages of New Testament Scripture which seem to disparage the Older Testamental law. The unity and consistency of Scripture would lead us to expect that Matthew 5:17 f. would not be contradicted elsewhere in the New Testament. Yet antinomians have made attempts to bolster their following by appealing to passages which are apparently negative to the thesis of this treatise. These texts require an answer from any scripturally oriented interpreter and theologian, and by and large one *has been* offered in our foregoing analysis. The apparently negative passages basically fall into three groups: (1) those which renounce the law as a means of justification, (2) those which point to the death-dealing nature of sin in relation to the holy law, and (3) those pertaining to the ceremonial law.

It is important for us to see that those passages which would be cited to contravene the Christian's obligation to the exhaustive details of God's law are negative to this position *in appearance only*. Further study of any of these passages will show them to fit the analysis offered thus far (i.e., the moral law has abiding validity and integrity under the New Covenant as a pattern not of justification, but of sanctification for the Christian believer). Unless the antinomian is prepared to undo all of the prior scriptural exposition, he must be guided by the assumption that those texts which have been used to support "lawless Christianity" have lawful explanations. In what follows, specific passages and subjects which might be erroneously held as supporting antinomianism are elucidated. (The reader can check the indices for treatment of other texts or subjects not treated in this section.)

Pauline Theology and Theonomy. Perhaps nothing has been appealed to more than the epistles of Paul in order to support a Christianity free of obligation to God's law. Dispensationalists fabricate a radical discontinuity between Paul and Moses, matched only by the discontinuity fabricated by the liberal and neo-liberal (alias, "neo-orthodox") between Jesus and Paul. Perhaps nothing has been more misconstrued, misunderstood, and warped than Pauline theology here; the thoroughly confused nature of the antinomian view of Pauline teaching on the law is demonstrated by the fact that in 1903 Geerhardus Vos defended Paul against the charge of *legalism (The Princeton Theological Review,* vol. I, no. 2) and in 1957 Herman Ridderbos protected Paul from appeal to him as an *antinomian* (*When the Time Had Fully Come,* chapter 4: "The Law of God in Paul's Doctrine of Salvation")! Paul was neither a legalist nor an antinomian; he condemned the use of the law as a way of justification, but magnified it as the perfect pattern of sanctification. Paul directly affirmed the law's holiness and goodness (Rom. 7:12), echoed Christ's words in saying that we establish the law (Rom. 3:31), appealed to the law as authoritative (e.g., 1 Cor. 9:8 f.), and exhorted Christians to keep the law (e.g., Gal. 5:13 f., Rom. 7:4 ff.; 13:8 ff.). In this light we must understand any apparently negative or disparaging remarks about the law that are found in Paul's writings. To see Paul's words in their proper setting we must remember the historical context: Jewish pride in the law, and Paul's struggle against Judaism (and the Judaizers in particular). Israel boasted in the law, used it to lay up merit in heaven, and snobbishly segregated herself from the nations as superior to them because the law was in her possession. Israel felt that her very *hearing* of the law was sufficient to exalt her above the barbarians (cf. Rom. 1:13), and Paul accurately described this Jewish pride in Romans 2:17-20, ". . . you bear the name 'Jew,' and rely upon the law, and boast in God . . . being instructed out of the law, and are confident that you yourself are a guide to the blind, a light to those who are in darkness, a corrector of the foolish, a teacher of the immature. . . ." The Hillel school was proud to recite "where much law is, there is much living." This Jewish pride led them to use the law as the instrument of works-salvation (cf. Rom. 3:27-4:25; 9:31-10:13). Paul himself could have boasted in this way as a Pharisee, as one who prided himself in the law (e.g., Phil. 3:4-6), for he too had once been a zealot for the halacha (Gal. 1:14); but now whatever gain he had is considered as loss and dung (Phil. 3:7 f.).

Having learned that the law could not justify and spiritually empower a man, Paul writes against Jewish legalism with strong disapprobation. Vos correctly notes:

> The Judaistic spirit made itself the end and God the means, gave to itself the glory and to God the part of subserving the interests of this human glory by His moral government; that it led the creature to regard itself as the active and God as the merely passive factor in the determination of eternal destiny; perhaps also that it conceived of God as by nature bound to reward man. It is this profoundly sinful specifically Jewish καύχασθαι, against which the religious spirit of Paul rises in protest, and which makes him so uncompromising in his repudiation of the legal system. Inspired by such motives, it becomes to him the absolute antithesis to the very idea of religion.[1]

Hence,

> Most of the Pauline formulas bear a negative character. The law chiefly operated toward bringing about and revealing the

[1] Geerhardus Vos, "The Alleged Legalism in Paul's Doctrine of Justification," *Princeton Theological Review*, I (April, 1903), p. 170.

> failure of certain methods and endeavors. It served as a pedagogue unto Christ, shut up the people under sin, was not given unto life, was weak through the flesh, worked condemnation, brings under a curse, is a powerless ministry of the letter. These statements of Paul were made under the stress of a totally different philosophy of the law-purpose, which he felt to be inconsistent with the principles of redemption and grace. This Pharisaic philosophy asserted that the law was intended, on the principle of meritoriousness, to enable Israel to earn the blessedness of the world to come.[2]

In promoting the righteousness of faith, Paul necessarily condemned the attempt to attain justification by the works of the law. This explains his disparaging remarks about the law. In making his point, Paul was led to write that the law became a hostile power to man as a result of sin; Paul did not regard the law *itself* to be hostile to man. The disability and problem are with sin, not the law (Rom. 7:7, 12 f.; 8:3; 2 Cor. 3:6; 1 Cor. 15:56; Gal. 3:21). Because Paul was seriously concerned with man meeting the legal demands of God, he speaks contemptuous words about Judaistic legalism and sinful man's relation to the law of *God; only* faith in Christ can impute to man *the righteousness which God demands.* Therefore, Pauline theology and almost any negative comment Paul makes about the law can be understood as harmonious with the thesis of this treatise once the context of Paul's writings is understood.

Statements in Galatians. Antinomians will often seize upon quotations from Paul's letter to the Galatians to uphold their disdain for the law in Christian living. However, such argumentation can be easily countered by reminding the antinomian of the purpose of Galatians and against whom it was written. Paul is dealing with heretical *Judaizers* who demanded observance of the Mosaic *ceremonial* law for salvation (e.g., 4:9 f., 21-31; 5:1-4). Both legalistic justification and continued observance of the ceremonies have been renounced in former sections of

---

[2] Geerhardus Vos, *Biblical Theology: Old and New Testaments* (Grand Rapids: William B. Eerdmans Publishing Co., 1948 [reprinted 1966]), p. 142.

this treatise. Hence Galatians is not antagonistic to the thesis that the Christian is responsible to the law as the pattern of sanctification. The present treatise is in agreement with Paul's disapprobation for the law as the way of justification (Gal. 2:19, 21; 3:10-12; 4:21; 5:4) and the condemnation which the law, in conjunction with man's sin, brings (Gal. 3:19, 22-29). The negative comments in Galatians are not contrary to, but rather compatible with Jesus' pronouncements in Matthew 5:17-20.

Romans 3:27. Paul's mention here of "a law of faith" in contrast to a law of works has been erroneously taken to indicate a moral code dictated by saving faith rather than by God's revealed law. Such an interpretation fails to note the fact that "law" means different things in various contexts and intents for Paul (cf. Rom. 3:21, 27; 4:14, 16). In this verse Paul is using "law" to indicate a principle, system, or rule. He is saying that the works-principle is in diametric contrast to the faith principle.

Romans 6:14. Here we come across the most "sloganized" verse in the dispensationalist's polemic. The antinomian must wrench the statement "you are not under law, but under grace" out of its textual and theological context in order to justify belief that one is no longer responsible to God's holy law. "You are not under law, but under grace" is the *reason* Paul offers for the declaration that sin shall not have dominion over the Christian; lawlessness shall not reign in the believer's life, for he is under grace, not law. Paul is referring to a *law-principle* or legalistic system, *not* the Mosaic law, for grace was *not* antithetical to those who lived under the Mosaic economy (as demonstrated above). In Romans 6:14 "grace" and "law" are strongly contrasted (note the use of ἀλλά). *Both* grace *and* law came to believers under the Older Covenant; yet the "law" which Paul refers to in Romans 6:14 *excludes* "grace" (and vice versa). To be under law is to take a legal system and its demands *for your reckoning* before God, but to be under grace is to be the recipient of God's mercy. The impotency of the law is indicated in that one who is "under law" is a bondservant of sin; by contrast, the power and guarantee that sin (i.e., lawlessness) shall not lord it over the

Christian is found in being "under grace"—having the resources of God's redeeming and regenerating power. The believer shall not have sin rule over him because he is *not* the slave of *legalism;* he is the renewed and obedient *servant of God.*

Verse 15 goes on to safeguard against any antinomian interpretation of verse 14. Shall our response to verse 14 be the breaking of the law (i.e., sin)? May it never be! To be "under grace" does *not* imply the irrelevance of the moral law; not being "under law"[3] cannot entitle one to *transgress the law.* Sin is transgression of the law, and being under grace is the guarantee that sin shall not have dominion in the believer's life. Paul, who was under the sovereign resources of God's grace, also characterized himself as "under the law of God and Christ" (1 Cor. 9:21). Romans 6:13 exhorted the Christian to present his members as the instruments of righteousness, and righteousness is defined by God's law (as seen previously). Verse 18 of Romans 6 says that the believer has been freed from sin to become the *slave of righteousness.* Hence the verses preceding and following Romans 6:14 reject the intolerable inference of antinomianism in the name of "being under grace." The verse simply declares that justification for the Christian is not *legalistically* procured.

Romans 7:4, 6. It should be obvious that when Paul says that the believer has "died to the law" and is "discharged from the law" he is referring, again, to the condemnation which the law brings, as well as its impotence and subsequent bondage to sin. The antinomian inferences grounded in these phrases are contravened by the verses in which they are found. The Christian has died to the law *in order that* (ἵνα) he might bear fruit to God, and he has been discharged from the law *with the result that* (ὥστε) he serves in the newness (power) of the Holy Spirit (cf. Rom. 8:4). Paul again safeguards himself from antinomian interpretations of these two verses by strongly declaring in verse 7 that

---

[3] Notice the omission of the definite article ("the") here. Paul is not speaking of *the* (well-known) law, but rather a legalistic orientation ("under law"); his reference is generic.

his reader must not conclude that the law is sinful. Being released from self-righteous complacency (Rom. 7:9) and condemned by the law, Paul found the grace of God and "died to the law, was released from its bondage"; thereby he was enabled to *keep* the law in service to God. He was freed from sin and the law's impotence; he became enslaved to God and lawful sanctification (see Rom. 6:22).

Romans 10:4. As indicated previously, this verse declares, not that Christ terminates any and all obligation to the law of God, but that Christ is the end of the law *as a way of righteousness.* The believer is imputed with the righteousness of Christ which comes by faith; he does not earn it by the works of the law, for if righteousness came through the law, then Christ died needlessly (Gal. 2:21). Law-righteousness is terminated by faith-righteousness, but Paul does *not* say that the law is terminated in *all* respects for the believer (only as a personal way to justification).[4]

2 Corinthians 3. In this chapter Paul does not despise the law, but exposes the error of exalting the law *at the expense* of the more glorious gospel. The law is associated with condemnation; however, this fact exalts the law and its sanctity rather than disparaging it. The fault lies with law *breaking,* not the law itself. God's grace transforms the letter

---

[4] For the previous verses in Romans, the reader can consult with profit: Charles Hodge, *A Commentary on Romans* (London: Banner of Truth Trust, 1835 [1972]), and John Murray, *The Epistle to the Romans* (Grand Rapids: Wm. B. Eerdmans, 1959).

NOTE: Bahnsen later wrote in *No Other Standard: Theonomy and Its Critics*, (Tyler, TX: institute for Christian Economics, 1991), pp. 26-27: "I have been persuaded by Daniel Fuller that Romans 3:31 ("we uphold the law" by faith) is better interpreted—better than I did in *Theonomy*—as Paul saying that his message of salvation through faith endorses or substantiates the same message as found in the Old Testament (the law): see *Gospel and Law: Contrast or Continuum?* (Grand Rapids: Wm. B. Eerdmans, 1980). Likewise, Fuller convinces me that I was wrong to say of Romans 10:4 that it sets aside the law as a way of attaining righteousness—since the law was never presented as such in the Bible anyway (even the Old Covenant). The other example is that I no longer believe (as was suggested on p. 213 [second edition—p. 211, third edition], in *Theonomy*) that the sanction of death in Lev. 10:8-11 or Num. 4:15 denotes capital punishment—but rather direct, divine intervention to punish the offender with death."

of condemnation into life and love; hence the glory of the New Covenant completely outshines that of the Old, just as the brightness of the sun supersedes that of the stars. The ministration of righteousness confirms the law, for that ministration is made possible by Christ's perfect obedience to the law thus becoming the believer's righteousness (1 Cor. 1:30), and the Holy Spirit sanctifies the believer in the likeness of Christ's obedience (Eph. 4:13, 15; Gal. 4:19). In verse 13 Paul refutes the rabbinic tradition of extolling the law, pointing out that the glory which shone in Moses' face in receiving the law was interrupted and concealed.[5] That which was fading is *not* the *law,* but the *glory* which accompanied it; Paul brings this out in order to *magnify* the contrasting glory of Christ's gospel which is *without* interruption throughout eternity. In honoring the gospel Paul did not find it necessary to discredit the law.

Titus 3:9. In this verse Paul commands Titus to shun disputes about the law. This might be taken on the surface to imply a depreciation of the law, but closer reading makes it clear that it is certain *disputes* about the law (and not the law itself) which Paul discredits. He is scorning those debates which were initiated by Jews, using the law as the pretext for their argument. The law does not give rise to these disputes. *Judaizers* who pretended to defend the law's ceremonies were disturbing the peace of the church with their absurd controversies. The *nature* of these disputers over the law is disclosed in Titus 1:10-11, 14, 16.

Acts 15 and 21:19-26. The decision of the Jerusalem Council in Acts 15 is no more contrary to the thesis of this treatise than is Paul's polemic in the book of Galatians; this is because both the decision of the Council and the epistle to the Galatians were directed against the

---

[5] See the excellent commentary of P. E. Hughes on this passage: *Paul's Second Epistle to the Corinthians* (Grand Rapids: Wm. B. Eerdmans, 1962), pp. 102-121. Because they were stiffnecked (cf. Ex. 32), the Israelites could not continually gaze upon *even* the non-permanent glory of the Mosaic administration without interruption. The veil was not a subterfuge to hide the fading (which was obvious anyway, for Moses eventually removed the veil), but rather a condemnation of those who could not look upon the *glory* (Ex. 34:30, cf. 2 Cor. 3:7).

same group: the Judaizers. As commented earlier, the decision of the Jerusalem Council also included expedient counsel to the Gentiles that they refrain from certain things in order to pave the way for table fellowship with the Jews; these items do not represent exceptions to an already abrogated moral law. Rather, these items are not morally prohibited for the Gentiles at all; they come from the social customs of the Jews, and the Gentiles are requested to refrain from them in order to smooth social relations with their Jewish brethren. It would be a great misunderstanding of the Jerusalem Council's decision to see it as abrogating the Mosaic law *except* in a few select points; the Council only depreciated the law as a *way of justification* for the Gentiles (as also the Jews). The Jewish customs, except when used as a way of justification before God, were religiously indifferent, as Paul's activity in Acts 21:19-26 proves. Certain Judaizers or converted Pharisees ("zealots for the law") were upset over rumors to the effect that Paul was dissuading Jewish converts from practicing their ancesteral traditions. It is suggested to Paul that, just as the advice of the Jerusalem Council encouraged expediency in order to smooth social relations, he join in a purificatory rite with four men who had taken a temporary Nazirite vow in order to demonstrate to the public that Paul was *not* antagonistic to the indifferent social traditions of the Jews. Paul's ceremonial participation, just as the Gentile abstinence recommended by the Jerusalem Council, had no justifying or religious significance. Paul's activity was certainly no compromise of his Christian principles (the text in no way indicates disapprobation for his activity). In fact, this was his stated policy (see 1 Cor. 7:19). Only when these customs are taken as justifying in their effect are they condemned (e.g., Galatians). Earlier Paul had taken a vow similar to the one he consented to in Acts 21 (see Acts 18:18); perhaps this was thanksgiving for God's protection of him at Corinth. Therefore, we should see Paul's activity in Acts 21 not as inconsistent with the thesis of this treatise and the decision of the Jerusalem Council, but as an attempt to set Jewish minds at ease by evidencing that his Gentile ministry had not destroyed his Jewish loyalty. We could say that Paul was "going the second mile" in order "to be all things to all men" *as long as* it did *not* entail a violation of God's law.[6]

Hebrews 7:11-12. Based on Matthew 5:17 f., the thesis of this treatise has been that the law is valid and unchanged until the end of the world. A shallow reading of Hebrews 7:11 f. might seem to contradict this, for it mentions a necessary "change of law" (NAS). The context makes it clear that this phrase does *not* have reference to a new moral code under the New Covenant. The preceding verses deal with the priesthoods of Melchizedek and Aaron (Christ being after the order of the former), and verse 13 explains this "change of law" (note the word "for") as referring to the fact that Christ, the great high priest, descended from Judah and not from Levi (the tribe specified in the Mosaic law as the priestly line). The phrase in verse 12 is a partitive genitive dealing with the ceremonial law: "a change in the law" occurred with respect to priestly qualification. Verse 18 indicates that it is only *one* commandment (singular) which has been set aside, and verse 16 teaches that this commandment was "a commandment with respect to flesh," that is, concerning the external qualification of physical descent for priests (see the rendering in the RSV and NASV). This change in stipulation is a confirmation of the law as expressed in Psalm 110:1, 4; while human priests were to be from the tribe of Levi, the great priestly-Messiah was to be after the order of Melchizedek. As this was already specified in the Older Testament, and since it deals with the ceremonial law, Hebrews 7:12 does not alter the present thesis.

John 1:17. This verse has been used at times to justify a termination of responsibility to the law after the advent of Christ. Those who argue this way see an absolute antithesis between Moses, who brings law, and Christ, who brings grace and truth. Closer examination shows this contrast to be erroneous. We have already seen that *grace* was an unmistakable element of the Older Testament and Mosaic period, and certainly *truth* was present in the Mosaic era. Law and grace-truth simply

---

[6] See F. F. Bruce's discussion of Acts 21 in his *Commentary on the Book of the Acts* (Grand Rapids: William B. Eerdmans Publishing Co., 1954).

cannot be viewed as compartmentalized counterpoints in the periods before and after Christ respectively. The proper contrast in John 1:17 is not between law and grace-truth, but between "given through" and "realized." The law was given through Moses (was not his own), but grace and truth were realized through Jesus Christ (they are his own personal, essential perfections: John 1:14). The law and Christ manifest God; the former indirectly, and the latter directly. In the same verse which says that Christ was full of grace and truth (John 1:14), it is also said that He *tabernacled* among us. We do well to remember that, just as the law was preserved in the Older Testamental tabernacle (Deut. 10:2-5), so also the Messiah preserved the law in His life and person (as Ps. 40:7 f. said that He would). Therefore, just as *grace* and *truth* were present in the age *before* Christ, so *law* remains in the age *following* Christ.

Luke 16:16. It is not immediately clear why the statement, "The law and prophets were, until John, since then the kingdom gospel is proclaimed," should be used to nullify one's responsibility to God's law. This simply tells us that the period of the Older Testament is now being followed with the New; the kingdom has superseded the time of expectation (the Older Testamental era). The age of the law and prophets is past; the age of the Son (and its fuller revelation) is here to stay (cf. Heb. 8:13; 1:3). In context this verse certainly cannot teach the termination of the law's validity, for verse 17 following declares that "it is easier for heaven and earth to pass away than for one stroke of the law to fail" (i.e., become invalid, come to an end; πίπτω is used here as it is in 1 Cor. 13:8, where it is said that, in contrast to other things, love never *ceases)*. The law and prophets were until John, yes, but the law will still never cease! (cf. Matt. 5:18 with Luke 16:17).

Mark 7:1-23 (cf. Matt. 15:1-20). This passage hardly needs comment. It could only be made to appear contradictory to the thesis of this treatise if wrenched from its context. This passage deals with the *tradition of the elders*, and not the written Older Testamental law (see Mark 7:3, 5, 7, 8, 9, 13; Matt. 15:2, 3, 6, 9). The main subject is eating with unwashed hands, not dietary prescription. Mark 7:19 is a parenthetical comment made in *retrospect;* it does not indicate the didactic intention of Christ *when He spoke* the words of this text, for His intention was to show that defilement is from the heart (not the stomach). Peter, who narrated the gospel for Mark's writing, has reflected his experience in Acts 10 (the dream which taught him that no longer is any meat unclean) back into this earlier gospel story. (Note that, *Matthew* does not include the parenthetical comment about all foods being declared clean—even though he *may* have followed the skeletal pattern of Mark's gospel in writing his own, thus consciously passing over Peter's *inference* in order to narrate the simple history of this encounter with the Pharisees.) Similar Petrine touches are discernable elsewhere in Mark's gospel. Finally, it is noted that the parenthetical inference of Mark 7:19 deals with the ritualistic law; hence this thesis suffers nothing in admitting that the ceremonies are no longer useful after Christ. The abiding validity of the *moral* law is our concern here.

The Sabbath. The Sabbath is a creation ordinance (Gen. 2:2, 3) which men were obligated to observe even *before* the coming of the Mosaic law.[7] Compare Exodus 20:10, 11 for its interpretation of Genesis 2:2, 3. *All* men are subject to the Sabbath law (note that Christ does *not* say that the Sabbath was made for *Israelites* in Mark 2:27, but for generic "man"). Man's moral obligation to Sabbath observance is placed right along side the nine other universally moral words of the Decalogue, which was written by the very finger of God. When man observes the Sabbath he is rightly imitating his Creator; the Sabbath rest is patterned after the creation rest of God. In the era of the New Covenant this creation rest becomes a sign of the Christian hope, his heavenly rest at the consummation of this age (Heb. 4). In the beginning God established His rest; Christ provides for and promises entrance to this rest, and in the eternal age we shall enjoy it. The Sabbath has universal extension and perpetual obligation. At the coming of Christ the Sabbath was *purged* of the legalistic accretions brought by the scribes and Pharisees (Luke 13:10-17; 14:1-6; Mark 3:1-6); the Sabbath had suffered corruption at the hands of the "autonomous"

---

[7] John Murray, *Principles of Conduct: Aspects of Biblical Ethics* (Grand Rapids: William B. Eerdmans Publishing Co., 1957), pp. 30-35.

Pharisees just as numerous other moral precepts had (cf. Matt. 5:21-48). Moreover, the *ceremonial and sacrificial aspects* of the Older Testamental cycle of feast days ("new moon, sabbath year, Jubilee, etc."), along with those cyclic observances of feasts, were "put out of gear" by Christ's work of redemption. Hence Colossians 2:16 f. looses us from the ceremonial elements of the sabbath system (the passage seems to be referring specifically to feast *offerings*),[8] and passages such as Romans 14:5 f. and Galatians 4:10 teach that we need not distinguish these ceremonial days any longer (as the Judaizers were apt to require).[9] As Christ provides for entrance to the eternal Sabbath rest of God by His substitutionary death upon the cross, He makes the typological elements (e.g., offerings) of the Sabbath system irrelevant (things which were a *shadow* of the coming substance according to Col. 2:17; cf. Heb. 10:1, 8). By accomplishing our redemption Christ also binds us to the observance of that weekly Sabbath which prefigures our eternal Sabbath (cf. Heb. 4).

Although ceremonial days are no longer to be distinguished, the New Testament does distinguish the *first* day of the week from the other six (1 Cor. 16:2; Acts 20:7) and denominates it "the Lord's Day" (Rev. 1:20). In observing the weekly Sabbath we honor Christ who is the "Lord" of the Sabbath (Mark 2:28), and we anticipate the coming Sabbath rest which our Lord has secured for us (in this, parallels can be seen with the "Lord's Supper"). In Mark 2:23-28, Christ and His disciples are accused of "doing what is not lawful" on the Sabbath, but

---

[8] Since one's interpretation of Colossians 2:16 must take account of "meat and drink" as well as the days mentioned, and since the dietary restrictions of the ceremonial law did not include "drink," it is best to see them as the *offerings* made on *special days* (feast days, new moons, and sabbaths)—just as the Older Testament correlates such offerings with these particular days (cf. Num. 28-29; 1 Chron. 23:31; 2 Chron. 31:2-3).

[9] That these verses do *not* mean that the Christian is under no obligation to distinguish *any* day from another is clear from John 20:19, 26; Acts 20:6-7; 1 Cor. 16:1-2; Heb. 4:9 with 10:25. Those who hold to absolutely no distinction of days and a completely internalized and individualized observance of any make Scripture to contradict itself.

because they had only violated a rabbinical tradition Christ does not bother to contest the accusation; it simply amounted to nothing. There was no contest, for Christ did not recognize the traditions of the elders as "lawful." However, Christ does take this as an opportunity to assert that He is "Lord even of the Sabbath." Thereby Christ definitely and positively confirmed the Sabbath; otherwise Christ would be grandly proclaiming His lordship over something which was nonexistent. The Sabbath did not pass away with Christ's advent or Messianic work; until our eternal rest the weekly Sabbath continues to be "lorded" by Christ and is a type of the coming reality. "The Sabbath was made for man" (Mark 2:27), and man still needs the benefit of it. The issue of the Sabbath poses no contradiction to the abiding validity of God's moral law.

The Penalty for Adultery. Reference should be made here to the treatment of the second and third antitheses of Matthew 5 earlier in this treatise as well as the later chapter on penology.

The Woman Taken in Adultery. The primary thing that must be said about John 7:53-8:11 is that it is of very doubtful authenticity. It is omitted by the majority of ancient Greek manuscripts and by the oldest representatives of every kind of evidence; notable witnesses against its inclusion in John's gospel are p^{66}, p^{75}, B, א, Θ, uncials N and W, and several codices and early Fathers. Several manuscripts of those which include this passage bear asterisks or obelisks, indicating some doubt about the passage. It appears in at least three other positions: after Luke 21:38, after John 7:36, and after John 21:24. The passage itself contains large numbers of variant readings, its style is not characteristically Johannine, and even stichometric information about John's gospel implies its absence. Every line of thought casts grave doubt upon the authenticity, and hence authority, of the passage. Hence this thesis is not seriously responsible to account for John 7:53-8:11. However, *even if* this passage be accounted as part of the infallible autograph of John's gospel, rather than weakening the present thesis, it strongly confirms it! Christ demands that the very *details* of the Mosaic law be followed in John 8:7. The Pharisees who brought the adulteress before

Jesus were more concerned with trapping Jesus in a statutory dilemma than in the sanctity of God's moral law; they intended to trap Him between upholding the Older Testamental law and submitting to Roman law which reserved for itself the sole right to inflict the death penalty. However, the scribes were the ones who ended up being caught by their own woeful ignorance of God's law. They came to test Jesus, but as elsewhere, *they* failed to know the law. God requires, in conviction for capital crimes, that the witnesses who bring the accusation against a person be innocent of that very same crime (Deut. 19:15); furthermore, the law specified that in the event of capital punishment the accusers had to cast the first stones (Deut. 17:7). Christ was merely enforcing the precise demands of God's holy law in John 8: 7; the one who was without sin should cast the first stone, Ὁ ἀναμάρτητος ("one who has not sinned") might possibly be taken as a reference to God (The Sinless One) or to any human executor that happened to be free from all sin; however, both of these interpretations are impossible. Christ is not saying that the only person who can execute a violator of a capital crime is one who has no sin whatsoever, for this would contradict Romans 13:4 (which, when written, applied to sinful Rome and its debauched emperors). And a reference to God casting a stone in order to punish a sinner in this passage would be absurd and irrelevant to the situation. Ὁ ἀναμάρτητος refers to one who has not committed the *particular* sin of adultery; the word is used to denote innocence of an individual type of sin (rather than *all* sin) in extra-biblical literature (e.g., 2 Macc. 12:42, where Judas prays that his men be kept free from particular sin after discovering that slain soldiers had been specifically unlawful by wearing idolatrous tokens). The woman's accusers, then, either were not witnesses or were not free of adultery; hence Christ dismisses her with the admonition to sin no more. The law protects the rights of accused individuals and demands that the case against them be solid and legal before they are deprived of their lives. John 7:53-8:11, even if authentic, does not support the relaxing of the details of God's law; it harmonizes with Christ's words in Matthew 5:17 f. to the effect that every jot and tittle of God's law remain valid until the end of the world.

Therefore, we now see that those passages and subjects which are most commonly appealed to in order to nullify the Christian's responsibility to the law of God disparage the law's validity *in appearance only.* What Christ asserted in Matthew 5:17-20 is not contradicted elsewhere in the New Testament. God's truth is *one.*

Chapter 11

THEONOMY AND GRACE, FAITH, LOVE

IT is an unfortunate sign of current-day confusion in theology that the principle of law is set forth as antagonistic to the principles of grace, faith, and love (witness the writings of most liberals and dispensationalists): salvation by grace is made out to exclude sanctification according to the law, faith is portrayed as the antithesis of Christian obedience, and love is used to suppress the demands of law. Unless we are prepared to see in God an inner dialectical tension, or unless we are prepared to deny His immutability, we must hold that the law which God authored and which reflects His moral character is perfectly harmonious with the grace He sovereignly administers, the faith which He gives as a gift, and the love which He embodies. God's authoritative word makes the point vivid and emphatic that grace, faith, and love are not at odds with God's law; in fact, they *require* obedience to it.

Grace and Law

Although two systems of justification, one based on law works and one rooted in God's grace, can be hostile to each other, nevertheless grace and law in their appropriate places are not contrary to each other. Paul does not consider it inconsistent to exhort the Christian to put on the *full* armor of God, which includes, among other things, exercising faith *and* public righteousness (Eph. 6:10-18). In Ephesians 2:8-10 Paul declares that we are saved by grace through faith, yet *unto* good works. May it never be that we see grace nullifying obligation to God's law (Rom. 3:31)! To follow Scripture is to see them as *correlative* to each other; God's grace is lawful, and His law is gracious. Paul teaches in Romans that the law promotes the fulfillment of the promise (5:20 f.) and that grace fulfills and establishes the law (3:31; 8:3 f.). The two support each other.

In granting favor to His covenant people God never violates His own holy nature or overturns His law; consequently, Paul can say that God is both *just* (lawful) and the *justifier* (gracious) of the one who has saving faith in Christ (Rom. 3:26). The law represents the holy behavior God requires of man, and when man transgresses that law, salvation is accomplished not by a capricious fiat, but by the substitutionary atonement by the perfectly *obedient* Son of God and *in accord* with the law's penal demands; the Saviour sends the Advocate into the believing church, and this Holy Spirit sanctifies God's redeemed people according to the law in order that they behave as God originally desired. Christ in His redemptive work is the grandest example of the amity that exists between law and grace; the Spirit who is graciously sent to bring new life is the power of obedience to the law. The grace of God works in accordance with, and toward the fulfillment of, the law; yet the law promotes the ends of grace and is itself an expression of God's grace.

To be the *creature* of the sovereign *Creator* directly implies the necessity of obedience; hence, for God to require obedience of man, that is, to be man's Creator (even before the fall into sin) is an expression of undeserved favor. Man could not require God to create him to enjoy God's fellowship; it is God's lovingkindness that brings man into a position which by its very nature requires obedience.

God could have justly left man in utter darkness and confusion after the fall into sin, but instead of abandoning man to moral chaos He mercifully reveals His law for right direction; the moral calamity caused by sin in its most dreadful extents has been postponed until the judgment and punishment of eternal hell. The law, both *prior* to and *after* the fall, is gracious. *Subsequent* to *salvation* the law shows us how to *respond* to God's grace and love.

Observing that God came from Sinai with a fiery law, Moses says that *indeed* God *loves* the people; the law with which Moses charged the people is a blessed inheritance (Deut. 33:2-4). The law has as its *weightier* matters mercy and faith (Matt. 23:23). Psalm 25:8-10 tells us that, because the Lord is good and upright, He instructs sinners in the way of justice, and these paths are lovingkindness and truth. The law is seen by the inspired Psalmist as an expression of God's grace; therefore, he says "At midnight I shall rise to give thanks to Thee because of Thy righteous ordinances. . . . The earth is full of Thy lovingkindness, O Lord; teach me Thy statutes" (Ps. 119:62, 64, NASV). The law is not the grievous burden that so many make it out to be in this day (1 John 5:3); it should be the delight of every believer saved by grace. All those who have been redeemed by God's mercy should be able to pray, as did the Psalmist, "*Graciously* grant me Thy *law*," (Ps. 119:29).

Law and grace are *correlative* to each other; the law is a manifestation of God's grace to His covenant people, and God's grace reigns in accord with His law, endorsing and promoting obedience. Both law and grace magnify and point us to the supremacy of God; they both have as their goal the personal righteousness which God requires of His creature and which reflects His holiness.

Because the believer is renewed in the image of His Creator (Col. 3:10) by God's redemptive grace (Titus 3:5), he must strive to reproduce his Creator's attributes on a creaturely level (cf. Jer. 9:24; John 17:26; Titus 2:10; 1 Peter 2:9). The moral attributes of God and creaturely reflection of God's righteousness are revealed in the law of God (see discussion above). The object of regeneration is obedience to God's law: "And I shall put a new heart within them . . . that they may walk in My statutes and keep My ordinances, and do them" (Ezek. 11:19 f.; cf. 36:26 f.). In his chapter on "The Life of the Christian Man" in the *Institutes,* Calvin says right at the start,

> The object of regeneration . . . is to manifest in the life of believers a harmony and agreement between God's righteousness and their obedience, and thus to confirm the adoption that they have received as sons (Galatians 4:5; cf. 2 Peter 1:10). The law of God contains in itself that newness by which his image can be restored in us.[1]

---

[1] Ford Lewis Battles (trans.), *Calvin: The Institutes of the Christian Religion*, ed. John T. McNeill, The Library of Christian Classics, Vol. XX. eds., John Baillie, John T. McNeill, and Henry P. Van Dusen (Philadelphia: The Westminster Press, 1967), Book III, chap. VI, section 1, p. 684.

The Heidelberg Catechism appropriately states that genuine repentance and conversion will effect obedience to God's law:

> Question 88: In how many things does true repentance or conversion consist? (Answer) In two things: the dying of the old man, and the quickening of the new.
>
> Question 89: What is the dying of the old man? (Answer) Heartfelt sorrow for sin; causing us to hate and turn from it always more and more.
>
> Question 90: What is the quickening of the new man? (Answer) Heartfelt joy in God; causing us to take delight in living according to the will of God in all good works.
>
> Question 91: But what are good works? (Answer) Those only which are done from true faith, according to the law of God, for his glory; and not such as rest on our own opinion or the commandments of man.[2]

Although awareness that the habitual practice of sin leads to spiritual death (1 John 3) promotes obedience in the Christian's life, his strongest motives for keeping the law are (1) *grateful love* to the Author of the law for His gracious salvation and (2) the subsequent desire to *glorify* His name. The man who has experienced God's gracious regeneration, who has been renewed in his Creator's image, who has responded to God's grace with genuine repentance, will have an overwhelming desire to please his Lord by meticulous observance of the law. Herein man glorifies God and enjoys Him forever.

Those liberal and dispensational interpreters who are prone to pit law against grace in the Christian life imprudently fail to notice

---

[2] *The Creeds of Christendom,* ed. Philip Schaff (Grand Rapids: Baker Book House, originally 1877), vol. III, pp. 339 f.

when they read the Older Testament that the *law primarily and functionally rests on the foundation of grace* [3] as the principle of the covenant between God and His chosen people (cf. Ex. 20:2 and 2:24-25). The law is detailed as part of a gracious covenant which is enacted following God's mighty work of redemption for His people, and (as we noted previously) holiness must be the character of any covenant relationship with God. Grace requires lawful obedience. The meaning of the commandments is redemption and sanctification (Deut. 6:20-25); hence lack of obedience is identical with forgetting God and His redemption (Deut. 8:11-17). Exhortation to law-keeping is based on first-hand experience of God's great acts of redemption and judgment (Deut. 7: 10 f.), and the enabled obedience to God's law follows His monergistic and gracious circumcision of the heart (Deut. 30:6-8). Based on God's sovereign personality and His redemption of us we owe Him obedience to His law: "I am the Lord your God who brought you out from the land of Egypt; you shall thus observe all My statutes, and all My ordinances, and do them; I am the Lord" (Lev. 19:36 f.; cf. Deut. 10:12-22; Ps. 105:37-45). The Psalmist requests that he be taught God's law *because* God has graciously saved him: "Make me know Thy ways, O Lord; teach me Thy paths. Lead me in Thy truth and teach me, for Thou art the God of my salvation" (Ps. 25:4 f.). In Psalm 103 David greatly magnifies and extols the mercy and gracious forgiveness of God and appropriately ends on the note of obedience to God's precepts: "Bless the Lord, O my soul, and forget none of His benefits; who pardons all your iniquities. . . . The Lord is compassionate and gracious, abounding in lovingkindness . . . the lovingkindness of the Lord is from everlasting to everlasting on those who fear Him . . . to those who keep His covenant and who remember His precepts to do them." Listen to this cantata from Psalm 119, which evidences that obedience follows grace:

[3] Recall that earlier we *correspondingly* argued that God's *gracious* atonement is according to the dictates of His *law*.

> Deal bountifully with Thy servant that I may live and keep Thy word. . . . Revive me according to Thy lovingkindness so that I may keep the testimony of Thy mouth. . . . Redeem me. . . . that I may keep Thy precepts. . . . save me and I shall keep Thy testimonies. . . . Great are Thy mercies, O Lord; revive me according to Thine ordinances. . . . I hope for Thy salvation, O Lord, and do Thy commandments. . . . I long for Thy salvation, O Lord, and Thy law is my delight (vv. 17, 88, 134, 146, 156, 166, 174, NASV).

The *law* has as one of its purposes to have *confidence* put in God, which shall be followed by sanctified *obedience* (Ps. 78:1, 5-7); and although God's covenant is *gracious,* it nonetheless demands *obedience* (Jer. 11:4).

Law promotes grace, and grace encourages obedience. The *law* is normative for those saved by grace (Rom. 8:4). Paul turns back the intolerable inference of antinomianism in the name of grace, telling us that we must be servants of obedience and righteousness because being under grace gives no license to sinful transgression of the law, but rather the power and desire to obey the law (Rom. 6:15-7:6). However, to miss the provision of *grace* makes one's attempted obedience to the law ignorant and unlawful (Rom. 10:2 f.). That God's mercy is no warrant for lawlessness is vividly and dramatically set forth by Paul in Titus 2:11-14; therein he says that *it is grace itself which directs us to live righteously and godly:* "For the grace of God has appeared to all men, bringing salvation, instructing us to deny ungodliness and worldly desires and to live sensibly, righteously and godly in the present age" and looking for the appearance of Christ who "redeemed us from every lawless deed. . . ." (NASV). It is not in some future age that we are to pursue obedience to God's law, but right now; and God's saving *grace* is that which declares this to us! Grace demands lawful obedience. Calvin comments upon this passage in Titus,

> God's grace should itself instruct us to order our lives aright. Some are quick to turn the preaching of God's mercy into an

> excuse for licentiousness, while carelessness keeps others from thinking about the renewal of their life. But the revelation of God's grace necessarily brings with it exhortations to a godly life. . . . In God's Law there is complete perfection to which nothing else can ever be added.[4]

We see, therefore, that Scripture teaches that God's grace is not antagonistic to His law. Grace and law are correlative to each other and support one another; God's law is gracious, and His grace is lawful. Just as grace *demands,* regeneration gives the *power* and *desire,* that we be obedient to God's law. "Do we then nullify the law through faith? May it never be! On the contrary, we establish the law" (Rom. 3:31, NASV). There is no scriptural basis for seeing a contradiction between God's law and God's grace. The biblical Christian who is saved by grace through faith will be earnest in his attempt to keep, as well as in his promoting of obedience to, the law of God.

Faith and Law

It should be perfectly clear that just as God's grace does not depreciate our obligation to God's law, neither does our saving faith. Faith establishes the law of God rather than voiding it (Rom. 3:31). The faith which is the instrument of our salvation from lawlessness and the guilt of moral rebellion can certainly not be ethically indifferent. Paul makes it clear in Galatians 5:6 that faith is not adverse to "working," and James hammers home the truth that "faith without works is dead" (James 2:26; cf. Deut. 8:2; 13:3 f. for the test of inner reverence).

This same viewpoint is expressed in the Older Testament; faith was to be followed by obedience and working. "Trust in the Lord and do good" (Ps. 37:3, NASV); "He who confesses his transgressions *and forsakes them* will find compassion" (Prov. 28:13; cf. Ezek. 18:30 f.). Whereas a "faith" which is not accompanied by the works of the law is

---

[4] *Second Epistle of Paul the Apostle to the Corinthians* et. al., *op. cit.*, p. 373.

useless and cannot save a person, faith which results in the works of the law is attested, perfected, and powerful to justify (James 2:14-26).

Faith is *not merely* the inner rehearsal of an assertion; if it does not also have an *accompanying disposition* to behave in accord with that assertion's truth, then it is nongenuine (insincere). Acting contrary to what we profess is evidence of hypocrisy in most cases. Obedience is implicit in faith; to believe an assertion one must know what the assertion means (i.e., its intention and proper application) and be disposed to act accordingly. To have faith in someone (i.e., to trust) is to heed his advice and direction; disobedience would be a sign that we had not truly entrusted ourselves to that person's care. Consequently, to trust in Christ (to have saving faith) necessarily binds one to the keeping of Christ's words and commandments.

Thus faith necessitates obedience to God's law. This fact is well understood in the Belgic and Westminster Confessions. Article XXIV in the Belgic Confession says:

> Therefore it is impossible that this holy faith can be unfruitful in man: for we do not speak of a vain faith, but of such a faith as is called in Scripture a faith that worketh by love, which excites man to the practice of those works which God has commanded in his Word.[5]

The clarion word of the Westminster Confession of Faith, chapter XVI ("Of Good Works"), section II is that "good works, done in obedience to God's commandments, are the fruits and evidences of a true and lively faith" and as such manifest thanks, strengthen assurance, edify, adorn profession, stop adversaries, and glorify God. Faith is not antithetical to obedience in the Christian life; rather it *impels* one to keep the law. The wise words of Dr. Machen should be seriously regarded:

---

[5] *Creeds*, p. 411.

> But it is quite inconceivable that a man should be given this faith in Christ, that he should accept this gift which Christ offers, and still go on contentedly in sin. For the very thing which Christ offers us is salvation from sin—not only salvation from the guilt of sin, but also salvation from the power of sin. The very first thing that the Christian does, therefore, is to keep the law of God . . . he keeps it joyously as a central part of salvation itself.[6]

The way to happiness in the Christian life, as the popular hymn puts it, is to "*trust and obey.*"

Love and Law

Whereas grace and faith necessitate obedience to God's law, love is *identical* with lawful obedience. Christian love, as biblically defined, is so totally unopposed to God's law that this law is actually the pattern and content of love. Believers are commanded to be like *God* (Matt. 5:48); God is love (1 John 4:8), and the commandments reflect God's moral perfection. Therefore, love and law must go hand in hand; to be loving as is God is to keep the commandments which transcribe God's holiness. Christian love is first love to God (Mark 12:29) and, therefore, love of *rectitude;* hence love's demands must never be taken by the Christian to abrogate the demands of rectitude which God's law contains.

Obedience to the commandments is the *test* of genuine love to Christ. Our Lord clearly states that if we love Him we are to keep His commandments; obedience to His commandments evidences our love for Him (John 14:15, 21, 23). The wise man and the brother of Christ is the one who does His word (Matt. 7:21 ff.; Luke 8:21). Abiding in Christ's love is dependent upon keeping His commandments (John 15:9 f.). The one who does not do whatsoever Christ commands him is

---

[6] Machen, *What is Faith?* (Grand Rapids: Wm. B. Eerdmans, 1925), p. 204.

not the friend of Christ, and if he claims to know Christ he is a liar (John 15:14; 1 John 2:4).

The theme of the Book of the Law is *also:* "If you love Me, keep My commandments." Deuteronomy 6:4-6 says that because the Lord is our God we must love *and* obey Him; God keeps His covenant and lovingkindness with those who love as well as obey Him (Deut. 7:9). God's covenant people are *commanded* to *both* love God and obey His commandments (Deut. 11:1). In Deuteronomy love for God is placed in apposition to keeping His law (e.g., 11:13, 22), and love is always closely related to obedience (e.g., 13:3 f.; 19:9). Moses concludes the heralding of God's law with these words: "I command you today to love the Lord your God, to walk in His ways and to keep His commandments and His statutes and His judgments, that you may live and multiply, and that the Lord your God may bless you" (Deut. 30:16, NASV).

Thus love and law sustain the same relationship to each other in both the Older and New Testaments. According to 1 Corinthians 13:8 and Luke 16:17, love and law are *equally* permanent; neither one shall cease or fail. Indeed, love is the *fruit* of that eternal *Spirit* who *fulfills* the law in us (cf. Gal. 5:22 with Rom. 8:4).

In Romans 13:8-10 Paul teaches that love does not replace, dispense with, or depreciate the law; on the contrary, love grants the law its full required measure. Love and law are mutually inclusive; Paul sees no incompatibility between them. In fact, the Older Testamental law is the norm for love's activity; the law shows one *how* to love his neighbor. Love is the *summation* or *recapitulation* of the law. This is parallel to what Christ taught in Matthew 22:37-40; the whole law hangs on the commands of radical love to God and neighbor. There is *no commandment* which is greater in its extension than *these* (Mark 12:31), and God's Older Testamental law was exceeding broad (Ps. 119:96). Love enforces the full details of God's law.

Here is one of the strongest affirmations of the abiding relevance and validity of God's law. It is *summarized* in love, and love is the Christian's *perpetual duty*. Certainly a summary does not nullify the *contents* of that which it summarizes! The law of God is the standard of Christian love, so that one who does not follow the law can never be said to love. According to Scripture the criterion of love to the *brethren* is observance of God's commandments, just as loving *God* means keeping His law. "By this we know that we love the children of God, when we love God and observe His commandments. For this is the love of God, that we keep His commandments" (1 John 5:2 f., NASV). The law is the confirmation and perfect expression of true love. Love cannot generate moral direction for life when taken by itself; men live by radically different ethical standards when allegedly under the sole guidance of "love." Ethical chaos and situational morality are inevitable when love is taken as a moral arbiter. The word of God tells us that *genuine love* is the keeping of God's law. Love and law are inseparable.

As explained by Jesus, love entails a totalitarian and all-embracing surrender to God (cf. Matt. 6:24; 10:37); as such it *corresponds* to the demand of radical obedience and service to God contained in the statutes of the law of God. The radicalism of Jesus' commandments, as concrete applications of the Older Testamental law, is identical with the radicalism of love as self-surrender and perfect willingness to serve God.

> This also implies that love is not a law unto itself. Love is the prerequisite and the root of the fulfillment of the law. But it is directed and guided by the divine law as the expression of God's will.[7]

Ridderbos also says about such passages as Romans 8:3 f.; 13:8, 10; 1 Corinthians 9:21; Galatians 5:14; 6:2,

> Some writers have endeavored to bring these passages into agreement with the exclusively negative view of the law by

[7] Herman Ridderbos, *The Coming of the Kingdom,* trans. H. de Jongste, ed. Raymond O. Zorn (Philadelphia: The Presbyterian and Reformed Publishing Co., 1962 reprinted 1969), p. 329.

> saying that love as the fulfillment of the law also makes the law superfluous. This is, however, clearly an argument resulting from embarrassment. Paul does not describe love as the termination of the law, nor does he assert that love makes the law superfluous. He speaks of love as the fulfillment of the law, a fulfillment which is demanded from the believer and which supposes the continuous commandment of the law. . . . The weight of Romans 13:8-10 and Galatians 5:14 is unmistakable. The love mentioned in these passages does not function in Paul's epistles as a new Christian ideal which replaces the law; rather, it is in fact the fulfillment of the law. It is also untrue that the law henceforth finds its criterion in love; rather the contrary: that which the demand of love implies and which makes this demand so imperative is to be found in the law.[8]

To hold that an inner moral disposition or the emotion of love is the compass of ethics has affinity with the philosophy of Hume or Ayer, not with the theology of Jesus and Paul. The law of God is the guide of love; the Bible knows no other understanding of love. Love is not autonomous; it is not a self-law. If it were autonomous, love would be identical in character with sin (cf. 1 John 3:4). When man becomes a law unto himself, then he rebels against the law of God; sin is essentially autonomy. Hence it is totally improper for a Christian to hold to any view of love which finally reduces to inner direction based on feeling, intuition, or emotion. Love is not autonomous because love is not sinful—"love is from God" (1 John 4:7). Following a survey and discussion of the relevant scriptural texts, John Murray concludes:

> When we examine the witness of the Scripture itself as to the origin of the canons of behavior which the Scripture approves,

[8] Herman N. Ridderbos, *When the Time Had Fully Come: Studies in New Testament Theology* (Grand Rapids: William B. Eerdmans Publishing Co., 1957), p. 74.

> we do not find that love is allowed to discover or dictate its own standards or patterns of conduct. We do not find that the renewed heart is allowed spontaneously to excogitate the ethic of the saints of God. We do not find that love is conceived of as an autonomous, self-acting agency which of itself, apart from any extraneous prescription or regulation, defines its own norms of behavior. We do find that, from the beginning, there are objectively revealed precepts, institutions, commandments which are the norms and channels of human behavior. Even man in his innocence was not permitted to carve for himself the path of life; it was charted for him from the outset.[9]

We cannot avoid seeing that the content and method of love is obedience to God's commandments. It should be obvious that a person cannot really "love" his neighbors to such a degree that he steals from them or commits adultery with their wives! For the Christian to do so (or to break any other stipulation in God's law) in the name of "love" would be a monstrous deception, for *love is not an outlaw.* "This is love, that we should walk according to His commandments" (2 John 6). The mark of our Christian faith is a brotherly love which is distinctive (John 13:35). It is distinctive because its guidelines are not *personal disposition;* while the world maintains a characterless "love" based on emotion, Christian love is guided by standards delivered from God and reflecting His character. Christian love involves the whole man (all your heart, soul, might, and mind: Deut. 6:5; Matt. 22:37). Christian love is distinctive because it does not *undercut* ethics. Because acts of Christian love are guided by godly morality, they support ethical living rather than altering moral standards and making situational ethics inevitable, as dispositional love does. Christian love is distinctive because its practical applications are not merely condescending, but embody

---

[9] John Murray, *Principles of Conduct: Aspects of Biblical Ethics* (Grand Rapids: William B. Eerdmans Publishing Co., 1957), p. 24.

discipline and *justice* for all. The dispositional and emotional love of the world is at best sympathy and at worst pity, but Christian love is therapeutic, guaranteeing the welfare of its recipient (see Josh. 1:7 f.; the Lord's statutes are commanded for His people's good, Deut. 10:13). What is true of our love to the Christian brethren is true also of our love for God: it demands lawful obedience.

The love of a son of God for his heavenly Father must be characterized by obedience. If our Lord, the unique Son of God, Himself loved the Father by obeying His commands (John 12:49; 14:31), how much more should we? Christ makes this very point in John 15:9 f. In Mark 3:35 He says that the one who does God's will is His brother (an adopted son of God). And just as a home is judged by the obedience of its children, 1 John 3:1 tells us that we manifest whose children we are by our righteous behavior. It is not surprising, therefore, that Scripture continually correlates and unites love with law (e.g., Deut. 5:10; 7:9; 10:12; 11:1; Josh. 22:5; Matt. 22:36 ff.; Mark 12:29 ff.; John 14:15 ff.; 1 John 2:5; 5:3). All believers are unified and fellowship together in a common life-style of loving obedience to God's law.

God's commandments must be taken by the Christian as his guide to genuine love. Any "love" which is based on inner disposition or which leads to the destruction of, or indifference to, godly morality is a monstrous and fraudulent substitute for Christian love which, in emulation of our Lord Jesus Christ, operates according to God's commandments. God's love is loving, and our love is to be lawful. Love is not an outlaw for the Christian, but the very fulfilling of the law by obedience to its every detail.

We must conclude, then, that the persistent witness of God's word is that the principles of grace, faith, and love are confirmations of the continual obligation the Christian has to meticulous observance of God's law. Grace is lawful and results in obedience to the law; faith establishes the law; and love is identical with keeping God's commandments. The God whom we love because He saved us by His grace and granted us faith as a gift makes an absolute demand upon us. The radical nature of God's demand upon our lives is seen in that it cannot be questioned (cf. James 4:11), it surpasses all other loyalties (James 1:8; 4:8; Matt. 6:22 f.), and it covers every area of life (1 Peter 4:10 f.; Col. 3:17; 1 Cor. 10:31; 2 Cor. 10:5; Rev. 12:11; 3:15 f.). The greatness of a man's faith and love is, consequently, unquestioning trust and obedience. The absolute demand of God upon our lives is expressed in His law: "And now, Israel, what does the Lord your God require from you, but to fear the Lord your God, to walk in all His ways and love Him, and to serve the Lord your God with all your heart and with all your soul, and to keep the Lord's commandments and His statutes" (Deut. 10: 12 f., NASV). Therefore, to call the law of God into question *under the guise* of grace or faith or love is nothing short of spiritual deception.

V. CONFIRMATION AND SUMMARY OF THE THESIS

Chapter 12

NEW TESTAMENT SUBSTANTIATION OF THE THESIS

Remonstrance to Antinomianism

THE thesis of this treatise finds confirmation throughout the pages of the New Testament. The previous sections of our study have adequately verified the thesis of pro-nomianism already. The thesis was laid out in Matthew 5:17-20; subsequently the law's divine integrity, the centrality of the law in the Messianic atonement, the necessity of the law as the proper pattern of Spiritual sanctification, the complete unity of theonomy between the two covenants, and our obligation to the law as entailed in grace, faith, and love, were all demonstrated. Thus consciousness of the covenant, or of grace, or of the Messiah's example, or of living faith, or of Spiritual sanctification, or of Christian love, or of the law's perfection *should each* be sufficient to bind God's law upon the heart of any genuine believer.

How much more should the believer be constrained to honor and obey God's law when he understands the scriptural *implications* of *all* these things! The very fabric of Christianity is woven throughout with God's law; the Bible never displays lawlessness as fundamental to, or implied by, true and godly religion. Hence any theological system or particular assertion which is *based* on a depreciation of God's law or which *results* in indifference to, or disobedience of, God's law must be viewed as diametrically opposed to the principle and ethic of Christianity of a biblical nature. *Lawlessness* must be reproved from the outset, for the Christian cannot sympathize with *sin*. Therefore, even without the following New Testament evidence, antinomianism must clearly be seen as out of character with scriptural Christianity and its principles;

the foregoing arguments of this treatise have already sufficiently established the abiding validity of God's law and hence, the heretical nature of antinomianism (in both licentious and legalistic forms).

The following considerations go over and above what is requisite to prove the present thesis. Having been scripturally explained and established, the thesis will now be shown to be substantiated as a *recurring* theme throughout the New Testament. Not only does the Bible teach that the believer should obey God's law, it *continually assumes* and *applies* this point.

Relevance of the Law

We find in reading *through* God's revelation that the law is as *unchangeable* as the justice of God which it embraces; God is immutable, and the law as a transcript of His holiness is never modified in its content and validity. It is obvious that the law did not *begin* to have relevance at Mt. Sinai. Murder, dishonesty, homosexuality, hatred, treachery, lying, adultery, etc., are all portrayed with severe disapprobation far *before* the Mosaic period. Consequently we should not *expect* that the law would decrease in its relevance at all due to the *passing* of the Mosaic period. As we read the New Testament we see that in fact the law *did not* lose obligation. The New Testament *never* says that we are *redeemed from the law* or released from its appropriate use and validity; instead, we are redeemed from the *curse* of the law and set free from sin *in order to* keep that law.

Renewed Call to Love

We are never delivered from the obligation to love God and our neighbor, and this love comprehends *the law* (Matt. 22:40; Rom. 13:10). The love commandments which Christ delivered were *summaries* of the law, *not replacements.* Significantly, these summary commands advanced by our Lord were direct *quotations* from the law of the *Older* Testament, and in both instances these citations appeared in contexts which stressed the keeping of *all* God's commandments:

> That thou mightest fear the Lord thy God, to keep all His statutes and His commandments . . . and thou shalt love the Lord thy God with all thine heart, and with all thy soul, and with all thy might. And these words, which I command thee this day shall be in thine heart . . . Ye shall diligently keep the commandments of the Lord your God, and His testimonies, and His statutes, which He hath commanded thee (Deut. 6:2, 5, 6, 17, AV). Ye shall do no unrighteousness in judgment . . . thou shalt love thy neighbor as thyself: I am the Lord. Ye shall keep my statutes (Lev. 19:15, 18 f.).

All men in *all* ages have been obligated to love their Creator by willing obedience to His commandments, and to love their neighbors by securing that esteemed and righteous society purposed in God's law. Meticulous obedience to God's law expresses gratitude for His grace and promotes the welfare of our neighbors; to keep the law is to love God and neighbor because "love is the fulfillment of the law" (Rom. 13:10). No commandment obligates us to *more responsible duty* before God and for neighbor than that of love (Mark 12:31). Love is a *perpetual* moral obligation placed upon men. Thus men are committed to keeping that law code which gives *expression* to genuine love.

Recipients of God's Favor

The coming of the promised Messiah did nothing to alleviate the aforementioned moral propriety and obligation of the divine law. The age of anticipation was superseded by the reign of Christ upon the throne of David (Luke 1:32 f.). Since godly kings of the older age were seriously responsible to the law of God in the exercise of their reign, *how much more* shall the perfect reign of the great King-Messiah be characterized by endorsement and application of God's law! (Heb. 1:8-9).

The various ways in which the law is commended to us as valid are numerous. Many of them have the force of an *implication; as* such they indicate that the presupposition of the law's validity was so strong and obvious that *unexplained* and *unargued* comments about it could *surface* as indications of the underlying theonomic foundation.

For example, in the gospels people are applauded for their lawfulness. Elizabeth and Zacharias were called "righteous before God" seeing that "they blamelessly walked in all the commandments and ordinances of God" (Luke 1:6), and the point is made about righteous Joseph and blessed Mary that they were ones who meticulously followed the law (cf. Luke 2:21-24, 27, 39). Going beyond mere explanation of their deeds and complimenting them, Luke 23:56 indicates that the Galilean women who followed Christ "indeed rested on the sabbath, *according to* the commandment."

The Law Presupposed By Christ

Christ appealed to the law in order to place authority behind His *teaching* (e.g., John 8:17); He said that His teaching was identical with that of the law (Matt. 7:12). Christ also appealed to the law in order to vindicate His *behavior* (see Matt. 12:5 and John 7:23). These appeals indicate the authority of the law. Christ referred men to the law to answer their theological questions (e.g., Luke 10:26 shows Christ answering a question about inheriting eternal life with the loaded words, "What stands written in the law?"). Christ expected men to know the law and to live it; He demonstrated rhetorical surprise at their ignorance of God's demands (e.g., "Haven't you read . . . ?"), and indicted men for breaking the law ("Did not Moses give you the law? And not one of you does the law!" John 7:19). In all this it must be tacitly understood that the law was viewed by our Lord and the writers of the gospels as bearing divine authority.

However, the gospels do not leave us with simple *implications* about the law; they clearly state its continuing normative character. In answer to the (so-called) rich young ruler's question, Christ was in no way obscure in stating, "If you wish to enter into life, then keep the commandments" (Matt. 19:17; cf. 1 John 2:17). Christ taught us to pray that God's will may be done on earth, just as it is followed in heaven.

Obviously this is a prayer that God's *prescriptive* will (which we know to be expressed in the law) be done, for there is *no question* of His *decretive* will being accomplished. The request that God's kingdom be actualized is followed by the facilitating petition that God's will (i.e., law) be done (Matt. 6:10). The kingdom and law-obedience go hand in hand.

A quick look at just the gospel of Mark broadly indicates Christ's endorsement of, and concern for, the law: He sends the leper to follow Mosaic command (1:44), is concerned to defend His own activity as lawful (2:25-28), defines His family in terms of those doing God's will (3:35), is agonized that the Pharisees make the law void by their traditions (7:1-13), answers moral questions by beginning with Mosaic law (10: 3), declares the obedience to law as essential to salvation (10:17 ff.), enforces the law in the temple (11:15-17), and is recognized as a master of the law who can answer interpretative questions concerning it (12:14 ff., 28 ff.).

The Law Applied By Christ

In John 10:35 Jesus affirms that "Scripture cannot be broken." How then could He be viewed as changing or abrogating the law? If the hold of the law is released, then it would certainly seem that Scripture had been "broken." The continuing validity, authority, and truth of Scripture as a *whole* is set forth in this declaration by Christ, and the law is included in that which cannot be broken. Everything written from God always binds man (2 Tim. 3:16 f.).

The Christian's obligation to every jot and tittle of God's law thus cannot be broken; our responsibility clearly extends beyond the Decalogue. So implicit was our Lord's endorsement of even the Older Testamental *case law*, holding it to be *as binding* as the Decalogue itself, that when He quoted from the Decalogue He could casually (and without explanation) insert a particular case law *along with*, and on a par with, the ten laws (see Mark 10:19, where "Do not defraud" from Deut. 24:16 in LXX—v. 14 in English versions—is appropriately adduced in dealing with a rich young ruler and placed on a par with "Do not kill," etc.).

In Matthew 15:3-9 and Mark 7:6-13, Christ strongly rebukes the Pharisees for failing to follow the law of God. He authoritatively quotes from two sections of the law: one from the Decalogue, and one *outside* the Decalogue. It was not simply the fifth commandment that Christ cites as binding, but even the *penal sanction* specifying capital punishment for incorrigible children is held forth by our Lord as an obligation. Christ made no artificial distinction between "moral" laws and their "civil" punishments. Whereas the Pharisees nullified God's law by their traditions, *Christ upholds its integrity and validity in exhaustive detail.* Whereas the Pharisees would easily let a son be released from his obligation to support his parents, Christ endorses the severity and strictness of God's law. The antinomian traditions of men cannot be used to "break" Scripture apart. Christ does not explain away His citation of the prescription of capital punishment for incorrigible children; in fact, He gives absolutely no indication that He feels it *needs* any argument at all. Its validity is simply assumed, and hence it is authoritatively pronounced in unadorned, clear terms. Every word of God, even every word of God's law, is upheld by our Lord; His coming effects no breaking of Scripture, no release from the rigid demands of the law.

That Christ taught the continuing validity of God's law is more than clear when He declares that He shall bring judgment and punishment upon those who commit "lawlessness" (Matt. 7:23; 13:41). We are obviously obligated to keep God's law if disobedience to it brings condemnation. Christ further confirms the obligation we have to the law in that He specifies as integral to the Great Commission the teaching of the nations to observe all that He has commanded (Matt. 28:19 f.); not only must the gospel be effectively preached, but it must be followed up with the exhortation to sanctification in terms of God's law. The Christian being condemned by the law, saved by Christ's obedience to the law, and sanctified by the Spirit in accordance with the law, is to propagate the Christian gospel *in conjunction with* pressing home the demands of God's holy law. Teaching the nations to observe the commandments of God is a definite obligation laid upon the Christian by Christ; if the nations are to be exhorted to obedience, how much more should Christians practice what they preach! (cf. Rom. 2:21). The central role which the law plays in the Christian life extends right from the basis for his guilt and salvation, through his sanctification, into his personal evangelism; the Christian life and God's kingdom are theonomic through and through, as evidenced by both the Lord's prayer ("Thy kingdom come, Thy will be done") and the great commission ("teaching them to observe all things whatsoever I have commanded you").

The gospels, as we have seen, support the abiding validity of God's law in a great variety of ways: by direct teaching, by complimenting obedience, by noting its use to underpin Christ's teaching and vindicate His behavior, by authoritative citation, by expected knowledge of and obedience to it, by prayer for obedience, by direct command to follow it, by judgment based upon it, and by its crucial place in the program of Christian mission. Ridderbos has good reason to say:

> The theonomy of the gospel is subjection to the law, and any attempt to eliminate the category of law from the gospel is frustrated by the continuous and undeniable maintenance of the law by and in the gospel.[1]

Pauline Theonomy

The New Testament writers take a stand along with Jesus *against* the Judaistic distortions of the law and its proper use. There is a profound agreement between the evaluation of the law made by Paul, for instance, and Jesus. Further, the New Testament writers are in complete harmony with the attitude exhibited in the gospels respecting the *obligation* which the follower of Christ has to the law of God. The law is again summarized in the demand of love (Rom. 13:8-10; Gal. 5: 14); the agape demanded of the believer is nothing short of keeping the law (cf. 1 John 5:2 f.; 2 John 6).

---

[1] Herman Ridderbos, *The Coming of the Kingdom,* trans. H. de Jongste, ed. Raymond O. Zorn (Philadelphia: The Presbyterian and Reformed Publishing Co., 1962 reprinted 1969), p. 307.

Paul adamantly opposes the law as a way of justification in the book of Galatians. However, coming to chapter 5, verse 13 ff., he goes on to stress the necessity of an ethical life *in accord with* the law. The abuse of the law is renounced; yet a proper use of it is demanded.

In 1 Corinthians 7:19 Paul clearly states that although circumcision is nothing, law keeping *is* greatly significant (note the strong adversative ἀλλά); what matters is whether one is following the commandments of God, and outside of that matters are indifferent.

Although the believer has been discharged from the law, has been put to death to the law, has died to the law (Rom. 7:4, 6) and is, therefore, *not* "under law" in the sense of *sin's dominion* (Rom. 6:2, 14), and although the believer is *not* under the Mosaic ceremonial economy and its ordinances but rather enjoys the unrestrained privilege and freedom of a Son, nevertheless, there is a sense in which the believer *is* "under law"; he is bound in law to God, and his very relation to Christ demands obedience to God's law.[2] This is the truth expressed by Paul in 1 Corinthians 9:20 f.; he clearly affirms that *he is not without the law of God,* and his Christian liberty does not annul this fact. Paul sees it as imperative that believers imitate the *obedient* attitude of their Lord and Savior (Phil. 2:5-13; cf. 1 Peter 2:21 f.).

Let us be reminded of the discussion of 1 Timothy 1:5-10 above. Paul exhorts Timothy to demonstrate that there is complete agreement between the gospel which he preached and the law—contrary to the commentary of the pseudo-rabbis. When the law is used "lawfully," that is, as it was intended to be used, then it forbids everything opposed to the orthodox, sound teaching of the gospel. Although Paul is not offering a treatise dealing with all the functions of the law, he does elaborate one use of the law which is relevant to his argument with the opponents, a characteristic description of whom is found in Titus 1:10-16. The pseudo-rabbis use the law for idle speculations rather than for the practical use which God intended: restraining and convicting evil. The law is quite obviously not laid down for a righteous

[2] Cf. Murray's discussion of "under law" in *Principles of Conduct: Aspects of Biblical Ethics* (Grand Rapids: William B. Eerdmans Publishing Co., 1957), pp. 183-190.

man, for he does not carry out the desires of a sinful nature and, hence, evidences character, attitudes, and deeds against which no law is needed (see Gal. 5:13 ff.). Paul makes this point for contrast and effect; his assertion is principial. However, "there is none righteous, no not one" (Rom. 3:10). Even Christians have indwelling sin (Rom. 6:20; 7:14-25; 1 John 1:8; 2:1) and have yet to put on incorruption (Phil. 3:21; 1 Cor. 15:54); consequently Christians must purify themselves just as Christ is pure (1 John 3:3), i.e., sinless (1 John 3:5). This purification implies conformity to the righteous standard of the law, for sinlessness demands the practice of the law (1 John 3:4). The believer is righteous in principle alone; he is not yet completely righteous in deed. Hence the New Testament exhorts believers to godly and righteous living; the Christian is not to let sin reign in him but to be an instrument of righteousness (Rom. 6:12 f.), he is to perfect holiness in the fear of God (2 Cor. 7:1; cf. the Westminster Confession of Faith, XIII, with Scripture texts). The law is still needed by the Christian as the pattern of holiness by which he shall conduct himself in the power of the Holy Spirit. The law is good, says Paul, and good men do not need it; but such we are not. The law was laid down for the lawless, rebellious, ungodly, sinful, unholy, or profane; these persons need restraint (socially), conviction of guilt (spiritually), and guidance in the paths of righteousness (subsequent to regeneration and conversion). We who are not yet perfect retain a need for God's law.

In Romans 12:1 f. Paul exhorts the Christian to approve God's will, that is, His law ("the good, the well-pleasing, the perfect"; cf. Rom. 7:12). In verse 9 of the same chapter Paul exhorts the believer to "abhor evil, cleave to *the good*"; it is God's law which defines both. The same exhortation, with its implied reference to God's holy law, is found numerous times in Paul. Christians are to reprove the works of darkness (Eph. 5:11), the man of God is to follow after righteousness and godliness (1 Tim. 6:11 f.), every Christian is to depart from iniquity (2 Tim. 2:19; cf. 1 John 3:4), to keep the charge of pursuing righteousness and godliness (1 Tim. 6:14). We have seen previously that it is the law of God which shows us righteousness and godliness on a creaturely level. In Ephesians 5:17 Paul exhorts his readers not to be foolish, but to understand the Lord's will (i.e., be wise). Proverbs 10:8 complements this by telling us that the wise of heart will heed commandments.

Just as in the case of Jesus, Paul's endorsement of the law extends *beyond* the Decalogue. Even the *case law* of the Older Testament is authoritative for Paul (so much so that he can extend its application; cf. 2 Cor. 6:14 with Deut. 22:10). He can cite it as binding upon his readers, as in 1 Corinthians 9:8 f. Elsewhere, Paul places this same quotation from Deuteronomy 25:4 side by side, and on a par with, a quotation from Matthew 10:10 when instructing Timothy (1 Tim. 5:18). What is remarkable here, for our purposes, is that Paul offers no explanation for his relying upon the Older Testamental case law—as if it were an *exception* to some rule. It is simply, silently, and forcefully, assumed that the law of God, even its jots and tittles, has contemporary obligation and value in the New Testament age. Every word which proceeds from God's mouth, whether in the gospels of the New Testament or in the case law of the Older Testament, binds the behavior of God's people.

The law is valid (indeed the whole of it) as Paul demonstrates and the words of our Lord confirm (Matt. 5:17 f.). Ridderbos again comments with insight:

> The anthropological and redemptive-historical way of approaching the law in Paul's doctrine is, therefore, not in conflict with the words which Jesus uses in His requisitory against the Pharisees: "Think not that I came to destroy the law or the prophets: I came not to destroy, but to fulfill" (Matthew 5:17). The servant is not above his Lord; Paul is merely preparing room for his Master in order that the Lord Himself may fulfill the law and the prophets, in the life of His congregation, too. Such, and none other, is the profound meaning of Paul's doctrine of the law, and in it all he is verily an apostle and witness of Jesus Christ the Lord.[3]

---

[3] Hermann Ridderbos, *When the Time Had Fully Come: Studies in New Testament Theology* (Grand Rapids: William B. Eerdmans Publishing Co.,) 1957), p. 77.

Pro-Nomian Attitude Exemplified

Paul does not stand alone in the New Testament as obedient to the theonomy of his Lord; there are indications throughout that the law of God was honored and applied by other saints of the New Covenant. Note the example of Stephen. In Acts 6:11-14 we read that the accusation against him was that he spoke *against* the law and made out Jesus to do the same. The inspired word tells us that this witness was *contrived* and *false*. The truth, by contrast, is that Stephen was holding to the law as did his Saviour and Lord; he did not depreciate its demands in the slightest. In his defense before the Sanhedrin, Stephen declares that Moses received living oracles at Mt. Sinai to pass on to "you," that is, Stephen's hearers (Acts 7:38); on the basis of this he indicts them for breaking the law (Acts 7:53). The demands of God's law were still endorsed and applied in the age following Christ's redemptive work; the earliest church knew that God's living law was valid still.

Taking Peter for another example, we see that he identified the way of righteousness with the holy commandment (2 Peter 2:21).

John pays great attention to the keeping of God's commandments *throughout* his gospel and epistles. In the Revelation of Jesus Christ, John writes that the "woman's seed," the saints, are those who keep God's law and keep faith in Jesus (Rev. 12:17; 14:12).

There is a highly significant text in James 4:11; in it James makes it clear that believers are not to speak against, or stand in judgment over, God's law. There is *only one* Lawgiver and Judge, and that is God. No Christian can presume to alter or criticize this Divine Lawgiver's commandments. The law must be kept and endorsed just as God imposes it, and thus it must be followed *in full*. Venturing to select some commandments as binding on the believer and some as not is to come into judgment upon God's holy law; *every* bit of it is authoritative and continues to bind God's people. No creature can turn back or modify the Creator's word. James herein condemns both antinomianism and subtle antinomianism (i.e., a smorgasbord approach to the law).

Appeal to the Law as Authoritative

Just as did Christ, the writers of the New Testament appeal to the law as an authority. We have already noted significant citing of the Older Testament case law by Paul in 1 Corinthians 9 and 1 Timothy 5. Paul cites Deuteronomy 30:12-14 in Romans 10:6-8, and he attributes these words about the law to the righteousness based on faith. Faith-righteousness itself speaks to us out of the law and tells us that the commandment of God, which is not too difficult, is in our mouth and heart (cf. Deut. 30:11, 14 with Rom. 10:8).

Another example of Paul authoritatively appealing to the Older Testamental law is in 1 Corinthians 14:34. There he commands the women to subject themselves "just as *the law* also says" that they are to do; Paul does not consider it illegitimate to apply the law of God from the Older Testament to his New Testament situation. His lack of *argument* for the validity of this move is noteworthy.

James does the same sort of thing as Paul when in James 2:9 he says that those who practice partiality are "committing sin and convicted *by the law* as transgressors." James condemns his hearers out of the law, which would necessarily imply that he considered the Older Testamental law still to be in force and that believers are obligated to it.

The list of New Testament *citations of the Older Testamental* law in a prescriptive sense, or to support an exhortation, or which implies the law's validity, is *extensive.* [4] There are also many indirect allusions to the law which have the same function as these direct quotations (e.g., 1 Tim. 5:19; James 3:18; 1 Peter 2:17; 4:18, etc.).

Paul's experience recorded in Acts 23:1-5 is very instructive with respect to the abiding validity of God's law. First we note that Paul was concerned to defend himself against the accusation that he had broken

---

[4] Read Matthew 4:4, 7, 10; 15:4; 18:16; 19:4 f., 18 f.; 21:13; Mark 7:10; 10:6 f., 19; 12:29 f.; Luke 4:4, 8, 12; 10:28; Rom. 12:20; 13:9; 1 Corinthians 6:16; 9:9; 10:6-11; 2 Corinthians 4:13; 6:17 f.; 10:17; 13:1; Galatians 3:10-13; 5:14; Ephesians 4:25, 26; 5:14, 31; 6:2 f., 14, 15; 1 Timothy 5:18; Hebrews 1:9; 3:7-11; 10:37-38; 12:5 f.; James 2:8, 11; 4:6; 1 Peter 1:16; 3:10-12; 5:5.

the Jewish law (which the Roman guards needed to ascertain); Paul did not want to be denominated a "law-breaker." He knew himself to be obligated to the law, and he strove to defend his innocence before it. Second, we see that Paul appeals to the law because of his abusive treatment, at the command of Ananias; Paul accuses Ananias of violating the law by having him smitten (cf. Deut. 25:2). Third we see that Paul himself is rebuked out of the law; he implies that he would not have spoken against Ananias if he had known that Ananias was high priest, for the law tells Paul not to speak evil of a ruler of the people (cf. Ex. 22:28). So Paul is concerned to be innocent before the law, reproves another out of the law, and is himself rebuked by the law. In these three points he should be our example.

We must contend, then, that the New Testament does not turn back the Older Testamental law of God in the slightest; rather, the New Testament *substantiates* the abiding validity of God's law. The law is not deprived of sanctity in the New Testament; it is intensified. Hebrews 10:26-29 is an exemplary teaching of this point. In this passage, sinning willfully is identical with sinning with a high hand as described in Numbers 15:30; the same judgment is pronounced in both cases: there shall be no pardon (cf. Heb. 3:12; 6:4-8; Mark 3:29). Although breaking the covenant law could make a person subject to the death penalty (e.g., Deut. 17:2-7), the apostate under the Newer Covenant faces much *sorer* punishment. The defiant sinner under the Older Covenant had to be utterly cut off from the people, and there could be no immunity (Deut. 13:6-9). However, under the new order the apostate cannot escape *God's* eternal wrath, for there is no more forgiveness for him at all. The *equity* of this harsh judgment is established by appeal to the Mosaic law. There is hardly a turning back of the judicial tone of the Older Covenant, for the Newer Covenant brings further and worse punishment for apostasy.

Based on all the foregoing lines of argument the conclusion is inescapably driven home that the New Testament *consistently* supports the Christian's obligation to God's law as expressed in the stipulations of the Older Testament, both inside and outside the Decalogue. Christ affirmed that He did not come to abrogate the law; the writers of the New Testament follow His example. Throughout the New Testament the validity of God's law is stated, assumed, appealed to, and acted upon. We must concur with the Westminster Confession of Faith, chapter XIX, section V:

> The moral law doth ever bind all, as well justified persons as others, to the obedience thereof; and that, not only in regard of the matter contained in it, but also in respect of the authority of God the Creator, who gave it. Neither doth Christ, in the Gospel, any way dissolve, but much strengthen this obligation.

Chapter 13

THE FUNCTIONS OF GOD'S LAW

IN the process of establishing the full validity of God's law in the New Testament era, the preceding portions of this treatise have touched upon various uses and abuses of the law. It would be well for us at this point to summarize these allusions into a list of uses and misuses of the law for the Christian who lives between the two advents of Christ.

It is specified that we want to summarize the functions of theonomy *in the age of the New Testament,* for the principle of obedience to God's law is qualified by its various roles in the history of redemption. The obedience-principle does not have one universal, axiomatic application that spans all ages and all relations of man to God. It is necessary to distinguish between the two epochs of *before* and *after* man's historical fall into sin, and between the spiritual conditions of being under God's *wrath* and under God's *grace* in that latter period.

Life, Death, Rebirth

Before Adam fell from his state of innocence, obedience to the stipulations of God would have led to life, based on God's equitable government; God's favor was the promised corollary to the perfect righteousness of full obedience. Observing the full extent of God's demand would bring justification, blessing, and life; the slightest divergence from His law would bring death. The obedience-principle no longer operates in this way after the fall into sin; man can no longer sustain the same relationship to God wherein the righteousness of personal obedience can effect justification and life. Man's acceptance with God can no longer depend on his own obedience to God's stipulations; man has been introduced into the terrible syndrome of sin, condemnation and death.

Before man experiences any transition from wrath to grace in his personal spiritual life, the obedience-principle, used as a way of earning justification, is diametrically and blasphemously opposed to gracious justification through faith. Now only God-righteousness can be effective; the gospel provision (both in the period when God's people *anticipated* the accomplishment of redemption—the objective, historical transition of wrath to grace—and when God's people *look back* upon that accomplishment while looking forward to the return of Christ in judgment) is *necessary,* not a mere second option. Obedience to the law can save no one living under God's wrath. However, when a subjective change from wrath to grace takes place (i.e., when the subject has moved from the realm of death into that of life), then the obedience-principle has a different application. The believer sees that life and righteousness are inseparable; his new spiritual life demands habitual obedience of God's law, considering his past redemption and his future sanctification. In the realm of grace, then, obedience is again a way of life.

Three Death-Dealing Errors

Our concern is to summarize the use and misuse of the law from the vantage point of a Christian living between the advents of Christ. We must be careful to avoid the three basic unlawful attitudes of man: *substituting* man's law for God's law, *misusing* God's law as a way of works-righteousness and justification, and knowing but *ignoring* God's law. The genuine Christian cannot be characterized by the spirit of humanistic autonomy, Pharisaism, or rebellion. And on the other hand, in our concern for the law, we must never fail to see obedience to law within the context of gracious redemption; the law cannot stand apart from the gospel. To depreciate God's provision of redemption and sanctifying strength which is received by faith tends to make one a pseudo-rabbi who uses the law *unlawfully* (1 Tim. 1:3-8) and who is a vain deceiver, making grand professions of knowing God yet being detestable and disobedient (Titus 1:10-16). Understanding the principle of obedience in relation to its place in the history of redemption (both cosmic and personal) and in its relation to the extremes of autonomy and legalism, we are ready to summarize the basic uses of God's law.

Declares God's Character and Demand

The law shows all men what God is like and what He demands. The law is the transcript of God's holiness; it shows man how he is to be holy like God his Creator. By its very character (revelatory of God's justice and perfection) the law lays down the stipulation for fellowship with God. In Christ this stipulation is satisfied, and we are united to Him—then to be required to grow up into His holy stature. The law reflects God and enunciates His demand; it changes not, for He does not change. God makes an absolute demand upon all men's lives; they are not to have any other god before Him. The authority of His demands is often expressed simply by the phrase, "I am the Lord." Man as man is obligated to God as God. The law has the moral attributes of God applied to it. It is the standard which defines those who are to be condemned by God for lack of compliance. To disobey the law is to follow other gods. To follow the living and true God requires an emulation of His perfection. Therefore, the law is first of all, by definition, the demand of God; it shows man how he is to behave and thereby imitate the righteousness of God on a creaturely level.

Defines Sin

In showing us the demand of God upon our lives, the law necessarily defines what rebellion against God is. By defining righteousness, the law also delineates iniquity. Consequently, where there is no law there is no transgression (Rom. 4:15; 5:13), and by the law is the knowledge of sin (Rom. 3:20; 7:7). Sin is simply defined as transgression or absence of law (1 John 3:4; cf. Josh. 7:11; Isa. 24:5; Hos. 6:7). Where there is no law, there is no sin, hence no need of salvation, and consequently no Christianity. Lawless Christianity is a contradiction. The law tells man what God demands of him; it instructs him in what he must avoid. The law is the criterion of righteousness and sin.

Exposes Infractions

By setting before man the objective standards of God's holiness, the law convicts man of his sinful rebellion by contrast. The law is spiritual (Rom. 7:14) and a living oracle (Acts 7:38); as such, it is part of that word of God which is living and active and sharper than any two-edged sword, piercing to the division of soul and spirit, and joints and marrow; it is able to judge the thoughts and intents of the heart (Heb. 4:12). The law convicts us of sin (Rom. 7:9-10).

Incites Rebellion

The law also exposes the true character of sin, for sin takes hold of the law and induces transgression. The law provokes sin, calls forth transgression (Rom. 5:20; 4:15: Gal. 3:19); sin is aroused by the law, it finds opportunity for rebellion in the commandment (Rom. 7:8, 11, 13). The very power of sin is the law (1 Cor. 15:56). So the law convicts man of sin and shows the true nature of rebellion; it excites transgression and spurs sin on to further disobedience. It must be remembered, however, that the law which carries out the judicial function of exposing sin, is not the factor which causes death. *Sin* is to blame, not the law (Rom. 7:13). Sin destroys the way of life intended in the law, and because the law cannot restore the sinner, it is a way of condemnation and death for him.

Condemns Transgression

This is the next function of the law. Having shown the absolute demand of God upon man's life, having defined what sin is, having convicted man of sin and shown him the nature of sinful rebellion, the law pronounces the just condemnation of God upon the sinner. The law shuts up all men under sin and seals off any escape to life for them in their own strength (Gal. 3:22). The sinner finds himself lost and sold under sin; the magnitude of his dilemma is revealed in the words, "It stands written that accursed is everyone who does not continue in all things having been written in the law-book to do them," and, "Whoever stumbles in one point has become guilty of all" (Gal. 3:10 with James 2:10). The inevitable outcome is that the law works wrath upon the sinner (Rom. 4:15); the law is an instrument of condemnation to sinners (Rom. 2:12).

Drives Us to Christ

Because the law condemns men for their sin, it operates as a tutor to lead them to Christ (cf. Gal. 3:24), the only one who can release them from sin's bondage and punishment. We must be careful to note, again, that the law is not to be looked down upon for its condemnation of sinners; it was not designed to kill, and condemnation is accidental to its true purpose (Rom. 7:10). Here the law is parallel to the gospel, for it too brings death even though life is its main aim (cf. Luke 2:34; 2 Cor. 2:16; 1 Pet. 2:8).

Restrains Evil

Not only does the law define, convict, and condemn sin, it also restrains sin. Paul can actually say that the law was made for (i.e., aims to hold back) the lawless, rebellious, ungodly, and sinful (1 Tim. 1:8-10). The law represses the rampage of sin in a person's life and in society; it halts the sinner with the authoritative demand of God, even if only for a while. So the law has a certain preservative effect, even when it is not a sanctifying one, in the life of sinners. Rightly has Calvin said:

> (The law restrains malefactors and those who are not yet believers. The law is protection of the community from unjust man:)
>
> The second function of the law is this: at least by fear of punishment to restrain certain men who are untouched by any care for what is just and right unless compelled by hearing the dire threats in the law. But they are restrained, not because their inner mind is stirred or affected, but because,

> being bridled, so to speak, they keep their hands from outward activity, and hold inside the depravity that otherwise they would wantonly have indulged. Consequently, they are neither better nor more righteous before God.[1]

Yet the law also acts as a restraining factor in the life of the regenerate. Heeding the voice of God in His law keeps one from sinning; "Thy word have I treasured in my heart in order that I might not sin against Thee" (Ps. 119:11, cf. 17:4 f.). When he feels the power of indwelling sin asserting itself, he can reflect upon the law of God which is written upon his heart and, thereby, resist.

Guides Sanctification

This leads us to the final function of God's law, and perhaps the most significant for the man who in faith repents of his sin and seeks to live a godly life. The law offers positive moral direction for the Christian believer; it is the pattern of his sanctification. Seeing that even Adam, before the fall, was given positive moral direction by divine revelation, we might view this directing function of the law as its principle use. Paul seems to indicate this in Romans 7:10; the commandment "was to result in life" but, for the sinner, proved to be death-dealing. The original purpose of the law was to direct and regulate man's life in the paths of righteousness. Calvin comments in this regard:

> The third and principal use, which pertains more closely to the proper purpose of the law, finds its place among believers in whose hearts the Spirit of God already lives and reigns.

---

[1] Ford Lewis Battles (trans.), *Calvin: The Institutes of the Christian Religion*, ed. John T. McNeill, The Library of Christian Classics, Vol. XX, eds. John Baillie, John T. McNeill, and Henry P. Van Dusen (Philadelphia: The Westminster Press, 1967), Book II, chap. VII, section 10, p. 358.

> . . . Here is the best instrument for them to learn more thoroughly each day the nature of the Lord's will to which they aspire, and to confirm them in the understanding of it. . . . Again, because we need not only teaching but also exhortation, the servant of God will also avail himself of this benefit of the law: by frequent meditation upon it to be aroused to obedience, be strengthened in it, and be drawn back from the slippery path of transgression.[2]

Proverbs 6:23 tells us, "The commandment is a lamp, and the law is light; and reproofs for discipline are the way of life" (NASV). The law offers us direction, reproof, and moral discipline for our Christian lives; it is the guide for holy living: "You shall keep My statutes and practice them; I am the Lord who sanctifies you" (Lev. 20:8).

Although what has been designated "the third use of the law" in traditional theological works now holds no important place in Lutheran theology (the law being used primarily in connection with human guilt), the Formula of Concord gives excellent expression to the law's directive function:

> We believe, teach, and confess that the Law is properly a doctrine divinely revealed, which teaches what is just and acceptable to God, and which also denounces whatever is sinful and opposite to the divine will.
>
> We believe, teach, and confess that although they who truly believe in Christ, and are sincerely converted to God, are through Christ set free from the curse and constraint of the Law, they are not, nevertheless, on that account without Law, inasmuch as the Son of God redeemed them for the very reason that they might meditate on the Law of God day and night, and continually exercise themselves in the keeping thereof (Psalm 1:2; 119:1 ff.). For not even our first parents,

---

[2] Calvin, *op. cit.*, Book II, chap. VII, section 12, p. 360.

> even before the fall, lived wholly without Law, which was certainly at that time graven on their hearts, because the Lord had created them after His own image (Genesis 1:26 f.; 2:16 ff.; 3:3).
>
> We believe, teach, and confess that the preaching of the Law should be urged not only upon those who have not faith in Christ, and do not yet repent, but also upon those who truly believe in Christ, are truly converted to God, and regenerated and are justified by faith.
>
> For, although they are regenerate and renewed in the spirit of their mind, yet this regeneration and renewal is in this life not absolutely complete, but only begun. And they that believe according to the spirit of their mind have perpetually to struggle with their flesh, that is, with corrupt nature, which inheres in us even until death (Galatians 5:17; Romans 7:21, 23). And on account of the old Adam, which still remains fixed in the intellect and will of man and in all his powers, there is need that the law of God should always shine before man, that he may not frame any thing in matter of religion under an impulse of self-devised devotion, and may not choose out ways of honoring God not instituted by the Word of God. Also, lest the old Adam be constrained against his own will, not only by the admonitions and threats of the law, but also by punishments and plagues, in order that he may give obedience to the Spirit, and render himself up captive to the same (1 Corinthians 9:27; Romans 6:12; Galatians 6:14; Psalm 119:1 ff.; Hebrews 12:1; 13:21).[3]

In the 119th Psalm the Psalmist sees God's law as his counselor, as that which brings good discernment and knowledge, as a lamp to his feet and light to his path (vv. 24, 66, 105). The believer should not be

[3] *The Creeds of Christendom*, ed. Philip Schaff (Grand Rapids: Baker Book House, originally 1877), vol. III, pp. 127, 131-133.

indifferent to the law after being redeemed from its curse; he should go back to the law and see that righteous behavior his God requires of him. The law is of great use to the Christian.

> Although true believers be not under the law, as a covenant of works, to be thereby justified, or condemned; yet is it of great use to them, as well as to others; in that, as a rule of life informing them of the will of God, and their duty, it directs and binds them to walk accordingly; discovering also the sinful pollutions of their nature, hearts, and lives; so as, examining themselves thereby, they may come to further conviction of, humiliation for, and hatred against sin, together with a clearer sight of the need they have of Christ, and the perfection of His obedience. It is likewise of use to the regenerate to restrain their corruptions, in that it forbids sin: and the threatenings of it serve to shew what even their sins deserve; and what afflictions, in this life, they may expect for them, although freed from the curse thereof threatened in the law. The promises of it, in like manner, shew them God's approbation of obedience, and what blessings they may expect upon the performance thereof: although not as due to them by the law as a covenant of works. So as, a man's doing good, and refraining from evil, because the law encourageth to the one, and deterreth from the other, is no evidence of his being under the law; and not under grace.
>
> Neither are the forementioned uses of the law contrary to the grace of the Gospel, but do sweetly comply with it; the Spirit of Christ subduing and enabling the will of man to do that freely, and cheerfully, which the will of God, revealed in the law, requireth to be done.[4]

[4] Westminster Confession of Faith, chap. XIX, sections VI and VII.

Abuses to Avoid

We can infer from what has been detailed as the proper functions of God's law what other uses of it are contrary and unlawful; such other uses of the law are abusive. There are many things which the law of God cannot do and for which it is not to be used. For instance: the law cannot justify the sinner since it has no expiatory power or immunity to offer the one who is under its curse. The law cannot enable obedience to itself nor relieve the bondage of sin. The law ought not be used to support self-righteous complacency, nor should it be worshipped as a lofty moral ideal apart from God, His glory and His purposes. The law ought not be supplemented by human traditions thereby nullifying it. What the law properly does is this: it propounds the will of God requiring obedience, approves and promises blessing for conformity with it, defines sin, guards and enunciates justice, convicts and exposes sin, condemns disobedience, incites sin and intensifies its bondage, leads sinners to Christ by showing their need, and directs regenerated believers in the paths of righteousness (operating as a rule and standard for grateful obedience in response to God's gracious salvation). These constitute the *lawful* uses of the law of God, the Christian should heed them all.

VI. ANTITHESIS

Chapter 14

THEONOMY VS. AUTONOMY

THE foregoing sections have explained the principle of theonomy in its covenantal context based on the special revelation of God. God's law has been shown to be indispensable to Christian biblical ethics. Based on the absolute authority of God, and in response to His gracious salvation, the Christian is taught what God requires and desires of him by the written law of God. Motivated by faith and enabled by the Holy Spirit, the Christian seeks to glorify and serve God in all his moral behavior by following the directives of God's law. Such is the Christian ethic: covenantal use of the law of God. Because the Christian has a personal relation with God established by His sovereign grace, wherein the Spirit of knowledge, power, and holiness enables him to understand and obey the moral stipulations of God, the Christian can live a life pleasing to his Lord. The biblical ethic is constituted by this covenantal theonomy. The *normative* center of Christian morality, then, is nothing other than the whole law of God as recorded in Scripture.

The direct antithesis of Christian ethics is sin or lawlessness. Covenantal theonomy is incongruous with autonomy, for self-law does not seek to conform the person's thoughts, words, and deeds to God's righteousness as learned in God's revealed word. The skills of godly living can only be acquired by Spiritual reception and obedience to the commandments of God's word. Thus only the Christian theonomic ethic is true and effective. Adam learned this hard lesson in the garden; we do well to learn from it also.

Adam

Even when man's life was untainted by sin, his moral consciousness was not ultimate, but derivative; Adam was receptively reconstructive of God's word, that is, he thought God's thoughts after Him on a creaturely level. Adam did not look to himself for moral steering; rather, he lived by supernatural, positive revelation. Adam was not without external moral dictate; he knew what was good and evil because His Lord told him. However, Adam fell from his state of blessing and moral uprightness when he succumbed to the Satanic temptation improperly to "be like God." Satan lured our original parents into thinking that they should know good and evil for themselves; they would be moral arbitrators determining good and evil. They decided that they could be self-sufficient in their moral consciousness and reasoning. They substituted *autonomy* for *theonomy*.

The dreadful results are all too well known to us. Man is *not* morally self-sufficient; when he tries to be he sins and rebels against God, and such is the *antithesis* of true ethics. Autonomy is inherently destructive of genuine morality; self-law makes ethics impossible. Although Adam's temptation and fall took place in calendar history, his pattern of autonomy has been recapitulated throughout the history of ethical philosophy. Biblical theonomy as the principle of Christian ethics is a resplendent sight in contrast to the wasteland of humanistic ethical philosophy.

In what follows we shall selectively explore, albeit briefly, the history of humanistic ethics that we might see the collapse of morality and ethic in its ungodly course.[1] Note should be made of the failure of

---

[1] The following treatment in this chapter is not intended to be the in-depth analysis which only a book (or series of books) could be. Philosophic detail-work and highly qualified argumentation have been relinquished in order to achieve a popular sketch of the high points of autonomous ethical systems. The discussion is thus non-expository as well as incomplete in its selection (e.g., the period spanning the third century B.C. TO the eighteenth century A.D. is completely untouched). My aim has simply been to set out an outline of approaches to ethics and present key critical questions for them, in order that some general comparative remarks and a fundamental conclusion can be reached in the end. Those wishing background to the history of philosophy can profitably pursue it in: Henry Sidgwick, *Outline of the History of Ethics,* (with an additional chapter by H. G. Widgery) (Boston: Beacon Press, 1886, reprinted 1960); Alasdair MacIntyre, *A Short History of Ethics* (New York: Macmillan, 1966); Mary Warnock, *Ethics Since 1900,* 2nd ed. (London: Oxford University Press, 1966).

autonomous ethics (i.e., anything outside of biblical theonomy) to answer the decisive questions of interpretation, direction, authority, motive, power, and goal for an ethical system. What is the meaning of "good"? What norms are to be used for choosing value? What is the right thing to do in a particular situation? Why should a person be obligated to act morally? In what is obligation grounded? What motivates moral behavior? Where does one get the ability to act rightly? What is the aim of moral conduct? Autonomous ethics, because it looks to sinful man rather than to the covenantal Lord and His law, is bankrupt before the demands of these questions. Only theonomy can render a genuine and effective moral system, for there is only one Lawgiver: the living and true God. Autonomy refuses to acknowledge this. The autonomous philosopher is misled in his metaphysical and, hence, epistemological presuppositions. Presuming autonomy he does not see the facts of God's self-sufficient authority *over* man and His self-attesting communication *to* man; it is only inevitable, then, that he will be misled in his ethics. In fact, the very presumption of self-sufficiency is evidence of immorality, sinful rebellion against the clearly revealed, living and true God. When man turns away from covenantal theonomy to supposed autonomy, ethics become a vain delusion.

Plato

Plato reacted to the moral relativism of the Sophists of his day; although denying their maxim "man is the measure of all things," Plato ended up reintroducing it in a different way. The Sophists were moral subjectivists who viewed value as relative to human tradition; of course their relativism made moral prescriptions (universal statements of obligation) impossible. Against this Plato developed a school of axiological realism (i.e., moral absolutism or objectivism); he held that moral values were independent of human relativities and acknowledgment. However, correlative to his axiological realism was the autonomy of ethics from religion (cf. *Euthyphro).* Plato maintained that there is right and wrong even if the gods do not exist, and he held that a person could get answers to his ethical questions without religious revelation. Plato posed this question: Is a certain behavior approved by the gods because it is good, or is it good because it is approved by the gods? All non-Christian ethicists have assented to the former alternative along with Plato. When it comes to deciding or knowing *what* is good, man is (eventually) the judge, not God. Plato and all subsequent ethical philosophy are indifferent to what God has to say about holiness; moral good will be discovered and analyzed by looking within, by looking to man's thought.

Of course Plato's question was a false antithesis; by setting it up in the way he did, Plato could make God look totally arbitrary or capricious in determining what is good and evil. The truth of the matter is that good is not independent of God. Certain behavior is good because God approves it, and God approves it because it is the creaturely expression of His holiness—in other words, it is good. To be good is to be like God, and we can only know what behavior is good if God reveals and approves it to us. The important point is that good *is what God approves* and cannot be ascertained independent of Him, but Plato and the history of ethics turned away from this and down the alley of autonomy.

By a very *unconvincing* line of reasoning (cf. *Republic)* Plato ends up asserting that man's particular virtue is justice, that is, to live the life of reason. (Does man *qua* man have one particular function? Must that function be tied up with reason and the intellect? Could not someone hold that the appetites should govern the reason just as capriciously as Plato asserts the opposite? Given that man's observed function *is* that of living reasonably, *ought* it to be? etc.) Plato *arbitrarily* posits "Good" above nonbeing and evil (and he would accuse the gods of this same caprice!). *Contrary* to moral experience Plato's ethical system requires him to hold that no man knowingly does evil (universal psychological egoism). And at base Plato's ethic turns out to be ignoble and *self-centered* hedonism, for the reason he offers that man ought to be "good" (have reason govern the appetites and spirit in order to gain a harmonious soul) is that it leads to a life which is happier, more satisfying, and richer. Plato's ethic is adrift from credibility, the facts of moral experience, genuine direction, and authority. Even if there are moral absolutes on Plato's basis, one has no assurance of *knowing* what they are: the testimony of the philosophical "priests" is hopelessly conflicting. After all, it is Plato's word against that of Protagoras.

Aristotle

In Aristotle's *Nicomachean Ethics* man's highest good is considered to be "well-being" or happiness; yet there can only be linguistic agreement on this point, for "happiness" is different from person to person. Aristotle made the same mistakes with respect to man *qua* man's "rational function" as did Plato. He also shared Plato's oblivion to the "forbidden fruit syndrome" (i.e., men often do what is immoral simply because it is enticingly against the law) and thereby held that no man knowingly does evil. Such moves were necessitated by his rationalistic system and false anthropology.

Even if we grant Aristotle that it is meaningful and true that "all men desire happiness as an end," he still commits a naturalistic fallacy by directly going on to say that "all men, therefore, *ought* to desire happiness as an end." (All descriptions do not in themselves yield prescriptions.) By the doctrine of the golden mean Aristotle held that the right thing to do was to choose a mediating course between excess and deficiency; due to varying situations the golden mean will not be the same for all men or for all time. However, a descriptive variety of situations does *not* imply that moral (prescriptive) absolutes cannot apply irrespective of circumstance.

Finally, Aristotle's attack on hedonism turns back on his own system. He rightly observed that some things which bring pleasure (hedonism holds that pleasure is the sole good) are still disgraceful and immoral; further, pleasure is not the supreme or "intrinsic" good because pleasure combined with something else (e.g., wisdom) is better than pleasure alone. These same comments could be made about "happiness," but Aristotle inconsistently failed to make them. We can only agree with Aristotle's own evaluation of ethics as based on his system: it is an inexact science—of little help or plausibility.

Butler

The humanistic nature of Bishop Butler's ethic is more than evident in that he grounded morality in man's *conscience.* The dictates of a calloused conscience will be different than those of a hypersensitive conscience, so what becomes of the universal obligation inherent in the "ought" of genuine morality? Furthermore, not being a universal psychological egoist, Butler is particularly responsible to explain how man can acquire the requisite *ability* to perform what he knows to be right (in the face of his despairing failure to do so in many instances). Denying God's sovereignty, Butler had no answer except to rely upon autonomous man's resources. The moral principles that Butler did enunciate were based on his observation and analysis of such things as self-love, benevolence, etc.; in basing moral prescriptions thereon he illegitimately moved from observation to obligation. By entrusting moral steering to each man's conscience Butler undermined the possibility of a self-regulating, objective norm; when each man is allowed to be a law unto himself, moral principles will be superfluous as far as correcting or restraining him are concerned. Each man can end up doing what is right in his own eyes. Or *one* man's conscience is arbitrarily selected to dictate standards for the others (depriving ethics of *moral* authority).

Hume

David Hume wielded his surgeon's knife of scepticism to cut the heart out of ethics just as he had done with science; both science and ethics were psychologically rooted according to him (cf. his discussion of induction). Moral judgments are based merely in moral sentiment; a person's approbation leads him to prescribe moral principle. The moral sentiment is a *given* of experience (as are desires, aptitudes, etc.) and so unanalyzable. One does not rationally support such a sentiment, he simply accepts it as a given part of his constitution or on the basis of sympathy. Hence, with Hume morality becomes noncognitive and closed to public examination for truth. Skepticism closes the door on universal moral absolutes. Hume "defended" ethics by making it as *tenuous* as science! Because Hume saw moral judgments as rooted in feelings of approbation and disapprobation, prescriptions are not statements about moral *truth* but statements about the moralist himself. And biography is a woefully inadequate substitute for ethics.

Utilitarianism

Utilitarianism, represented by a man like J. S. Mill, is a form of hedonism; to be exact, it is universal ethical hedonism. The concern of morality in utilitarianism is the man-centered goal of the production of the greatest happiness for the greatest number; good is identified with that which maximizes happiness. Of course, to make sense of this position "happiness" must be computable; yet no one has been able to do this. Morality with its universal prescriptions is again lost in this system, for nobody can condemn anyone else's pleasures; to do so the critic would have to appeal to a value separate from pleasure, but in utilitarianism this is illegitimate. Moreover, no behavior is intrinsically right or wrong in utilitarianism; relativism and the loss of ethics results.

The attempt to bolster utilitarianism with *rule utilitarianism* (i.e., the test of utility is applied to general rules instead of specific acts) is futile since rule utilitarianism simply *collapses* into act utilitarianism in the long run (by extensive specification of one's rule). The principle of utility can be cleverly manipulated to sanction almost any act, even those which are universally abhorred; hence utilitarianism is inherently immoral. As with other ethical systems, utilitarianism also commits the naturalistic fallacy; it moves from the observation that all men seek happiness or pleasure to the dictate that men ought to do so. This expression of autonomous ethics is obviously self-serving and duty-dissolving. Although utilitarians have held that man ought to work toward the happiness of others, one can critically inquire as to *why* he should be thus obligated (especially if *he* gets more pleasure out of *exploiting* than the *victim* gets out of being *helped)*. Mill is especially vulnerable here since the obligation to maximize the happiness of others is rooted by him in the *assumption* that it is pleasurable for the individual to seek the happiness of the group or others. At base, then, utilitarianism is simply egoistic hedonism. To calculate one's conduct always for his own welfare is merely prudent self-interest, an abandonment of morality and principle. Inclination, not obligation, prevails.

Kant

Immanuel Kant represents the very opposite of utilitarianism, for he viewed ethics as *deontological* rather than teleological; intrinsic good, rather than instrumental good, was for Kant the only proper subject of morality. Hence certain acts have intrinsic rightness which is not determined by their consequences. Kant wanted to get completely away from an ethic of inclination; this he did by drawing a radical bifurcation between facts and values (between *scientific* assertions which convey information that is true or false about the phenomenal world and *moral* judgments relating to the noumenal dimension). Facts have no bearing on morality; only duty is to be heeded—duty determined by man's moral consciousness apart from God. God is a noumenal object for Kant; hence God cannot enter the phenomenal world to deliver propositional, informative, true moral commandments. Yet the only area in which man has any right to be absolutistic, according to Kant, is in the area of practical morality, for god is found *in our experience* of ethics. God is not revealed, but is the projection of the morally autonomous man; God is *postulated* as the ultimate moral enforcer. It is not "true" that God will judge the lawless in a final day of judgment, but nevertheless the moral obligations given in conscience can be "considered as" commands from a God who will redress moral imbalance beyond phenomenal history. We might say that for Kant, although it is not "true" that God is genuine Law-giver and Judge, it is *helpful* to think of Him as such. The absoluteness of God is found within the moral experience of man; the moral dictates of man's self-sufficient ethical consciousness are dignified by referring them to a (superfluous) "god." Having drawn a hard and fast distinction between facts and values, Kant maintains that the only thing which is "good" without qualification is a good will; acts are morally right when joined with this good will, and agents are morally good only if they act *from duty*. It is not enough that the moralist acts in accord with his duty; he must act solely *because* it is his duty. Kant continues (with his faulty faculty psychology) to say that a good will acts in accord with *reason,* for man's sole obligation is to reason. Reason shall excogitate objective maxims with which the moral agent is to align his subjective maxims. The requirements of reason must be met in the objective maxim, and Kant revealed (based on what authority?) that a maxim is in accord with reason if universalizable with consistency and reversability: that is, if atuned with Kant's categorical imperative. The categorical imperative is the necessary and sufficient criterion of right behavior. If the moralist can take his proposed behavior and imagine that everyone followed the same course of behavior, and if that universalized activity were not inconsistent, and if the moralist could allow anyone else to do as he plans to do irrespective of his position, then that behavior is right. It should be done from duty, with a good will. Even overlooking the fact that this is simply Kant's word (and view of reason, etc.) against someone else's, that moral judgments have been deprived of the qualities of truth and falsity, that Kant's view is built up on an erroneous faculty psychology, that Kant cannot supply the power to effect what reason prescribes as a moral obligation, that Kant's view of duty-motivation is somewhat artificial, still Kant's ethic faces insurmountable problems.

The rationalistic formalism of Kant sought to objectivize morality; yet it turned out making all value relative to the rational will. Kant's view that man's one and only value is loyalty to his obligation to be rational is contrived and arbitrary (Why should man have only *one* value? Why should that value be found in rationalism rather than its opposite?). How does Kant derive obligation from rationalization? Most everyone can see that morality is far more than logical consistency; on Kant's basis a sternly self-sufficient person would never need to help others as long as he could *consistently* cling to his cherished self-sufficiency in time of need. In the categorical imperative there is a measure of ambiguity as to what will count as a contradiction when a maxim is universalized; hence ethics is deprived of clear direction. Kant made the categorical imperative the sufficient test for rightness; yet acts which everyone considers to be amoral can pass the test and come out being obligatory (e.g., wearing blue socks can be consistently univeralized irrespective of a person's position in life, hence it becomes man's duty to wear blue socks!). Maxims which are generally agreed to as morally binding are abrogated by Kant's principle; for instance, "honesty is the best policy" does not universalize with reversability, that is, it does not necessarily apply irrespective to circumstance. "Honesty is the best policy" is a conditional, not a categorical, imperative; under the condition that a business is running short of capital and manpower, cheating could be viewed as the best policy, especially if feeding the family is held in more esteem than a good reputation. On the other hand, if someone did not need profits at all, honesty might be indifferent to him altogether. The duty to honesty is categorical only if Kant can specify some universal, value-oriented end for man; rational consistency fails to guarantee categorical obligations. A clever person could use Kant's categorical imperative principle to legitimize his immorality (e.g., everyone who has a certain set of fingerprints can steal; since the "moralist" is the only one who has those fingerprints, he can continue with his nefarious deeds). Qualifications can be built right into the rule which the categorical imperative legitimizes; self-interest and inclination can be reintroduced therefore. The categorical imperative permits of *contrary* maxims being universalized, which is ironical since Kant exulted in rational consistency as a supreme value!

Kant never explained why it was better to be moral than economic; and although he would have repudiated it, it is hard to see how relativism could be prevented from entering Kant's ethic given the incommensurability of different scales of values. Kant's notion of a good will acting from duty was muddled; he held that the virtue of certain acts lies in acting in such a way because it is dutiful. Hence, being-honest is not virtuous in itself or on some other grounds; what is virtuous is being-honest-because-honesty-is-virtuous. When this concept is analyzed it is seen to be virtuous because of the duty attaching to it also; hence, what is virtuous is being-honest-because-honesty-is-virtuous *because*-being-thus-honest-is-virtuous. The infinite regress entailed is obvious—and deadly. In later development of his ethic Kant came to emphasize the value of free and autonomous personality. But what justifies personality as a value? A scientist might just as arbitrarily posit impersonalism as valuable. In appealing to the "noumenal self" (or transcendent personality) of man Kant inevitably ran into insuperable difficulties with explicating this notion. Furthermore, the determinism inherent in Kant's discussion of the phenomenal realm contradicts his view of human freedom in the ethical sphere; in his useless attempt to reconcile the contradiction he ended up bifurcating man and using an ambiguous notion of "freedom." In working from a false metaphysics (view of God and man) and a false epistemology Kant could not avoid destroying the credibility of ethics.

The Modern Shift

In a world dichotomized between facts and values axiology has come to the foreground in modern philosophy. Due to scepticism with respect to questions about the nature and basis of moral judgment, contemporary moral philosophy has been considerably narrowed in its scope. Also there has been an ironic return by those who followed in the autonomous footsteps of Kant precisely to the ethic of inclination which Kant was trying to avoid. In modern ethics there has been a definite turn toward voluntarism, intuitionism, and noncognitivism. There has also been an interesting turn made to questions of metaethics and away from the field of normative ethics (which is significant commentary in itself). Instead of seeking to answer the questions, "What is really right and wrong?" and, "Why?" contemporary axiology has inquired into the logical structure of moral discourse; rather than attempting to understand the validity, content, order, consistency and universality of morals (i.e., ethical system), the current ethicist studies the *language* of ethics in order to ascertain its function and logical status. What does a valuational word such as "good" mean? Metaethics seeks to answer this question.

Naturalistic Objectivism

We consider first those philosophies which have held that moral discourse has an *informative* function, that is, conveys cognitive propositions which can be verified or falsified. The informativist school is divided between the objectivists and subjectivists, between those who see moral discourse as giving information about objective moral good and those who see it as giving information about the likes and dislikes of the subject who is speaking. The *naturalistic* objectivist holds that "good" applies to some discernable or empirical quality in the appraised item (e.g., pleasure for Epicurus and Bentham, maximized group happiness for J. S. Mill, or harmony with nature for the Stoics and Aquinas). Normative terms are definable and, when applied, open to examination. This naturalistic approach has the effect of reducing ethics to a branch of empirical science where the proper method of study would include statistics, induction, and descriptive generalization; however, this method by itself is irrelevant for arriving at moral conclusions. "Ought" must play a distinctive role from "is." Descriptive truths of this sort about the world or society cannot reasonably convince anyone of a prescriptive truth without the naturalistic fallacy being committed; to observe what *is* the case has nothing to do with what *should* be the case. It is always *meaningful* to ask *if* a pleasure, for instance, *is* good; yet on the naturalist's basis such a question would have to be nonsensical.

Intuitionism

The nonnaturalistic objectivist asserts that "good" applies to some nonnatural or undiscernable quality in the thing appraised; this position is also known as intuitionism, for it claims that "good" is indefinable yet denotes an intrinsic, objective quality (or relation) which is apprehended intuitively (e.g., G. E. Moore, W. D. Ross). "Goodness" is a simple, unanalyzable concept (like "yellow"); hence it can be recognized only by an immediate insight or intuition. The consequence of this is that ethical principles lose all relation to the realm of fact (even facts about God). The intuitionist holds that moral judgments are synthetic *a priori* assertions, yet indefinable; however, he fails to answer the common autonomous criticism that only experience can yield synthetic statements. Moreover, these moral judgments do not show common characteristics of a priori truths such as universality, necessity, and self-evidency; disagreements between people on their intuited moral judgments is an insurmountable difficulty for intuitionism. Another difficulty with nonnatural objectivism is that it is not clear what a "natural" property is for the intuitionist, and so it is not clear what he is denying. The intuitionist's thesis that goodness is simple and unanalyzable is not argued, but assumed; apparently, this characterization of goodness must *itself* also be intuited! The moral intuitions described by men like G. E. Moore have failed to have the cogency which is claimed for them as far as most people and their ethical experiences are concerned (these intuitions seem to suffer the same fate as Descartes' "clear and distinct ideas"). The whole appeal to intuition must acquiesce in the face of many of the same arguments which are raised against mysticism. In the long run it is simply unclear what authority or obligation can attach to one's closed-to-investigation intuition, what help in making moral decisions this offers, and how this intuition helps one to enact what is "good" behavior. The "odd facts" of moral intuitions render moral theory undiscussable. The content, grounds, and significance of ethics was lost to inexplicable intuitions which rendered it impossible to even define valuational terms in moral discourse.

Subjectivistic Schools

Others who hold that "good" is used in an informative way in ethical judgments are subjectivists. The private subjectivist maintains that the predication of "good" to anything simply asserts the speaker's personal approbation for it (e.g., Hume) or that it contributes to fullest satisfaction (e.g., Santayana). If this is the case, however, then moral judgments are never false unless the speaker is mistaken about his own psychology; at least all moral utterances are incorrigible. This is certainly a strange state of affairs; moral discourse is informative according to the private subjectivist and thereby capable of being true or false—yet it is never false! Also, two people could never mean the same thing even though there might be a linguistic agreement on a moral appraisal, for in "agreeing" that X is "good" the two speakers are not attributing to it the same property. All predications of "good" are statements about the *speaker*, not about the object under consideration. Furthermore, the private subjectivist could not reasonably answer to a question asking why he approves of X as "good," for he would either make an illegitimate reference to the goodness or value of the object independent of his feelings toward it or he would end up reasoning in a vicious circle. It is also meaningful for us to ask whether what the private subjectivist approves is *actually* good or not; yet on his basis such a question would be ridiculous. Although the private subjectivist holds that ethical discourse is informative and definable, oddly enough ethics is still not open to discussion. "Good" is simply relative to each moralist; therefore, ethics is destroyed because the notion of obligation cannot be derived from this conception of "good."

A modification of the above proposal is found in the "interest theory" of R. B. Perry, who defines "good" as an object of interest to someone. In this way Perry seems to deny that there is anything which is intrinsically good; for anything to be good it must sustain a certain relationship with a mind outside of it. Yet it certainly seems that when most people attribute goodness to something they are viewing that object as being in some way valuable for itself; at least what they appear to intend is something stronger than simply "someone has an interest in X." To hold that X is "good" in customary discourse usually implies that others *should* value it. It is normally not muddled to appraise someone's interest as bad or evil; however, Perry's construction would make it so. How does Perry's relational view of "good" account for this stronger use of the term at all? Unless an intrinsic notion of goodness came into being as an apprehension of some objective reality, it would seem to be senseless; yet most people do not consider that it is absurd to view certain items or behavior as good *irrespective* of what people may think about them. Perry's view must stretch the general limits of plausability in order to account for the "forbidden fruit syndrome" (i.e., seeking the immoral for immorality's sake). To explain this facet of moral experience by reference to ignorance or a confusion of priorities is simply not accurate or true to human nature at all. Perry's view falls into the same pitfalls as subjectivism; there is no moral authority, universal obligation, or concrete direction offered by a theory which is at root nothing more than moral relativism.

Another form of subjectivism is *societal* subjectivism; it holds that "good" applies to those things of which the group approves (e.g., Durkheim) or which is the law of the land or which has the sanction of tradition. Yet to say that something is "good" because it evokes the approval of most people has blatant difficulties. Obviously the majority is not always right; moving from 49% to 51% in the opinion polls does not make a certain behavior right. Again, it is not meaningless to ask whether what the group decided upon was in fact "good"; yet on this view the majority or common law or tradition would be right by definition! Furthermore, if this social approval view were correct, then all obligations could be removed by secrecy—which from an ethical viewpoint seems nonsense. All forms of subjectivism inherently destroy what ethics strives to attain: objective standards which can properly correct and direct man's behavior. If moral principle has no restraining or corrective element, why should one bother to enunciate it?

Process Schools

Others who have held that "good" is informative in moral discourse have not been naturalistic objectivists, or intuitionists, or subjectivists of a private or societal brand; rather, they have viewed good instrumentally or from the standpoint of a *process*. A broad evolutionary theory says that "good" applies to that which is conducive to the development of new values (e.g., Julian Huxley). Marxism holds that those ideals are good which are adapted to the needs of a particular stage in economic-social, dialectical process (e.g., Marx, Engels). Men like Hegel and Bradley identified good with that which contributed to the realization of true selfhood, man's ultimate aim. But *is* change, or a classless society, or selfhood (whatever that means) genuinely "good"? How does one calculate moral directives or get the ability to follow them? Is there anything to recommend these aims over competing ones? Can obligation be derived from such notions of "good"? Such questions serve to undermine the ethical authority of process theory ethics and underline the arbitrariness of their standards. It would seem that any man could claim that his behavior represented the pioneering newness of the evolutionary process, or the appropriate expression of dialectical materialism, or the true realization of genuine selfhood. Who could gainsay him? On the other hand, what besides coercion could motivate a person who is recalcitrant to the process? Since the only intrinsic good is that toward which the process is moving, is it not accurate to say that coerced behavior is just as morally praiseworthy as willing behavior since both further the process? Since any means can be justified by the end, and since no person can presume to speak authoritatively as to what behavior will actually promote the realization of the desired end, ethics is once again adrift from universal obligation and concrete directives and correctives.

Pragmatism

Voluntaristic pragmatism asserts that "good" applies to whatever promotes our course of action or desired ends. Men like Dewey and James, building on the same concerns as the utilitarians, sought to make ethics relevant to man by associating it with human projects or goals. In the long run it turns out that there are only successful and less successful types of behavior; the evaluative difference between various activities is only one of degree, not one of quality or kind. Hence there is really no moral system at all, unless one posits that all men are obligated to act in a way which maximizes success—a principle which is as dubious as it is arbitrary. Pragmatism is not immune from the same type of criticisms which have been leveled against subjectivism and utilitarianism. In pragmatism moral obligation is out of place, an intrinsic good is unknown, authority is lacking, and selfish motivation is the only one known. Pragmatism is simply an unsuitable counter-intuitive foundation for morality.

Emotivism

All of the preceding schools of thought have in some way viewed the function of ethical discourse as informative; however, in the face of the verifiability criterion (which, in passing, nobody has been able to formulate adequately and consistently), commonly recognized moral judgments are *neither* empirically verifiable nor analytic truths. Hence a major new approach to the metaethical question was developed. It fundamentally held that, although valuational utterances have a grammatical similarity to factual assertions, the function of moral discourse is *noncognitive* or noninformative. *Emotive* function was attributed to ethical language by men like A. J. Ayer and C. L. Stevenson; according to them moral statements were really only expressive of feeling and personal approval (e.g., "Hurray for chastity!"). Moral utterances are not credited as being genuine judgments; so emotivism is concerned to deal only with the perlocutionary effects of ethical language. This approach does not take moral discourse seriously enough, however, for it is quite apparent that a person also uses moral utterance to recommend to others that they also follow this action (indeed, that they are obligated to do so). The emotivist has nothing to contribute as far as what moral locutions are or say or mean; it is difficult to analyze spontaneous, gut-level, bursting-forth expressions of feeling. Emotivism deprives ethics of any genuine directive value and places a great strain upon moral principles: how are they derived? what legitimizes them? why are they proper or improper? The moralist's given attitude cannot be open to discussion since it is noncognitive. So it seems that one is thrown back again upon an ethics of inclination, which (as we have previously observed) is really a nonethic. Emotivism can only have significance in an ethical discussion as a version of private subjectivism, and the inadequacies of that philosophy have already been demonstrated.

Prescriptivism

Another noncognitivist reply to the metaethical question has been that of R. M. Hare who heads the school of imperativism or *prescriptivism*. According to this line of thought moral utterances are really veiled commands; hence ethical language has a directive or commending function. The prescriptivist differs from the emotivist in that he is concerned with the illocutionary "speech-act" which moral utterances perform rather than their perlocutionary effect. Prescriptivism is afflicted with much of the same problem facing emotivism since they are both noncognitivist answers. The grounds for ethical prescriptions and the meaning of moral principles have been abandoned, leaving the central concerns of morality behind and future considerations of ethical direction closed to any discussion or investigation. Furthermore, both emotivism and imperativism dissolve any distinctiveness which moral language once had, for the central functions of moral utterance on the noncognitivists' view are also performed by other kinds of language which are completely indifferent to questions of morality. So not only is ethics undiscussable, it is simply not a separate discipline or concern of man. The imperative intrinsic in a moral utterance does not even have the arrogance of authority which is customarily associated with ethical commandments; imperativism reduces ethics to simple personal commendations or advice. That is, according to imperativism the veiled command inherent in moral utterance does not have the force of universally valid, authoritative command dictated by objective moral principle; rather, it is merely a personal expression of a desire to have others conform to a subjectively approved course of action. So although imperativism might seem to offer more hope for the ethical endeavor than emotivism, it actually leaves ethics as rootless, subjective, and nonobligatory as emotivism. This approach also fails to do justice to the seriousness with which people use their ethical language; they seem to imply that true *obligation* attaches to their moral judgments so that they are offering something stronger than a recommendation to others. The sheer relativism inherent in the imperativist's position is exhibited in his asserting that the descriptive meaning of "good" or any other ethical language can be completely different in every case of its usage; the only thing which is constant is the directive element. No objective qualities can be made the criteria for the application of "good." When pressed for justification for his moral utterances, the moralist cannot appeal to any inherent value (i.e., "goodness") in his recommended behavior; he could never say that it was *virtuous* to act in a particular way but only that it was *imperative!* If the prescriptivist supported his utterances by appealing to ascertainable values he would be forsaking his position, and if he said that a person should act in the way recommended because it was "good" (or any other valuational adjective) he would be reasoning in a vicious circle (e.g., "Jones is commanded to be truthful because it is commanded"). The imperativist can tell us what we *should* do, but he cannot tell us *why*. In the long run the imperativist even fails to offer guidance, for in situations of moral complexity or where there are conflicting recommendations, reasons cannot be urged for or against the given attitude of any moralist. Imperativism is another reversion to the nonethic of an ethic of inclination. All that which is customarily of distinctive moral interest has been eliminated from the picture.

Analytic Approach

Ethics fares no better under the analytic school, for the analyst restricts his attention to studying the role of moral language in common life circumstances. His job is merely that of analyzing and describing; he can offer no directive help or moral principle for situations in which one is morally uncertain. Moreover, there is no guarantee that the situations which he analyzes are instances of valid or genuine moral behavior or applications of true moral principle; hence, *if* the analyst laid down moral directives based on his study of the actual use made of moral language, he would be open to criticism for committing the naturalistic fallacy.

Existentialism

Existentialism is preoccupied with ethical situations where genuine decisions must be made by the "free" man. Being disenchanted by the total lack of help the noncognitivist schools offer one in making difficult moral decisions, and being entirely sceptical of all the solutions offered by the informativist schools of ethics, the existentialist centers on the moral psychology which comes to play in profoundly complex and extraordinary circumstances requiring definite ethical decision. The virtues of authenticity and radical freedom are extolled; this fact, coupled with the existentialist emphasis that all human situations are morally unprecedented (a man cannot look to previous answers) and that each man chooses for *all* men in his moral decisions, puts an intolerable strain upon the moralist. He is to consider himself completely alone and without any moral guidance whatsoever; the dreadful responsibility he has leaves him in the anguish of moral paralysis. Out of such a situation authentic decisions can be made by the radically free man. This is the one virtue: that the moralist *acts*. The direction he takes in his behavior is irrelevant; what counts is that *he* alone made the bold decision and dramatically acted. He can help the man who is being mugged, or he can help mug him; either act, if an authentic choice, would be moral. Ethical decisions must be spun right out of thin air, for the man who makes the "authentic" decision must be free from his passions (for *he chooses* whether to resist or give in to them), from motives (since there is *no* psychological centrum or ego to which motives could adhere, and since the agent himself must *first decide* what kinds of reasons he will allow to have weight *before* he begins to rationally deliberate), from reality-in-itself (since man, who is being-for-itself, lies outside the causal series altogether), and from any human essence (since existence precedes and formulates essence). Existentialism, then, does not even have the advantage of being an unethical ethics of *inclination* (like emotivism, etc.); it is simply an ethics of pure volition (or *alleges* that it is anyway). Man is free from any antecedently fixed values according to the existentialist; value is *defined* as it is *chosen*. Jean-Paul Sartre says that the very starting point of existentialism is Dostoyevsky's words, "If God did not exist, everything would be possible"; based on the absence of God, says Sartre, man has nothing to cling to and all values disappear. Every choice is consequently as justifiable as it is absurd; there are not good and bad choices, but just choices. Sartre has the protagonist, Orestes, say in *The Flies,* "I am doomed to have no other law but mine." Sartre says of Mathieau, the protagonist of *The Age of Reason,* "There would be for him no good nor evil unless he brought them into being." Obviously existentialism is the complete annihilation of ethics, for within that school of thought it is impossible to make a *wrong* free choice. Responsibility and ethic are appropriate only to a world in which there are objective moral principles which can be accepted or rejected, followed or violated. There is nothing ethical at stake in a "moral decision" for the existentialist; hence, negative ethical judgments are impossible and positive ones are superfluous.

Evaluation and Comparison

Such then is the graveyard of autonomous ethics; each gravestone reads the Satanic temptation, "Ye shall be as gods, knowing good and evil." When man turns away from covenantal theonomy to autonomy, when he despises God's law in favor of humanistic self-law, the inevitable result is spiritual death for man and the loss of any hope for ethics. The autonomous philosophies of man have failed to answer the crucial questions of both normative ethics and metaethics; they have thus failed because each has assumed a nonbiblical anthropology wherein man is not the creature of an authoritative and sovereign Lord-Creator who has placed His indelible image in man and has perspicuously revealed Himself to each man in every fact of man's environment. Rather man is taken to be, as Sartre unpretentiously puts it in *Being and Nothingness,* "the being who tries to become God." Rather than submitting himself to God and God's self-attesting word, man has attempted to deify himself; the consequence of this in the area of ethics is that God's law is rejected or ignored in favor of a moral law which man himself will devise or validate. Man is *culpable* for trying to develop his own ethic, for God's image and revelation are inescapable; man *knows* himself to be a creature accountable to God and responsible to God's demands. Theonomy condemns autonomy. The very fact that *God* has uttered the law makes man obligated to it since he is the creature of God. God's law is ethically self-attesting; as such it cannot be questioned, appealed, ignored, or replaced.

Autonomous ethics has failed to supply an adequate meaning for "good." It has failed to supply any genuine *authority* for ethics. All of the autonomous schools of ethics finally fall short of providing actual moral direction and correction; they do not supply the *guidance* which man longs for in studying morality. An effective *motivation* is not suggested in the ethics of autonomy; nor is ethical *power* provided. A final *goal* or aim of ethics is either unknown or open to question in autonomous ethics. In one or all of these vital elements of a genuine ethic the philosophies of autonomy let man down.

By contrast, the ethics of theonomy is a genuine ethic. "Good" is identified with God; anything which is good is God-like. God reveals to man *what* is God-like behavior; He tells the creature how to practice holiness. The law of God is good, for its Author is good; the law is the transcript of God's holiness. This law is very explicit with respect to moral directives and correctives; man is given concrete ethical guidance by the law of God. This law is also authoritative, for the Lord-Creator stands behind it and will judge on the basis of it. All men have a clear revelation of God and know that they are obligated to keep His word; there is no epistemological skepticism with respect to morality. Ethics has a definite relation to *facts*; the same God who created and defined the material world is the Law-giver who demands the obedience of man. Because the world is as it is, because God is who He is (Creator and Lord), man must behave as prescribed in God's law. Obligation can be derived from the facts of God's character and existence. Because the biblical God is the living and true God who shall hold man accountable, man *is* accountable to God and obligated to keep God's law. Man should be motivated to keep this law by faith in God and reverence for His Person; in the light of God's grace and/or coming judgment, a person is impelled to obey the commandments of God. The enabling power of obedience to God's law for the believer and the effective agent which restrains the unbeliever from being as unlawful as he could be is the Holy Spirit; God supplies His Spirit, who exercises the power of common grace and sanctifying grace. The power of obedience is most intensely and genuinely known by the Christian who, under the New Covenant, has the law written upon his heart by God; the Spirit causes him to grow up into the obedient stature of Christ, thereby fulfilling the law in the believer. The goal of theonomic ethics is the glory of God and service of His kingdom; by obeying God's law the Christian honors and magnifies God's name, bows to His authority, extols His wisdom. Through obedience to God's law the believer is an effective servant of the kingdom by promoting and seeking its righteousness, by enforcing its demands in the world, by spreading its bounds; the demands of God's kingdom are applied to self, family, society, and church. This then is the only true ethic for man; to follow another is to deny God His due. Commitment to an autonomous ethic (any moral system which does not fully acknowledge and promote the law of God) is a choice of death and curse in the face of blessing and life.

All non-Christian ethics ultimately seek information and a standard for ethics in man's moral consciousness; it attempts to divorce the metaphysical question from the ethical. The nature and authority of morality must exist independently of God for the unbeliever; the "good" must be *impersonal.* Man is forced to find direction for himself; and the inevitable outcome is subjectivism or relativism. There is no hope in non-Christian ethics; there is no promise of enabling power, of sure direction, of the victory of the right. Having no grounds for ethical responsibility and no justification for the consistency and validity of moral demands, the non-Christian ethic becomes ego-centric rather than ego-regulating. Man is not dealt with as a unity by the autonomous ethicists; he is dichotomized into phenomenal/noumenal categories, and there is a one-sided stress on his intellect, or emotions, or volitions.

How totally different is the biblical ethic of theonomy! Christian ethics is bound to an absolute, objective authority in God; good does not exist independently of Him and cannot be discussed without bringing Him into the picture. The moral principles followed by the Christian are *personal* imperatives, not abstract ideals; they can only be learned by revelation, never by man's own searching. The Christian does not assume that the present state of the world is normal or that his moral consciousness is normal; this is the fatal presupposition of autonomy. The believer knows that he needs to be corrected and directed, for he cannot trust his own reasoning or inclinations; even God's general revelation must be seen through the corrective lenses of Scripture. Evil is not inherent in the world; so the Christian has the bright hope of its defeat and judgment. The power of the Spirit and pattern of the law are sufficient to destroy the bondage and effects of Satan in a person's life and world conditions. Although perfection is not possible until final glorification, and although a thoroughly righteous society will not exist until the establishment of the eschatological new heavens and earth, nevertheless God is at work in the Christian and in His Church even now; sanctification is taking place, and the forces of evil can be reproved and nullified by the positive forces of God's Spirit in accordance with His holy law. The Christian is never left in situations of moral perplexity; everything he needs to be perfectly equipped for all good works has been supplied to him ((2 Tim. 3:16 f.) and there is no situation in which he is left in utter moral insolubility (1 Cor. 10:13). Obligation to God's law is grounded in His authority as Creator; His final judgment will punish all disobedience and redress all moral imbalance. God, through His law, deals with man as a unified personality; He makes an absolute demand upon man's thinking, feeling, and willing, for His law touches upon every area of life. The ethics of theonomy is God-centered, then, rather than man-centered; it will regulate and correct man in order to bring glory to God. Only the ethics of theonomy can supply man with his needed moral system.

The main problem with autonomous ethics is that it ignores God's authority and revealed will; this in itself is immoral and rebellious. It should be rather clear, therefore, that genuine Christian ethics must not align itself with the autonomous methodology and systems of unbelieving philosophy. The Christian should *never* attempt to find out the principles of morality outside of God's revelation and direction; the neutrality proposed by Plato in the *Euthyphro* is sin. The Christian is not relieved of his obligations as a *son of God* when he studies ethics; God's clear revelation is the light in which all moral questions (as with *all* questions) must be answered. Theonomy must be *central* in Christian ethics. We do not decide to follow God's law after it has been validated by the categorical imperative or paralleled by any other secular philosophical ethic; we do not demand autonomous justification for God's commandments. We obey because we love, revere, and trust our Creator, never questioning His wisdom. No apostate standard shall be allowed to evaluate and pass judgment upon God's law. Theonomy, and theonomy alone, must be the standard of Christian ethics. The sole Law-giver and Judge is God. Hence God's law must be *the* criterion by which we evaluate the secular systems of ethics. The "goodness" of God and absolute authority of His word are *a priori* presuppositions for the Christian. The clay cannot talk back to the potter (Isa. 45:9), and the vassals have no right to question the Lord (cf. Matt. 20:1 ff.). We will be blessed only if we *faithfully* obey the directives of our God without questioning His word, just as Abraham did (Gen. 22:1 ff.; Heb. 11:17 ff.). When Job demands an interview with God, it is *God* who does the questioning, thereby asserting His sovereign Lordship and affirming that man cannot call Him into question (Job 38-42). "Let God be true and every man a liar" (Rom. 3:4), for "His work is perfect, for all His ways are just; a God of faithfulness and without injustice, righteous and upright is He" (Deut. 32:4, NASV). The only foundation for a Christian ethic, and hence the only foundation for any genuine and true morality, is the holy law of God.

Theonomy is pitted against autonomy; no man can take stand in between, for no man can serve two masters (Matt. 6:24). The authority and righteousness of God must be asserted against any and all serpents who question His goodness and veracity. Even if God should ask that we sacrifice the only son of promise, we must never demur or question; His revealed will alone defines the righteousness which is becoming of the believer (cf. Gen. 22; Heb. 11:17-19). We do not attempt to be as God, determining good and evil; rather, we gladly take our place beneath the sovereign Lordship of the Triune God. His word, not our autonomous reasoning, is our law. Theonomy is the *exclusive* normative principle, the only standard, of Christian ethics. It is all or nothing, ethic or non-ethic, obedience or sin.

Chapter 15

LATENT ANTINOMIANISM

Two Lines of Resistance

THERE are two types of antinomianism which threaten the ethic of theonomy in the Christian Church: outright and latent. Those who hold to the former brand see any kind of external authority which is applied to the Christian life as repugnant to their "spiritual" freedom; the law of God, therefore is *not* the principle used for knowing God's will, but instead a vague notion of the Spirit "realizing" itself in the human will is the standard of moral direction. For these antinomians maintenance of the law is legalism of the letter rather than living in the Spirit; they would replace the objective authority of God's revealed law with Christian self-determination, conscience, and "freedom" (to call this a misnomer would be an understatement). This position is contravened by all which has been written above; it represents a substitution of autonomy for theonomy. Hence this brand of antinomianism is out of accord with what we have found God's word to teach about the law, sanctification, the Spirit, the covenant, grace and love; it is simply a non-Christian ethic baptized with Christian terminology. What has been said previously about autonomy and its character as totally opposed to the biblical ethic must also be applied to this mistaken idea of the Christian life. Although many in Christian churches propound it, such a "morality of the Spirit" is no more genuinely Christian than is "the morality of the Serpent" which we read of in Genesis 3. Satan's advice is, "Look to yourself, make up your own mind; don't lose your freedom by legalistically following God's command"; he urged this upon our first parents, and he urges it upon many in the church today. The supposedly "Christian" ethic of self-determination suffers the same fatal defects as any non-Christian ethic of inclination, but an even more serious problem is that it simply fails to square with God's authoritative word (see previous sections of this treatise).

By not attempting to follow and do the *Lord's sayings*, the antinomian has founded his house upon the sand (Luke 6:46 ff.); although he may honor God with the lip, his heart is far from the Lord since that which he teaches is the precept of *men*. Lest we deny the Lordship of Christ in ethics by turning the grace of God into licentiousness (cf. Jude 4) and thereby show ourselves to be slaves of sin rather than servants of righteousness (cf. Rom. 6:16-18), we must endorse the holy and authoritative law of God in life and word and mind. "O how love I thy law! it is my meditation all the day" (Ps. 119:97, AV); by faith that law is established in our lives (Rom. 3:31). The Spirit witnesses to the law and empowers our obedience; thereby all humanistic morality and every competing authority is chased away. The dark night of sin must yield to the Light.

The latent brand of antinomianism is also quite prevalent today among Christians. Although there is an evident concern for God's law, this attitude still feeds upon the polluted stream of autonomy. Latent antinomianism gladly accepts the place of God's law in the Christian life, and so on the surface it does not *appear*—and in many cases is not *intended—to* be antinomian in its outlook. Then enters the difficulty. Having paid courtesy to the law of God, the latent antinomian proceeds to arbitrate *which* of God's laws he deems appropriate to the Christian life today. That is, the latent antinomian agrees that a Christian must follow God's law, but he looks to himself to choose *how much* of God's law he will consider as binding. In the final analysis the latent antinomian is actually his own moral authority; in taking upon himself to delimit the extent to which the Older Testamental law applies to him he is not really submitting to God's will but rubber-stamping it where it parallels his own feeling. This brand of antinomianism is subtle, for its proponent will defend the sanctity of God's law; however, he will not recognize *all* of God's law as his obligation. *Without clear scriptural justification* he will presume to nullify portions of that law. This is eventually (even if unwittingly) nothing other than self-law; the difference between it and non-Christian autonomy is that "latent antinomians" take their moral principles from among the set of commandments given by God, but they take a smorgasbord approach to that set.

Two points should be noted here. *First,* the type of antinomian we are referring to here should be distinguished from Christians who legitimately see that not every ordinance of the Older Testament applies in the same manner to the New Testament Christian (i.e., the ceremonial law). These two are distinguished by the fact that the latter bases his qualified circumscription on the immediate teaching and direction of God's word, while the former goes *beyond* this and uses the razor of his own ratiocination to shave off *further* demands of God's revealed law.

Second, not all Christians are as conscious as they should be that their moral reasoning is subtly antinomian. In fact, *every* believer must be careful to correct himself from time to time as he catches himself rationalizing away God's demands on his life (it is easy to fall into excuse making: "That law does not apply to these unique circumstances," "This command does not apply to me," "That ordinance is not relevant in our age," etc.). Self-examination is constantly called for in the Christian life; we must review our motives, our moral calculations, our handling of God's word. Recognizing that "latent antinomianism" is theoretically as autonomous as "outright antinomianism," the Christian must seek to purge it from his life with the help of God's Spirit.

If we are to submit to God's law, then we must submit to every bit of it *(as well* as its *own* qualifications). God cannot be taken as a *general* moral authority with Christians presuming to have the authority of *specification*, for no man can serve two masters (Matt. 6:24). In such a situation the Christian's own moral consciousness will end up being lord in his life; the only alternative is whole-hearted submission to the whole of the Lord's law as laid down in Scripture. Every jot and tittle of the law must be as jealously guarded as Christ guarded it (Matt. 5:17-20); if we do not defend and live by *every* word that proceeds from God's mouth (Matt. 4:4), then we will end up using God's law for our own selfish advantage, just as did the Pharisees.

Unwarranted Compartmentalization

Latent antinomianism expresses itself in different ways. Sometimes it comes in the form of multiplying distinctions and qualifications which are not enumerated in God's word. Some people (e.g., Charles Hodge)[1] try to draw a line between "moral" and "civil" laws with the intention of giving the impression that the latter class are mere matters of time-bound administration which are irrelevant today; in this way they can shave off those laws of God which have social and punitive application. Yet Scripture recognizes no such demarcation. God's law *does* and *should* have public implications, for He alone can be the sole legislator with respect to issues of crime and punishment. When people get so *accustomed* to doing things in a secular way because they live amidst a secular society, they bring themselves to believe that there simply is no other way to do things; it is not surprising, then, they are recalcitrant to having God's law transform the society and its traditionalism or "progress" (take your pick). The concealed presumption in eliminating commandments from God which directly apply to social matters (e.g., the execution of certain types of criminals) is that a law from God is only valid if I can find a good reason for it or if it does not shock my general "Christian" feelings. Such an approach does not live under the sovereign authority of God but is a reversion to rationalism and inclination.

Another way of nullifying the full force of the biblical ethic is by distinguishing between different facets (call them "modal spheres") of life and then declaring that Scripture applies directly only to matters of

---

[1] Cf. *Systematic Theology* (Grand Rapids: Wm. B. Eerdmans, reprinted 1968), vol. III, pp. 268-269. Regrettably, Hodge left his customary cogency here and used some of the most infelicitous reasoning imaginable in moral philosophy or scriptural exegesis (of which he offers none). At best, he offers a modified dispensational approach (except that most dispensationalists are more thorough or consistent) and at worst an explicit foreshadowing of situationism in ethics. At either rate, one must shudder when Hodge unreflectingly says that the "degree of punishment may vary with the varying condition of society." Such is to allow God to be viewed as arbitrary and to allow man an open door to totalitarian persecution and cruelty.

"faith." God's written law is useful in the religious life and devotion of a Christian, but it cannot be used in the outside pursuits of politics, law enforcement and penology, sociology, economics, etc.—so we are told. For the Bible is a book about "faith," not having theoretical relevance for natural science, philosophy, or social science. Such a dichotomizing of life, and such an arbitrary restriction of the Bible's scope and application, are in open discord with Scripture's own witness to itself: "All scripture is given by inspiration of God, and is profitable for doctrine, for reproof, for correction, for instruction in righteousness: that the man of God may be perfect, *thoroughly* furnished unto *all* good works" (2 Tim. 3:16 f., AV); "The anointing which you received from Him abides in you, and you have no need for anyone to teach you; but as His anointing teaches you about all things, and is true and is not a lie, and just as it has taught you, you abide in Him"(1 John 2:27, NASV); "I (the Lord) will put My laws into their minds, and I will write them upon their hearts" and "out of the heart are the *issues of life*" (Heb. 8:10, NASV; Prov. 4:23, AV).

Extraneous Rules of Interpretation

Latent antinomianism also appears in the garb of alien and unwarranted hermeneutical principles. A common approach is to say that only those commandments which are *repeated* in the New Testament are binding today. However, is this what Scripture says? Is there biblical justification for such an interpretative rule? No, in fact there is strong presumption in favor of the *very opposite* approach. When we read through the New Testament we see that its writers presupposed *continuity* with the Older Testamental Scriptures (and not merely in matters of prophecy). The section on New Testament substantiation in a former portion of this treatise cited numerous Scriptures where a New Testament author appeals to, alludes to, or quotes the prescriptions of the Older Testament, and this is done with no apology or rationalization for violating a general policy of discontinuity with the Older Testament. The New Testament writers assumed that they built upon the foundation of the Older Testament teaching; Christ definitely ratified such an assumption by saying, "Do not begin to think that I came in order to abrogate the law or prophets, I came not to abrogate but to confirm; for until heaven and earth pass away not one iota or one horn shall become invalid, not until everything has taken place" (Matt. 5:17 f.).

Only God has the authority and prerogative to discontinue the binding force of anything He has revealed; man, therefore, must live by everything which proceeds from God's mouth (Matt. 4:4) without diminishing it (Deut. 4:2). Since the law is *not* against the promises (Gal. 3:21), we are not warranted to affirm discontinuity with the Older Testament except where expressly indicated otherwise; such a method would be backwards. We must live by every Scripture, not just those which God has spoken *twice* (and in the right places). The Christian is not to wield an "unwritten Torah" in opposition to God's clearly revealed word. *Continuity* between the Testaments, not discontinuity, *must* be presupposed.[2] "Whatever was written in earlier times was written for our instruction" (Rom. 15:4). If the Scriptures are seen as a progressive revelation, then the New Testament must be used to understand, not undermine, the Older Testament; again the *presumption* would have to be continuity, not contradiction. The attempt to cancel the obligation which Christians have to *all* of God's law by introducing a hermeneutical principle not justified by the teaching of Scripture is simply an imposition of an autonomous requirement upon the canon of God's word. "The supreme judge by which all controversies of religion are to be determined . . . can be no other but the Holy Spirit speaking *in the Scriptures.*"[3]

Disregarding Details

Latent antinomianism works through the multiplication of illegitimate distinctions, through the introduction of an alien hermeneutic,

---

[2] The great *contrast* between the Older Testament and the New is the contrast between *anticipation* and *realization in the historia-salutis.* A little reflection here will show that even this contrast presupposes *continuity.*

[3] Westminster Confession of Faith, chap. I, section X.

and often through *oversimplification.* This third approach is found in those who will accept that the Older Testamental law binds the Christian being sanctified in this age, but who balk before the *extent* of God's law and decide to recognize only the Decalogue as applicable. Now the Ten Commandments are an *excellent* summary of God's law, but a summary does *not cancel the content* of that which it summarizes. Love summarizes the law, but it does not replace it; the Decalogue summarizes the biblical ethic, but it is not a substitute for the whole. The Ten Commandments cannot be understood and properly applied without the explanation given them throughout the case laws of the Older Testament. The case law illustrates the application or qualification of the principle laid down in the general commandment. The case law elaborates the commandment by means of a concrete illustration (e.g., the word of Ex. 20:13 is partially explicated by the case mentioned in Deut. 19:4-6). The sixth commandment is of particular interest here, for standing alone the law, "Thou shalt not murder," constitutes an ethical tautology since "murder" means "illegitimate killing" (thus: "Thou shalt not do the killing which thou shalt not do"). However, given the extended series of case laws for this commandment throughout the Scriptures, the law has information and direction to impart; its summary nature is not disquieting.

Obviously, then, the biblical ethic could not be limited to the Decalogue—or else men would end up being their own moral authorities, extracting from broad general principles of morality what their own particular ethic shall be. Each man would give the Ten Commandments an interpretation which is fit in his own eyes (and, at base, we have returned to an ethic of inclination). All interpreters of Scripture need biblical cross-references to aid them, and the Lord provides needed interpretive guides in the case law. Furthermore, the New Testament definitely gives us examples of authoritative use and application of Older Testamental law which does *not* come specifically from the Ten Commandments (see previous discussion). Does Scripture, then, limit the law which is binding upon Christians to the Ten Commandments? Our Lord definitely did not; according to His word, *every jot* and *every tittle* has abiding validity (Matt. 5:18). To follow the *Lord's sayings* is to be founded upon the rock (Matt. 7:24); only that moral edifice which takes the whole of God's law for its foundation will stand.

Just as the Christian ethicist may not overtly pit theonomy against autonomy, neither can he be *subtly* antinomian. A smorgasbord approach is illegitimate. Matthew 5:17-18 condemns both autonomy and latent antinomianism in the Christian life; verse 17 confirms the validity of *the law*, and verse 18 confirms the validity of *all* the law.

VII. APPLICATION OF THE THESIS TO THE STATE

Chapter 16

THE RESPONSIBILITY OF CIVIL MAGISTRATES: INTRODUCTION

BECAUSE Christ confirmed every stroke of God's law in the Sermon on the Mount and that law includes direction for the civil magistrate (especially with respect to penal sanctions), a *prima facie* answer to the question, "Ought the civil magistrate to obey and enforce the Older Testament law of God (particularly its penal sanctions)?" is disclosed to us:

> The purity and holiness of Moses' social and civil law is amply vindicated in the Sermon on the Mount. This sermon is the final word on Morals. But its utterances are not new. The Pharisees by their traditions had made void the law. . . . The law-giver on Mt. Sinai and the law-expounder on the mount in Galilee exposed and swept away their false philosophy and morals and restored Old Testament morality to its true place in all social and civil relations.[1]

Every detail of God's law has abiding validity from the time of Christ's advent to the time of His return (i.e., the passing away of heaven and earth). Therefore, we are instructed that responsibility to all of God's commandments continues in this present age. Just as the magistrate of the Older Testament had divine imperatives which he was responsible to carry out, so also magistrates in the era of the New Testament are under obligation to those commands in the Book of the Law which

---

[1] J. B. Shearer, *Hebrew Institutions, Social and Civil* (Richmond: Presbyterian Committee of Publications, 1910), p. 45.

apply to civil affairs and social penology. Christ affirms that not even the least of the commandments of God's law has lost its binding character, in which case His disciples must not teach the relaxation or breaking of any law from God. Because the penal sanctions of God's law are imperatives delivered with divine authority and approval, the follower of Christ should teach that the civil magistrate is yet under moral obligation to enforce the law of God in its social aspect.

Clearly the blanket endorsement of every jot and tittle of God's law by Jesus Christ in Matthew 5:17-19 puts the burden of proof on anyone who would hold that the civil magistrate is *not* to carry out the law's demands to demonstrate from Scripture itself that an exception is distinctly enunciated by God. No one but God Himself has the prerogative of diminishing from His law (Deut. 4:2); as creatures of the sovereign Creator men must live by every word from God's mouth (Matt. 4:4). Consequently neither imaginative models brought to bear upon Scripture nor arguments from silence can contravene the explicit teaching of Matthew 5:17-19. Any rationale aside from the authoritative declarations of God's inscripturated revelation can only function as a procrustean bed when used to eliminate current day observation of some portion of God's law. Hence the question posed by this chapter (viz., ought the civil magistrate today carry out the penal sanctions of God's law?) receives a *prima facie* affirmative answer from the Sermon on the Mount.

However, that affirmative answer is further corroborated when one examines the specific teaching of Scripture on the nature and responsibility of the civil magistrate. While the general principle of continuity between the Older and New Testaments is established in Matthew 5:17-19, the particular doctrine of rulership in society as set forth throughout the Bible teaches that all magistrates, past and present, Jewish and Gentile, are responsible to God for their rule and required to enforce the law of God.

In the following chapters the general conclusion as to the magistrate's theonomic responsibility which derives from Matthew 5:17-19 will be studied with respect to the scriptural doctrine of social rule, the separation of church and state, the relevance of Theocratic considerations, and the question of penology.[2] The attempt will be made to see whether the Bible's teaching in these areas modifies the initial answer which has been suggested above for the problem posed in this chapter. The next chapters are devoted to an analysis of the civil magistrate according to the Older and New Testaments. Should general discontinuity be established between the doctrine of the state as it applies to Older Testament Israel and the doctrine of the state applying to either (1) the nations outside of Israel during the former dispensation or (2) the civil governments of the New Testament era, then there would be reason to question whether the law binding Israelite rulers properly continues to direct civic leaders today. Thus the following inductive analysis of the civil magistrate in Older Testament Israel, the Gentiles of the Older Testament, and the New Testament, has a direct relevance to the question at hand.

---

[2] While the literature available on these topics has played a role in the development of my treatise, very little of that literature is distinctive enough to be footnoted. Moreover, the material in print is generally not geared toward answering the question posed in this thesis.

Chapter 17

THE MAGISTRATE IN OLDER TESTAMENT ISRAEL

God Sovereignly Appoints and Removes Rulers

IT is a well-established doctrine of the Older Testament that God made and unmade the rulers over Israel; there was no authority except by God, and the existing authorities were ordained by God. Saul was appointed by God (1 Sam. 9:16; 10:1) and subsequently rejected by God (1 Sam. 16:1). David was chosen and made king over Israel by God (1 Chron. 28:4). It was also from God that the kingdom came to Solomon (1 Kings 2:15; 1 Chron. 28:5). First Kings 14:7-8 tells us that God tore the kingdom away from David's house and gave it to Jeroboam, whom He had exalted to be prince over Israel. So also God exalted Baasha from the dust (1 Kings 16:1-2), anointed Jehu over Ahab (2 Kings 9:6-9), and established by His sovereign control over any and all rulers in Israel (or Judah). The political movements of the people had full reality (e.g., they selected and acknowledged their leaders; cf. 1 Kings 12:20; 2 Kings 9:13) yet even as they were the ones who made the individual king, so there was the corresponding divine sovereignty in establishing the ruler (e.g., 1 Kings 11:31, 37; 2 Kings 9:1-2).

The relationship which a ruler sustains to those whom he ordains (LXX: τάσσω; e.g., appointing army captains, 1 Sam. 22:7; appointing a court recorder, 2 Sam. 23:23; or appointing Levites to minister in the Temple, 1 Chron. 16:4) is precisely the relationship which is described as holding between God and earthly rulers. God "ordained" the angel with a flaming sword (Gen. 3:24, LXX) just as He "ordained" judges over His people Israel (2 Kings 7:11; 1 Chron. 17:10, LXX). Moreover, the authority or dominion which civil rulers have is called ἐξουσία (e.g., 2 Kings 20:13; Isa. 39:2; Ps. 113:2; Ezra 7:24; Neh. 5:15; 9:37;

Eccl. 7:20; 10:4-5; Jer. 28:28, Alexandrian ms., LXX), as in the phrase "even as a king having power" (Eccl. 8:4, LXX). Such ἐξουσία is given or withheld by God (e.g., Eccl. 5:18; 6:2, LXX), can apply to God's own powerful dominion (Dan. 3:33; 4:23, LXX), that of the Messiah (Dan. 7:14, LXX), and that which is given to the saints (Dan. 7:27, LXX). Consequently, according to the Older Testament (LXX) it can properly be said that the οὖσαι ἐξουσίαι (powers that be) are ὑπο θεοῦ τετάγμεναι (ordained by God), which corresponds to Paul's assertion in Romans 13:1.

The principle of God's sovereign appointment of rulers in Older Testament Israel is clearly exemplified in the statement of Hosea 13:11, "I have given thee a king in mine anger, and have taken him away in my wrath" (ASV). God ordained and removed the civil magistrates of Israel. The ruler had a higher Ruler over him, a Ruler who appointed him, and who gave him his power or authority.

Rulers, as God's Appointees, Are Not to Be Resisted

Because of the close association of rulers with God's appointment it was forbidden that the people should revile God or curse the ruler (Ex. 22:28; cf. Eccl. 10:20), a principle to which Paul appealed in Acts 23:5. Honor must be given to whom it is due (cf. Rom. 13:7).

Thus death was prescribed for anyone who rebelled against Joshua's command (Josh. 1:18), and David had the Amalekite who lifted his hand against the Lord's anointed king, Saul, executed (2 Sam. 1:14-16). It was precisely because Saul was the *Lord's anointed* that David would not lift his hand against him (1 Sam. 24:7, 11; 26:23); nobody could attack the Lord's appointed leader and be guiltless because that is forbidden by God (1 Sam. 26:9, 11). Even failure to protect the king from attack (1 Sam. 26:16) or cursing him (2 Sam. 19:21) are considered crimes worthy of death. Because the king's word has power and because he does whatsoever he pleases (in these respects he resembles God, whom nobody can interrogate; cf. Dan. 4:35), one should obey his command, not oppose sore rebuke, not defy his power, and not throw off allegiance (Eccl. 8:2-5).[1]

Thus by refraining from cursing and reviling the civil magistrate, by not defying him or attacking him, the Older Testament citizen was subject to the higher powers and mindful not to oppose the ruler ordained of God (cf. Rom. 13:1-2).

Rulers Bear Religious Titles

In 2 Samuel 8:18, at the end of a list of David's chief officers, David's sons are designated "priests" (using the common Hebrew word, כֹּהֵן, for that cultic office). Not being from the tribe of Levi, but Judah, these sons could not be cultic functionaries. The parallel passage from 1 Chronicles (18:17) helps us to understand this designation, for in its place is substituted "heads with respect to the (hand) power of the king." The Septuagint also explains the designation, rendering "court princes" in 2 Samuel (Kings) 8:18 and "chief deputies (successors) of the king" in 1 Chronicles 18:17. Therefore, David's sons were political officials, probably being counselors at the king's side (based on the fact that "the king's sons" are placed together with a list of counselors and "the king's friend" in 1 Chron. 27:32-33).[2] What is significant here is that political office bearers should receive the honorific and religiously connotative title "priests."

The same phenomenon is found in 1 Samuel 20:26. There Ira the Jairite (possibly one of David's mighty warriors; cf. 2 Sam. 23:38) is named in a later list of David's officers (in the same position of "David's

[1] Christian D. Ginsburg, *The Song of Songs and Coheleth (Commonly Called the Book of Ecclesiastes): Translated from the Original Hebrew, with a Commentary, Historical and Critical*, ed. Harry M. Orlinsky, The Library of Biblical Studies (New York: KTAV Publishing House, Inc., 1857 [reprinted 1970]), pp. 391-395.

[2] Roland de Vaux, *Ancient Israel*, Vol. I (Social Institutions), trans. Darton, Longman & Todd Ltd. (New York: McGraw-Hill Book Co., 1965) says that this possibly denotes police officers (pp. 119-120); however, the (allegedly) *technical* designation, "king's sons," does not appear in 2 Samuel 8:18, but instead we find the personal identification, "*David's* sons."

sons" from the earlier list) as "priest unto David." Again, Ira could not qualify for cultic service since he descended from Manasseh (cf. Num. 32:41; Deut. 3:14; 1 Kings 4:13) and thus was not a member of one of the Levitical families. Evidently he was a chief minister or counselor unto David; in his governmental role he received a religious title.

In the list of Solomon's officers found in 1 Kings 4:2-6, David's grandson (through Nathan; cf. 2 Sam. 5:14), Zabud, is designated as a "priest." In this place, however, the text goes right on to explain, by means of an appositive phrase, that Zabud was "the king's friend" or his confidential counselor. Hence we have three definite instances where the political cabinet of the king in the person of his counselors was considered to have such responsibility to God that its members were called "priests." It seems quite likely, also, that the prime administrator of the kingdom (the first among the king's confidential advisors) is, in 1 Kings 4:2, being designated a "priest." Azariah, son of Zadok, is called *the* priest (rather than reading: "Azariah, son of Zadok the priest"—which leaves Azariah without any designated office). The definite article before "priest" would indicate foremost status among the other "priests" (which, as explained in v. 5 following, must be taken as denoting king's counselors or "friends").[3] Therefore, the prime minister and chief counselors of the king had political positions which, due to their service before God, were assigned the religiously significant label of "priests." These rulers in Israel had such dignity that they were considered authorized *ministers of God* (cf. Rom. 13:4, 6).

Hence Rulers Are God's Vicegerents, Avengers of His Wrath

The sword of judgment and punishment is predominantly associated with God in the Older Testament. The Angel of the Lord is often portrayed as carrying a sword (e.g., Num. 22:23, 31; Josh. 5:13; 2 Kings 19:35; 1 Chron. 21:16, 27, 30). Contrary to the imaginations of

---

[3] C. F. Keil, *The Book of the Kings,* trans. James Martin, Biblical Commentary on the Old Testament, by C. F. Keil and F. Delitzsch (Grand Rapids: William B. Eerdmans Publishing Co., [reprinted 1970]), pp. 44-45.

humanism, Scripture boldly and frequently speaks of the sword of the Lord God which falls in judgment upon sinners.[4] God sovereignly uses history for history's judgment, raising nation up against nation to effect His punishments. Revelation 6 graphically depicts this by saying that a great sword is given to the rider upon the red horse who takes peace away from the earth (v. 4); so also Death—Hades is given the sword to kill a quarter of the earth (v. 8). God's historical judgments, then, are described under the imagery of a sword. The sending of this avenging sword or its restraint is determined by the nation's relation to the law of God. Israel's obedience to God's commandments would be rewarded by the fact that no sword will come against the nation, but instead it shall put all enemies to flight (Lev. 26:6-7). By contrast, if Israel breaks the law of God, they will be punished by the sword (Lev. 26:25, 33, 36-37),[5] the climax of that judgment being revealed in Christ's declaration that Jerusalem shall fall by the edge of the sword (Luke 21:24).

Although the sword of punishment against disobedience is predominantly wielded by God in the Older Testament, the avenging sword is also associated with human government. It symbolizes the power and authority of both Pharaoh (Ex. 18:4) and Saul (2 Sam. 1:22), and thus could be generalized to stand for the executive power of the state (cf. Rom. 13:4). In the hands of human rulers the sword is used for lawful execution of criminals (1 Kings 1:51; 2:8; 2 Kings 11:15, 20) as well as the punishment of disobedient nations (Deut. 13:15; Judg. 20). Here it can be seen that the *magistrate's* use of the sword for punishment of those who disobey God's holy word reflects the punishment

---

[4] Cf. Ex. 5:3; 22:24; Deut. 32:41-42; Judg. 4:15; 2 Kings 19:7; 1 Chron. 21:12; Ps. 7:12; 17:13; 45:3; Isa. 27:1; 34:5-6; 41:2; 66:16; Jer. 9:16; 12:12; 24:10; 25:16, 27, 29, 31; 27:8; 28:17-18; 32:17; 44:13; 47:6; 49:37; 50:35-37; Ezek. 5:12, 17; 6:3; 11:8; 12:14; 14:17; 21:3-5; 21:15; 28:23; 29:8; 30:24; 33:2; Amos 4:10; 7:9; 9:1, 4; Nah. 2:13; Zeph. 2:12.

[5] Cf. Num. 14:43; Deut. 28:22; 32:25; Ezra 9:7; Ps. 78:62; Isa. 1:20; 3:25; 65:12; Jer. 5:17; 11:22; 14:12; 15:3; 16:4; 19:7; 20:4; Ezek. 6:11; Hos. 13:16; Amos 9:10; Zech. 11:17.

of law-breakers which has already been seen as represented in the imagery of *God* wielding a sword. The sword is God's to use for punishment, but it is obvious that the state also uses the sword to that end. We should conclude that the magistrate's authority to punish by the sword has been delegated to it by God. One way in which God realizes His justice upon those who are disobedient to His law is through the agency of the state. The sword it wields is thereby His sword and must be used according to His direction. When the use of the sword comes under Israel's own autonomous direction the nation sins against God. Saul killed the Lord's priests at Nob for aiding David, the Lord's anointed (1 Sam. 22:19)—an act so flagrantly sinful that Saul's guard would not carry it out against Jehovah's priests (v. 17). David set up Uriah to be killed in battle, and in consequence of this sin the sword would never depart from David's house (2 Sam. 12:9-10)—an example of the principle that all who take up the sword perish by the sword (Matt. 26:52). Israel took to the battlefield without the ark of the covenant and suffered defeat (1 Sam. 4:1-3). But the depth of Israel's depravity in autonomously using the sword is reflected in the fact that, just as Saul killed God's priests by the sword, Israel killed the prophets by the sword (e.g., 1 Kings 19:10; Jer. 2:30; 26:23) according to Hebrews 11:37. From these examples we learn that the magistrate's use of (God's) sword of judgment was to be at His direction and according to His will; the state had no independent right to slay men but had to be the avenger of God's wrath.

Similar conclusions result from an examination of *wrath* (ὀργή, LXX) and *vengeance* (ἐκδίκησις, LXX) in the Older Testament. Both are predominantly associated with God's response to disobedience to His holy will. God's "wrath" is occasioned by transgressions against His law[6] —which is to say that it is sin and evil against which God expresses His wrath.[7] His wrath is retribution against those who

---

[6] Cf. Deut. 11:17; 33:10; 2 Kings 22:13; 23:26; e.g., Ex. 32:10, 12; Num. 25:4; Deut. 13:17; 32:19; 1 Chron. 13:10; 2 Chron. 24:18; Ps. 105:23; 2 Sam. 6:7; Neh. 13:18, LXX.

[7] Cf. Num. 11:1; 12:9; 14:34; 16:22; 32:14; Deut. 9:19; 29:20, 24-28; Josh. 7:1; 2 Kings 1:18; 2 Chron. 28:13; 29:8; Ps. 37:3; 58:13; Dan. 9:16, LXX.

profane His covenant (Ps. 54:20-21, LXX). Thus when the civil magistrate punishes violations of the law of God in society that magistrate is expressing God's wrath. At Joshua's command Achan was executed to alleviate the Lord's wrath (Josh. 7:25; 22:20, LXX), and ten chiefs of the tribes went to warn the other tribes of the Lord's wrath against their rebellious sin (Josh. 22:18, LXX). We could note also that Saul was to execute God's fierce wrath against Amalek (1 Kings 28:18, LXX) and King David's judicial wrath against the criminal in Nathan's parable (2 Kings 12:5, LXX). Artaxerxes' command was for the people to obey God's law and avoid wrath (Ezra 7:23, LXX); in restored Jerusalem the princes and elders were to lead the way in alleviating the wrath of God due upon their disobedience (Ezra 10:14, LXX). Hezekiah also commanded Israel to serve Jehovah and thereby turn away His wrath (2 Chron. 30:8, LXX). When, by contrast, the king helped a sinner, God's wrath was then directed against the king (2 Chron. 19:2, LXX). By judging in accordance with God's commandments the judges could prevent God's wrath from coming upon themselves or their brethren (2 Chron. 19:10, LXX).

The Older Testament clearly declares that "vengeance" belongs to the Lord, and He will be one who repays or recompenses for wrong (Deut. 32:35, 41; cf. Ps. 94:1; especially at the great Day of Vengeance, Isa. 35:4; 61:2; 63:4; 66:15; Ps. 36:28, LXX). Vengeance is the Lord's, and it is based upon His holiness (Ps. 98:8; cf. Jer. 11:20, LXX). He renders vengeance as He recompenses justice (Deut. 32:43, LXX). God's vengeance or punishment is meted out according to a man's ways or practices (Hosea 12:2, LXX), and so only righteousness alleviates divine punishment (Ezek. 14:21, LXX). God's vengeance, like His wrath, is occasioned by iniquities, ungodliness, or sin against His law (Ezek. 7:27; 9:1; 20:4; Hos. 1:4; 2:13; Zech. 5:3, LXX)—indeed, bringing the two terms together, God is said to punish (avenge) with His wrath (Ezek. 5:15; 24:8; 25:11, 12, 14; Mic. 5:15; Nah. 1:2, LXX). However, while vengeance is the *Lord's,* the civil *magistrate* was still said to punish disobedience against God's law. The God who avenges blood (cf. Deut. 32:43, LXX) appointed Jehu as king and sent him to avenge (procure justice) for the blood of God's servants (2 Kings 9:7, LXX). The magistrate was to carry out punishment (vengeance) for specific violations of the law (e.g., Ex. 21:20-21; Deut. 18:19; Ezek. 23:45, LXX). But when kings and princes themselves are ungodly transgressors of the law God's vengeance will come against them (Zeph. 1:8, LXX). Thus the civil magistrate represents God's vengeance when He punishes law violations in society. Bringing together the facts that the magistrate can *express* God's *wrath* and *represent* God's *vengeance* against the disobedient, it would not be inappropriate to say that He is ἔκδικος εἰς ὀργὴν τῷ τὸ κακὸν πράσσοντι, "an avenger for wrath against the one practicing evil" (cf. Rom. 13:4).

Quite clearly the civil magistrate and judge are considered the vicegerents of God in the nation; as He judges in righteousness, according to law, so also they are to judge the people by means of God's righteous law. While the gods of the heathen acted in arbitrary and capricious fashion, the God of the Bible, the divine Judge, is a God of law. Thus Abraham declared, "Shall not the Judge of all the earth do right?" (Gen. 18:25). God's judgment is defined as the right, and His actions are always viewed as in accord with law: "All His ways are justice . . . just and right is he" (Deut. 32:4). Judgment and righteousness are essential to God's nature; "Thy righteousness is like the mountains of God; Thy judgments are a great deep" (Ps. 36:6). God says of Himself, "I am the Lord which exercises lovingkindness, judgment, and righteousness" (Jer. 9:24). Jehovah, who "administers judgment to the peoples" is the "righteous God" (Ps. 7:8, 9). Consequently He prepared His throne for judgment and will judge the world in righteousness, administering judgment to the peoples in uprightness (Ps. 9:7, 8). When God judges the earth He does so with righteousness (Ps. 96:13; cf. 50:6). Being the "God of recompenses" (Jer. 51:56), a righteous Lord who loves righteousness (Ps. 11:7), Jehovah judges in terms of His holy law. But Jehovah is not the only one who judges; He also requires men to exercise judgment (e.g., Ps. 33:5; Prov. 21:3; Isa. 5:7; 56:1). Their judgment should be an image of His own. Consequently God is a "lawgiver" (Isa. 33:22), and His law is the standard of righteousness and judgment for men. "Keeping the way of Jehovah" is "to do righteousness and justice" (Gen. 18:19). "The righteousness of

Jehovah" is placed in poetic parallel to "His ordinances" according to the Blessing of Moses (Deut. 33:21). Earlier in the Book of the Law Moses had declared, "And what great nation is there that hath statutes and ordinances so righteous as all this law which I set before you this day?" (Deut. 4:8). "It shall be righteousness unto us if we observe to do all this commandment before Jehovah our God as He hath commanded us" (Deut. 6:25). Now then, if God is the great Judge, if it is His judgment which is righteous and His law which defines justice, then by placing the civil magistrate and judge under obligation to carry out His commandments in the nation God constitutes them His deputies upon earth. The civil magistrate is the vicegerent under the righteous Judge. Thus they are forbidden to condemn the righteous (Isa. 5:23; Prov. 17:15; cf. Eccl. 5:8); instead, "Let judgment run down as waters and righteousness as a mighty stream" (Amos 5:24)—that is, "establish justice in the gate" (Amos 5:15). To do this the magistrate or judge must enforce the law of God (Deut. 17:9-11; cf. Ex. 18:16), and such is what he is commanded to do: "Ye shall do no unrighteousness in judgment . . . but in righteousness shalt thou judge thy neighbor" (Lev. 19:15, ASV; cf. v. 35). The Book of the Law prescribes that "Judges and officers shalt thou make thee in all thy gates. . . . and they shall judge the people with righteous judgment" (Deut. 16:18). In carrying out the penal sanctions of God's law the magistrate is "God's image" (cf. Gen. 9:5-6), for his judgment reflects that of the Lord. Just as God "will not justify the wicked" (Ex. 23:7), even so "If there be a controversy between men, and they come unto judgment, and the judges judge them, then they shall justify the righteous and condemn the wicked" (Deut. 25:1, ASV). As the divine Judge righteously judges, so must the vicegerent.

There is yet another way in which we can see that the civil magistrate is God's deputy or representative in matters of civic righteousness and social law. Jehovah was the covenant Lord in Israel (cf. Ex. 19:3-8), and His covenant had a definite legal basis (cf. Josh. 24:25) as is clear from the poetic parallelism between "statute" and "covenant" in 1 Chronicles 16:17. Therefore, God was the true king over Israel (Judg. 8:23; 1 Sam. 8:7; 12:12; Isa. 41:21; 43:15; 44:6; 47:6). The throne of

Israel was actually "the throne of Jehovah" (1 Chron. 29:23; 28:5), and He is represented as enthroned at the mercy seat of the ark of the covenant (Ps. 80:1; cf. Ps. 24:7-10 which refers to the bringing of the ark to Jerusalem). Thus God is the enthroned King over Israel, and of His rule we read, "righteousness and justice are the foundation of His throne" (Ps. 89:14; 97:2), referring to His righteous character and the tables of the law (which reflected that character) under the mercy seat in the ark of the covenant. So also the *earthly* king's throne was to be established on justice and righteousness (Ps. 72:1-2), for he was obligated to read the law of God daily as he sat upon the throne of the kingdom in order that he would not turn aside from the commandment (Deut. 17:18-20). The judges over the people had to rule according to the statutes of God's law (Ex. 18:20-22), and only when such judges are restored in Jerusalem will it truly be "a city of righteousness" (Isa. 1:21-26). If God's covenant is interchangeable with His law, the law which is the foundation of His kingly rule, and if the rule of earthly magistrates must be established upon, and directed by, the law of God, then the magistrate rules as God's representative and deputy. The earthly ruler is actually established *in* God's domain (1 Chron. 17:14) and made to sit upon the throne of *Jehovah's* kingdom (1 Chron. 28:5; 29:2); the king of Israel, their shield, actually belongs to Jehovah (Ps. 89:18). And thus in the words of the Queen of Sheba, "Blessed be Jehovah thy God, who delighteth in thee, to set thee on his throne, *to be king for Jehovah* thy God . . . to do justice and righteousness" (2 Chron. 9:8, ASV). The Lord is with the earthly judge (Judg. 2:18), and the ruler's judgment comes from Jehovah (Prov. 29:26). The magistrate's judgment is *God's*. Jehoshaphat instructed the judges that he appointed: "Consider what ye do, for ye judge not for man but for Jehovah; and he is with you in the judgment" (2 Chron. 19:6). When men stand before the judges, Scripture appositionally says that they "stand before Jehovah" (Deut. 19:17); this is quite appropriate since the reason that the judges are charged to "judge righteously" and not respect or fear persons is declared to be: "for the judgment is God's" (Deut. 1:16-17). It is for this reason that the judges of the nation are actually designated "gods" (Ps. 82:1, 6; cf. Ex. 21:6; 22:8).

The rulers and judges, therefore, who punish evil according to the law of God are the image of God (cf. Gen. 9:5-6), His vicegerents in society and representatives of His justice. From a study of the sword, wrath, vengeance, judgment, righteousness, and the kingly throne, we must conclude that the civil magistrate is to rule under God, being an avenger of His wrath (cf. Rom. 13:1, 4).

The Magistrate Must Deter Evil but Honor the Good

According to the Older Testament there was to be two sides to the magistrate's task. On the one hand he was to requite the wicked (Job 31:11, 28), but on the other he was to justify the righteous (2 Chron. 6:23). Proverbs 16:14-15 expresses this dual effect of proper rule in society: "The wrath of the king is as messengers of death. . . . In the light of the king's countenance is life, and his favor is as a cloud of the latter rain" (ASV). Solomon's word about Adonijah carried the same import; the one who shows himself worthy is safe, but the wicked shall die (1 Kings 1:52). Consequently, according to the teaching of the Older Testament rulers are not a terror to good work but to evil; to avoid fear of the ruler one needs to do the good, and then he will have the magistrate's praise (cf. Rom. 13:3).

The Magistrate Must Rule, then, According to God's Law

If, as we have seen, the rulers in Israel stood under the authority and ordination of God, were to avenge His wrath, and were obligated to deter evil as well as promoting the good, then it must be quite evident that they were required to follow the law of God, for therein the ruler could find authoritative direction from his Sovereign, the occasions of God's wrath, the proper way of executing punishment for social disobedience, and the criteria of good and evil. Responsibility to God's law is, in addition to being established *ipso facto* from the revelation of that law to God's people, the clear implication of the preceding considerations (especially the fact that the magistrate is God's vicegerent as discussed above).

The magistrate was required to judge righteously, which must mean according to God's law since justice is perverted when the law is slackened (Hab. 1:4) in the place where judgment is executed (cf. Eccl. 3:16). Hence the ruling judges should be honest and God fearing men (Ex. 18:21-22), wise men who can rule with just judgment (Deut. 1:13; 16:18; cf. 27:19). Judges were to be appointed who do not distort justice (Deut. 16:18-20) but who judge righteously because the judgment is for God (Deut. 1:16-17; 2 Chron. 19:6). The judges were required to make diligent inquisition (Deut. 19:18) in order that their judgment will be according to truth (Isa. 42:3). Justice in trials was never to be perverted (Lam. 3:36; Ex. 23:2, 3, 6; Deut. 16:19; 24:17; 27:19), for judgment must be righteous (Lev. 19:15, 35; Deut. 1:16-17; 2 Sam. 15:4; 2 Chron. 19:6-7, 9-10; Prov. 31:9; Isa. 10:1-2) and justice established in the law courts or gates (Zech. 8:16; Amos 5:15): "Thus saith Jehovah: Execute ye justice and righteousness, and deliver him that is robbed out of the hand of the oppressor: and do no wrong, do no violence to the sojourner, the fatherless, nor the widow; neither shed innocent blood in this place" (Jer. 22:3; cf. Ezek. 45:9). The judges would be unable to do this if the standard of righteousness were not known from the law of God. To command them to judge righteously is tantamount to requiring them to judge according to the law: "And in a controversy they shall stand to judge; according to mine ordinances shall they judge it: and they shall keep my laws and my statutes . . ."(Ezek. 44:24, ASV).

What applies to the judges is also true with respect to kings and princes in Israel. The king is bound to God's law and must carefully observe all of its statutes without swerving to the right or the left says the Book of the Law (Deut. 17:18-20). The law of God binds kings to carry out true justice and scatter evil without oppression (cf. Prov. 20:26; Ezek. 45:8); they are forbidden to frame mischief by a law (Ps. 94:20). In passing the kingship unto Solomon, David charged his son to "keep the charge of Jehovah thy God, to walk in his ways, to keep his statutes, and his commandments, and his ordinances, and his testimonies, according to that which is written in the law of Moses . . . (1 Kings 2:3, ASV); he also prayed to God that the king should effectively rule in terms of the Lord's judgments and thereby crush the oppressor while encouraging the righteous to flourish (Ps. 72). As David intended for Solomon to rule under the direction of God's law, Josiah "made a covenant before Jehovah, to walk after Jehovah, and to keep his commandments, and his testimonies, and his statutes, with all his heart, and with all his soul, to perform the words of the covenant that were written in this book [of the Law]" (2 Chron. 34:31, ASV). This sounds very much like the charge delivered by David to Solomon and thus represents something more than an idosyncratic notion of statesmanship; it is the pervasive understanding of what God's word requires of the magistrate. Hence at the time of Ezra's reform, after years of exile, we find that the leaders of the community again dedicated and bound themselves to obeying the revealed law of God. *Throughout* Israel's history this obligation to enforce the law of God was taken to be essential to the function of the civil magistrate. A wise king is one who is willing to receive instruction (Eccl. 4:13), and so when it comes to leadership the exemplary king is one who trusts in the strength of the Lord (Ps. 21:1, 7). Because God's kingdom sceptre is uprightness and because the Lord loves righteousness while hating wickedness (Ps. 45:6-7), the king is instructed to ride on for the cause of truth and righteousness (Ps. 45:4); as obligated to God, the king should be righteous as the Lord is righteous—in accordance with His law (cf. Ps. 119:137-138, 142, 160).

A guideline for godly government can be sketched from the book of Proverbs. Therein we learn the foundation, task, and indispensable ingredient of civil government; they are, respectively, God, then the enforcement of God's law, and consequently godly rulers. "By me kings reign and princes decree justice. . . . The throne is established by righteousness" (8:15; 16:12). Rulers must be sober "lest they forget the law and pervert the judgment" (31:5). Anyone who provokes the magistrate's anger actually sins against himself (20:2), for the king is preserved by mercy and truth (20:28). Thus it is an abomination when the wicked rise to power (28:28; cf. 16:12). The just king is one who scatters evil, executes the wicked, and founds his throne upon righteousness (20:8, 26, 28), all of which require the heeding of God's instruction and standards. So then, all who judge rightly and decree justice rule by means of godly Wisdom (8:15-16) and in accordance with righteousness (8:7-8, 17, 20, 35-36). The man who is wise fears God and hates evil, walking in the paths of righteousness (1:7; 8:13); but the ruler who distorts justice is cursed and abhorred by the nations (24:24). Such a king's reign must be short-lived, but by contrast the throne of that king who judges with truth is said to be established forever (29:14). Take evil away from before the king and his throne will be established in righteousness (25:5). Therefore, the duty of the king could be summarized as "judge righteously and minister justice" (31:9).

This injunction is the fundamental responsibility of a magistrate, for it is this which he must perform *daily* (just as daily he reads God's law, cf. Deut. 17:19). David's resolution for an upright society is for the king to judge and punish the wicked and workers of iniquity "morning by morning" (Ps. 101:8), thereby purging the nation of criminals but showing favor to the faithful who walk in a perfect way (vv. 2-7); all of this presupposes a heeding of *Jehovah's* justice (v. 1). If the magistrate does not follow David's word and does not "administer justice every morning," then it is the magistrate himself who must face God's punishment (Jer. 21:12; 22:2-9). Our conclusion must be that all who are entrusted with rulership must personally behave in accordance with God's righteous law (e.g., Lev. 19:15; Deut. 19:18-19; 27:19; Ps. 82:2; Prov. 10:16-17; 17:7; 24:23-26; 25:2; 28:15-16; 29:12; 31:4-5; Isa. 5:22-23; etc.) and, in recognition of their personal responsibility to those commands binding civic officials, enforce God's law within their domains by exacting its penal sanctions.

Therefore, the Magistrate Is Subject to Criticism and Judgment for Lawlessness

It naturally follows that, if magistrates are responsible to obey and enforce God's law, their failure to do so merits criticism based upon the standard of God's word and deserves judgmental punishment from the hand of God (whether executed temporally or eternally). The prophets of the Older Testament were paradigmatic of disapprobation toward disobedient rulers. Isaiah declared, "Woe to those who enact evil statutes, and to those who constantly record unjust decisions" (10:1, NASV), and Hosea rebuked Israel for trespassing against God's law (8:1) and rebelling against the need for His sanction upon the rulers who are appointed (v. 4). Amos pronounced God's judgment upon Israel because they hate those in the gate who would reprove by speaking uprightly; hence they afflict the just and turn aside the needy in the gate (5:10-12). All of these cases are instances of sinful disobedience to God's law and commandments in civic affairs.

With respect to judges in society Psalm 82 says that God stands in the law court of the "gods" (judges) and rebukes unjust judgment which is passed there. These men are called "elohim" because they judge for God (v. 6). When these judges are not just in their doings (v. 2), then all the foundations of society are shaken (v. 5); the civil order's foundation is undermined because the judges do not properly discern between good and evil (cf. 1 Kings 3:9). When those who are to judge *for* God fail to judge righteously, then they must be judged *by* God, who will impeach lawless judges just as surely as He enters into judgment upon unrighteous rulers (cf. Isa. 3:13-15).

Scripture is replete with God's judgment upon kings and rulers in Israel, thereby implying their obligation (though unfulfilled) to God's law. The wickedness of kings is reproved; for instance: Saul's transgression in consulting the medium (1 Chron. 10:13-14), David's adultery and homicide (2 Sam. 12:13-18), Solomon's alien wives (1 Kings 11:1-12), Jeroboam's idolatry (1 Kings 14:9) and Ahab's false witness, theft, and murder (1 Kings 21:1-22). God's temporal judgment upon wicked kings brings their downfall. Because Jeroboam has not kept the Lord's commandments God will bring evil against the king's house (1 Kings 14:8-10). Jehu made the people to sin against God, and so Jehu will be swept away (1 Kings 16:2-3); in like manner, Ahab worked evil and made the nation to sin, so he will be swept away (1 Kings 21:20-22). When the king is made glad with wickedness (Hos. 7:3-7) there is nothing but detestable sin in the nation (Hos. 4:1-2); when the princes are rebellious against righteous judgment, then sinners are lodged in the city and the whole town becomes unrighteous (Isa. 1:21-28), calling for Jehovah's judgmental intervention. The prophets condemn corruption in magistrates (e.g., Mic. 7:3; Ezek. 43:7-9) and thus pronounce the fall of princes and the punishment of rulers (e.g., Hos. 7:16; 8:10; 10:15; cf. v. 7). The Book of the Kings condemns nearly every king of both the Northern and Southern kingdoms. And it is particularly the iniquity of rulers which is condemned by the prophets at the time of Israel and Jerusalem's fall.[8] Subsequently when the Jews returned from exile, the sin that they confessed was that their kings had not kept the law of God (Neh. 9:34-37). Therefore, in restored Jerusalem the magistrates were to execute true and peaceful judgments in the law courts (Zech. 8:16).

The general responsibility of Israel's rulers to promote the good (obedience to God's law) and punish the evil (social crimes against God's law) comes to telling expression in the fact that they are criticized and condemned for failing to promote justice in the nation and for ruling in lawlessness.

---

[8] Cf. Isa. 1:23; 3:12-15; 10:1-3; 28:14-15; 29:20-21; 52:5; 59:14-15; Jer. 5:28; Hos. 5:1, 10; 7:3; Amos 3:10-11; 4:1-2; 5:11-12; 6:12-13; Mic. 3:1-3, 9-11; 7:3-4.

Chapter 18

THE MAGISTRATE IN NATIONS SURROUNDING ISRAEL

IT might be supposed that because God was dealing with Israel in a covenant context of blessing (i.e., redeeming and intending to redeem these chosen people) and did not set His electing love upon all the other nations (cf. Amos 3:2), the standard of ethical obligation and moral uprightness differed between Israel and the nations. Should this be the case, then general discontinuity between the law governing Israel and the law governing her neighbors might extend even to matters of social morality and the magistrate's duty to promote justice. In that supposed case there would be a divergence of ethical standard at the civic level, and this could have bearing upon the answer to the question "ought the magistrate today (i.e., non-Israeli rulers) obey the law of God as revealed in the Older Testament?"

Now the first thing that must be said respecting this supposition is that, without explicit scriptural teaching, it would be a mere argument from silence and thus could not be authoritative in arriving at doctrinal or ethical conclusions. However, even if it were the case that Scripture is silent as to the ethical standard which applied to the ancient nations (which it is not), there would be strong *prima facie* reason to suppose continuity (rather than discontinuity) between the moral obligations which applied to Israel and those which applied to the other nations. That *prima facie* case flows from the following considerations. Since God is the living Lord over all creation and immutable in His character, and since all men are His creatures and morally accountable to Him, we are led to believe that God's law (as reflecting the righteousness of God) applies to every man irrespective of his position in life, situation in the world, nationality, or place in history. Moreover, Romans 2:11-12 tells us that God is no respecter of persons; He will apply the same absolute criteria of holiness to each person whom He creates, irrespective of who, what, or where they are. This is possible because even the Gentiles know God's judicial ordinance that certain crimes are worthy of death (Rom. 1:32) and have the works of the law written on their heart (Rom. 2:14-15). Even though they do not have the advantage of a *written* (and hence, redemptive) revelation of this law as did Israel, nevertheless no Gentile can claim ignorance or exemption from responsibility to God's law. Paul's argument in Romans 1-3 is precisely that the *whole* world, Jew and Gentile alike, fall under the judgment of God's law since all live in the sphere of responsibility to it. Because all men do not live up to the obligations of the law, the law condemns all men; Paul lays to the charge both of Jews and Gentiles "that they are all under sin" (Rom. 3:9)—which is to imply, under the law (cf. 1 John 3:4).

All those who wander from God's statutes, yes all the wicked of the *earth* are condemned by God (Ps. 119:118-119). The Father, who is without respect of persons, will judge according to *every* man's work (1 Peter 1:17). Christ Himself will judge *all* those who behave lawlessly (Matt. 13:41); "Behold, the Lord comes with ten thousands of His messengers to execute judgment upon all, and to convince all that are ungodly among them of all their ungodly deeds which they have impiously committed" (Jude 14-15). There is no escape for anyone from accountability before the standard of God's law.

The universality of responsibility to God's holy commandments is reflected in the fact that men are not to show partiality or grant immunity in their judgments. Immunity could not be granted for an infraction against God's law, not even to a cherished relative or friend (Deut. 13:6-9). To show partiality to the rich is to act in opposition to God's law (cf. James 1:8-9). Even official rank does not keep one from having the demand of the law imposed on his behavior (cf. Luke 3:10-14; 19:8; Rom. 13:4). "Ye shall do no unrighteousness in judgment; thou shalt not respect the person of the poor, nor honor the person of the mighty" (Lev. 19:15, ASV). Because God's law *cuts across all social distinctions* nobody is free from its demands. The conclusion must be, then, that God's law was binding upon the Gentile as well as the Jew in the age of the Older Testament. Thus the law itself specified that even the alien was to be judged by the magistrate in accordance with the standard of God's law (Deut. 1:16-17). "There shall be *one standard* for the stranger as well as the native, for I am the Lord your God" (Lev. 24:22, NASV; cf. Num. 15:16, "one law and one ordinance"). The words of Ecclesiastes 12:13 are appropriate here: "The conclusion, when all has been heard, is: fear God and keep His commandments, because this applies to every person" (NASV).

Therefore, one should not come to the testimony of Scripture predisposed toward the idea that there is discontinuity between the ethical standards governing Israel and those which God uses to judge the nations. Had the law not been specially revealed to Israel, its inhabitants would nevertheless have been culpable (as in the case of its neighbors) for rebelling against the clear revelation of God (and His requirements) in nature and conscience (Rom. 1:18 ff.; 2:14-15). Thus the fact that the written law was *primarily* addressed to Israel certainly cannot be used to imply a double standard of morality between her and the surrounding nations! What is sinful within the borders of Canaan is not condonable outside, and this is because the Mosaic law does not represent the ethic of a few Palestinian tribes but the universal and divine standard of righteousness. The deliverance of the law to Israel in *written* form will not hinder God from punishing sin in *non*-Israelites (or even non-Israelite rulers), nor should it be thought to contradict its worldwide application. After all, the benefit granted to Israel of having laws which excelled the *de facto* ethical standards of the other nations (cf. Deut. 4:8) cannot be considered something Israel was to keep to itself; just the opposite is true: "Attend unto me, O my people; and give ear unto me, O my nation; for a law shall go forth from me, and I will establish my justice for a light of the peoples" (Isa. 51:4, ASV; cf. Matt. 5:14). Such a blessed lamp as God's law (cf. Prov. 6:23) should not be put under a bushel but allowed to shine into the world so that other men would come to glorify God and serve Him. Consequently, the norm of the law should be seen as applying to those living outside the borders of Israel; otherwise God would be represented as having a double standard of judgment—something which

He clearly forbids in His people and their judges (Deut. 25:13-16; Lev. 19:35-37).

Therefore, there is no initial reason why we should expect there to be ethical discontinuity between the divine norms God will use in judging Israel and those in judging the other nations. His law has *international* relevance and binding force (as it comes by means of general revelation to the Gentiles, special revelation to the Jews, and indirectly through the Jews to the Gentiles). If His law has this absolute character (drawing the whole world under its authority), then the justice required in social affairs in Israel will be the same justice required in other nations; the Jewish magistrate is to judge righteously by following God's law, and so also is the Gentile ruler morally responsible to enact justice according to God's law. With this general background in mind we can proceed to examine the Older Testament's teaching with respect to the civil magistrate in Gentile nations. Before doing so, however, note should be made of the fact that the following examination presupposes the general validity of interpreting passages in the Wisdom literature of the Older Testament as having universal application or bearing. It is generally conceded that the scope of the Wisdom literature opens up onto the whole world and is not restricted to what is true only in Israel; thus we find axiomatic and categorical truths throughout a book like Proverbs, truths which lack distinctive nationalistic traits. The wisdom literature stems from and intends to be used in cultural interplay, and hence it is concerned with all nations. In particular, the Wisdom literature of the ancient world is concerned with, as Derek Kidner says, the moral government of the world.[1] In light of these facts it is not without

---

[1] Derek Kidner, *The Proverbs: An Introduction and Commentary,* ed. D. J. Wiseman, The Tyndale Old Testament Commentaries (Downers Grove, IL: InterVarsity Press, 1964), pp. 16 ff.; Gleason L. Archer, *A Survey of Old Testament Introduction* (Chicago: Moody Press, 1964), p. 454; R. K. Harrison, *Introduction to the Old Testament with a Comprehensive Review of Old Testament Studies and a Special Supplement on the Apocrypha* (Grand Rapids: William B. Eerdmans Publishing Co., 1969), pp. 1007-1008, 1020; F. F. Bruce, "The Wisdom Literature of the Old Testament," and W. A. Rees Jones and Andrew F. Walls, "Proverbs" in *The New Bible Commentary,* 2nd ed., ed. F. Davidson, A. M. Stibbs, and E. F. Kevan (Grand Rapids: William B. Eerdmans Publishing Co., 1954 [reprinted 1965]), pp. 42-43, 516.

significance for the present thesis that God's word says of God's commandments delivered by the hand of Moses, "Keep therefore and do them; for *this* is your *wisdom* and your understanding in the sight of the peoples" (Deut. 4:6, ASV). We turn, then, to investigate the teaching of the Older Testament on the subject of the civil magistrate as found in the nations surrounding Israel.

God Sovereignly Appoints and Removes Rulers

The Older Testament consistently views the heads of foreign powers as the servants of God's will, just as the New Testament also teaches (for instance: Pharaoh, Rom. 9:17; Herod and Pilate, Acts 4:25). Pharaoh had to learn the lesson that God is unsurpassed in all the earth when it comes to power and authority (Ex. 9:14-16), and even pre-Mosaic kings were subject to God's reproof (Ps. 105:14; e.g., Gen. 12:17; 20:3, 7). Thus the civil magistrates who ruled prior to the establishment of Israel as a nation owed their authority to divine sovereignty and were clearly subject to God's rule. Metaphorical expression is given to the truth that God brings down kings and sets up rulers at His sovereign will in Ezekiel 17:24. The nations of Israel's *own* day were certainly subject to this description.

Jeremiah declares that God tells the local kings that He is the one who gives them power, for He gives the earth to those unto whom it seems right to Him (27:5). In the case at hand God has *given* the lands to Nebuchadnezzar, who is appropriately described as God's "servant" (v. 6; cf. Ezek. 29:18-20; Jer. 21:7; 22:25). Jeremiah also reveals that it is God who will either break the yoke of the Babylonian king or establish it as iron (28:1-14). Thus the Older Testament would clearly teach the nations that Jehovah is "Most High" over the earth (Ps. 9:2; 83:18), determining the course of nations and bringing them under His rebuke and judgment (Ps. 9:4-8; 83:9-12).

It is especially in the book of Daniel that these truths come out. When Daniel speaks of the "power-authority" (ἐξουσία, LXX) of the beast, he says that it is *given* to him (7:6). As all kinds of rulers have "authority" (ἐξουσία, 3:2-3, LXX) and a strong king obtains great "dominion" (ἐξουσία, 11:5, LXX Alexandrian ms.), still Daniel maintains that all of this comes by the ordination of God. "He removeth kings and setteth up kings" (2:21, ASV); such is Daniel's teaching. And such is the lesson that Nebuchadnezzar had to learn; to that end God punished the great monarch until he knew "that the Most High ruleth in the kingdom of men, and giveth it to whomever he will" (4:25, ASV). Nebuchadnezzar is told that the God of heaven gave him the kingdom (2:37), and it is just at the time that Nebuchadnezzar praised his own might, glory, and majesty that the prophecy began to be fulfilled that he should learn that God gives political rule to men of His own sovereign choice and it is He who establishes them over the kingdom (4:28-32, cf. v. 17). When Nebuchadnezzar finally recovers from the punishment he praises "the Most High" because "His dominion is an everlasting dominion. . . and He does according to His will . . . among the inhabitants of the earth" (4:34), and the response is appropriately that *God returns* the kingdom to Nebuchadnezzar. The previously self-sufficient king now honors "the King of heaven." Therefore, Daniel emphatically teaches that the powers that be are ordained of God (cf. Rom. 13:1). The parallel to Paul's teaching at a later time is striking since Babylon (Nebuchadnezzar) in Daniel's day was in the same position as Rome (Caesar) in the days of Paul. No sooner has the fourth chapter of Daniel finished teaching this lesson with respect to Nebuchadnezzar than Belshazzar is set before us as needing to learn that *God* rules over earth and gives power unto whom He will. Belshazzar had been mocking God's rule (cf. 5:2-4) when a message was written to him upon a wall by hand. In the course of interpreting that divine oracle for the king, Daniel reminds him that the Most High gave Nebuchadnezzar the throne and deposed him for his pride (vv. 18-20). Since Nebuchadnezzar was punished until he learned that the Most High sets whomever He will over the kingdom (v. 21), Belshazzar his son should have humbled himself and not lifted himself up against God (v. 22). Therefore, as positive proof of the principle that Belshazzar had spurned, God decisively puts an end to his kingdom (vv. 25-28).

Hence God is seen by the Older Testament as the One who sovereignly appoints and removes rulers. This is not just a Jewish perspective which interprets the autonomous experience of the Gentile nations. But the surrounding nations themselves were to know that God rules in the kingdom of men. This is perhaps nowhere revealed more clearly than in the fact that Nebuchadnezzar, having learned his lesson, sends a decree to *all* the nations that they might also recognize the truth about God's dominion (Dan. 4:1, 3).

Rulers, as God's Appointees, Are Not to Be Resisted

In discussing the civil magistrate in Israel it was noted that, because God ordained such a ruler, the king or judge was not to be opposed by rebellious words or actions. The same is found to be true with the magistrate in the other nations. God also forbids resistance against their proper authority.

It is the authority of God's ordinance which stands behind the civil magistrate and explains why he is not to be resisted. This close association of God with the ruler of the nation was not restricted to Israel. Because it is Jehovah who *gave* the kingdom and rule to Cyrus (Isa. 41:2, 25; Ezra 1:2; 2 Chron. 36:23), Cyrus serves God's ends by being under His control; thus Cyrus is the Lord's appointed "shepherd" (Isa. 44:28), performing all His pleasure. To rise up against the one whom God Almighty calls "My shepherd" is tantamount to rising up against the ordinance or appointment of God (cf. Paul's logic in Rom. 13:2). Those who respect God should, then, also respect the king. Such is the message of Proverbs 24:21, "reverence (fear) Jehovah and the king." Peter alludes to this verse at the end of his exhortation to be subject to the authorities as sent by God (1 Peter 2:13-14); since rulers are ordained of God, "Fear God. Honor the king" (v. 17). Proverbs 24:21b-22 goes on to apply this imperative, paralleling the message of Paul in Romans 13:2, 4 (cf. 1 Peter 2:14)—viz., opposition to the ruler ordained of God will bring God's punishment plus that of the ruler. Although the Hebrew in verse 21b is difficult, both of the possible interpretations [2] result in the same message for the passage as a whole. Either do not company with "dissidents (revolutionaries)"

---

[2] E.g., Franz Delitzsch, *Biblical Commentary on the Proverbs of Solomon,* Vol. II, trans. M. G. Easton, Biblical Commentary on the Old Testament by C. F. Keil and F.

because their calamity will come as destruction from both Jehovah and the king, or do not disobey "either of them" (God or king) because of the calamity and destruction which comes from them both. Thus one is required to show respect for the civil magistrate or face God's condemnation, and this is categorically true (i.e., not restricted to rulers chosen by God for leadership in Israel).

The Psalmist instructs the people to "seek peace" (34:14). In Jeremiah 29:7 we learn that this commandment applies even to the political situation where a Gentile ruler is in power: "seek the peace of the city whither I have caused you to be carried away captive, and pray unto Jehovah for it; for in the peace thereof shall ye have peace" (ASV). Here God's elect people are instructed to have the same attitude toward the Gentile magistrate as is expected toward their own Jewish king and capital city. The imperative delivered by Jeremiah corresponds to Paul's exhortation that prayer be offered for kings and for high officials in order that a peaceful life be possible (1 Tim. 2:1-2). In the face of imminent persecution by the Roman high command (cf. 1 Peter 1:6; 4:12; 5:13), the responsibility for seeking peace which was found in Psalm 34:14 is applied in 1 Peter 3:10-14 (using a direct quotation) to the people of God in "Disperson" (cf. 1:1), so that they would not suffer for anything but righteousness. The peacefulness of Christians should be evidence to the government that they are not revolutionaries. A prime example for New Testament believers on this score, then, can be found in Jeremiah's earlier word from God that His dispersed people are to seek the peace of even a city where a Gentile ruler is in command.

Honor, obedience, and spiritual support are required of people for their magistrates, whether they be Jewish kings or Babylonian emperors. It is not merely of God's people that this subjection to the ruler is required; all men must honor and obey the powers that be (cf. "every soul" in Rom. 13:1). In demonstration of this point one can

---

Delitzsch (Grand Rapids: William B. Eerdmans Publishing Co., [reprinted 1970]), pp. 137-139; Kidner, *op. cit.,* pp. 155-156; cf. translations in ASV and RSV.

look at Jeremiah 27:1-8. Jeremiah had a message from God for all the kings of those nations surrounding, and including, Israel. The message is that God ordains the existing political authority by His great power, giving it to whomever He pleases (v. 5; cf. Rom. 13:1). Therefore, resisting the power will bring divine judgment: "And it shall come to pass, that the nation and the kingdom which will not serve the same Nebuchadnezzar king of Babylon [to whom God had given all the lands], and that will not put their neck under the yoke of the king of Babylon, that nation will I punish, saith Jehovah" (v. 8). This even applies to the theocratic king, Zedekiah, and the nation of Judah (vv. 12-17). Thus Jeremiah emphatically teaches that rulers, as God's appointees, are not to be resisted, or else they that resist shall receive to themselves judgment (cf. Rom. 13:2). The obligations of subjection to political authority in Israel are the same moral responsibilities for submission to political authority in any nation.

Rulers Bear Religious Titles

With respect to the rulers in Israel it is widely recognized that the titles given them, such as "My servant" and "My shepherd," have strong typological significance. The coming Messiah could also be designated the Lord's "servant" and a "shepherd" (e.g., Isa. 53:11; Ezek. 34:23); in the person of Jesus Christ the New Testament finds the Messianic servant, the good shepherd, as well as the Holy One of Israel. The disciples of Christ and officers in the church are subsequently spoken of as "servants" and "shepherds." Therefore, while "shepherd" or "servant" could bear simple mundane denotation in the Older Testament, the terms could also, in the context of consecration or appointment by God, bear religious connotation. Now it should be observed that these titles are not only applied to the theocratic rulers raised up by God, but also to political leaders outside of Israel. Nebuchadnezzar, king of Babylon, is spoken of by Jehovah as "My servant" (Jer. 25:9; 27:6; 43:10), and Cyrus, king of Persia, is called by God "My shepherd" (Isa. 44:28). However, the outstanding example of a political figure outside of Israel receiving an honorific, religiously significant title is found in Isaiah 45:1 where Cyrus is termed by Jehovah as "My anointed" ("My Christ," LXX). Such is the designation for the High Priest in Israel and for the King over the people; especially is it known as the title for the coming deliverer, the righteous "Messiah." Hence the rulers of the nations are given titles which clearly indicate that they are considered by God's word to be *ministers of God* (cf. Rom. 13:4, 6).

Hence Rulers Are God's Vicegerents, Avengers of His Wrath

That kings and judges are to represent God and execute His justice upon earth was demonstrated with respect to Israelite rulers above by an examination of God's wrath, vengeance, kingly throne, and righteous judgment; it became evident that the magistrates over the people were God's delegates in carrying out a portion of His wrath and vengeance, that their own thrones had to represent the just rule of the great King over them, and that their judgment had to reflect the judgment of God which is according to righteousness, in other words, His law. This study need not be rehearsed here but only shown, by particular examples, to apply to the civil magistrates of the Gentile nations as well. The conclusion flowing from the previous study with respect to Israel must then be derived with respect to the other nations as well.

The Older Testament speaks of God's "vengeance" or punishment coming upon the sinfulness of the nation Israel (e.g., Lev. 26:25; Isa. 57:16; Jer. 5:9, 29, LXX). Throughout the Older Testament, based upon the curses of the covenant, Israel had to understand that God would bring other nations against His people in order to punish their disobedience to His ethical stipulations (e.g., Lev. 26; Deut. 32:25; Jer. 5:17; Ezek. 6:11; Hab. 1:1-11; etc.). The other nations thereby became avengers sent by God to deal with Israel's lawlessness. So also God's "wrath" is said to be meted out against Israel when their lawlessness is no longer tolerated (e.g., Isa. 5:25; Jer. 7:20, LXX). Again, the other nations will be agents of God in this respect (e.g., "Ho Assyrian, the rod of mine anger, the staff in whose hand is mine indignation" Isa. 10:1, ASV). Therefore, the nations outside of Israel can properly be considered "avengers of God's wrath." To this end, for instance, Assyria was commissioned or "sent" by God (Isa. 10:6). And this activity of *punishment* by Assyria should not be considered simply an incidental perspective, a way of looking at the political movements of a warlike empire that were in progress anyway; God's punishment of Israel *by* Assyria is not merely a matter of His foreordination of all things. God can be said to have given a "command (charge)" to Assyria to do this judgmental work of seizing, plundering, and treading down. *Assyria* was to *understand* that it was doing God's work of vengeance, being a servant of His will, and an executioner of His temporal penalty against sin in Israel. Thus there is an element of morality and responsibility involved in Assyria being the "avenger of God's wrath." This is demonstrated by the fact that God says He will punish the stout heart of the Assyrian king for his self-sufficient pride and arrogance (Isa. 1:12-13); obviously this magistrate is held accountable for not going to war against Israel in the proper attitude of carrying out God's bidding. Assyria should have *known* that it was judging *for* God. In this case the Assyrian magistrate, with respect to the norm that God expected to be followed (yet was not), is seen as a vicegerent of God upon earth—sent to perform His command of vengeance.

Earlier it was observed that, since God was enthroned as King over Israel, its leaders were to be His deputies; furthermore, because God's throne has righteousness and justice for its supports, these deputies were required to make the foundation of their own rule the justice of God's law. It must now be emphasized that God is not declared to be King enthroned over Israel only, but He is heralded in the Older Testament as King over *all* earthly kingdoms. "He is a great King over all the earth. . . . God is the King of all the earth. . . . God reigns over the nations; God sits upon His holy throne" (Ps. 47:2, 7, 8). Consequently all earthly kings must be thought of as God's delegated authorities; their rulership and authority is subsumed under the Kingship of God. They *represent* His throne. That is why the Psalmist declares both that *Israel's* shield (king) belongs unto God (89:18) *and* that "the shields of the *earth* belong unto God" (47:9). All civil magistrates, whether in Israel or among the nations, are God's officers, under His Kingly authority, and morally responsible to His throne. Jehovah is a great King *among* the nations, not simply in Israel (Ps. 22:28; 83:18; 99:2; 113:4; Mal. 1:14). Human kingship in these nations, then, is secondary to God's rule; it is derived from God's own authority. God's throne is established of old, and He reigns among the nations in righteousness (Ps. 93:1-2; 45:6; 96:10; Lam. 5:19; Ps. 97, 98, 99). That this rule is not merely a matter of sheer power or amoral sovereignty is evidenced in the fact that it brings the nations under requirement to praise and reverence God. Moreover, based on this kingship of God the nations are exhorted to reflect His justice and holiness. God will judge the nations with righteousness, for "His *holy* throne" (Ps. 47:8) is the place from which the Lord reigns; "righteousness and justice are the foundation of His throne" (Ps. 97:2). Those who rule under Him as earthly magistrates must, therefore, represent this same righteous basis for judgment and direction. "The throne is established by righteousness" (Prov. 16:12), and "the king by justice establishes the land" (Prov. 29:4). The throne of the magistrate (any magistrate) is to be *like God's* (characterizing righteousness and justice); in that God has ordained the kings of the earth, they must represent His interests and be His faithful servants. Just as their subjects must give account when they have disobeyed His commands, even so the earthly magistrate will have to give account of his own reign when he appears before the divine King, the righteous Judge. All rulers must appropriately deal with wickedness in society, and the standard by which they judge and penalize should then be that which reflects God's conception of justice for social relations; for this reason magistrates are culpable for violating the dictates of God's law in the exercise of their official duties. Their purpose is to deal with public disobedience to God's law ("For the transgression of a land many arc the princes thereof" Prov. 28:2), and so "he who justifies the wicked, and he who condemns the righteous, both of them alike are an abomination to the Lord" (Prov. 17:15, NASV). God does not judge in this fashion, therefore, the magistrates who rule in the nations of the world must be seen as responsible to behave as vicegerents for the divine King who sits upon a holy throne; they are obligated to be avengers of His wrath when they pass social judgment (cf. Rom. 13:4).

The Magistrate Must Deter Evil but Honor the Good

If the magistrate is truly to reflect the righteous rule of God and be the Lord's servant in matters of crime and punishment, then his rule must be according to the *Lord's* way. This would give his leadership a dual character and effect, for "the way of Jehovah is a stronghold to the upright, but it is destruction to the workers of iniquity; the righteous shall never be removed, but the wicked shall not dwell in the earth" (Prov. 10:29-30). When the magistrate judges righteously, following God's law, then naturally there will be the two-fold effect of terrifying violators of that law and honoring those who strive to keep it; this truth is axiomatic. It not only pertains to Israel, but instructs all nations. Indeed, this law of God, as noted earlier, was intended to be Israel's very wisdom before the nations (Deut. 4:6). In heeding the inspired direction of God's Proverbs the statesmen of the nations around Israel would deter evil and promote good (cf. Prov. 10:9; 13:6; 28:18). By following the statutes of God, a king correctly punishes criminals and commends the obedient, thus being a "terror" where he ought to be a terror: "the execution of justice is joy to the righteous, but is terror to the workers of iniquity" (Prov. 21:15, NASV). Years after the penning of these words the Apostle Paul would reiterate the same truth: "rulers are not a terror to good work *but* to the evil. And do you wish not to fear the authority? Then do the good and you will have from him praise" (Rom. 13:3).

The Magistrate Must Rule, then, According to God's Law

The fact that civil rulers among the nations were to align their thrones with the throne of God and to govern, as Wisdom would instruct them, in such a way that criminals were terrified but the righteous praised has already indicated that these rulers were required to carry out their official functions according to the direction of God's law. Further evidence of that obligation can now be set forth.

In the first place it would be wrong to suppose that God's law did not morally bind the nations outside of the covenant community, Israel.

That God's law did not have such a geographical delimitation is clear from the fact, if nothing else, that David would make the surrounding nations surrender to his own theonomic rule (2 Sam. 22:21-25, 44-50; Ps. 18:43-50). David clearly intended that the sway of God's law should be extended beyond the mere boundaries of Israel, and he looked forward to praising God *among* the nations because of the Lord's plan to make the other countries obey David (and his seed) as head of the nations. It is evident that the rulers of the earth need not be Jews in order to come under theonomic dominion. God's law was not meant to be restricted to the Hebrew nation but had international application. J. H. Bavinck has discerned this scriptural truth well:

> It is striking how frequently the other nations are called upon in the Psalms to recognize and to honor God, and how complete is the witness of the prophets against the nations surrounding Israel. God does not exempt other nations from the claim of his righteousness; he requires their obedience and holds them responsible for their apostasy and degeneration.[3]

The cities of Sodom and Ninevah provide adequate proof that nations which have not been corporately selected by God for special care and that have not been granted a special, written transcript of God's law are nevertheless fully responsible to God's standard of holiness as revealed in the law. Being a city full of exceedingly wicked sinners (Gen. 13:13; 18:20) Sodom was justly destroyed for its "unlawfulness" (2 Peter 2:6-8). For that reason it is paradigmatic throughout Scripture for God's judgment upon iniquity.[4] Sodom was destroyed for breaking

---

[3] J. H Bavinck, *An Introduction to the Science of Missions,* trans. David Hugh Freeman (Philadelphia: The Presbyterian and Reformed Publishing Co., 1960), pp. 12-13.

[4] Cf. Deut. 19:23; 32:32; Isa. 1:9-10; 3:9; 13:19; Jer. 23:14; 49:18; 50:40; Lam. 4:6; Ezek. 16:46-56; Amos 4:11; Zeph. 2:9; Matt. 10:15; 11:23-24; Jude 7; Rev. 11:8.

God's law; the ethical presupposition of this historical event was the responsibility of that non-Jewish nation to God's righteous requirements. And this was not simply a vague, general responsibility (e.g., to the broad guidelines of only the Decalogue), for the statute that Sodom was specifically guilty of violating is not one of the Ten summary Commandments but a specific and particularized case law: the prohibition of homosexuality (Gen. 19:4 ff.; Lev. 18:22; 20:13; cf. Deut. 23:17; 1 Kings 14:24; 15:12; 22:46; 2 Kings 23:7). Hundreds of years *before* the constitution of Israel as a nation under the written law of God that same law had ethical authority; if there had been no binding law, there could have been no sin and hence no justified vengeance of God against the Sodomites.

Hundreds of years *after* the formation of the Israelite nation it is clear that the law of God was still binding upon the nations outside of Israel, for Jonah was sent to preach God's imminent wrath upon the great city of Nineveh unless it should repent. The demand for repentance surely presupposes a violated moral dictate and so also prior obligation to obey the dictate. In contrast to the outcome of Sodom, Nineveh repented of its unlawful wickedness at the preaching of Jonah (Jonah 3) and thereby became an example of a heathen city (to whom the written law was not primarily addressed) submitting to God's word (cf. Luke 11:30, 32). Therefore the binding authority of God's law, from before its Sinaitic revelation to Israel until many years thereafter, must be viewed as holding for the nations outside of Israel's covenant community.

However, the most dramatic illustration of the law's validity outside of Israel comes from the period immediately following its deliverance through Moses to God's elect people. Following a list of prohibitions Leviticus 18:24-27 declares: "Defile not yourselves in any of these things: for in all these the nations are defiled which I cast out from before you; and the land is defiled: therefore do I visit the iniquity thereof upon it, and the land vomiteth out her inhabitants. Ye therefore shall keep my statutes and mine ordinances, and shall not do any of these abominations . . . for all these abominations have the men of the land done, that were before you, and the land is defiled" (ASV). Here is sufficient evidence that the same law delivered to Israel is the law to which the other nations were subject. It is the same law given through Moses which defines the defilement and abominations of the people upon whom Israel will bring God's temporal retribution. The striking thing is that verse 28 following this passage asserts that the punishment exacted against the Canaanites (the land vomiting them out) is precisely the punishment that shall be enacted against Israel if it commits the forbidden abominations. As Israel was subject to God's law, so also were the nations who did not receive it in written form. Otherwise God's judgment would have been unfounded—a thought which is precluded by the Lord's justice and equity.

The book of Deuteronomy, a book reflecting the marks of a specific covenant document, persistently teaches that responsibility to God's law extends *beyond* the covenant community. That Israel was instructed to destroy the ungodly nations in Canaan implies that those nations bore a prior responsibility to, and were consequently guilty for violation of, the law of God (Deut. 7:5-6, 16, 25; 12:1-4). Since these nations did not heed God but forgot Him they must perish (8:19-20; cf. vv. 11-19), and it is their wickedness which explains their being dispossessed from the land (9:4-5). The opposite of that abomination which brought vengeance upon the Canaanites is obedience to God's law (12:29-32); this is what the nations should have been striving after. Israel was told, then, not to imitate the pagan practices of the Canaanites because they (by contrast) were to be a holy people (14:1-2). The detestable practices of the nations constitute sin (20:18) and of necessity cannot be imitated by *law*-abiding Israel (18:9, 12). Should Israel depart from the law and become lawlessly idolatrous, they would likewise perish (30:17-18). Instead, Israel's obedience to God's law was intended to be an example to the nations (4:5-8). Hence we see that the covenant document itself plainly teaches an international responsibility to the stipulations of God's law, and that responsibility has full force even in the non-elect nations who did not have the advantage of the law in *written* form. The fact that God did not have a *redemptive* purpose in mind for the Canaanites themselves does not contravene the unity of *moral* standard and obligation between the elect and non-elect nations.

Thus it is not surprising that the Older Testament definitely states the inclusion of *all* nations under God's righteous judgment, a judgment *not* limited to crimes committed against His chosen people (e.g., Ps. 9:4-5, 7-8; 98:9; Amos 1:3-2:3, etc.). The whole world shall be judged by the same righteous, absolute moral standard: God's law. Therefore, there is scriptural reason to deny the premise that God's law did not morally bind the nations outside of Israel's covenant community. This being the case, the civil magistrates outside of Israel were required, no less than the rulers of Israel, to carry out their functions by following the righteous law of God. The law clearly prescribes numerous things of a social character, and the law lays it upon the civil magistrate to honor and enforce those things. Therefore, as the law of God binds the nations outside of Israel, so their *rulers* are under obligation to rule according to that law. The laws binding magistrates are just as much *commandments* from God as are the laws binding farmers, merchants, parents, women, men, children, or any other distinct class of person instructed by the Lord's commands. *The law* morally binds the nations, and that means that the magistrates of the world kingdoms are as much under ethical obligation as the fathers, craftsmen, or children of those nations. The fact that the socio-civil commandments of God's law are as binding upon the nations outside Israel as they are upon Israel itself receives confirmation from a comparison of Habakkuk 2:12 with Micah 3:10. Habakkuk declares, "Woe to him that buildeth a town with blood, and establisheth a city by iniquity!" (ASV). Although the assertion itself is general enough to be a universal axiom, in its particular context in Habakkuk it is a reference to the Chaldeans. What is significant is that the *same* pronouncement is spoken against the Israelite city of Jerusalem by Micah the prophet, and the context (cf. vv. 1-3, 9-11) clearly is one of rebuke for sins of the civil magistrates. Thus the same judgment against sin in national leaders is entirely possible between the Jewish and Gentile nations, and this is grounded in the fact that the Lord *universally* does not honor a city which fails to be founded upon, or acting in accord with, the justice of His law. When the rulers ignore

God's law, whether in Babylonia (Hab. 1:4) or in Jerusalem (Mic. 3:1-12), the result is always that justice is perverted and not upheld; instead the wicked abound. It is for the restraint of this social evil that God ordains magistrates and expects them to keep His righteous law. *"Righteousness exalts a nation, but sin is a disgrace to any people"* (Prov. 14:34, NASV). The international scope, civic emphasis, and theonomic theme of that inspired declaration should be unmistakable. Here is straightforward and indisputable confirmation of our thesis.

The obligation of non-Jewish magistrates to honor and obey God during the Older Testament era can also be supported by positive example. Huran, king of Tyre, recognized the divine appointment of Solomon (2 Chron. 2:11-12), and the queen of Sheba acknowledged Solomon's appointment by God as well as his just and righteous government (1 Kings 10:9). Cyrus of Persia obeyed the Lord's command to have the Jerusalem temple rebuilt (Ezra 1:1 ff.). Darius commanded *all* the *nations* to serve the God and Lord of Daniel (Daniel 6:25 ff.), and Nebuchadnezzar instructed the *nations* that God rules over all and expects righteousness of kings because His own ways are just (Dan. 4:esp. 1, 25-27, 37). If civil obedience to the law of God were to be restricted to Jewish government, then Scripture is strangely silent in disapprobating the previous examples. When the Israelite, Daniel, assumed civil office in a nation which was not Jewish or located in the promised land, he apparently did not feel that the rules for leadership had changed from what God would have expected of a civil magistrate in Israel. Daniel sat as an official in the court of the king in Babylon (Dan. 2:49), and was well known for his close adherence to the law of God (cf. Dan. 6:5). The ancient Jews certainly thought of Daniel as a ruler who applied God's law to civil affairs, as is evidenced in the book of Susanna 5:60-62 (cf. Deut. 19:16-19; Prov. 19:5, 9). Thus we have an example of a godly Jew bringing the law of Jehovah to bear upon the government of a Gentile nation. Furthermore, we have, on the other hand, an example from Scripture of a Gentile monarch decreeing the application of God's law. Ezra 7:11-28 is highly instructional at this point. Artaxerxes sent Ezra to inquire about Judah's and Jerusalem's adherence to the law of God (7:14). Artaxerxes honors God as God and knows that he is under responsibility to God and subject to divine judgment (7:15 ff., 21, 23). Most notably Artaxerxes commands Ezra to appoint magistrates and judges that will judge *all* those "beyond the River" (i.e., the whole territory between the Euphrates and the Mediterranean Sea).[5] Those who were ignorant of God's law were to be taught it (7:25), and the judges were to go so far as to punish offenders against God's law—even to the point of execution (7:26)! Artaxerxes as a non-Israelite ruler thus applied the whole law of God in its social and penal details, and he applied it to areas far exceeding the boundaries of Israel! However, the factor which cannot be overlooked in the narrative is Ezra's blessing of the Lord for putting such a thing in the king's heart (7:25-26). However one humanly accounts for the involvement of Artaxerxes in sending this decree, the fact stands that the action itself is the sort of thing which meets with approval in Scripture. Therefore, by both negative and positive *illustration,* in addition to consideration of ethical *principles* as revealed in Scripture, one must conclude that the civil magistrate in even non-Israelite countries was under moral obligation to obey God's commandments in the official and social capacities of national leadership.

"It is an abomination for kings to commit wickedness, for a throne is established on righteousness" (Prov. 16:12, NASV). The foundation of all civil rule according to the Wisdom literature of the Older Testament is righteousness, the righteousness of God's law. Thus when *any* king commits violations of God's law it is detestable in God's sight. The comments which have been made on the nature of civil rule according to the Wisdom literature (especially Proverbs) of Scripture could be introduced again at this time as demonstrating the universal validity of God's law for political matters; however, it will only be observed that the ancient Jews certainly understood their Wisdom literature and law

---

[5] F. F. Bruce, *Israel and the Nations: from the Exodus to the Fall of the Second Temple* (Grand Rapids: William B. Eerdmans Publishing Co., 1963), p. 102.

to be normative for Gentile magistrates. That they did not restrict the civil morality of God's law merely to Israel is evidenced in Wisdom of Solomon 6:1-5:

> Listen therefore, O Kings, and understand; learn, O judges of the end of the earth. Give ear, you that rule over multitudes, and boast of many nations. For your dominion was given you from the Lord, and your sovereignty from the Most High, who will search out your works and inquire into your plans. Because as servants of his kingdom you did not rule rightly, nor keep the law, nor walk according to the purpose of God, he will come upon you terribly and swiftly, because severe judgment falls on those in high places.[6]

While it may be incorrect, at least the interpretation of the Torah and the attitude of the Jews themselves toward their law was that it *bound* the kings of all the nations. Wisdom 6:17-21 says rulers must honor God's law if they value their thrones and scepters.

The *inspired* and canonical Wisdom literature of God's word would not appear to differ in outlook at this point. No king is allowed to establish his throne on unrighteousness, as observed just previously (Prov. 16:12). Also we read that all who judge rightly and who decree justice (as every leader *should)* do so by means of godly Wisdom (Prov. 8:15-16), but all those who hate godly Wisdom (and its righteousness, even as applying to the civil courts, vv. 3, 7, 8, 13, 20) are lovers of death (v. 36). Consequently the king who rules a people who walk in God's righteousness is said to belong to God (Ps. 89:15-18), but the ruler who condones wickedness by calling it "righteous" will be cursed and abhorred by the nations (Prov. 24:24). It is not merely magistrates in Israel, but all kings, princes, judges, and people of the earth who are instructed to praise the Lord (Ps. 148:11, 13).

---

[6] Bruce M. Metzger (ed.), *The Apocrypha of the Old Testament: Revised Standard Version with Introductions,* et. al. (New York: Oxford University Press, 1965), p. 108.

When in Psalm 119:46 David declares that he would speak God's law before kings, it is clear that he did not refer to the civil magistrate in Israel, for he himself was that magistrate. Therefore, David infallibly considered the commandments of God as binding upon the Gentile kings and urged the communication of that law to those who ruled in the nations. Thus the words of 2 Samuel 23:3 speak directly to the point presently at issue: "the God of Israel said . . . *he who rules among men must be righteous, ruling in the fear of God.*" The throne of civil power is established on righteousness (cf. Prov. 16:12), and hence earthly rulers must be just and God fearing in the performance of their official task. The verse does not distinguish Jewish leaders and the Jewish people from Gentile leaders and the Gentile nations; it simply asserts that *any* person who has authority to rule among a body of people must do so in accordance with godly righteousness and reverence. This truth applies to those who rule באדם, not simply to those who rule among Israel of God's elect people. The ideal leader is righteous, God fearing, and a blessing to his people (cf. 2 Sam. 23:4), and that ideal does not shift once one passes from Israel to other nations. The reason David would speak God's law to the kings of the nations is because that law was as binding upon them as it was upon David, for it is the pattern of *righteousness* which is required for the *establishment* of any earthly *throne* as well as for the concrete leadership of anyone who would *rule* among men.

The conclusion of the matter about obedience to God's law by magistrates who rule in the nations can be taken from Psalm 2, one of the clearest teachings about the responsibility of world rulers to God's lawful and righteous direction. The Psalm is dealing with the nations, the kings and rulers of the earth, the peoples, the very ends of the earth, and the judges of the earth (vv. 1, 2, 8, 10); the context of David's words here is obviously international. The kings and rulers of the earth counsel together against the Lord and His Messiah in order to cast God's rule and authority off themselves (vv. 2-3; cf. Jer. 5:5); the civil magistrates try to rid themselves of their obligation to obey God and His commandments (note how the Psalm simply assumes that obligation to be upon the world rulers without offering any argument or explanation). However, the Lord laughs at them and holds their vain attempts in derision. All the nations, even the ends of the earth, are given to God's Messianic Son so that they are "herded" and ruled with a rod (or scepter) of iron. Throughout Scripture the rod represents an instrument for guidance and punishment, connoting power and authority.[7] In the book of Revelation John applies this same imagery to Jesus Christ, saying that He shall *rule the nations* with a rod of iron (Rev. 12:5; 19:15; cf. 2:26-27). Thus the Lord's Messiah has absolute, firm, and autocratic authority over all the magistrates of the nations; they are guided, directed, and chastised by Him.

The practical application of David's words is stated in his conclusion: "Now therefore, O kings, be wise; accept instruction, judges of the earth" (v. 10). Both wisdom and instruction are to be found in the commandments or law of God (e.g., Deut. 4:6; Prov. 10:8; Rom. 2:18, etc.). Thus the Psalmist counsels the kings and rulers to "serve the Lord with fear . . . (and) do homage to His Son" (vv. 11-12). World leaders are to be servants of God, ministers of the Lord (cf. Rom. 13:4), and consequently they are constrained to *obey* Him since obedience is the characteristic gesture of those who serve another.[8] The directives from God which show kings how they are obliged to obey the Lord are found in God's law, and the servant of God needs to be taught God's statutes (Ps. 119:124). Moreover, if the kings are *in fear* to serve the Lord, then again they must serve Him by obeying the law of God, for it is that which inspires reverence (Ps. 119:38, 63, 79). What God the Lord requires is that men fear Him and keep His commandments (Deut. 10:12-13). "The fear of the Lord is to hate evil" (Prov. 8:13) and wickedness consists in forsaking God's law (Ps. 119:53); therefore, the one who genuinely fears the Lord delights in His commandments (Ps. 112:1) and keeps His precepts (Ps. 119:63).

---

[7] Cf. Lev. 21:20; 2 Sam. 7:14; Job 9:34; Ps. 120:2; 125:3; Prov. 10:13; 13:24; 29:15; Isa. 11:4; Jer. 10:16; 48:17; 51:19; Ezek. 20:37; Mic. 7:14.

[8] Cf. Josh. 22:5; Ps. 119:124-126; Matt. 6:24; Eph. 6:5; Col. 3:22; Titus 2:9; 1 Peter 2:18.

It is quite plain what David means, then, by telling earthly magistrates to *serve* the Lord with *fear*. This imperative is very similar to the imperative delivered by Moses to Israel after he had explained to them that they must keep all of God's statutes and commandments: "You shall fear the Lord your God, and you shall serve Him" (Deut. 6:13). Psalm 2 says that the magistrate's obligation to obey God's rule in His law is so serious that, if the magistrate does not submit, then the Son's wrath will be kindled and the magistrate will perish in the way (v. 12). By contrast, earthly rulers are advised that all who put their trust in the Son are blessed. The wrath of God is kindled when those who have been ordained to civil rule do not serve Him with fear but refuse to enforce His righteous law as the only proper standard of social morality and order. The ancient nations of the world were under the authority of God's law, and their magistrates were obligated to rule accordingly.

Therefore, the Magistrate Is Subject to Criticism and Judgment for Lawlessness

Since the magistrates of countries outside of Israel were morally responsible to rule in accord with God's law these rulers were subject to reproof and punishment (from God's hand) if and when they departed from the course of genuine justice. Psalm 94 teaches that God chastens the *nations*, and His instruction is out of the *law* (vv. 10, 12); so then a *throne* of iniquity cannot be allied with God, and He will destroy such in its evil (vv. 20-23). A city must not be founded in iniquity (cf. Hab. 2:12), and "it is an abomination for kings to commit wickedness" (Prov. 16:12). In the perspective of these principles we can understand Jeremiah's word from God as appointing the prophet over the earthly nations and kingdoms (Jer. 1:9-10) and his message that the kings of the pagan nations will be punished for the iniquity of their hands (25:12 ff.). The kings of these Gentile nations are especially brought into particular judgment for their lawlessness and ungodly rule. Holding all nations responsible to Himself, God will not hesitate to overthrow kingly thrones and the power of the kingdoms of the nations (cf. Hag. 2:22). The fact that God will judge and punish statesmen from all over the world for their disobedience is demonstration of their accountability to His law. The Lord is to be feared as the great King over all the earth (Ps. 47:2); even the kings of the earth fear this King, for He cuts off the spirit of princes (Ps. 76:12). The Lord breaks the scepter of rulers for their wickedness and iniquity, and the kings of the pagan nations are themselves liable to the punishment of hell for their sinful rule (Isa. 14:5, 9). The king of Babylon is condemned for trying to make himself like the Most High, for trying to raise his throne above the stars of God (Isa. 14:9 ff.). Egypt is judged for its idolatry and punished for the ungodly rule of its princes (Isa. 19:1, 13-14); yet it will be a partaker of the worldwide salvation to be sent by God (Isa. 19:22) just as it also stands under the universal scope of responsibility to God's law. In judging the Assyrians God singles out their king for special mention; the idolatrous place of human sacrifice, Topheth, has been prepared for him (Isa. 30:33; cf. Prov. 28:10). The king of Tyre is condemned for lifting up his heart against God and trying to sit in the seat of God (Ezek. 28:1-10); there is only one Law-giver and Authority, but rather than submitting to Him the king of Tyre tried to usurp His rule. Because Belshazzer lifted himself up against the Lord of heaven and did not glorify Him, Belshazzer is judged wanting by God and subsequently punished (Dan. 5:22-28). And thus there is a long list of concrete examples which only confirm the accountability of those national leaders outside of the Jewish theocracy to God and God's authoritative law.

In summation of the Older Testament's teaching on the civil magistrate outside of Israel, the evidence has strongly indicated that there is continuity between Israel and the other nations on the essential outline of the magistrate's nature and duty. Although in terms of history there would be a radical difference between the actual performance of God's law (or intent to do so) and understanding of it on the part of Israel and the nations, nevertheless the *moral obligation* for rulers to guide and judge in terms of the holy law of God remains identical for both Israel and the world nations.

Chapter 19

THE CIVIL MAGISTRATE IN THE NEW TESTAMENT

IN an important sense the question of whether today's civil magistrate ought to obey the law of God has received a solid affirmative answer from the preceding investigations. The root question is actually whether the geographical and temporal separation of the civil magistrate today from that of Older Testament Israel effects a separation in *moral duty* as well. Matthew 5:17-19 has indicated that the temporal separation of the magistrate today from the Israelite rulers of the Older Testament does not modify or invalidate the law of God which bound the past Jewish authorities, and the comparative investigation of the doctrine of the civil magistrate in Israel with that of the civil magistrate in the other nations has revealed that geographical separation does not alter the moral obligation of Gentile magistrates to obey the same law that Israel's rulers were responsible to obey. Therefore, one could liken the *situation* of, say, the Roman Emperor of Paul's day (with respect to the revelation of God's law) to that of the (Older Testament) ruler who governed in a country outside of Israel. From the essential identity of what was required of magistrates in Israel and of rulers in the other nations one then would, by transition, liken the Roman Emperor's moral obligations to those of the Older Testament king. At this point the question would be whether the *historical* distance between the Jewish King and the Roman Emperor makes for a divergence of ethical requirements between them. Christ authoritatively speaks to such a question and says that the full details of the Older Testament law are confirmed until the physical universe is destroyed (Matt. 5:17-18). Thus: the law which was valid for Israel was valid also for outsiders; it furthermore remains valid for all of *history*. The conclusion of such a line of thought would be that since God's law binds all men for all time, the Roman Emperor *ought* to carry out the social prescriptions of God's law.

However, there is good reason to go ahead with an analysis of the New Testament's direct teaching on the civil magistrate. The evidence of Scripture supplies concrete connection and continuity between the doctrine of the civil magistrate in the Older and New Testaments, thereby confirming the inferential argument rehearsed above. This continuity is so plain to some writers that they have said, not without good warrant, that the same admonition which is recorded by Paul in Romans 13 about the state could also have been written by a contemporary Rabbi.[1] This is not to say that there are no radical differences between Judaism and Christianity but is only a recognition of how well Paul's outlook on the state harmonizes with that of the Older Testament.

Since Romans 13 has generally been taken as the *locus classicus* of the New Testament doctrine of the state the concentration of the following examination will be upon that passage. Before delving into its particular assertions, however, a few words to set the framework within which one should approach this passage are called for. Romans 13 has been one of the most misused portions of the New Testament because Christians have often mistaken it to be an endorsement of indifference to concrete political wrongs.[2] Thus there have arisen two schools of thought in the interpretation of this passage. They can be summarized as the *normative* and *descriptive* views; the former sees Paul as prescribing what proper government is, while the latter maintains that the Apostle was simply giving an inspired description of the actual government with which he was familiar.[3]

---

[1] E.g., Hans von Campenhausen, "Zur Auslegung von Röm. 13: Die damonistiche Deutung des ἐξουσία-Begriffs," *Festschrift Alfred Betholet zum 80. Geburtstag*, ed. W. Baumgartner (Tübingen, 1950), pp. 100-105.

[2] F. F. Bruce, *The Epistle of Paul to the Romans: An Introduction and Commentary*, ed. R. V. G. Tasker, The Tyndale New Testament Commentaries, Vol. VI (Grand Rapids: William B. Eerdmans Publishing Co., 1963), p. 237.

[3] While both of these schools have long histories, a modern statement of the debate between them can be found in: W. Mögling, "Ursprung Grenze und Aufgabe

The positivistic approach to Romans 13 has been found to produce highly suspect conclusions in the past, some being willing to go so far as to grant *autonomy* to the state.[4] Others have maintained that Paul is saying that *all* governments have divine *approval* of such a character that the Christian would be morally culpable for disobeying the government except where preaching the gospel was prohibited. Beyond that no ethical criteria can be laid upon the state, and the believer has a strong obligation to have a positive and patriotic attitude toward whatever government is in power. The argument put forward is usually a variety of the following example. Since it was Nero, infamous Nero, who was in power when Paul wrote Romans 13, saying that this ruler was ordained of God and could be resisted only at the peril of eternal damnation from God, the Christian must be willing to support actively even the most unethical or dictatorial governments. Secondly, it is urged, even a corrupt Nero should be looked upon by Christians as the "minister of God" who *in fact* does promote good and restrain evil, for the text of Romans 13 says that he "*is*" the minister of God to us for good. There are glaring difficulties with such an approach. With respect to the first argument, not only does it rest upon an extra-scriptural premise to gain its strength, but its premise is historically inaccurate. It might well be questioned whether Nero was at the forefront of Paul's thinking while composing Romans 13 (if he was, then it is at least strange that Paul did not more dearly indicate that fact), but even granting that he was, the fact of the matter is that the book of Romans seems to have been written in the period between 54 and 57 A.D.[5] which

des Staates," *Kirchenblatt für die reformierte Schwiez*, 101 (1945), 162-6, 178-80, 194-8, 212-16; and C. Eggenberger, "Der Sinn der Argumentation in Röm. 13.2-5," ibid., 243-244.

[4] Cf. the references to this phenomenon in Nazi Germany: Oscar Cullmann, *The State in the New Testament* (New York: Charles Scribner's Sons, 1956), pp. 55-56; Helmut Thielicke, *Theological Ethics,* Vol. I, ed. William H. Lazareth (Philadelphia: Fortress Press, 1966), pp. 364, 367; Warren A. Quanbeck (ed.), *God and Caesar, A Christian Approach to Social Ethics* (Minneapolis: Augsburg Publishing Home, 1959), p. 3.

[5] Robert H. Gundry, *A Survey of the New Testament* (Grand Rapids: Zondervan Publishing House, 1970), p. 384; Everett F. Harrison, *Introduction to the New Testament*

would date it either in the year that Nero came to power or shortly thereafter. Historians of the New Testament age attest that at least the first five years of Nero's reign (under the influence of Burrus and Seneca) were marked by enlightened government which became famous in the provinces.[6] If Paul were thinking especially of Nero while he wrote, then since Nero's personal debauchery was as yet not public, we would have to conclude that Paul is approving, not of oppressive and immoral government, but only of the enlightened kind of government for which Nero was then famous! The tables would then, with respect to what is a fundamentally questionable style of argument anyway, be completely turned on the disputer. And with respect to the second argument (viz., the magistrate "is" a minister for our good) one should note that it completely overlooks the logic of value-laden substantives. When someone is said to *be* something which carries a connotation of some sort of value judgment, such descriptions do not function like empirical observations or the attribution of a necessary essence in an object. To say of a student that he *is* a "clown," of a ballplayer that he *is* a "powerhouse," of a professor that he *is* an "intellectual," or of a Christian that he *is* a "saint," is *not* to say that the student is never serious, that the ballplayer never strikes out, that the professor never gets his information wrong, or that the Christian never commits sin. These are value-laden substantives which variously generalize about, set goals for, or state one perspective on, an individual's behavior. It is especially important that one observe the logic of value-laden substantives when it comes to the description of someone as God's "minister." This is an honorific description of the person as ministering to God or for God. However, the fact that someone comes into the recognized station (or even office) of a "minister" does not

(Grand Rapids: William B. Eerdmans Publishing Co., 1964), p. 285; Donald Guthrie, *New Testament Introduction*, rev. ed., (Downers Grove, IL: InterVarsity Press, 1970), pp. 396-397.

[6] F. F. Bruce, *New Testament History* (New York: Doubleday & Co., Inc., 1971), p. 310; E. M. Blaiklock, *The Century of the New Testament* (Chicago, IL: InterVarsity Press, 1962), p. 45.

guarantee that the evaluation "minister" is appropriate. For instance, from the fact that gospel "ministers" are described as not handling the word of God deceitfully (2 Cor. 4:1-2) we are not to be so foolish as to think that every ordained "minister" in a "Christian church" anywhere is above deceit in his use of Scripture. Not everyone who claims to be a "minister" really is! In the same way, not every man who seizes power in a nation will *ipso facto* "minister" for God there. There are criteria that are expected to be, or have been, satisfied when a value-laden substantive is applied to a man. In this case a national ruler might be called a "minister" as a matter of course, but he would not actually be such a minister unless he matched up to particular criteria. Just as Paul can think of a "gospel which is no gospel" (Gal. 1:6-7) he certainly can think of a "minister which is no minister." And then it also should be observed that the suggested argument for a descriptive reading of Romans 13 which is under consideration here overlooks the logic and grammar of category or class descriptions. When it is said of a class that it "is" such and such, the very fact that the statement is categorical should prevent one from understanding it as a factual description of each member of the category. For instance, Paul's categorical statement that no one who warreth entangleth himself with the affairs of this life (2 Tim. 2:4) serves its proper function as a class generalization without intending to deny that particular soldiers very often do become intimately involved in the matters of regular life in the cities near their post of duty; they may be worse soldiers for that, but still there are individuals who participate in the class of soldiers or warriors who have not remained within the bounds of Paul's categorical description. Thus it is very important to note that in Romans 13:3 Paul is dealing with "rulers" (plural) as a class, not as separate individuals. What is true of the class or category of rulership, namely, that it should be a fear only to evil-doers, does not mean that specific rulers have not sinned in becoming a fear to those (e.g., Christians) who do the good. The fact that Paul uses value-laden substantives and category descriptions in Romans 13 should indicate to us that he is at least describing what government's *proper* function is and not rendering an affirmative moral judgment on any *particular* ruler or political policy. Moreover, the descriptive interpretation of Romans 13 engenders a number of unnecessary conflicts in evaluation of the then present government on the part of the New Testament writers (e.g., Rom. 13:4 vs. Rev. 13:1, 7; 1 Peter 2:13-17 vs. Acts 5:29; Luke 20:25 vs. 13:32); a great deal of work is then called for to explain these alleged divergences (e.g., only later when the evil side of the government started to assert itself, did the negative evaluations receive expression).[7]

The normative interpretation of Romans 13 would then seem to have some strength. Paul's words have definite bearing on what governments *ought* to be and do, and his words can hardly be construed as offering unqualified acceptance of every specific human ruler. The repeated subordination of the political order to God by Paul certainly suggests that Paul is speaking *theologically*[8] placing government in proper relation to other relevant factors, and not simply giving the believer practical direction (what to do in his own personal situation and from the perspective only of his own individual relation to the state). To say that the political authority is a "minister of God" is, by the very designation, to say something about what rulers ought to be about in their labors. However, while there is truth in this approach to Romans 13, the normative interpretation is wrong if taken to be an entire account of Paul's intended message. Paul gives no indication that he has taken up the topic of "the state properly so called," and one would struggle to fit such a teaching into the context of Romans 13 with any sense of harmony or literary continuity; a discourse on the state *per se* would be quite abrupt in terms of the book of Romans as a whole. Furthermore, if Paul were digressing into a political treatise at this point it is strange that he does not go into more detail work and explanation, answering some of the most obvious questions that have arisen in the history of biblical interpretation and Christian ethics in relation to this passage. The historical context has to be accounted for as well. Paul is

---

[7] Cf. Clinton Morrison, *The Powers that Be: Earthly Rulers and Demonic Powers in Romans 13:1-7*, ed. C. F. D. Moule, et. al., Studies in Biblical Theology, No. 29 (London: SCM Press Ltd., 1960), pp. 12-13.

[8] Ibid., p. 112.

writing to Christians in the imperial capital, those who might very easily be in a position to give the magistrate the wrong impression as to the nature of Christ's kingdom and kingship. In terms of literary context one can hardly avoid seeing that Paul's main point in Romans 13 was of a practical nature: "be in subjection!" And in terms of this specific exhortation, propounders of the normative interpretation have been just as prone as their opponents to create, by overlooking the serious commands to obey those in authority, a conflict in outlook on the state between different New Testament passages.

It is quite clear that Romans 13 has *two elements* in it: practical ethics and normative description. When both are not respected then the church ends up either with the distortion that the practical command to be subject means that normative authority is granted to anything the state might do (with minor qualifications), or with the distortion that the normative role of the state laid out by Paul must override the duty to be submissive and grant the right of violent revolution. However, full justice must be done to both elements without subsuming one under the other. It is not the *via media* but the very wording of Romans 13:1-7 which should lead one to see that Paul's teaching is *twofold* here: what is expected of the Christian and what is expected of the state. (After all, it would be initially peculiar if the Christian and the state were to be responsibly related to each other by Paul, but with the effect of laying duties upon the one while leaving the other free to act merely as it pleases.) Some help is found in looking at the place Romans 13 has in literary history. The maxims of Romans 13 are common to Jewish literature (cf. Wisdom 6:1-3; Baruch 4:25 ff.; Enoch 46:5; Josephus, *Jewish Wars* II, 8.7; etc.) where they are used to indicate the *ruler's* obligation to act responsibly before God (who is over them), even as the Jews endure with obedience the ruler's command (which is over them). The literature of the early church also alluded often to Romans 13 (cf. Polycarp, Justin Martyr, Athenagoras, Theophilus, Tertullian, Dionysius of Alexandria, Eusebius, and many liturgies), and again these maxims went beyond the Christian's duty to the state and summoned magistrates to righteousness (cf. especially Clement's letter to Corinth). Thus bracketed within literary history, Romans 13 would not implausibly be interpreted as stating what God requires of *both* believers and magistrates. This double thrust of the believer's duty to the state and then, in explanation, the state's duty to God is expressed in the commentary on Romans by H. C. G. Moule:

> . . . in this brief paragraph we see and touch as it were the cornerstone of civil order. One side of the angle is the indefeasible duty, for the Christian citizen, of reverence for law, of remembrance of the religious aspect of even secular government. The other side is the memento to the ruler, to the authority, that God throws His shield over the claims of the state only because authority was instituted not for selfish but for social ends.[9]

When the duty of both believer and ruler are seen to be the expressions of Paul's theonomic ethic, then Romans 13:1-7 fits its literary context within the book, and the apparent conflicts of evaluation of the state which are engendered by the descriptive and the (exclusivistic) normative interpretations of Romans 13 need not arise as in any way troublesome or in need of (behind-the-scenes) explanations at all.

On the first point, Romans 13:1-7 arises in a context of ethical instruction (note the long list of moral exhortations in chapter 12 and the discourse on love and law in 13:8-10), and for Paul Christian ethics is directed by God's law (cf. Rom. 3:31; 7:12; 8:4; etc.). Thus when he has instructed believers to avenge not themselves because vengeance is God's (12:19), it is not unnatural that he should go on to explain how God's vengeance is expressed in social relations by means of the state's sword (13:4) and also what the Christian's relation is to that state (13:1-2). In both these areas Paul's teaching is from the law of God. And then, by taking a theonomic approach to the state, there is no difficulty in

---

[9] Handley C. G. Moule, *The Epistle of St. Paul to the Romans*, ed. W. Robertson Nicoll, The Expositor's Bible, Vol. V (Hartford: The S. S. Scranton Co., [n.d.]), p. 354.

the fact that the state is both honored in its authority or functions and criticized in its actual disobedience or over-extension of authority. In terms of God's law both of these attitudes are consistent and called for by the circumstances in the biblical passages where they appear. Therefore, by seeing in Romans 13:1-7 an expression of both the lawful duty of Christians to the state and the lawful duty of the state to God, one can do justice to the wording of the passage (in both its call to subjection as well as its normative understanding of the state), harmoniously fit the passage into its literary context within the book, and avoid making the New Testament appear to contradict itself in the attitude expressed toward civil rule.

It is within this framework that we can now examine the doctrine of the civil magistrate as presented in the New Testament, noting especially the continuity with what was taught in the Older Testament.

God Sovereignly Appoints and Removes Rulers

Paul affirms that government is a divine institution: "there is no power but of God" (Rom. 13:1). The existing "powers" are "ordained by God." The word Paul uses for "ordain" (τάσσω) is the same as that which was observed earlier to be used in the Septuagint for God appointing judges in Israel. And the word for the government's authority (ἐξουσία) is used in the Septuagint of the power of dominion of various political figures; perhaps of great interest at this point is the recollection that Daniel spoke of the "authority" of even the beast (in his vision) being granted to it from God. Given this Older Testament background and Septuagint vocabulary there would not seem to be any necessity, as recent writers from Dibelius on (e.g., Oscar Cullmann, Clinton Morrison) have thought, of relating ἐξουσία to the cosmological world spirits.[10] There is no contextual reason to go beyond the mere thought of political rulers. (In *other* contexts the word "powers" is used with a string of synonyms and referred to the angelic world, but that string of synonyms is absent in Romans 13; there would then be

---

[10] Cf. Morrison, *op. cit.*, passim.

no warrant for importing a cosmological meaning into Paul's words at this point unless one illegitimately treats a word like a concept and thinks that a word carries the accumulation of its various senses in every instance of its appearance.)

The fact that the magistrate has been ordained by God places stress upon the supremacy of God, not that of the state. The same *root* for the key words Paul uses in telling *believers* to be in subjection and not resist the authority of the state is used by Paul to speak of the *state* being "ordained" by God. The subjection of the Christian unto the state's authority, then, should suggest the corresponding appropriateness of the state being subject to God's authority. And just as a person does not need to be a Christian to be under moral obligation to obey the state (note "every soul" in Rom. 13:1), so also unbelief does not rid the magistrate of his obligations to God.[11] The fact that the magistrate has been ordained by God implies that he has functions for which he is responsible before the Lord. John Murray observes that:

> The civil magistrate is not only the means decreed in God's providence for the punishment of evildoers but God's instituted, authorized, and prescribed instrument for the maintenance of order and the punishing of criminals who violate that order. When the civil magistrate through his agents executes just judgment upon crime, he is executing not simply God's decretive will but he is also fulfilling God's preceptive will, and it would be sinful for him to refrain from so doing.[12]

The ordination of God puts the magistrate under moral obligation to the Lord and His prescriptions. This might also be inferred from the fact that Paul tells believers to "be subject" to the magistrate, for

---

[11] Cf. the teaching of Luther as cited in Philip S. Watson, *The State as a Servant of God: A Study of its Nature and Tasks* (London: Society for Promoting Christian Knowledge, 1946), p. 25.

[12] John Murray, *The Epistle to the Romans: The English Text with Introduction, Exposition and Notes*, Vol. II, ed. F. F. Bruce, The New International Commentary on the New Testament (Grand Rapids: William B. Eerdmans Publishing Co., 1965), p. 149.

elsewhere when the New Testament admonishes a class of people to "be subject" to someone else the writer turns around and also calls upon these masters, husbands, and parents to demonstrate equal responsibility (e.g., Eph. 5:22-6:9). Thus it would not be unreasonable to expect that Paul, having told believers to be subject to rulers, would turn around and expect responsible obedience of rulers—indeed, this is precisely what we find in verses 3 and 4.

Therefore, in agreement with what the Older Testament teaches, the New Testament declares that God sovereignly appoints rulers and that this appointment by God puts the magistrate under responsibility to reverence and obey God. God also removes rulers from their thrones and punishes their disobedience. When Herod received praise as a god he was smitten by an angel of God; God both deposed this ruler from his powerful position and brought vengeance upon his immoral rule. That God's ordination and removal of magistrates entails their obligation to serve Him and obey His will is an outlook which seems to have been recognized even by Pilate. When Jesus stood before Pilate Jesus declared that Pilate would have no power at all against Him unless it had been given from above, and at this word from Christ, Pilate (it might be implied) realized that he was thereby responsible to the Heavenly Sovereign to be just in his dealings as a ruler and so sought to release Christ (John 19:11-12; cf. Matt. 27:19, 24). Whether or not this message from Christ motivated the next mentioned activity of Pilate, it is plainly taught in the New Testament that all earthly rule is the result of God's appointment.

Rulers, as God's Appointees, Are Not to Be Resisted

"The one resisting the authority has opposed the ordinance of God, and they who oppose will receive to themselves judgment" (Rom. 13:2). Little needs to be said of this assertion since its Older Testamental background is adequate commentary upon it. Paul found it an important principle since he reiterated it again in Titus 3:1, instructing this pastor also to "put them in mind to be in subject to rulers." Peter declares that believers must "be subject to every ordinance of man . . . whether to the king, as supreme, or unto governors. . ." (1 Peter 2:13-14).

Earlier it was seen that God's people were required to seek the peace of Babylon when under its control, and this same attitude of seeking peace is required by Paul (cf. Rom. 12:18; 14:19); it is part of the "good" which believers should do in order to have the magistrate's praise (cf. 13:3, 13). Paul's respect for authority is indicated in his repentance for speaking evil of a ruler unwittingly (Acts 23:5), a repentance grounded in the law of the Older Testament (Ex. 22:28). In Romans 13:7 he indicates that honor is to be rendered to whom honor is due, which on Older Testament background would include the king (cf. Prov. 24:21). As the people of the Older Testament were required to pray for even their Gentile rulers (cf. Jer. 29:7; Ezra 6:10), Paul exhorts the church to pray for kings and all that are in high place (1 Tim. 2:2). The continuity between the Older and New Testament attitudes toward the state are thus again seen to be evidenced.

It is worth noting that, just as the section above indicates that the magistrate is under moral responsibility since ordained by God, the premise at hand (viz., not resisting but rather respecting the authorities) also points in an *indirect* way to the state's obligations to God. The idea of rendering unto the state the things which are its due (e.g., honor and tribute) in Romans 13:7 has as its background the statement of Jesus to "render unto Caesar the things that are Caesar's and unto God the things that are God's" (Matt. 22:21). This definitely implies a restriction of state authority within certain prescribed limits.[13] Thus the state has a specifically assigned task. Furthermore, Caesar is required to render to God those things which belong to God; this includes the life and service of Caesar to God since the person of Caesar bears the "image of God," just as citizens must render their taxes to Caesar because their coins bear the image of Caesar (cf. Matt. 22: 20). So again it seems that the state or magistrate is viewed by God's word as being responsible to God. In Romans 13:7 "that which is due" has the same root as "to owe" in verse 8. Verse 7 says to render to each his due, and verse 8 says nothing is due to anyone except love—that is, the fulfilling

[13] Cullmann *op. cit.*, p. 36; cf. John H. Yoder, *The Politics of Jesus* (Grand Rapids: William B. Eerdmans Publishing Co., 1972), p. 211 (on Rom. 13:7).

of God's law (v. 10). The conclusion should be that what is due to the state is obedience to God's law, and if this is what is its due, then the law of God is the area of the state's assigned function. What Caesar must render unto God as the things which are God's includes his obedience to, and enforcement of, God's law within the nation.

Rulers Bear Religious Titles

The responsibility of the civil magistrate to God is evidenced in the fact that Paul views him as the *minister of God,* a prescribed instrument for the maintenance of order and the punishment of evildoers (Rom. 13:4, 6). Twice the magistrate is called "minister of God," an appellation which functionally parallels the giving of religiously significant titles to magistrates in the Older Testament. In verse 6 the term λειτουργός is used; it is a term denoting the enhanced dignity of the highest forms of service to God. In the ancient world it was a plainly religious term used to speak of work done to promote the social and natural order in service to the divine-state. Paul uses the term, then, with a twist; rather than being a minister of the divine-state, the state is a minister of the divine Creator. The term strongly connotes obligation to divine orders. It is used of the Levites who perform priestly services as the Lord commanded (e.g., Num. 8:22; 18:4; 2 Chron. 31:2; Ex. 28:34-45; 29:30, 35, 44, LXX); it is also used in Daniel 7:10 (LXX) of the thousands who attend the Ancient of Days. It is used in the Older Testament for service to a prophet, such as Samuel (1 Kings 2:18; 3:1; 2 Kings 8:11, LXX) or Elijah (2 Kings 19:21, LXX). Of importance as background to Paul's use of the term in Romans 13 is the Older Testament usage of it for political service.[14] It applies to Joshua as a servant of the leader, Moses (Josh. 1:1), of the service given by family heads to the captains (1 Chron. 27:1, LXX), of service to the king (2 Kings 1:4, 15, LXX), of the officials, princes, commanders, and

[14] This, as well as the wealth of *Older Testament background* to the relevant terms, demonstrates why Morrison's approach to the phrase "minister of God" in Romans 13 is both unnecessary and misleading; he thinks a worldview which does not distinguish myth, history, and the spiritual realm from each other is the background to Paul's designation, cf. *op. cit.*, pp. 98-99, 102-103.

attendants of the king (2 Chron. 17:19; 22:8; 2 Kings 10:5; Esther 2:2, LXX). It is specifically correlated with doing the Lord's commandments (Ps. 102:19-22, LXX). In the New Testament the strong association with cultic service is present (Heb. 9:21; 10:11; Luke 1:23) and again applies to angels (Heb. 1:7) as agents of God's will. It is even used of Christ as minister of the heavenly sanctuary and new covenant (Heb. 8:2, 6). It can be applied to Christian service of teaching (Acts 13:2; Rom. 15:27; 2 Cor. 9:12; Phil. 2:25, 30), and Paul uses it of himself as a minister of the gospel, one poured out in service to the faith (Rom. 15:16; Phil. 2:17). In the early Fathers the word is applied to righteous conduct.[15] This survey indicates the sort of value-laden substantive λειτουργός is. Being applied to the civil magistrate in Romans 13:6 (and to the work of the Apostle and Christians in the same book, just two chapters later) the "ministry" expected by God of the civil magistrate carries high responsibilities before the Lord and suggests obedience to His revealed will.

In verse 4 of Romans 13 Paul also says that the magistrate is a "minister of God," and here he uses the term "deacon" (διακονός). The word appears outside the New Testament; "the statesman rules as διακονός τῆς πολέως. . . for the sake of the service laid upon him, which consists supremely in the education of good citizens."[16] It appears in the sense of obedience, even political obedience (e.g., "obedience to the king's command"),[17] Paul now applies it to the civil magistrate as one who obeys the Great King's command, obedience which consists supremely in meting out the punishments of God's wrath against the wicked in society, thus preserving justice. Just as God has ordained this "deacon" (Rom. 13:1, 4), Christ established Paul in the "deaconate" (ministry, 1 Tim. 1:12; Acts 20:24). A deaconate received from the Lord

---

[15] H. Strathmann, "Λειτουργός," et. al., *Theological Dictionary of the New Testament,* Vol. IV, ed. Gerhard Kittel, trans., and ed. Geoffrey W. Bromiley (Grand Rapids: William B. Eerdmans Publishing Co., 1967), p. 228.

[16] Hermann W. Beyer, "Διάκαινος" et. al., *Theological Dictionary, op. cit.*, Vol. II, p. 82.

[17] Ibid., pp. 14-15.

is to be obediently fulfilled (Col. 4:17). Christ our Lord is a "deacon," one who came to serve in accordance with God's command (Matt. 20:28; Mark 10:45), and the Bible says that "service" done unto the Lord is honored by God (Rev. 2:19), but He despises the bad ministry of a Judas (Acts 1:16-17) or the ministry given to Satan by false teachers (2 Cor. 11:15). The term applies to the ministry of the word (Acts 6:4; 1 Peter 4:11), the gospel (Eph. 3:7; Col. 1:23), the church (Col. 1:25), the New Covenant (2 Cor. 3:6), of Christ (2 Cor. 11:23; Col. 1:7; 1 Tim. 4:6), of God (2 Cor. 6:4; cf. 1 Thess. 3:2 with 1 Cor. 3:5), to the needy (Phil. 1:1; 1 Tim. 3:8, 12; cf. Acts 6:1-6), and in the social state (Rom. 13:4). Responsibilities before God in obedience to His dictates are high in all these areas or respects. As a minister of God the political ruler is afforded the same dignity as Older Testament magistrates in the respect that he too is a *servant of the King and is commissioned to obey and carry out the King's Law.* This "service" is not *automatically* rendered, for there are *criteria* to which it must conform.

Hence Rulers Are God's Vicegerents, Avengers of His Wrath

The civil magistrate is to be "an avenger for wrath to the one practicing evil" and thereby does not "bear the sword in vain" (Rom. 13:4). The parallel in 1 Peter 2:14 is instructive here; it says of kings and authorities that they are δὶ αὐτοῦ πεμπομένοις εἰς ἐκδίκησιν κακοποιῶν "through Him being sent for vengeance on evildoers." The civil magistrate has been commissioned by God to punish workers of evil in society; this is his task and proper function. His ministry is not in vain as he executes penal justice on criminals, for he has been "ordained" and "sent" by the Lord of Justice Himself.

Verse 2 of Romans 13 represents the civil magistrate as a substitution instance for God; that is, to resist the former is to resist the latter. "The one resisting the authority has opposed the ordinance of God." Here the magistrate represents the rule of God, and an offense against God's representative is an offense against the rule of God. Because the magistrate has been sent and ordained by God, and because one who opposes the magistrate will be accounted as opposing God, it is properly said that the civil ruler is a vicegerent for God.

God has equipped the magistrate with the sword, the power of execution. As was noted above, God is primarily the one who has the right to punish with the sword; He is the one who throughout Scripture wields it against the disobedient. However, the magistrate has the approval of God's word to use the sword as well, and in such a case must express the punishments of God; God's sword finds partial expression in the sword of the state when the magistrate obeys the Lord who sent him. The magistrate, as John Murray was quoted as saying above, is God's prescribed instrument for punishing criminals who violate God's order for society; he is to execute, not simply God's decretive will, but God's preceptive will—and he sins should he fail to do so. No man has the right to take another man's life or carry out punishment upon another without the approval of God, and thus the autonomous use of the sword in Israel was grave iniquity, as discussed earlier. The magistrate cannot presume to take just anybody's life at his own whim (i.e., murder), but must execute criminals and punish evildoers *as God so sanctions* these punishments—in His law. When the magistrate punishes violators of God's law his use of the sword has God's sanction; it is not vainly used. In Romans 13 Paul draws particular attention to the punitive aspect of the ruler's authority: he is a terror to evil works (vv. 3-4). We must notice that the magistrate's punishment pertains to "works," or *outward behavior*—not all sin (e.g., sins of the heart). The ruler punishes all sin that is actively committed against God's righteous order for society and interpersonal relations; he punishes crimes that are publicly expressed, but not personal sins entertained privately. Since only God can read the heart, only God is in a position to judge and punish internal or personal sins; He will certainly punish *social* transgressions at the day of judgment also, but in this area He has sent, ordained the magistrate to preserve justice and peace in human society and thus temporally to punish these offenses *as well.* Calvin notes this distinction, saying:

> Because the mortal lawgiver's jurisdiction extends only to the outward political order, his ordinances are not violated, except when actual crimes are committed. But God, whose eye nothing escapes, and who is concerned not so much with outward

> appearance as with purity of heart, under the prohibition of fornication, murder, and theft, forbids lust, anger, hatred, coveting a neighbor's possessions, deceit, and the like.[18]

When the magistrate uses the sword against public crime he must follow *God's direction and definitions* with respect to crime; he, as a vicegerent, must obey and enforce the Lord's law—even to the point of capital punishment where God calls for it to be used. God does not grant the magistrate the right to judge men's hearts, evaluate their motives, or bind their consciences. Luther was right in saying:

> For over the soul God can and will let no one rule but himself. Therefore, where temporal power presumes to prescribe laws for the soul, it encroaches upon God's government and only misleads and destroys the souls.
>
> Human ordinance cannot possibly extend its authority to heaven and over souls, but belongs only to earth, to the external intercourse of men with each other, where men can see, know, judge, sentence, punish and acquit.[19]

It is in the *public* realm of human society that the magistrate bears not the sword in vain. It would be vain for him to assume the prerogative of judging and punishing any and all sins, as if he were like God and could know men's hearts.

However, there is firm grounding and good purpose in the magistrates' use of the sword for *those crimes* against which God prescribes it; *here* the magistrate does *not* use the sword in vain, but as God's vicegerent. As the civil magistrate in Israel was ordained to preserve

---

[18] Ford Lewis Battles (trans.), Calvin: *The Institutes of the Christian Religion*, ed. John T. McNeill, The Library of Christian Classics, Vol. XX, eds. John Baillie, John T. McNeill, and Henry P. Van Dusen (Philadelphia: The Westminster Press, 1967), Book II, chap. VIII, section 6, p. 372.

[19] Cited in Watson, *op. cit.*, p. 19.

peace and justice in society and thereby allow for the development of the redeemed community and the progress of redemptive history, so also the civil magistrate today must preserve peace and justice in society in order that God's will be done (on earth as it is in heaven) and to provide an environment conducive to the spread of the Christian gospel by the church and the progress of redemptive history (particularly in the application of redemption) until the consummation and regeneration of all things.

Therefore, the civil magistrate is "an avenger of wrath." In Romans 12:19 we are told not to *avenge* ourselves, for "it stands written, vengeance is mine, I will repay, says the Lord." The believer is told to "give place to *wrath*." The Lord prohibits personal retribution and claims the right to punish as His own. How does this work? Paul goes on in Romans 13:4 to say that the *magistrate* (with his sword) is the "*avenger* of *wrath*." This is the important syntactical connection between Romans 13 and what immediately precedes.[20] And in that connection the relationship between the civil ruler and judge becomes quite evident. The magistrate is expected to rectify justice and recompense for evil deeds.

> The authorities are recognized (13:4) as executing the particular function which the Christian was to leave to God, It is inconceivable that these two verses, using such similar language, should be meant to be read independently of one another.[21]

The Lord claims that vengeance is His, and then He delegates (a portion) of that vengeance to the civil magistrate. God will not wait to the Last Day before seeing to it that justice is maintained in human society. He has commissioned magistrates to maintain social justice by expressing the wrath of God against public evil. There is *temporal* punishment for crime as well as *eternal* punishment for crime, and the reality or

---

[20] This demonstrates that Morrison is mistaken in his denial of any connection, *op. cit.*, p. 104.

[21] Yoder, *op. cit.*, p. 199.

validity of neither can be impugned. The magistrate is to act in such a way that he represents the proper vengeance of God against social impurity and injustice. In the future Christ will return from God's right hand in the "*vengeance*" of flaming fire against all those who know not God and obey not the gospel (2 Thess. 1:8), and truly the Lord is an avenger (1 Thess. 4:6; Heb. 10:30). Still, justice is to be procured by earthly judges who avenge for those who have been wronged (cf. Luke 18:3, 4, 7, 8). God has instituted that proper authorities have the power to express His vengeance on crime; He has ordained and sent a "punisher" with a "sword." The vengeance of the Last Day is *not contradictory* to, or a *substitute* for, the temporal punishments God ordains His earthly vicegerent to execute.

The magistrate is "an avenger for wrath." Whose wrath? Generally in New Testament usage human "wrath" is a passion to be avoided (Matt. 5:22; Eph. 4:31; Col. 3:8; 1 Tim. 2:8; Titus 1:7) or held in check (Eph. 4:26; James 1:19). Thus the magistrate is not set free to express *his own personal* anger or vindictiveness against individuals. He is commissioned to apply *God's* wrath where it is appropriate to do so (cf. Rom. 13:4 with 13:2). "Wrath" nearly always refers to God's wrath in the New Testament, as it does eleven times in Romans itself. Thus the wrath which is applied by the magistrate—as well as the "fear" which belongs to him (cf. vv. 3, 7 with Isa. 8:13)—must be the wrath of God against disobedience. The magistrate ministers for the Lord, the Lord's vengeance, the Lord's wrath, and the Lord's fear; he represents the justice of God and its appropriate expression against civil unrighteousness. The magistrate is far from wielding arbitrary power, then, but must follow the norm of God's law (as the standard and source of information on justice and penology). This wrath which the magistrate demonstrates is consonant with the fact that there is a day of wrath *to come* (cf. Matt. 3:7; Rom. 2:5; 1 Thess. 1:10; 5:9); God has ordained *both* temporal punishments for unrighteousness in society at present as well as eternal damnation for all sin and iniquity at the Great Tribunal when all shall stand directly before His judgment seat. What is it that merits God's wrath (either now from the earthly judge or later from the divine Judge)? The New Testament strongly teaches that it is the law of God which works "wrath" (Rom. 4:15); God's wrath is due to the lusts of the sinful flesh (Eph. 2:3), to the sins of the children of disobedience (Eph. 5:6; Col. 3:6), or simply to sin (1 Thess. 2:16). The conclusion must be then that it is violation of *God's law* (cf. 1 John 3:4) which provokes and warrants the expression of God's wrath. Those for whom the magistrate's sword is to be a source of fear, and those against whom the magistrate is to apply the wrath of God are the violators of God's law as it pertains to social and civil affairs. The magistrate's throne, like that of God's, is to be established on righteousness and justice, for he represents God in matters of civil judgment and social uprightness.

The Magistrate Must Deter Evil but Honor the Good

The eyes of the Lord are upon the righteous, but His face is against them that do evil (1 Peter 3:12). As God's vicegerent the magistrate must reflect the same two-fold attitude; he must be fearful to those who do evil, but a blessing to those who are righteous. If he is this way and not a persecutor of the righteous or distorter of justice (cf. 1 Peter 3:14), then there is real strength in the question: "who is he that will harm you if you are zealous for that which is good?" (1 Peter 3:13). The people of a country can feel secure when they know that their leaders are men of righteousness and integrity, those who vindicate the offended and punish the offender.

In harmony with the Wisdom of the Older Testament as it was discussed previously, and according to the dual effect the magistrate is to have in society according to the doctrine of civil rule in the Older Testament, Paul says "Rulers are not a fear to the good work but to the evil. And do you wish not to fear the authority? Then do the good and you will have praise from the same" (Rom. 13:3). The magistrate must, therefore, be concerned not with his own selfish interests but with "the good." *A standard is laid upon him.* He must be a terror to evildoers, his eyes scattering evil (Prov. 20:8) and his fear being as a lion's roar (Prov. 20:2). Note must be made of the fact that according to Paul the magistrate is not simply a negative force in history or society; he is not simply the one who minimally protects human life against aggravated murder and otherwise has no interest in social justice. The magistrate, in scriptural perspective, not only deters evil (*all* public expressions thereof) but "praises" and promotes the good. He aims at a maximization of social justice in his domain, and thus is not reluctant to justify the righteous against the offenses of the wicked or to enter into severe judgment against all public unrighteousness. While his judgment is based upon and hemmed in by the law of God, the magistrate must attempt to do everything within his power to see to the public and corporate sanctifying of civil society. He seeks the social justice prescribed by the penology of God's law for as many crimes legislated against by God and placed under public sanctions, for his aim is not that of doing as little as one can in the face of crime (restraining only the most dangerous, and selected crime) but everything that the Lord demands by His law. He *promotes the good* while deterring the evil—not simply deters a few selected evils. This maxim of Paul's could only seem to be out of the spirit of Christ if one *fails* to distinguish between the *preservation* of the world from the *salvation* of the world. While the church propagates the gospel of God's grace, the state maintains the standards of God's justice in social matters (matters of outward behavior, but not matters of the heart, conscience, or belief).

The Magistrate Must Rule, then, According to God's Law

That civil magistrates ought to obey and enforce the appropriate commandments of God (viz., those dealing with social relations and civil justice) in their official functions has been demonstrated already in the preceding sections.

Paul does not neglect to indicate this directly when he says that the magistrate is a minister of God "for the *good*," but an avenger of God's wrath "to the one practicing *evil*" (Rom. 13:4). Since magistrates are sent and *ordained by God, represent* the rule of *God*, are *ministers* of *God,* execute the *vengeance* of *God,* and show the *wrath* of *God,* it is *not* the case that "good" in Romans 13 is whatever the rulers recognize or take to be good.[22] "Evil" and "good" must be understood as presented in Scripture.

"The good the magistrate promotes is that which subserves the interests of piety."[23] The terms "good" and "evil" are defined in Scripture *with reference to the law of God.* Good is that which is in accord with the commands of God (Deut. 12:28; Mic. 6:8; Ps. 119:68; Luke 8:15; 1 Tim. 1:8); in fact, Paul says in the book of Romans itself that God's law is "the good" (7:13, 12; cf. vv. 16, 19). And in the local context of Romans 13:4 it is clear that Paul is thinking of "good" as observance of God's law; the law is taken up for discussion immediately following Paul's words on the civil magistrate, showing what duty men are under obligation to render to others.[24] If the magistrate is to promote the good, then he is to promote obedience to the law of God.

On the other hand, the one who does evil is one who has not seen God, is not godly (3 John 11); evil is the opposite of God's nature (James 1:13-15), and so to act out of accord with the righteousness of God (which is expressed in the law of God) is to be evil. Evil is contrasted quite sharply with obedience, good, and righteousness (Rom. 12:21; 16:19; 1 Thess. 5:15; 1 Peter 3:10-12; Heb. 5:14) which are all known by the standard of God's law. In Mark 3:4 evil is contrasted to what is "lawful," and in Luke 6:9 it is contrasted with doing good. In Romans 7:21-23 Paul directly identifies evil with war against the law of God, and in Romans 13:10 itself (the local context for 13:4) evil is seen as the violation of God's law. An evildoer would be one who is thought of as having broken the law of God (cf. John 18:30), even the law as calling for the death penalty (John 18:31). Hence an "evil doer" can stand for someone who is held as guilty of committing a capital crime according to God's law (cf. Matt. 26:57-67, esp. 66; 27:22-23). The same conclusion is reached when we consider Paul's trial before the Sanhedrin; once the Pharisees became willing to defend Paul's cause they claimed

---

[22] As suggested by Morrison, *op. cit.*, p. 107.

[23] Murray, *op. cit.*, p. 152.

[24] Cf. Yoder. *op. cit.*, pp. 198-199.

that he had done nothing evil, which in context means worthy of capital punishment according to the Jewish law (Acts 21:28; 22:1, 22, 30; 23:1-5, esp. 9). Therefore, those who have done "evil" and are to be apprehended by the civil magistrate according to Romans 13 are those who have violated the law of God (local context especially demands this conclusion: cf. 7:21-23; 12:21; 13:10; 16:19). Against such criminals the magistrate must wield his sword, the tool of God's righteous vengeance and retributive justice.

The magistrate can only maintain his prescribed relation to the good and to the evil if he attunes his behavior and official policies in the government to the law of God. The magistrate has the particular function of promoting social righteousness and peace, which can only be obtained through obedience to God's law—outward behavior being the proper sphere of concern for the civil magistrate. The sword must only be used when it represents the direction and sanction of God; otherwise it is used autonomously and, thereby, sinfully. God alone can define justice and prescribe the *proper* response to injustice in social matters. Therefore, the use of the sword must be informed by God's law.

Everything in Romans 13:1-4 points to the civil magistrate's undaunted responsibility to obey and enforce the law of God: he is ordained by God, rules for God, is a minister of God for "good," and avenger of God's wrath against those practicing "evil." All men who are given the duty of ruling over a society of men must reign under the authority and direction of God, aiming to establish *justice* in the land. Augustine's rhetorical question in *The City of God* (IX:4) is right to the point: "If justice be taken away, what are governments but great bands of robbers?" God has not established human government simply that some may take advantage, in the name of sheer power, of others; government should be a ministry pleasing to God and beneficial to the people. The throne must be established on righteousness and justice, as Luther correctly declared: "Human law, when it does not agree with the divine, is unjust."[25] God's law must be enforced as the law of the

[25] Cited in Watson, *op. cit.*, p. 64.

land. As Calvin aptly put it, "Accordingly, nothing truer could be said than that the law is a silent magistrate; the magistrate, a living law."[26]

The fact that Christians are commanded to obey the civil magistrate is another indication that human government is obligated to follow God's holy law. Scripture clearly teaches that God's people must obey and respect civil magistrates. And yet in the book of Revelation men are indicted and held culpable for following the dictates of the "beast," that is, sinful Rome and its emperor. Moreover, those who followed the beast are *contrasted* with those who, instead, kept the *law of God* (Rev. 14:9-12). Rulers are consequently expected to follow the law of God so that Christians can obey them—or else those who are punished for obeying sinful Rome according to Revelation 14 would be exonerated by Romans 13! The way to reconcile Romans 13:4, where the state is spoken of as in the service of God, and Revelation 13:2, where the state is said to be in the service of Satan, is by viewing the former as the norm for government and the latter as indictment for deviation from that norm. Outside of that one must either forfeit the unity of Scripture or appeal to principles (e.g., Rom. 8:28) to explain Romans 13 which that passage itself gives no hint of utilizing as necessary for understanding its message. Thus the civil magistrate *ought* to promote obedience to God's law (the good) and to punish with God's wrath (i.e., according to the just penal sanctions for society) those who publicly perform evil deeds (violations of God's laws). Toward this end believers are exhorted to pray for all kings and authorities: *in order that* they might lead peaceful lives *in all godliness and holiness* (1 Tim. 2:1-3). The tranquility which the magistrate should establish and protect in society must be characterized by justice and civic righteousness, for his reign should enable Christians to live in peace (which does not mean, in this passage, that believers have "personal" peace while nevertheless under public persecution) and should provide for, and promote, an environment characterized by justice and righteousness (which, as in the case of tranquility, does not simply mean that believers have personal

---

[26] Calvin, *Institutes, op. cit.*, Book IV, chap. XX, section 14, p. 1502.

or private godliness in the midst of complete social unrighteousness and public injustice). The peace which the believer wants to have, and also the godliness which the believer wants to express, should be made possible by the civil magistrate's proper administration of government; toward that end Christians are told to pray.

According to the New Testament doctrine of the civil magistrate, his primary responsibility is public morality or justice, lawfulness, and the punishment of offenders. Commenting upon 1 Peter 2:13-14, Stibbs provides a concise summary of the matter:

> Civil rulers are explicitly commissioned to represent God as the Judge. They give active expression to His righteousness and His wrath by inflicting just retribution on wrongdoers, and by publicly commending and rewarding those who do well (cf. Romans 13:3-4). All to whom such divine authority is thus delegated ought in its exercise to be like God, by whose commission and in whose service they act; i.e., they should love righteousness and hate iniquity (see Hebrews 1:8, 9).[27]

Therefore, the Magistrate Is Subject to Criticism and Judgment for Lawlessness

Because the New Testament, no less than the Older Testament, requires civil magistrates to rule in a just and God-honoring fashion, the state and rulers thereof come under disapprobation and final punishment for defiance of God's law.

Revelation plainly teaches that the kings of the earth who cooperate with, and participate in, the immoral practices or policies of Rome will be judged of God (cf. Rev. 14:8, 15-20; 17:1-2; 18:2-3, 9-10). The state is not free to run its affairs autonomously and pragmatically; moral demands are laid upon it by God, and judgment awaits those officials

---

[27] Alan M. Stibbs, *The First Epistle General of Peter*, ed. R. V. G. Tasker, The Tyndale New Testament Commentaries, Vol. 17 (Grand Rapids: William B. Eerdmans Publishing Co., 1959), pp. 110-111.

who turn aside from ruling according to the just standards established by the Lord. For this reason the New Testament and its preaching is not apolitical.

When the Pharisees brought a threat of death to Christ in the name of Herod Antipas (Luke 13:31) He contemptuously called Herod "that vixen" and strongly responded that He would continue the work that God had called Him to do—irrespective of Herod's desires (Luke 13:32 ff.). The feminine form of the word "fox" was a cutting way to denounce the fact that Herod was dominated by his unlawful wife, Herodias, the same woman who had demanded the head of John the Baptist.[28] In Jewish usage the designation "fox" had the double sense of typifying low cunning (instead of upright dealing) and disdainful weakness (instead of the significant power and greatness of a lion).[29] Thus Jesus sends back this message to Herod: "you are a dishonorable ruler, one who is neither lawful nor respectable in his activities." In the discourse on forethought (Luke 14:25-35) Jesus uses two rhetorical questions to illustrate the need to count the cost of one's proposed projects. These questions play on the foolishness of someone not being able to finish the building of a tower after starting the work and the foolishness of a king going to war rashly. Since Herod had been involved in both these mistaken ventures, it seems that Jesus was indirectly involved in political preaching against the king's foolishness.[30] And so Jesus, whether by passing allusion or direct confrontation, was not unwilling to bring the magistrate under criticism. Nor was John the Baptist. In his preaching against sin John indicted the illegality of the magistrate's behavior, specifically mentioning Herod. The summary of his indictment is given in Mark 6:18: "it is not lawful for you to have your brother's wife." One must not think that John's word was tempered

---

[28] Gundry, *op. cit.*, p. 167.

[29] Norval Geldenhuys, *Commentary on the Gospel of Luke: The English Text with Introduction, Expositions, and Notes*, ed. F. F. Bruce, The New International Commentary on the New Testament (Grand Rapids: William B. Eerdmans Publishing Co., 1951), p. 384.

[30] Yoder, *op. cit.*

to the point of mere advice or only casually spoken on one occasion; apparently his political excoriation was adamant enough that word actually came to Herod and Herodias of it. Not only did it come, but it came with such persistence that they would not let it pass by unavenged—for John later lost his life over the matter (Mark 6:19-29). Such preaching and results are hardly apolitical.

The lesser officials in government are also, when they appear in the New Testament, represented as under obligation to God's law. When soldiers[31] came to John the Baptist he spoke to them of their responsibility to obey the law of God: in particular, prohibiting unwarranted violence, false accusation, and coveting (Luke 3:14)—the sixth, ninth, and tenth commandments of the Decalogue respectively. The publicans or tax-collectors who had come to John previous to the appearance of the soldiers had been told of their obligation to exact no more money from the people than what was appointed to be collected (Luke 3:13)—the eighth commandment.

Not only were public officials to obey the law of God, but it is clear that even the sanctions of the law were to be observed. For instance, if a tax collector were to steal from the people, God's law would require restitution of him (cf. Ex. 22:1). And this is actually what we find in the case of Zacchaeus, an official state tax gatherer who confessed his crime and restored fourfold whatever he had exacted by false witness (Luke 19:1-10).

Moreover, the judges were required to enforce the sanctions of God's law according to Christ, for He definitely condemns the judge who will not avenge (the same word as in Rom. 13:4) for the widow, in other words, secure justice for her against her opponent; thus he is "unjust" or "unrighteous" (Luke 18:2-6). The central thing wrong with this magistrate, according to Christ's word, was that he did not reverence God or have any respect for man (v. 2). The one leads immediately to the other according to the continual teaching of the Older

[31] Probably these were enforcers of the tax collection; cf. Geldenhuys, *op. cit.*, p. 139.

Testament on the civil magistrate; when rulers do not submit to God's law, then justice is perverted and the magistrate fails to have any genuine concern for human life, dignity, honesty, purity, and the like.

When the state refuses to honor and obey the law of God in social matters, then it fails to be what God requires: His delegated representative or vicegerent in the social realm, one who rules under His authority and direction. The outcome of such disobedience against its responsibility to the law of God is that the state substitutes its own law for God's and arrogates to itself the prerogatives of God. That is, it ceases to be *a servant* of God for good; it assumes the function and place in ethics which alone belongs to God. The servant usurps the place of the true King. The results are dreadfully sinful, and the New Testament unflinchingly condemns the state for them. Such a government as this is represented in Revelation 13, and its decisive punishment is related in Revelation 16:11-12, 19-21 and 18:1-24. God's condemnation rests upon a government which does not realize that its authority is derivative and that its law must not supplant God's own law. The government against which God's judgment comes according to Revelation is no longer the "image of God" as God originally intended for human government to be (cf. Gen. 9:5-6) but a *beast* which requires men to worship *its own* image (Rev. 13:1, 14). Here is civil government degraded and deified. As such it represents the work of Satan according to Revelation 13:4 (cf. 12:9), and Satan's work from the beginning has been that of leading men astray into disobedience against God's commands. The obvious disapprobation of such a government by God's word implies that the government should, *by contrast,* function under the genuine authority of God and in obedience to the just law of God. When the state presumes to sit in the place of God, then naturally the law of the state becomes absolute, thereby replacing the proper moral authority of God's law. The law of God, according to Deuteronomy 6:8, was to be bound upon the hand and upon the forehead (between the eyes); this indicated metaphorically that God's commandments guided a man's thoughts and actions. However, the totalitarian state demands that *its own* law be supreme, and thus it is symbolically represented as placing the mark of the beast upon the hand and forehead of those who follow it (Rev. 13:16). Those who submit to the beast in this fashion are destined to experience the "wrath" of God, which indicates (as the discussion above has shown) that God's law has been spurned. In contrast to those who have the mark of the beast upon their hand and forehead stand those who "keep the commandments of God" (Rev. 14:12). Therefore, Revelation condemns human government (e.g., imperial Rome) that replaces the law of God with the law of the state. The law which a man submits to as ultimate indicates his religious commitment. Those who keep the law of God (thus having it written upon their forehead and hand) belong to the living and true God, for in honoring His authority they can be said to have His *name* (the name of the Father and the Son) upon their foreheads (Rev. 14:1). But those who submit ultimately to the beast's authority and direction (having his mark upon their forehead and hand) actually bear, in contrast to the godly, *his name* upon their foreheads (Rev. 13:17-18). The judgment which befalls the city that usurps the moral authority of God and replaces His law with its own is a clear declaration that God ethically requires that the state operate on just the opposite basis—in other words, submission to His authority and law.

A final example can be taken from the life and writing of Paul. In Acts 17:7 Paul is accused by name before the rulers of Thessalonica for acting "contrary to the decrees of Caesar, saying that there is another king—Jesus." Paul, who in Romans 13 declared that the magistrate was a "servant" of the true Lord and King, preached the gospel of the Messiah in such a way that political implications were involved; he subordinated the authority of Caesar to that of King Jesus (cf. Col. 1:16). Thus Caesar's laws would be required to conform to the laws of God, and Caesar would be lawless in God's eyes otherwise. Therefore, by his teaching of the Kingship of Christ Paul was opposing the decrees of autocratic Caesar. For this Paul was banished from the city by the rulers (17:9-10). This incident is *in itself* significant: Paul's message had implications for Caesar and his laws, and Paul was known to subordinate the magistrate to the authority of Christ.

However, when Paul writes back to the church at Thessalonica the significance of his message as it touched upon the state and his attitude toward rulers needs even further attention. In 1 Thessalonians 2, Paul reflects upon his ministry in Thessalonica and mentions the opposition of the Jews (who are filling up their sins that wrath might come upon them to the uttermost) which precipitated his banishment from the city. Although he wants very much to return (v. 17) he cannot because of the magistrate's sentence against him. However, instead of saying that the rulers in Thessalonica prevent him from returning, Paul says, "Satan hindered us." This is a strong indictment against the rulers, saying that they represent the working of Satan.[32] The Thessalonians were expected to catch the allusion.[33] Paul's writing and apostolic outlook, then, are not immune from bringing magistrates under severe moral censure.

That this is the case, and the nature of such censure, is exhibited in 2 Thessalonians 2. Here Paul rehearses a portion of that teaching which he delivered to the Thessalonians before his banishment (v. 5). His point is to refute the idea that the coming of Christ is immediately at hand (vv. 1-2); this he does by reminding his readers that certain things must happen before the day of the Lord becomes historically imminent. Although he gives no indication of the time span separating these events from the final coming of Christ, the fact that they have not as yet occurred is evidence enough to halt false expectations. The two things which must happen are: the apostasy, and the coming of the man of lawlessness. The language and content of Paul's words parallel the Olivet Discourse of Christ, both passages being rooted in the prophecy of Daniel. The referent of these passages is the wrath of

---

[32] F. F. Bruce, *Commentary on the Book of Acts: The English Text with Introduction, Exposition, and Notes*, ed. F. F. Bruce, The New International Commentary on the New Testament (Grand Rapids: William B. Eerdmans Publishing Co., 1954), p. 345.

[33] Leon Morris, *The First and Second Epistles to the Thessalonians: The English Text with Introduction, Exposition, and Notes*, ed. F. F. Bruce, The New International Commentary on the New Testament (Grand Rapids: William B. Eerdmans Publishing Co., 1959), p. 95.

God which will be poured out upon the Jews (cf. 1 Thess. 2:15-16) in A.D. 70 at the fall of Jerusalem.[34] Thus the apostasy of 2 Thessalonians 2:3 and the desecration of the temple mentioned in 2:4 pertain to the sinfulness of the Jews (especially in opposing the Messiah and His gospel) and the destruction by the Romans of Jerusalem (God's subsequent judgment upon the apostasy). This enables us to identify the "man of lawlessness" in verse 3; he is the Roman emperor, as Warfield correctly concludes from a comparison of the relevant texts.[35] This is confirmed by the fact that the specific principle of lawlessness embodied by the "man of lawlessness" was at work already in Paul's day (v. 7), simply waiting to be revealed (v. 6). Furthermore, the description of this individual matches up with other passages where the Roman emperor or government is under discussion (cf. v. 9 with Rev. 13:4, 13-14; 17:8-10; cf. v. 4 with Rev. 13:12, 15). Finally, this interpretation of the passage is confirmed by the events which took place with respect to Jerusalem within two decades of Paul's writing.[36] Now what is important for the present thesis is the way in which Paul speaks of the civil magistrate. Paul says that the emperor's coming is in accordance with the working of *Satan,* a strong moral indictment. In particular, though, Paul's criticism of the magistrate centers in his "*lawlessness.*" He has refused to be ruled by God or to conform to the standards of God's law. In consequence he, not being content with supreme political position, demands even religious veneration—arrogating to himself the

---

[34] The connection of 2 Thessalonians 2 with the Olivet Discourse is discussed by B. B. Warfield, "The Prophecies of St. Paul," *Biblical and Theological Studies*, ed. Samuel G. Craig (Philadelphia: The Presbyterian and Reformed Publishing Co., 1952), pp. 470-475; and the interpretation of the Olivet Discourse can be found in J. A. Alexander, *Commentary on the Gospel of Mark*, Classic Commentary Library (Grand Rapids: Zondervan Publishing House, 1864 [reprinted]), and J. Marcellus Kik, *Matthew Twenty-Four: An Exposition* (Philadelphia: The Presbyterian and Reformed Publishing Co., 1948).

[35] Warfield, *op. cit.*, p. 472.

[36] Ibid., p. 475. For the point relevant to this thesis, however, it is not necessary to demand this interpretation of the passage. Even those who hold that the events of 2 Thessalonians 2 are yet future will grant that the "man of lawlessness" is a *political* figure.

exalted position and law-decreeing function of God. Thus Paul was involved in asserting the ultimate Kingship of Christ over Caesar and the culpable disobedience of Caesar to *God's law*. Certainly this presupposes the magistrate's moral *obligation* to rule in *theonomic* fashion.

Summation

Perhaps more important than any *particular* datum in the previous investigation is the fact that the *overall* view of the civil magistrate according to Scripture (whether Older Testament, New Testament, Israelite or Gentile) has been found to be *uniform and unchanged*. The same basic propositions apply to any and all governments. They are ordained by God and not to be resisted; rulers bear religiously significant titles as they carry out the function of avenging God's wrath against social violators of His law. They are required to deter evil and honor the good, ruling in obedience to the direction of God's law; when they fail to do this, criticism of them is well founded, and divine judgment of them is certain. Thus the doctrine of the state presented by Paul in Romans 13 is a *reaffirmation of the essential Older Testament conception of the civil magistrate*. There is fundamental continuity between the responsibilities of the Older Testament king and the New Testament magistrate, and this is highly relevant for answering the question posed by this thesis. There is good reason to hold that, just as God required obedience of rulers to His law during the era of the Older Testament, so today the *standards of justice have remained immutable*, and God continues to expect rulers to honor and obey His law.

The question of whether statesmen today *ever will* come to recognize their obligations to God's law is another issue altogether. God is able to bring about lawful obedience from the ruler if He so wishes (Prov. 21:1). But whatever God's *decretive* will might be, His *prescriptive* will alone is that for which we are responsible. Therefore, the question to be answered is "*ought* the ruler to obey and enforce God's law?" At this point we find that there is continuity between the law of God in the Older Testament and New Testament morality: Christ has confirmed every jot and tittle of the law. This fact *alone* could establish that the social prescriptions of God's law have a continuing validity, and therefore, that the magistrate is morally responsible to rule in accord with those sections of God's law that bear upon his office and task. *Beyond this*, Scripture shows that there is continuity between the *doctrine of the magistrate* throughout history, including the present era between Christ's advents. God still expects the same sort of service as He always has from magistrates, and God still holds men accountable for obeying the entire law as revealed in the Older Testament. Therefore, there is *doubly* strong reason to maintain that the magistrate today continues to be responsible to enforce the law of God. The continuing validity of the law and the uniform doctrine of the civil magistrate make it nearly impossible to drive a wedge between the moral obligations of the civil magistrate now and those of the civil magistrate in the Older Testament. Thus the *prima facie* answer given above to the question posed by this thesis has been *substantiated* by the doctrine of the civil magistrate itself.

The obligation of the civil magistrate to perform his official functions in accord with God's law can be seen from one other angle. It has been demonstrated in the preceding sections of this chapter that the state is *going to be judged by God.* Now since this is true, there must be *criteria* or a standard for this judgment (i.e., a law the magistrate is responsible to obey). If this law is *not* God's law, then it must be one of five alternatives. It might be *natural law,* but this is simply a projection of autonomy and satisfaction with the status quo. It might be the law of the *people,* but then abortion, or racism, and any number of other things could be voted in by the population. It might be taken as the *politician's own* law to which he attributes absolute authority, but this is simply autonomy writ large. Thus the proposals of the Roman Catholic Church, the Enlightenment, and the ancient totalitarian states are unacceptable as explaining the basis on which God will judge civil rulers. Others have gone on to maintain that *natural revelation* will be the standard of judgment. However, this either amounts to preferring a sin-obscured edition of the same law of God or to denying the unity of natural and special revelation (and being willing to pit the one against the other). Not only this, but in fact natural revelation is suppressed in unrighteousness by the sinner, and this should dissuade us from thinking that it can be the recognized, functional measure of his ethical obligation. Finally, someone might suggest that the civil magistrate rules by means of continuing *special revelation,* each decision being founded upon a direct word from God. This proposal is in contradiction to the closed nature of the canon, but even if it were not it would fail to eliminate the necessity for having the state obey God's law since every new revelation must be judged, says Deuteronomy 13:1-4, as to its harmony with the *previous* revelation and law from God.

Thus there would appear to be no alternative to God's own written law as the suggested norm by which rulers must govern. If, as Scripture says, the magistrate will be judged by God in his official capacity, then one must grant that the magistrate is responsible to obey and enforce the law of God in its entirety (including penal sanctions). The only escape from this conclusion is to take some form of a dispensational approach to Scripture and morality. However, Matthew 5:17-19 confutes a dispensational approach to God's word and its ethical teaching. Therefore, there is no alternative but to maintain that the civil magistrate is responsible to the entire law of God as a direction for his government and judging.

Chapter 20

SEPARATION OF CHURCH AND STATE

BRIEF consideration must now be given here to the relation of church and state as it bears upon the question of the magistrate's responsibility in the current age to obey and enforce the law of God. This matter comes up in conjunction with two ways in which the magistrate's moral obligation to God's law is either questioned or denied. On the one hand, some will hold that the magistrate cannot be ethically bound to God's law because that would break down the standing *distinction* between church and state; on the other hand, appeal to the alleged *union* of church and state in the Older Testament is often thought to be a factor sufficient to deny the magistrate's current obligation to God's law.

The Separation Recognized in Old Testament

However, the Older Testament indicates a standing separation of church and state, and this fact should be recognized. There was a distinction between the work of Moses and that of Aaron (cf. Ex. 16:33-34; 29:1 ff.), for Aaron represented the people in distinctly cultic matters while Moses rendered general, civil leadership for them (functioning a king over the gathered heads of the tribes, Deut. 33:5). So also in restored Jerusalem there was clearly a distinction between Nehemiah the "governor" and Ezra the "scribe"; it is specifically *because* the civil governor could *not* regulate the religious life of the people that Nehemiah called for Ezra to return to Jerusalem.[1]

---

[1] F. F. Bruce, *Israel and the Nations: From the Exodus to the Fall of the Second Temple* (Grand Rapids: William B. Eerdmans Publishing Co., 1963), p. 107.

At the time of the Exodus the people were divided into tribes having one prince each and heads over the families (cf. Deut. 29:10);[2] the princes were civil governors and military leaders (cf. Num. 1:1-16; 2:3-29; 7:2; 10:14-27; 13:3; 17:6; Josh. 9:15; 22:14; 23:2; 24:1), and the heads of the families under them were captains and then judges or officers (Num. 1).[3] During the time of the Judges executive and judicial power stayed in the hands of the family and tribal heads (e.g., Judges 11:6 ff.; the elders' transactions with Samuel);[4] each city had a council of elders (Deut. 21:6; 25:8; Judges 8:6, 8, 14; Ezra 10:4) who worked separately but sometimes joined efforts (Judg. 1; 4:10; 6:35; 11).[5] They were thus governed by the judges (1 Chron. 17:10; e.g., 1 Sam. 8:1) for 450 years until the last judge, Samuel (cf. Acts 13:20). Local affairs were in the hands of the elders who settled town disputes.[6] With the institution of kingship the kings served as judges (1 Sam. 8:5; 1 Kings 3:16-28; 1 Chron. 18:14; cf. 2 Sam. 15:1-6) in addition to the other judges (Ex. 18:14-26; 2 Chron. 19:5, 8; Ezra 7:25). In fact, the kings do not seem to have had legislative power,[7] but they were essentially judges or governors (the two being virtually synonymous: 2 Kings 15:15; 2 Sam. 15:41; 1 Kings 7:7; e.g., 2 Sam. 12:6; 14:4-11; 1 Kings 3:16-28; 2 Kings 8:3). Under Saul there was "no central government and the tribes, or rather the clans, retained their administrative autonomy."[8] Thus while *cultic* duties were assigned to the *priests* (Ex. 28-29), *judicial-executive* power resided in *tribal heads* (cf. 1 Sam. 8:4 ff.; 10:20 ff.; 2 Sam. 3:17 ff.; 5:1 ff.) who were later seriously consulted by kings (e.g., 1 Kings

---

[2] E. W. Hengstenberg, *History of the Kingdom of God Under the Old Testament,* Vol. I (Cherry Hill, NJ: Mack Publishing Co., 1871 [reprinted 1972]), p. 235.

[3] J. B. Shearer, *Hebrew Institutions, Social and Civil* (Richmond: Presbyterian Committee of Publication, 1910), p. 81.

[4] Hengstenberg, Vol. II, *op. cit.*, p. 67.

[5] Shearer, *loc. cit.*

[6] Roland De Vaux, *Ancient Israel,* Vol. I (Social Institutions), tran. Darton, Longman, and Todd, Ltd. (New York: McGraw-Hill Book Co., 1965), pp. 93, 138, 152-153.

[7] Ibid., pp. 150-151.

[8] Ibid., p. 95.

8:1; 20:7; 2 Kings 23:1) and exercised influence over them (e.g., 1 Kings 12). Internal administration and guidance of the cities or tribes remained vested in the hands of the elders even after the exile (Jer. 20:1; Ezek. 14:1-5; 20:1). Now in these matters (i.e., pervasively the function of civil judgment) legislation originally came from Moses and not through priests; when it was adjudicated, the elders and judges are prominent. Therefore, the priests seem to be completely taken up with religious service and not leaders in the political order.

The Levites

At this point a few words should be said about the involvement of Levites in civil affairs. The Levites were members of the tribe of Levi who had no direct hand in the priesthood, the priesthood belonging to *one special family* of Levi. The Levites were as independent of the *priesthood,* then, as were rulers, judges or the king (who was not elevated or directed by priests).[9] This is evident from the conflict that could develop with the priestly line (e.g., Num. 16:8-11). The nonpriestly Levites were involved in the things of the religious cult or the things of God's law. They helped in the administration of the Temple services, and so forth (1 Chron. 15-16, 23-26; 2 Chron. 24:6, 11; 29:34; 31:11-15; 35:11). But they could be instructors in God's law instead (Lev. 10:11; Deut. 33:10; cf. 31:9 ff.; 2 Chron. 17:8-9; 35:3; Neh. 8:7-9). It is in connection with this last function, and as experts in the law of God, that Levites were involved in the administration of justice as their only political function.[10]

Therefore, priests were not political, for political power was in the ruler's hand. Yet priests could be consulted,[11] or more specifically (with historical development) Levites could be consulted (1 Chron. 26:29-32) in matters of civil judgment that were difficult cases (Deut. 17:9, 12; 19:17; 21:5; Ezek. 44:24), matters of cleanliness (Lev. 10:10;

---

[9] Ibid., pp. 366-367.

[10] Hengstenberg, Vol. I, *op. cit.*, pp. 362-363.

[11] Ibid., p. 316.

13-14; Hag. 2:11-13; Ezek. 44:23) or questions of ritual (Zech. 7:3)—that is, in cases which called for *expertise in the law* of God. Because of their close relation to the law of God, then, Levites had roles in both areas of life: the cultic and the political. Their advisory overlap into civil affairs is illustrated in 1 Chronicles 23-27. Here the offices of the Levites are laid out in chapters 23-26, and the civil officials are laid out in chapter 27. At the very end of chapter 26 (i.e., the list of Levitical offices) verses 29-32 explain that some Levites would have functions extending into the civil realm. These were appointed as scribes and judges (26:29) and were six thousand in number (cf. 23:4). Apparently there was some degree of specialization involved, for while the other Levitical offices were filled on a rotating basis by men from all the families of the Levitical tribe, in this case the office was filled from only two fathers' houses of the Kohathites (viz., Izhar and Hebron). They appear to have been minor officials assigned to help the actual judicial head or elder in the various cities of Israel; they receive little if any mention beyond their assignment. De Vaux had this to say about these Levites involved in matters of civil justice:

> In the absence of any concrete examples no certain conclusions can be drawn. It seems that the priests were authentic interpreters of the law, that they judged all strictly religious matters, the "affairs of Yahweh" (2 Chron. 19:11), and intervened in civil cases at least when these involved some religious law or procedure. . . . They seem to have been clerks of the court, and more generally, clerks attached to the judges (cf. Deut. 16:18; 1 Chron. 23:4; 26:9).[12]

According to Josephus (*Ant.* IV, viii, 14) every town had a tribunal consisting of seven judges and fourteen Levite assistants. Therefore, we would conclude from the available evidence that the Levites were not the cultic leaders of Israel (the priests), nor were they civic leaders in

---

[12] De Vaux, *op. cit.*, pp. 362-363.

the nation (magistrates and kings); instead they were a group specially trained in God's law and thereby useful as aids to both the officers of the cult and the officials of the state (this function as deputies in both areas is reflected in 2 Chron. 19:8, 11; "the Levites served as notaries")[13] The Levites (as trained teachers in the law), then, do not disturb the separation between civic and cultic realms.

Normal and Extraordinary Circumstances

With respect to the relation of cult to state the division between priests and judicial magistrates (elders, heads, judges, kings) remains clear. Civil legislation was handled by the state, and religious practices performed by the priests. While the priest might have been consulted for advice, there was no blurring of the distinction between him and the civic official. When the priest was called on to interpret the law in a difficult case, the distinction between judge and priest was sharp, for only then would the conjunction of the two be meaningful (cf. Deut. 17:9). Israel was unique among the other ancient Canaanite countries in that her executive leader was the king and not the priest.

> In striking contrast to the priests in the surrounding areas who at certain times and places were very powerful and influential, the priests in ancient Israel hardly had a very important historical or even political role.[14]

The only times that the *priests*[15] were involved in *political* [16] matters were *exceptional* cases. When God sent Israel to destroy Jericho He

---

[13] Ibid., p. 154.

[14] Martin Noth, *The Laws in the Pentateuch and Other Studies,* tran. D. R. Ap-Thomas (Edinburgh: Oliver & Boyd, 1966), p. 234.

[15] The bringing of judgment against idolotrous Israel by the Levites with the sword in Exodus 32:27 takes place before they have been given the priestly function (cf. Deut. 10:8); at this stage they were simply one tribe like any other.

[16] When certain rituals had to be performed involving a test-ordeal or sacral lots in order to ascertain God's judgment, the priest was involved; however, as De Vaux

intended to perform a miracle in order that His people might get into the great walled city; this miracle would make use of the ark of the covenant. Thus the priests were called upon and used in the performance of God's special instructions as precursory to the miracle. Not only must it be noted that the priests were involved since they had to care for the ark of the covenant, but it is also necessary to remember that all of the possession of the promised land (including Jericho) was done by special, "positive" direction by God. The destruction of the Canaanites was commanded for a particular instance or circumstance; it is not *standing* law, but extraordinary law for the performance of God's special purpose or judgment at a specified point in history. Thus the priestly involvement before the battle of Jericho must not be viewed as normative for future priestly duties.

When the priest was a participant in the installment of a king (e.g., Zadok anointed Solomon, 1 Kings 1:38-40, and Jehoida crowned Jehoash, 2 Kings 11:12) it was under circumstances where there was illegitimate usurption of authority by a rival (e.g., Adonijah, Athaliah). Now since the Lord intervened in Israel's history in a *special* way at times to indicate who should be king by His choice, illegitimate usurption by another leader would not be known to the people *as* illegitimate without an *indication from God.* In the nature of the case, then, the priest could redress the situation, thereby showing God's sanction of the proper leader; this would be communicated to the people by the intervention of the permanent religious authority, the priest. In the case of Athaliah's usurption, she had come to power by means of murdering the royal seed (2 Kings 11:1); God's law then demanded her execution for the crime. However, being the highest magistrate and a cruel ruler in the land, no one would resist her *without* divine sanction; hence again the involvement of the priest of God (cf. 11:4 ff., 15-16) in order to indicate the special direction of God for this situation. Finally, in the case where Phinehas executed the outrageous adulterer (Num. 25:6-9), the circumstances were particularly dire; Jehovah's wrath was kindled against the idolatry of His people. Consequently Phinehas was not merely

---

points out, these events are properly considered *extra-judicial* (i.e., religious, not civil in nature): *op. cit.,* pp. 157-158.

performing the ordinary role of executioner in the state for a particular violation of the law. Scripture teaches that his activity in executing the blatant sinner was a specifically priestly act of *intercession,* securing *atonement* for the people (vv. 10-13). Thus the people, and the history of redemption, were preserved from termination. However, this act by Phinehas, no more than that of Jehoida, was not to be taken as establishing the *normative* or *standing* rule for priests in Israel. It was a specific, extraordinary work done by the priest, not a pattern for future office bearers to carry out as part of their normal functions or duties—in contrast to the normal, customary, standing law inscribed for kings from God.

Extended Differences Between Cult and State

The separation of church (cult) from state in Israel can be seen by a *number of differences* between the priest and the king. The officials of the king included cherethites and pelethites (2 Sam. 15:18; 20:7), commander of the army, commander of the body guard, recorder, scribe (2 Sam. 8:16-18; 20:23-26; 1 Chron. 27:32-34; 1 Kings 4:1-6), counselors (1 Chron. 18:17; 1 Kings 12:6; 2 Kings 25:19; Jer. 52:25), overseer of public works (1 Kings 5:16), royal treasurer (1 Chron. 27:25-31), official tax collectors (1 Kings 4:7-19), and marshall of the court (1 Kings 4:5). Mettinger lists the major officials in Solomon's court as: royal secretary, royal herald, friend of the king, house-minister, chief of the district prefects, and superintendent of the forced levy.[17] These officers are clearly distinct from the officials of the temple priesthood,[18] which were: high priest, suffragan priest, chief treasurer, overseer, gate-keepers, under-treasurers (these preceding being the

---

[17] Tryggve N. D. Mettinger, *Solomonic State Officials: A Study of the Civil Government Officials of the Israelite Monarchy,* Coniectanea Biblica: Old Testament Series, No. 5 (Lund, Sweden: CWK Gleerups Förlag, 1971).

[18] The listing of the priests in 1 Kings 4:4 does not indicate that they were princes in the royal family, but simply among the chief officials in relation to the people. Mettinger does not treat them as state officers at all.

council of the temple), heads of each course, heads of families of each course, and finally overseers of gates, guards, lots, and so forth.[19] Therefore, the *officials* of the church did not overlap with the officials of the state but differed in each realm.

So also did the *duties* and *regulations* differ between the ecclesiastical and executive realms of the Israelite state. The king tended to administration, justice, war, safety, foreign affairs, and commerce, while the priests were busy with consecration, the holy place and courts, ceremonial cleanness, sacrifices, cultic observances, and the like. Nowhere are the priests given *rights* like those of the king: to take a general levy and appoint officers thereunto (1 Sam. 8:11-17; 14:50; 2 Sam. 8:16; 20:23; 1 Kings 4:4), to take over property or oversee estates (1 Kings 4:6; 21:15; 2 Sam. 8), to lay levies on property owners and to tax agriculture and animal husbandry (2 Kings 15:20; 1 Sam. 8:15, 17; 1 Kings 4:5, 7; 5:2 ff.), to constitute the highest court of legal appeal (2 Sam. 8:16; 14:2 ff.; 15:2 ff.; 20:24; 1 Kings 4:3), to require forced labor or use conscription (2 Sam. 20:24; 1 Kings 4:6; 5:27 ff.; 9:21-22). However, the king was very certainly *limited* in his activities by the law of God (cf. Deut. 17:14-20). Consequently he could *not* carry out the functions of a *priest*. When the king takes it upon himself to ordain priests, they are idolatrous priests that need to be put down (cf. 2 Kings 23:5). When the king presumes to offer sacrifice to God he is condemned. Saul offers sacrifice against the command of God and thus must suffer the termination of his kingdom (1 Sam. 13:9-15). Uzziah trespassed the Lord's commandment and offered incense upon the altar, and for this he was struck with leprosy (2 Chron. 26:16-21). When Jeroboam offers sacrifice at the new altar he is judged by God and stricken (1 Kings 12:32-13:5). And when Ahaz offers sacrifice upon the altar, it is the new altar made after the pattern of an altar in Damascus—the altar to a *pagan* god (2 Kings 16:12 ff.). The only places where a king is said to offer sacrifice and the passage does not either have a *causative* sense ("had sacri-

---

[19] Merril F. Unger, "Hebrew Priesthood," *Unger's Bible Dictionary,* 3rd. ed. rev. (Chicago: Moody Press, 1961), p. 884.

fices offered") or *disapprobate* the behavior are: David's sacrifice at the coming of the ark to Jerusalem and Solomon's sacrifice at the dedication of the temple. Both of these instances are laden with strong typological value, pointing to the work of the Messianic *Priest-King,* Jesus Christ, who is God come to His people to dwell among them (the symbol of the *temple).* Thus, these two incidents must be viewed as "positive" law or activity again; they quite clearly do not sanction the priestly activity of the king as a general or standing rule (witness Saul and Uzziah). Indeed, what gives these incidents their noteworthy and special nature is precisely the *extra*ordinary character of the events.

Therefore, it is proper to see a normal distinction between the duties and rights of the king and those of the priest, which in turn points to the separation of church and state. While the priest had to satisfy purity *requirements,* among which entailed no touching of dead bodies or drinking wine, the king was allowed both to engage in war and drink alcoholic beverage. The priest had to be a Levite, the king did not; in the Southern Kingdom he had to be from Judah.

The *succession* of high priests always passed from father to son (cf. Neh. 12:10-11), but the succession of kingship did not automatically go to the son. Sometimes it went outside the royal line by popular choice (cf. 1 Maccabees 9:30-31; 13:8-9) or by usurption (Judg. 9) or to a queen (2 Kings 11:1-3; 2 Chron. 22:12). The will of the people or human arrangements were foundational to the selection or election of a king (1 Sam. 11:14-15; 2 Sam. 2:4, 8-9; 5:3; 1 Kings 1:11 ff.; 12:1, 20; 2 Kings 11:12; 21:24; 23:30). David made a mutual obligation covenant between himself and the tribes who chose him as king, based on negotiations with the elders. The elders laid down legal conditions for the king (1 Kings 12:3 ff.), and a new king would be elected when there was dissatisfaction with the present ruler (1 Kings 12:16-20). Thus although Israel's rulership was always subject to the will of God as spoken by the prophet (cf. 1 Sam. 9:26-10:1; 2 Sam. 7:8-17; 1 Kings 11:29 ff.; 16:1; 2 Kings 9:1 ff.), it was nevertheless true that there was reality in the political movements of the people or elders in establishing what is basically a constitutional monarchy in Israel. While the priesthood was based upon strict family descent, the heads of the tribes (Deut. 1:13), some of the judges (e.g., Judg. 11:4-11), and a significant number of the kings in Israel were elected or representatively selected by the people. As Martin Noth aptly puts it, the Israelites were "king-makers." However, the people *never* had the prerogative to be "priest-makers"!

The king's *palace* was differentiated from the temple (and priestly residence; cf. 1 Kings 6-7). The draftee *servants* of the king were separate from the temple servants (cf. 1 Sam. 8:11-17; 1 Kings 5:13; Ex. 28-29; Num. 3:28, 32; 8:18). The Levites were *exempt* from the census and draft (Num. 1:48-49). And at the most practical level, the temple tax and tithes were distinct from the *tributes* paid to the king. While the priests were supported by the voluntary contributions of the people, the magistrate could lay taxes upon the population and enforce them. First Kings 14:26 clearly indicates a distinguishing between state revenues and religious revenues. The Older Testament recognizes an offering on the firstborn (Ex. 12:17 ff.; 13:13; 15:19 ff.; Num. 18:15 ff.; Lev. 28:26), an offering of first-fruits (Ex. 23:19; Num. 18:9, 12 ff.; Deut. 26:2 ff.; 18:4), a tithe (Lev. 27:30-33; Num. 17:21-24; Deut. 12:6 ff.; 14:22-27; 26:13 ff.), atonement money (Ex. 30:11-16), and a temple tax (Ex. 38:25 ff.; 2 Chron. 24:6-11; Neh. 10:33). All of these went to the priests and are distinct from the king's own taxation tithe (1 Sam. 8:14-17), import tax (1 Kings 10:15), vassel tributes (2 Sam. 8:2, 6; 1 Kings 5:1), gifts (1 Kings 10:2, 10, 24-25; 2 Kings 5:5; 20:12; 1 Sam. 10:27; 16:20; 2 Sam. 8:10), taxes levied on the people (2 Kings 15:19-20; 23:33-35; 2 Chron. 17:5; Amos 5:11; 1 Sam. 8:15, 17), and appropriations (Amos 7:1). Were there no separation of church and state, all collections from the populace would go into one coffer and be allocated by a single administrator, but this is not what we find in the Older Testament. When Israel was under foreign control at the time of Artaxerxes there was still a distinction drawn between church and state, for while tax was paid to the king (Neh. 5:4, 14-15) he recognized Levite-priestly exemptions (Ezra 7:24).

Another separation of church from state had to be observed with respect to the *penalties* imposed for violations of God's law. While the magistrate had the power of the sword to execute appropriate criminals, the most extreme punishment imposed for the breaking of ecclesiastical law (i.e., ceremonial commandments) was excommunication.[20] This did not belong in any sense to the civil arm to inflict.

Was there a separation of church and state in Israel then? It appears that evidence supports an affirmative answer.

> The true view is that church and state were in equilibrio, and the Lord was the head of both. He was the civil head of the republic, and was also the head of the ecclesiastical system or hierarchy. These both had access to him by prophet and oracle, and found their only unity in him. Under his administration neither state nor church could dominate the other. . . . Two features are obvious. Neither church nor state derived its rights and franchises from the other, nor over the other. Neither could fill official positions in the other, or usurp the functions of the other . . . each had its own revenues.[21]

There was also a recognized distinction between the *personnel* who comprised the national state and those in the spiritual church. This is evidenced by the doctrine of the remnant in the Older Testament (cf. Lev. 26:40-44; Isa. 1:9; 6:3; 8:16-20; 10:20 ff.; 14:21-27; 28:5; 37:30-32; 41:8-9; 42:18-43:13; 44:15; Jer. 3:12, 14; Ezek. 11:14 ff.; 33:24; 37:12; 36:26-27; Hos. 1:9-10; 2:23; 5:15-6:3; Amos 3:12; 4:11; Zeph. 3:9-13; Hag. 1:12; Zech. 8:6, 11-15). A person could have civic membership and rights (as well as social responsibilities) in the national state without being accounted as a good covenant-keeping child of God; the mention of the remnant draws a line between those who were in the state *and* church and those who were in the state only. As Paul explains it, "they are not all Israel which are of Israel," and only a remnant of

[20] Shearer, *op. cit.,* pp. 146-147.

[21] Ibid., p. 96.

those who are numbered as the sand will be saved (Rom. 9:6, 27). So we conclude that there was a distinction drawn between the personnel as well as the officials of the state and church. As to the officials, there was an obvious separation between church and state regarding qualification, function, locale, support, organization, and servants.

The Unity Amid Differsification

The unity which brought church and state together was the Lordship of Yahweh over every facet of life; God ruled via His revealed law. Since both the king and the priest were under God's law, unity existed between them. Hence also, the prophet could rebuke both. The prophet was not an officer of the state [22] nor was he an intervener *to* God for the people; rather, he was a prosecutor of the law *from* God who called down Israel's sin (e.g., Isa. 58:1; Ezek. 22:2; 43:10). He indicted both king (as Nathan did David, and Elijah did Ahab) and priests (as with Eli, 1 Sam. 2:27-36, and others: e.g., Hos. 6:9; Mic. 3:11; Zeph. 3:4; Jer. 5:31; 6:13; Ezek. 22:26; Mal. 2; Jer. 2:8; 8:1-2; Ezek. 44:12, 17; Isa. 28:7-8; 56:10-12). The union of church and state, then, was found in *God* as King, Lawgiver, Judge, Shepherd, and Lord. This is demonstrated by the fact that when Judah and Israel were divided *politically* into two separate national kingdoms (which were sometimes enemies and which were pervasively treated as separate entities by the other nations), and when Israel had two separate temples (one in the North and one at Jerusalem), nevertheless the whole people of Israel and Judah were united by

---

[22] When the Lord's prophet executes the punishment by sword (e.g., 1 Kings 19:17) it is only in extraordinary circumstances justified by a direct imperative from God. Thus Elijah executes the prophets of Baal by the sword when the state government under Ahab would not (1 Kings 19:1) and God so decrees. This is parallel to Israel's aggressive warfare at God's command; it is not establishing a principle to be emulated as a matter of normal course. Only when there is direct divine revelation warranting it can those who have "ecclesiastical status" use the sword. More often than not, the weapon actually used by the prophets is the word of God preached against the people; towards this end Isaiah's mouth was made like a sharp sword (Isa. 49:2).

their God—He was reverenced as God over "*both* the houses of Israel" (Isa. 8:13-14).

The Genuine Separation

So we conclude that there was a *functional* separation of church and state in the Older Testament. An illustration of this can be found in 2 Chronicles 19:11. When Jehoshaphat brought the people back to Jehovah their God and set judges in the cities of the land, he told them that they must judge *for Jehovah* (vv. 4-7). When then he comes to the capital city of Jerusalem where there are to be found the priests of Jehovah, *who* will have the upper hand in judgment and rule? The civil officers or the priests? The question of religious *or* civil authority is natural here. Jehoshaphat sets for judgment those from among the priests *and* the heads of the father's houses (i.e., the cultic class and the ruling class).[23] He answers the question regarding the relation which is to hold among them by separating the matters of the church from the matters of the state. "The chief priest is over you in all matters of Jehovah, and . . . the ruler of the house of Judah in all the king's matters" (v. 11). And so it is throughout the Older Testament, apart from "positive" law with its typological or redemptive significance. From the delivering of the law to both the priests *and* the elders (Deut. 31:9) to the parabolic olive trees signifying God's *twin* channels for governing authority among his people (i.e., the king and the priest; cf. Zech. 4:10-14), the Older Testament consistently represents the function of the church from the functions of the state. Hence when the kingship and priesthood are to be represented as brought together (Ps. 110:4), the Scriptures have no illustrative model from Israel to use; hence it goes *outside* of Israel to the Canaanite king, Melchizedek, to find this pattern (for outside of Israel kings *were* priests: e.g., Egypt, Assyria, Phoenicia).[24]

---

[23] The dual function of the Levites has been discussed above.

[24] De Vaux, *op. cit.*, p. 113.

The New Testament Parallel

With the separation of church and state in the Older Testament plus the affirmation that God rules in both realms a parallel can be found with the New Testament on church and state as they both related to God. In the Older Testament God ordained the priests and the kings, choosing whom He would (cf. Num. 16:7; 18:7; Ex. 28:1; cf. 1 Sam. 2:28; 10:16). And in the era of the New Testament God sets rulers in the church (cf. Eph. 4; Acts 1, 6) and ordains the civil magistrate (Rom. 13). There is still a separation of church and state functions, the one dealing with God's law of social justice, the other dealing with Christ's gospel of eternal grace; however, both are unified under the authority and direction of God.

The Two Swords

The seed which the Old Testament plants is harvested in the New Testament teaching with respect to the *sword.* Christ our Lord did not come in order to impose or cast peace upon the earth, contrary to the Jewish expectation, but He brought a sword (Matt. 10:34). The result of Christ's advent, work, and word would be the splitting up of families and friends. But is the sword with respect to which they would fight to be a physical or iron sword? No. The kingdom of Christ would not be one which comes with swords loud clashing. Still, there is a proper place for the use of the iron sword, as there was in the Old Testament; yet there is the assured hope that the sword of Christ's kingdom shall cause the iron sword to be finally laid to rest. So we look to the teaching of Christ and the New Testament for the distinctions which must be drawn in the elaboration of the Old Testament themes of church and state.

What was the mission of Christ upon the earth? As the Messiah, did He have earthly political aspirations? The New Testament teaches that although the kingdom of Christ has political implications, Christ was not interested in entering national politics. His personal mission was to provide a vicarious sacrifice for His elect people; hence His kingdom has spiritual roots and devices. A sword must pierce through Mary's soul, for her son must be taken and crucified. Although one should use a sword in an effort to prevent Christ from drinking the cup of suffering associated with God's wrath (cf. Ps. 75:8; Isa. 51:17, 22; Jer. 25:15; Ezek. 23:31-33; cf. Rev. 14:10; 16:19), He is not prevented from finishing the work which the Father gave Him to do. Christ wins for His people spiritual salvation from the bondage and punishment of sin. Although the Jews in their delusions prided themselves in political freedom (John 8:33) and sought after a political liberator (John 6:15; cf. Acts 5:36-37), Christ the true Messiah promised in the Old Testament liberates men by the truth, not a sword (John 8:32); this Truth is embodied in His own person (John 14:6). In contrast to a kingdom like unto what Pilate knew, Christ came as a king who bears witness to the truth; those who are members of the kingdom of truth hear His voice, the Truth's message (John 18:37), the word of The Word (cf. John 1:1). He is the life-light of men (John 14:6; cf. 1:4) who makes men members of God's household by means of their faith in Him (John 1:7, 12-13). To *this end* He became Incarnate (John 1:14) so that God's grace would triumph by His death upon the cross as the King of the Jews (John 19:19). His resurrection assures the victory over the kingdom of Satan to which all men are enslaved; by it He is declared Lord, Christ, and Son of God (Acts 2:36; Rom. 1:4), and all believers are justified before God (Rom. 4:25). Flesh and blood cannot inherit this kingdom of Christ, for one must be spiritually reborn into it, exercising repentance, faith, and obedience.

It is no surprise, then, that Christ declares that the *iron* sword is not appropriate for use in the advance of His kingdom. In the garden of Gethsemane Peter presumed to smite the servant of the high priest with a sword in defense of Christ (Matt. 26:57; Mark 14:47; Luke 22:50; John 18:10), but Christ rebuked him sternly (Matt. 26:52; John 18:11) and healed the ear of the high priest's servant (Luke 22:51). Christ's followers are not to establish His kingdom or carry on His work with carnal weapons—regardless of provocation. The victory of the kingdom is won by deeds of truth and love, by the heralding of the gospel, by obedience to God and His law. The employment of political and physical weapons to advance the kingdom of Christ is suicidal, for "all they that take the sword shall perish with the sword" (Matt. 26: 52)—as the history of Christendom has borne out. Christ's truth is not defended by violence; by taking up the sword, the Christian will not establish the faith but will simply perish with the sword. Revelation 13:10 says that it is the saint's patience to recognize this principle of Christ. Peter did not have such patience in the garden. He was *not alone* in his misunderstanding, for the other disciples asked whether they should use the sword (Luke 22:49). The disciples should have known better by that time, but instead they misunderstood a statement of Christ in the upper room (Luke 22:36, 38). Christ taught them that, in contrast to their previous experience (note the strong adversative in the Greek; cf. Luke 9:3; 10:4, 17), they were about to start facing persecution for their faith. Hence they must be just as *determined* in their endeavors as is a soldier who gives up even his garment in order to have a sword with which to carry on the campaign; that is, the disciples must be ready now to exercise great courage. His meaning was clearly figurative as He made reference to a sword (as later events in the garden bear out), but the disciples missed the figure. They mistook the spiritual sword which they would need for an iron sword which could not but defeat them. When they assert that they have two swords with them, Jesus ends the discussion sorrowfully. Disappointed at their obtuseness, He uses a formula of dismissal (see LXX for Deut. 3:26) and breaks off the conversation, letting the subject drop. He certainly did not mean that the two swords would be "enough" to counter the forces which would rise against Him in the ensuing hours! Overlooking the disciples' mistaken impression, we do learn quite positively from this passage that when Christ's follower faces scorn and hate, he must remain firm by equipping himself with a sword not made of iron—but which is the word of God. The kingdom of Christ is entered by faith-response (repentance, belief, obedience) to the word of the heralded gospel; it is advanced without the instrumentality of a warrior's sword.

In making clear that His disciples were not to use the iron sword Christ was not denying His kingship over the nations, nor was He repudiating the rights of civil government. Tribute *was* to be paid to Caesar (Matt. 22:21), and Christ's apostle *could* legitimately appeal *to* Caesar (Acts 25:11). The effect of Christ's teaching with respect to the kingdom and the sword was simply *the reaffirmation and confirmation of what the Old Testament so clearly laid out: the separation of church and state functions.*

Christ repudiates the use of the sword in spreading the gospel of the kingdom because this task belongs to His church, and the church and state are *separate* (as the Old Testament taught and Christ confirmed). The civil magistrate may use the sword as a proper means of enforcement, but the church may not. Christ's endorsement of the church's separation from state is found in a well-known, but often abused, verse from Matthew's gospel (22:21). The Herodians and Pharisees attempted to trap Christ into either renouncing Caesar's authority or submitting everything to it; they asked if it was permissible to pay the tax to Caesar. We have already seen that the Old Testament clearly distinguishes between the tribute paid to the king and the temple tax and so forth given to the priests; moreover, there was ample guidance offered to the Pharisees on this question from the example of tax being paid to Artaxerxes while the Jews were under his subjugation. So Christ can answer them in terms of a principle *already laid down* in the Older Testament (thereby showing their own ignorance of the law in which they so self-righteously prided themselves). "Render to Caesar the things which are Caesar's, and to God the things which are God's." The type of separation of church and state here affirmed by Christ does not set the state loose to be autonomous, any more than the separation of priest and king in the Old Testament gave the king any moral right to depart from the law of God (cf. Deut. 17:18-19). Rome occupied Palestine, and Caesar was the civil magistrate; under these circumstances the people must pay their taxes in submission to the authority—for it is his right. But it was no more Caesar's right to flaunt the law of God than it was David's. Christ's statement in Matthew 22:21 cuts *two* directions; not only must citizens obey the magistrate, but *all* men must obey *God.* Just as the coin bears Caesar's image and therefore must be rendered to him, so Caesar bears *God's image* and must give himself to God; "render unto Caesar the things which are Caesar's, and to God the things which are God's." Caesar must render unto God the things which God demands, even obedience to His righteous law. So, in reiteration, this verse does not set the magistrate free to be autonomous; it merely confirms the well-established separation of church and state as recognized in the Older Testament.

Now then, when Christ appears before Pilate, Christ declares that His kingdom was not of this world (or from this world). The kingdom of Christ is not like unto the old Israelitish kingdom which was identified with earthly Palestine. The gospel is a universal message, and the kingdom formed by those who embrace the gospel message cannot be restricted to a geographical boundary. Christ posits discontinuity between the *way* in which the kingdom is *measured* or *identified* as a *type* and as a *reality*. The Old Testament typological kingdom entailed the soil of Palestine but the person to whom this land was promised looked for a city whose architect and builder was God (Heb. 11:10)—thereby understanding the genuine importance of the promise. Christ brings in the reality, the fulfillment of the Old Testament hope; now that the real kingdom of God is among men we see that its essence is spiritual (with practical outward manifestations to be sure) while the truths about it in the Old Testament were built upon a physicalistic model. Moreover, Christ's kingdom does not receive its authority from below but from God above. His kingdom is not of this world. Therefore, as He goes on to declare before Pilate, His servants do not fight. As the conquering Israelites entered the promised land, the characteristic thing about them is that they won the land *by the sword* and battle.[25] By contrast, the kingdom of Christ is not advanced by such weaponry or methods; the servants of Christ do not wage war on a physical plane—because, after all, the kingdom of Christ is not derived from this world. In speaking to Pilate, Christ taught that the church does not look for a this-worldly geographic realm which has authority from below, and it does not take up the iron sword to defend and advance the cause of Christ. Christ

[25] Cf. Ex. 17:13; Num. 21:24; 31:8; Deut. 20:13; Josh. 6:21; 8:24; 10:11; 10:28, 30, 32, 35, 37, 39; 11:10-14; 13:22; 19:47; Judges 1:8, 25; 4:15-16; 18:27; 21:10.

affirmed that, *indeed, He was a king* (John 18:37; 19:10-11) although His royal authority was *over* this world, *not of it.* Christ's rule is not a political kingship among politicians, but entails authority over all worldly leaders. Even though all authority is His (Matt. 28:18), and He is able at any time to call His angel-servants to fight at His command (Matt. 26:52-53), He does not show His power by means of coercive political pressures. Nevertheless, *Pilate* would have no power unless given him from above, for all government rests upon the shoulders of Christ (cf. Isa. 9:6-7). The kingdoms which *are* of this world still owe their allegiance to Christ; they are not laws unto themselves.

We can summarize Christ's teaching with respect to the sword at this point. The iron sword is not part of the believer's armour. That kind of sword is the instrument of the political state, and Christ's kingdom is not world-derivative. Christ draws the customary line between the domain of the state and the domain of the church; thereby the church learns that it does not use political pressure in the work of advancing Christ's saving kingdom. To use the sword is to die by the sword. In the upper room Christ intimates that His followers must acquire a different kind of sword than that of a warrior; in the garden He emphatically confirms that the sword of iron is not the appropriate instrument of defense in His kingdom. In His coming Christ accomplished salvation for God's elect nation from all over the world by allowing the sword of God's judicial wrath to strike against Him. In accordance with the type of salvation He brought, Christ refused to have the people make Him their revolutionary king (John 6:15). He could admit to His band of disciples both Matthew, supporter of the established system, and Simon Zealotes, revolutionary against the system. He taught them both that one enters the true kingdom of God by repentance, faith, and obedience. He declared that the *heralding* of God's *good news* was the way to win men over to this kingdom. He taught that His followers must not use the sword of war.

Christ brought no *new* program for social-political affairs because the Old Testament pattern for social affairs as found in God's holy law was already sufficient and grandly beneficial if only followed. Note its *perfections* (Ps. 19, 119; Rom. 7:12, 14) and note its *promises* (Deut. 6:24; 7:12, 15; 10:13; 11:14-15; 13:17-18; 15:4-5; 28:1-14; 30:6-10, 19-20; Lev. 16; Isa. 26:3). Nothing more was needed here as far as the plan was concerned. Instead men desperately need *remission* from their sins against that perfect order, as well as the subsequent *power* of obedience. Christ need not bring a political kingdom; yet mankind superabounds in need for Christ's dominion in forgiveness and power. Before the Old Testament laws could be obeyed *in fact* (the *obligation* always being there to comply) one must enter the kingdom of Christ by means of repentance and faith; then the influence of kingdom-obedience can be felt in all areas of life—even the state.

The church and state are separate domains in Christ's thinking, but both are under the authority of God. Both church and state have their legitimate functions and authorities, and the sword belongs to the state while being banned in the church—reflecting the normal situation of the Old Testament theocracy (wherein execution, for example, could not take place in God's temple).

In the New Testament, then, we can ascertain a doctrine of *two swords:* one belonging to the church, and separate from the one belonging to the state. Romans 13 is the key passage for the doctrine of the *state's* sword. There we read that human government is a *divine* institution made up of authorities who have the right to rule and to require every person's subjection (see discussion of Romans 13 in the section on the civil magistrate above). We learn from Paul in Romans 13 that the civil magistrate has a right to use an iron sword; this is the sword of the *state* (not the church) which has been delegated the task of restraining evil by punishing violators of God's holy law as it touches upon matters of social concern (i.e., outward deeds). That Paul is in harmony with Christ's teaching about the state is evidenced by the obvious parallel between Romans 13:7 and Matthew 22:21. The church and state are separate realms with different functions; only the state has a warrant to use violence and the iron sword, but then it is *not* autonomous in so doing. All who use the sword must submit to *God's* direction.

The contrast between the state sword and the sword which has been given to the church for its use could not be greater. One is physical, the other is spiritual; one restrains the hand, the other converts the heart. In Ephesians 6:12 Paul explains that our Christian struggle is not against flesh and blood enemies, but against spiritual forces of wickedness. The kingdom of Christ, which is not of this world, is set in direct opposition to the kingdom and Satan. Hence the Christian needs a weapon suited to his kingdom and its foe; the one and only weapon of the Christian panoply which Paul exhorts believers to put on is the *"sword of the spirit*, which is the word of God" (Eph. 6:17). This sword has true power from the Holy Spirit; we can have complete faith in its vitality and virtues. The sword of the Spirit, God's word, harkens back to the Old Testament where Isaiah's mouth was sharpened as a sword (Isa. 49:2), where the Lord is said to slay the wicked by the words of His mouth (Hos. 6:5), and where it is said that "He will strike the earth with the rod of His *mouth,* and with the *Spirit* of His lips will He slay the wicked" (Isa. 11:4). In 2 Thessalonians 2:8 Paul assures us that the lawless one who opposes the kingdom of Christ will be slain with the Spirit of the Lord's mouth. The word of God was written by the agency of the Holy Spirit; He is the one who gives internal conviction of its truth, and He is the one who can assure the efficaciousness of its preaching. This is the sword to be used by Christ's church: the gospel of Christ preached (based on the word of God written). This preaching of the gospel can bring life (John 6:63) or can induce spiritual death (2 Cor. 2:14-17; cf. 1 Peter 2:8); as such it is a "sword" which functions as the "keys" of the kingdom (Matt. 18:18)! Hebrews 4:12 elaborates upon the power of the Christian sword: "the word of God is living and active and sharper than any two-edged sword, piercing to the division of soul and spirit, and joints and marrow; it is able to judge the very thoughts and intents of the heart." This sword *surpasses* the sharpness and ability of the state sword. The word of God can bring conviction of sin (John 16:8), salvation (Rom. 10: 8-10), and power (Rom. 1:9). It is not a dead letter but a living oracle (cf. Acts 7:38) which abideth forever (1 Peter 1:23). This word of the gospel has the power of the New Covenant in it: it proclaims an accomplished redemption, writes the law of God upon the inner heart, and guarantees its own worldwide prosperity (cf. Jer. 31:31-34; Heb. 8). Nothing is hidden from the probing light of this word, for it penetrates to the deepest parts of man's person (cf. 1 Cor. 14:24-25). The word of God is glorious for its efficacious power (cf. Isa. 55:11; 1 Thess. 2:13); it is an eschatological word, for it, as the coming day of the Lord, can bring to light the hidden works of darkness (cf. 1 Cor. 4:5). Like God its author, the word is "heart-knowing" (cf. Acts 1:24; 15:8). By contrast to the sword of the state, which slays the body of the sinner, this word of God works akin to the circumcision knife of the Old Testament priest (cf. Josh. 5:2 ff.) by circumcising the sinner's heart.

The imagery of Christian warfare is not foreign to the New Testament; Paul can exhort us to put on the whole armour of God (Eph. 6), can liken the Christian minister to a soldier (2 Tim. 2:3 f.), can encourage Timothy to fight the good fight (1 Tim. 6:11-12). He makes it clear, however, that it is the "prophecies" which enable Timothy to war the good warfare (1 Tim. 1:18). The word of God is the power and weapon of the Christian as he advances the kingdom of Christ; this harmonizes completely with what we have observed Jesus to teach about the weaponry and nature of His kingdom. "The weapons of our warfare are not of the flesh, but divinely powerful for the pulling down of fortresses" (2 Cor. 10:4). Because the Christian's foe is not fleshly, neither is the weapon of his warfare. In this battle only a spiritual weapon empowered by the Spirit of God will do. Even the strongholds which are hostile to Christianity can be destroyed by the Christian's spiritual sword, the word of God. Although this weapon may be scorned by the world, it is fearful to the powers of darkness (Eph. 6:14 ff.; cf. 2 Cor. 6:7). So, again, Christ's church is admonished not to meet the challenge of the world with carnal weapons, but to rely upon the powerful word of God; when it does, the church is assured of victory (cf. 2 Tim. 4:7-8). The forces of evil which parody Christianity (cf. Rev. 13:3) can be mortally wounded by a sword of iron (e.g., Nero, who stabbed himself to death) and yet recover (e.g., the line of deified emperor; Rev. 13:14). However, the preached word of Christ's gospel destroys completely the foes of the kingdom (cf. Rev. 19). Neither Herod the Great, the

Jewish pseudopatriots of Caesar (John 19:12), Satan himself (Matt. 4), nor a great red dragon (Rev. 12) can destroy the spiritual kingdom of Christ. Herod may ill treat the church by killing James with the sword (Acts 12:1-2), but not even the sword can separate us from the love of Christ (Rom. 8:35). For even without a sword of iron we are more than conquerors (Rom. 8:37).

Victory for the kingdom of Christ has been assuredly promised in God's word. Because all power and authority have been given to Christ who is present with us always, the *nations* will indeed be discipled and taught to observe God's *law* (Matt. 28:18-20). The victory which overcomes the world is, indeed, our faith (1 John 5:4), for Christ our Lord has Himself overcome the world (John 16:33). The promise of God is the worldwide dominion of the kingdom of Christ. "All the earth shall be filled with the glory of Jehovah" (Num. 14:21); all nations shall come and worship and glorify the Lord's name (Ps. 86:9). All the ends of the earth shall turn unto Jehovah (Ps. 22:27); the nations and the uttermost parts of the earth are given to Christ for His kingdom (Ps. 2:8).

> In His day shall the righteous flourish and abundance of peace till the moon be no more. He shall have dominion from sea to sea, from the River unto the ends of the earth. They that dwell in the wilderness shall bow before Him, and His enemies shall lick the dust. . . . Yea, all kings shall fall down before Him; all nations shall serve Him. . . .and call Him blessed (Ps. 72).

Jehovah shall make the Lord's enemies His footstool (Ps. 110:1); He shall stretch forth His strong scepter and rule among His former enemies (v. 2). In the latter days all nations shall flow unto the church (Christ's body) where the word and law of Jehovah will be taught (Isa. 2:2-3). In Daniel's interpretation of Nebuchadnezzar's dream a stone made without hands representing a spiritual kingdom is established by God and becomes a great mountain filling the whole earth. Jeremiah promises a coming time when evangelism will no longer be needed, for everyone (from least to greatest among a man's neighbors and relatives) shall know the Lord (Jer. 31:34). "For the earth shall be filled with the knowledge of the glory of the Lord, as the waters cover the sea" (Hab. 2:14).

In that day the Lord's Servant, upon whom He puts His Spirit, will bring forth justice among the nations (Isa. 42:1). The parable of the leaven in the New Testament teaches the universal extension and triumph of the gospel. Salvation is destined for the ends of the earth (Acts 13:47). In Revelation 7:9-10, John beholds a multitude from every nation and tribe which could not even be numbered for its vastness praising the Lamb and clothed in white array. The secular world kingdom will assuredly become the *kingdom of our Lord and of His Christ* (Rev. 11:15; prophecy placed in the past tense! cf. Rev. 15:3-4; Heb. 1:13; 2:8; 10:13). And this spiritual kingdom will come to triumph even among the *political* kingdoms of the earth, for all rulers, dominions and authorities have been created *for* Christ (Col. 1:16). The ruler of all earthly kings is Christ (Rev. 1:5), and these kings fear the wrath of the lamb (Rev. 6:15-16). The ten rebel kings are overcome by the King of Kings and His faithful elect (Rev. 17:14; cf. v. 18). And earthly kings will bring their glory into the heavenly Jerusalem (Rev. 21:24). The triumph of Christ's kingdom will be worldwide! God has put all things in subjection under Christ's feet and has given Him as head over *all* things for the benefit of the church (Eph. 1:22; dative of advantage). Therefore, Paul writes to us "The night is almost gone, and the day is at hand. Let us therefore lay aside the deeds of darkness and put on the *armor of light*" (Rom. 12:12). *The Christian is assured of victory when he uses, not the iron sword of the state, but the powerful weapons of the Spirit—in particular, the word of God.* When this is done Paul can promise in Romans 16:20 that "the God of peace shall bruise Satan under your feet shortly."

Application of the Separation

Therefore, an investigation of the Older and New Testaments reveals that they *both separate* the functions of the state from those of the church; however, they both maintain also the *authority of God over* church as well as state. In the era of the New Testament this means that the sword of the state is under moral responsibility to the law of God without being confused with the sword of the church. The state has recourse to capital punishment as a penal sanction, but the church's severest punishment is that of excommunication. The state is an agency of justice in social matters, but the church is an agency of mercy. Thus the state cannot be a promoter of the gospel or personal Christian faith, and the church cannot use the sword of the state in its evangelism. The state does not operate in the name of the Redeemer or as an organized expression of the redeemed community. However, this does not mean that the state is not morally responsible to God and His justice. The state is a "minister of God for the good" and "an avenger of wrath against those practicing evil." It does these things under the authority and direction of God, especially as found in God's law. In this way it protects the sanctity of God's name, human life and its sources, plus proper authority in society. The aim of punishment in the state is the maintenance of equity and justice, and the scope of such discipline is coextensive with the population of a nation. The aim of church discipline, on the other hand, is repentance and restoration; the scope of this discipline is restricted to those who have made public profession of faith, "for what have I to do with judging those without?" (1 Cor. 5:12).

The point, then, is that church and state can be *separated* with respect to function, instrument, and scope and yet *both* be responsible to God. The Lord rules not only His church but also His world. While we might legitimately expect more ready obedience from the former, the fact remains that God has established standards for the latter as well. To argue that the state should divorce itself from God in order allegedly to protect the separation of church and state is in reality an argument for a kind of nature/grace dichotomy which grants autonomy to the state. So then, if the state is *not* autonomous, where does it learn its proper bounds and obligations? Clearly the answer must be that it learns them from the Lord who ordained the state. "When the righteous are in authority, the people rejoice: but when the wicked beareth rule, the people mourn" (Prov. 29:2, AV). It is simply unscriptural to argue that the state should be indifferent to God's righteous direction, and that direction is found in His law. The law does not grant the state the right to enforce matters of conscience (thus granting "freedom of religion"), but it *does* have the obligation to prohibit and restrain *public* unrighteousness (thus punishing crimes from rape to public blasphemy). The state is not an agent of evangelism and does not use its force to that end; it is an agent of God, avenging His wrath against social violations of God's law. If one's outward behavior is within the bounds of the law he has nothing to fear from the civil magistrate—even if one is an idolator, murderer, or whatever in his heart.

Theocratic Considerations

In the process of investigating the scriptural view of the separation of church and state it was observed that the sword of the church (viz., God's word) is *not* of second-rate power just because it does not operate like the sword of the state (viz., physical punishment, even execution). In particular the power of the church sword is evident from the success that is promised to its preaching. In this prosperity that the gospel has been assured by God's sovereign word there is the indication that the Older Testament "Theocracy" is now a "Christocracy" intended to become worldwide in its scope. However, caution must be exercised in understanding the previous assertion. Much rests upon how one defines "theocracy" (a word originating in Josephus, not Scripture).[26] In its simplest form, a "theo-cracy" would be the rule of God in a particular country—that is, the *moral* rule of God (for in the sense of God's *sovereign,* providential government of whatsoever comes to pass in history *everything* would be "theocratic," and it would serve no useful distinction to use the word). Hence a "Christocracy" would be the moral (i.e., *Messianic,* in distinction from sovereign or providential) rule of Jesus Christ. In this sense the Great Commission (Matt. 28:18-20) intends for the nations to become a Christocracy. Psalm 110 has Christological reference; in it we read that the Lord will stretch forth His strong scepter in order to rule amidst His enemies who shall be for

---

[26] Hengstenberg, *op. cit.*, p. 312.

Him a footstool (vv. 1 f.). The Lord judges among the nations and shatters kings (vv. 5 f.). Psalm 67 declares that God will indeed *govern* the nations upon earth (v. 4), and all the ends of the earth will *fear* Him (v. 7); the kings of the Gentiles will come to the light of God's kingdom and minister unto it, or else they will utterly perish (Isa. 60:3, 10, 12). Psalm 72 speaks of the reign of the righteous king; it is a reference to *both* Solomon's accession (vv. 1, 20; cf. 1 Kings 1:30 ff.)—thus an exhortation by godly example—*and* to the rule of Jesus Christ, God's Messiah. He will reign in accordance with God's righteous law (vv. 1 f.) and thus honor, integrity, prosperity, and peace shall permeate His dominion (vv. 2 ff.). All nations and kings, from sea to sea, are to serve Him and bless Him (vv. 8-11; 15-17); the whole earth is to be filled with His glory (v. 19). The Messiah will bring justice to the *nations* and will *establish* justice in the *earth;* even the coastlands (i.e., the nations on the very perimeter) wait for God's law (Isa. 42:1-4). To this end God's covenant people are to be a light to the *nations,* for they have been called in righteousness (Isa. 42:4; cf. Matt. 5:14!). "Many *nations* will come and say, Come let us go up to . . . the house of the God of Jacob in order that He may teach us His ways and in order that we may walk in His paths, for out of Zion will go forth the *law* . . . " (Mic. 4:2). The zeal of the Lord of hosts will accomplish Isaiah's promise from God that the *government* will rest upon the shoulders of the Messiah, and that there will be no end to the increase of His government, which shall be characterized by justice, righteousness, and peace (Isa. 9:6 f.). All things are being put in subjection under the feet of Christ (Heb. 2:8; cf. 1:13; 10:13; 1 Cor. 15:24 ff.), even world dominions and thrones; there is no area of God's creation where Christ is not the Lord. His rule is to be authoritative in church *as well as* state. Christ is seated above *every rule and authority*: since He is the Head of all things, all things are subjected under His feet (Eph. 1:21 f.; cf. Matt. 28:18). The book of Revelation makes it clear that Christ is the ruler over kings, that the kingdoms of this world have become the kingdom of our Lord and of His Christ, that consequently, the Lamb on David's throne (the King over kings) will be the judge of the kings of the earth (Rev. 1:5; 6:15 f.; 11:15; 15:3 f.; 17:14). The only ultimate King in civil government is Christ, and all rulers of the nations derive their authority from Him; hence all magistrates are subject to Christ's word, even Christ's confirmation of every bit of the law (Matt. 5:17 f.). National leaders have no exemption from the law of God just as they have no escape from the universal Lordship of Christ. All thrones, dominions, rulers, and authorities were created by Him and *for Him* (Col. 1:16). *If* the Kings in Older Testament Israel were responsible to God's law *because* of the "Theocracy," then also magistrates today are responsible to God's law because of the "Christocracy."

What we learn from the preceding is that neither considerations with respect to *separation* of church and state nor considerations pertaining to the *word* "Theocracy" are sufficient to dissolve the civil magistrate's duty to obey and enforce the law of God. Every argument advanced against the theonomic responsibility of the civil magistrate that attempts to impose discontinuity between the social standards of justice in the Older Testament and those of the New Testament (i.e., the specific obligations of political leaders) by use of the word "Theocracy" collapses for two reasons: it conceives of "Theocracy" in such a way that it either (1) *fails* to *apply* to Israel exclusively, or (2) *fails* to be argumentatively *relevant* since the magistrate's theonomic responsibility was never grounded in, or legally dependent upon, such a consideration.

For instance, the idea that a "Theocracy" is where there is no separation of church and state[27] would fall under condition (1) above since it simply does *not apply* to Israel (as the foregoing examination has indicated).

The same disqualification holds for the idea that a "Theocracy" is where God is the *sole* ruler of a people;[28] with this outlook Israel would

---

[27] E.g., Oscar Cullmann, *The State in the New Testament* (New York: Charles Scribner's Sons, 1956), p. 10; H. B. Clark, *Biblical Law: Being a Text of the Statutes, Ordinances, and Judgements Established in the Holy Bible, etc.* (Portland, Oregon: Binfords & Mort, 1944), p. 57; A. A. Hodge, *The Confession of Faith* (London: Banner of Truth Trust, 1958), p. 255—a corrective interpretation of the Westminster Confession can be found in Appendix 2.

[28] E.g., De Vaux, *op. cit.*, p. 99.

have ceased being a "Theocracy" at the anointing of Saul! However, Saul was clearly under theonomic responsibilities; thus Israel was either *not a* "Theocracy," or the "Theocracy" was not the ground of the magistrate's theonomic responsibility (number [2] above).

If a "Theocracy" is seen as a country where God intends the people to be a "nation of priests unto Him,"[29] then we must remember that God now intends the *whole world* to become a nation of priests—that is, the church is to permeate the world. Therefore, in this sense, Israel was not *exclusively* a "Theocracy" (number [1] above). If a "Theocracy" is where God is the King of the commonwealth,[30] then Israel was not exclusively a "Theocracy" because God is and was declared to be King over the whole world (number [1] above). If a "Theocracy" is where the King not only rules but also delivers the people from oppression, then not only are most nations of the world such "Theocracies" (the executive head being military leader), but this consideration is argumentatively irrelevant since Israel's kings were under theonomic responsibility irrespective of their military prowess (number [2] above). If a "Theocracy" is where direct divine revelation can be sent to the king, [31] then this is argumentatively irrelevant since the king was obligated to enforce God's law based on an *abiding* theonomic responsibility, *not* the current presence or absence of a message from God (number [2] above). Further considerations that present what are legitimate and noteworthy discontinuities between Older Testament Israel and a national government today could be mentioned (e.g., the anointing of kings at God's direction, the presence of the temple, etc.), however they all fail to be directly germane to the present thesis since they were not given (or scripturally expounded) in the Older Testament *as the ground for* the magistrate's theonomic responsibility.

---

[29] E.g., Clark, *op. cit.*, pp. 54, 57; Alexander Jones, *Gospel According to St. Matthew: A Text and Commentary for Students* (New York: Sheed and Ward Inc., Publishers, 1965), p. 195.

[30] Shearer, *op. cit.*, p. 88.

[31] Ibid., pp. 104-105.

Hence their current absence says nothing about ethical *obligation.* Finally, if someone were to argue *against* the theonomic responsibility of today's leaders by referring to Israel's "Theocratic" character, meaning by "Theocracy" a nation obligated to keep God's law, then he could arrive at the conclusion that magistrates today are not under theonomic responsibility by sheer question-begging. *If* a "Theocracy" is a nation under *obligation* to enforce God's law, then Scripture teaches, according to the thesis presented herein, that *all* nations are "Theocracies." Hengstenberg claims that David's highest honor was to be the servant of God; here, said Hengstenberg, was theocracy in its deepest reality.[32] In terms of this outlook Romans 13 would teach that every magistrate, as a servant of God, participates in a theocracy.

Other senses for the word "Theocracy" might be, and have been, suggested, but the lesson that should have been learned by this point is that one needs more than simply a word or label to nullify the theonomic responsibility of the civil magistrate. Only the explicit teaching of Scripture can turn back the *continuity* which holds with respect to moral obligation and ethical standard in the Bible. The magistrate today, no less than in Older Testament Israel, is required by God's abiding law to enforce justice and righteousness in social affairs. This conclusion has the weight of *specific and extensive* biblical teaching in its favor; thus the *burden of proof* would have to lie on anyone who wishes to contradict the conclusion on the basis of "Theocratic" considerations.

Conclusion

Therefore, in this chapter we have found two things. First, the objection that the civil magistrate's enforcement of God's law would be a violation of the separation of church and state is unfounded. Church and state are separated as to their functions in *both* Testaments of God's word; thus the law which was valid in the Older Testament cannot be invalidated in the New Testament on the basis of the principle of church/state separation. Scripture does not view the magistrate as au-

---

[32] Hengstenberg, *op. cit.*, p. 320.

tonomous even though it does view the state as separate from the cult or church. The church and state, though separate from each other, are united *under the authority of God.* The second thing which the present examination has indicated is that the power of the church sword is such that God's word will see worldwide prosperity, the reign of Christ being extended to earth's remotest ends. *All authority* in heaven and earth is His, and thus all "authorities" (civil magistrates) are subject to His rule. Since Scripture speaks of Christ establishing justice in the earth we can speak of the Older Testament Theocracy becoming in the New Testament a Christocracy with international boundaries. There is no reason why the "Theocratic" character of Israel should prevent the application of God's law to the civil magistrate today. If, as Morrison maintains, eschatology and Christology ultimately shape the Christian view of the state,[33] then the same conclusion that has been derived from a study of the scriptural view of moral obligation, law, and civil authority would follow here as well. The magistrate today *ought* to obey and enforce God's law in society. A nature/grace dichotomy in the area of civil government is totally alien to the scriptural outlook; Christ does *not* merely rule in His church, leaving the world governments to Satan. Moreover, a further way in which God's word teaches us that magistrates are to obey His direction is the indication that Christ is to rule them Himself. All authorities, whether ecclesiastical or civil, are under His divine rule. Therefore, state leaders are just as obligated to follow Christ's direction *as the church elders* are required to obey the *Head of the Church.* The Word has commandments relevant to both church and state.

---

[33] Clinton D. Morrison, *The Powers That Be: Earthly Rulers and Demonic Powers in Romans 13:1-7,* ed. C. F. D. Moule, et al., Studies in Biblical Theology, No. 29 (London: SCM Press Ltd., 1960), p. 35 n. 1.

Chapter 21

PENOLOGY

THE binding force and authority of any particular commandment always lies in its penal threat; if no punishment is to follow the violation of a law, then the law is merely a suggestion. A person is not *demanded* to act in a certain way unless his disobedience is followed by the application of a penal sanction.

> Law without sanctions is not law. Here the mutual obligation of law and political authority becomes quite obvious. Though political authority exists for the sake of the Law, the Law is only real if enforced through political authority. Though the Law does not receive its validity, it does receive its power from the political authority, and the government must not bear the sword in vain.[1]

The law of God contains both positive demands and penal sanctions; it not only commands the full discharge of its precepts but also the infliction of appropriate penalty for all infractions. Both of these elements must be heeded or else the law of God is *not* being kept.

Dual Sanction

God has delivered not only commandments relating to how we are to behave, but also commandments to the civil magistrate specifying what is to be done when we do not. God's law contains a *double*

[1] George W. Forell, "The State as Order of Creation," *God and Caesar: A Christian Approach to Social Ethics,* ed. Warren A. Quanbeck (Minneapolis: Augsburg Publishing House, 1959), p. 50.

sanction: penalty is to be inflicted in order to guard the justice and order of the state, and eternal penalty is inflicted to guarantee the holiness and righteousness of God. Hence the Older Testament details civic punishments (even execution for capital crimes) for violations of God's law as it applies to society; yet it also fully recognized that the punishment for breaking a commandment of God extended *beyond* this temporal sanction to God's eternal punishment. There was recognition of an afterlife (e.g., Gen. 5:24; Lev. 19:28; Num. 16:30; Deut. 26:14; Ps. 55:15), that the Lord Himself would judge iniquity (e.g., Ps. 1:5 f.; 96:13; 98:9; Eccles. 12:14; cf. 11:9), and that His judgment could lead to eternal damnation (Job 18; Ps. 49:12-15, 19; 69:28; 104:35; Prov. 11:7; 14:32; 15:24; Isa. 33: 14; 66:24; Dan. 12:2; Mal. 4:1). Yet the Older Testament *also* demanded civil punishment for wrongdoers, even execution—fully realizing that another punishment followed this life. Since a violation of God's law has detrimental effect upon both the welfare of society and the spiritual welfare of the offender, punishment according to the law was appropriately *two*-edged: civil and divine. It is perhaps helpful to distinguish between "sin" and "crime."[2] While all crime is sinful, not every sin is a crime. An offense against God's law is a crime when it is a *social* misdeed punishable by the governing authorities; sin, on the other hand, is always judged and punished by God. The magistrate cannot presume to punish a man's sin, but he is obligated to enforce penal sanctions against a man's crime. Thus a crime bears two punishments: one before the magistrate (as a social misdeed), one before God Himself (as a sin). God's law designates what the penal sanctions in both areas are. God's law deals with holiness in society as well as holiness in one's personal life. God is concerned that a man walk upright before Him as well as in society. Hence the social punishments detailed in God's word are as authoritative as any other command He sets down to be obeyed. Intrinsic sanction belongs to civic retribution as a dictate of divine justice.

---

[2] Cf. J. B. Shearer, *Hebrew Institutions, Social and Civil* (Richmond: Presbyterian Committee of Publication, 1910), p. 144.

Equity in Punishment

The main underlying principle of scriptural penology (whether civic or eternal) is not reformation or deterrence, but *justice.* The outstanding characteristic of theonomic punishment is the principle of *equity;* no crime receives a penalty which it does not warrant. The punishment for a violation of God's law is always appropriate for the nature of the offense; "an eye for an eye, and a tooth for a tooth." Here is the most blessed standard of *social* retribution that man's civilization has ever seen. That the Older Testament law sets forth humane and just punishments for crime is immediately apparent when one compares it with the legal codes of the nations around Israel.[3] God's penal sanctions are not overweighted, cruel, unusual, or excessive; a criminal receives what he deserves: no more, no less. It is especially important for Christians to recognize this fact, for it is the underlying principle at work in the atoning death of Jesus Christ upon the cross; He is the sinner's *substitute* in order to effect atonement. Sin must meet divine judgment (e.g., Nah. 1:2, Hab. 1:13), and God can only forgive sin in a manner consistent with His holiness (Ps. 85:9 f.). Hence a sacrifice had to be offered to placate divine wrath occasioned by sin.

> Sin involves a certain liability, a liability arising from the holiness of God, on the one hand, and the gravity of sin as the contradiction of that holiness, on the other. The sacrifice was the divinely instituted provision whereby the sin might be covered and the liability to divine wrath and curse removed. The Old Testament worshipper when he brought his oblation to the altar substituted an animal victim in his place. . . the sin of the offerer was imputed to the offering and the offering bore as a result the death-penalty. It was substitutive endurance of the penalty or liability due to sin.[4]

---

[3] Roland De Vaux, *Ancient Israel* Vol. I (Social Institutions), tr. Darton, Longman, & Todd, Ltd. (New York: McGraw-Hill Book Co., 1965), pp. 149-150.

[4] John Murray, *Redemption: Accomplished and Applied* (Grand Rapids: William B. Eerdmans Publishing Co., 1955), p. 25.

Within this framework Christ came as our sacrificial substitute; He is the Lamb of God who brings redemption by His sacrifice upon the cross (John 1:29; 1 Cor. 5:7; Heb. 9:11-15; 10:3-18; 13:10-12; 1 Pet. 1:18 f.) and thus substitutes Himself for the sinner by taking God's wrath upon Himself (Col. 2:14; 2 Cor. 5:21; Gal. 3:10, 13; cf. Deut. 21:23; 27: 26; Jer. 11:3). The Lord has caused the iniquity of us all to fall upon Him (Isa. 53:6). Christ laid down His life to atone for the sinner's life; Christ took the punishment warranted by the sinner's violation of God's law upon Himself. Therefore, the sinner need not fear God's eternal punishment, for his sin has been atoned. The principle of retribution is prominent in man's salvation. This illustrates the importance of the scriptural penal system: "an eye for an eye, a tooth for a tooth."

This principle of equity applies to civic punishments imposed by the civil magistrate; there must be equity in punishment, even at the *social* level. God operates on the basis of retribution (Job 34:11; Ps. 18:25 f.; Ezek. 18:4, 20; Gal. 6:7—and even restitution, Job 42:10), and the penalties which He prescribes for social sins are based on the same principle of *retribution, restitution* and *compensation* (Ex. 21:18-22:7; Lev. 6:4 f.; 24:17-21; Deut. 19:21). None of God's penalties are excessive or lenient; hence the Older Testament does not detail *arbitrary* punishments for crimes (as with the varying fines for traffic violations from state to state in our modern day), but the punishment was made to correspond to the social heinousness of the offense so that the culprit receives what his public disobedience merits (e.g., Deut. 19:19). The penalties imposed upon social crime are just as appropriate, equitable, and just with respect to their sphere of reference (civil society) as the eternal punishment for that crime (considered now as sin) is just with respect to its sphere of reference (the God-man relation with respect to eternity).

The Necessity of Punishment

In the scriptural outlook civil punishment is needed (1 Tim. 1:9-10) in order to protect the godly (Prov. 12:21; Ps. 125:3) and to destroy the wicked (Ps. 101:8). The rationale behind it, then, is that evil must be rooted out (Prov. 2:21-22; Deut. 17:12, 19:19). As an indirect result of this, punishment becomes a deterrent to crime in others (Prov. 21:11; Deut. 17:13; 19:20). The design of the penal sanctions in God's law, then, is not the rehabilitation or amendment of the criminal. Instead of being pragmatic, the punishment was to fit the crime. Thus man is said to be punished "according to his fault" (Deut. 25:2), "according to his wickedness" (2 Sam. 3:39), "according to his ways" (Jer. 17:10; Ezek. 33:20), "according to the fruit of his doings" (Jer. 17:10; 21:14). This comes to expression in the civil realm as *just recompense* (Heb. 2:2), as in the *lex talionis* (Ex. 21:23-25; Lev. 24:19-20; Deut. 19:21). Consequently the death penalty is to be viewed as the appropriate response of the magistrate to violations against the purity of the God-man relation (e.g., idolatry, witchcraft, etc.), the sanctity of life and its sources (e.g., murder, adultery) or authority (e.g., striking one's parents). In the areas of theft and property damage, then, full restitution or compensation is the standard of punishment (e.g., Ex. 21:22; Lev. 24:21). An insolvent debtor would not be thrown in prison (a punishment extraneous to biblical law), for that serves no dictate of justice; instead the man was allowed to work off his debt.

Not only was punishment according to an equitable standard in the Older Testament, but such punishment (in order to remain just) had to be certain (Prov. 11:21) and without mercy or pity to the criminal—no matter who he was (Heb. 10:28; Deut. 19:13, 21; 25:12; cf. James 2:13). Offenders were not to be helped, justified, or praised (2 Chron. 19:2; Prov. 17:5; 28:4; Isa. 5:20; 26:10; Mal. 3:17). The nations need leaders who will not praise wickedness but rebuke it (Prov. 24:24-25). And even the altar (which was to be undefiled: Num. 19:20; Ezek. 5:11; 23:38; Zeph. 3:4) could not protect those who had murdered with guile (Ex. 21:14; cf. 1 Kings 2:5, 28-31, 34). All those who committed capital crimes (as defined in God's law) had to be executed or else the magistrate would have been sinfully judging *against the victim* and *in favor of the offender;* this is the sign of wicked judgment. Hence the ruler was prohibited from respecting persons or showing mercy to criminals. Luther has properly commented:

> For in this case a prince and lord must remember that according to Romans 13 he is God's minister and the servant of his wrath and that the sword has been given him to use against such people. If he does not fulfill the duties of his office by punishing some and protecting others, he commits as great a sin before God as when someone who has not been given the sword commits murder. If he is able to punish and does not do it—even though he would have had to kill someone or shed blood—he becomes guilty of all the murder and evil that these people commit *(Against the Robbing and Murdering Hordes of Peasants).*
>
> If he (God) will have wrath, what business do you have being merciful?. . . What a fine mercy to me it would be, to have mercy on the thief and murderer, and let him kill, abuse, and rob me! (*Open Letter on the Harsh Book Against the Peasants*).

The *civic* punishment upon a man's crime could not be eliminated even though he was required to make atonement and find God's ultimate forgiveness by means of sacrifice for sin (cf. Lev. 4-6). Social restitution (the penal sanction) was not incompatible with being forgiven by the trespass offering (Lev. 6:4-7; Num. 5:5-8). Therefore, the *civil* punishment was required to be executed upon every criminal unconditionally—without consideration of his status, without mercy, without cancellation through atoning sacrifice. Such are the demands of justice in the realm of civil judgment; a crime always receives what it, with respect to the context of social life, deserves as equitable for the nature of the offense.

Divine Desert in Punishment

We are to understand the prescription of the death penalty on the basis that such a civic punishment is what the crime *warrants* in God's eyes. And God's standards are not subject to a popular vote or alteration by human opinion. When God says homosexuality (for instance) warrants capital punishment, then that is what social justice demands; that is how heinous with respect to social relations the crime is in God's judgment. Those who are put to death according to the law of God are described in Deuteronomy 21:22 as ones who have "committed a sin *worthy of death*." The God-given authority of the law is established in the penalties incurred by its violators. Hebrews 2:2 declares that the word of the law is unalterable. Such is the logic of ethics. If some action is ethically good or right, then the change of time will not *per se* alter the rightness of that action. That which is morally binding has an absolute character about it: it is a *standing* obligation. This verse also affirms that "every transgression and disobedience received a *just recompense*," that is, an equitable punishment or appropriate penalty. Those crimes which are punishable by death according to God's law receive a just recompense. The converted criminal who was crucified at Christ's side recognized that he received just retribution for his crime under the sanctity of justice; he asserted, "We die justly, for we receive the *due reward* of our deeds" (Luke 23:41).[5] Even the Gentiles know the judicial commandment of God that they who commit certain things (homosexuality in particular) are "worthy of death" (Rom. 1:32).[6]

Knowing that God's standard of righteousness (which includes temporal, social relations) is as immutable as the character of God

---

[5] Although these criminals who were crucified with Jesus have come down to us through history designated as "thieves," the language and context of the gospel passion narratives indicate that they were more than mere robbers. According to Arndt and Gingrich, κακοῦργος (cf. Luke 23:32-33, 39) is a "criminal" or "evildoer," one who commits *gross* misdeeds and *serious* crimes. λῃστῆς (cf. Matt. 27:38, 44; Mark 15:27) basically meant "robber" or "bandit," but its meaning had been expanded to signify "revolutionary" or "insurrectionist" (when John 18:40 is compared with Mark 15:7 we can see this point; it is further implied in Matthew 25:55). The two criminals who were crucified with Christ were guilty of serious crimes, even murder or insurrection. (See "malefactor" in *Unger's Bible Dictionary*, 3rd. ed. (Chicago: Moody Press, 1961), p. 686.

[6] John Murray correctly comments on this passage that "death" cannot be reasonably *restricted* to temporal death; cf. *The Epistle to the Romans: The English Text with Introduction, Exposition and Notes,* Vol. II, ed. F. F. Bruce, The New International Commentary on the New Testament (Grand Rapids: William B. Eerdmans Publish-

Himself, we should conclude that crimes which warrant capital punishment in the Older Testament continue to *deserve* the death penalty today. So we ask ourselves at this point whether there is any agency in the New Testament era that has the *right* to carry out God's sentence upon such criminals. Romans 13:1-4 (cf. Prov. 21:15) answers the question; Paul definitely places the right of punishment, even capital punishment, in the hands of the civil magistrate (an avenger who brings God's wrath upon one who practices evil). The civil leader "does not bear the sword in vain"; this reference cannot possibly be restricted to lesser forms of punishment but expressly authorizes the most extreme penalty: death. The "sword" properly symbolizes the *death* penalty (cf. for what the "sword" represents: Matt. 26:52; Acts 12:2; Heb. 11:37; Rev. 13:10; Ulpian, *Digest* 1.18.6; Tacitus, *Hist.* 3.68; Dio Cassius 42.27). Therefore, civil magistrates today are under obligation to execute all those who commit capital crimes as defined by God's authoritative law. Paul's word in Romans 13 is sufficient to demonstrate to us that the magistrate *does* have the obligation and authorization to inflict the death penalty upon certain violators of God's law.

The Agency of Punishment

However, if the question, "Why does *man* have the right to require and exact the death of another *man?*" is raised, Scripture gives us the rationale in Genesis 9:5 f. The reason offered is that man is the *image of God:* man can accordingly carry out God's judgments on a creaturely level. Thinking God's thoughts after Him, man judges and penalizes after the commandment of God; man is properly *like God* his Father and Judge when he too judges crimes as God does. God judges with righteousness and truth (Ps. 96:13), meting out equal retribution (Ps. 9:16;

---

ing Co., 1965), p. 51. It is important to note that temporal death is the *primary* and obvious referent. Other allusion to the "second death" is built upon the primary allusion and comes in by inference. The Gentiles know God's ordinance making particular crimes (notably homosexuality) punishable by execution, although one can hardly keep from going on to see that eternal death is also involved.

cf. 7:11-17; Obad. 15; Heb. 2:2), repaying according to man's deeds (Isa. 59:18); God requites men according to their work and according to the evil of their practices (Ps. 28:4; 62:12; Jer. 17:10; Matt. 16:27; Rom. 2:6; 2 Cor. 5:10; 1 Pet. 1:17; Rev. 22:12). Man should do this as well on his level as a creature, not in personal vindictiveness (i.e., such judgment does not apply to interpersonal affairs: 1 Thess. 5:15; 1 Pet. 3:9; Matt. 5:39; Rom. 12:17 ff.) but as a matter of *social justice* (i.e., it is the *magistrate's* duty to punish criminals for the good of society: Rom. 13:1-4). The man created in God's image who has the responsibility of rule in human government (not citizens, not the church) is required to punish violators of God's law for the welfare of his country; he has the right to do this because he is the image of God and has God's law to direct him. The rationale which was given in Genesis 9:5 f. is neither indicative prose nor poetry;[7] it is a serious and straight-forward imperative. "The one shedding the blood of man by man his blood is to be shed, for in the image of God He made man." The reference to man being made in God's image is given in order to explain the *human infliction* of the death penalty, not so much the *penalty* of death itself. In the verse emphasis lies on "by man" since it is placed outside normal and expected sentence order. Instead of smoothly saying "his blood is to be shed by man" the verse reads "*by man* his blood is to be shed." We stumble over the "by man" due to its obtrusion and conspicuousness. Man's being made as God's image explains the infliction of the death penalty *by man.* Historical and textual contexts support this interpretation as well. Genesis 4:14 shows us that Cain realized an innate law of retribution in human nature, but God did not sanction its use at that time (Gen. 4:15). Lamech had far *exceeded* just recompense (Gen. 4:23). And God *Himself* had just executed men for their violence (Gen. 6:11 ff.) by means of the flood. But God now explains to Noah that in the

[7] Cf. John Murray, *Principles of Conduct: Aspects of Biblical Ethics* (Grand Rapids: William B. Eerdmans Publishing Co., 1957), pp. 110-111. Plus note that the Hebrew text does not set verse 6 in poetic line structure. Any supposed poetic chiasm is read into the verse (as the NASV apparently does) with no ready explanation for an abrupt interruption of the prose going before and after—only two short and notably serious verses being selected amidst the run of prose.

new post-flood world the law of retribution *would* come into play for and by man (in the likeness of God). In Genesis 9:5 God says that *He* will require the life of the murderer, but in verses 5 and 6 the idea is introduced that "*by man*" the murderer's blood is to be shed. This could seem contradictory, and certainly needs explanation; the explanation God gives is that man is His image so God can require the murderer's life *through* the agency of man. The emphasis in verse 5 is upon the exacting of punishment by each man's brother; verse 6 reiterates this emphasis. Furthermore, the mention of capital punishment does not seem to force the question of "why?" upon us here at this stage of revelation; after all, given Lamech why *not?* Remember also the flood! Cain knew what he had coming; his brother's blood cried out from the ground for revenge (Gen. 4:10 f., which is akin to Gen. 9:5). However, God did not allow capital punishment to be inflicted upon him. So the proper question at Genesis 9:5 f. is: what *right* has *man* to retaliate against the murderer? Genesis 9:6 gives the rationale: man is God's image. The later Jews apparently understood the civil magistrate in this light; Philo says that the king is to be honored as "an image of God."[8] And Hengstenberg's comment upon Romans 13 is germane here: "all supremacy is of God, Rom. xiii.1. Every king bears His image, and this alone gives him the right to rule and makes it the duty of subjects to obey."[9] When the magistrate follows God's law in executing criminals he has the approval and authorization of God. The authorization is that he rules as a representative of God and that his judgment be according to God's law-judgment; thus is he God's image. This interpretation of Genesis 9 is drawn out through the Scriptures where he is presented as God's vicegerent who can actually be designated a "god" since he judges the judgment of God upon criminals (cf. the appropriate sections in the earlier discussion of the civil magistrate).

---

[8] Cited in Clinton D. Morrison, The *Powers That Be: Earthly Rulers and Demonic Powers in Romans 13:1-7,* ed. C. F. D. Moule, Studies in Biblical Theology, No. 29 (London: SCM *Press,* 1960), p. 96.

[9] E. W. Hengstenberg, *History of the Kingdom of God Under the Old Testament,* Vol. I (Cherry Hill, N. J.: Mack Publishing Co., 1871 [reprinted 1972]), p. 316.

Effects of Punishment

When the magistrate carries out the dictate of justice in executing one who has committed a capital crime according to God's law, this has the effect of *purging* the land of evil and *restraining* others from committing similar crimes (Deut. 13:5, 11). Scripture lists the following as capital offenses against God: murder (Ex. 21:12; Num. 35:31), adultery and unchastity (Lev. 20:10; Deut. 22:21, 23), sodomy and bestiality (Lev. 18:23; 20:15; Ex. 22:19), homosexuality (Lev. 18:22; 20:13), rape (Deut. 22:25), incest (Lev. 20:11, 14), incorrigibility in children (Ex. 21:15, 17; Deut. 21:20 f.), sabbath breaking (Ex. 31:14; Num. 15:32 ff.; Ex. 35:2), kidnapping (Ex. 21:16; Deut. 24:7), apostasy (Lev. 20:2; Deut. 13:6-17), witchcraft, sorcery, and false pretension to prophecy (Ex. 22:18; Lev. 20:27; Deut. 13:5; 18:20), and blasphemy (Lev. 24:10-16). With respect to social affairs the Lord looks with so much scorn upon these crimes that He commands the state to execute those who commit them. Christians do well at this point to adjust their attitudes so as to coincide with those of their Heavenly Father. Remember the seriousness of the penal law. Not even refuge sought by the altar could protect those who were guilty of capital crimes (Ex. 21:14; cf. 1 Kings 2:28, 34); not even cherished friends or relatives are exempt from the death penalty when they have violated God's law (Deut. 13:6-9). The application of capital punishment to appropriate criminals contributes to the expiration of evil and produces reverence for God's righteousness; it demonstrates and preserves the sanctity of life, truth, family, sex, property, and authority. It is not without significance that the major problems facing society today are listed among those things which God adjudges to be things worthy of capital punishment.

A Call for Justifying Evidence

In light of the above comments and references to God's word, we must ask *where* is scriptural support for the position that the stipulations respecting capital punishment in God's law no longer have application? Such a position seems to diametrically contradict a good and necessary deduction from Scriptures based on Matthew 5:17 f. If every jot and tittle of the Older Testamental law is confirmed for the New Testament era, and if God commands that certain criminals be executed according to His law, then those criminals *are* to be executed during the New Testament era (by the civil magistrate—Rom. 13:1-4). The necessity of the penal sanction in the death penalty is not removed except in a righteous society, for "the law is not made for a righteous man" (1 Tim. 1:8); hence we should not expect the cessation of capital punishment for appropriate crimes until we reach the "new heavens and new earth wherein righteousness dwells" (2 Pet. 3:13)—which shall appear *after* the Great Day of Final Capital Punishment (2 Pet. 3:7-10; Acts 17:31; Rom. 2:5-16; 2 Thess. 1:7 f.; Heb. 10:26-29; Jude 14 f.; Rev. 20:11-15).

A Consistent Conclusion

Those who propose the abolition of the death penalty (in apparent opposition to God's word) should also carry out the logic of their position: if the gravest punishment (death) is abolished, *how much more* the lesser penalties! The result would have to be *no* punishments at all. Thus, the magistrate could no more impose a traffic fine upon someone for speeding than he could execute someone for murder! Without the "political use" of the law wickedness is unrestrained in the social order. The weakening or abrogation of some of the penal sanctions of God's law is a major step in that direction. When the death penalty is removed, society is allowed to run completely amuck in unrighteous behavior, for there will be *no* legitimate penal sanctions left to God's law. Only those illegitimate and arbitrary punishments imposed by the humanistic state would remain.

Furthermore, if it is the case that there has been a cancellation of God's law with respect to capital punishment, have God's standards changed or have such crimes become less reprehensible in the New Testament era? The former answer is heresy, and the latter is incredible. Sins which are punishable by execution do not become any less heinous under the New Testament. With increased revelation concerning God, His righteous character, and His demand for holiness, these crimes acquire (if anything) *greater* culpability and appear even more dreadful. The gravity of sin is magnified by the light of progressed revelation. The atrocity of capital crimes is, therefore, intensified in the New Testament age. God's standards for public and civil justice have *not* changed, for God is immutable (as is His law, Matt. 5:17-18). Thus the death penalty for certain crimes is not simply a suggestion from God but a formal *command.*

The suggestion is sometimes made that capital punishment is inconsistent with the Christian's interest in evangelism. However, this suggestion, if pressed, could only lead to the pitting of God's love against His justice or the unfounded idea that no Israelite (for whom, all will grant, the law respecting capital punishment held) was ever unsaved or subject to the death penalty. However, God calls men to be part of His redeemed community and uses the church to proclaim the gospel without any indication in Scripture that God has made the dishonoring of His law for society the necessary condition for evangelism. One must then hold to the authority of the law as well as submitting to the commission of the gospel. The implausibility of the suggestion that God's law is inconsistent with the evangelistic task of the church is nowhere more pronounced than in the Great Commission itself (Matt. 28:18-20), for therein the church is sent both to disciple the nations *and* to teach them to observe the law of God. The Gospel and the Law are both elements of the church's commission then. Moreover, the honoring of the Lord's command to us that certain crimes be punished by death is simply *not* an inhibition to evangelism. If a man is condemned to die there is nothing to stop the believer from going to him and witnessing the gospel; the evangelism of men on death row has long been an activity of the church. But the objection might arise that by putting a man to death you cut off all further possibility of evangelism, and that extra time might be just the time needed for his conversion. Now while it is a possibility that the man would repent in the future if not executed, "there is a great difference between what Providence and the secular magistrate may do."[10] It is presumptuous

---

[10] John David Michaelis, *Commentaries on the Laws of Moses,* Vol. III, tr. Alexander Smith (London: D. Chalmers and Co., 1814), p. 402.

for the believer to set aside obedience to God's law on the basis of what might or might not happen in the future. The fact of the matter is that only God knows who will be saved; yet He has given to us His law with the *expectation* that it be observed. "The secret things belong unto Jehovah our God; but the things that are revealed belong unto us and to our children for ever, that we may do all the words of this law" (Deut. 29:29, ASV). The Christian's duty is to obey all the commands of God, not picking and choosing which to follow and which to set aside. In God's grace there will be criminals who are converted, but their conversion or possibility thereof must not hinder the application of God's law as the standard of justice for society. Needless to say, if someone who is a capital criminal should be converted *before* God's law is recognized and enforced as the law of the land, then he would be a member of the church just like any other forgiven sinner (cf. 1 Cor. 6:11). The state would be operating on an improper *ex post facto* basis if it later submitted to God's law and began executing converted criminals for their past lives. If the criminal is converted *after* the law of God is recognized by a country as binding, and *if* the magistrate has *a lawful* case against the criminal (two witnesses, etc.), then the converted criminal should: (1) as Paul, say "If I am an evildoer and have committed anything worthy of death, then I refuse not to die" (Acts 25:11), for a born-again believer will respect the law of God, and (2) rejoice in his soon departure to be with the Lord, no longer fearing death as the greatest of enemies. Notice that there is no tension in the account of the dying revolutionary caused by the fact that, although Christ had forgiven his sins, he was nonetheless to be executed; rather, that converted criminal rejoiced in the words, "Today thou wilt be with me in paradise" (Luke 23: 43).

Parallel to Ceremonial Law?

Attempts might also be made to nullify the penal sanctions of God's law (in qualification of the broad endorsement of the law in Matt. 5:17-19) by likening them to the ceremonial law which is no longer observed today as it was during the Older Testament era. The argument can take two forms here: (1) it might be said that the ceremonial/moral law distinction is *illegitimate* and thus the nonobservance of the ceremonial law today forces us to re-evaluate the *whole issue* of ethical *continuity* between Older and New Testaments, or (2) it might be argued that a ceremonial/moral law distinction *warrants a further* ceremonial/judicial/moral law distinction, leaving only the last category with binding force in the New Testament dispensation. First let it be observed that the distinction between moral and ceremonial laws, as was demonstrated in a previous chapter, is *not* arbitrarily imposed on the Older Testament by modern theology. The distinction is a moral and scriptural necessity, was anticipated in the Older Testament itself, was expected by the pre-Christian rabbis, and recognized in the early church based on solid New Testament teaching. Moreover, the distinction is rule-governed and consistent, not *ad hoc* —guided by the distinction between God's justice and God's mercy; what counts as restorative (ceremonial) law is determined by scriptural exegesis, not social conditioning. The distinction, then, is *not* illegitimate or arbitrary.

Therefore, the ceremonial (i.e., restorative) law does not give support to the invalidation of the law's penal sanctions today. First, the penal sanctions are *not* in the same category as the ceremonies. Second, there would appear to be no ground for assigning the sanctions to a *historically qualified* form of expression (as with the ceremonies). Thirdly, since the ceremonial (restorative)/moral distinction is not arbitrary, one does not have grounds for *simply positing* a third category (viz., judicial laws) which is comprised of laws not to be observed today as they were in the Older Testament.

Wherein is Capital Punishment Confirmed?

Given the authority of God's word at Matthew 5:17-19 it is imperative for any who would today nullify the penal sanctions of God's law to show how those Older Testament sanctions are *confirmed* in this age. We can see how the Decalogue is confirmed (e.g., murder is still murder) and how the restorative law is confirmed (e.g., Christ is the true temple, the Lord's supper functions like the Passover celebration, etc.). But for the person who puts aside the use of the penal sanctions today, how are *those* laws confirmed? Are they rather not simply *abrogated?* Three possible confirmations come to mind, but they are all unsatisfactory. First, it could be suggested that the penal sanctions are confirmed in the crucifixion of Christ. However, Christ did not take the *civic* penalty for criminals upon Himself, but rather the eternal penalty for sinners. Christ cancels the second death, but His atoning work does not abrogate the inducement of the first death for certain social crimes. A sacrificial substitute was offered during the Older Testament for the matter of sin and eternal punishment; however, there was also a civic penalty for crimes that was to be imposed—even when sacrifice was made for the sin involved in that crime. Moreover, the law states in Deuteronomy 24:16 that with respect to social punishments everyone must be executed *for his own transgression.* This did not apply to eternal judgment (witness the sacrificial system) but to the penal sanctions to be applied by the civil magistrate (check context). Consequently, unless Christ's death is a violation of the law of God (which would then invalidate its effectiveness), His atonement must be seen as relating to *eternal* judgment before God and *not* the *social* penalties of the law—otherwise not every man would be bearing his own social responsibility. Christ died to release men from their doom to hell, not that they would be extricated from the penal obligations of the social state in which they live. Furthermore, *if* the cross confirmed the penal sanctions of the law, then all criminals would be exempt from any punishment at the hands of the state. If Christ bore the civic penalties due to a man, then the Christian who is stopped for speeding could rightfully tell the officer that Christ had already paid the penalty for crimes, thus freeing him from further punishment. But of course this is absurd, and it would spell the moral degeneration of society. The fact is that Christ did not, and legally could not, remove the penal sanctions of the law as they apply to inter-social relations and history. Finally, *if* the cross cancelled the civil magistrate's authorization to impose the death sentence, then Paul was unaware of that fact even under inspiration (Rom. 13:1-4) and Matthew 5:17-19 is misleading.

A second suggestion would be that the penal sanctions of the law are confirmed in this age by the church's use of excommunication (which spells eternal death for the apostate). However, the judgment of eternal death held for those who were *also* executed by the state in the Older Testament. And the sanction of excommunication was used in the Older Testament for cultic violations (i.e., a "cutting off" which was not in some cases the same as physical execution, but rather exile). Therefore, excommunication in the New Testament could hardly be the confirmation of execution in the Old Testament. Instead this would amount to collapsing execution into excommunication—that is, dropping it altogether. That would be abrogation, not confirmation. Furthermore, there are major discontinuities between excommunication in the New Testament and execution in the Older Testament. Repentance can secure release from church discipline (for the church is an agent of God's grace), but repentance could not secure release from civic punishment in the Older Testament—indeed, it would be immoral for magistrates to be respectors of persons or judges of mens' hearts according to the law. Their function is simply to carry out fairly and fully the sanctions of God's law against a convicted criminal (for the state is an agent of God's justice in social matters). Then again, the magistrate in the Older Testament took as the scope of his jurisdiction the whole populace, but the elders of the New Testament church cannot judge those who are without; their discipline is to a restricted body of individuals (thus not even touching upon the many criminals who operate outside of concern for the church altogether). For these reasons then, excommunication cannot be the confirmation of the penal sanctions of the Older Testament law; instead this would amount to abrogation of that portion of the Older Testament altogether.

A final suggestion is that the confirmation of the Older Testament punishment laws is found in the final judgment. However, in the Older Testament a criminal faced the threat of final judgment *as well as* the civic penalty for his crime. Thus, to postpone the penal sanction of the law with respect to social affairs to the Day of Judgment (of course, then it is no longer the *civic* punishment of the law dealt with by ordained magistrates at all) is not fairly to "postpone" it—it is simply to "drop" it altogether. There would be no confirmation of the social penalty for crime from the Older Testament, but only a confirmation of a different aspect of the law: its eternal threat. This suggestion also has the effect of suspending *all* civic punishment (or else bears the burden of proof in showing a nonarbitrary principle of selectivity or discontinuity as to which crimes will be punished and which will not) and, therefore, making it hard to understand the legitimacy of Romans 13:4 or civil magistrates at all. Moreover, this suggestion does not satisfy the conditions of Matthew 5:17-19. In that passage Christ speaks of the law being confirmed at His "coming" (first advent) and remaining valid until heaven and earth pass away (His second advent in judgment). Thus it is specifically *between* the advents, in this present era, that every jot and tittle of the law (including the commandments pertaining to civic punishment) are confirmed. However, the suggestion that final judgment is the confirmation of the Older Testament penal sanctions renders this age a parenthesis (in contradiction to Scripture's own testimony) and places the confirmation of the law beyond the specific scope of Christ's words in Matthew 5:17-19. Hence, once again we do not find confirmation of the law at this point (viz., its penal sanctions in the social sphere) but *abrogation.* Because God is concerned for righteousness on the personal level (the relation between God and individual man) as *well as* on the social level (the relation between man and man) one cannot allow the penalties which are appropriate to the latter to be absorbed into the former; instead, *every jot and tittle* of the law must receive confirmation in this age while we await the return of Christ and the Great Day of Judgment from God. Crime must be properly handled by the civil magistrate today, not leaving it to be handled as sin by God in the future. While God's judgment is certainly the most ultimately dreadful of the two, nevertheless His will is that the magistrate also punish the criminal in this life and during this age.

Ethical Arbitrariness

At this point our argument might well end. On the basis of Matthew 5:17-19 and the foregoing exposition with respect to the civil magistrate, and in the absence of any suitable explanation of how the penal sanctions of God's law are confirmed in this age, we must conclude that it is the moral responsibility of all magistrates to obey and enforce the law of God as recorded in the Older Testament (including its penal prescriptions for crime). The notion that the death penalty has been abrogated is clearly contrary, then, to the teaching of God's word. If the various methods and suggestions examined above have turned out to be infested with difficulties in an attempt to put aside capital punishment in this age, then how much more riddled with problems is that position which appeals to these same methods or makes the same suggestions in order to argue for the abrogation of capital punishment for all crimes *except one!* The person arguing according to the above patterns commits himself (if consistent) to the abrogation of all the penal sanctions of the law, providing his argument could be sustained. However, if the principle used in the argument abrogates the death penalty, then let it be. The death penalty is abrogated. It would be overt special pleading at this point to try to rescue the death penalty for one crime of the many to which it applies. Therefore, those who disagree with the confirmation of the penal sanctions of the Older Testament and desire to lay aside the death penalty *except* for murder have taken on a much harder task than may have been envisaged. Not only must they deal with "every jot and tittle" of Matthew 5:17-19, but they must then turn around and argue with cogency and solid *scriptural* warrant for a special *exception.* The only Scripture-oriented attempt to perform this prodigious task will be dealt with below. It remains now only to conclude that the nullifying of the penal sanctions of the Older Testament law cannot be reconciled with the authoritative declaration by Christ of their *confirmation* (Matt. 5:17-19). In this present age the civil magistrate ought to follow the law of God and its commandments pertaining to punishment for social crimes.

Before bringing this chapter to an end, however, there are two last attempts to contravene the use of the Older Testament penal sanctions in the present age that need to be mentioned. The first attempt is based in a hypothetical argument from typology; the second has been advanced by John Murray.

"Arguments" from Typology

With respect to typology it might be suggested that Israel as a nation is a type of the church of Christ. There is certainly scriptural warrant for that comparison. However, the argument might continue that, for this reason, whatever *is said to Israel* in the Older Testament applies today only to the church. This would clearly be wrong. The God who revealed himself to Israel is also the God who created, sustains, and will judge those outside of the church. Modifying the conclusion then, the person thus arguing from typology might say that the things *Israel was to do* only apply to the church today. But again this is certainly wrong. Israel was to repent of sin, and today God commands all men everywhere to repent; thus it is not the case that everything Israel was to do applies only to the church today. Modifying the conclusion again, the typologist might suggest that *the moral standards* which held in Israel only apply to the church today. Here again Scripture does not support the inference, for not only did God hold the nations outside of Israel accountable for their violations of His law (e.g., Sodom, the Canaanites, etc.) but today that same law is the basis for the universal condemnation of sin (cf. Rom. 1-3).

Shifting positions again, the typologist might argue that *the penal sanctions* of the law which were used by Israel only apply to the church today; yet this premise is not only *mistaken* (the church today does not have the right to execute murderers, etc.) but it now reduces *the argument against* the use of the penalties of the law today to *question-begging.* Moreover, since the argument from typology would appear to contradict the direct assertion of Scripture (cf. Matt. 5:17-19), then much more than a typological connection must be mentioned. It must be demonstrated that *Scripture warrants* the suggested inference from the typological connection to the argumentative conclusion. The artistic and pedagogical designs inherent in the Scriptures certainly must not be ignored or despised; however, neither must they be abused by trying to make them say something which Scripture itself does not say. The infallible interpreter of Scripture is not an imaginative model brought to bear on the data of the Bible (thus threatening to operate like a Procrustean bed) but is the Scripture *itself* (Westminster Confession of Faith, I.IX). Without *specific biblical* moorings and key *didactic* confirmations, from point to point, typology degenerates either to *allegory* or a mere *projection* of the *typologists* clever or artistic imagination.

A second kind of typological argument against the use of the Older Testament penal sanctions today might run like this. Since Israel's government was peculiarly tied up with its *redemptive-historical* functions, perhaps it had to apply a *distinct* principle of justice, a peculiar kind of cleanness, in society. Perhaps also, crimes received in Israel a kind of *heightened* retribution, and these penal sanctions were intended to *instruct the* people of God in a *later* day of the purity of God's kingdom. Now the first thing to be noted about this consideration is that, even *if* it turns out to have biblical warrant, it does *not* nullify the penal sanctions for today. The premise that must necessarily be added in order to bring down the conclusion that the penal sanctions have been put aside is that God does *not* any longer want the kind of purity He required of Israel. Such a premise needs explicit scriptural backing, and it is not likely to be found (cf. Matt. 5:17-19). God's moral nature has not changed, for He is immutable; thus it is difficult to see justification for presuming that His moral requirements would have changed from Older Testament to New.

But even aside from this response there is more to be said about the suggested argument. The penal sanctions of the Older Testament may well have had a teaching aspect to them, but the *Israelites* themselves were being taught by them. Consequently, the pedagogical element *per se* in the penal sanctions does *not* require the nullification of their application; they were executed according to, *as well as* learned from, the Older Testament. So why should not the same state of affairs hold today? The penal sanctions could *continue* to teach men of God's righteousness while nevertheless being applied by the civil magistrate. Romans 15:4 says that everything written aforetime was written for our present day instruction, but we would consider it completely illegitimate to conclude from that fact that *everything* in the Older Testament is abrogated or laid aside. Clearly then, the typological or pedagogical value of the Older Testament penal sanctions cannot be used as an argument against their application today. One would have to demonstrate that these punishments were typological in value and *only* typological in value (i.e., that their function is exhausted in typology) before he could argue against their use today.

Moreover, it needs to be demonstrated *from Scripture's explicit teaching* that the Older Testament penal sanctions *were* in fact *heightened* in their severity or intensity. The testimony of Scripture would seem to be quite otherwise: every violation of the law received a *just recompense,* a punishment *appropriate* to the crime with respect to social relations. Also, scriptural testimony is required that warrants the premise that the penal sanctions were only *temporary,* that they were *not intended* to be applied today or that the Bible expressly says that they *do not* apply today. If such an intimation could be found, then again the matter of confirmation in Matthew 5:17 needs to be explained. And then finally, if the penal sanctions of the Older Testament were *only* intended as a "heightened" punishment for the civil magistrate to execute *in Israel,* what are we to make of the magistrate's being granted the sword to be an avenger for God's wrath in *this* age (Rom. 13:4)? If he is not to apply the sanctions laid out in Scripture, then what guidance does he have? More importantly, what limits and responsibilities are laid upon him by God—standards that will be the basis for God's later judgment of that ruler?

Critique of Murray's Position

It is plain, then, that typology cannot be used to contradict the direct teaching of Scripture. Therefore, if there is to be an argument against the theonomic responsibility of the civil magistrate it will have to be grounded in more immediate scriptural considerations. For this we turn to the position espoused by John Murray. Murray contends that the penal sanctions of the Older Testament law have been abrogated in this age. His argument is simply this: in the divorce discourses of Christ, our Lord gives divorce as the proper recourse of a spouse who has been wronged by the adultery of his or her mate. "By implication our Lord abrogated the death penalty for adultery."[11] Elsewhere Murray says that when there is no scriptural warrant repeated in the New Testament for certain regulations of a preceptive and punitive nature, then they do not bind us today,[12] Now with utmost respect for Murray's scholarly contributions as an orthodox theologian, I must point out, nevertheless, that *this* argument is directly contradictory to the way Murray argues elsewhere. With respect to penal sanctions he has said that *silence abrogates* the unmentioned principle. However, when he is comparing the various versions of our Lord's discourse on divorce Murray strongly maintains that the fact that Luke and Mark do not mention the exceptive clause found in Matthew does not mean that the various gospel writers are in contradiction with each other; *here* silence is *not* taken to oppose the unmentioned principle.[13] Of course it is this second approach to the matter of silence which is legitimate. The reason that not everything is mentioned or every related matter exposited in someone's discourses is to be explained by the intention of the author to deal only with some particular aspect of a subject; in terms of his context or purpose in speaking, certain things are said and certain other things are left out as failing to be germane to the topic or conclusion. Murray should have taken this approach to Christ's silence about the death penalty for adultery as well. The topic for elaboration pertains to *divorce* and its proper grounds in Matthew 19:3-9, not all the details and enactments with respect to adultery. Thus Jesus speaks to the question at hand, not another question that some interpreters have forced the text to answer, even though it is patently silent on the subject (e.g., capital punishment). Jesus did not need to give any explanation or elaboration on the subject or sanctions against adultery because these things were perfectly clear from the law. What

---

[11] Murray, *Principles of Conduct, op. cit.*, p. 54.

[12] John Murray, *The Sabbath Institution* (London: Lord's Day Observance Society [1953]), pp. 9-10.

[13] John Murray, "Divorce," *The Encyclopedia of Christianity*. Vol. III ed. Philip E. Hughes, et al. (Marshalltown, Delaware: The National Foundation for Christian Education, 1972), pp. 420-424.

the Pharisees wanted to know, and what is not obvious to all, is what are the grounds for *divorce.* To *this* question Jesus speaks, saying that the only thing serious enough to warrant a legal separation of man and wife is fornication. This should indicate how serious the marriage bond is in God's eyes. Christ is reproving the Pharisaical interpretation of Deuteronomy 24 and their loose policy on divorce. It is clear that He did *not* say "adultery no longer warrants execution," but that only fornication is a legitimate cause for divorce. Jesus confirmed the Older Testament attitude toward divorce (Gen. 2:24 and Mal. 2:16).

In passages such as Matthew 5 and 19 Christ is not instituting a new penalty for adultery (it is hard to see how divorce itself *punishes* an already adulterous spouse, except in a *possible* economic sense). Adultery is not any less heinous in God's eyes after the advent of Christ; consequently, its penalty is not lightened. Jesus is not intending here to make a legislative pronouncement about the law containing penal sanction against adultery; this law does not even come into the scope of the discourse. Consequently, Murray's argument is overtly an illegitimate (Deut. 4:2) *argument from silence.* (The kind of argument utilized here is rehearsed and refuted in the discussion of the antitheses of Matthew 5 above; the reader is directed there for more extensive treatment.)

Murray makes the same mistake with reference to 1 Corinthians 5 where, according to him, Paul's silence respecting the Older Testamental penalty for fornication implies that it is revoked, and that the sanction has been changed from the corporeal to the spiritual. However, these implications simply *do not follow from silence.* Neither Jesus nor Paul revoke the death penalty in this case; neither one even mentions it! Paul does not charge the church at Corinth (to whom the letter is addressed) to execute the fornicator because the *church* does *not* bear the sword (as Paul definitely taught: Rom. 13). Only the civil magistrate could execute; so there is *no reason* for Paul to discuss *execution* when giving advice to the church on how to handle this particular situation. And certainly there has been *no change* with respect to bodily and spiritual punishments from the Older Testament, for *both* features were *present in Older Testamental* jurisprudence and literature. If Paul were denying that capital punishment by the state would be appropriate, he certainly would have been *diminishing* the former sanction. It is precisely this kind of argument from silence which Murray (appropriately) *rejects* elsewhere. His inconsistency is evident when one looks at Murray's argument for infant baptism. While he has been seen above to require that an Older Testament principle be expressly repeated if it is going to be binding today, in the case of baptism he maintains that the Older Testament must be *expressly revoked* if its principles are *not* to be kept or followed by the church today[14] Quite obviously one cannot have it both ways: assuming a principle of continuity with the Older Testament unless explicitly rescinded, but assuming a principle of discontinuity with the Older Testament unless explicitly repeated. Matthew 5:17-19 shows us which general principle is to be followed (viz., continuity) when the New Testament is silent on something. Murray's argument against the penal sanctions of the Older Testament as being binding today then must be rejected. The abrogation of God's law cannot be built on a hiatus; only God's explicit authority is sufficient to nullify what He has previously spoken. As Murray himself is willing to say elsewhere, the moral law of God does not change but shows a standard of unchanging justice.[15]

If one were to follow the (erroneous) principle that what is not reiterated from the Older Testament in the New Testament is abrogated, one would have to conclude that the penal sanction of capital punishment for *murder* has also been abrogated since it is *not* reaffirmed. However, this raises a very difficult problem. If murder does not warrant capital punishment today (since the New Testament does not tell

---

[14] John Murray, *Christian Baptism* (Philadelphia: The Presbyterian and Reformed Publishing Co., 1970), pp. 48, 52, 53.

[15] John Murray, *The Sanctity of the Moral Law* (Philadelphia: Committee on Christian Education, The Orthodox Presbyterian (Church, [n.d.]), p. 11. Note well Murray's own accurate declaration: "We may not take away from God's law. When we do we open wide the way of license" (*Principles of Conduct,* p. 54). Would that we as well as our neighbors were thus guarded against the *license* of *civil* authorities, and not just our own private proclivity to sin.

us that it does), then most people will be inclined to say, "well then what does?" The point is that nothing, then, seems to be punishable by death. After all, the New Testament does not lay down any particular penal prescriptions for the civil magistrate. And yet Romans 13 shows that the magistrate clearly has the right to execute criminals. Could this then be taken as justification for the continuation of the penal sanction against murder? Many individuals treat it in just that way. However, if Romans 13 justifies the continuation of the death penalty for murder, then it just as much confirms the death penalty for all the other capital crimes mentioned in the Older Testament, for no principle of discrimination is established in that passage (or anywhere else for that matter).

Is Murder Relevantly Unique?

It is at this point that the second step in John Murray's argument enters the discussion. Not wanting to give up the death penalty for murder, Murray has to find some rationale for keeping it while rejecting the validity of execution for the other capital crimes of the Older Testament. Although we have already seen that his argument for the *general repeal* of capital punishment is invalid, we should observe that the next step of his argument is faulty as well. The way that Murray hopes to maintain the death penalty for murder alone is by going behind Romans 13 to the Noahic covenant and skipping over the Mosaic law altogether.[16] By doing this Murray claims to put murder in a *unique category* all its own, for in Genesis 9 it is only murder that is mentioned as a capital crime and this because man is said to be the image of God. In response to this, one must first ask what *right* anyone has to discriminate in this manner, choosing the Noahic covenant over the Mosaic covenant instead of accepting them both. While one might appeal to the fact that the Noahic covenant was made with all the living creatures as well as Noah and his seed (thus having universal scope), someone else could just as well appeal to Romans 1-3 to show that the

---

[16] Murray, *Principles of Conduct, op. cit.*, pp. 118-119.

whole world is also under the Mosaic law (thus having universal scope as well). And when one looks to Matthew 5:17-19 there seems to be no grounds for choosing one of the covenants over the other anyway. Since man is to live by *every* word from God's mouth (Matt. 4:4, a quotation from the Mosaic covenant, Deut. 8:3), then the question arises: who has the right to follow a particular Scripture passage and be indifferent to another? Certainly a *covenant* theologian who does not break the unity of God's covenantal dealings with man throughout the history of redemption should be the last, with respect to ethical authority, to discriminate between the covenants of the Older Testament! Secondly, Genesis 9:6 does not attribute the image of God to man as an explanation of an alleged uniqueness of murder. As has already been pointed out earlier, this passage explains why it is that *man* has the right to carry out the death penalty. Thirdly, if Murray is going to be consistent, then he would not only have to restrict the scope of capital crimes to the Noahic covenant, but he would have to maintain that *all* abiding validity in *morality* as a whole (personal and civic) would also have to be limited to the Noahic covenant. Yet Murray clearly recognizes that it would be unbiblical to do that, for the Mosaic law is just as binding in ethics today as it was in the Older Testament. Thus the restricting of the one question of capital punishment to the Noahic covenant is *arbitrary* special pleading. In terms of the scriptural outlook on penology, the punishments designated in the Mosaic law are perfectly just and equitable. So why should they be overlooked and the law of Genesis 9:6 alone be recognized as binding today? As a fifth problem with Murray's argument it can be noted that Genesis 9 does *not* give the right of taxation to the civil magistrate but Romans 13 *does*. Therefore, it is quite evident that Paul is *not* restricting the principles which govern the civil magistrate today to the Noahic covenant. Not only is the supposition of such a restriction unwarranted from the standpoint of what the whole Bible has to say about ethics, but in particular it is unwarranted when one looks at Paul's specific teaching in Romans 13. And then finally, contrary to Murray's argument, God's law does *not* place murder in a unique category all its own. Murray thinks that it is unique by reason of the *character* of murder and by reason of the *time* of its penal sanction's institution. Murder is an assault against God's image says Murray; now while this is not the force of Genesis 9:6, nevertheless this point can be indirectly granted. However, as Hengstenberg so properly observed, in a sense *all* sin is against the image of God.[17] Therefore, the uniqueness of murder cannot be established on this point. Even if Murray's approach to Genesis 9:6 could be supported contextually, and so forth, still there would be no reason for not seeing it as the *typical* explanation that God would give for any capital crime (viz., it is an assault on His image). Therefore, one cannot find strong enough evidence in Genesis 9 for abrogating capital punishment in the case of all crimes except murder (as they are defined in the Mosaic law). Next, the consideration of the time in which the death penalty for murder was instituted is irrelevant to the rightness of the moral dictate. Man is to live by every word from God—without consideration of the time when it was revealed. There is nothing new about the heinousness of murder as soon as the flood water subsided; Cain innately recognized and feared the law of retribution, and the flood itself was evidence of God's hatred for violence. Moreover, the detailing of the penal sanction against murderers took place at no more epochal a time than the coming of the law at Sinai—when Israel had been called out as a nation, at the beginning of the prophets, priests, and kings, at the time of entrance to the promised land, during a time replete with redemptive typology of Christ and His saving economy, and so forth.[18] If one is to pay attention today to laws which came at the beginning of significant epochs in salvation history how could he ignore the Mosaic legislation? But if one does not want to limit recognition of divinely valid moral prescriptions to the Noahic

---

[17] Hengstenberg, *op. cit.*, pp. 314-315.

[18] Although I do not find it in Murray, some might argue against the Mosaic laws being applicable today since they, as reflecting God's redemptive kingdom at the *consummation,* are a special case in history and not normative (e.g., an "intrusion" ethic). Yet in terms of typology how could one dismiss the image of a "new heavens and earth" after God's great judgment which we find in the account of Noah and the flood? On such a (extra-biblical) typological basis one would have to give up the penal sanction against murder just as surely as against anything else.

covenant altogether, then the Mosaic commandments (with their divinely valid moral prescriptions to judges and magistrates) should be recognized as binding today—just as the law given to Noah. I submit that *any legitimate principle* which is used to endorse the Mosaic law today will endorse *its penal injunctions at the same time.* Contrawise, any principle (aside from question-begging) used to *eliminate* the Mosaic *penal* sanctions will *also* cover the *other* commandments. God's moral law is a garment without seams.

Murray suggests that murder has a unique character and gravity about it since it is a violation of the summary command to love and is irremediable. However, *all* sins are violations of the commandment to love (1 John 5:2-3; Rom. 13: 8-10). And besides being extra-scriptural (just like many of the preceding considerations) the consideration of irremediability is in fact not unique, for pregnation by rape is also irremediable (unless sinful abortion is condoned).

John Murray's argument, then, began with an illegitimate argument from silence—an argument he rejects elsewhere, and an argument which cancels the death penalty for murder as much as it cancels it for adultery, and so forth. Then for the sake of argument we granted his (unsupported) repeal of capital punishment in general for the New Testament and turned to see whether Murray could salvage the death penalty for murder in the New Testament. It was then noted that his discrimination of the Noahic covenant from the Mosaic was, with respect to the argument at hand, not legitimate. Moreover, even *if* it were legitimate, the exegesis Murray needs to get out of Genesis 9 in order to make his point is not the strongest exegesis (as shown earlier in the chapter).[19] Then it was noted that consistency would demand that Murray limit all morality to the pre-Mosaic, Noahic covenant (which he will not do). Also, Romans 13 (which is needed to have New Testament endorsement of capital punishment) is clearly not being governed exclusively by the principles of Genesis 9. And then, finally,

[19] And even *if* otherwise, the exegesis is *surely not strong enough* to bear the enormous weight of justifying an abrogation of God's authoritative commands. A much less ambiguous appeal is needed for that (e.g., Heb. 6:19-7:28).

Murray's extra-scriptural arguments for the uniqueness of murder were found to be unconvincing. Therefore, we have yet to find a legitimate argument against the *confirmation* (cf. Matt. 5:17-19) of the penal sanctions of God's law as applying to the New Testament era.

The Justice of Every Stroke of God's Penal Code

Because all sin is defined by God, all sin must receive the punishments assigned by God, for *this* Judge will certainly do right. A smorgasbord approach to penology is just as wrong as personal selectivity in one's personal obedience to God's commandments. Thus, we should accept God's direction with respect to crime in order that our earthly magistrates maintain genuine justice and righteousness in society; otherwise, whether we want to be or not, we are afloat in a sea of autonomy. If the magistrate is to have direction from God, if the magistrate is to be limited in what he can legitimately do, and if there is to be any court of appeal above the magistrate to which the Christian can plead against abuse, then the magistrate should be seen as bound by the law of God and obligated to enforce it.

That there is no cancellation of the death sentence for those crimes which are specified in the Older Testament is indicated in Acts 25:7-11. In harmony with the implication of Matthew 5:17-19, Paul's words have the effect of showing that there are a *plurality* of crimes (vv. 7, 9, 11) for which the death penalty is valid in the New Testament age—crimes as prohibited in the Jewish law (vv. 8, 10, 11). Paul declared that he refused not to die if he were guilty of any of the capital accusations against him, thus recognizing the sanctity of God's penal law. In verse 11 Paul demonstrates to us that the death penalty is still a proper penalty as demanded by God's justice; the state, as Paul indicates, had the authorization to execute him if he had violated any of the commandments warranting capital punishment of which the Jews had accused him—and he *demanded* to be executed if he had. If this standard of judgment held in Paul's case, then it holds for everyone (since God is no respector of persons: Rom. 2:11; 10:12 cf. 2:9; Eph. 6:9; 1 Tim. 5: 20-21; "He who does wrong will receive the consequence of the wrong which he has done, and that without partiality" [Col. 3:25, NASV]). If the death penalty had been abrogated for all but one capital crime in the Older Testament, then Paul was either not aware of that fact or unwilling to take a stand for it—and Matthew 5:17-19 needs to be qualified by God's word elsewhere in order that we be not misled. One would certainly think that "every jot and tittle" covers the numerous penal laws of the Older Testament just as it covers all else.

> But, says the critic, did not Christ set aside this barbarous code in the sermon on the mount? By no means. He did set aside the doctrine and practice of private revenges as taught by the Pharisees, but he nowhere interfered with or even criticized the due processes of law as set up by himself at Mt. Sinai, and as administered by himself as Theocratic King and supreme judge for fifteen hundred years.[20]

Therefore, if rulers are to follow the whole law of God as they are responsible to do, then they must execute the punishments God has prescribed. In this way the law of God can act as a restraining force on the unrighteousness of society. As we have seen from Scripture it is the clear duty of civil magistrates to duly enforce this law—not with their own estimates of proper penology, but with God's true and proper judgments. Then every crime will receive its perfectly equitable recompense; the magistrate, as God's minister for avenging wrath against evildoers, does not have the right to enforce *any other* but *a just penalty.*

> Valid law is always divine Law; it is expression of the righteousness of God. The authority of the law does not derive from the political authority, or from "reason" or "nature," but from God Himself. Furthermore, as we noted above, political authority has been created for the sake of civil righteousness, i.e. for the sake of the law. Because of the

[20] Shearer, *op. cit.*, p. 138.

righteousness of God authority has been ordained. Thus political authority does not determine the nature of right and wrong, as positivism would have it, but as we indicated above, its relation to right and wrong determines the validity of political authority. . . .

But what is this Law of which "political authority" is a part and which it is called upon to enforce? It is the Law which the Jews received in the Ten Commandments and which God has written in the hearts of all men.[21]

---

[21] Forell, *op. cit.*, p. 48.

Chapter 22

SUMMATION

WE are now in a position to answer the question posed in the introduction to this section: ought the civil magistrate to obey and enforce the law of God as found in the Older Testament (particularly the penal sanctions)?

It has been observed that every detail of the law of God as it was revealed in the Older Testament has abiding validity today, for Christ has confirmed that law in exhaustive detail for the age between His advents (Matt. 5:17-19).

It has also been observed that the doctrine of the state or civil magistrate is uniform throughout Scripture. What Paul says of rulers in Romans 13:1-7 is a confirmation of the Older Testament outlook on civil authority. Because God sovereignly appoints magistrates they are not to be resisted; bearing religious titles, the magistrates are God's vicegerents—sent to be avengers of His wrath. Their duty is to deter evil and promote the good. Therefore, they must rule according to God's law (and be subject to criticism or judgment when they do not) in order that God's wrath be expressed against those who genuinely do evil (i.e., violate the law of God).

Consequently the law for society today is the same as that in the Older Testament, and the officials of the state are responsible today, just as in ancient Israel, to enforce God's law.

For them to do so is not a violation of the principle of separation between church and state. That separation is seen to be, in both Older and New Testaments, a division as to function. The state is an agent of social justice, while the church is a propagator of God's grace to sinners for eternal salvation. However, while divided with respect to their goals and methods, church and state are both united under the single authority of God and His law. If this is what is meant by calling the nation of Israel in the Older Testament a "Theocracy," then the whole world during the age of gospel prosperity is conceived of as a "Christocracy" in Scripture.

Finally, in confirmation of what is implied in the foregoing observations, the civil magistrate is obligated to follow the penal sanctions of God's law, for those sanctions are neither arbitrary nor temporary. Reflecting the justice of God for inter-social relations, these sanctions set forth an equitable recompense for every crime forbidden in the law of God. Indeed, these sanctions are as much a part of the law as the other commandments found therein. The death penalty continues in full force during this age, and it applies to more than simply murder. The magistrate is under moral obligation, then, to apply death to those who transgress God's law at places where God requires the life of the criminal. While God will judge all sin with eternal damnation, He nevertheless requires justice in temporal society as well. Hence the magistrate's responsibility to follow the penal sanctions laid down by the Lord.

One must not get the false impression, however, that the foregoing study makes everything in civil government a simple matter or that finding out what the whole Bible has to say on any one particular law of God can be done without running into difficult questions of exegesis and application in the modern world. Indeed, there will even be problems in understanding whether a law is basically moral in character or restorative, and so forth. However, as Shearer has properly noted, "there is no problem so difficult that we cannot afford to wait for light, rather than impugning the 'wisdom, power, holiness, justice, goodness, and truth' of God."[1] While many specific questions need to be answered in particular situations, the *basic or fundamental principle of social morality and state responsibility* has been answered. The magistrate must

---

[1] J. B. Shearer, *Hebrew Institutions, Social and Civil* (Richmond: Presbyterian Committee of Publication, 1910), p. 147.

rule according to the law of God as revealed in Scripture. Our *categorical assumption must* be that of *continuity* with Older Testament morality.

Jacques Ellul has said that politics "is the sphere of the greatest affirmation of man's autonomy, of his revolt, of his pretentious attempt to play the role of God."[2] It is for this reason that the present thesis has a practical importance in the current world. The alternative to God's law is not *no law at all*, but *human* law; governments which do not guard the majesty of God and His righteous law have no alternative and choice but to uphold the majesty of their own human authority. When crime is not viewed as an offense against the moral order of God, it becomes viewed as an offense against the arbitrary power of the state. If no higher law is adhered to, then the law of man is absolute; there is no logical barrier to stop such a state from becoming totalitarian. When the state's will is substituted for God's will, then the only real crimes become crimes against the state (as in Imperial Rome, present day Russia, and much of the United States), for example, treason, defection, and so forth. Men die for resisting the absolute will of the state, then, and not for crimes against a holy God. There is no appeal beyond the state and its rulers when God's law is put aside; man has no realm of justice to which he has recourse in opposing the will of the state. Here we have the "beast" of Revelation who executes all those who will not worship his image or receive his sign; when God's law is made irrelevant to state government, then untrammeled human will comes to rule insanely where God's will ought to be followed. For Christians the choice is between a law order based on God or the potentially tyrannical oppression of a law order resting in the arbitrary will and power of the secular state. Although we must insist on a proper separation of church and state, we must insist that both be subject to God's holy and authoritative law; both church and state, as well as the home, should be under the sovereign domain of God. Civil government must enforce God's law, the whole of that law, and rest its authority thereupon. Christ said that every stroke of the Older Testamental

---

[2] Jacques Ellul, *The Politics of God and the Poetics of Man,* tr. and ed. Geoffrey W. Bromiley (Grand Rapids: Eerdmans Publishing Co., 1972), p. 14.

law remains in force for the New Testament era; that includes the stipulations having social and penal relevance.

Man's fallen nature, his spiritual depravity, makes civil government a necessity; it is through the agency of the state that God restrains human evil to some measure. The magistrate must dignify the good and deter the evil if he would properly carry out his God-ordained function. But how is the ruler to know what is good and what is evil? What standard does he have for righteousness? The ruler who does his proper duty must have authoritative direction from God in order that he deter those activities which are actually unrighteous and promote those which are truly godly. That direction is found in God's revealed law. Therefore, the biblical Christian must hold to the *theonomic responsibility of the civil magistrate.*

J. B. Shearer provides an apt summary: "governments are good or bad according as they approximate or diverge from the 'Pattern showed in the Mount.' "[3] Whether one looks to Mount Sinai or to the sermon on the Mount, the criterion of good government is the same: obedience to, and enforcement of, the law of God.

[3] Shearer, *op. cit.,* p. 64.

VIII. INDIFFERENCE TO THE THESIS DISPELLED

Chapter 23

OUR DUTY TO PROMOTE OBEDIENCE

THE Christian's ethical responsibility to the law of his God extends beyond the simple personal observation of those stipulations. More than just obeying God's commandments personally, the Christian is expected to promote the keeping of God's law (and every detail thereof). The person who loves and obeys the Lord cannot indifferently tolerate the breaking or ignoring of God's law on the part of others. It is clear from Scripture that corporate responsibility and punishment applies in the area of ethics; we see this in the case of Adam's fall into sin (Rom. 5:12-19), in the case of Abimelech (Gen. 20:7), Achan (Josh. 7:1, 10), and David's census (2 Sam. 24:17). The law itself indicates that God deals with respect to corporate guilt (e.g., Ex. 20: 5). The Israelites were accountable for their own city's obedience to the law as well as the punishment of disobedient cities (Deut. 13:12-16). If a God-fearing Jew found or heard of any person committing detestable evil in violation of God's covenant, he was responsible to search out the matter thoroughly, seek out the offender, and bring him or her to the city gates (i.e., law court) in order that they be executed (Deut. 17:2-5). In fact, so important is the principle of corporate responsibility that when a dead body was found in the open country, the elders of the nearest city had to verify that they had neither *seen* nor done the crime before they are accounted as innocent (Deut. 21:1-9). The Christian must take it upon himself to encourage, exhort, and demand obedience to God's holy standards of morality in home, church, society, place of employment, and nation; otherwise these institutions or groups will be progressively degraded by sinful rebellion against God and His law. The Christian shares responsibility not only for promoting obedience to God's law but also for its enforcement. If the punishments attaching to God's laws do not follow their infraction, then in reality there is *no law* on the social level at all! To maintain that punishment for crimes against the law of God as it applies to public morality will come only in the eschaton is: (1) simply to gloss over the law of God as Scripture presents it (for many infractions have social penalties to be imposed in this life), (2) to relegate God's moral concern for righteousness to the unseen future, and (3) to abandon this present world and human society to antinomian anarchy in pious vindictiveness. It is true that a murderer (for instance) will suffer the second death, but it is likewise true that God's law stipulates that he shall suffer the first death by induction thereunto in order to preserve righteousness in human affairs.

Believers must exhort their neighbors to know God through His Christ and to follow His ethical direction, showing what benefits flow from such behavior. They must also exhort governmental officials to enforce God's righteous law by imposing divinely prescribed punishments upon violators of God's law. One of the accusations from God against His people which is depicted of the final judgment is found in Psalm 50:18, "When thou sawest a thief, then thou consentedst with him," and the implication of verse 21 following is that this consent resides in their *keeping silent.* Failure to reprimand the thief or to report his crime to the magistrate results in the witness being as guilty as the criminal; by not promoting God's law, he broke it. The biting indictment of Luke upon Saul is unmistakable in that brief clause referring to the time when Stephen was stoned to death: "Saul was consenting" (Acts 8:1). As a witness to a crime, the believer is publicly responsible for the arrest, prosecution, and testimony against the violator of God's law. Corporate responsibility is typified in that the law requires that everyone in a city take part in the stoning of a criminal; in this way they take responsibility and a direct hand in the execution of criminals according to God's demands. If the Christian does not urge the *full* keeping of God's commandments he becomes a consenter to the crimes which are allowed to follow. The believer must have hot indignation and loathing for those who break God's law (Ps. 119:53); the unjust man must be abominable in the sight of the righteous (Prov. 29:27).

Psalm 139:21 gives us the example of David's proper attitude of hating those wicked men who hate His Lord and God; Psalm 97:10 commands those who love the Lord to hate evil (i.e., to reverence the Lord, Prov. 8:13). Then they will not be ashamed, as the Psalmist was not, to promote God's law publicly (Ps. 119:13).

> The least of God's commandments, if they bind us, bind others. We must resist the virulent poison of individualism which tolerates in others the indifference and disobedience which we cannot justify in ourselves, just as we must resist the tendency to tolerate in ourselves the disobedience which we condemn in others. The moment we become complacent to the sins of others then we have begun to relax our own grip on the sanctity of the commandments of God, and we are also on the way to condoning the same sin in ourselves.[1]

All Christians must do whatever they can to facilitate the keeping of God's law in his society. If the believer simply accepts the antinomian situation surrounding him without any recourse, he has willingly subordinated himself to the Satanic power and direction of that environment. "Restore unto me the joy of thy salvation, and uphold me with thy free spirit. *Then will I teach transgressors thy ways,* and sinners shall be converted unto thee" (Ps. 51:13, AV).

It is quite clear that if the Christian is not exhorting others to obey the law of God and promoting such obedience in every way he can, then he is not fulfilling the Great Commission delivered to him by His Lord and Saviour: "Therefore, having gone, disciple the nations. . . *teaching them to keep everything I commanded you*" (Matt. 28:19 f.). This charge is given on the basis of the authority of Jesus Christ and in recognition of His powerful presence; the church is assured of victory on these terms (cf. Rev. 19). Christians are to make disciples for Christ; such

---

[1] John Murray, *Principles of Conduct: Aspects of Biblical Ethics* (Grand Rapids: William B. Eerdmans Publishing Co., 1957), p. 154.

disciples will place their saving trust in Jesus Christ and endeavor to live in obedience to His word. This is what the Christian must aim for and be diligent in prayer about. The restoration of man and his civilization is not to be accomplished by antagonism or indifference to God's laws but by a return to covenantal obedience in terms of the biblical law. In accord with Christ's Great Commission, believers must teach the observance of God's law; evangelism does not end with repentance and faith on the part of the hearer, but it extends into obedience to the commandments of the Lord.

Ephesians 5:11 commands the believer to *reprove* the unfruitful works of darkness. No Christian can be silent in the face of violation against God's law and the ungodly direction of his society. The responsibility of rebuking sin (based upon the prior rebuking of sin in one's own life—Matt. 7:1-4) is repeated over and over again in the New Testament. We are to rebuke a *trespassing* brother (Luke 17:3), and those who *sin* (1 Tim. 5:20); ungodliness is to be authoritatively reproved (Titus 2:14; cf. 2 Tim. 4:2). Men must be urged to obey God's moral direction, to submit to the covenantal theonomic ethic. Such a reproof is actually a sign of kindness and a blessing to the one reproved (Ps. 141:5); it should be highly valued (Prov. 25:12) and gladly accepted (Prov. 10:17; 12:1; 15:5; 29:1; Eccl. 7:5; Heb. 12:5). However, even when their theonomic exhortations are not joyfully received, believers must be steadfast against the sinful behavior. When their witness has been silenced, the society has been turned over to Satanic and antinomian sway. Christians must "warn them that are unruly" (1 Thess. 5:14), for although others are not, *they are* "able to admonish" (Rom. 15:14), being filled with all knowledge. Only the man who has submitted to the moral standards of God's word is in a position to give genuinely sound exhortation in ethical matters. The law of God is the authoritative foundation and substance of biblical counseling; with it the Christian can offer concrete direction to men having personal problems due to moral dilemmas, and with it the believer has the right to rebuke all ungodliness in behavior. The law of God and its promotion also offers an answer to the current social-political irrelevance of the orthodox churches of Christ; rather than choosing between pietistic withdrawal from social issues or public morality and the politicized gospel (which is no gospel at all) of the revolutionary liberals, the true church of Christ can have a solidly beneficial and truly significant influence on social and political matters by exhorting society and national leaders as well as all individual citizens to obey the righteous law of God. Then health can return to a torn and troubled nation.

With a view toward their corporate responsibility, Christ's Great Commission, and the sanctification of individuals as well as nations, all genuine believers in Jesus Christ must demonstrate their love to Him by obeying and promoting obedience to His law, every jot and tittle of the Older Testamental commandments as well as every New Testament ethical exhortation.

And though this world with devils filled,
Should threaten to undo us,
We will not fear, for God has willed
His truth to triumph through us,
The prince of darkness grim,
We tremble not for him;
His rage we can endure,
For lo! his doom is sure;
One little word shall fell him.

(Martin Luther, "A Mighty Fortress is our God," stanza 3)

Chapter 24

THE BLESSEDNESS OF THE LAW AND THE BLESSING OF OBEDIENCE

CONTRARY to contemporary opinion, the Lord's commandments are neither burdensome (1 John 5:3) nor too difficult (Deut. 30:11). In fact, a consideration of how the Scriptures extol the law of God and exult in it is enough to prove that one should obey it—even if it were not the case that obedience had already been demanded. The law is of great value in the esteem of Christ's disciple. The commandments were originally ordained for *life* (Rom. 7:10); the law *is* our life (Deut. 32:47), for obedience to it leads to life and well-being (Deut. 30:15, 19 f.). The law was delivered for the *good* of God's people (Deut. 10:13; cf. 6:24). "How blessed are those whose way is blameless, who walk in the law of the Lord. How blessed are those who observe His testimonies, who seek Him with all their heart" (Ps. 119:1 f., NASV). The one who walks in the Lord's ways and reveres Him is highly blessed (Ps. 128:1); "Blessed is the man whom Thou dost chasten, O Lord, and dost teach out of Thy law" (Ps. 94:12, NASV). Psalm 112 also declares that the man who fears the Lord and greatly delights in His law is blessed (v. 1); his descendants are mighty in the land (v. 2; cf. Ps. 128), it is well with him (v. 5), he is not moved (v. 6), and he is not troubled with fear, for his heart is strong in the Lord (v. 7; cf. Prov. 1:33). *Paul's* deepest delight was in the law of God (Rom. 7:22); the law is also the delight of the *Messiah* (Heb. 10:7). The delight of the *righteous man* is in God's law (Ps. 1:2), and he is blessed for that (Ps. 1:1). According to the first Psalm, that man is blessed who does not adopt the principles or practice of the wrongdoer, or associate with wicked, ungodly sinners; by contrast "his delight is in the law of the Lord, and in His law he meditates day and night" (v. 2). The wicked will perish while the righteous prospers. The Psalmist expressly declares that God's law is his *"delight"* at least nine times in the 119th Psalm (vv. 14, 16, 24, 35, 47, 70, 77, 92, 143); according to the inspired writer, God's law is *wondrous* (Ps. 119:18), the basis for both *hope* (Ps. 119:43, 49, 114) and *comfort* (Ps. 119:50, 52; cf. Ps. 23:4). The Psalmist exults in *revival* in, according to, and unto obedience to the law of God (Ps. 119:25, 37, 40, 50, 88, 93, 107, 149, 156). God's statutes are his song (Ps. 119:54; 51:14), are sweet to his taste (Ps. 119:103), and are the joy of his heart (Ps. 119:111).

Righteousness guards those whose ways are blameless (Prov. 13:6), and the law of God prevents the believer from perishing in his affliction (Ps. 119:92). Hence to *do* the Lord's sayings is to be founded upon the *rock* (Luke 6:46-48; cf. Matt. 5:17 f.). Speaking of the righteous man, Psalm 37: 31 says, "The law of his God is in his heart; his steps do not slip" (NASV). The work of righteousness produces peace and security (Isa. 32:17; cf. Ps. 85:5). "Those who love Thy law have great peace, and nothing causes them to stumble" (Ps. 119:165, NASV). The law is the basis for *strengthening* (Ps. 119:28), *help* (Ps. 119:175), *understanding and wisdom* (Ps. 119:98-100, 104). So while disobedience to God's law leads to great remorse and crying (Ps. 119:136), he who pursues righteousness finds life, uprightness, and honor (Prov. 21:21). Obedience to, and reception of, the law of God results in divine mercy, compassion, and love (Deut. 13:17 f.; 33:2-4). The Lord's *lovingkindness* is upon those who obey His precepts (Ps. 103:17 f.), and the Lord does good to those who are upright in their hearts (Ps. 125:4). When we have respect for all of God's commandments, then we will have no cause for shame (Ps. 119:6); hence we should call upon God to teach us His ordinances (Ps. 119:108). We should follow the example of the Psalmist and firmly resolve to obey the Lord's law (Ps. 119:44, 109 f.)—even amidst sorrow and persecution. The law of God is very pure and more highly valuable than the finest gold (Ps. 119:127, 140). Therefore, the servant of God should *love* it and *meditate* upon it (Ps. 119:47, 48, 78, 97, 113, 127, 140, 159, 167). God should be *praised* for His righteous law and for teaching it to man; even seven times a day we could extol and thank Him for His commandments (Ps. 119:164, 171).

To use the works of the law as a means of self-justification is to be yoked to the slave principle (Gal. 4:21-31); Christ has liberated us from such subservience to the law by saving us in grace (Gal. 5:1). Having redeemed us from the curse of the law, Christ gives us the freedom we need: ethical ability to keep God's law in grateful love to Him—not the commonly urged type of "freedom" which turns God's grace into licentiousness (Jude 4). Christ sends His Spirit to regenerate our hearts and empower our obedience to God's will as expressed in the law. Where the Spirit of the Lord is, there is true liberty (2 Cor. 3:17) and progressive growth in holiness (Rom. 8:4). The Spirit does not bring liberty *from* the law but liberty *in* the law so that we can fulfill the royal law according to Scripture (James 2:8). The *law is* the pattern of true Christian *freedom* when it is used as a guide to sanctification; if a man is to please God and to live in harmony with the image of God within him, then he must be the "slave" of righteousness rather than the slave of sin. The freedom of Christian righteousness is found in the law. James calls God's commandments "*the perfect law of liberty*" (James 2:25); this coincides with the inspired words of the Psalmist: "The law of the Lord is perfect, restoring the soul" (Ps. 19:7); "*I will walk at liberty, for I seek Thy precepts*" (Ps. 119:45, NASV). Under the New Covenant God grants believers living power to walk in His law (Jer. 31:33), for true Christian freedom is found in service to God's holy will. "The man who looks into the perfect law of freedom and abides by it, not becoming a forgetful hearer but an effectual doer, this man is blessed in his doing" (James 1:25).

> Christian freedom therefore means freedom from the condemnation and death which the law works without Christ. It means acquittal from God's judgment; it means, even here and now, a good and sanctified conscience. It means, moreover, the freedom, the possibility, to live with the aid of the Spirit in agreement with God's demands as expressed in the law. It is the freedom, moral freedom, to do what God requires. There can be no greater error than using Paul for an

> appeal to the autonomy of Kant . . . Christ, the Spirit, and love form a unity in Paul, and therefore Christ, the Spirit and the fulfillment of the law are not to be separated.[1]

When we come to view the law as do the inspired writers of Scripture, we will treasure it and revere it as they do, rather than reacting in adversion like so many individuals do today. When we see that the law of God is wondrous, pure, sweet and golden, that God's commandments are accompanied with genuine life and divine lovingkindness, that the statutes of the Lord are the source of good, blessedness, stability, peace, understanding, comfort, strength, honor, hope, integrity, protection, great delight, and true freedom, then we will appropriately respond to the law with joyous song, meditation, love, praise and dedication. This must be the outlook of one who has been saved by God's sovereign grace. When such an evaluation is held of the law, when such an esteem is felt for it, then one can understand and emulate the Psalmist's overwhelming desire for the law of God. In Psalm 119 alone we read that his soul is crushed with longing for God's ordinances (v. 20); he longs for God's precepts, even with panting! (vv. 40, 131). He beseeches the Lord not to hide the commandments from him (v. 19), but rather to teach the law to him and make him understand it (vv. 26 f., 33 f., 73, 124, 135). The Psalmist resolves, promises and swears to keep God's law and righteous ordinances continually (vv. 44, 57, 106). He is steadfast in his determination not to turn aside from God's law even in the face of arrogant derision and assault (vv. 51, 78, 87, 157). His prayer is, "Make me walk in the path of Thy commandments, for I delight in it" (v. 35, NASV). Such should be the Christian's attitude as well.

The law itself is blessed, and obedience to it brings great blessing for that people who honor God by heeding His commandments. When the law is ignored by a nation, then justice is perverted and wickedness

---

[1] Herman N. Ridderbos, *When the Time Had Fully Come: Studies in New Testament Theology* (Grand Rapids: William B. Eerdmans Publishing Co., 1957), p. 76.

abounds (Hab. 1:4). By contrast, an abundant, prosperous and holy people is the goal of a God-directed state (cf. Prov. 14:28-35). "Righteousness exalts a nation, but sin is a reproach to any people" (Prov. 14:34). A king can give his land stability by administering justice (Prov. 29:4), for the effects of righteousness are peace and assurance (Isa. 32:17; cf. Ps. 37:30-37). There are great national blessings for that society which follows the moral directives of God; however, the alternative is not indifference but disobedience. A nation will receive a blessing *or* curse from God's law based on their obedience or disobedience thereof (Deut. 11:26 ff.). The book of the law is emphatic that the Lord will greatly bless a nation for careful obedience to all His commandments (Deut. 15:4 f.). If a nation will respond properly to God's prescriptive will, then the law will not bring death, evil and a curse upon them, but rather it will promote their life, blessing and good (Deut. 30:15, 19). If a nation keeps the commandments and statutes of God, He will love them, bless them, and multiply their children, crops, and herds; furthermore there will be no barrenness or sickness among them (Deut. 7:12-15). The nation which hearkens to God's commands will be prospered with rain, crops, grass, and fatted cattle (Deut. 11:13-15). If the nation obeys all of God's law it will be exalted with blessed cities, fields, children, crops, herds, rain, labor and economy (Deut. 28:1 ff.). If the nation hearkens to God's commandments and statutes in the book of the law with their whole heart God will bless their labor, procreation, crops, and herds (Deut. 30:6-10). If a nation will walk in God's law, then it will have rain, abundant crops, plenty of food, peace, no warfare, no ravaging beasts, fruitful multiplication, and—most blessed of all—the *Lord will be their God* (Lev. 26:3-13). See also Psalm 112 for indications of the prosperity of one who fears God and keeps His commandments. Certainly we must concur with Moses when he says that the law of God was given for the people's *good* (Deut. 10:13; cf. 6:24).

Quite obviously the conditions promised to a nation which obeys God's law sound very much like heaven itself (paradise regained!), and indeed they shall only be perfectly fulfilled in that new heavens and earth which will come in the eschaton. But the fact that heavenly conditions can prevail in a nation where God is obeyed should certainly not discourage or dissuade one from looking for the realization of God's promises in this life to a great extent. God is faithful to His word and will abundantly bless that nation which honors Him and His law. To refuse to be blessed by God, saying, "No! there will be no such blessing before we reach heaven!" is manifestly absurd; it represents pessimistic recalcitrance. Why should a people refuse to be blessed? Why should they so refuse especially since God's word promises a full blossoming of gospel prosperity and blessing before the return of our Lord? (e.g., Num. 14:21; Ps. 2:8; 22:27; 47:2-8; 72:7-11, 17; 86:9; 110:1; Isa. 2:2 f.; 11:9; 35:1; 45:22; 65:20; Jer. 31:34; Ezek. 47:1-5; Dan. 2:35, 44; Zech. 9:10; Matt. 6:33; 13:33; 28:18-20; Rev. 19). The believer cannot hold that God will bless obedience to His word *only* in a coming heaven. "Godliness is profitable for all things, since it holds promise for the present life and also for the life to come" (1 Tim. 4:8). Although full realization of God's gracious blessings will come only in heaven (just as perfect obedience to Him will come only at that time), and although a nation's obedience to God's law cannot set up heaven on earth, nevertheless we are instructed by Christ our Lord to pray, "Thy kingdom come; Thy will be done *on earth as it is in heaven*" (Matt. 6:10). To some degree the blessings which accrue to a nation which obeys God's law are a foretaste of the heavenly kingdom. Not only is God's law blessed *in itself,* obedience to its stipulations results in magnanimous blessing for its adherents as well. This law is in no way a burden to those who are graciously redeemed by Jesus Christ, for He is their Savior as well as their *Lord.*

Chapter 25

CONCLUSION

WE are now in a position to answer those initial questions which were raised in the introduction to this treatise and which provoked our investigation. The biblical Christian knows that society's crying demand for "love" as well as "law and order" is only satisfied in a genuine sense by the law of God. Christian love is guided by the Lord's commandments and thereby gives direction for man and society, and obedience to God's law is the supreme demonstration of love to both God and fellow man. The congregation of God's people, the disciples of Jesus Christ, are shown how to be the preservative agent in a wicked society ("the salt of the earth") by God's moral law; as sons of the Light, believers are themselves the light of the world, reproving the darkness of sin (i.e., lawlessness). The serious alternative which the church offers to a dying world is to turn in faith to Christ and keep His commandments; both elements are demanded by the Great Commission. As obedience to it is empowered by the Holy Spirit, the law of God establishes righteousness in human affairs and human hearts. The ethical dilemmas facing individuals and nations are resolved by the Christian, not by searching for answers based on his autonomous reason, but by going to the authoritative law of God; there alone are adequate answers found for the moral anarchy of his day. The lawless assumptions of humanistic man are countered by the theonomic direction of God's word. The written word of Christ does in fact offer the needed practical direction for establishing righteousness in interpersonal relations, imperatives to guide one in making ethical decisions, and concrete directions for producing a more decent world in which to live. Covenantal theonomy provides both the power and direction for a valid and beneficial ethic; biblical morality is both effectual and upright. The Holy Spirit grants the ability to follow the road map of divine law; His influence brings holiness into individual and corporate life in accordance with the commandments of God. The Holy Spirit inspired the writing of the law, regenerates the man who has died through violation of the law, and sanctifies that man unto new obedience to the law. God's inscripturated revelation, therefore, alone offers the moral direction which man needs; it is the necessary and sufficient rule for life.

The extent to which men must follow the law of God is exhaustive, but not exhausting; the Christian must observe even the minutial details of God's law, but the strength to do so is received from the Spirit of Christ. Having declared in Matthew 5 that His hearers are the salt of the earth and light of the world, Jesus immediately went on to confirm every jot and tittle of God's law. New Testament believers are responsible to keep the Older Testamental law, for it has abiding validity until the world passes away. Because abiding validity applies to even the smallest points of God's law. Hence civil magistrates *are* obligated to enact and enforce the ethical stipulations of social character from the Older Testament. Only then will the evil of a society be restrained and rectified; only then will divine blessing and moral integrity come to characterize that nation. The criterion of individual Christian discipleship is following the commandments of Christ, and those commandments are identical with the Older Testamental statutes of God. If the believer does not aim at full obedience to, and promotion of, the whole law of God as revealed in God's word, then he is unwise, and does not really know and love Christ. Christian disciples must be obedient to their Master, and that Master saves His friends in order that they glorify God in gratefully following His will. Antinomianism is inherently destructive of the Christian faith; it is the nature of sin (which is not to have dominion over the believer) to oppose God's law—any part of it. Genuine Christian living is defined by God's word, and that word contains authoritative prescriptions for moral behavior; the man who disregards those commandments is (in terms of scriptural logic) by definition not a follower of Christ. The Christian's attitude toward the Older Testamental law should coincide with that of his Lord; Christ honored and defended the validity of God's righteous commandments.

Man-centered and autonomous morality must be shunned as abhorrent by the disciple of Christ; he must strive to conform to every detail of the theonomic ethic—only then will holiness come to characterize individual Christians and their societies (like leaven in the lump). The controlling norm of Christian ethics is the whole law of God as revealed in Scripture: nothing more and nothing less. The alternative is moral anarchy or humanistic totalitarianism. The only valid and genuine ethic is the biblical one; individualism and moral tolerance are alien to the ethical paradigm of the Christian faith. Just as autonomous reason has produced the collapse of Western thought, even so autonomous moral philosophy has brought about the death of personal and social ethics; the answer in both cases is the same: *sola scriptura!*

The declaration of Christ in Matthew 5:17 f. is that He confirms every jot and tittle of the Older Testamental law; the criterion, then, of standing within the kingdom is the doing and teaching of that law. However, the legalism of the Pharisees is in reality antinomian; they misuse and distort the law of God so that they have no affinity with the kingdom of God. The law is abused when man tries to justify himself thereby; the law simply does not have the ability to enable the obedience it demands. Consequently, before a man's regeneration the law is a dead letter of condemnation written on exterior tablets of stone.

Yet the Scriptures uphold the absolute integrity of the law. Man's spiritual death is due to his own sinfulness and not to God's holy law. The law is the transcript of God's righteousness; and thus the standard of human holiness after the likeness of God. The obedience of the Messiah to this law is integral to atonement; those who have been atoned should imitate His righteous behavior. The Holy Spirit enables us to be conformed to the holiness of our Savior and Lord by sanctifying us according to the inscripturated law of God. The promise of the New Covenant is that the Older Testamental law would be inscribed on the heart of the believer. The theonomy of the Older Covenant differs from that of the New Covenant, not in material content, but only in the power granted to obey God's law.

Even the ceremonial law is confirmed, being typological of Christ and His saving economy; however, the older ways of observing the ritual law have been put out of gear by the appearance of the reality which they foreshadowed. The person who opposes theonomic ethics has a great deal more to justify and explain in the teaching of Scripture than one who adheres to God's law exhaustively; given the above principles, all passages which seem to disparage God's law are really negative to it in appearance only. The biblical concepts of grace, faith, and love ratify the believer's responsibility to God's commandments rather than loosening the law's hold in any way.

The theonomic ethic is substantiated in multiple ways throughout the pages of the New Testament. The law of God is scripturally described as having numerous functions, prominent among which is that of giving ethical direction for believers.

All autonomous attempts to establish an ethical system have looked to man's moral consciousness (as if it functioned normally and normatively) rather than to God's revelation for authority and direction; the inevitable result has been their utter failure to answer the questions of normative ethics and metaethics, while covenantal theonomy is adequate to the task. The error of subtle antinomianism is, at root, autonomy; it presumes to take a smorgasbord approach to God's revealed ethical system.

All men are held responsible by God to obey *all* of His law in every area of their lives. Even *Gentile* magistrates living outside Canaan in the *post*-Older Testamental period are obligated to conform to God's righteous standard of morality! The magistrate's duty as uniformly taught in both Testaments is to enact and enforce the law of God as it pertains to social affairs; his duty also extends to God's penal demands, even that of capital punishment. All rulers of the earth are subject to the law of God, for Christ is the King over kings. Christians are commanded to obey their magistrates but not therein to violate God's law. Scripture indicates that rulers will be liable to God's sure judgment if they do not justly rule according to the perfect law of God. God's concern for holiness extends to society; hence there are appropriate punishments attached to violations of the commandments from God applying to public morality. The magistrate, and he alone, is to execute these punishments of God. Those who are subsequently subject to capital punishment are executed because they have committed a crime warranting such a stringent penalty. That such is done is consistent with the separation of church and state.

All Christians share corporate responsibility for the righteousness of their society and are expected to obey Christ's Great Commission. Therefore, they must rebuke all offenses against God's law and promote obedience to the same. That law is highly valued in Scripture and should be similarly esteemed by Christ's disciples. Obedience to it produces personal holiness and social uprightness, not to mention prosperity and noteworthy blessing from God upon the obedient nation. The responsibility men have to God's law is solemn, unquestionable, and all-encompassing; the blessing of obedience to it is resplendent and broad, far surpassing human expectations.

The benefits of having a society which endeavors to observe all the commandments of God can only be properly appreciated when one becomes thoroughly familiar with the Lord's law. Even beginning this long process soon fills one with the excitement of knowing the good gifts delivered by our loving Father—including His law. The law is the pattern of sanctification for individuals; it protects their rights even amidst the stability of a godly and lawful state which observes the commandments of God. When this is not the case due to rebellion, then a state or individual is headed for ruin. "Where there is no vision the people perish; but he that keepeth the law, happy is he" (Prov. 29:18, AV). Christians have a vision and ideal set before them by Christ's Great Commission and confirmation of the exhaustive details of God's law; by actively keeping God's law and promoting such obedience in the world the reward of life is ours and our society's—"He that feareth the commandment shall be rewarded. The law of the wise is a fountain of life, to depart from the snares of death" (Prov. 13:13 f., AV). By stark contrast, those who despise God's rightful rule over them are committed to the ways of death; "All they that hate me love death"

(Prov. 8:36, AV). To attempt to build and sustain a social order, nation, home, or spiritual life apart from God is self-defeating and futile; "Except the Lord build the house, they labor in vain that build it" (Ps. 127:1, AV). "Be wise now therefore, O ye kings: be instructed ye judges of the earth. Serve the Lord with fear, and rejoice with trembling" (Ps. 2:10 f., AV). Hopefully as a result of studying the issues discussed in this treatise the reader can say, "I delight to do thy will, O my God: yea, thy law is within my heart" (Ps. 40:8, AV), and will pray, "Teach me, O Lord, the way of thy statutes; and I will keep it unto the end. Give me understanding, and I shall keep thy law; yea, I shall observe it with my whole heart. Make me to go in the path of thy commandments; for therein do I delight" (Ps. 119:33-35, AV). Whenever Christians face moral questions or consider matters of ethical import, these words of Christ should be ringing in their ears: "Think not that I came to abrogate the law or prophets; I did not come to abrogate *but* to *confirm* them. For truly I say to you, not one iota or one stroke of the law shall become invalid until heaven and earth pass away, until all things have passed" (Matt. 5:17 f.).

IX. APPENDICES

APPENDIX 1

AN EXEGETICAL STUDY OF GALATIANS 3:15-18

BECAUSE the apostle Paul acknowledged the unity of God's covenantal dealings throughout the Older Testamental period he could speak of the "covenants of the promise" (Eph. 2:12). Covenantal grace was central to all of God's administrations. There was one underlying promise which formed the core for all the diverse administrations of covenant relationship; God's purpose was not divided, His intentions were not dichotomized, as the modem day dispensationalist wants to maintain. Paul declared that "as many as are the promises of God, their affirmative is in Him (Jesus Christ)" (2 Cor. 1:20). Whatever promises God delivered to His people in the Older Testament all point to and center in the person and work of Jesus Christ. The covenantal promises of God are not distributed toward two ends, one spiritual, the other physical (as though God had special designs for ethnic Israel and Palestine, in and of themselves); every promise of God concerns His Messianic Son. We read of Paul's Christological analysis of the Davidic Covenant in Acts 13; his discussion of the Mosaic and New Covenants (and their relationship) is found in 1 Corinthians 3. In Galatians 3:15-18 the argument concerns the Abrahamic covenant and its relationship to the Mosaic administration; here again Paul's covenant theology is seen to be singularly Christocentric.

The fundamental concern of the book of Galatians is the gospel of justification by faith alone; it is this gospel which Paul was maintaining against the influence and teaching of the Judaizers who would place an unbearable yoke upon the neck of Christians (Acts 15:10) by requiring that faith be placed on equal footing with meritorious law-works, especially circumcision (Acts 15:5). Because Paul held that salvation was wrought only through the grace of Jesus Christ and that this salvation was intended for the Gentiles as much as for the Jews, the Judaizers would allege that Paul's gospel entailed God's abandonment of His people and the breaking of His covenant with them (cf. Rom. 9:6; 11:1-2); they would argue that if salvation is by faith alone, then what advantage has the Jew? But Paul responds as an accurate ecclesiastical lawyer that it is rather the Judaizers who fail to defend the fidelity of God by representing Him as going back on His promise. In the midst of his defense of his own apostleship Paul begins his structured polemic against the Judaizers by referring to his rebuke of Peter for withdrawing from the Gentiles; this transition is effected in the second chapter of Galatians, and the third chapter begins Paul's heaviest argumentative appeal to the Galatians. He first refers to their experience of faith (verses 1-5) and then declares its harmony with Scripture (verses 6-9); next Paul discusses the impotence of the law to secure God's promised salvation (verses 10-14). At this point, and before Paul's well-known discussion of bondage and freedom, Paul argues from the history of salvation and the law's relation to the promise that no one can make fulfillment of the promise dependent upon law-keeping.

Speaking to an imagined or real Judaizing opponent, Paul argues in Galatians 3:15-18 that the law would *not* have annulled any earlier arrangements made with Abraham due to *priority* of the Abrahamic covenant and the irrevocability of covenant arrangements; and if the law of Moses did not supplant or alter the promise-principle in the covenant with Abraham, then the principle of gracious promise and not that of meritorious law-works must still be in effect. If one does not see this, then the unconditional character of a promise would be violated and a covenant lawlessly altered. Paul's line of thought in Galatians 3:15-18 has significant ramifications for contemporary evangelical theology, in particular dispensational theology in its treatment of the validity of God's law in an age of grace (promise) and its anticipations with respect to the land promised to Abraham. With this brief introduction to the passage we turn to an analytic treatment of Galatians 3:15-18.

Paul begins with the vocative, ἀδελφοί which represents a change of mood from his designation "O foolish Galatians" in 3:1; though he may scold them, nevertheless he loves them and addresses them now as his fellow Christian brethren (for the use of this family designation as applied to fellow believers see 1 Cor. 5:11; 6:5-8; 8:12; 1 Thess. 1:4; 2:1; James 1:2; 1 Peter 5:12; 1 John 3:13; Rev. 12:10; also Clement of Rome 1:1; Ignatius, *Philad.,* 5:1). Whereas Paul had been dealing with the Judaizers in the preceding paragraph, he now addresses the Galatian Christians more directly. This same affectionate approach continues through the epistle (cf. Gal. 4:31; 6:1).

Κατά ἄνθρωπον λέγω uses a simple present tense and an accusative of general reference to indicate that Paul is going to indulge his readers with a human example. He will speak to them by means of an illustration from human life in order to make his readers understand him better. Κατὰ ἄνθρωπον after a verb regularly means "as men do." It was not uncommon for Paul to draw upon an aspect of law in common human affairs that would be familiar to laymen (e.g., Rom. 7:1-3), and in the passage under discussion Paul uses words common to Greek legal documents (e.g., κυρόω, ἀθετέω, ἐπιδιατάσσω). Although Paul is not here referring to simple human authority, κατὰ ἄνθρωπον can have this sense (e.g., 1 Cor. 9:8—a reference to Paul's apostolic authority and not direct verbal revelation spoken by the Lord Himself on some occasion); however, more commonly it means "in accordance with men and their ways" (cf. Rom. 6:19; 1 Cor. 3:3; 15:32; Gal. 1:11). This latter sense fits the circumstance of Galatians 3 better than does the former since Paul would not likely derogate the authority of his argument at such an important juncture in his argument with bitter opponents. What Paul is doing is laying the groundwork for an *a fortiori* argument. Since the state of affairs to which he will refer is in accord with the will and ordinance of God, Paul can make use of it to prove divine matters—his point being that God's sacred covenant should not receive less deference than is commonly yielded to ordinary human transactions.

῞Ομως gives Paul's consideration its *a fortiori* character, although some have been inclined to deny it. There are those who see Paul as saying that "when confirmed, no one *yet* disannuls a covenant"; others think Paul's thought is that *although* he speaks from a human standpoint, *yet* what is said is not without force. However, there is no good argument against taking ὅμως in trajection. The classical writers' displacement of this word often takes place so that it must (in translation) be put with a later word or phrase, especially when it occurs in a participial environment (which it does in Galatians 3:15). Those who have not endorsed this possibility have overlooked the unusual syntax which results from placing ἀνθρώπου up toward the head of the clause; "of man" is placed there in order to emphasize it. This fact fits in well with the *a fortiori* direction of Paul's argument as introduced by "I speak from a human standpoint." Hence Paul is emphasizing what is true in human affairs: "Even though it is a *human* covenant which has been ratified, no one sets it aside or adds to it." The implication would then be clear: *how much more* shall a *divine* covenant be irrevocable! The same treatment of ὅμως can and should be given to Paul's use of it in 1 Corinthians 14:7 (the only other passage in which Paul uses the word)—even lifeless things must give a distinct sound, so how much more the living preacher! Hence the adversative force of ὅμως should be maintained as it is found in the Authorized Version.

The argument which follows is based on what is true of a human covenant; once it is legally ratified men cannot annul or amplify it. The implication is that the immutable divine covenant also cannot be annulled or amplified (this is directly stated for those who miss the inference in verse 17). Jesus Himself had endorsed such *a fortiori* argumentation (e.g., Luke 11:13; 18:1; cf. Heb. 6:16). Josephus *(Antiquities* xvii, 9.4; *Jewish Wars* ii, 2.3) tells us that Herod the Great had more than one will, and hence his son Antipas was burdened with the decision as to which one was valid. God is not this kind of arbitrary human monarch; He does not have two plans of inheritance, and He does not alter His immutable promises. The Judaizers did not take their example from God, for while He is abidingly faithful, they will amazingly observe civil customs and punctiliously keep human promises but then violate God's covenant by altering it!

Διαθήκην, in accordance with Paul's consistent usage, means "covenant," not "testament or will." This word regularly translates *berith* in the Septuagint; it is selected over against the more readily available word, συνθήκη, in order to better express free grace and monergism. The covenant of God is not a two-sided agreement but a one-sided grant; this is clear throughout the various stages of covenantal development in the Older Testament. Though the covenant may involve the responsibility to certain stipulations, still these stipulations are not agreed upon by equal parties but decreed by God alone. The διαθήκη of the LXX, then, taught Paul of the special bond between God and man and the unconditional guarantee involved therein; his use of the word is quite in line with this background, but gives no evidence of being tied to the hellenistic concept of a last will and testament. Even if Galatians is addressed to those of general Gentile background, still it is addressed *against* the Judaizers who cannot be doubted to have a thorough acquaintance with the Older Testament. The hellenistic notion of a last will and testament was staked on the ideas of inheritance and death (of the testator); since Galatians 3 makes absolutely no mention of God's death (a notion we should expect that Paul would have gone to pains in explaining and making clear to his readers), we cannot see here "testament" as the translation for διαθήκη. Moreover, anyone can read into the background and character of Greek wills and will see that they were *not* considered irrevocable; yet the διαθήκη which Paul is speaking of in Galatians 3:15 is specifically said to be unalterable and inviolable. Furthermore, in verse 16 the word ἐπαγγελίαι ("promises") takes the place of διαθήκη of verse 15, which again favors the notion of a "covenant" (on the Older Testamental background) rather than "testament or will." Also verse 17 uses the word διαθήκη in a clear reference to "covenant" and not "testament." So local context would lead us to translate the word as "covenant" in verse 15. Finally, note should be made of the fact that the word διαθήκη never takes the translation of "testament" in the New Testament; it always means "covenant." This statement is not altered, contrary to common opinion, by the wording of Hebrews 9:16. Although the burden of this appendix is not to exegete this passage in Hebrews, it will be noted that: (1) the author of Hebrews never departs from the LXX rendition of Older Testamental quotations (hence always uses διαθήκη in the sense of "covenant"), (2) the word φέρω can be translated "bring in" (in which case "it is a necessity that the death of the testator be *brought in*"—i.e., brought into the picture, or *represented),* (3) the covenants of God in the Older Testament are uniformly bonds *in blood* (the issue of death is always entailed), and especially does the Abrahamic covenant include the self-maledictory oath of Yahweh (thus the death of the testator is brought into the picture), (4) the ἐπί of verse 17 in Hebrews 9 can only fit the idea of last will and testament if it is translated "after" (a sense which can only be imposed upon the word), but more legitimately means "upon, over"—a covenant made over dead bodies is firm (just as the Abrahamic covenant was made over the slain bodies of animals). Therefore, since Hebrews 9:16 should be translated as referring to "covenant," the uniform rendition of the entire New Testament for διαθήκη would be "covenant"—leaving the burden of proof upon those who want to take διεθήκη of Galatians 3:15 as "testament." For all of the above reasons, then, we translate this verse as making mention of a "covenant," not a last will and testament. A qualitative genitive, *ἀνθρώπου,* is attached to διαθήκη, thereby indicating that a *human* covenant is in view (rather than the idea of a testament *from a* man).

Κεκυρωμένην is an intensive perfect whose root is cognate to that of "previously ratified" in verse 17; the covenant in view in Paul's argument is said to be a past matter which is closed and established. He is not referring to the drafting of a covenant but to its actual execution, that is, to its actually being in force and thus not subject to modification. Κυρόω is a technical term meaning "confirm, ratify or validate"; it is found used as such in extrabiblical authors like Aeschylus, Herodotus, and Josephus, and it is applied to the ratification of a bargain (e.g., Gen. 23:20, LXX), a public measure (Thucydides viii.69), a peace treaty (Polyb. i.6) and more generally to laws. Paul says that such a covenant which is in the abiding state of ratification "no one sets aside or adds thereunto." These represent the two ways of superseding a covenant. Ἀθετεῖ is a gnomic present meaning to render something ἀθετός—without place or standing; thus it can mean "to reject or rebel" (e.g., Deut. 21:14; Isa. 1:2, LXX) or "to abrogate" (e.g., 1 Maccabees 11:36; 2 Maccabees 13:25, LXX). In Scripture the Pharisees are said "to set aside" God's commandment (Mark 7:9), "to reject" God's counsel (Luke 7:30). Just as "setting aside" one's first faith leads to damnation (1 Tim. 5:12), so also the "disregarding or nullifying" of Moses' law leads to death without mercy (Heb. 10:28). By refusing to hold that righteousness must be gained by the law, Paul declares that he does not "set aside" or "declare invalid" God's grace (Gal. 2:21). Thus we see by this brief background what Paul is getting at in Galatians 3:15 when he says that a ratified covenant is not "invalidated." With respect to such a covenant neither does one ἐπιδιατάσσεται, another gnomic present which is based upon a legal term nowhere else found in Scripture. Διατάσσω is frequently used to mean "to arrange or prescribe"; the compounded form, ἐπιδιατάσσω, then signifies "to make *additional*, further prescriptions." Not only can a ratified covenant not be set aside, it cannot be amplified without violating it. Thus the Judaizers are prohibited from viewing the Mosaic law as a superimposition or addition to the promise given unto Abraham; if it were such, the latter would be deprived of its due effect.

Paul now proceeds to apply the general observation he has made in verse 15. Before showing the binding character of God's promises (v. 17), Paul parenthetically makes clear just who the proper recipients are of those promises; he does this in order that the declaration of the inviolability of these promises can be more specific. As verse 16 declares, the promises were delivered to Abraham and to his seed, who is the Messiah. The covenant privilege of having Yahweh as one's God and being a part of His people, as well as blessing to the Gentiles, and even the promise of the land of Canaan, are all tied up with Jesus Christ and fulfilled in Him. The dispensationalist must see this. Just as Jacob's dream indicated, the promised land (from which he was about to depart) was not an end in itself, but was only the base for the ladder to heaven—it was a *means* to an end. Thus Paul can clearly see that even the promise of Palestine was made to Christ, and is fulfilled in the incarnation, obedience, death, resurrection, and economy of Jesus. The Christian inheritance is the living hope of heaven (1 Peter 1:3-4), not the sandy soil of Israel, an inheritance which is secured by the redemptive work of Jesus Christ (as 1 Peter says) and given its down-payment (in same kind) by the granting of the Holy Spirit unto us (Eph. 1:14). Because the promise was made to Christ and thereby He is heir of all things (e.g., Col. 1:12-18), we who are in union with Him are joint-heirs (Rom. 8:15-17). We are of the household of God, being the family of Christ—the true "seed" of Abraham says Paul in Galatians 3:7. The promises were made to Christ as *the* seed of Abraham, thus they accrue to us, Christ's brethren, as also Abraham's seed and heirs of the promise since we are Christ's (Gal. 3:29). Therefore, right from the start, the promises and their recipients did not coincide with fleshly Israel—a point which undercuts the whole outlook and circumcision requirement of the Judaizers!

Oὐ λέγει in verse 16 might refer to God or to Scripture as the subject of the speaking (cf. Rom. 15:10; Eph. 4:8; 5:14), but on any orthodox understanding of the nature of Scripture, this will not make any difference. "Scripture says" equals "God says." Probably Paul is using this phrase impersonally like the Attic form, φησί, which is often used in quoting legal documents (see also 1 Cor. 6:16; 2 Cor. 10:10). "It does not say" begins Paul's clarification of his point that the promises were made to Abraham and his seed. Paul makes the point that Scripture does not say the promises are for the "seeds" of Abraham, but only for his "Seed" (singular). Thus the "seed" referred to in the Older Testament is not ὡς ἐπὶ πολλῶν ("as concerning many") using an adverb of general reference and using ἐπί to introduce the object which is to be discussed or acted upon (cf. Jer. 35:8, LXX; 1 Esdras 1:22; John 6:2). This sort of construction is found only here in Scripture. Paul is not using a bit of rabbinical casuistry here at all. Although "seed" is a *collective* noun in both Hebrew and Greek (cf. Gen. 15:5; 16:10; 22:17; 46:6; 2 Kings 11:1; 2 Chron. 20:7; Mal. 2:15; Matt. 22:24; Rom. 4:18; Acts 7:6; 2 Cor. 11:22), the singular form can certainly also refer to one individual (cf. Gen. 4:25; 21:13; 1 Sam. 1:11; 2 Sam. 7:12; 1 Chron. 17:11; Gal. 3:19; Acts 3:25; Rom. 9:7-8; Heb. 11:18). Although the Hebrew plural for "seed" is never used in the Older Testament in referring to one's descendants, the Greek form, σπέρματα, *is* used for a plurality of descendants (e.g., Dan. 11:31), indeed we even read "τῶν 'Αβραμιαιῶν σπερμάτων" ("of Abraham's *seeds*") in 4 Maccabees 17:1. What Paul means then is that we should take note of the singular form of the noun which is used in the promise of Abraham; God did *not* refer to τὰ τέκνα or οἱ ἀπογονοί or even σπέρματα. Instead the promise is unto the singular seed of Abraham. Most commonly in Hebrew "seed" has reference to one's posterity, but by the time of the LXX the word had taken on the sense of a race, nation or group of people without distinct reference to their common ancestor (e.g., Prov. 11:18; Isa. 57:4; 65:25; Song 17:8, 11). The seed motif in the Older Testament expresses the positive values of salvation and blessing (e.g., Jer. 31:27). The Dead Sea community at Qumran seldom made use of the imagery at all. However the New Testament uses "seed" in the sense of "race, posterity" (Mark 12:20 ff.; John 7:42; 8:33; Rom. 1:3; 4:13), qualitatively for a single individual (2 Cor. 11: 22), and Paul always uses the word in the context of the descendants of Abraham, Isaac or David. What Paul is saying in Galatians 3:16 is that not all of Abraham's seeds (i.e., "families of descent") are granted the promises of the covenant. Indeed Paul is exegetically and historically correct; he is not straining after a point based on grammar alone. Abraham had to regard his "seed" which would be blessed of God as *one*—Isaac and not Ishmael. See Genesis 17:19-21; 21:12. Paul's distinction between the one and the many is objectively contained, then, in God's address to Abraham (cf. Rom. 9:7 for similar usage). Throughout the history of salvation we observe the narrowing of the promised covenantal line which shall be blessed; Isaac is chosen over Ishmael, Jacob over Esau, Judah over against the eleven, and so forth. The culmination of this narrowing process is found in the person of Jesus Christ: ὅς ἐστιν Χριστός is an adjectival clause modifying σπέρματι, defining this substantive more pointedly. Abraham must have understood that Isaac himself was not the hope of mankind (cf. John 8:56; Heb. 11:13, 17-19).

Micah's prophecy in 5:2 had been given a *personal* interpretation even by the Sanhedrin (cf. Matt. 2:4-6), and Micah's contemporary, Isaiah, had rendered a personal understanding of the suffering servant of the Lord (Isa. 53). We should note 2 Samuel 7:12-13 refers beyond Solomon, just as Genesis 49:10 is not exhausted at the time of its occurrence. All these points, including the promise to Abraham and to his *seed,* are based upon Genesis 3:15. In the protoevangelium the enemy is a definite individual, so also must be his destroyer; such is intimated in the head/heel contrast and the Hebrew demonstrative pronoun which is used. The echo of Genesis 3:15 which is found in Revelation 12:1-6 again points to two personal antagonists: Satan and Christ. The promised seed is indeed Jesus the Christ; He was promised to Adam and Eve as a savior, to Abraham as a seed, to David as a royal-family successor, and to Mary as a virgin-born son. However, just as in Genesis 21:12 Isaac is designated as "seed" in distinction from Ishmael but not in exclusion of Isaac's descendants, so also Paul singles out the reference to Christ in Galatians 3:16, although not in exclusion of those bound to Christ by faith (Gal. 3:26-29). Hence there is still a collective overtone possibly seen in "seed" as used by Paul in Galatians 3:16; he would be referring to that one, elected seed (i.e., "family") which comes from Abraham (the father of the faithful and ancestor of Jesus). There are not *many* corporations of the redeemed (remember, Ishmael was cast out)—that is, there are not many ways of salvation (faith, works, faith plus works, etc.)—but there is only the *one family* which shall be saved: that family which is *Christ's.* Christ is their representative head. Just as the "seed" of the woman in Genesis 3:15 refers to Christ and all those in union with Him by faith, so also the "seed" of the Abrahamic promise which is explicated in Galatians 3:16 is Christ and all those in union with Him by faith. Only Christ is mentioned in verse 16 since He is the important figure through whom blessing flows to us—thus the promises are affirmed *in Him* (2 Cor. 1:20). It is interesting that this same emphasis is found elsewhere in Paul. Galatians 3:16 is paralleled in Romans 9:7, 8, 24 (also in the discussion of Sarah and Hagar of Gal. 4; cf. Gen. 21:12), and Galatians 3:28-29 is paralleled in 1 Corinthians 12:12 and Romans 9:6-7, 13, 31. "Neither because they are the seed of

Abraham are they all children, but in Isaac shall thy seed be called. That is, they which are the children of the flesh are not the children of God, but the children of the promise are accounted as the seed" (Rom. 9:7-8). It is interesting to note that in Galatians 3:16 Paul speaks of Χριστός and not "Jesus" or "Jesus Christ"; the office of Messiah rather than the person of Jesus is given slight emphasis. In the Older Testament the redeemed people of God are corporately identified with their Messiah who is to come, and this organic unity is evidenced also in the New Testament (e.g., Isa. 6:13; Hos. 11:1; Acts 9:4; 1 Cor. 12:12; 2 Cor. 1:5; Eph. 1:23; Col. 1:24; Heb. 11:26). Hence, in Galatians 3:7 and 16 Paul declares that the promises of God's covenant were never intended for all the fleshly descendants of Abraham, but rather these promises were delivered to the one singular "family-seed" of Abraham who is Christ (the Messiah). Whatever benefit a man is to have from God must be derived via Jesus Christ, in whom and to whom are all the promises of God. One can be part of this blessed family which is Christ's only by faith. In discussing verse 16 we should note, finally, that Paul is quoting from either Genesis 13:15 or 17:8 (both these are spoken to Abraham, and both include the quoted καί), and in both cases the reference is to the *promise of Canaan as a land.* Even this "physicalistic" promise is fulfilled in Jesus Christ, and hence we do not wait for a restoration of that plot of ground to the apostate, fleshly-descendants of Abraham. Paul undisputedly "spiritualizes" this promise of the land, and he does it under the infallible direction of the Holy Spirit!

Having laid the general principle which is the foundation for his *a fortiori* argument in verse 15, and having specified who the proper recipient of the Abrahamic promises is in verse 16, Paul plainly states his inference in verse 17. Τουτο δὲ λέγω ("Now this I say") signalizes that a further explanation of a phrase or thought already used is about to be given (cf. 1 Cor. 1:12; 7:29; 10:29; 16:50). Paul is going back to the principle stated in verse 15 and comes to his real, fundamental purpose; both verses 15 and 17 speak of διαθήκη and thus are tied in with each other. Paul applies the truths mentioned in verse 15 about human covenants to the very covenant of *God* (which verse 16 had parenthetically defined in terms of for whom they are valid). "The law which appeared four hundred and thirty years later does not abrogate a covenant (having been) previously ratified by God." A covenant is unalterable and so the Mosaic law cannot turn back the promissory character of God's covenant with Abraham; this Paul has argued by inference, but now he states that because the law came much later in time than the promise it cannot affect the way of our salvation. This verse evidences that "promise" (v. 16) is convertible with "covenant" (cf. Rom. 1:20; 1 Thess. 2:16). Paul perhaps omits the article before διαθήκη in order to stress the qualitative character of the Abrahamic covenant as a guaranteed divine dispensation. προκεκυρωμένην is a consummative and intensive perfect tense, ascriptive, adjectival participle; rather than designating a separate act of subsequent confirmation (cf. Heb. 6:17-18), it (like the ὑπὸ τοῳ θεοῳ) serves to emphasize the absoluteness of the covenant. Such a covenant which has been previously ratified by God cannot be "made invalid" (i.e., by rescinding or overriding as verse 15 mentioned) by a later law. ᾿Ακυρόω is a legal term found in the writings of Philo, Josephus, and others. Matthew 15:6 reminds us that it is the Pharisees who "make void" the word of God by means of their traditions. Paul re-emphasizes this point by appending a phrase beginning with an ecbatic εἰς which repeats the denied result. "So as to abolish the promise." Καταργέω refers to making something inoperative or ineffective (cf. Luke 13:7; Heb. 2:14), thus in legal contexts takes the meaning "to nullify or abolish." At this point Paul uses the definite article before "promise" thereby indicating that all along he has been dealing with the specific covenant delivered to Abraham. That which cannot effect the mentioned abrogation and abolition is described as νόμος (in its *legalistic* aspect, as in Gal. 3:10, 12, 13) "having come" or "having appeared (in history)" 430 years after the promise delivered to Abraham. Γίνομαι is used in the same sense in passages like Mark 1:4; John 1:6, 17; and 1 John 2:18; in Galatians 3:17 it appears as a restrictive adjectival participle (telling *which* law is being discussed) in the perfect tense—thus indicating that there is a remaining effect of this appearance of the law even at Paul's time. Thus Paul is not completely deriding the law of God; he hints that it is still in effective operation during the age of gospel proclamation (a theme he elaborates elsewhere, e.g., Romans 3: 31; 7:12; 8:4). This description of the law as appearing 430 years after the covenanted promise to Abraham can be seen as forming the minor premise to a syllogism which takes verse 15 as the major premise; the resultant, good and necessary consequence would be that the Abrahamic covenant cannot be set aside by a subsequent law. Such argumentation characterizes Paul's theology elsewhere as well (e.g., Rom. 5). Ironically, the Judaizers had placed the law (which was 430 years later) *above* the original promise! This turns the world upside-down. By contrast Paul claims that the law cannot contribute to the inheritance of salvation, nor can it, in competition, subtract from the full effects of the promise. Those to whom the promise was granted will unconditionally receive it.

In verse 18 Paul sums up his line of attack by setting forth the diametric contrast between the promise-principle and the law-principle; since they are directly contradictory (one being conditional, the other being unconditional), and the promissory covenant preceded (at least) the stipulations of the law, therefore the Mosaic law *could not* abrogate the principle of blessing through promise; neither can merit and grace be combined in any way. This point is stressed by the use of the words κληρόνομαι ("inheritance"), ἐπαγγελιας ("of promise"), and κεχάρισται ("graciously granted"). An inheritance is a gift which is neither bought or earned; it is inalienable (cf. 1 Kings 21:3) and for the Christian it is given a first installment (cf. Eph. 1:13 f.). In classical Greek the term can refer to a *possession* without the idea of inheritance, but in the LXX it usually translates *nachalah*, "gift, possession, share." It is thus used of Canaan (Deut. 12:9; 19:14; Judg. 20:6; Isa. 58:14; 1 Chron. 16:16-18), the share of a particular tribe (Josh. 19), Israel as God's possession (Deut. 4:20; Ps. 78:1), property received as an heir (Num. 27:7-11; 36:2-4, 7-8) and (rarely) of land which is willed to someone else (Job 42:15). In the New Testament the term designates property which is transmitted by inheritance (only Luke 12:13), possessions (Matt. 21:38; Mark 12:7; Luke 20:14; Acts 7:5; Heb. 11:8), but in specifically Christian theological vocabulary it designates the blessing from God upon the faithful (cf. Acts 20:32; 1 Cor. 6:9-10; 15:50; Gal. 5:21; Eph. 5:5; Col. 3:24). As already noted, this peculiar "inheritance" is granted as a down-payment in the Holy Spirit (1 Cor. 1:22; 5:5; Eph. 4:30). Paul saw the promise to Abraham (including the land) as fulfilled in the sending of the Holy Spirit (cf. Gal. 3:14). Paul states that if such an inheritance is ἐκ νόμου (a genitive of source or cause—the explanation of something's existence), then it is οὐκέτι (which should be taken logically, as in Rom. 7:17, 20; 11:6, rather than temporally—"no more," by force of inference) of promise. The "promise" obviously points to God's blessing and grant to Abraham, as the next clause specifies, but for Paul it must be seen as referring to the Holy Spirit mentioned in verse 14 immediately preceding. Both "law" and "promise" are anarthrous, so should be taken in a qualitative sense most directly: the promise principle is antagonistic to the law principle. Indirectly Paul is saying that the (incorrect) Judaizing interpretation of the Mosaic covenant is antagonistic to the correct interpretation of the Abrahamic covenant. By adding works to promise the Judaizers thereby annulled the promise. It is either-or, not both-and. Paul uses the singular form of "promise" to denote the substantial identity of the promises made on several occasions. The principial argument of verse 18 is paralleled elsewhere in Paul (particularly in Romans 4:13-16—"for if they which are of the law are heirs, then faith is made void"), and it was foreshadowed in this chapter of Galatians at verse 12 ("the law is not of faith"). The principle is Paul's major premise; what follows is the minor premise: the inheritance was granted to Abraham through promise. The indubitable conclusion, then, is that the inheritance for Christians can be by no other agency than unconditional promise! "To Abraham" is given strong emphasis by the syntax of the clause, thereby showing that the hypothesis of verse 18a was surely unsound. Διά is used with the genitive when the object is the medium through which the original cause has effected the action expressed by the passive verb (cf. John 1:3; Matt. 1:22); hence the means by which God has caused the gift to come is promissory. The ἐπαννελία is the medium of inheritance, not meritorious law-works. He hammers this point home again when using the verb χαρίζομαι, which without mention of a specific object is a technical term drawn from the laws of inheritance and meaning "make a grant, deed something by will." The deeper sense of "grace" is expressed to the Christian by the root of this verb. The perfect tense of κεχάρισται denotes the fact that the grant is still in force, thus indirectly telling us of the once-for-allness of God's grace in Christ, such that no later system or law-principle of the Judaizers can alter. The duration of the gift, then, is permanent (cf. Rom. 8:32; 1 Cor. 2:12; Phil. 1:29). It has also been suggested that in Galatians 3:18b we find a "perfect of allegory," denoting that a fact stands recorded in the abiding Christian tradition and viewing the Older Testamental narrative as contemporary and relevant in its effect for the believer. Overall, Paul's point is that the grace motif militates against the soteriological legalism of the Judaizers and utterly excludes the thought of a conditional inheritance. This gracious grant from God has no commercial character and is not based on strict compliance with legal stipulations. Paul's own personal experience had shown him that this was the case (cf. Phil. 3:1-6).

Looking back over Paul's argumentation in Galatians 3:15-18, we must submit to the authoritative word of God by refusing to see any possibility of altering or annulling the covenant of God, we must see that all the promises of God (even that of a land) are fulfilled in the person and work of Jesus Christ, that the law of God can in no proper way be brought into conflict with the promises of God and salvation by grace, and that our redemption has a completely unconditional, gracious and promissory character. Paul would have our Christian experience to be Christocentric, rooted in God's stable covenant, engendered by grace yet not indifferent to abiding law. The Judaizers failed to be covenant theologians when it came to the ceremonial law of circumcision (not seeing the Christological focus of the covenants of God) and they proved themselves to be really antinomian when it came to the moral law of God (for instead of using the law as it was intended—a pattern for sanctification—they abused it by treating it as a way of justification). When confronted by such erroneous theologies, the Christian believer must turn to the experience of Abraham, the father of the faithful (Rom. 4:11-12), and the interpretation of it given by Paul, a foundational apostle of Christ's church (Eph. 2:20).

APPENDIX 2

THE CIVIL MAGISTRATE ACCORDING TO THE WESTMINSTER CONFESSION OF FAITH

THE particular concern of this essay will be to ascertain the specific doctrine of civil government set forth in the Westminster Confession of Faith. Of key importance in this examination will be the question of church and state separation and the question of the civil magistrate's relation to the law of God. The Westminster doctrine of civil rule is set forth in chapter 23 of the Confession as adopted by the General Assembly of the Church of Scotland in 1647.

I. The Origin of Civil Rule (section 1a)

The Confession presents the framework in which Christians are to understand the nature and function of civil rule by declaring in the first place that magisterial authority is from God: "God, the supreme Lord and King of all the world, hath ordained civil magistrates, to be, under Him, over the people. . . ." The true magistrate over the world is actually God, and thus any who rule upon earth must be viewed as His delegates. As supreme ruler God ordains the civil magistrate, setting him in office to be over the general populace. However, the statement of the Confession imposes a limit upon the magistrate even while granting divine sanction to his operations. In the course of saying that the magistrate is ordained by God to be over the people, the Confession intrudes these words immediately before saying over the people: "under

Him." It was not to be forgotten that the magistrate is limited in his control of a country by the governing authority of God. The ruler is first to be seen as under God and responsible to Him, and *then* to be accounted as over the people and in civil control. Therefore, the Confession immediately rejects despotic absolutism in civil government. The ruler must govern as the vicegerent of God, and thus the people always have a realm of appeal above the temporal king when he abuses his authority and rights.

In this declaration the Confession forthrightly rejects the view that God and morality are the tools of an absolute state, used to further only the desires of an autocratic ruler (such as portrayed in Machiavelli's *The Prince)*. Instead, the ruler is the tool of an absolute God and His moral demands according to the Westminster doctrine. And in opposition to theories which were currently taking seed, the Westminster divines firmly stood for the view that the source of all government is the divine will—not a primal "social contract," or the "consent of the governed," or the "will of majority." Since the ruler's authority stems from God, it is to God that the ruler is responsible for his official actions. And while God has not prescribed any particular form of government or plan of lawful succession, the citizens of a country are to consider "the powers that be" as ordained of God. The people are accountable to the ruler, and the ruler is accountable to God. This means that the ruler should follow the moral direction of God. The earthly king should be obedient to the King of kings:

> In the development of the plan of redemption the God-man as mediatorial King has assumed the government of the universe. Matt. xxviii, 18; Phil. ii. 9-11; Eph. 1. 17-23. As the universe constitutes one physical and moral system, it was necessary that his headship as Mediator should extend to the whole and to every department thereof, in order that all things should work together for good to his people and for his glory, that all his enemies should be subdued and finally judged and punished, and that all creatures should worship him, as his

> Father had determined. Rom. viii. 28; 1 Cor. xv. 25; Heb. x. 13; i. 6; Rev. v. 9-13. Hence the present providential Governor of the physical universe and "Ruler among the nations" is Jesus of Nazareth, the King of the Jews, to whose will all laws should be conformed, and whom all nations and all rulers of men should acknowledge and serve. "He hath on his vesture and on his thigh a name written, KING OF KINGS, AND LORD OF LORDS." Rev. xix. 16. (A. A. Hodge, *The Confession of Faith: A Handbook of Christian Doctrine Expounding the Westminster Confession.* London: reprinted by The Banner of Truth Trust, 1958, pp. 294-295.)

The fact that civil magistrates are not unlimited in their authority but are responsible to God's revealed will is further indicated in the next assertions of the Westminster Confession.

II. The Purpose of Civil Rule (section 1b)

Not only does the person who rules in a nation have his appointment from God, but also the special end of his rule is appointed by God: ". . . for His own glory, and the public good." Here then are two aims of civil rule: proximately, the public good, and ultimately, the glory of God. The ruler cannot do just whatever he pleases to do; he must do that which advances the proper ends of his ordained government. That public good which reflects the glory of God is justice and righteousness in social affairs. Therefore, the King of kings will have His name honored by having His will obeyed. This promotes the public good, for God's law was given for our benefit and good (cf. Deut. 6:24; 10:13); the godliness defined therein is profitable even in this life (cf. 1 Tim. 4:8).

By closely defining the ordination of the civil magistrate as including the proper ends of temporal government the Westminster Confession is simply following the example of Paul (Rom. 13:1-7) and Peter (1 Peter 2:13-14) who do not give a blank check authority to the ruler, but who specify that the ruler is to be of a certain kind: promoting good and avenging evil (both of these terms are strongly associated with obedience to, or rebellion from, the law of God in Scripture). Thus the Westminster divines, by seeing both the man and his function as ordained by God, would recognize legitimate power as that which fulfills the duty of the office as scripturally defined. Thus later in section 4 the Confession will delineate the magistrate's *lawful* demands as those to which the Christian is obligated.

III. The Means of Civil Rule (section 1c)

Having laid down the proper origin and purpose of civil government, the Confession finally explains the character of civil rule or its method of operation: "and, to this end, hath armed them with the power of the sword." The state is an institution of force; it accomplishes its ends by police and military operations. This is clearly taught in Romans 13:4 and endorsed by the writers of the Westminster Confession. Consequently the Confession teaches against those points of view which promote complete pacificism and the abolition of capital punishment. Included in the power of the sword is obviously the ability and right to take human life. Now the granting of that right to a fallen man would be immediately distressing and problematic in terms of a scriptural view of sin and violence; however, the Confession adequately provides limits to the state's use of violence by means of the very statement in which it acknowledges the state's right to use it. It is "to this end" (viz., God's glory and public good) that the state has been granted the weapon of death. Therefore, the magistrate does not have unbridled use of violence nor the prerogative of private revenge. In Romans 12:19 Paul instructs Christians not to avenge themselves because vengeance belongs to God; then in 13:4 Paul elaborates, saying that the magistrate is an avenger of God's wrath. The ruler can use the sword, then, only as God's word and law direct him so to use it. The Confession goes on to define the end for which the temporal governor has been armed with the sword: "for the defense and encouragement of them that are good, and for the punishment of evildoers."

By transition through the phrase "to this end" (which looks back to the words "for His own glory, and the public good") these last mentioned clauses also explain the previously cited divine glory and public good which the magistrate promotes. "For His own glory, and the public good" then, are epexegetically rendered "for the defense and encouragement of them that are good, and for the punishment of evildoers."

The church is separated from the operations of the state in that "the keys of the kingdom" are separated from the "sword" with which the state is armed. The power of the sword is not granted to the church of Christ, and thus is not (in the Westminster outlook) a proper agency for spreading the gospel or church discipline. The sword is not the way of entrance to God's kingdom, and thus the state is delimited to a ministry of social justice (not divine grace). The use of the sword by the state must be to one of two ends: defending and encouraging the good, or restraining and punishing the evil. The former of these functions is often overlooked in this day by those who assert that the state's only task is to remain neutral toward Christ's kingdom while preserving peace (negatively defined as the absence of warfare or violence) in the land—thus providing conditions under which the gospel can be preached. Neither Romans 13 nor the Westminster Confession agree with that outlook. Instead, the state is to have a positive concern with righteousness and promoting good. It is not content merely to preserve a negative peace or restrain only violence in society, for the state is to punish evil (which certainly includes more than violence) and to encourage the practice of good. The Larger Catechism parallels this concern of the Westminster divines. One of the duties which is required of superiors toward inferiors is listed in question 129 as "commending, and rewarding such as do well." The sole scriptural backing which is adduced is the example of kings and governors: 1 Peter 2:14; Romans 13:3; Esther 6:3. Governors have been "sent" by God for the praise of those who do well, and Paul promises that those who do good will have praise of the authorities. An example of this is King Ahasuerus' concern that Mordecai be honored and dignified for saving the king's life (by revealing the plot of Bigthana and Teresh to assassinate the king). The same question in the catechism provides that the superior is to be concerned for "protecting" his inferiors; one of the scriptural proofs cited is Isaiah 1:10, 17—an exhortation to the national leaders to heed God's law, relieving the oppressed, fatherless, and widow. Therefore, the Confession brings in the law of God as a guide to the ruler as to his duty to promote good in his society. On the other hand, the ruler is to be "a terror" to those who practice evil (cf. Rom. 13:3-4). His attitude toward the evil must be just the opposite of that toward the good. Larger Catechism question 129 states that superiors are to discountenance such as do ill, and Romans 13:3-4 is the biblical backing cited for this point. It follows from the fact that rulers must punish evildoers that rulers are wrong to command, counsel, or encourage evil. This inference is borne out in question 130 of the Larger Catechism, wherein we read that it is a sin when superiors are "commanding things unlawful . . . counseling, encouraging . . . them in that which is evil." The Scripture citations for these points all deal with magisterial violations of the law of God: Nebuchadnezzar commanded the nations to worship his image, the Sanhedrin commanded the apostles not to preach the gospel, Herodias counseled her daughter to ask for the head of John the Baptist, and Absalom commanded his servants to kill Amnon. Here are illegitimate uses of state authority and power of enforcement according to the Westminster divines. It is clear, then, that the Westminster outlook on civil rule requires that the magistrate refrain from evil himself and punish those who do evil. Evil is considered to be "things unlawful," and this obviously refers to the law of God (since it is the law of the magistrate which is said to be "unlawful" by the catechism). Therefore, the use of the sword by the civil magistrate must be directed toward obeying and enforcing the law of God according to the Westminster teaching; in this way the ruler will fulfill his two-fold task of promoting good and punishing evil. In chapter 20, section 4 of the Confession we find confirmation of the fact that the writers of the Westminster standards viewed the civil magistrate as having the duty to punish violators of God's law. In that section it is asserted that those who maintain practices which are contrary to the light of nature (i.e., the law of God inwardly revealed to all men, as the citation of Romans 1:32 demonstrates), the principles of Christianity, or the power of godliness may be *lawfully* proceeded against by the power of the civil magistrate. The Scripture proofs include the citation of the Old Testament law about willful seduction to idolatry in Deuteronomy 13:6-12 as well as the command from Artaxerxes to Ezra that magistrates and judges should be appointed who will punish violators of the law of God—even punishment with the death penalty (Ezra 7:23, 25-28). The reforms of Josiah and Asa according to God's law are also cited. Hence the statement in chapter 23, section 1 about the magistrate's duty to promote good and punish evil should be understood as instructing the magistrate to use the sword in promotion of the social righteousness of God's law. As Hodge rightly noted, magistrates should seek to promote piety as well as order (1 Tim. 2:1, 2) . . .

> by the explicit recognition of God and of Jesus Christ "as Ruler among the nations"; and by the enactment and enforcement of all laws conceived in the true spirit of the Gospel, touching all questions upon which the Scriptures indicate the will of God specifically or in general principle, and especially as touching questions of the Sabbath-day, the oath, marriage and divorce, capital punishments, etc., etc. (ibid., p. 295).

In section 1 of chapter 23, then, we find the fundamental doctrine of the civil magistrate as taught by the Westminster divines. There we learn of the origin, purposes, means, and specific tasks of civil rule. In the remaining sections of this chapter in the Confession specific applications and relational questions of this fundamental doctrine will be taken up.

IV. The Christian's Relation to the State (section 2)

Two separate and conflicting attitudes form the polemical background to section 2 of chapter 23 in the Confession. It was the common view of the Roman church that the civil state was a department of the church and thus under ecclesiastical direction. Consequently a Roman Catholic was ready and willing to take civil office, but perhaps more than willing—for Romanists often were appointed to office by the bishop or pope, thus intruding themselves into the temporal government. This practice tended to result in absolutism in Roman Catholic lands. On the other hand the Anabaptists refused to take public office or even recognize the legitimate authority of civil and military arrangements. Ironically, however, the Anabaptists were often quite willing to form their own political and martial forces and then use them against the duly established government of a country. This practice naturally tended toward anarchism. Now driving a straight course through the implicit absolutism of Romanism and the implicit anarchism of Anabaptism was a delicate assignment, but one which the Westminster divines did well. Their resolution to the tension between Romanist and Anabaptist outlooks came in the espousal of two principles. Against the Anabaptists the Westminster Confession maintains that the office of magistrate has divine appointment (section 1) and therefore "It is lawful for Christians to accept and execute the office of a magistrate. . . ." Against the Roman Catholics the Westminster Confession adds ". . . when called thereunto"; hereby the divines indicated that a Christian could not foist himself upon a populace as their ruler by implicit ecclesiastical right. The officers of the state had to be called by the people, as Rutherford declared in his famous treatise, *Lex Rex* (1644): "The power of creating a man a king is from the people." Therefore, chapter 23, section 2 plainly sets forth the view that a Christian has standing in both the church and the state. The Christian, by virtue of his allegiance to Christ's kingdom, is not excluded from active participation in the affairs of the states and kingdoms of this world. He may even exercise magisterial power in such states when properly called to do so.

When the Christian exercises civil rule his aim should be to apply righteous laws to the commonwealth; he should be interested in seeing justice promoted, peace maintained, and piety encouraged. This is far from the ideal of neutrality endorsed by some Christians in their attitude toward civil affairs today. The Westminster Confession maintains that the Christian *as a Christian* can influence civil affairs when he holds the office of magistrate: "in the managing whereof, as they ought especially to maintain piety, justice, and peace, according to the wholesome laws of each commonwealth." This calls for ruling in the fear of God (2 Sam. 23:3), doing justice (Ps. 82:3-4), and being instructed by the Lord (Ps. 2:10-12). It is of interest to note that the divines took 1 Timothy 2:2 to teach that the goal of supporting the magistrate was his support of believers in living quiet and godly lives; thus when one prays for the magistrate he does not simply request escape from persecution, but he petitions God that the magistrate would promote the causes of godliness and peace in a positive fashion.

The Confession then goes on to list one major implication of the preceding teaching: "so, for that end, they may lawfully, now under the new testament, wage war, upon just and necessary occasion." Similar to the granting of the sword in section 1, section 2 now grants the powers of war to the magistrate—over against the claims of the Anabaptists that it was illegitimate. However, the lawfulness of warfare is (as with the power of the sword) delimited by two clauses: "for that end" (viz., the maintenance of piety, justice, and peace) and "upon just and necessary occasion." When these conditions are combined it is evident that the Westminster Confession sanctions only defensive warfare: that is, warfare which is strictly for the end of preserving peace, which is according to justice (thus not aggressive or provoking another to violate peace), and which is the last resort left to a nation (and consequently necessary to engage in). The Confession does not give a blanket approval to all warfare, and this grounds the right of selective conscientious objection in this day. No man, even the magistrate, has the right to take the life of another without explicit warrant from God Himself; that warrant is given in the case of capital offenses and in the case of self-defense. The warrant for aggressive warfare came only to Israel by direct revelation and upon special circumstances (God's temporal judgment upon an abominable society). Since such direct revelation has ceased today, no nation can claim the right to aggressive warfare or to policing the world (for whatever proffered rationale: e.g., "to make the world safe for democracy," "to end all wars," "to guarantee the right of national self-determination"). When a magistrate goes to war for an unjustified cause, then the Christian who follows the Westminster Confession has the duty (not merely the right) to resist this practice of murder. However, when the state fights wars of self-defense it has divine approval, and the Christian should support such a cause (since pacificism is an unwarranted demand according to the Westminster Confession). Finally, observe that the Confession goes to specific lengths to indicate that warfare is not against the New Testament dispensation or its ethic. Not only could war be sanctioned in the Old Testament, but magistrates can *lawfully* "now under the new testament" wage war as well. The writers of the Confession felt that there was continuity between the ethical standard of the Old Testament and that of the New; therefore, even after the advent of Christ a just war remains a lawful possibility to the civil magistrate.

V. The State's Relation to the Church (section 3)

In section 3 of chapter 23 we come to an area of the Confession which is greatly misunderstood today. But it has been misunderstood in the past as well, thus occasioning certain interpretative declarations and even amendments in order that people not abuse the Confession by putting its language to a misuse. The contention by some has been that the Confession here departs into Erastian notions, giving the civil magistrate some jurisdiction in the church. That this is, whatever initial impression the section may make, contrary to sound interpretation and contrary to the facts of the matter can be demonstrated in the following list of arguments.

(1) This section cannot be interpreted as an Erastian assertion since the few Erastians in the Westminster Assembly argued strongly against it (cf. Gordon Clark, *What Do Presbyterians Believe? The Westminster Confession: Yesterday and Today*. Philadelphia: Presbyterian and Reformed Publishing Co., 1965, p. 212).

(2) Since the Confession teaches elsewhere that only ecclesiastical (and not civil) office holders bear rule in the church, this must be the interpretation given to chapter 23, section 6, or else the Confession is made to set forth a blatant and open-face contradiction with itself. The Westminster divines were most decidedly against any blending of temporal and spiritual authority. God has ordained a *civil* ruler in society,

and respecting the *church:* "The Lord Jesus, as King and Head of His Church, hath therein appointed a government in the hand of Church officers, distinct from the civil magistrate" (chapter 30, section 1). A distinct government (which was not to be confused with civil rule) has been appointed in the church, and thus the Confession maintains the separation of church and state. Chapter 31, section 3 asserts that "It belongeth to synods and councils, ministerially to determine controversies of faith, and cases of conscience; to set down rules and directions for the better ordering of the public worship of God, and government of His Church. . . ." Here it is decreed that matters pertaining to Church government, worship, and belief are assigned to synods and councils; these things are defined and designated to be ecclesiastical concerns. So again the Confession guards the separation of church and state by keeping the civil magistrate out of ecclesiastical business and jurisdiction. Moreover, the Confession protects the state from authoritative intervention or intrusive jurisdiction by the church: "Synods and councils are to handle, or conclude nothing, but that which is ecclesiastical: and are not to intermeddle with civil affairs which concern the commonwealth, unless by way of humble petition in cases extraordinary; or, by way of advice, for satisfaction of conscience, if they be thereunto required by the civil magistrate" (chapter 31, section 5). The magistrate may appeal to the church for advice, or in extraordinary cases the church may out of conscience rebuke the actions of the magistrate (with humility); but the church is prohibited from meddling, handling, or concluding matters which pertain solely to civil affairs. It should be noted that certain matters of public morality are *not* solely the concern of the commonwealth. Therefore, having observed these clear declarations of the Confession which separate the jurisdiction of church and state, the burden of proof must rest upon those who wish to interpret chapter 23, section 3 in an Erastian fashion to show convincing reasons why the writers of the Confession set forth there a bald contradiction with what they said elsewhere.

(3) The first clause of chapter 23, section 3 governs the rest of the section since that first clause ends in a full colon ("The civil magistrate may not assume to himself the administration of the Word and

sacraments, or the power of the keys of the kingdom of heaven:"). What follows that colon must be interpreted in light of the declaration that the "power of the keys" (i.e., the ordinary government and administration of church affairs as distinguished from administering word and sacrament) is not allowed to the civil magistrate. Again we can see that the Confession is cautious to separate the ecclesiastical realm from the sphere in which the magistrate has jurisdiction; his authority does not extend over the church. Not only is he prohibited from handling the sacraments and preaching the word (a prohibition with which Coleman, an Erastian spokesman at the Westminster Assembly, expressly concurred), but the civil magistrate is also forbidden to meddle in the governmental affairs of the church. As the Confession goes on to explicate what the magistrate *may* do with respect to the Christian religion, the former prohibitions expressed in the opening clause of section 3 must be held as determinative for interpretation.

(4) The nature of those things in which the magistrate may become involved according to the Confession at 23.3 demonstrates that his involvement must be circumscribed by Scripture (since it is "the truth of God" and "all the ordinances of God" with which he is concerned). Gillespie, who was very influential at the Westminster Assembly, is also known for his book dealing with questions of church and state government, *Aaron's Rod Blossoming.* In this volume Gillespie expresses a point of view which had formative effect in the writing of the Confession. He says, in good anti-Erastian fashion, that the church must be kept separate from the state and that this separation pertains to the *functions* of magistrate and minister; while their jurisdictions are coordinated, being set side by side, their authority and responsibility trace back to God in both cases. Thus the magistrate cannot meddle in the church, but he does have obligations under God to care in a particular way for the church. Gillespie says in *Aaron's Rod Blossoming* that the civil magistrate's disposal of causes which touch upon ecclesiastical areas must be tied to the rule of God's word (and that even the Erastians admitted this principle). Thus the Confession should not be read in any way but to indicate that the civil ruler's concern for religion is

bounded and controlled by the explicit teaching of Scripture. This fact is quite evident when one notices that section 3 of chapter 23 in the Confession states that the magistrate's provision for the transactions in synods must be "according to the mind of God." The magistrate cannot do anything with respect to the church except that which is in conformity to God's will as found in the Bible. The civil ruler has overextended and violated his duty when he cannot show that his actions are in accord with Scripture. The only functions which bear on religion that the Westminster Confession grants to the civil magistrate are those which God's word will grant to the civil magistrate. If the ruler does not heed Scripture and exegesis he is not executing the function given to him in chapter 23 of the Confession. Here is the most adequate provision one could want that the magistrate not intrude himself illegitimately in matters of the Christian religion and its practice.

(5) It is necessary to distinguish between the object of someone's *care* and the sphere of his *jurisdiction;* the former is an object in which he has interest and which he aims for (being "a nursing-father" as the Scripture proof for this section, citing Isa. 49:23, says), while the latter is a realm where one has the right of authoritative interference. The civil magistrate may care for the church, but he has no jurisdiction therein; he is a nursing-father, but not an overlord. Those objects for which the *magistrate is to aim* according to section 3 (viz., "that unity and peace be preserved in the Church, that the truth of God be kept pure and entire, that all blasphemies and heresies be suppressed, all corruptions and abuses in worship and discipline prevented or reformed") are the very matters which the Confession elsewhere puts within the sphere of *ecclesiastical jurisdiction.* Thus the Confession must be understood as saying that the civil ruler should conduct his office in such a way that Christianity can prosper, yet without assuming to himself ecclesiastical functions or authority. These functions and authority belong, according to chapters 25, 30, and 31, to church office bearers; consequently, they are not under civil control or direction, but are simply the things which the magistrate promotes by the godly execution of his own duties.

(6) The former point is confirmed when the actual language of the Confession at 23.3 is properly interpreted. The Confession says that the magistrate has authority "to take order" with respect to the items already listed (preach in the Church, etc.). This phrase, "to take order," was commonly used at the time of the writing of the Confession in the sense of "to attend to, to aim at, to see about, to provide for, to labor to effect." That the phrase must be interpreted in this way, and not in the sense of sovereign jurisdiction, is proved by the Latin translations made of the Confession at the time of its original writing. The Latin translation prepared under Presbyterian direction in 1656 at Cambridge University renders "to take order" as "*providere*" ("to see to it" or "to make it an object of attention"), and Brown of Wamphray, a minister of the church when the Confession was adopted, rendered it "operam dare" ("to pay or give attention to"). These Latin translations help us to understand the actual sense intended by the words "to take order" in the Confession. It should be clear that, consonant with all the above points, the writers of the Confession did not grant the magistrate any authority in the church by this phrase, but only indicated that he was required to care for the church of Christ by the godly exercise of his own duties.

(7) The only specification of means by the Confession for the magistrate's promotion of church welfare clearly indicates that he does not gain jurisdiction in the church thereby. It would be illegitimate to hold that the Confession grants the magistrate means beyond those specified, and the ones actually listed reveal that he does not have the right to assume authoritative control of the church or to claim veto power over the decisions of synods. Such things would indicate a seizing of the power of the keys—which has already been forbidden. The magistrate may only "call synods," "be present at them," and "provide that whatsoever is transacted in them be according to the mind of God." With respect to the first item it should be noted that the "synods" called by the magistrate apparently include both civil and ecclesiastical synods; this is indicated in the Scripture proof cited, where (according to 2 Chron. 19:8-11) Jehoshaphat established both civil and ecclesiastical judges for the people (and, notably, with a separation of

the matters of the king from the matters of Jehovah). The reason that civil synods may be included here is that the Confession introduces this power to call synods with the words "For the better effecting whereof," and that which is to be better effected includes the enforcement of God's law in society—one of the duties assigned to the magistrate, but not yet discussed in this essay. But whether the power to call synods includes civil counsels (one would certainly think that this would be, especially in a chapter explicitly dealing with the civil magistrate, the most obvious power of a magistrate) or not, the important thing to observe is the nature of those *ecclesiastical* synods called by the magistrate. The Scripture proof cited for this element in the Confession (viz., Matt. 2:4-5) pertains to the magistrate calling an ecclesiastical synod for the purposes of advice or interpretation of Scripture; this exactly parallels the teaching of the Confession in chapter 31, section 5 where synods are instructed not to meddle with civil affairs except when the civil magistrate requires advice of them. Therefore, it is proper to see the magistrate's power to call ecclesiastical synods according to chapter 23, section 3 as pertaining (in the intention of the Confessional writers) to scriptural advice requested from the church by the civil magistrate. The Confession made a special point of listing this prerogative of the magistrate because it was commonly understood that the *ordinary* right to call church synods was reserved to the *officers of the church,* Christ's appointed "government" for His church—which "government" properly includes Synods and Councils (cf. 30.1 with 31.1; also 31.2). Rutherford maintained in *Lex Rex* that the church has the liberty to convene synods whenever necessity arises and *without* an act of Parliament to that effect. And in the adopting act of the Assembly of the Church of Scotland when the Westminster Confession was accepted (1647) it was explicitly affirmed that a synod could *not* be called in a constituted and settled kirk on the authority of the magistrate *alone* (but only in as yet unsettled kirks). It is in light of these things that the power to call ecclesiastical synods which is given the magistrate by the Westminster Confession must be understood. There is no ground here for maintaining that the Confession gives jurisdiction or authority in the church to the civil ruler. With respect to the second means granted to the magistrate in chapter 23, section 3 (viz., to be present at synods) we need only observe that the Confession refrains from saying that the magistrate has the right to govern or preside in the synods. It is only granted that he has the right to attend the synods of the church that he might be pleased to call for advice (or in unsettled kirks). And then with respect to the third means put at the magistrate's disposal (viz., to provide that whatever is transacted be according to the mind of God) one should note that the Latin translation of "provide" is *"prospicere"* ("to make it an object of concern"). The magistrate promotes and seeks godly and biblical decisions or answers from ecclesiastical synods, but chapter 23 of the Westminster Confession does not go beyond that; it does not extend the proper jurisdiction of the magistrate in civil affairs to authoritative intervention in the church. The magistrate's interest and concern for the welfare of Christ's church is exercised within his own designated realm of control.

(8) It should also be clear that the objects for which the magistrate is to aim (basically: the welfare of the church) are also the objects for which every private individual is to aim. Thus there is no more ground for holding that the Westminster Confession is Erastian than there is for holding that the Confession favors democratic congregationalism over presbyterianism. The magistrate, like all men in general, is to use his properly delineated power and authority (which is ascertained from other sources than chapter 23, section 3 of the Confession itself) in such a way that Church peace and unity, the purity of God's truth, and the suppression of abuses and heresies be advanced. He must act upon his own responsibility in these areas (just as all men are required to do), not intervening in the lawful authority of others (especially the power of synods which are "an ordinance of God appointed . . . in His Word" chapter 31, section 3). Only the church has God's authority and jurisdiction in ecclesiastical matters, and yet it is left to all men (including magistrates) to judge for themselves the meaning of God's word and accordingly give sanction or disagreement to the decrees of church courts; following from this, all men (including magistrates) must work

within the legitimate bounds of their authority and duties to promote the causes of Christ. (Much of what has been presented in points [2]—[8] above is derived from William Cunningham's "The Westminster Confession on the Relation Between Church and State," in *Discussions on Church Principles: Popish, Erastian, and Presbyterian.* Edinburgh: T. & T. Clark, 1863, pp. 211-234.)

(9) The foregoing anti-Erastian interpretation of section 3 of chapter 23 in the Westminster Confession is confirmed by literature from the period in which it was composed and from explicit statements from its writers. In 1660, Brown of Wamphray expressed (in his *Apologetical Narration)* what he says the position of the Puritan and Covenanting party was with respect to civil interference in ecclesiastical matters; this position is epitomized, according to him, in the declaration of James VI (1585) to the effect that a king should never apprehend any pastor for matters of doctrine in religion or salvation, heresies, or the true interpretation of Scripture, for these things are purely ecclesiastical and impertinent to the king's specific calling. That this was the attitude of the Westminster divines is even more strongly indicated in the "Hundred and eleven propositions concerning the ministry and government of the Church" drawn up by Baillie and (especially) Gillespie which they were appointed to do by the Church of Scotland. Since these men had a prominent role in the Westminster Assembly these propositions certainly represent the best direct evidence we have for correctly interpreting the Confession on these points. These two men were appointed to prepare these propositions against "the errors of Erastianism, Independency, and what is falsely called liberty of conscience," and the propositions were published by the 1647 Assembly of the Church of Scotland (the same Assembly that adopted the Westminster Confession of Faith). The following specimens from those propositions will sufficiently prove that the Westminster Confession, chapter 23, section 3 cannot be read in Erastian fashion; the Confession does not sanction any ecclesiastical jurisdiction by the civil magistrate nor his authoritative intervention in the concerns of the church.

4. The Church ought to be *governed by no other persons than ministers and stewards preferred and placed by Christ, and after no other manner than according to the laws made by Him*; and, therefore, there is no other power on earth which may challenge to itself authority or dominion over the Church.

6. The same Lord and our Saviour Jesus Christ, the only Head of the Church, hath ordained in the New Testament not only the preaching of the Word and administration of baptism and the Lord's Supper, but also ecclesiastical government, distinct and differing from the civil government; and it is His will that there be such a government distinct from the civil in all His Churches everywhere, as well those which live under Christ, as those under infidel, magistrates, even until the end of the world.

41. The orthodox churches believe, and do willingly acknowledge, that every lawful magistrate . . . ought first and chiefly to take care of God's glory, and (ACCORDING TO HIS PLACE, OR IN HIS MANNER AND WAY), to preserve religion when pure, and to restore it when decayed and corrupted. . . .

95. Christian magistrates . . . defend, stand for, and take care to propogate the true faith and godliness . . . turn away injuries done to it [the Church], restrain false religion, and cherish, and underprop, and defend the rights and liberties of the Church. . . .

96. Wherefore seeing these nursing-fathers, favourers and defenders, can do nothing against the truth, but for the truth, nor have any right against the gospel, but for the gospel; and their power in respect of the Church whereof they bear the care, being . . . cumulative and auxiliary, thereby it is sufficiently clear that they ought to cherish . . . ecclesiastical discipline; but yet not with implicit faith or blind obedience;—for the Reformed Churches do not deny to any of the faithful, much less to the magistrate, the judgment of Christian

prudence and discretion concerning those things which are decreed or determined by the Church.

97. *Therefore, as to each member of the Church respectively, so unto the magistrate*, belongeth the judgment of such things, both to apprehend and to judge them; for although the magistrate *is not ordained and preferred of God, that he should be a judge of matters and causes spiritual, of which there is controversy in the Church*, YET IS HE QUESTIONLESS JUDGE OF HIS OWN CIVIL ACT ABOUT SPIRITUAL THINGS; namely, of defending them in his own dominions, and of approving or tolerating the same; and if, in this business, he judge and determine according to the wisdom of the flesh, and not according to the wisdom which is from above, he is to render an account thereof before the supreme tribunal.

98. However, the ecclesiastical discipline, according as it is ordained by Christ, whether it be established or ratified by civil authority or not, ought to be retained and exercised in the society of the faithful . . . ; as it [civil authority] superaddeth nothing more, so it takes nothing away.

51. The magistrate calleth together synods, not as touching those things which are proper to synods, but in respect of the things which are common to synods with other meetings and civil public assemblies,—that is, not as they are assemblies in the name of Christ, to treat of matters spiritual, but as they are public assemblies within his territories.

(In these citations I am following the text as provided by William Cunningham, ibid., pp. 232-234.)

Therefore, Macpherson is quite correct in saying that the Westminster Confession of Faith, at chapter 23, section 3 "must be understood of moral support and encouragement to ecclesiastical officers in the administration of doctrine and discipline" (John Macpherson, *The Westminster Confession of Faith: With Introduction and Notes.* Edinburgh: T.

& T. Clark, 1882, p. 137). This section does not grant authority in the church to the civil ruler at all.

(10) Finally it can be observed that both the Scottish and American Presbyterian Churches authoritatively declared that any Erastian interpretation of section 3 of chapter 23 in the Westminster Confession is improper to its actual teaching. This is clear from the short discussion of Gillespie's propositions as published by the Church of Scotland at the same time as it adopted the Confession, as well as from Act 12 of the 1846 Assembly of the same church which reaffirmed the anti-Erastian understanding of the section, disclaiming all intolerant and persecuting practices of the civil ruler. In 1729 when the Synod in North America adopted the Westminster Confession and Catechisms as its ecclesiastical standard it declared that it did not receive this section "in any such sense as to suppose the civil magistrate hath a controlling power over synods with respect to the exercise of their ministerial authority."

Having then established that the Westminster Confession protects the proper separation of church and state with respect to their functions and jurisdictions, and having shown why chapter 23, section 3 cannot be interpreted in any Erastian fashion, we can consider the teaching of this section as a whole. It begins with a prohibition which bars the civil magistrate from assuming the administration of the Word and sacraments or the power of the keys of heaven; here is the well guarded separation of church and state. However, the Confession then goes on to list the positive responsibilities of the civil magistrate; they are two basically. The first has already been elaborated above. Separation of church and state should not, according to the Confession, lead one to think that the magistrate may be indifferent to God's word, for the civil ruler is obligated (1) to promote conditions in which the church can function prosperously (being concerned with its unity, peace, purity, etc.) by being a nursing-father unto it, and (2) to enforce the law of God (". . . all the ordinances of God duly settled, administered, and observed"). An examination of the scriptural proofs offered for this second duty makes quite clear that the Westminster divines expected the civil magistrate to rule according to the law of God (including its Old Testament stipulations), even to the point of its penal sanctions. In the Scripture texts adduced the magistrate is instructed to put blasphemers and idolators to death; clearly then, it was the *whole* law of God which the magistrate, as God's vicegerent, was to maintain and enforce according to the Westminster Confession. Whether this outlook is endorsed today or not, it surely has the support of orthodox Presbyterian heritage and confessional standards. As Gillespie accurately put it in proposition 41 of the "Hundred and eleven propositions concerning the ministry and government of the Church" (therein revealing the position maintained by the writers of the Westminster Confession): "The orthodox churches believe, and do willingly acknowledge, that every lawful magistrate, being by God Himself constituted the keeper and defender of both tables of the law, may and ought first and chiefly to take care of God's glory. . . ." The magistrate was not artificially restricted to the last six areas of the Decalogue, but he was viewed as under serious responsibility to carry out the prescriptions of the whole law (the ten words and their case law elaborations). Proposition 5 in Gillespie's list plainly states that "the law of faith commandeth the counsel and purposes of men to be framed and conformed" to the rule of Christ, laid open in His Holy Word. When the magistrate carried out capital punishment against violaters of the first four areas of the Decalogue he did so as a protector of public or social righteousness and peace; he did not presume to judge the secret thoughts of the heart, but only to restrain the actual outward manifestations of law-breaking. This is evident from Gillespie's proposition 41: ". . . as likewise to restrain and punish as well atheists, blasphemers, heretics, and schismatics, as the violators of justice and public peace." It should be observed also that the Westminster Confession (as evidenced in the proof texts for chapter 23, as well as the comments of Gillespie just mentioned) considers there to be more than simply one capital crime (viz., murder); there are a number of social crimes (as indicated in the law of God) which receive this due recompense. That this has been understood throughout subsequent church history as being taught by the Confession is illustrated in the quotation from A. A. Hodge's commentary on the Confession that was recorded earlier in this essay; Hodge points out that chapter 23 of the Westminster Confession requires magistrates to promote piety and social order by the enactment and enforcement of laws conforming to the specifically revealed will of God in Scripture, and especially as touching (among other things) "capital punishments" (plural). So then, the civil magistrate is obligated to keep and enforce the whole law of God, including its penal sanctions (capital punishment for a plurality of crimes), according to the Westminster doctrine of civil rule. Chapter 23, section 3 binds the civil authority to all the ordinances of God; his rule in society was to be upright and just. This is paralleled in the Larger Catechism, where, according to the statement of questions 129 and 130 as well as the relevant Scripture proofs adduced, the magistrate is obligated to judge according to the wisdom of God (1 Kings 3:28) and sins when he violates the law of God by seeking ease, profit, or selfish pleasure from his position (Deut. 17:17) or by unjust, rigorous, or remiss behavior (1 Kings 12:13-16). From question 145 and its Scripture citations we learn that the Westminster divines viewed God's word as prohibiting the ruler from doing unrighteousness in judgment, such as is done when the law of God is slackened and thereby wrong judgment proceeds from the magistrate (Lev. 19:15; Hab. 1:4); the law of God must be enforced or else the magistrate will sin in "passing unjust sentence, calling evil good, and good evil; rewarding the wicked according to the work of the righteous, and the righteous according to the work of the wicked" (cf. Prov. 17:15; 1 Kings 21:9-14; Isa. 5:23). Therefore, the Westminster view of civil authority requires all magistrates to observe and carry out the whole law of God as the standard of social justice and public righteousness.

The above conclusion is helpful in clarifying an often misunderstood portion of the Westminster Confession: chapter 19, section 4. Chapter 19 deals with the law of God, and in section 4 of that chapter we read that the sundry judicial laws given by God to Israel as a body politic have expired with the state of that people and thus bind us today no further than the general equity of those laws may require. This statement is sometimes interpreted as saying that the penal sanctions and case laws of the Old Testament no longer bind people, and thus that the civil magistrate is freed from the obligation to enforce public justice by executing those criminals specified in God's law. However, it is sufficiently clear from chapter 23, section 3 of the Confession that this was *not* the Westminster position. To attribute the abolition of the case laws and penal sanctions of God's law to chapter 19, then, would be to accuse the Westminster divines of blatant self-contradiction (even though the Confession is recognized as the most cautiously worked out and carefully worded creed of the evangelical church). In the Westminster outlook civil magistrates have not been given autonomy in their various tasks, but are obligated to observe *all* the commandments of God (23.3), even those which elaborate and illustrate the Decalogue. Therefore, whatever 19.4 may mean, it cannot be understood as abrogating, say, the death penalty for blasphemers, and so forth. This is evident from chapter 19 itself when one examines the Scripture proofs cited at section 4; they include not only Matthew 5:17 (Christ's statement that He did not come to abrogate the law) but also Paul's utilization of the case law of the Old Testament in a way which shows that it was still authoritative and binding after Christ's advent (cf. 1 Cor. 9:9-10; in verse 10 Paul says that God's word specifies this law "for our sakes," meaning Paul's contemporaries).

Perhaps the best interpretation of 19.4 is to see it as affirming the necessity to apply the illustrations given in the Old Testament case laws to changed, modern situations and new social circumstances. For instance, the law requires that fencing be placed around your roof in order to provide safety and protect human life; however, current American society does not ordinarily use the rooftops of homes for entertaining guests (as did the Israelites). But this does not mean that modern America is freed from that case law of God's word, for the Westminster Confession asserts that the general equity of such a law is still binding. Thus the underlying principle (of which the case law was a particular illustration) of safety precautions has abiding ethical validity. "It is very evident that the circumstances of modern society demand very different regulations from those which suited national conditions under the Jewish monarchy" (Macpherson, *op. cit.,* p. 119). Still, God has not stopped requiring social righteousness and justice; the law which He gave to define this justice has permanent validity. "Yet whatever principles of eternal justice appeared in those laws are now obligatory. The adventitious, circumstantial, formal, perishes; the substantial endures" (ibid.). So the civil magistrate is still required to execute just recompense upon criminals as dictated in the law of God (cf. Heb. 2:2), even if the crimes committed may have to be understood within a different set of social circumstances that obtain in modern America. This appears to be the best reading of 19.4. Others may be possible, but whatever view is taken cannot result in the civil magistrate's release from obligation to the Old Testament laws, as 23.3 lays down.

Before going on to discuss the last section of chapter 23 in the Confession a word of commentary upon the revision of section 3 made by the Presbyterian Church in America is appropriate. It was noted above that the Presbyterian Church in America, when it adopted the Westminster Confession in 1729, declared that the Confession could not properly be interpreted in an Erastian fashion. However, by 1788 this Presbyterian body was willing to amend 23.3 so as to avoid all possibility of misreading and, thereby, misunderstanding of the Church's stand. The newly adopted form of this section (which reads as the version accepted by the Orthodox Presbyterian Church, except for punctuation) opens with the same words as the original (except that the singular, "magistrate," has been altered to the plural, "magistrates," to fit better the American concept of political organization if not also the plurality mentioned in Romans 13:1): "Civil magistrates may not assume to themselves the administration of the Word and sacraments, or the power of the keys of the kingdom of heaven. . . ." At this point the American revision inserts another clause and then finishes out the section with completely different wording from that found in the original; the clause which is inserted characterizes well the thrust of the remaining alteration: ". . . or in the least interfere in matters of faith." From that point the revision goes on to elaborate the intended separation of church and state. The interesting thing about the altered form of the orthodox version of the Confession is that the very thing guarded (viz., that the magistrate should not interfere in the church or matters of faith) by the revised form was already guarded by the orthodox version itself (as we saw above). The original Westminster Confession did not allow for a blending of church and state authority, but rigorously separated the two. Now, while later readers may have stumbled over the form of expression in 23.3, the orthodox version of the Confession did not need alteration from the standpoint of its actual teaching. Thus it is best to regard the 1788 rewriting of that section as a recasting of the earlier doctrine in language which would more clearly express the separation of church and state which was implicit all along (and explicitly asserted in the opening words of the section). Just as with the original version of the Confession, the revised version did not take the separation of church and state to imply that the magistrate was indifferent to the Christian church. The original statement of the Westminster Confession taught that the magistrate should promote (within his proper bounds and duties) the well-being of the church, and the revised form continued this teaching, speaking of magistrates as "nursing fathers" to the church who must "take order" to protect that church. Thus the new outlook was not significantly different from the older viewpoint. However, in their attempt to emphasize the intended separation of church and state, the writers of the new version dropped the entire last portion of the original version and then filled in their clear sentiments on church-state separation. In so doing they did not attempt to parallel the original version, element by element, but only to make sure that Erastianism could not be wrested from the Confession. The inevitable result of such a strong, singular aim in rewriting was that some important features of the orthodox statement were overlooked and, thus, not reflected upon (one way or the other) in the revised version. In particular we should observe that the American rewriting of the Westminster Confession at 23.3 did not bring over the statement of the civil magistrate's obligation to observe all the ordinances of God. It does not seem that one could fairly interpret this omission as an intentional repudiation of that aspect of the Westminster teaching, seeing that the Puritans clearly took the Old Testament law of God as the basis for the magistrate to execute various sorts of criminals, for instance witches (cf. Matthew Henry's scriptural explanation of this practice in his commentary on the Bible at Exodus 22:18). While holding to the magistrate's responsibility to enforce the law of God and be governed by the same, the Presbyterians who re-wrote the Westminster Confession at 23.3 emphasized the matter which they felt needed clarification and did not attempt to completely parallel the original statement of the Confession—thus overlooking to republish the statement of the magistrate's obligation to God's law. In evaluation of the revised version of 23.3, then, we can see how it was, and was not, necessary; also we can see how it helped to clarify the original teaching, but also failed to clarify it. The implicit separation of church and state could have been more clearly expressed in the latter portion of 23.3 in the original version, but the rewriting done by the American church did not result in the all-around improved statement that should be expected when someone puts his hand to revising the Church's doctrinal standards. The American revision did stress the separation of church and state in a clear fashion, but it failed to include the important statement of the orthodox version to the effect that the magistrate must govern in accord with God's law. Hence there was some gain, but a significant loss in the rewritten form of 23.3.

VI. The Individual's Relation to the State (section 4)

Chapter 23 closes out its discussion of the civil magistrate by rehearsing the "duty of people" toward the civil magistrate and then rejecting two errors of Romanism.

The Westminster Confession, in accordance with Scripture, requires people to pray for the civil ruler and to honor his person (cf. 1 Tim. 2:1-2; 1 Peter 2:17). The Larger Catechism reiterates the responsibility of inferiors to pray for superiors in question 127, where the Scripture text cited is again 1 Timothy 2:1-2. In these requirements the Westminster divines were dealing with the very realistic problem that people may refrain from outward violence against the magistrate and yet despise him in their hearts. The Westminster outlook is not simply that one must tolerate the magistrate (as a necessary evil, say) but that one must have a positive attitude of reverence and prayerful support for the ruler. Indeed, the Larger Catechism goes on to say that inferiors are duty bound to defend and fight for the safety of the magistrate (cf. question 127; 1 Sam. 26:15-16; 2 Sam. 18:3; Est. 6:2). Also the Confession says that people are required by God to pay their taxes to the government. Thus prayer, reverence, and support (defensive and financial) are due to political authority.

The Confession continues to list the duties of people to the magistrate by mentioning obedience to "their lawful commands." The Larger Catechism, question 127, speaks of "willing obedience to their lawful commands." Now although the Scripture texts cited speak only of the responsibility of obedience to the word of the magistrate, the Confession and Catechism modify this to obedience with respect to the ruler's *lawful* commands. The divines could have cited passages which clearly indicate this (e.g., Acts 5:29), and so their omission of such Scripture proofs would indicate that they felt such an understanding (viz., that we need only obey the magistrate when his commands are lawful) was implicit in the Scripture texts that were in fact adduced. Here is another line of evidence that shows the Westminster outlook to require the magistrate to follow the direction of God's word; even when the Bible does not explicitly say this, such obedience to God's direction must still be understood according to the divines. And what "law" is it that the magistrate must conform to in order that his commands be "lawful"? It certainly is not the law of the state, for then his commands would always be "lawful" (and if the country is under constitutional rule, then the question simply shifts to the "lawfulness" of the constitutional commands). The Westminster divines did not expect *natural* law to be a *moral* authority, and they viewed natural revelation as identical in its demands with special (redemptive) revelation. Thus it was the law of God which, according to the Westminster Confession, determined the "lawfulness" of the magistrate's commands; "the moral law doth ever bind all . . . to the obedience thereof," for it is "a perfect rule of righteousness" (cf. 19.5, 2). The citizen must obey the magistrate, just as the magistrate must obey God. The magistrate's commands must be "lawful."

It is interesting that the immediately preceding teaching should come before the next obligation of individuals to the state (viz., to be subject to its authority). This suggests the order of priorities in the thinking of the Westminster divines. It needed to be made clear first that the obedience due to the magistrate was conditioned upon the lawfulness of his commands before it could be asserted that subjection to his authority was required of the people. However, the Westminster divines did take such a requirement of subjection seriously. In chapter 20, section 4, the Confession prohibits the use of "Christian liberty" to resist or oppose any lawful civil power; such resistance is tantamount to resisting God Himself (cf. Rom. 13:1-8); rebellion can rightly be punished, the Confession goes on to say, by the power of the civil magistrate. The Larger Catechism lists rebellion against the magistrate (illustrated in the history of Absalom, 2 Sam. 15:1-12) as *sin* (question 128). Therefore, the citizens of a country are put under serious obligation to obey the civil authorities by the Westminster Confession. Since it is sinful to disobey or rebel against the magistrate, such opposition on the part of a Christian can appropriately bring church discipline. Hence there is two-fold sanction in the Confession against civil disobedience: as a crime it can be punished by the magistrate, and as a sin it can be disciplined by the church.

The Confession now ends the discussion of the civil magistrate by mentioning two erroneous ideas about the magistrate that had been fairly prevalent in church history. First, the Confession declares that citizens must respect the rights of the civil magistrate even if he differs with them in religion; even infidelity does not cancel his legal authority. Such a viewpoint undermines the error of the Levellers who opposed kingship and advocated complete freedom in religion. The Confession does not contradict its previous teaching that the magistrate is obligated to observe all the laws of God, but it does make clear that the magistrate need not be a Christian and do such before the citizens are responsible to obey him. Even if he be reprobate, as long as his commands are lawful he is to be obeyed. While infidelity would cancel the authority an officer has in the church, it does not have similar results in the state. Thus again the Westminster divines protected the proper separation of church and state; the principles governing the church (in particular, its rulers) are not the same as those governing the state. It would be wrong to make Christian profession a requirement for civil rule, for that would make the state blend into the church. The magistrate has certain moral responsibilities (viz., God's law); however, conversion unto salvation and orthodoxy in matters of the faith are *not* among them. That the state was not to be blended into the church is strongly taught in the last portion of chapter 23. Here we find a dual rejection of the error of Roman Catholicism in its view of the civil magistrate. In the first place, there is no privileged status for church officers in civil matters, for "ecclesiastical persons are not exempted" from obedience to the civil authority. The Roman Church had held that priests could not be tried in civil court for their crimes; the Westminster Confession forthrightly rejects such a notion. To hold that ecclesiastical officers were free from civil prosecution would imply that the church had higher jurisdiction over the state (thus providing that the higher officials—e.g., priests—not be tried by lower officials—e.g., magistrates). The church and state are separate jurisdictions standing side by side in the Westminster outlook, not somehow arranged in a hierarchy of authority. *A fortiori* the Confession held that the Pope did not have any power or jurisdiction over civil magistrates in their dominions. Here the error of the Ultramontanes was condemned. They held (from the time of Hildebrand in the 11th century) that the spiritual power of the Pope assumed absolute supremacy over the state. They went so far as to say that the prince had to acknowledge himself and his treasury at the disposal of the Roman pontiff, who could otherwise release his people from allegiance to the magistrate and the protection afforded to the magistrate under the law. The Confession unequivocably denies all this: the Pope has no authority "least of all, to deprive them [rulers] of their dominions, or lives . . . upon any pretence whatsoever." Therefore, under the general responsibility of people to obey the civil magistrate the Westminster Confession includes the responsibility of all ecclesiastical officers to obey the ruler, prohibits the Pope from interfering with the ruler's authority, and specifies that even infidelity in the ruler does not warrant civil disobedience. The Confession not only puts civil authorities under great responsibility (viz., to enforce God's law), then, but it also affords the magistrate the right to demand obedience and sanctions his authority with far reaching creedal provisions.

In closing we can summarize the teaching of the Westminster Confession with respect to the civil magistrate.

1. The magistrate's rule originates from God and serves two divine purposes: God's glory, the public good.

2. The magistrate has the right to use the sword in order to encourage good and punish evil, as well as to fight defensive wars.

3. The magistrate is required to obey and enforce the law of God (even its penal sanctions), and the commands of the ruler are to be obeyed to the extent that they do not violate the law of God.

4. The magistrate's authority and jurisdiction is separate from that of the church; he may not administer the word or sacraments, handle the keys of the kingdom. And on the other hand orthodoxy or Christian profession are not required for civil authority.

5. This separation of church and state, however, does not render the two indifferent to each other: the ruler is to be a "nursing-father" to the church, and Christians are to pray, reverence, and support the magistrate.

6. All men are obligated to be subject to civil authority, for rebellion and disobedience are sins against God.

7. The Christian may participate in civil rule, but he has no inherent right to it; moreover, church officers are not exempt from civil obedience, and no ecclesiastical personage (e.g., the Pope) has authority over the magistrate.

APPENDIX 3

A HISTORICAL SPECIMEN OF THEONOMIC POLITICS

Cotton's *Abstract of the Laws of New England*

IT is well known that the rise of Puritanism in Britain led to the founding of America's New England some three and a half centuries ago.[1] "Under the leadership of William Laud . . . friends of the king deprived Puritan ministers of their pulpits and moved the church of England even closer to Rome in its ceremonies, vestments, and doctrines. . . . In despair and hope [the Puritans] too turned their thoughts to America, where they might escape God's wrath, worship in purity, and gather strength for future victory."[2] In 1630 a thousand people sailed with John Winthrop to Massachusetts; soon they were joined by twenty thousand others.

The attitude of the Puritans in founding this new land was governed by the model set by Calvin in Geneva. They were convinced of the dire need for godly politics and determined to let God's infallible word guide their endeavors. The renewed emphasis we see in this day on the application of Christianity to every area of life and human activity is the heritage of Reformed theology; much can be learned from the New England Puritans in this regard. Their goal was to see the kingdom of Jesus Christ come to expression in society as well as the private, inner heart of man. Due to their zeal for a righteous political

---

[1] Cf. William Haller, *The Rise of Puritanism* (New York: Harper Torch-Books, 1938, reprinted 1957), p. 5.

[2] J. M. Blum, *et. al., The National Experience* (New York: Harcourt, Brace, & World, 1963), pp. 21, 22.

structure they "preferred a wilderness governed by Puritans to a civilized land governed by Charles I. . . . Here in truth, was a self-governing commonwealth, a Puritan Republic. . . . The New England Puritans agreed on a great deal. . . . They wanted a government that would take seriously its obligation to enforce God's commandments."[3]

The Puritans were foremost men of the word of God written. They acknowledged the authority of Scripture for all things, and this naturally led to their affirmation of the full validity of God's law. A dispensational antagonism between law and grace was abhorrent to them. Hence Samuel Bolton wrote in the Epistle Dedicatory for this 1645 masterpiece, *The True Bounds of Christian Freedome,* that his purpose was "to hold up the Law, as not to intrench upon the liberties of Grace, and so to establish Grace, as not to make void the Law, nor to discharge beleevers of any dutie they owe to God or man." The law was integral to every area of theology. Sin is the transgression of God's law, for the law itself reveals the holiness of God. Christ's death was the satisfaction of the law; justification is the verdict of the law, and sanctification is the believer's obedience to the law.

Since God's law reflects His immutable character it was impossible that the law should be abrogated; to speak of the law's abrogation, said the Puritans, was to dishonor God himself. Thus in *Regula Vitae, The Rule of the Law under the Gospel* (1631) Thomas Taylor said "A man may breake the Princes Law, and not violate his Person; but not Gods: for God and his image in the Law, are so straitly united, as one cannot wrong the one, and not the other." The moral law was viewed as "consonant to that eternall justice and goodness in [God] himself" so that God could turn it back only if He would "deny his own justice and goodnesse" (Anthony Burgess, *Vindiciae Legis,* 1646). Ralph Venning expressed the view succinctly, declaring "To find fault with the Law, were to find fault with God" (*Sin, the Plague of Plagues,* 1669).

Therefore, in Puritan theology the law of God, like its Author, was eternal (cf. e.g., William Ames, *The Marrow of Sacred Divinity,* 1641,

---

[3] Ibid., pp. 22, 23.

or Edward Elton, *God's Holy Minde Touching Matters Morall*, 1625). Every jot and tittle of it was taken as having permanent validity. John Crandon stated in 1654, "Christ hath expunged no part of it" *(Mr. Baxters Aphorisms exorcized and Authorized)*. Christ's confirmation of the law of Moses was likened to a goldsmith newly-minting a valuable coin (Vavasor Powell, *Christ and Moses Excellency*, 1650) or a painter who works over and recovers the glory of an older picture (Anthony Burgess, *Vindiciae Legis*). "Every beleever . . . is answerable to the obedience of the whole Law" said Thomas Taylor *(Regula Vitae)*. Unlike modern theologians the Puritans did not seek clever schemes for shaving the law of God down to the preconceived notions of man or society. The validity of the law meant the validity of *all* the law.

Without doubt this had tremendous implications for their approach to civil government. One of the key functions of the law was that of restraining sin (cf. the works by Burgess and Powell mentioned above). The law does this by means of its sanctions. Thomas Manton noted that "a law implies a sanction," and Burgess commented that such sanction is imposed "that the Law may be the better obeyed." Consequently, the penal commandments of the law of God needed to be enforced by godly magistrates, for to fail in this matter was to violate God's righteous demand. The positive attitude of the Puritans toward every stroke of God's law led them to oppose antinomianism in *both* theology and politics. Indeed, as Henry Burton recognized in 1631, theological antinomianism leads to political antinomianism (*Law and Gospel Reconciled*). Therefore, a proper political order had to conform to the dictates of God's law. As Ernest F. Kevan says in his brilliant study, *The Grace of Law, A Study in Puritan Theology*, "This acknowledgment of the authority of the Law of God affected the attitude of the Puritans to the civil law."[4]

---

[4] (Grand Rapids: Baker Book House, 1965), p. 21. This was Kevan's doctoral dissertation at the University of London and is well worth the reader's full examination. The preceding quotations from the Puritan writers have been derived from Kevan's study.

Because the Puritans were students of God's word and held to its unity and abiding authority, their thinking and living aimed to be governed by the principle that only God can diminish the requirements of His law (Deut. 4:2). Not one jot or tittle of it was abrogated by the Messiah (Matt. 5:17-19), and hence no man dare tamper with its full requirements. The law is to be used as a social restraint on crime (1 Tim. 1:8) as well as guidance in holy living for individuals. The state, no less than any other area of life, was taken to be subject to God's authority via His written revelation. The magistrate could not escape his obligation to be "a minister of God" appointed as an *avenger* of God's *wrath* against *evildoers*—that is, against transgressors of God's law (Rom. 13:1-7; cf. vv. 8-10). The civil leader was called to be a blessing to his public, which could mean nothing other than following God's prescribed moral pattern. The magistrate was required to establish justice in the gate (Amos 5:15), and justice was preeminently defined by the law of Moses given to Israel (Deut. 4:8). Thus when the statesman forgets the law of God, he inevitably perverts justice (Prov. 31:5) and thereby betrays his vocation. The Puritans took seriously the magistrate's responsibility not to swerve to the right or left of God's revealed law (Deut. 17:18-20). This law was not a standard of righteousness merely in Israel; it was universal in its application and demand, for God does not have a double standard (cf. Deut. 25:13-16). The justice of God's law has been established as a light to the peoples (Isa. 51:4; Matt. 5:14, 17); it should guide their steps just as it was intended to guide the steps of Israel in ethics. God's law binds all nations and their leaders, for sin is a disgrace to *any* people (Prov. 14:34). This truth led David to promote God's law before kings (Ps. 119:46) and to declare that all rulers must fear the Lord in their government and become thereby a blessing to the people (2 Sam. 23:3-4). The kings and judges of *all the earth,* then, are called upon to serve the Lord with fear (Ps. 2:10-12). Having learned these truths well, the Puritans had to conclude that it was an abomination for kings to violate the law of God, for in so doing justice was perverted and the people were brought under oppression (Prov. 16:12; 28:28). Therefore, the New England Puritans sought a government which would enforce God's commandments, knowing that the sure word of the sovereign Lord required, endorsed, and undergirded this project.

Among the Puritans who came to America, John Cotton (1584-1652) stands out as one of the very most prominent and influential pacesetters and theologians of the Massachusetts Bay Colony. A convert under the ministry of Richard Sibbes, Cotton created enough of a reputation and stir in England that he was summoned before the High Court to answer to William Laud in 1632. However, the well organized Puritan underground concealed him and enabled him to take flight to New England, where his presence was eagerly anticipated. In Boston Cotton was a leader in Christian doctrine and ecclesiastical polity. His political influence is here to be noted. In his work, *A Discourse about Civil Government in a New Plantation whose Design is Religion* (published in Cambridge, 1663), Cotton (perhaps in association with John Davenport) wrote that a theocracy was the proper and best form of government to endorse, and he defined a theocracy as where the Lord God is our Governor and *where the laws by which men rule are the laws of God* (pp. 14-15, original edition). A theocracy did *not* mean the erasing of the distinction between church and state:

> The best form was theocracy, which for Cotton meant separate but parallel civil and ecclesiastical organizations framed on the evidence of scriptures. Church and state, he believed, were of the same genus, "order," with the same author, "God," and the same end, "God's glory." On the level of species, however, the two diverged. Here the end of the church was salvation of souls while that of the state was the preservation of society in justice.[5]

The law of God was binding on the civil magistrate, then, and the government of the state ought to be molded in conformity to God's

[5] Larzer Ziff, *The Career of John Cotton: Puritanism and the American Experience* (New Jersey: Princeton University Press, 1962), pp. 97-98.

revealed direction. "The laws the godly would rule by were the laws of God, and in all hard cases, the clergy could be consulted without danger of a confusion of church and state." [6] Cotton's attitude was that "the more any law smells of man the more unprofitable." Cotton and his Puritan contemporaries applied the revealed law of God to the state's constitution and stipulations. If any provision of the civil code was not warranted by God's word, then it had to be looked upon with great suspicion and accepted only with great caution. It should be remarked here that, just as Cotton's theocratic ideal did not confuse church and state, neither did it blur the difference in Scripture between cultic or *restorative* laws which anticipated the redemptive economy of Christ and *moral* laws with eternal rectitude or holiness as their essence. "Moses' laws, Cotton affirmed, were ceremonial as well as moral, and the former were to be considered dead while the latter were still binding in a civil state."[7]

In May of 1636 Cotton was given his greatest opportunity to exert his theological influence on the framing of the commonwealth when he was appointed to the constitutional committee charged with drafting laws agreeable to God's word for the new plantation. Cotton's contribution to the effort was his work, *Moses His Judicials;* the chapters on crime and inheritance were drawn directly from the Scriptures.[8] The other chapters followed the existing civil code, with Cotton providing the biblical support for its various articles. Cotton's excellent work in this regard had effect beyond Boston, being influential in the settlements at New Haven and Southampton, Long Island. Later, on December 10, 1641, the Massachusetts Bay Colony adopted a biblically based civil code authored by Nathiel Ward (another Christian pastor) and given scriptural annotations by John Cotton.[9] It was called the

---

[6] Ibid.

[7] Ibid.

[8] Cf. Isabel M. Calder's study in *Publications of the Colonial Society of Massachusetts* XXVIII (Boston, 1935), pp. 86-94.

[9] George L. Haskins, *Law and Authority in Early Massachusetts* (New York: Macmillan Co., 1960), pp. 130, 199.

Body of Liberties, and it explicitly provided that no law was to be prescribed contrary to the word of God. [10] The 1648 *Massachusetts Code* was based upon the *Body of Liberties,* and in turn it became the prototype for the legislation of every other state constitution in the early days of America.

A further manuscript written by John Cotton, but difficult for most readers to obtain, is his *An Abstract of the Laws of New England, As They Are Now Established,* which was originally published in London in 1641. William Aspinwall republished it in 1655, unequivocally attributing it to John Cotton in the printer's foreword to the reader. A copy of the manuscript by this title was found in Cotton's study after his death; it was handwritten and agrees by and large with the Aspinwall publication. In the early archives of the Massachusetts Historical Society the work was bound along with *Mr. Cotton's Discourse on Civil Government in a New Plantation whose Design is Religion.* Thus there is every reason to assign its authorship to Cotton, even though the original publication was anonymous. It is quite likely that Cotton was assisted in this work by Sir Henry Vane, the Massachusetts governor in 1636 whom Milton highly commended for properly seeing the bounds of civil and religious power. Vane was a great friend of Cotton's and shared the same political and religious principles with him.

The character of this important historical piece is evident from its lengthy subtitle: "wherein, as in a mirror, may be seen the wisdom and perfection of Christ's kingdom, accommodable to any state or form of government in the world, that is not antichristian and tyrannical." Cotton was convinced that believers ought to promote the pattern of justice embodied in God's revealed law as the guideline for any civil community. Indeed, God's law was the only alternative to despotism as he saw it. A godly state will bring its laws into conformity with God's, thereby serving His just ends in society.

A copy of this document is reprinted below, serving as an illustration of a civil code which attempted to be founded upon the word of

[10] Cf. *Puritan Political Ideas,* ed. Edmund S. Morgan (Indianapolis, 1965).

God. It is taken from the *Collections of the Massachusetts Historical Society For the Year 1798,* volume 5 (Boston: Samuel Hall, 1798, reprinted 1835), pages 173-187. It deserves the serious attention of all those concerned with the Christian reconstruction of society along godly and God pleasing lines. Today we are seeing a renewed interest in the Christian's obligation to be the light of the world and salt of the earth—in seeing the influence of Christian faith permeate every aspect of life and effect a widespread cultural renovation. As usual, history has instructive lessons for us here. The seventeenth century Puritans have laid a groundwork and forged a path to which today's Christian should pay attention.

This is not to say that everything which we find written in Cotton's work should meet with our approval. Indeed, a disclaimer is necessary. There are matters which today's Bible student may wish to dispute in Cotton's analysis (e.g., in Chapter 7, article 24, Cotton appears to make all perjury punishable by death, whereas the law of God more strictly says that the false witness is to receive *whatever* punishment would have been due to the accused—and that was not always death). There is surely room to challenge some of his conclusions or applications (e.g., price and wage controls in chapter 5). Thus the reader should not understand that the reprinting of Cotton's work constitutes a blanket endorsement of each of his various positions.

Nevertheless, the document is of significant weight in the history of Christian thought, and it should not be lost from sight. Its noble attempt to bring God's law to bear in a real historical situation on the civil magistrate should serve as an encouragement, a rebuke, and an ideal for us today. By the way, given this document's publication in London in 1641, it also provides valuable background to Reformed thought at the time of the Westminster Assembly, which convened just two years later; reflecting popular Reformed sentiment with respect to civil government at that time, this work can be of hermeneutical benefit when it comes to present day understanding of the Westminster Confession's declarations about God's law and the civil magistrate.

A further observation should be made for the reader prior to reproducing Cotton's *Abstract* here. Although it is quite evident at many specific points that the author was grounding his legislation in the law of God since he gave concrete scriptural citations along with his articles, the reader must not overlook the fact that in many other places Cotton simply quoted the Mosaic law and, expecting his reader's acquaintance with God's word, did not attach a scriptural citation. For instance, chapter 6 in the Abstract ("Of Trespasses") has no biblical citations listed, and yet it comes right out of Exodus 22. The effort to build on God's revealed law is evidenced, then, throughout the work.

Finally, we can introduce John Cotton's *Abstract of the Laws of New England* by quoting from Aspinwall's "Address to the Reader" in the 1655 reprinting of it:

> [This model] far surpasseth all the municipal laws and statutes of any of the Gentile nations and corporations under the cope of Heaven. Wherefore I thought it not unmeet to publish it to the view of all, for the common good. . . . Judge equally and impartially, whether there be any laws in any state in the world, so just and equal as these be. Which, were they duly attended unto, would undoubtedly preserve inviolable the liberty of the subject against all tyrannical and usurping powers. . . . This Abstract may serve for this use principally (which I conceive was the main scope of that good man, who was the author of it) to shew the complete sufficiency of the word of God alone, to direct his people in judgment of all causes, both civil and criminal. . . . But the truth is, both they we, and other the Gentile nations, are loth to be persuaded to . . . lay aside our old earthly forms of governments, to submit to the government of Christ. Nor shall we Gentiles be willing, I fear, to take up his yoke which is easy, and burthen light, until he hath broken us under the hard and heavy yokes of men, and thereby weaned us from all our old forms and customs. . . . So that there will be a necessity, that the little stone,

cut out of the mountain without hands, should crush and break these obstacles, ere the way can be prepared for erecting his kingdom, wherein dwells righteousness.— And verily great will be the benefit of this kingdom of Christ, when it shall be submitted unto by the nations. . . [Ps. 95:10; Isa. 66:12]. All burdens and tyrannical exactions will be removed; *God will make their officers peace, and their exactors righteousness,* Isa. 60:17.

AN ABSTRACT OF THE LAWS OF NEW-ENGLAND, AS THEY ARE NOW ESTABLISHED. PRINTED IN LONDON IN 1641.

Chapter I.

Of Magistrates.

1. ALL magistrates are to be chosen. Deut. 1:13, 17, 15.

First, By the free burgesses.

Secondly, Out of the free burgesses.

Thirdly, Out of the ablest men and most approved amongst them. Ex. 18, 21.

Fourthly, Out of the rank of noblemen or gentlemen among them, the best *that God shall send into the country,* if they be qualified with gifts fit for government, either eminent above others, or not inferior to others. Eccle. 10:17. Jer. 30:21.

2. The governor hath power, with the assistants, to govern the whole country, according to the laws established, hereafter mentioned: he hath power of himself, and in his absence the deputy-governor, to moderate all public actions of the Commonwealth, as

First, To send out warrants for calling of the general court. Josh. 24:1.

Secondly, To order and ransack all actions in the court where he sitteth: as, to gather suffrages and voices, and to pronounce sentences according the greater part of them.

3. The power of the governor, with the rest of the counsellors, is

First, To consult and provide for the maintenance of the state and people. Num. 11:14-16.

Secondly, To direct in all matters, wherein appeal is made to them from inferior courts. Deut. 17:8, 9.

Thirdly, To preserve religion. Ex. 32:25, 27.

Fourthly, To oversee the forts and munition of the country, and to take order for the protection of the country from foreign invasion, or intestine sedition, as need shall require, with consent of the people to enterprise wars. Cor. 19:32; 23:6. Prov. 24:5.

And because these great affairs of the state cannot be attended, nor administered, if they be after changed; therefore the counsellors are to be chosen for life, *unless they give just cause of removal,* which if they do, then they are to be removed by *the general court.* 1 Kings 2:6.

4. The power of the governor, sitting with the counsellors and assistants, is to hear and determine all causes whether civil or criminal, which are brought before him through the whole Commonwealth: *yet reserving liberty of appeal from him to the general court.* Ex. 18:22. Deut. 1:16, 18.

5. Every town is to have judges within themselves, whose power shall be once in the month, or in three months at the farthest, to hear and determine both civil causes and pleas of less value, and crimes also, which are not capital: yet reserving liberty of appeal to the court of governor and assistants. Deut. 16, 18.

6. For the better expedition and execution of justice, and of all affairs incident unto every court; every court shall have certain officers, as a secretary to enrol all the acts of the court; and besides ministers of justice, to attach and fetch, and set persons before the magistrates; and also to execute the sentence of the court upon offenders: and for the

same end it shall be lawful for the governor or any one or two of the counsellors, or assistants, or judges, to give warrants to an officer, to fetch any delinquent before them, and to examine the cause, and if he be found culpable of that crime, to take order by surety or safe custody for his appearance at the court. Deut. 16, 18. Jer. 36:10, 12. 1 Sam. 20:24, 25. Acts 5:26, 27.

And further for the same end, and to prevent the offenders lying long in prison, it shall be lawful for the governor, with one of the council, or any two of the assistants or judges, to see execution done upon any offenders *for any crime that is not capital,* according to the laws established: *yet reserving a liberty of appeal from them to the court, and from an inferior court to a higher court.*

Chapter II.

Of the free Burgesses and free Inhabitants.

1. FIRST, all the free burgesses, excepting such as were admitted men before the establishment of churches in the country, shall be received and admitted out of the members of some or others of the churches in the country, such churches as are gathered or hereafter shall be gathered with the consent of other churches already established in the country, and such members as are admitted by their own church unto the Lord's table.

2. These free burgesses shall have power to choose in their own towns, *fit and able men out of themselves,* to be the ordinary judges of inferior causes, in their own town; and, against the approach of the general court, to choose two or three, as their deputies and committees, to join with the governor and assistants of the whole country, to make up and constitute the general court.

3. This general court shall have power,

First, By the warrant of the governor, or deputy-governor, to assemble once every quarter, or half a year, or oftener, as the affairs of the country shall require, and to sit together till their affairs be dispatched.

Secondly, To call the governor, and all the rest of the public magistrates and officers into place, *and to call them also to account for the breach of any laws established, or other misdemeanor, and to censure them as the quality of the fact may require.*

Thirdly, To make and repeal laws.

Fourthly, To dispose of all lands in the country, and to assign them to several towns or persons, as shall be thought requisite.

Fifthly, To impose of monies a levy, for the public service of the Commonwealth, as shall be thought requisite *for the provision and protection of the whole.*

Sixthly, To hear and determine all causes, wherein appeal shall be made unto them, or which they shall see cause to assume into their own cognizance or judicature.

Seventhly, To assist the governors and counsellors, in the maintenance of the purity and unity of religion; and accordingly to set forth and uphold all such good causes as shall be thought fit, for that end, by the advice and with consent of the churches, and to repress the contrary.

Eighthly, In this general court nothing shall be concluded but with thc common consent of the greater part of the governors, or assistants, together with the greater part of the deputies of the towns; unless it be in election of officers, *where the liberty of the people is to be preferred,* or in judging matters of offence against the law, wherein both parties are to stand to the direction of the law.

4. All the householders of every town shall be accounted as the free inhabitants of the country, and accordingly shall enjoy freedom of commerce, and inheritance of such lands as the general court or the several towns wherein they dwell, shall allot unto them, after they have taken an oath, or given other security to be true and faithful to the state, and subject to the good and wholesome laws established in the country by the general court.

Chapter III.

Of the Protection and Provision of the Country.

1. FIRST, a law to be made (if it be not made already) for the training of all men in the country, fit to bear arms, unto the exercise of military discipline and withal another law to be made for the maintenance of military officers and forts.

2. Because fishing is the chief staple commodity of the country, therefore all due encouragement to be given unto such hands as shall set forwards the trade of fishing: and for that end a law to be made, that whosoever shall apply themselves to set forward the trade of fishing, as fishermen, mariners, and shipwrights, shall be allowed, man for man, or some or other of the labourers of the country, to plant and reap for them, in the season of the year, at the public charge of the commonwealth, for the space of the seven years next ensuing; and such labourers to be appointed and paid by the treasurer of the commonwealth.

3. Because no commonwealth can maintain either their authority at home, or their honor and power abroad, without a sufficient treasury: a law therefore to be made for the electing and furnishing of the treasury of the commonwealth, which is to be supplied and furnished,

1st. By the yearly payment,

First, Of one penny, or half a penny an acre of land to be occupied throughout the country. Land in common by a town, to be paid for out of the stock or treasury of the same town.

Secondly, Of a penny for every beast, horse or cow.

Thirdly, Of some proportionable rate upon merchants.—This rate to be greater or less, as shall be thought fit.

2d. By the payment of a barrel of gunpowder, or such goods or other munitions, out of every ship that bringeth foreign commodities.

3d. By fines and mulcts upon trespassers' beasts.

4. A treasurer to be chosen by the free burgesses, out of the assistants, who shall receive and keep the treasury, and make disbursements out of it, according to the direction of the general court, or of the governor or counsellors, whereof they are to give an account to the general court. It shall pertain also to the office of the treasurer, to survey and oversee all the munitions of the country, as cannons, culverins, muskets, powder, match, bullets, &c. and to give account thereof to the governor and council.

5. A treasury also, or magazine, or storehouse, to be erected, and furnished in every town, [as Deut. 14:28.] distinct from the treasury of the church, that provision of corn, and other necessaries, may be laid up at the best hand, for the relief of such poor as are not members of the church; and that out of it such officers may be maintained, as captains and such like, who do any public service for the town. But chiefly, this treasury will he requisite for the preserving of the livelihood of each town within itself. That in case the inheritance of the lands that belong to any town, come to be alienated from the townsmen, which may unavoidably fall out; yet a supply may be had and made to the livelihood of the town, by a reasonable rent charge upon such alienations, laid by the common consent of the landowners and townsmen, and to be paid into the treasury of the town. This treasury to be supplied,

First, By the yearly payment of some small rate upon acres of land.

Secondly, By fines and amercements put upon trespassers' beasts.

A town treasurer to be appointed for the oversight and ordering of this, chosen out of the free burgesses of the same town, who is so to dispose of things under his charge, according to the direction of the judges of the town, and to give account, at the town's court, to the judges and free burgesses of the town, or to some selected by them.

Chapter IV.

Of the right of Inheritance.

1. FIRST, forasmuch as the right of disposals of the inheritance of all lands in the country lyeth in the general court, whatsoever lands are given and assigned by the general court, to any town or person, shall belong and remain as right of inheritance to such towns and their successors, and to such persons and to their heirs and assigns forever, as their propriety.

2. Whatsoever lands, belonging to any town, shall be given and assigned by the town, or by such officers therein as they shall appoint, unto any person, the same shall belong and remain unto such person and his heirs and assigns, as his proper right forever.

3. And in dividing of lands to the several persons in each town, as regard is to be had, partly to the number of persons in a family—to the more, assigning the greater allotment, to the fewer, less—and partly by the number of beasts, by the which a man is fit to occupy the land assigned to him, and subdue it; eminent respect, in this case, may be given to men of eminent quality and descent, in assigning unto them more large and honorable accomodations, in regard of their great disbursements to public charges.

4. Forasmuch as all civil affairs are to be administered and ordered, so as may best conduce to the upholding and setting forward of the worship of God in church fellowship; it is therefore ordered, that wheresoever the lands of any man's inheritance shall fall, yet no man shall set his dwellinghouse above the distance of half a mile, or a mile at the farthest, from the meeting of the congregation, where the church doth usually assemble for the worship of God.

5. Inheritances are to descend naturally to the next of kin, according to the law of nature, delivered by God.

6. Observe, if a man have more sons than one, then *a double portion* to be assigned and bequeathed to the eldest son, according to the law of nature; unless his own dermerit do deprive him of the dignity of his birth-right.

7. The will of a testator is to be approved or disallowed by the court of governor and assistants, or by the court of judges in each town: yet not to be disallowed by the court of governors, unless it appears either to be counterfeit, or unequal, either against the law of God, or against the due right of the legators.

8. As God in old time, in the commonwealth of Israel, forbade the alienation of lands from one tribe to another; so to prevent the like inconvenience in the alienation of lands from one town to another, it were requisite to be ordered:

1st. That no free burgess, or free inhabitant of any town, shall sell the land allotted to him in the town, (unless the free burgesses of the town give consent unto such sale, or refuse to give due price, answerable to what others offer without fraud), but to some one or other of the free burgesses or free inhabitants of the same town.

2d. That if such lands be sold to any others, the sale shall be made with reservation of such a rent charge, to be paid to the town stock, or treasury of the town, as either the former occupiers of the land were wont to pay towards all the public charges thereof, whether in church or town; or at least after the rate of three shillings per acre, or some such like proportion, more or less, as shall be thought fit.

3d. That if any free burgesses, or free inhabitants, of any town, or the heir of any of their lands, shall remove their dwelling from one town to another, none of them shall carry away the whole benefit of the lands which they possessed, from the towns whence they remove: but if they still keep the right of inheritance in their own hands, and not sell it as before, then they shall reserve a like proportion or rent charge out of their land, to be paid to the public treasury of the town, as hath been wont to be paid out of it to the public charges of the town and church, or at least after the rate of three or five shillings an acre, as before.

4th. That if the inheritance of a free burgess, or free inhabitant of any town, fall to his daughters, as it will do for defect of heirs male, that then if such daughters do not marry to some of the inhabitants of the same town where their inheritance lyeth, nor sell their inheritance to some of the same town as before, that then they reserve a like proportion of rent charge out of their lands, to be paid to the public treasury of the town, as hath been wont to be paid out of them, to the public charge, of the town and church; or at least after the rate of three or five shillings an acre; provided always that nothing be paid to the maintenance of the church out of the treasury of the church or town, but by the free consent and direction of the free burgesses of the town.

Chapter V.

Of Commerce.

1. FIRST, it shall be lawful for the governor, with one or more of the council, to appoint a reasonable rate of prizes upon all such commodities as are, out of the ships, to be bought and sold in the country.

2. In trucking or trading with the Indians, no man shall give them, for any commodity of theirs, silver or gold, or any weapons of war, either guns or gunpowder, nor swords, nor any other munition, *which might come to be used against ourselves.*

3. To the intent that all oppression in buying and selling may be avoided, it shall be lawful for the judges in every town, with the consent of the free burgesses, to appoint certain selectmen, to set reasonable rates upon all commodities, and proportionably to limit the wages of workmen and labourers; and the rates agreed upon by them, and ratified by the judges, to bind all the inhabitants of the town. The like course to be taken by the governor and assistants, for the rating of prizes throughout the country, and all to be confirmed, if need be, by the general court.

4. Just weights and balances to be kept between buyers and sellers, and for default thereof, the profit so wickedly and corruptly gotten, with as much more added thereto, is to be forfeited to the public treasury of the commonwealth.

5. If any borrow ought of his neighbour upon a pledge, the lender shall not make choice of what pledge he will have, nor take such a pledge as is of daily necessary use unto the debtor, or if he does take it, he shall restore it again the same day.

6. No increase to be taken of a poor brother or neighbour, for any thing lent unto him.

7. If borrowed goods be lost or hurt in the owner's absence, the borrower is to make them good; but in the owner's presence, wherein he seeth his goods no otherwise used than with his consent, the borrower shall not make them good; if they were hired, the hire to be paid and no more.

Chapter VI.

Of Trespasses.

1. IF a man's swine, or any other beast, or a fire kindled, break out into another man's field or corn, he shall make full restitution, both of the damage made by them, and of the loss of time which others have had in carrying such swine or beasts unto the owners, or unto the fold. But if a man puts his beasts or swine into another's field, restitution is to be made of the best of his own, though it were much better than that which were destroyed or hurt.

2. If a man kill another man's beast, or dig and open a pit, and leave it uncovered, and a beast fall into it; he that killed the beast and the owner of the pit, shall make restitution.

3. If one man's beast kills the beast of another, the owner of the beast shall make restitution.

4. If a man's ox, or other beast, gore or bite, and kill a man or woman, whether child or riper age, the beast shall be killed, and no

benefit of the dead beast reserved to the owner. But if the ox, or beast, were wont to push or bite in time past, and the owner hath been told of it, and hath not kept him in, then both the ox, or beast, shall be forfeited and killed, and the owner also put to death, or fined to pay what the judges and persons damnified shall lay upon him.

5. If a man deliver goods to his neighbour to keep, and they be said to be lost or stolen from him, the keeper of the goods shall be put to his oath touching his own innocency; which if he take, and no evidence appear to the contrary, he shall be quit: but if he be found false or unfaithful, he shall pay double unto his neighbour. But if a man take hire for goods committed to him, and they be stolen, the keeper shall make restitution. But if the beast so kept for hire, die or be hurt, or be driven away, no man seeing it, then oath shall be taken of the keeper, that it was without his default, and it shall be accepted. But if the beast be torn in pieces, and a piece be brought for a witness, it excuseth the keeper.

Chapter VII.

Of Crimes. And first, of such as deserve capital punishment, or cutting off from a man's people, whether by death or banishment.

1. FIRST, blasphemy, which is a cursing of God by atheism, or the like, to be punished with death.

2. Idolatry to be punished with death.

3. Witchcraft, which is fellowship by covenant with a familiar spirit, to be punished with death.

4. Consulters with witches not to be tolerated, but either to be cut off by death or banishment.

5. Heresy, which is the maintenance of some wicked errors, overthrowing the foundation of the christian religion; which obstinacy, if it be joined with endeavour to seduce others thereunto, to be punished

with death; because such an heretick, no less than an idolater, seeketh to thrust the souls of men from the Lord their God.

6. To worship God in a molten or graven image, to be punished with death.

7. Such members of the church, as do wilfully reject to walk, after due admonition and conviction, in *the churches' establishment*, and their christian admonition and censures, shall be cut off by banishment.

8. Whosoever shall revile the religion and worship of God, and the government of the church, as it is now established, to be cut off by banishment. 1 Cor. 5:5.

9. Wilful perjury, whether before the judgment seat or in private conference, to be punished with death.

10. Rash perjury, whether in public or in private, to be punished with banishment. Just is it, that such a man's name should be cut off from his people, who profanes so grosly the name of God before his people.

11. Profaning of the Lord's day, in a careless and scornful neglect or contempt thereof, to he punished with death.

12. To put in practice *the betraying of the country,* or any principal fort therein, to the hand of any foreign state, Spanish, French, Dutch, or the like, contrary to the allegiance we owe and profess to our dread sovereign, lord king Charles, his heirs and successors, whilst he is pleased to protect us as his loyal subjects, to be punished with death. Num. 12:14, 15.

13. Unreverend and dishonorable carriage to magistrates, to be punished with banishment for a time, till they acknowledge their fault and profess reformation.

14. Reviling of the magistrates in highest rank amongst us, to wit, of the governors and council, to be punished with death. 1 Kings 2:8, 9, 46.

15. Rebellion, sedition, or insurrection, by taking up arms against the present government established in the country, to be punished with death.

16. Rebellious children, whether they continue in riot or drunkenness, after due correction from their parents, or whether they curse or smite their parents, to be put to death. Ex. 21:15, 17. Lev. 20:9.

17. Murder, which is a wilful man-slaughter, not in a man's just defence, nor casually committed, but out of hatred or cruelty, to be punished with death. Ex. 21:12, 13. Num. 35:16, 17, 18-33. Gen. 9:6.

18. Adultery, which is the defilng of the marriage-bed, to be punished with death. Defiling of a woman espoused, is a kind of adultery, and punishable, by death, of both parties; but if a woman be forced, then by the death of the man only. Lev. 20:10. Deut. 22:22-27.

19. Incest, which is the defiling of any near of kin, within the degrees prohibited in Leviticus, to be punished with death.

20. Unnatural filthiness to be punished with death, whether sodomy, which is a carnal fellowship of man with man, or woman with woman, or buggery, which is a carnal fellowship of man or woman with beasts or fowls.

21. Pollution of a woman known to be in her flowers, to be put to death. Lev. 20:18, 19.

22. Whoredom of a maiden in her father's house, kept secret till after her marriage with another, to be punished with death. Deut. 22:20, 21.

23. Man-stealing to be punished with death. Ex. 21:16.

24. False-witness bearing to be punished with death.

Chapter VIII.

Of other Crimes less heinous, such as are to be punished with some corporal punishment or fine.

1. FIRST, rash and profane swearing and cursing to be punished,

1st. With loss of honour, or office, if he be a magistrate, or officer: meet it is, their name should be dishonoured who dishonoured God's name.

2d. With loss of freedom.

3d. With disability to give testimony.

4th. With corporal punishment, either by stripes or by branding him with a hot iron, or boring through the tongue, who have bored and pierced God's name.

2. Drunkenness, as transforming God's image into a beast, is to be punished with the punishment of beasts: a whip for the horse, and a rod for the fool's back.

3. Forcing of a maid, or a rape, is not to be punished with death by God's law, but,

1st. With fine or penalty to the father of the maid.

2d. With marriage of the maid defiled, if she and her father consent.

3d. With corporal punishment of stripes for his wrong, as a real slander: and it is worse to make a whore, than to say one is a whore.

4. Fornication to be punished,

1st. With the marriage of the maid, or giving her a sufficient dowry.

2d. With stripes, though fewer, from the equity of the former cause.

5. Maiming or wounding of a freeman, whether free burgess, or free inhabitant, to be punished with a fine; to pay,

1st. For his cure.

2d. For his loss. Ex. 21:18, 19. And with loss of member for member, or some valuable recompence: but if it be but the maiming or wounding of a servant, the servant is to go forth free from such a service. Lev. 24:19, 20. Ex. 21:26, 27.

6. If any man steal a beast, if it be found in his hand he shall make restitution two for one; if it be killed and sold, restitution is to be made of five oxen for one; if the thief be not able to make restitution, then he is to be sold by the magistrate for a slave, till by his labour he may make due restitution. Ex. 22:1, 4.

7. If a thief be found breaking a house by night, if he be slain, his smiter is guiltless; but in the day time, the thief is to make full restitution as before; or if he be not able, then to be sold as before. Ex. 22:2.

8. Slanders are to be punished,

First, With a public acknowledgment, as the slander was public.

Secondly, By mulets and fine of money, when the slander bringeth damage.

Thirdly, By stripes, if the slander be gross, or odious, *against such persons whom a man ought to honor and cherish;* whether they be his superiors, or in some degree of equality with himself and his wife.

Chapter IX.

Of the trial of causes, whether civil or criminal, and the execution of sentence.

1. IN the trial of all causes, no judgment shall pass but either upon confession of the party, or upon the testimony of two witnesses.

2. Trial by judges *shall not be denied,* where either the delinquent requireth it in causes criminal, or the plaintiff or defendant in civil causes, partly to prevent suspicion of partiality of any magistrates in the court.

3. The jurors are not to be chosen by any magistrates, or officers, but by the free burgesses of each town, as can give best light to the causes depending in court, and who are least obnoxious to suspicion of partiality; and the jurors then chosen, to be nominated to the court, and to attend the service of the court.

4. The sentence of judgment given upon criminal causes and persons, shall be executed in the presence of the magistrates, or some of them at least.

5. No freeman, whether free burgess or free inhabitant, to be imprisoned, but either upon conviction, or at least probably suspicion,

or some crime, formerly mentioned; and the cause of his imprisonment, be declared and tried at the next court following, at the furthest.

6. Stripes are not to be inflicted, but when the crimes of the offender are accompanied with childish or brutish folly, or with lewd filthiness, or with stubborn insolency, or with brutish cruelty, or with idle vagrancy; but when stripes are due, not above forty are to be inflicted.

Chapter X.

Of causes criminal, between our people and foreign nations.

1. IN case any of our people should do wrong to any of another nation, upon complaint made to the governor, or some other of the council or assistants, the fact is diligently to be inquired into, and being found to be true, restitution is to be made of the goods of offenders, as the cause shall require, according to the quality of the crime.

2. In case the people of another nation have done any important wrong to any of ours, right is first to he demanded of the governor of that people, and justice upon the malefactors, which if it be granted and performed, then no breach of peace to follow. Deut. 20:10, 11. 2 Sam. 20:18, 19.

3. If right and justice be denied, and it will not stand with the honour of God and safety of our nation that the wrong be passed over, then war is to be undertaken and denounced.

4. Some minister is to be sent forth to go along with the army, for their instruction and encouragement. Deut. 20:2, 3, 4.

5. Men betrothed and not married, or newly married, or such as have newly built or planted, and not received the fruits of their labour, and such as are faint-hearted men, are not to be pressed or forced against their wills to go forth to wars. Deut. 20:5, 6, 7, 8; 24:5.

6. Captains are to be chosen by the officers.

7. All wickedness is to be removed out of the camp by severe discipline. Deut. 23:9, 14.

8. And in war men of a corrupt and false religion are not to be accepted, much less sought for. 2 Chron. 25:7, 8.

9. Women, especially such as have not lain by man, little children, and cattle, are to he spared and reserved for spoil. Deut. 20:14.

10. Fruit trees, whilst they may be of use for meat to our own soldiers, are not to be cut down and destroyed, and consequently no corn. Deut. 20:19, 20.

11. The spoils got by war are to be divided into two parts, between the soldiers and the commonwealth that sent them forth. Num. 31:27.

12. A tribute from both is to be levied to the Lord, and given to the treasury of the church; a fiftieth part out of the commonwealth's part, and a five hundredth part out of the soldiers' part. Num. 31:28, 29, 47.

13. If all the soldiers return again in peace, not one lacking, it is acceptable to the Lord if they offer, over and above the former tribute, a voluntary oblation unto the treasury of the church, for a memorial of the redemption of their lives by the special providence and salvation of the Lord of Hosts.

Isaiah 33:22.
The Lord is our Judge,
The Lord is our Law-giver,
The Lord is our King: He will save us.

APPENDIX 4

A CRITIQUE OF M. G. KLINE

IN the preface to this work the problems of M. G. Kline's outlook as it touches on the subject of ethics were alluded to; since his position is relevant to the subject matter of the present study, and since the entire line of thought worked out above constitutes an indirect contradiction of Kline's view of the validity of the Older Testamental penal sanctions, it would be appropriate here to digress into a short critique of the relevant aspects of Dr. Kline's *The Structure of Biblical Authority* (Grand Rapids: Eerdmans, 1972). While the study of theonomy presented above is the most adequate case against Kline's point of view, a few direct observations about his methodology and his views on double canon and "intrusion" ethics might fill out the critique and show where the wrong turns were made.

As is clear to anyone who has read Kline's materials, he builds extensively upon research into the treaty forms of the ancient Near East for his views, seeing the form and content of Scripture as interestingly analogous to these treaties. Some notes should be made, then, on the use of analogies. There are three basic kinds of analogy: explanatory, argumentative, and hypothesis-suggestive; the first and second types of analogy are used in Scripture. An example of an explanatory analogy would be describing God as a father. This raises a question however: in what respects is God fatherly? What characteristics of earthly fathers can be appropriately applied to the heavenly father? A number of things come to mind when we think of fathers: they are responsible for our birth, provide for our needs, rebuke our disobedience, express love and affection to us; however, they also return home weary from work, sleep with mother, require respect even when they make a mistake, are obligated to make amends for our mischievousness, need care when elderly, and so forth. Thus when Scripture calls God "our heavenly father" we must use discretion in understanding that appellation, depending upon Scripture itself to *explain* the explanatory analogy! Through reading the Bible it is made clear in what fashion God can be considered analogous to a father.

Moreover, when Scripture uses an argumentative analogy (e.g., Christ's appeal to David's eating of the shewbread in order to defend His own sabbath activity; cf. Mark 2:23-28), it again must *specify* what the analogy is intended to prove (e.g., is Christ saying that He was using deception like David did before Ahimelech? cf. 1 Sam. 21:1-6). Thus we see that analogical inference proceeds from the similarity of two or more things in one or more respects to the similarity of those things in some further respect, and when Scripture uses such analogical inference it must be depended upon to indicate the respects in which the two analogues are similar and what further similarity can be drawn between them. Scripture clarifies its analogies so as to prevent illegitimate inferences.

Hereby we can understand why Scripture does not use hypothesis-suggestive analogies. Just as Scripture is an authoritative revelation of truth (not a proposal of hypotheses for our pondering), so also it does not offer analogies from which doctrinal hypotheses are expected to be derived. The sufficiency of Scripture is such that hypotheses which go beyond the written word are not necessary. Based on 2 Timothy 3:16-17 we know that any question pertaining to belief and behavior can be answered by *applying* the word of God (whether deductively or inductively) to our situation; however, what we apply is the *word* of God, *not hypotheses* built up from analogies. That is, I may need to draw parallels between my situation and the assertions of Scripture, but I do not derive new *doctrinal understanding* by expanding a hypothesis-suggestive analogy that I imagine Scripture uses, or import extraneous teaching material to make Scripture appear to suggest a hypothesis. Scripture clarifies its analogies for us, thus rendering them revelational and not hypothetical. From this an important hermeneutical principle arises. It will be illegitimate to infer doctrinal truths from historical analogies, in other words, analogies drawn from one's research into historical background and imposed on biblical terms or concepts. To do so would be to use a hypothesis-suggestive analogy which takes us *beyond* the statement of Scripture which is alone authoritative for the Christian. Moreover, there may be every reason why Scripture *excluded* the hypothetical inference (which is drawn from historical analogy) in the detailing of the truth from God. The possibility of *uniqueness* in biblical concepts is present! There are proper and improper elements in any conceptual model; the matter of distinguishing them in Scripture has not been left to human conjecture. Although the knowledge of historical parallels (e.g., with Hittite treaties) may be an interesting literary supplement or apologetic tool which accompanies the direct work of exegesis, the hermeneutical principle which must be *authoritative* for us (even with respect to canons and covenants) is that set forth in the Westminster Confession of Faith, chapter I, section 9—Scripture is its *own* infallible rule of interpretation.

The notion of a covenant, like that of fatherhood, was known by the people living at the time of divine scriptural revelation; thus it was profitable in aiding them to learn their relationship to God (and it may be necessary for Christian missionaries to rehearse something about covenants, etc. in order to help a completely different culture understand God's word). Yet as a conceptual model, neither a covenant nor a father was to be taken as an exhaustive parallel. The analogies are good only insofar as God intended particular characteristics to be drawn, and that divine *intention* can only be ferreted out of the divine *word.* Because scriptural analogies do not demand one-to-one correspondence between every conceivable characteristic of the prime analogue and the inferred characteristic of the secondary analogue, we must closely adhere to the teaching of the Bible itself in order to know what the analogies teach us. The knowledge which Scripture presupposes on our part in drawing an analogy may be less than many people seem to think; literary context (which is very broad in the case of the Bible) is the indispensable and best tool for interpretation. However, even in determining whether a researched item of historical information has, or has not, been presupposed by Scripture (and is, therefore, significant for interpretation) it will be the reading of *Scripture* in terms of Scripture itself (albeit in a highly scrutinizing manner) that determines relevance. For example, historical research has pointed out some interesting features about the prerogatives of an "apostle" according to Rabbinic literature; yet the way in which Christ's church knew to take this Rabbinic background as appropriate in interpreting the New Testament mention of the "apostles" was tied to the fact that it had *already* recognized these features (e.g., representative authority) *to some degree* based upon contextual reading and cross-referencing the mention of "*apostle*" throughout the New Testament. What Scripture teaches need never be mediated through some special "knowledge" (gnosis) of the "experts" (whether they be neo-platonic mystics, Roman Catholic magisterium, or historical researchers). As John Knox declared:

> The Word of God is plain in itself; and if there appear any obscurity in one place, the Holy Ghost, who is never contrary to himself, explains the same more clearly in other places; so that there can remain no doubt, but such as obstinately remain ignorant (*History of the Reformation in Scotland,* edited by Dickinson, II, p. 18).

Therefore, whatever conclusions M. G. Kline may come to which are to have *doctrinal authority* must ultimately be related to the assertions of *Scripture itself,* not inferred from hypothesis-suggestive analogies built upon extrabiblical information about ancient treaties. This point is, in addition to being destructive of Kline's methodology and thereby his conclusions about God's law, especially important to set forth because of *Kline's understanding of the significance of his work* with extrabiblical treaties and the scriptural covenants: "For our aim here is simply to make available a hermeneutical tool, to develop the conceptual apparatus . . ." (*The Structure of Biblical Authority,* p. 109).

Before going on to examine more pointedly the position Kline sets forth, a further discussion of his methodology should be inserted. It is distressing to see that he, in common with many modern theologians, uses words in a quite *extraordinary* way in order to make certain scriptural statements conform to his position. Only two of many examples will be given. He states that the conquest of Canaan was neither murder nor robbery, "but the meek inheriting the earth" (p. 163). Now one may legitimately see that the execution of the Canaanites was not immoral, and one may legitimately wish to tie the Old Testament in with the New Testament, but to call the warring Israelites "meek" calls for a linguistic renovation that strains the limits of imagination!—especially when the beatitudes of our Lord to which allusion is made would seem to imply a *contrast* between the way in which His kingdom is to be spread in the new age and the manner in which it was extended in the previous age (cf. "The Two Swords" *supra)*. Another example of this method of semantic deviation, but now where it is a matter of serious import, is Kline's mention of "revision which does not destroy but fulfills" (p. 97) the norms of the covenant with God. To "fulfill' a legal statute by *altering it* certainly does not conform to any of the usual senses of the word "fulfill"; to substitute one piece of legislation for another and then to call this "fulfillment" amounts to making "fulfill" a substitute for "abrogate"! We do not ordinarily consider amendments to the United States Constitution as *fulfillments* of that document's stipulations! In addition to this extraordinary use of words in his argument, Kline can make an appeal to the "obvious" at very crucial junctures. For instance, he alleges that it obviously is not normative for civil governments to actively support the religion of God's people in the New Testament dispensation; yet since this is precisely the point at issue (both in his notion of "intrusion" and in the conflict between his thesis and that of the present volume) his reference to what is "obvious" is more than a trifle question-begging. Connected with this same example we see a tendency for Kline to import unwarranted assumptions in order to make his scheme of things work out. He says the Old Testament state of affairs wherein the civil government endorsed the religious establishment is a case of "intrusion" of the ultimate state of affairs, since (by contrast) in the New Testament the Christian church must take a place of only common privilege along with other religious institutions (p. 167); this last clause is merely assumed without argument. In both what he sees as obvious and what he simply assumes there are scriptural considerations weighing exactly contrary to Kline's line of thought (this treatise is given to exploring such biblical considerations). Finally it is observed that Kline tends to pull back from affirming the inferences that naturally flow from his discussion and point of view; yet he does so without much explanation as to why such inferences do not rightly follow (e.g., p. 160). To assert a point of view, and then to deny *without* further elaboration that it implies what it appears to imply, gives an unavoidable impression of arbitrariness (or the attempt to make your position unassailable to *reductio* counter argumentation).

There are two fundamental ways in which Kline argues against the application of the penal sanctions of God's law in the current age: (1) his discussion of canon and (2) his discussion of "intrusion."

In the former case his analysis of canon and covenant in light of Hittite treaty patterns leads him to declare "that the Old Testament is not the canon of the Christian church" (p. 99). Instead there are two different canons found within Scripture (p. 97) because there are two different covenants. What is initially odd about this argument is that it moves in a direction diametrically opposite of that usually found in "covenant" theologians. Normally those who subscribe to the continuity of covenantal history and development, thus allowing for a thorough-going pattern of foreshadowings of the New Testament reality to be found in the Old Testament, view the New Covenant (and its concomitant scriptures) as the maturity or fruition of the Older Covenant (and scriptures)—and they do so with good scriptural warrant (cf. Luke 24:44 f; John 5:38; 8:56; 12:41; Acts 3:18, 24; 10:43; 13:27; 17:2 f.; 26:22 f.; 2 Cor. 1:20; 1 Peter 1:10-12; plus the chapter on "Covenantal Unity" above). And the prophetic terms given in description of the New Covenant make it clear that it will be the law of the *previous* covenant which receives internalized power in the new age. Hence the idea of two covenants with two canons is *prima facie* out of tune with the view of the New Testament as organically and progressively related to the Older Testament. The notion that the Older Testament is not "normative measuring rod" or "catalogued standard" (i.e., canon) for the New Testament believer is manifestly out of accord with the witness of the New Testament itself (e.g., 2 Tim. 3:14-17; Rom. 15:4; Matt. 5:17 f.; 1 Cor. 10:11; etc.). All the various covenants pertain to the *one* sovereignly administered promise (cf. Eph. 2:12), and we are instructed to live by *every* word from God's mouth (Matt. 4:4), which means all of Scripture (cf. 2 Tim. 3:16; 2 Peter 1:21); therefore, there is ample reason to see *one* basic covenant and *one* central canon for God's people, contrary to Kline's scheme. However, by extensive qualification Kline retrieves the typological history and cult, the faith-norms and the personal life-norms of the Old Testament from his scheme of two canons and announces them as normative for the New Testament church. That is, he substantially reduces the distinguishing characteristic or defining mark of a covenantal canon simply to community life norms:

> However, the *sine qua non* of biblical canonicity, canonicity of the covenantal type, is not a matter of faith-norms but of life-norms. More specifically . . . canonicity precisely and properly defined is a matter of *community* life-norms (pp. 101 f.).

Using this approach Kline thinks to guard himself from the obvious error of saying that the Older Testament is not canonical—in the sense of normative—for the New Testament era while enabling himself to dispense with socially-oriented commandments (e.g., the penal sanctions of God's law) as abrogated. The problem, though, is obvious: Kline no longer has an *argument* in appealing to the canon concept to demonstrate the inapplicability of certain laws in the age of the New Testament, for that is precisely how he *defines* the canon! Thus he still has the responsibility of proving his point, since appeals to the canon concept will (in Kline's special sense of canon) amount to reasoning in a vicious circle.

Therefore, with respect to Kline's discussion of canon and covenant we see that he needs to show that the Old Testament and New

Testament are dealing with fundamentally different covenants. His case in *By Oath Consigned* (Grand Rapids: Eerdmans, 1968) is faulty because: what he designates as "law" covenant contains *both* divine and human oaths. The fact that only one party took the oath or that they took the oath prior to the other party's oath does not imply or convey the distinctive of either law or grace. The parallels with Hittite treaties are overworked. He erroneously assumes that grace must be subsumed under the law (or that law must be prior to grace) instead of being correlative to it. The compatibility of sovereignty and responsibility does nothing to indicate the formal structuring principle of covenant. Rather than synthesizing elements in various covenants Kline just selects one particular covenant and uses that as the model. The preredemptive covenant is not solely a matter of law. In terms of Kline's criteria there was no genuine oath-covenant in Eden anyway. And his interpretation of Galatians 3 has more adequate alternatives. Returning to the canon-covenant question, then, Kline has not shown that there are two fundamentally different covenants in the Old and New Testaments. Furthermore, he has truncated the essence of canon in a way which appears suspect. In addition, he is now left with the task of demonstrating the point which originally was to be established by discussing the concept of covenantal canon. We conclude, hereby, that his first argument has failed.

A few adjoining criticisms of his first argument can also be mentioned here. It is not at all insignificant that Kline's discussion of the Old Testament's not being canonical for the church is *not* accompanied with any *scriptural* backing or exegesis; the only place where any Scripture is brought in (p. 108) does not pertain to the central thesis of distinguishing Old and New Testament canons (and even the use of Scripture for illustrating the subsidiary point Kline is discussing here does not establish his point since these verses are adequately explained on a basis other than Kline's conceptual outlook). Without scriptural arguments Kline's viewpoint cannot help looking a bit speculative. Next, even granting that Kline can show that certain elements in covenant administration are transitory, he has yet to apply this principle to the socially-oriented Mosaic laws of penology in an argumentative fashion; establishing that a certain phenomenon exists is far from showing that the penal sanctions of God's law are instances of that phenomenon. Further, the distinction which Kline wishes to draw between "faith-norms" and "life-norms" in his discussion of the normative element which abides from the Old Testament canon (cf. 101-102, 109) is one which is not immediately clear or cogent; is it not the case that life is a matter of faith and that faith involves a form of life? Finally, it is interesting to note with respect to Kline's tendency to make his positions pivot on the use of analogies that he admits significant elements of dissimilarity between Old and New Testaments pertaining to his notion of canonical polities (cf. pp. 106 f.); this is an indication that, even outside of the methodological problems inherent (which were discussed above), the approach by means of analogies to the questions at stake itself breaks down when made to deal with the materials of Scripture.

Since a discussion of covenantal canon fails to dispense with the penal sanctions of the Older Testament, we turn to Kline's second way of attempting to demonstrate this point: the concept of "intrusion." Kline notes that the Old Testament gives a divinely sanctioned pattern of action (which would include the penal sanctions of the law, cf. p. 166) which is not consonant with the customary application of the law of God (p. 158). Based on this observation he feels a need to show that the Old Testament ethical pattern, nevertheless, is congenial to biblical religion. From that point Kline hopes to give some justification for the ethical pattern God used in the Old Testament by appealing to a notion of eschatological anticipation (p. 164). He sees the Old Testament ethic as an earlier edition of the final reality, "an anticipatory exercise of the ethics of the world to come," an intrusion of consummation ethics into history (cf. pp. 157, 160, 170). Before going any further we must question two assumptions that Kline has made.

First, based upon the discontinuity between Old Testament practice and the "customary application" of God's law, Kline has assumed that it is the Old Testament that needs some explanation or justification when in fact it should be the *customary practice* that is called into question; we should not assume that our ways are normal and that

God's ways are an abnormality which needs vindication. Second, the assumption that God's ways ever need justification according to some rationale or plan discernable and explicable by human intellect or patterns of thought needs to be challenged; simply in virtue of His status as Lord Creator our God has the prerogative to lay down commandments to which we are obligated and for which He need give no explanation. His ways are just by definition and so need not be related to an eschatological order to be congenial to us; even His "positive" commands (e.g., the conquest of Canaan) must be viewed as righteous in terms of the Lawgiver that stands behind them. Even if typological anticipations are appropriately found in God's "positive" commands, such typology does not constitute legal justification for them; rather, one need only understand God in His person and authority—not God in His eschatological plans—to submit gladly to His stipulations. His goodness and justice have a presuppositional, and hence unquestionable, status (cf. Deut. 32:4; Isa. 45:9); that God offers us evidence of His goodness in Scripture and history does not justify the assumption that we must seek out and find some way to justify certain of His ways as congenial to the Christian religion!

Because we should *not* begin with the premise that God's laws are in some places odd (in virtue of current practices) and thereby in need of some rationale (beside His own status) Kline will have to establish from *Scripture itself* that the Older Testament penal sanctions are intruded into the permanent moral order which applies throughout history by God's prescription; that is, he must demonstrate that the New Testament views the Older Testament penology as having only temporary validity. The course of this present study has argued to the opposite conclusion, and again we must note the absence of pertinent scriptural considerations in Kline's presentation; he has not shown that the New Testament *abrogates* the Older Testament law or that the Older Testament law is *merely* typological. The law which God reveals in Scripture reflects His unchangeable holiness; consequently, unless *He* places limitations upon its application (e.g., telling *these* Israelites to execute *those* Canaanites at *this* time) the commands of Scripture reveal abidingly proper ethical relationships.

Before concluding, a few subsidiary comments upon Kline's discussion of "intrusion" ethics might be recorded. *First,* it seems that one could see a contradiction in what Kline says about the penal sanctions of the Older Testament. He alleges that these penal sanctions are instances of intrusion ethics and as such cannot be applied today (p. 166); on the other hand he asserts that (as he sees it) "an analogy exists between the state's judicial use of the sword and Israel's conquest of Canaan" (pp. 165 f.). Now the book of Deuteronomy (as discussed above in this treatise) explains that the Canaanites were to be dispossessed and executed for reason of their violations of the righteous law of God; so in terms of Kline's analogy, the magistrate today should use the sword to execute those who deserve such judgment by reason of their violation of God's law. Thus Kline would appear to be inconsistent in his view of the state's use of the sword—although it is clear upon which side of the inconsistency he would resolve to stand. *Second,* in speaking of an underlying *immutable* principle or standard of morality which has *changing* (differing) applications (p. 160) Kline brings a few questions to mind. Such a construction looks odd on the surface; why would two conflicting moral instructions *not* be different ethical standards? If the two different instructions are contradictory, in what way could the principle be said to be immutable? When Kline says the application or moral rule changes in accord with different conditions (p. 160) has he not implicitly endorsed elements of truth in situation ethics? Could Kline distinguish his position in principle from that which is affirmed in "The Nature and Extent of Biblical Authority" of the Christian Reformed Church or that of *Understanding the Scriptures* by De Graff and Seerveld (i.e., differing time and place prevent God's commands from being normative in the same way as they were when originally given)? When Kline says that "Just because the grand principle . . . is immutable, the application . . . must be changed . . ." (p. 160), is he not again involved in strained linguistic renovation? *Third* we would note that Kline's examples of commands having limited application are readily explained without dependence upon his scheme of thought. The conquest of Canaan has been explained above; in order to become aware that God's command in this regard does not have universal application one need only read the command itself, for it does *not* claim to enunciate a general policy or abiding principle of morality (i.e., it is a "positive" command). It should also be observed that the Canaanites had brought this judgment upon themselves by their wickedness, just as Israel later called for such punishment by her own sinfulness; it is *not* a suspension of God's ethical principles to raise up nations in judgment upon other nations. Moreover, it is not a suspension of ordinary moral standards for Israel (or any nation, for that matter) to hearken to any particular command of God when He specially reveals it to her. Kline also speaks of the "neighbor relationship" as ending at Judgment Day (p. 159), thus illustrating a change of moral practice. Of course what he fails to mention in conjunction with this is that *the law* of God which commands us to love our neighbors holds validity up to the point when heaven and earth pass away (Matt. 5:18)—which is to say that God's law prescribes proper ethical relationships for the period from creation to consummation. Since the law itself obtains a different status when the period for which it specifies moral guidance has ceased, the alteration of relationships which ensues at the end of history simply does *not* amount to a change in the law. The end of the period in which the law is to be used does not constitute an amendment of the law. Moreover, it would be illegitimate to infer that because the law will not be used when history ends, we are not obligated to keep a portion of the law while history is still in process! If an employee argued that he could lay off work a few hours early because he knew that the workday was going to end anyway, it is doubtful that we would honor his reasoning by paying him for the missing hours! To show that the penal stipulations of the law are inapplicable today Kline must do more than point to the law being set aside at the consummation—specifically, he must demonstrate this point directly from Scripture. Remembering God's declaration that He would not alter His covenant words and His prohibition against altering the words that He has spoken, remembering Christ's exhaustive confirmation of the law of God, we are skeptical that Kline will be able to demonstrate his point from Scripture alone.

As we conclude it is well to remind the reader that this short critique of M. G. Kline's position (as found in *The Structure of Biblical Authority)* pertains specifically to his view of the validity of the Older Testamental law (especially its penal sanctions). The value of his position and benefits of his research *as a whole* are certainly not in question. It is the bearing of his thinking on ethics in particular with which we are forced to disagree. However, one should not hereby fail to go on and appreciate those points in Dr. Kline's studies which have genuine scriptural backing. This said, we would conclude this critique by noting that Kline's methodology as well as his views on double canon and intrusion ethics have been found unacceptable; therefore, his conclusion that the Older Testamental penal sanctions are invalid today must also be held unacceptable. By means of his analogies and eschatological assumptions Kline has assumed the prerogative to abrogate the principles of creaturely holiness revealed by God, norms of morality which must obtain until the heavens and earth pass away and we are ushered into the New Jerusalem wherein righteousness dwells. Until that day God has blessed us with civil government to restrain the unrighteousness of men by punishing their infractions of God's law; this restraint of evil by means of human government is a sure example of God's common grace. In annulling those principles whereby civil government can enforce the law of God in the social realm, that is, in canceling the current use of the penal *sanctions* of God's law, M. G. Kline becomes the one who is unwittingly guilty of assuming the prerogative of God to abrogate the functions of common grace (cf. his corresponding statement which forms the background for the wording of this conclusion: p. 171).

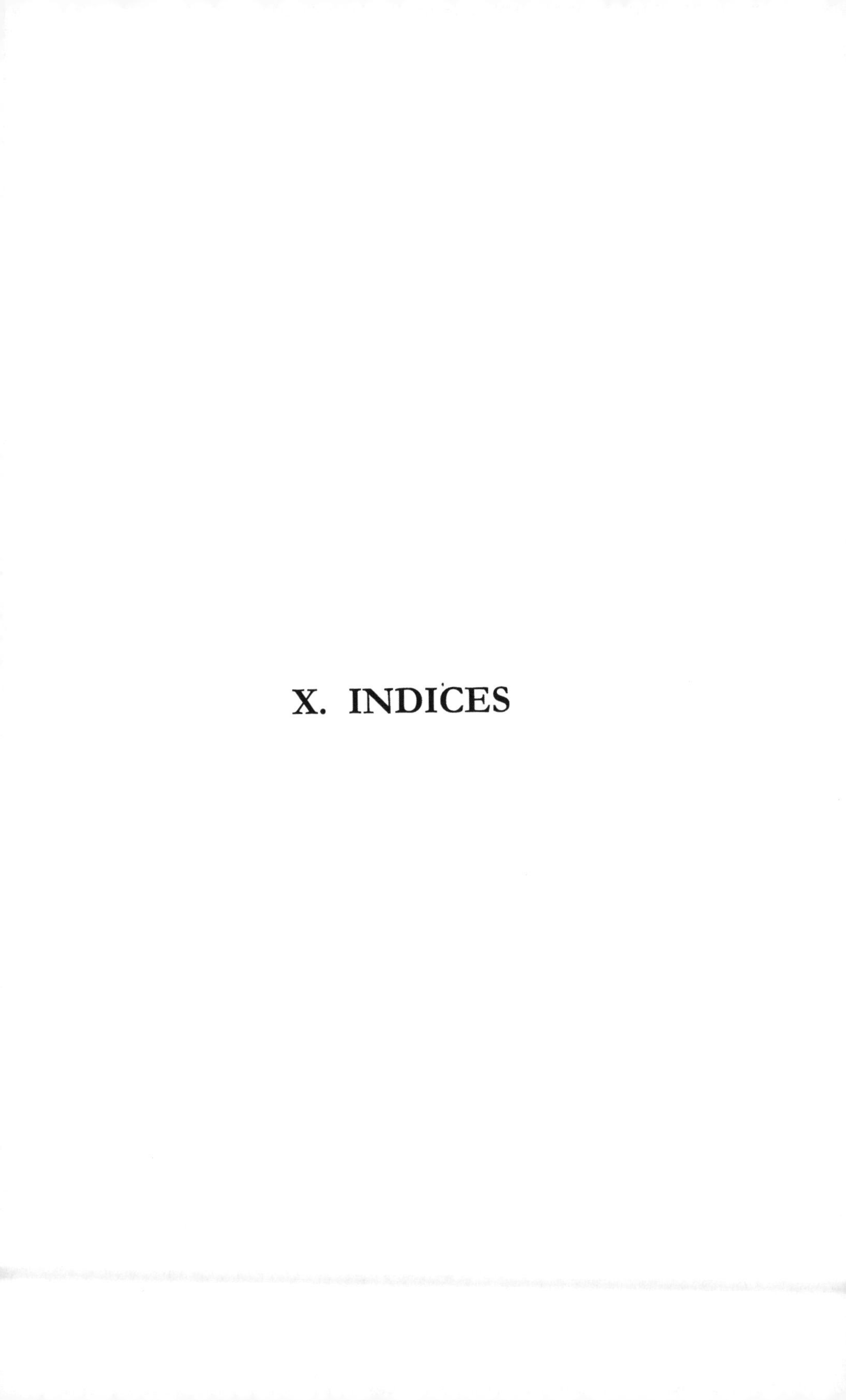

X. INDICES

INDEX OF SUBJECTS

A

B

C

J

K

L

M

N

O

P

Q

R

S

T

U

V

W

INDEX OF NAMES

INDEX OF SCRIPTURE TEXTS

Leviticus

Lamentations

Ezekiel

Micah

Nahum

Habakuk

Zephaniah

Haggai

Zechariah

Malachi

Matthew

1 Corinthians

Hebrews

James

1 Peter

2 Peter

1 John

Made in the USA
Middletown, DE
02 November 2021

51535705R00364